THE
CHESTER MYSTERY
CYCLE

VOLUME II · COMMENTARY AND GLOSSARY

EARLY ENGLISH TEXT SOCIETY

S.S. 9

1986

THE CHESTER
MYSTERY CYCLE

EDITED BY

R.M. LUMIANSKY

AND

DAVID MILLS

Published for
THE EARLY ENGLISH TEXT SOCIETY
by the
OXFORD UNIVERSITY PRESS
LONDON   NEW YORK   TORONTO

OXFORD

UNIVERSITY PRESS

Great Clarendon Street, Oxford OX2 6DP
United Kingdom

Oxford University Press is a department of the University of Oxford.
It furthers the University's objective of excellence in research, scholarship,
and education by publishing worldwide. Oxford is a registered trade mark of
Oxford University Press in the UK and in certain other countries

© The Early English Text Society 1986

The moral rights of the authors have been asserted

Database right Oxford University Press (maker)

First Edition published in 1986

All rights reserved. No part of this publication may be reproduced,
stored in a retrieval system, or transmitted, in any form or by any means,
without the prior permission in writing of Oxford University Press,
or as expressly permitted by law, or under terms agreed with the appropriate
reprographics rights organization. Enquiries concerning reproduction
outside the scope of the above should be sent to the Rights Department,
Oxford University Press, at the address above

You must not circulate this book in any other form
and you must impose this same condition on any acquirer

Published in the United States of America by Oxford University Press
198 Madison Avenue, New York, NY 10016, United States of America

British Library Cataloguing in Publication Data
Data available

Library of Congress Cataloging in Publication Data
Data available

Supplementary Series, 9

ISBN 978-0-19-722408-3

CONTENTS

PREFACE	vii
CORRIGENDA TO VOLUME I	ix
SHORT TITLE INDEX	xi
BIBLIOGRAPHY	xvi
COMMENTARY	1
APPENDICES	377
NOTE ON 'DR. MATTHEWS'	407
LIST OF LATIN ERRORS	411
ENGLISH GLOSSARY	419

PREFACE

In 1974 the Society published the first volume of our edition of the Chester Mystery Cycle, containing text, variant readings, textual notes, and descriptions of the manuscripts. In this, the second volume, we complete the edition by providing Explanatory Notes and an English Glossary, together with a Select Bibliography, Corrigenda to Volume I and a list of the errors in the Latin of the various manuscripts.

In the Preface to our first volume we described our projected second volume, then in preparation. But in the past ten years, as the cost of publications has risen regularly and rapidly, our original ambitious plan has had to be modified at the Society's request. Hence we had to abandon plans for an edition of the Banns and for extended discussions of the history, sources, and manuscript-relationships for the Cycle since these would have been beyond the scope of a second volume. Fortunately, the University of North Carolina Press expressed interest in publishing a collection of essays on the Cycle, and we are happy to refer readers to their 1983 publication, *The Chester Mystery Cycle: Essays and Documents*, by R.M. Lumiansky and David Mills, which includes essays and material of the kind which we had hoped to publish as part of our edition, together with edited transcripts of documents, and an essay on 'Music in the Cycle' by Richard Rastall.

Limitations of space further curtail the textual apparatus and, most reluctantly, we have felt compelled to omit a full Latin glossary. In its stead we have supplied a list of Latin errors in the manuscripts which we hope will help readers at particular points of difficulty.

Our intention to produce a modern English version of the Cycle, which we stated in our Preface to Volume I, remains firm. We are convinced of the urgent need for student-texts of this and of the other English play cycles.

In accordance with our previous practice, we take collective responsibility for this volume. Each of us has overseen the other's work as the typescripts have been prepared.

Although we would not deny the frustration which we have often felt since we first submitted a typescript for this volume to the

Society in 1978, we recognise the difficulties faced by the Society and the Press. The Society, through its readers, has taken considerable care in checking and correcting our work. In particular, we acknowledge the work and advice of Dr. P.O.E. Gradon. Mrs. Ruth M. Keane undertook the thankless task of verifying all references in the Explanatory Notes and performed it with efficiency and accuracy. We deeply appreciate the excellent work of Annette Butler, Barbara Henning, Catherine Rees and Joan Welford in the preparation of the typescript. The work was expedited by the grant of a year's study-leave to David Mills by the University of Liverpool.

As we indicated in the Preface to Volume I, we are grateful for the patience of our wives — Janet and Joy — through the long years of work on the Cycle. And for this volume we must express gratitude to them and to two others, Ian and John Mills, who have shared their whole lives with this Chester edition.

THE EDITORS

CORRIGENDA TO VOLUME I

Preface, line 5 from end: change *Skalaroff* to *Sklaroff*.

page xxviii, line 6 from bottom: change *better 'text'* to *'better' text*.

page xxxvi, line 12: supply period after *anye*.

2/208 + SD: delete comma after *volucris*; add semicolon after *penna* and after *forma*.

3/34: change [*rowfed*] to *ronett*.

3/34, VR: change *rowfed*]*ronett HmAB, rounde R* to *ronett*]*rounde R, rowfed H*.

3/page 52, VRs: reverse positions of the first two variant readings; change *GOSSIP H* to *om H*; before 243 insert *After 242*]*GOSSIP H*.

3/280–1: delete period in 280; change first comma in 281 to a period; change *all* to *All* in 281; delete second comma in 281.

3/318, VR: change *rainebow* to *raine*.

4/104 + SD: VR: after *AR* add a comma and *rec B*.

4/page 63, VRs: add *145* before *to*]*unto AR* and place this variant reading after *DEUS*]*GOD AR*.

5/90–1: add a semicolon at end of 90; delete dash in 91.

6/207, VR: move *ARH* to left.

9/248, VR: change *you* to *you (2)*.

11/12–4: delete the period; change *But* to *but*, dash to period, and *tyll* to *Tyll*.

13/*Before* 1, Latin, VR: reverse the order of *non*]*no B* and *sequitur*]*sequitor A*.

13/332 + SD: change *sit* to *ait*.

14/page 262, VRs: change first *276* to *266* and *260* to *270*.

15/118: omit question-mark.

15/190: add comma after *crowen*.

15/page 282, first VR: change *243* to *324*.

16A/212 + SH, VR: delete *om B*,.

16A/page 319, VRs: change *After 344* to *After 344 + SH*.

16A/page 321, VRs: change font for *LONGEUS*.

17/52–4: in 52 change comma to semicolon; in 53 and 54 change commas to dashes.

17/70: capitalize initials of *mercye* and *ryghtwisenesse*.

18/58: change exclamation-mark to comma.

18/page 343, VRs: delete VR beginning '*to left of 125*'. On p.344 insert VR, emended to begin '*to left of 126*', before VR 127.

18/133, VR: change *in charge A, in chare R* to *incharge A, inchare R*.

19/273, VR: change *that* to *that (1)*.

20/19, VR: change *ame* to *am*.

20/29–31: in 29 add comma after *weare*; in 30 change dash to comma; in 31 change comma to dash.

22/VRs, *After Guild-ascription* H: add a colon after *Secunda*; delete the semicolon after *Prophetantibus*; change semicolons after *Novissimo* and *Antechristo* to commas.

22/186: change semicolon to comma.

23/197–8: change exclamation-marks to commas; change *This* to *this*.

23/474: add comma after *Forsoothe*.

23/511, VR: change *anAR* to *an AR*.

23/529: add comma after *you*.

23/553–4: change second comma to exclamation-mark; change *but* to *But*.

23/621: add a comma after *other* and after *sight*.

24/2: change comma to semicolon.

24/302: delete bracket.

24/347: change *Hyse* to *hyse*.

24/508 + SD: change comma after

domino to period and add quotation-mark after *domino*. Change *salvator* to '*Salvator*.

24/588, VR: change *brune* to *breme*.

24/603, VR: change *her*]a *H* to *lure*]a *lurr H*.

App IA/headnote: change *forty-eight* to *forty-seven*.

App ID/first SD: add comma after *obviam*.

App IIB/356: add comma after *whyle*.

App IIB/358: change second comma to exclamation-mark; change *lowdelye* to *Lowdelve*.

App IIB/501: change comma to exclamation-mark; change *therefor* to *Therefor*.

page 537, Play V, 160–71: change *fonne* to *fanne*.

page 541, Play XIII: change *48–51* to *48–50*.

page 548, Play X: change 71^v, $312 + SH$–60 to 71^v, $320 + SH$–60.

page 579, Play VI, first line: delete period after *Above*.

page 596, Play XIV: change 74^r, 277–312 to 74^r, 281–312.

SELECT LIST OF WORKS TO WHICH REFERENCE IS MADE

Space prevents the inclusion of a full list of the analogues and works of reference and criticism mentioned in the Explanatory Notes. A few, to which reference is repeatedly made in the Notes, are included in this short bibliography.

Dictionaries, Encyclopaedias and Works of Reference
The Oxford English Dictionary (Oxford, 1884–1928), and Supplements.
The Middle English Dictionary (Ann Arbor, 1954–).
T.F. Mustanoja, *A Middle English Syntax: Part I. Parts of Speech* (Helsinki, 1960).
Encyclopaedia Judaica (The Jewish Encyclopaedia), 16 vols. (Jerusalem, 1972).
The New Catholic Encyclopaedia, 17 vols. (Washington DC, 1967).
The Oxford Dictionary of the Christian Church. 1st ed., edited by F.L. Cross (Oxford, 1958); 2nd ed., edited by F.L. Cross and S.A. Livingstone (Oxford, 1974).
C.W. Bardsley, *A Dictionary of English and Welsh Surnames* (London, 1901).
P.H. Reaney, *A Dictionary of British Surnames* (London, 1st ed., 1961).
E.G. Withycombe, *The Oxford Dictionary of English Christian Names* (Oxford, 1st ed., 1950).
E.C. Brewer, *The Dictionary of Phrase and Fable* (New York, 1978 ed.).
C.F. Brown and R.H. Robbins, *The Index of Middle English Verse* (New York, 1943), and Supplements.

Major Latin Analogues
The Vulgate Bible.
Evangelia Apocrypha, edited by C. Tischendorf (Lipsiae, 1853).
Apocalypses Apocryphae Mosis, Esdrae, Iohannis, edited by L.F.C. Tischendorf (Lipsiae, 1866).
Acta Sanctorum.

Legenda Aurea, edited by J.G.T. Graesse (3rd ed., Vratislava, 1890; repr. Osnabruck, 1969).
St Augustine, *De Consensu Evangelistarum*. Patrologia Latina (PL) 34. cols. 1041–1230.
The Venerable Bede, *In Matthaei/Marci/Lucae/S Johannis Evangelium Expositio*. PL 92.
Peter Comestor, *Historia Scholastica*. PL 198. cols. 1045–1722.
Walafrid Strabo, *Glossa Ordinaria*. PL 113. col.67 — 114. col.752.
St Thomas Aquinas, *Summa Theologiae*, edited by T. Grilby *et al.* 60 vols. (London & New York, 1963–5).
Vincent of Beauvais, *Speculum Maius IV: Speculum Historiale* (Austria, 1965 — facsimile of 1624 edition).

Translations of Latin Analogues
The 'Authorised Version' of the Bible (AV).
The Apocryphal New Testament, edited by M.R. James (corr. ed., Oxford, 1953).
The Book of Common Prayer. (BCP).
The Works of Flavius Josephus, translated by William Whiston (London & Edinburgh, n.d.).

Dramatic Analogues
The Cornish Ordinalia, translated by M. Harris (Washington, 1969).
Two Coventry Corpus Christi Plays, edited by H. Craig. EETS e.s. 87 (2nd ed., 1957).
The Digby Plays, edited by F.J. Furnivall. EETS e.s. 70 (1896).
Ludus Coventriae, or the Plaie called Corpus Christi, edited by K.S. Block. EETS e.s. 120 (1922).
The Macro Plays, edited by M. Eccles. EETS o.s. 262 (1969).
Non-Cycle Plays and Fragments, edited by N. Davis. EETS s.s 1 (1970).
The Towneley Plays, edited by G. England and A.W. Pollard. EETS e.s. 71 (1897).
York Mystery Plays, edited by L. Toulmin Smith (London, 1885).
Le Mystère du Vieil Testament, edited by Baron J. de Rothschild. 5 vols. (Paris, 1878–91).
David Bevington (ed.), *Medieval Drama* (Boston, 1975).
Karl Young, *The Drama of the Medieval Church*. 2 vols. (Oxford, 1933).

Middle English Non-dramatic Analogues
The Works of Geoffrey Chaucer, edited by F.N. Robinson (2nd ed., London, 1957).
Cleanness, edited by J.J. Anderson (Manchester, 1977).
Cursor Mundi, edited by R. Morris. 7 vols. EETS o.s. 57, 59, 62, 66, 68, 99, 101 (1874–93).
The Early South-English Legendary, edited by C. Horstman. EETS o.s. 87 (1887).
The Middle English Genesis and Exodus, edited by O.S.A. Arngart (Lund, 1968).
John Mirk: Festial: A Collection of Homilies, edited by T. Erbe. EETS e.s. 96 (1905).
The Northern Passion, edited by F.A. Foster. 3 vols. EETS o.s. 145, 147, 183 (1913–30).
Patience, edited by J.J. Anderson (Manchester, 1969).
Piers Plowman: The B Version, edited by G. Kane and E.T. Donaldson (London, 1975).
The South English Legendary, edited by C.D. Evelyn and A.J. Mill. 2 vols. EETS o.s. 235–6 (1957–9).
The South English Nativity of Mary and Christ, edited by O.S. Pickering (Heidelberg, 1975).
A Stanzaic Life of Christ, edited by F.A. Foster. EETS o.s. 166 (1926).
The Three Kings of Cologne, edited by C. Horstmann. EETS o.s. 85 (1886).
Select English Works of John Wyclif, edited by T. Arnold. 3 vols. (Oxford, 1869–71).

List of Works in Patrologia Latina series
Alcuin: *Opera Omnia*. vol. 2. 'Opera Supposita'. *Adsonis Abbatis Monasterii Dervensis: Libellus de Antichristo*. PL 101/1291–8.
St Ambrose: *Expositiones in Evangelium Secundum Lucam*. PL 15/1603–1944.
St Athanasius: 'Spuria'. *Homilia in Occursum Domini*. PG 28/973–1000.
St Augustine: *De Genesi ad Litteram*. PL 34/219–466.
De Consensu Evangelistarum. PL 34/1041–1230.
In Johannis Evangelium: Tractatus 33, 44, 49, 114, 117, 119, 120. PL 35.
Sermones. Sermo 163, 'De Verbis Apostoli', Sermo 199, 'In Natali Domini'. PL 38/889–95; 1007–9.

De Civitate Dei. PL 41/13–804.
De Trinitate. PL 42/819–1098.
Contra Judaeos, Paganos et Arian. Sermo de Symbolo. PL 42/1177–30.
De Anima et Eius Origine. PL 44/475–548.
Pseudo-Augustine: *Sermones. Sermo 33 'De Balaam et Balak'.* PL 39/1809–11.
Sermo 231; Sermo 241, 'De Symbolo'. PL 39/2190–1; 2171–2.
The Venerable Bede: *Hexameron, sive Libri Quatuor in Principium Genesis usque ad Nativitatem.* PL 91/9–190.
In Pentateuchum Commentarii. PL 91/189–394.
In Matthaei Evangelium Expositio. PL 92.
In Marci Evangelium Expositio. PL 92.
In Lucae Evangelium Expositio. PL 92.
In S Johannis Evangelium Expositio. PL 92.
Homelia. PL 94.
St Bernard: *Vitis Mystica, seu Tractatus de Passione Domini.* PL 184/635–740.
St Chrysostom: *Homiliae in Genesin.* PG 53/21 — 54/586.
In Matthaeum: Homiliae XC. PG 57/21–472.
In Matthaeum Homilia 76 al 77. PG 58/693–702.
Pseudo-Chrysostom: *De Beato Abraham.* PG 50/737–46.
In Matthaeum Homilia. PG 56/611–946.
Clement of Alexandria: *Stromatum. Liber IV.* PG 9/207–402.
Peter Comestor: *Historia Scholastica.* PL 198/1045–1722.
St Cyril: *Catecheses. Catechesis XV: 'De Secundo Christi Adventu'.* PG 33/869–916.
Peter Damian: *Sermo 61: Anonymi Cuiusdiam Sermo: 'De Nativitate Salvatoris et Praeclaris Miraculis in ea Factis.* PL 144/848–55.
Pseudo-Dionysius: *De Coelesti Hierarchia.* PG 4/29–184.
St Fulbert: *Sermones ad Populum.* PL 141/317–38.
St Gregory the Great: *Homiliae XL in Evangelia.* PL 76/1075–1312.
St Hildegard: *Scivias sive Visionum ac Revelationum.* PL 197/383–738.
Honorius of Autun: *Elucidarium, Liber 3.* PL 172/1157–1176.
Hugh of St Victor: *De Arca Noe Morali; De Arca Noe Mystica.* PL 176/618–704.
Hugo Eterianus: *Liber de Animo Corpore Iam Exuta sive De Regressu*

Animarum de Inferis. PL 202/167-226.
St Jerome: *Commentarium in Evangelium Matthaei.* PL 26.
Pope Innocent III: *Sermo II.* PL 217/319-24.
St Isidore: *Quaestiones in Vetus Testamentum.* PL 83/207-424.
St Jerome: *Epistolae: Epistola LXXIII, ad Evangelium Presbyterum.* PL 22/676-81.
Liber De Nominibus Hebraicis. PL 23/817-904.
Commentaria in Isaiam Prophetam. PL 24/17-704.
Commentariorum in Danielam Prophetam. PL 25/491-584.
Commentariorum in Zachariam. PL 25/1417-1542.
St Martin: *Expositio Libri Apocalypsis.* PL 209/199-424.
St Maximus: *Sermo 114.* PL 57.
Nicephorus Callistus: *Liber Ecclesiasticae Historiae.* PG 145/559-1332.
Origen: *Contra Celsum.* PG 11/637-1632.
Homilia in Numeros. PG 12/583-806.
Peter the Lombard: *Sententiarum Libri Quatuor.* PL 102/520-962.
Remigius: *Homilia 2.* PL 131/872-8.
Rufinus: *Commentarius in Symbolum Apostolorum.* PL 21/335-86.
Walafrid Strabo: *Glossa Ordinaria.* PL 113/67 — 114/752.
Tertullian: *Liber de Baptismo.* PL 1/1305-34.
Adversus Judaeos. PL 2/633-82.
St Theophilus: *Libri Tres Ad Autolycum.* PG 6/1023-1168.
Theophylactus: *Enarratio in Evangelium Matthaei.* PG 123.

COMMENTARY UPON THE CHESTER CYCLE
A SELECTED BIBLIOGRAPHY

Note A bibliography concerning the text of the Cycle was presented in Volume I of this edition. To this should be added *The Chester Mystery Cycle: A Reduced Facsimile of Huntington Manuscript 2*, Leeds Texts and Monographs, Drama Facsimiles IV (Leeds, 1979), introduction by R.M. Lumiansky and David Mills; Brownstein, Oscar L., "Revision of the 'Deluge' of the Chester Cycle", *Speech Monographs*, xxxvi (1968), 55–65; and Mills, David, "Edward Gregorie — a 'Bunbury scholar'," *REED Newsletter* (1982), no.1, 49–50.

The revision of J.Q. Adams, *Chief Pre-Shakespearean Dramas*, referred to in the Bibliography to Volume I, has appeared: David Bevington, *Medieval Drama* (Boston, 1975); it includes Play V (MS. H, with two additions from MS. Hm) and Play XIX from the Chester Cycle.

The final item under Discussions of the Texts in that bibliography appeared in *Leeds Studies in English*, vii (1974), 95–9.

The listing in the following Bibliography is chronological within each category.

A. *Books*

Ormerod, George, *The History of the County Palatine and the City of Chester* (London, 1819).
Morris, Rupert, *Chester in the Plantagenet and Tudor Reigns* (Chester, 1895).
Chambers, E.K., *The Medieval Stage* (Oxford, 1903).
Harper, C.A., *A Comparison Between the Brome and Chester Plays of Abraham and Isaac* (Radcliffe College Monographs, 1910).
Cornelius, Brother Luke, *The Role of the Virgin Mary in the Coventry, York, Chester, and Townley Cycles* (Washington, D.C., 1923).

Mathews, G.W., *The Chester Mystery Plays* (Liverpool, 1925). Reprinted from *Transactions of the Historic Society of Lancaster and Cheshire*, volume lxxvi.
Young, Karl, *The Drama of the Medieval Church* (Oxford, 1933).
Deasy, C.P., *Saint Joseph in the English Mystery Plays* (Washington, D.C., 1937).
Lucken, Brother Linus Urban, *Antichrist and the Prophets of Antichrist in the Chester Cycle* (Washington, D.C., 1940).
Gardiner, H.C., *Mysteries' End* (New Haven, 1946).
Craig, Hardin, *English Religious Drama in the Middle Ages* (New York, 1955).
Salter, F.M., *Medieval Drama in Chester* (Toronto, 1955).
Wickham, Glynne, *Early English Stages* (London, 1959–).
Prosser, Eleanor A., *Drama and Religion in the English Mystery Plays: A Re-evaluation* (Stanford, 1961).
Williams, Arnold, *The Drama of Medieval England* (East Lansing, Michigan, 1961).
Anderson, M.D., *Drama and Imagery in English Medieval Churches* (Cambridge, 1963).
Hardison, O.B., *Christian Rite and Christian Drama in the Middle Ages* (Baltimore, 1965).
Kolve, V.A., *The Play Called Corpus Christi* (Stanford, 1966).
Woolf, Rosemary, *The English Mystery Plays* (London, 1972).
Nelson, Alan H., *The Medieval Stage: Corpus Christi Pageants and Plays* (Chicago, 1974).
Clopper, L.M. (ed.), *Records of Early English Drama: Chester* (Toronto, 1979).
Dutka, JoAnna, *Music in the English Mystery Plays* (Early Drama, Art and Music Reference Series 3, Kalamazoo, 1980).
MacLean, Sally-Beth, *Chester Art: A Subject List of Extant and Lost Art Including Items Relevant to Early Drama* (Early Drama, Art and Music Reference Series 3, Kalamazoo, 1982).
Davidson, C. *et al.*, *The Drama of the Middle Ages: Comparative and Critical Essays* (New York, 1982). Reprints a number of articles originally published in *Comparative Drama*. Abbreviated to *DMA* for specific articles below.
Lumiansky, R.M. and Mills, David, *The Chester Mystery Cycle: Essays and Documents* (Chapel Hill, 1983). Includes an essay on "Music in the Chester Cycle" by Richard Rastall besides essays on the texts, sources and development of the cycle.

B. *Articles*

Hohfeld, A.B., "Two Old English Mystery Plays on the Subject of Abraham's Sacrifice," *MLN*, v (1890), 222–37. Examines the Brome and Chester versions.

Baugh, Albert C., "The Chester Plays and French Influence," *Schelling Anniversary Papers* (New York, 1923), 35–63.

Fort, Margaret D., "The Metres of the Brome and Chester Abraham and Isaac Plays," *PMLA*, xli (1926), 832–9.

Foster, Frances A. (ed.), *A Stanzaic Life of Christ*, EETS, o.s. 166 (1926 for 1924). Introduction treats relation of this poem to Chester Cycle.

Dustoor, P.E., "The Origin of the Play of Moses and the Tables of the Law," *MLR*, xix (1929), 459–63.

Wilson, R.H., "The 'Stanzaic Life of Christ' and the Chester Plays," *SP*, xxviii (1931), 413–32.

Greg, W.W., "'Christ and the Doctors' and the York Play," *Chester Play Studies* (The Malone Society, 1935), 101–20.

Greg, W.W., "The Lists and Banns of the Plays," *Chester Play Studies* (The Malone Society, 1935), 121–71.

Wells, M.E., "The Age of Isaac at the Time of Sacrifice," *MLN*, liv (1939), 579–82.

Severs, J.B., "The Relationship between the Brome and Chester Play of 'Abraham and Isaac'," *MP*, xlii (1945), 137–51.

Bryant, J.A., "Chester's Sermon for Catechumens," *JEGP*, liii (1954), 339–402. Concerns "Abraham and Isaac".

Woolf, Rosemary, "The Effect of Typology on the English Medieval Plays of Abraham and Isaac," *Speculum*, xxxii (1957), 805–25.

Lumiansky, R.M., "Comedy and Theme in the Chester 'Harrowing of Hell'," *Tulane Studies in English*, x (1960), 5–12.

Bland, D.S., "The Chester Nativity: One Play or Two?" *N&Q*, x (1963), 134–5.

Taylor, Jerome, "The Dramatic Structure of the Middle English Corpus Christi or Cycle Plays," *Literature and Society: Nineteen Essays* (Lincoln, Nebraska, 1964), 175–86.

Brown, Arthur, "The Study of English Medieval Drama," *Franciplegius: Medieval and Linguistic Essays in Honor of F.P. Magoun* (New York, 1965), 265–73.

Carpenter, Nan Cooke, "Music in the Chester Plays," *Papers on English Language and Literature*, i (1965), 195–216.

Robinson, J.W., "The Late Medieval Cult of Jesus and the Mystery Plays," *PMLA*, lxxx (1965), 508–14.
Coffee, Bernice F., "The Chester Play of Balaam and Balak," *Wisconsin Studies in Literature*, iv (1967), 103–18.
Stemmler, Theo, "Zur Datierung der Chester Plays," *G-RM*, n.f., xviii (1968), 309–13.
Powlick, Leonard, "The Staging of the Chester Cycle," *Theatre Survey*, xii (1970), 119–50.
Diller, H.J., "The Composition of the *Chester Adoration of the Shepherds*," *Anglia*, lxxxix (1971), 178–98.
Langoon, H.N., "Staging of the Ascension in the Chester Cycle," *Theatre Notebook*, xxvi (1971/2), 53–60.
Davis, Ruth Brant, "The Scheduling of the Chester Cycle Plays," *Theatre Notebook*, xxvii (1972/3), 49–67.
Clopper, L.M., "The Chester Plays: Frequency of Performance," *Theatre Survey*, xiv (1973), 45–58.
Hanning, R.W., "'You Have Begun a Parlous Pleye': The Nature and Limits of Dramatic Mimesis as a Theme in Four Middle English 'Fall of Lucifer' Plays," *Comparative Drama*, vii (1973), 22–50. Reprinted in *DMA*, 140–68. Includes the Chester 'Fall of Lucifer'.
Mills, David, "The Two Versions of Chester Play V: Balaam and Balak," *Chaucer and Middle English Studies* (London, 1973), 366–71.
Mills, David, "Some Possible Implications of Herod's Speech: Chester Plays, VIII. 153–204," *Neuphilologische Mitteilungen*, lxxiv (1973), 131–43.
Clopper, L.M., "The Rogers Description of the Chester Plays," *LSE*, vii (1973–4), 63–94.
Clopper, L.M., "The Staging of the Medieval Plays of Chester: A Response," *Theatre Notebook*, xxviii (1974), 65–70.
Campbell, T.P., "The Prophets' Pageant in the English Mystery Cycles," *Research Opportunities in Renaissance Drama*, xvii (1974), 107–21.
Travis, Peter W., "The Dramatic Strategies of Chester's Passion Pagina," *Comparative Drama*, viii (1974), 275–89.
Munson, W.F., "Audience and Meaning in Two Medieval Dramatic Realisms," *Comparative Drama*, ix (1975), 44–67. Reprinted in *DMA*, 183–206. Includes the Chester 'Shepherds' Play'.

Harty, Kevin J., "The Chester Fall of Lucifer," *McNeese Review*, xxii (1975–76), 70–79.

Travis, Peter W., "The Credal Design of the Chester Cycle," *MP*, lxxiii (1975–6), 229–43.

Harty, Kevin J., "The Unity and Structure of the Chester Mystery Cycle," *Medievalia*, ii (1976), 137–58.

Staines, D., "To Out-Herod Herod: The Development of a Dramatic Character," *Comparative Drama*, x (1976), 29–53. Reprinted in *DMA*, 207–231. Includes Chester's Herod.

Harty, Kevin J., "The Identity of 'Freere Bartholemewe', Chester Play VI.565: A Suggestion," *American Notes and Queries*, xvi (1977), 18–9.

Marshall, John, "The Chester Whitsun Plays: Dating of Post-Reformation Performances from the Smiths' Accounts," *LSE*, ix (1977), 51–61.

Clopper, L.M., "The History and Development of the Chester Cycle," *MP*, lxxv (1977–78), 219–46.

Ashley, Kathleen M., "Divine Power in the Chester Cycle and Late Medieval Thought," *Jnl of the History of Ideas*, xxxix (1978), 387–404.

Clopper, L.M., "The Principle of Selection of the Chester Old Testament Plays," *ChauR*, xiii (1979), 272–83.

Harty, Kevin J., "'Unbeleeffe is a Fowle Sinne': The Chester Nativity Play," *Susquehanna University Studies*, xi (1979), 35–41.

McGavin, J.J., "Sign and Transition: The *Purification* Play in Chester," *LSE*, xi (1980), 90–104.

Mills, David, "Stage Directions in the MSS of the Chester Mystery Cycle," *METh*, iii (1981), 45–51.

COMMENTARY

HEADNOTE

1. *Format:* The material in the Commentary section is presented play by play in the order in which the plays appear in the cycle texts. Notes relating to the Appendices follow the notes on the cycle.

Within each play, the material is presented as follows:

(a) *Internal evidence relating to production:* At the start of each set of notes are the following sections:-

Dramatis Personae — a list of all speaking characters in Hm in order of appearance, listed under the form of the first Hm SH;

Locations — a list of all locations specified in the Hm text, with line-references;

Properties — a list of all movable objects specified in the Hm text, with line-references;

Costume — a list of all articles of dress specified in the Hm text, with line-references.

Although only specific references are quoted, attention is drawn in supplementary notes to each section to passages from which further inferences may be made. Only the first three occurrences of any word are noted. References are, however, grouped together, so that different and widely-separated words for the same location, property or costume appear together in the lists.

(b) *Analogous Material:* After the production-material, analogous material appears in two sections:

Sources: In this section are listed passages of primary analogy. The section-title does not imply that the play derives directly from the material cited, nor does it imply that these will be the only analogues invoked in the notes;

Play-heading: This section contains textual notes on the words of the heading where necessary; but it also includes references to plays on similar subjects in the other English cycles, in other vernacular drama, and in the Cornish Ordinalia (cited in the English translation by Markham Harris).

(c) *Explanatory Notes:* Points requiring elucidation are presented under the appropriate line-number and, where more than one point is considered within a line, in the order of occurrence in the line. Notes relating to rhyme are placed within stanza-references, in the form *1-8, stanza 1*.

2. *Content of the Notes:* The primary purpose of the Notes is to further the reader's understanding of the Hm text. To this end, they attempt to discuss all instances in which the meaning of the Hm text is not immediately apparent. These discussions may also involve the evaluation of alternative readings in the other manuscripts and some consideration of the possible origins of the difficulty in the transmission of the cycle; they may also involve comparison of the text with other versions of the same material.

(a) 'difficulties of meaning' comprehend problems of semantics, syntax, stanza-form, and the continuity of action. They also include the identification of characters and places whose names and biographies or locations may no longer be familiar. But four areas are excluded from the Notes — difficulties of vocabulary (as opposed to semantics), which are covered by the *English Glossary* and *List of Latin Errors*; problems of guild-ascription; detailed explanation of the music in the cycle; and the stylistic evaluation of 'better' readings.

(b) in determining 'meaning', we have applied primarily to MED and OED. We have cited the date for a word or its usage whenever it seems possibly significant for scribal confusions or uncertainties, or an indicator of the *terminus a quo* or *ad quem* for the text; the dates in such instances are based on OED exemplification.

(c) in discussing stanza-form, we have generally assumed that corruption may be suspected when a stanza diverges in a limited number of respects from a 'standard' Chester stanza. We define the latter as $aaa^4b^3aaa^4b^3$ or $aaa^4b^3ccc^4b^3$. We have not made assumptions about the metre of the lines, feeling that this is often a subjective matter.

(d) we have included in the Notes comments on all instances in which, at EETS' request, we emended the Hm reading. No attempt is, however, made to discuss errors or equally possible readings in other manuscripts unless these are felt to be particularly significant for an understanding of the Hm text or its development.

(e) in citing analogues we have frequently made comparisons with primary analogues listed under *Sources* and have on occasion expressed preferences for readings which more accurately reproduce the meaning of those analogues. In addition, standard works are cited to suggest widely current interpretations of episodes — in particular, *Glossa Ordinaria* and Comestor's *Historia Scholastica*; such citations do not imply any direct link between the cycle and the works cited but merely indicate the conformity to or divergence from a commonly held interpretation of the scene. Quotations from Josephus are from the English translation by William Whiston; Vulgate quotations are followed by AV equivalents. In addition, the notes also reproduce passages cited by critics in support of the cycle's direct reliance upon particular texts — e.g. *A Stanzaic Life of Christ*, the Brome *Abraham and Isaac*; the inclusion of such passages does not imply any acceptance of the conclusions drawn from the parallels by other critics.

(f) The music in the cycle has been fully discussed by Richard Rastall in his essay 'Music in the Cycle', No. 3 in R. M. Lumiansky and David Mills. *The Chester Mystery Cycle: Essays and Documents* (Chapel Hill, 1983), pp.111–164, to which the reader is referred. Accordingly, the Notes contain no detailed comment on the music. References to the essay in the Notes take the form: Rastall, p.161, etc.

3. *Terminology:* The following conventions should be noted:

(a) By *exemplar* is meant "the latest postulated antecedent form of the cycle common to all the cycle-manuscripts".

(b) A distinction is made between a reading which clearly corrects an error in another manuscript or other manuscripts, and one which has less objectively-definable advantages. For the former, the formula "X *is* to be preferred to Y" is used, while for the latter "X *may* be preferred to Y".

(c) For the purpose of economy of space, arabic numbers have in all cases been preferred to roman. Also, / is used to separate a part from a subsection. For play-references / separates the play-number from the line-number; for biblical references, the chapter-number from the verse-number; for patristic references, the book-number from the chapter-number; for PL and PG references, the volume-number from the column-number.

PLAY I

Dramatis Personae Deus, Luciffer/Primus Demon, Angelie, Arckeangelis, Lighteborne/Secundus Demon, Vertutes, Cherubyn, Dominaciones, Principates, Thrones, Potestates.

NOTE 1. On the probable speaking role of the Seraphim, see 153 + SH note.
2. *Ruffyn* 260 seems to have a non-speaking role.
3. No numbers for the angels in each order are specified.
4. No change of actor is assumed for the fallen angels.

Locations
Heaven — a biglie blesse 38, heaven 39, this blesse in every tower 111
Hell — a dongion of darkenes 74, dungeon 235; the deepe pitt of hell 229; helle full lowe 269.

NOTE 1. The *worlde* 73 may also be represented; see also *the same stydd* 289 and note.
2. *fall* 228, *fell* 262, etc. indicate that Hell is located beneath Heaven.

Properties
Heaven — God's cheare 88, throne 91, 130, 159; *angels'* seates 139, 206
Hell — Lucifer's cheare 271.

NOTE 1. On *helle fier* 248, see note.
2. Lucifer is *fast bounde* 271; but see note.

Costume
God — the beames of my brighte face 116; *Angels* — gayer then goulde 104
Lucifer — wounderous brighte 126 et seq.; bearer of lighte 101, of all heaven I beare the lighte 128
Devils — two feeyndes blacke 251.

NOTE The repeated image-patterns of darkness and light characterising the bad and good angels were evidently translated into visual terms throughout the play.

Sources There is no complete biblical account of the Fall of the Angels. Biblical authority is provided by passages such as Job 4/18,

PLAY I 5

Isaiah 14/12–5, Ezekiel 28/11–9, Apocalypse 12/7–9. The treatment in Chester is influenced by theology concerning the Trinity, for which Augustine's *De Trinitate* and the opening of the Athanasian Creed provide analogues; and by the theology concerning the nature of the angels and devils, for which Augustine's *De Civitate Dei*, especially bks 9–12, and Aquinas' *Summa Theologiae*, especially 1a/50–64, provide analogues. Some details of creation are taken from Genesis 1/1–2. For a fuller list of possible analogues, see P. E. Dustoor, 'The Chester "Fall of Lucifer"', *Allahabad University Studies* vi, Pt. 1 (1930), 19–57, where additional material is cited in his notes.

Play-heading The Fall of the Angels is dramatised also in Wakefield 1/1–161 (Lucifer's expulsion itself is omitted through scribal error), York 1 and *Ludus Coventriae* 1.

RB indicates the play as one of Creation, H as the Fall of Lucifer; compare 2/*Play-heading*, which in HmARB indicates the Creation of the World, whereas H also adds the Temptation of Man.

The B variants are to be preferred for morphology and meaning to R. R's errors in Latinity may derive from the misinterpretation of contracted forms in the exemplar.

Before **1** SH *Deus* evidently represents the Trinity at this point; see 9–10, 24–31, 67, 200 and 213 + Latin, and compare 116–21 note. Contrast 286 and see 286 note. The opening speech (1–35) defines godhead as a prelude to the creation of Heaven and the universe with which the action begins. Similar definitive speeches occur in Wakefield 1/1–18, York 1/1–21, *Ludus Coventriae* 1/1–28. The nature of the godhead is the preliminary subject of theological works (e.g. Peter Lombard's *Sententiae*, Aquinas' *Summa Theologiae*) and of the Athanasian Creed 1–25. The latter is required in the *Book of Common Prayer* (BCP) in place of the Apostles' Creed at morning prayer on a number of days, including Whit Sunday and Trinity Sunday. Since the Chester cycle was performed in Whit week, the services of those two days might lend added significance to the opening speech here.

1–2 Apocalypse 22/13: AV "I am Alpha and Omega, the beginning and the end, the first and the last." Compare. 2/*Before* 1 Latin and 24/*Before* 1 Latin, and notes. This quotation, or a variant of it, introduces play 1 in the other three cycles. The text in Apocalypse is in the context of the Last Judgment.

3–4 Despite a lack of precision in the reference of *soe* 3, *thus* 4, the general meaning that all things exist at God's will is clear. With 3, compare Wakefield 1/16: "Hit shall be done after my will"; with 4, compare the doxological formulae of the type made familiar by the *Gloria*: *Sicut erat in principio, et nunc, et semper, et in saecula saeculorum* (BCP "As it was in the beginning, is now and ever shall be; world without end"). See also 8/181–2 and note.

The verb-sequence in 4 ARB suggests a viewpoint from the present to past and future; that at 4 H suggests a chronological progression, and would seem more probably derived from the ARB pattern than vice-versa.

5–51, stanzas 2–4   No manuscript has the correct arrangement of these lines for all three stanzas, although H correctly presents stanzas 3 and 4 and is to be preferred to ARB there. The stanzas should appear as three eight-line stanzas, consisting of five-stress lines rhyming abababab; viz:
   stanza 2: 5+6, 7+8, 9+10, 11+12, 13+14, 15+16, 17+(17+1VR), 18+19;
   stanza 3: 20+21, 22+23, 24+25, 26+27, 28+29, 30+31, 32+33, 34+35;
   stanza 4: 36+37, 38+39, 40+41, 42+43, 44+45, 46+47, 48+49, 50+51.
The misdivision of the lines seems to have existed in the exemplar; after stanza 2, H seems to have recognised the error and corrected it, while B sporadically produces complete lines (see TNs). The manuscript-arrangement attests formally a strong medial caesura and it is possible that the misdivision could have arisen in the misinterpretation by the exemplar-scribe of some scribal indication of this caesura (e.g. by a diagonal stroke).

A number of errors occur in stanza 2 and evidently arise from the exemplar. No manuscript has *mea essentia* for *my essention*, required by rhyme at 8; *assention* B may be a scribal error or a deliberate attempt to substitute a more familiar form for *essention*; *licentia* H represents the substitution of the rhyme-word of 19 — H gives sense, but has no rhyme-word at 19, where its use of *my* for *mea* may perhaps indicate an influence on the pronoun from 8. The BH line after 17 is required for stanzaic completeness, and BH is therefore to be preferred to AR; the AR omission may have resulted from an eye-slip in A, transmitted by R, whereby *all meirth lyeth in ma....* 17 has been confused with *all lyes in my* 17+1. *licentia* 19 B is to be preferred for rhyme to the scribally erroneous *licencill* AR and to H's omission (on which see above).

exelencie 31 AR is to be preferred for rhyme to *excellence* BH; it is recorded by OED as the equivalent of *excellence* 2, "that in which a person excels", to 1601, but acquired the modern use as a title of honour (3b) from 1532. BH's substitution may indicate that the latter sense had become dominant and that the word was no longer felt to be semantically appropriate.

5–6   Compare 2/1–3, 6/329–32; also Wakefield 1/7–8, York 1/1–2, *Ludus Coventriae* 1/4. The idea of the uncreated creator is embodied in Athanasian Creed 21: *Pater a nullo factus, nec creatus, nec genitus*; similar ideas are expressed in, e.g., Rufinus, *Commentarius in Symbolum Apostolorum* (PL 21/341), Theophilus, *Ad Autolycum* (PG 6/1030) 1/4; *Cursor Mundi* 277–8.

7–8   "The whole progeny of parents (*or* of our first parents) has its basis in my essential being." *foode* 7 seems to combine the sense of "offspring" (cf. MED *fode* (2), 2) with the senses of "nourishment or sustenance for the human body" and "spiritual sustenance, comfort, support" (cf MED *fode* (1), 1 and 2). The idea of God as origin of life in every sense may be compared with passages such as Theophilus, *Ad Autolycum* 1/4 (PG 6/1030).

wholl 7 ARB may be preferred for meaning to *holy* H in stressing Man's total dependence in all things upon God. *parentes* 7 BH is to be preferred for meaning to the scribally erroneous *parente* AR; the AR form may reflect a misreading of a contracted *-es* ending in the exemplar or a confusion in the combination *-es is*.

PLAY I

9 *tryall* Compare the same word at 28. OED does not record the word in any comparable contexts, and the two occurrences seem contradictory. Here it seems the equivalent of *triune* (OED 1605–), "a group of three things united"; possibly it is an error for *triad* (OED 1546–). At 28, however, it seems to have the sense of "a third part". Compare modern *triplet*, which can be used of "a set of three", and also "one of three at birth". Although the meanings are clear from the context, the word seems unlikely to have been current or familiar.

11–2 The creative power of a personified Wisdom is stressed in biblical passages such as Proverbs 8/23: *Ab aeterno ordinata sum, et ex antiquis, antequam terra fieret* (AV "I was set up from everlasting, from the beginning, or ever the earth was"), and Ecclesiasticus 1/5: *Ego ex ore Altissimi prodivi, primogenita ante amnem creatorem*. For a similar linking of power and wisdom, compare the description of Christ in 1 Corinthians 1/24: *Dei virtutem et Dei sapientiam* (AV "The power of God and the wisdom of God"), and Augustine's gloss, *De Trinitate* 6/1 (PL 42/923).

23–7 Compare Athanasian Creed 11: *Et tamen non tres aeterni sed unus aeternus*; also Augustine, *De Trinitate* 8/1 (PL 42/947). See also 13/7–12, 23/484–97.

36–41 Compare Genesis 1/1: *In principio creavit Deus caelum et terram* (AV "In the beginning God created the heaven and the earth"). Chester interposes the creation of the angels between the two acts. Augustine, *De Civitate Dei* 11/9 (PL 41/323): "*Ubi de mundi constitutione sacrae Litterae loquuntur, non evidenter dicitur utrum vel quo ordine creati sint Angeli: sed si praetermissi non sunt, vel coeli nomine ... vel potius lucis hujus, de qua loquor, significati sunt*. Here creation of Heaven involves the creation of angels of light. See 292 note.

37 *solation* BH is to be preferred to the scribally erroneous *solatacion* AR. *solation* is recorded only three times by OED, the first occurrence being in Caxton's *Golden Legend* in 1483.

40–1 *compasse* 40 may simply indicate "a bounded area", MED *compas* 3 (b), in contrast to *a heaven without endinge* 39, thus perhaps limiting its reference to the universe; but it may, more specifically, refer to "a circle, circular area, or a sphere", MED 2(a) — compare illustrations such as "God as Architect of the Universe" (*The Flowering of the Middle Ages*, ed. Joan Evans (London, 1966) p.83) where God traces a circular universe using a pair of compasses (MED 5(a)). The word also perhaps connotes its sense of "ingenuity, subtlety, cunning", MED 1 (a).

my 41 BH may be preferred to its omission in AR in producing a more regular sequence of strongly and weakly stressed syllables.

42–3 *nyne* 42 ARB is the usual number of orders created; compare York 1/23, *Cursor Mundi* 430–1. It reflects the number in Pseudo-Dionysius, *De Coelesti Hierarchia* (PG 4/119–370), the standard treatise on angels; see 52–60 note. But *ten* H has support in, e.g., Wakefield 1/142: "Thou has maide [neyn], there was [ten]", and *Genesis B* 248. This figure is reached by including as a separate order the angels who fell; see also 53 H, 63 H, 65 H, and compare especially *this order cleare* 218. The H reading seems to be an independent substitution.

attendinge 43 H may be preferred for meaning to *defendinge* RB (and perhaps A). God has no need of defence, and traditionally the angels were created to serve him —

compare York 1/24: "In louyng ay lastande at lowte me", and *Ludus Coventriae* 1/33: "My servauntys to be." See also 68–78 and note below.

46–7   The lines have been lost in the damaged A.

48–9   "For all the delight in this noble company should take the form of praise to my glory." B and H seem uneasy at this use of *laude* R and substitute the inappropriate *lawe* and *love* respectively. *laudacion* is first recorded by OED in 1470; it shares with *laud* the sense of "act of praise", which may account for the uneasiness of B and H, but also has the passive sense of "the condition of being praised".

51 + SH   *Luciffer* See Isaiah 14/12: *Quomodo cecidisti de caelo lucifer, qui mane oriebaris?* (AV "How art thou fallen from heaven, O Lucifer, son of the morning!"); the image is used of the King of Babylon. But taken with Luke 10/18: *Videbam Satanam sicut fulgur de caelo cadentem* (AV "I beheld Satan as lightning fall from heaven"), the reference was construed as a name for the devil by influential writers such as Jerome. Its etymological sense of "light-bearer" is here translated into a dramatic image; see 101.

52–60   Pseudo-Dionysius, *De Coelesti Hierarchia* (PG 4/119–370), proposes a triple hierarchy with three orders of angels in each rank; viz: Seraphim, Cherubim, Thrones; Dominations, Virtues, Powers; Principalities, Archangels, Angels. Thrones, Dominations, Virtues, Powers and Principalities derive from a conflation of Ephesians 1/21: *Supra omnem principatum et potestatem et virtutem et dominationem, et omne nomen quod nominatur non solum in hoc saeculo sed etiam in futuro* (AV "Far above all principality, and power, and might, and dominion, and every name that is named, not only in this world, but also in that which is to come") and Colossians 1/16: *Quoniam in ipso condita sunt universa in caelis et in terra, visibilia et invisibilia; sive throni sive dominationes, sive principatus sive potestates: omnia per ipsum et in ipso creata sunt* (AV "For by him were all things created, that are in heaven, and that are in earth, visible and invisible, whether they be thrones, or dominions, or principalities, or powers: all things were created by him and for him"). To these are added the Seraphim of Isaiah 6/2, the six-winged creatures who stand above God's throne and sing his praises; the Cherubim of Genesis 3/24 and Ezekiel 1/5ff, beings with four wings and four faces, looking like fire; and the Angels and Archangels.

There seems no attempt here to reproduce the Dionysian hierarchy. But some idea of hierarchy seems intended by *more and lesse* 139. Compare the distinction in 20/104 + Latin and see note.

In Wakefield, only Cherubim speaks, in York Cherubim and Seraphim, of the orders here specified.

52   *grace and* H destroys metre but may reflect a compounding of alternatives in the exemplar, since R originally wrote *grace* after *thy* but cancelled it (see TNs). A destroys rhyme at 54 by substituting *grace* for *thought*.

56–9, stanza 6   The stanza rhymes aaab, in contrast to the abab rhyme-scheme of stanzas 5 and 7. It is tempting to postulate that *Arcangeli* 59 BH should be preferred to *Arkeangelle* AR, and that *lighte* 57 is an exemplar substitution for *lee* (cf 2/7). An abab pattern would result, thereby also permitting a rearrangement of stanzas 5–8 as two stanzas, 5 + 6 (ababcbcb) and 7 + 8 (ababbaba). Some plausibility is lent to the proposal by the fact that, of the orders, only *Angell* and *Arkeangelle* occur in anglicised form, and those only in AR. A also anglicises *archangely* at 81 + SH, and R has an erroneous from there.

63   *the principall* Lucifer is similarly established as next below God in Wakefield 1/138-41, York 1/33-40; *Ludus Coventriae* 1/40-4 is more ambiguous. Aquinas, reviewing Satan's prelapsarian status in *Summa Theologiae* 1a/63, art.7 cites Ezekiel 28/14 as evidence that Satan was a cherub, but cites to the contrary Gregory, 'De centum ovibus', (*In Evang.* II, hom.34 — PL 76/1250).

67   *with* BH may represent independent scribal insertion or an exemplar insertion. It is, however, less probable than its omission in AR, partly because it suggests an equality of angelic orders with the Trinity, and partly because its inclusion disrupts the regular sequence of strongly and weakly stressed syllables.

68-78, stanzas 9-10   The inclusion of *atending* 68 BH is to be preferred to its omission in AR, since the word is required as the a-rhyme of the stanza. Its omission in AR suggests confusion with the b-rhymes of stanza 8.

comprehending 70 BH is to be preferred for rhyme to *comprehension* AR, which suggests influence from the b-rhymes of the stanza.

76-7, although here regarded as an independent stanza, could equally be taken as a final couplet of stanza 9, giving a stanza-form ababababcc.

68   *Lightborne*   Wakefield and York provide unidentified Good and Bad Angels, the latter serving as interlocutor for the fallen Lucifer; only Chester names Lucifer's sycophantic deputy and gives him a prominent role in inciting his master; compare Octavian and Preco, play 6; Herod and the Doctor, play 8; Antichrist and his Doctor, play 23. The name seems etymologically significant, suggesting "born of light" or "borne by light"; compare also the surname *Lightburn*, "active or little child" (P. H. Reaney, *A Dictionary of British Surnames* (London, 1958) p.200).

69   "I give to my first act the blessing appropriate to the start of my work". The sense of *begyninge*, "start, onset" (MED 2(a)), is supported by *first operacion*. But Deimling cites *benignitie* H as evidence of that manuscript's superiority, regarding *begyninge* as "unintelligible"; and H perhaps provides a more readily acceptable reading.

71   "Do not raise yourselves too splendidly into the highest position." The line presents two difficulties. *exelente* does not give good sense; as absolute, it does not admit the gradation implied in *to. exellency* H seems to be an independent substitution — "Do not raise yourself to a position of honour"; but the sense is again unsatisfactory, unless the word is taken as equivalent to *excellence*, "greatness". The phrase *high exaltation* is tautologous since *exaltation* means "the zenith or culmination (of power, fame or fortune); a high or supreme degree of power or fame, exalted position"; R alone treats *exaltation* as a noun of rank, however, since *in no* BH for *into* R suggests that the noun is there taken with verbal force — cf. OED *exaltation*, "the action of lifting up or raising on high" — a reading which is possible in the corrupt A text. In H, therefore, the line would read: "Do not raise yourselves to a position of excellence by any haughty act of advancement."

73-4   The creation of the earth corresponds to Genesis 1/1-2; *voyde and vayne* 73 ARB reflects Genesis 1/2, *inanis et vacua* (AV "without form, and void"), and *vayle*

H (presumably "veiled") would seem to be an erroneous substitution based on a misunderstanding of *vayne*.

The creation of Hell, which is not mentioned in the other cycles, seems to correspond to Genesis 1/2: *Tenebrae erant super faciem abyssi* (AV "Darkness was upon the face of the deep"). But it serves here more particularly to suggest preparation for Lucifer's inevitable and foreseen fall.

75–6 The similar openings of these two lines perhaps contributed to the interchange of *wrought* 75 and *donne* 76 in ARB and H.

iwrought 75 B seems to correspond to *I wrought* 76 H. But H is metrically and syntactically acceptable because of H's other variants — the omission of *is* and the reading *these workes* for *this worke*: "I did these works well"; the loss of a syllable compensates for the addition of *I*. In B, the scribe originally wrote capital *I* after *nowe* 75, perhaps indicating an initial intention to establish *I* as subject as does H (see TNs); B then cancelled the reading and, without further syllabic loss, inserted the *i* as participial prefix, to the detriment of metre.

85 + Latin The antiphon is based on Apocalypse 4/11. *domine* in B is to be preferred to *Dei* AR in reflecting the form in the antiphon; AR perhaps misinterpret an exemplar contracted form. B is further to be preferred in supplying the opening words of the antiphon.

H gives no indication of what is to be sung at this point; compare 213 + Latin and note.

The creation of Heaven is marked by the singing of *Te Deum* at York 1/24, and *Sanctus* at York 1/41 and *Ludus Coventriae* 1/39.

87 Compare 71 and note.

88 *cheare* The throne of God, looking like a sapphire, is described in Ezekiel 1/26. The throne symbolises God's supremacy and becomes a means of dramatising Lucifer's sinful desire as indicated in Isaiah 14/14: *Similis ero Altissimo* (AV "I will be like the most High"). The act of usurpation thus replaces the idea of a "war in Heaven". The throne is similarly important in the other cycles — in Wakefield 1/104–5 and *Ludus Coventriae* 1/56–61 Lucifer also occupies God's throne, while in York 1/89–91 he is expelled either as he sits, or as he announces his intention to sit, in it. The image is an extension of Isaiah 14/13: *In caelum conscendam, super astra Dei exaltabo solium meum* (AV "I will ascend into heaven; I will exalt my throne above the stars of God"), where the words could also imply the establishment of a rival throne.

94–101, stanza 14 The stanza rhymes ababcbab instead of the expected ababab (cf. stanzas 13, 15, 16). Possibly *mayne* 98 is an exemplar error originating in the mechanical transmission of a common collocation; some other word (e.g. *meed*) may perhaps have existed in rhyme-position at an earlier stage.

94–101 The contrast of Lucifer's initial obedience and subsequent rebellion may perhaps reflect the sense that Lucifer was created good and continued for a while in the state of grace before electing to sin. Compare Augustine, *De Civitate Dei* 11/15 (PL 41/330): *Non ab initio ex quo creatus est peccare putandus est; sed ab initio peccati, quod ab ipsius superbia coeperit esse peccatum*; Aquinas, *Summa Theologiae* 1a/63, art. 5: *Agens autem quod angelos in esse produxit, scilicet Deus, non potest esse causa peccati. Unde non potest dici quod diabolus in primo instanti suae creationis fuerit malus.* No

PLAY I

similar pledge of obedience is made by Lucifer in the other three cycles, suggesting that he may there be corrupt from the start, a heretical postulation.

96 Although a more regular sequence of strongly and weakly stressed syllables results from its omission by R, *will* is attested by ABH and may well represent the exemplar reading. *aye* BH also probably represents the exemplar form; *ever* AR is a frequent substitution for *aye* by Bellin.

101 See 51 + SH note and compare 128 and Wakefield 1/71–2, York 1/36.

110–3 There is no counterpart in the other cycles to this formal delegation of authority by God to Lucifer. In York and *Ludus Coventriae* there is no clear indication of God's withdrawal, and in Wakefield 1/76 + SD it occurs without explanation. God's withdrawal here seems to constitute a form of test.

114–5 "I now command that the ground of grace should be established with my order." The exact reference of *grounde of grace* 114 and of *my order* 115 is not clear. Possibly the former refers to Heaven itself, while the latter refers to the hierarchy represented by the angels. H, however, seems to regard *grounde of grace* as figuratively referring to the angels, and hence reads *they* for *yt* 115 and *in* for *with*: "Now I command here the angels, the foundation of grace, that they should be fixed within the order that I have established."

116–21 Deus here describes the Beatific Vision, the reward of the redeemed and hence the vision forfeited by sin. See *Catholic Encyclopaedia* 7, p.171, 'Heaven': That the blessed see God is a dogma of faith expressly defined by Benedict XII (1336): "We define that the souls of all the saints in heaven have seen and do see the Divine Essence by direct intuition and face to face [*visione intuitivâ et etiam faciali*] in such wise that nothing created intervenes as an object of vision, but the Divine Essence presents itself to their immediate gaze unveiled, clearly and openly." The *Oxford Dictionary of the Christian Church* (ed. F. L. Cross, 2nd. edn. London, 1974, p.146) cites the Council of Vienne (1311) that this sight is possible by the divine gift of *lumen gloriae*.

122–5 As here punctuated, 123 represents the purpose-clause explanatory of 122, and 124 the purpose-clause explanatory of 125: "I will stay here now in this place to be a comfort to the angels. It is my will in this same hour to become visible again in a short space of time." But both 123 and 124 could be taken with 125: "I will stay here now in this place. It is my will in this same hour to be a comfort to the angels, to be visible again in a short space of time."

comforture 123 is recorded only once by MED and described as "formed for rhyme's sake"; possibly here it is to be regarded as a form of *comfortour*, MED 1(a), "one who gives spiritual strength or solace."

revisible 124 is the only example cited by OED. While it clearly means "visible again", it is not certain whether God is off-stage in the ensuing action; or hiding and watching; or actually invisible and present.

128–31 Compare Aquinas, *Summa Theologiae* 1a/63, art.3 (p.256). As here punctuated, the concessionary clause at 129 is to be taken with 128; but it could also be taken with 130–1; "Even though God himself were here, if I were on this throne, then I should be as wise as he." 129 has a double conditional, *though* and *and*.

Lucifer evidently believes that the attributes of God proceed from the trappings of position and not from divine essence, in contrast to 5–35. For parallel with Adam, compare 131 and 160–1 with 2/224.

132–3   On the use of the imagery of coronation and usurpation, see further Ruth M. Keane, *The Treatment of Kingship in the Chester Cycle with particular reference to Play 6* (unpublished M.A. thesis, University of Liverpool, 1977) pp.142–56.

With 133, compare 123.

134   *pride* Compare 166–78, 274–81. On pride as the devil's sin, see Augustine, *De Civitate Dei* 14/3 (PL 41/406); Aquinas, *Summa Theologiae* 1a/63, art.2 (*op.cit.* p.254) sees the devil's sins as envy and pride.

139   *there seates* Compare 112. With *his hestes* H compare 282. Deimling regards the ARB reading as "unintelligible" and considers H superior, but either reading is acceptable.

153 + SH   *Ceraphine* B may be preferred to *Cherubyn* R, *Cherub:* H since the Cherubim have already spoken at 138–41 while the Seraphim, listed in 54, would otherwise have no speech assigned to them in the play. *Cheraphin* A indicates an intermediate form, although seemingly supporting B rather than RH. Possibly the confusion in ascription arose in an exemplar reading resembling that of A.

159   *arte cleane and cleare* The phrase is not syntactically integrated within the sentence-structure, although it forms part of a metrically regular line. *arte* is a second person singular form, appropriate in number insofar as the person addressed is Lucifer, but inappropriate in number-concord because the subject is *you*, not *thou*. The form may be an error for *are*; or have been adopted deliberately to indicate a personal subject, since *you* 158 is widely separated from the verb; or be an unthinking substitution, since hitherto the distinction of *thou* for singular and *you* for plural address has been fairly consistently observed (cf. 78, 95, 140 as opposed to 134, 146, 150). Whatever the cause, a subject and syntactical link must be supplied: "Because you are pure and bright." A simpler solution, however, is to regard *cleane and cleare* as an adjectival phrase qualifying *throne*, as in A and BH; A replaces *arte* by a metrically unwieldly relative construction, while BH replace it by *both*. It seems probable that *both* BH was the exemplar form which for some reason displeased the AR scribe who attempted to provide a different construction.

162   H erroneously and inexplicably omits the line, writing 163–5 in a quatrain-space. Possibly the scribe was uneasy at, or misled by, the repetition of the 161 rhyme-word, although Deimling postulates that the omission indicates derivation from an exemplar lacking the line.

165 + SH–77 + SH   The ascription of speeches in AR to *Thrones* and *Potestates* is to be preferred. H omits the latter and substitutes *Angeli* for the former, apparently intending to make 166–77 a collective address comparable with 274–81; but the change leaves Thrones and Potestates without speeches. B wrote *Potestates* after 173, but then moved directly and erroneously to the start of the following speech, 178; it does not, therefore, share H's omission after 173 in the way that the VRs might suggest.

172 'And preserve the brightness that is made for you'; on the non-expression of the relative subject pronoun in a relative clause see T. Mustanoja, *A Middle English Syntax*, I (Helsinki, 1960), pp.204–5.

174–7, stanza 24   *bodye* 176 AH is to be preferred for rhyme to *bodyes* RB. The latter perhaps derives from a sense that the subject is plural; compare *thoughtes* 170 B.

174   "Alas, that the spiritual barrier created by beauty is pride." *wall*, in the sense of "well, spring", seems improbable here, and *lewtye* H does not give good sense, perhaps arising from scribal confusion of exemplar *b* and *l*.

178   H's omission of *goe hense* is to be preferred to its retention in ARB in producing a more regular sequence of strongly and weakly stressed syllables. The ARB reading seems to have been that of the exemplar and perhaps reflects a scribal failure to observe line-division, later partially corrected by restoring the phrase to 177, but without the cancellation of the inclusion at 178.

178–93   Compare 187 with 71, 192 with 123, 193 with 20. With 188–9, compare 19/180–1, 19/244–5, 24/425–8.

195   "Perfect, as all can see." Although *replete* is not recorded in this sense by OED before 1601, some finite quality seems required here — contrast 211, where it has the more usual sense of "filled". With the meaning of *experience* proposed, compare *experience* MED 2(a) "what is found out by investigation or experiment" and 3 "what is observed or experienced by the sense, sense perceptions". H's reversal of *by all* suggests that in H *all* is an adverb — "completely by observation".

207–9   *playe* represents a pun on the senses of the word, as "activity" and also "mimetic action", since Satan's act here initiates both the action of the conflict of good and evil and also the action of the Chester Cycle itself. *daunce* 209 seems an almost jocular understatement; compare *daunce* MED 4a *Fig.* (b) "a situation or predicament".
subsequence 208, "sequel", is first recorded by OED only in 1500.

213 + Latin   This Vespers antiphon for Trinity Sunday is omitted in H, which has a SD at 212; with the failure to specify an antiphon, compare 85 + SD note. The omission may, however, be a scribal error occurring in the change from fol.3^r to fol.3^v in H.
212 + SD H seems to be misplaced, since Lucifer sits on the throne at 183.

216   "I made you, angel, and [you], Lucifer." *thee* refers to Lightborn; the pronoun reference changes to Lucifer at *thou* 217, but a pronoun should be understood before *Lucifer* 216. H, perhaps troubled by the shift in pronominal reference, reads *an angell* for *angell and*, thereby making 216 refer solely to Lucifer.

223–5   223 and 225 H suggest a partial transposition of the ARB lines, with change of pronoun and the substitution of *trespast* for *offended* 223.

226–7   *were* 226 ARB indicates a plural subject, all the rebellious angels, comprehended under *you* 228; *was* H suggests that the subject is Lucifer alone, as at 224–5.
sate 227 H is to be preferred for tense to *sitt* R, *sett* B; compare *were* 226. The verb is lost in A.

232 Sorrow is the sole torment of the devils; compare Aquinas, *Summa Theologiae* 1a/64 art.3 Comparable recriminations occur in Wakefield 1/132-61, York 1/97-120.

236 "You have sought out all this sorrow for us." *us* ARB is dative; *yt* H is a pronoun object, referring to *sorrowe*.

240 Both *cumber* (MED *combren* 1(a) "to trouble, vex (sb)") and *congere* (MED *conjuren* 1(b) "beseech or beg (sb.), implore") seem attested only in transitive use. *canker* H seems to be a substitution acknowledging the marginal semantic appropriateness of *congere*. The words are evidently used loosely for alliterative effect.

246-9, stanza 35   The stanza rhymes abcb, instead of the expected abab (cf. stanzas 33, 34, 36, 37, 38). *pine* 248 BH supplies the required a-rhyme and is to be preferred to *fier* AR, the mechanical transmission of a common collocation. The AR reading is the only evidence of a fiery hell in the play. The image is rather of a castle with a dungeon below; compare 74, 235, and *Piers Plowman* B Text, Prologue 14-5.

249 *beames* ABH is to be preferred for meaning to the scribally erroneous *beanes* R.

249+SH H omits this and the subsequent *Demon* SHs at 253+, 265+, 269+. Since these omissions continue through fols. 3^v-4^r and normal practice resumes at 273+SH, the omissions seem to be deliberate. They have the effect of making 246-73 an extended speech by Lucifer, balancing the final extended speech by Deus.

251 *blacke* The loss of spiritual illumination is symbolised by the change of outward appearance and prepares for the later separation of light and darkness. Compare Augustine, *De Civitate Dei*, 11/19 (PL 41/333).

254-65 This is the first reference to the future creation of Man. Lucifer appears to know God's immediate intention, although it has not been announced; compare *Ludus Coventriae* 2/317-24 and *Genesis B* 364-8. Lucifer lacks Adam's wider knowledge — see 2/449-72 and 2/436-72 note.

260 *Ruffyn* Compare 5/213. The name is well attested in Middle English, though unbiblical and of unknown etymology. OED records it to 1500 as the name of a devil, and to 1641 as *"Cant.* The Devil". 2/165-8, however, indicates that the temptation of Man is undertaken by Lucifer himself.

262 "[The bliss] from which I and my fellows fell [and will remain separated from] for ever." As here punctuated, *that* is relative pronoun, and *downe* conveys a sense of separation suggested in modern English by the preposition *from*; *for aye* indicates continuation of the state of separation, not of the action of falling. Alternatively, 262 could be taken with 263, with *that* 262 as pronoun object of *ordeyne* 263: "What I and my fellows fell from [and remain separated from] for ever, he will ordain again to mankind."

270-3 Compare *Genesis* B 378-88. Lucifer is presumably not physically bound to his chair but condemned to eternity in Hell wherever he is; compare Aquinas, *Summa Theologiae* 1a/64, art.4.

274-81, stanza 42   *blisse* 277 BH is to be preferred to *blesse* AR for perfect rhyme. Such formal variants in this word are common and will not be consistently noted in rhyme-position.

PLAY I

286–9 *I and two persons* 286 suggests that *Deus* no longer speaks as the Trinity, but in the person of God the Father, responsible for the creation of natural things. Compare Comestor, *Historia Scholastica*, 'Liber Genesis' 9 (PL 198/1063): *Deinde subditur de creatione hominis sic: "Faciamus hominem"* etc (Gen.1). *Et loquitur Pater ad Filium, et Spiritum sanctum. Vel est quasi communis vox trium personarum, "Faciamus", et "nostram"*.

288–9, like 2/81–8, derive from Genesis 1/27–8; *image* specifically recalls Genesis 1/27: *Et creavit Deus hominem ad imaginem suam* (AV "So God created man in his own image"). In context, *the same stydd* 289 could refer to the places vacated by the fallen angels — cf. 264–5; but it also corresponds to God's injunction at Genesis 1/28: *Replete terram* (AV "Replenish the earth"), and Adam is set in the earthly paradise, 2/171, so that the reference may also be to the earth, created at 73.

291 "Here I begin the first [of a series of acts] which shall be to my pleasure". *first* ARB continues the sense of series suggested by *begyne*; H supplies a noun object, to the detriment of metre.

292–3 Based on Genesis 1/4–5; compare 2/9–16, where the creation of light is followed by the separation of light and darkness again. Although H adds Genesis 1/3 beside 290, that text has no direct counterpart in play 1; the creation of light is here included in the creation of heaven and the separation of light and darkness has symbolic force. As the creation of the bright angels precedes and involves the creation of light, so the separation of the damned and blackened angels 251 in the dungeon of darkness 74 precedes and involves the separation of light and darkness. See Augustine, *De Civitate Dei* 11/9 (PL 41/325 and 333), also Comestor, *Historia Scholastica*, 'Liber Genesis' 3 (PL 198/1057). See also 1/294 and 2/9–10 and notes, and *ME Genesis and Exodus* 57–76.

294 The metaphysical separation of light and darkness, Genesis 1/4–5, is followed by the creation of the sun and moon, Genesis 1/16. Some overlap of the two acts may be implied by *keepe your course*; see *cours* MED 8, and compare *courses of planets* 2/53.

295 *suffer not* The construction is elliptical and requires an infinitive construction to be understood: "And I say to you, do not allow yourselves to do otherwise". Taken with 294, this represents an injunction to obedience; taken with 296, it introduces an address to the angels and audience, with a change of pronoun reference from *yow* (i.e. darkness and light) 294 to *yourselfe* (i.e. angels and audience) 295.

With 297, compare 3.

300 Based on Genesis 1/5. The metaphysical extension of the creation and separation of light and darkness to the creation and separation of the angels limits the action of the play to the first day of Creation. Only Wakefield of the English cycles places the fall of the angels on the fifth day.

PLAY II

Dramatis Personae Deus, Adam, Demon/Serpens, Eva, Primus Angelus, Secundus Angelus, Tercius Angelus, Quartus Angelus, Cayne, Abell.

NOTE Minstrelles are required at 112+SD, 280+SD, 384+SD.

Locations
the place where he [God] was — 80+SD
the place where he [God] createth Adam — 80+SD
paradice 112+SD, 207, 384+SD, yeartly paradice 171, this wyninge 404, this dwellinge 415, this cyttye 411, this wonninge 420; *containing* beastes and fowles 125, trees 280+SD; the tree of knowledge 112+SD, the tree of paradice 197, tree 119, 121, 187, *bearing* fruit 123, 190, 233, one/this apple 240, 245, 250.
earth 6, 81, yearth 93, 381.
the fyeld 595.

NOTE 1. The items created by God, 1–80, are not listed above.
2. *herbes, trees. fruite, seede* 90, *beastes* 92, *fowles in the ayre flyinge* 94 are mentioned in the context of paradise, but not necessarily realised visually.
3. The relation of earth to paradise is indicated by *thyder* 381; that of the field to the place of sacrifice by *a little froo* 595.
4. The serpent comes up from a *hole* 160+SD.

Properties
ribbe 128+SD, 136+SD, a bone 134; fleshe 135; this figge-leaves 274, leaves 280+SD; sharpe swordes 389, swordes of fyer 413, 422, flame of fyer 390; spade 494; plough 516+SD; wooll 503
Abel's sacrifice — the comlyest beaste 523, the beste beaste of all my flocke 557-8
Cain's sacrifice — corne 517, *of three kinds* — those fayre eares 538, such as the fruite is fallen froo 531, this earles corne 541
God's acceptance — a flame of fyer 560+SD, 565, 571.

NOTE 1. God's fire comes *from heaven on high* 566.
2. 496+SD H specifies *colum* for Eve.

Costume
Serpent — wynges 194, feete as an edder, a maydens face 195; the edders coate 206; suprema, volucris penna; serpens pede; forma, forma puella 208+SD.

PLAY II

Fallen Man — deade beaste skynes 363, such clothes 367, garmentes of skynnes 368 + SD.

Sources The play falls into three sections — creation of the universe, the world and natural things 1–128, based on Genesis 1/1–2/2; the creation and fall of Man, 129–424, based on Genesis 2/4–3/24; and the murder of Abel by his brother, Cain, 425–*Finis*, based on Genesis 4/2–15. A. C. Baugh, 'The Chester Plays and French Influence', compares the play with the corresponding portion of Greban's *Passion*, claiming "The succession of events and even of speeches is in general remarkably alike" (p.51), in support of the thesis of the presence of French influence in the Chester Cycle.

Play-heading Compare 1/*Play-heading* and note. No manuscript indicates that the play consists of the three episodes listed above; HmARB suggest it is about the creation of the world, to which H adds the temptation of Adam and Eve. Cain and Abel are not mentioned.

All three episodes have counterparts in the other English cycles; viz:
Creation of the universe — Wakefield 1/1–60, 162–4; York 1–2; *Ludus Coventriae* 1/30–9, 2/83–93 (1–2 are numbered continuously in Block's edition).
Creation and fall of Man — Wakefield 1/165–249 (the episode of the fall and expulsion from Eden is lost), York 3–6, *Ludus Coventriae* 2/96–*Finis*.
Cain and Abel — Wakefield 2, York 7, *Ludus Coventriae* 3.

Two versions of the Norwich *Fall of Man*, A and B, are extant. No other English cycle combines "Cain and Abel" with the accounts of creation and Man's fall, but since the pattern is chronological, the episodes follow in continuous action in the Cornish *Ordinalia*, pp.3–19, and the AN *Adam* 1–744. In *Mistere*, some apocryphal material intervenes.

be H is evidently an error for *de*; *creavit* B is a substitution, B perhaps not recognising *docuit*.

Before **1** *Latin* Compare 1/1–2, 24/*Before* 1 *Latin*, and notes. The quotation is as appropriate to the physical creation of play 2 as to the metaphysical creation of play 1. Norwich A and B have comparable quotations at line 1 and also had a preceding play of the creation of the universe, now lost. In 1, God, who is without beginning 1/6, creates a heaven that has beginning but no ending; here, God, who is without beginning or ending 2–3, creates a universe which is finite. Hence there is paradox in the presentation of God from the human viewpoint here and from the divine in 2-3, the latter reversing rather than translating the Latin.

The force of *1* is not clear. Possibly it represents a mark of division (compare the division of the quotation in 1/1-2) which has been incorporated into the text erroneously by Hm.

H's omission of the Latin may indicate unease at the repetition of the text from play 1.

1-16   The lines echo lines in play 1 — compare 1-4 with 1/3-4, 5-6 with 1/73, 11-14 with 1/292-3, 15-16 with 1/300-1. The creation of heaven and earth at 1/39-41 is presupposed in 5; but the creation of light at 1/36-41 is repeated at 9-10 and the events of the first day are recapitulated (cf. 161-70). If a shortened version of the cycle was required, it would be possible to omit play 1.

3   *endles* ARBH is to be preferred for meaning to the scribally erroneous *enlesse* Hm.

8   *liever* MED does not record a verb-root *lever*, formally required by rhyme, and no manuscript contains such a form. *liver* AR suggests *liveren* MED 1(a) "to procure freedom or deliverance for"; *liever* Hm probably represents the same word, with some formal modification in acknowledgement of its rhyming function. *be ever* B is an inappropriate substitution, perhaps arising from unease at the form and/or meaning of HmAR. *kever* H represents *coveren*, MED v. (2), 5(a), "to acquire, obtain or secure (sth)" and may be preferred for form, rhyme and meaning; scribal confusion of *k* and *l* may be postulated to explain the variation, but it seems most probable that the exemplar-reading was indistinct or erroneous and that H has substituted the most probable form.

The H verb should be read in conjunction with H's *crafte* for *might* HmARB, since H contains an alliterative phrase. It is impossible to assign priority to the readings, though *crafte* would be more probable if the verb was *kever* and its additional sense of "skill or art designed to deceive or overreach" (OED *craft* 4) could lead to its substitution by *might*.

12   *thestearnes* This is the latest occurrence of the word cited by OED; see also 14. *the steres/stares*, B's substitutions for the two occurrences, destroy the biblical sense, but may reflect unfamiliarity with the word.

18   *watters* ARBH is to be preferred to *water* Hm in reflecting Genesis 1/6: *Fiat firmamentum in medio aquarum* (AV "Let there be a firmament in the midst of the waters"). Compare *waters* 20, 25, 30.

23   *thus* AH may be preferred for meaning to *this* HmRB. It is, however, notable that R does not here follow A. The sentence differs in construction from the comparable sentences at 15, 39, 55, 69, all of which appropriately begin with *this*; the reading here may therefore be mechanical, or even indicative of a changed word-order.

morne and even Here, as at 15, 39, 55, 69, the text reverses the biblical word-order; compare Genesis 1/8: *Et factum est vespere et mane, dies secundus* (AV "And the evening and the morning were the second day"). Although *even and morrow* H restores the biblical sequence, it cannot here be preferred since it is the only instance in which H does this.

25–8 "Now I will that all the waters that are in great abundance under heaven gather into one, and dry land at once appear." The construction at 28 is not clear; presumably *them* is a reflexive pronoun and *drynesse* regarded as a collective noun with plural force: "And areas of dry land show themselves". *him* H provides the more expected singular reflexive: "And dry land show itself".

together 27 H may suggest an incompleted intention to write *gather together*, corresponding to Genesis 1/9, *congregentur* (AV "be gathered together").

31 *name* H is to be preferred for meaning to *man* HmAR, *men* B. Compare Genesis 1/10: *Congregationesque aquarum appellavit maria* (AV "And the gathering together of the waters called he Seas"). The exemplar perhaps read *nam*, which H has correctly taken as *name* but which HmAR have understood as *man* and B, perhaps influenced by *men* 32, has further modified to *men*. The sense of the resulting construction in HmARB is obscure, except perhaps in R, where *shewe* restores sense at the expense of rhyme: "They shall reveal seas to Man". In Genesis 1/10, God merely bestows the names — compare Genesis 1/5 and lines 13–4 — and some confusion has resulted from the dramatist's introduction of a reference to human language at this point.

35 *frutes* ARBH is to be preferred for morphology to *fruite* Hm. Although Genesis 1/11 employs collective singular forms here (*herbam virentem, lignum*), its *fructum* cannot be used to support the Hm reading since Hm has in other cases plural nouns (*yerbes* 33, *trees* 34).

39 No manuscript has *day* for *dayes*, required for meaning. *dayes* was evidently the exemplar form, perhaps influenced by the use of *three*; in all other cases, the ordinal form of the number is used (cf. 15, 24, 56, 70).

41–4 Compare Genesis 1/14–6. *lightninges* 42 Hm corresponds to *luminaria*, Genesis 1/14 (AV "lights"), but *light(e)ning* does not seem to be recorded in exactly this sense by OED or MED. *lightninge* ARBH may indicate unease at this form, but the result neither conveys the biblical sense nor gives good sense in context. The biblical account merely refers to the lights as *luminare maius* and *luminare minus*, Genesis 1/16 (AV "the greater light" and "the lesser light"); contrast 46–8.

45 *also, make* H may be preferred to their omission in HmARB in producing a more regular sequence of strongly and weakly stressed syllables.

52–3 "And by that [i.e. the positions of the stars] the movements of planets may be known". The passage has no direct biblical counterpart, but compare Genesis 1/14: *Et sint in signa et tempora, et dies et annos* (AV "And let them be for signs, and for seasons, and for days, and years"). The dramatist seems to distinguish the fixed stars from the moving planets which constitute the 'fingers' of the sideral clock and provide *signa* not only of time but of human events. Compare Comestor, *Historia Scholastica*, 'Liber Genesis' 6 (PL 198/1060–1).

60 The means of creation is not mentioned in the biblical account. The line suggests, however, that matter originates in the mind of God and probably reflects the standard medieval concept of visible matter as the manifestation of divine ideas; compare Aquinas, *Summa Theologiae* 1a/44 art.3 (p.16). Compare also 1/7–8 and note.

61–5 *beastes* 61 apparently refers to the *great whalles* 59, the sea-creatures distinct from the *fowles* 58; but at 65 *beastes* seems to refer to both land- and water-creatures, although the land-based animals are not created until the sixth day, 73–80. It might be possible to read into *by and by* 66 an indication that the injunction comprehends not only creatures already created but also those still to be created. Although such a reading seems tenuous, since at Genesis 1/22 the injunction to multiply is directed only to sea- and air-creatures, the injunction was commonly interpreted with wider application. Compare Comestor, *Historia Scholastica*, 'Liber Genesis' 8 (PL 198/1063).

61 seems to contain five strongly stressed syllables instead of the expected four. H's omission of *fruit* produces a four-stress line, although *stone* is the item not previously mentioned.

64 *this worke* HmAR seems to refer collectively to all that has been created; *thees work* B is clearly singular, but the preceding demonstrative may suggest an initial intention to substitute a plural form, as in *these workes* H. Compare *these workes* 62.

74 *helpely beastes* Compare Genesis 1/24: *Iumenta et reptilia et bestias terrae secundum species suas* (AV "Cattle, and creeping thing, and beast of the earth after his kind"). It seems unlikely that the phrase here is equivalent to *iumenta*, despite Comestor, *Historia Scholastica*, 'Liber Genesis' 8 (PL 198/1062): *Dedit ei iumenta, quasi adjuvamenta, ad opus, vel ad esum*. More probably, in view of the universal reference of 75, it suggests the pre-lapsarian state in which all beasts served the will of Man — compare 2/83–4, 89–96. *kindes of* H, for *helpely* HmARB, seems to be suggestive of the biblical *secundum species suas*.

81–5 Compare 1/286–9 and note. With the sequence *fishe, fowle, beast* 83, compare Genesis 1/26: *Et praesit piscibus maris, et volatilibus caeli, et bestiis* (AV "And let them have dominion over the fish of the sea, and over the fowl of the air, and over the cattle"). Although 83 appears to have five strongly stressed syllables instead of the expected four, A's omission of *beast* is clearly erroneous; *beastes* B corresponds to *bestiis*, but must be considered an error in view of the preference for collective singulars in *fishe fowle; both* H is an unnecessary substitution which destroys correspondence with the biblical text.

90 Compare Genesis 1/29: *Ecce dedi vobis omnem herbam afferentem semen super terram, et universa ligna quae habent in semetipsis sementem generis sui* (AV "Behold I have given you every herb bearing seed which is upon the face of all the earth, and every tree, in the which is the fruit of a tree yielding seed").

91 H erroneously and inexplicably omits *put* HmARB, thereby reducing the number of strongly stressed syllables from the required four to three.

101 "Heaven and earth is completed in the time indicated by the sixth day." *within* is best taken as a temporal adverb, gaining its full sense from the reference to *the sixt day*, 99; the ARB variant is possible, but gives weakened sense and has no scriptural basis. *wrought all*, "made entirely", corresponds to *perfecti* in Genesis 2/1: *Igitur perfecti sunt coeli et terra, et omnis ornatus eorum* (AV "Thus the heaven and the earth were finished, and all the host of them"). The passage, alone of those mentioning the completion of a day, has no counterpart to the reference to morning and evening, Genesis 1/31.

PLAY II

103-4 Genesis presents two versions of Man's creation; at 1/26-7 God first announces his intention, then creates Man, male and female. At 2/7, after the account of God's sabbatical rest, Adam is created from dust, vital spirit breathed into him, and he is established in Eden, where Eve is formed from his rib. Chester combines the accounts — announced intention 82-6, creation of Adam's inanimate body 85, animation of body, 105-10. God's sabbatical rest is not shown, but reference is made to it in *tomorrowe, the seaventh day* 103; *but* 105 suggests that the animation of Adam will be carried out before this rest, and it may therefore be assumed that Chester follows the Jewish and early patristic tradition that Adam fell on the day of his creation — compare Pseudo-Chrysostom, *In Sancta et Magna Parasceve*, which links the traditional Friday of the Fall with the Friday of the Crucifixion. Hence, God's rest would follow 384, the end of day six. In York, God creates both Adam and Eve before announcing his intention to rest at the end of Play 3 (3/90-2) and begins Play 4 by establishing them in Paradise. In *Ludus Coventriae* God creates Adam and Eve and places them in Paradise, admonishing them, before retiring to Heaven and, by implication, leaving Man at the mercy of the devil.

105-12, stanza 14   The stanza rhymes aabcbdbc; 108 seems to contain four strongly-stressed syllables instead of the expected three. The indentation-pattern of 107-12 Hm (see TNs) provides additional evidence that this section of the stanza had been mistaken for an independent unit which, in Hm, would rhyme abacab; this misunderstanding may have generated or been the result of the HmAR rhyme-pattern.

  rade 107 H is to be preferred for rhyme to *ryse* HmAR; B has erroneously omitted *rise* (2), but confirms *ra(y)de* as the rhyme-word. The last example of *rade* adv. cited by OED is c.1525; *ryse* may represent an alteration in the exemplar, whereby an obsolete form has been cancelled and the verb repeated. At 108, a regular three-stress line would result from the omission of *full*, attested by all manuscripts and evidently the exemplar reading. *delice* 110 BH is to be preferred for rhyme to *delite* HmAR, the latter apparently resulting from independent scribal confusion of *c* and *t* and perhaps also formal preference.

109   *paradice* Compare 171, 16A/323-4, 17/229-52, 23/253-84ff. A distinction is here clearly made between earthly and heavenly paradise; compare Augustine, *De Genesi ad Litteram* 8/1 (PL 34/371).

113-120, stanza 15   *saye* 116 ARBH is to be preferred for rhyme to the erroneous *bydd* Hm.

119   *this tree* i.e. *the tree of knowledge*, 112 + SD, although the H form of the SD does not specify the tree; although its function is defined, the audience is given no name for it apart from the devil's *the tree of paradyce* 197. Compare Genesis 2/9: *Lignumque scientiae boni et mali* (AV "The tree of knowledge of good and evil"). Although Eve knows of God's prohibition, 219-20, she is never seen to be warned — compare York, where God warns both Adam and Eve, 3/56-9; *Ludus Coventriae*, where Eve's creation, 2/100-1, precedes God's warning of 2/120; and Norwich A, 31-4 where God warns Adam and commands him to warn Eve.

123   *thee thou* ARB suggests that the construction in this line is a noun-clause with *that* suppressed, and that 124 is a parallel construction: "Therefore I will that you avoid this fruit and be not too presumptuous". *thee* Hm suggests that the construction at 123 is an infinitive phrase and that 124 is independent: "Therefore I desire you to avoid this fruit, and do not be too presumptuous." *not* H is an erroneous substitution, perhaps influenced by *not* 124.

128 + SD   The SD relates to the actions accompanying 129–36, as indicated by the SD at 130 H. The bone removed from Adam is identified as a rib only in the SD.

131–3   Compare Genesis 2/21: *Immisit ergo Dominus Deus soporem in Adam* (AV "And the Lord God caused a deep sleep to fall upon Adam"). *excite* 131 BH is to be preferred for meaning to the scribally erroneous *excice* Hm and the semantically inappropriate *excesse* AR. The AR reading may originate in a misreading of the exemplar similar to that in Hm, where *t* and *c* have been confused; that the scribe was conscious of the error may, however, be inferred from his substitution of *to make one,* ?"to make whole", for *anon in* 132 HmBH, since the latter yields no sense with the replacement of *excite*.

On the sleep, see further 139–40, 145–60 and note, 441–7 and note.

135   Compare 145. The reference to flesh may anticipate Genesis 2/23 or represent a misunderstanding of Genesis 2/21: *Replevit carnem pro ea* (AV "Closed up the flesh instead thereof").

145–60   Adam's words are uttered through God's *grace* 145 because he has no means of recognising that Eve is of his bone and flesh; compare Chrysostom, *In Cap 2 Genesim Homilia*, 15/13 (PG 53/122). Augustine, *De Genesi ad Litteram* 9/19 (PL 34/408), notes that Adam's words at Genesis 2/23 (145–9) are ascribed to God by Christ in Matthew 19/4, and suggests that this indicates a further prophetic revelation resulting from Adam's sleep. See 441–7 and note.

bones 146 is to be preferred to *bone* H in reflecting the biblical *ossibus*.

149–52   So Genesis 2/23: *Haec vocabitur virago quoniam de viro sumpta est* (AV "She shall be called Woman, because she was taken out of Man"); compare 269–72. Of dramatic analogues, only Cornish Ordinalia (tr. Markham Harris, Washington, 1969, p.5): "I will name her Virago", uses the text, and without explanation.

The woman does not receive the name Eve until she has fallen; compare Genesis 3/20: *Et vocavit Adam nomen uxoris suae Heva, eo quod mater esset cunctorum viventium* (AV "And Adam called his wife's name Eve, because she was the mother of all living"). But no cycle follows this sequence. *Ludus Coventriae* alone assigns no name to the woman in the spoken text. In York 3/44 and AN *Adam* 10 God gives Eve her name soon after her creation; compare Trevisa's translation of Methodius, *þe bygynnyng of þe World*: "And [God] cleped þe names of hem Adam and Eve." In Cornish Ordinalia, p.6, the serpent first addresses her as Eve. Here Adam calls her Eve at 253; the name is unexplained.

157–60   Compare Genesis 2/23. The text is cited in support of the divine institution of marriage in Matthew 19/5, Mark 10/7 and by St. Paul, Ephesians 5/31; compare BCP, 'The Form of Solemnization of Matrimony': "Almighty God, who at the beginning did create our first parents, Adam and Eve, and did sanctify and join them together in marriage." Here, the suggestion seems to be that sexual union in marriage constitutes the natural (*kyndely* 157) and joyful (*for to glad* 160) recreation of the original unity created by God (*as thou can make* 159) before its dispersion into male

PLAY II

and female. Similar ideas, though depending more directly upon Ephesians 5, occur in AN *Adam* 9–24; with the stress on mutual delight, compare *Cleanness* 697–708.

169–76, stanza 22   *weene* 172 Hm gives imperfect rhyme; *wen* A is apparently a scribal variant of the same word. *wyne* R suggests the forms *win(n)* and *wyn(n)*, listed as seventeenth-century by OED, and is to be preferred. *mynne* BH is also acceptable for rhyme. The choice semantically lies between "surmise" (*ween* OED1) and "remember" (*min* V² OED 26).

169–72   See 109 note.

179–88   No reason is given in the biblical account for the serpent's approach to Eve, but Jewish legend, followed by the Church Fathers (e.g. Augustine, *De Genesi ad Litteram* 11/30 (PL 34/445)), affirmed that the serpent approached her because she was the more gullible. Such an approach accords well with medieval antifeminist literary tradition. Compare also 271–2, 349–52.

193–6   Compare Comester, *Historia Scholastica*, 'Liber Genesis' 21 (PL 198/1072): *Et hoc per serpentem, quia tunc serpens erectus est ut homo, quia in maledictione prostratus est, et adhuc, ut tradunt, phareas erectus incedit. Elegit etiam quoddam genus serpentis, ut ait Beda, virgineum vultum habens, quia similia similibus applaudunt, et movit ad loquendum linguam ejus.* In York the devil is a *worme*, 5/54–5; in *Ludus Coventriae a worme with an aungelys face*, 2/302; in Norwich an angel, A74, B40; in the Cornish Ordinalia variously, a serpent, an angel, and an evil bird. Chester finds a convenient solution to the dramatic problem of the transformation of the devil. See 206 note and 208 + SD note.

203   *valley baylie* H, *baille*, MED n.2(a), "the wall surrounding a castle or fortified city", may be preferred as continuing the castle-image from play 1 and suggesting a walled fortification — compare *cittye* 411; H's use post-dates the last instance in OED (a.1325) and MED (a.1500) of the word before the nineteenth century. *valley* contradicts the probability that Eden was on a high site so that the rivers could flow out from it.

208 + SD   "Upper part of the body with feather of a bird; serpent, by shape in the foot; in figure, a girl." If the Latin is indeed a version of 193–6, it should read: *Volucris penna, serpentis pede, forma puellae*. HmARB seem in error in repeating *forma*, and *fronte* H gives rather better sense. *supremus* presents a difficulty, capable of a number of resolutions. A misread contraction of *serpens, spns*, could provide a basis for all the readings; or *supremus/superius* may be intended, to suggest that the wings are "on top, higher up"; or *superius* may suggest that the Latin is to be placed higher in the text, i.e. beside 193–6 — an editorial comment in the exemplar comparable with *Versus* H. *spinx* H suggests comparison with the sphinx, a mythical being with maiden's face and bird's wings but a lion's body.

209–10   "Woman, why was God so foolish as to give you permission for your delight and yet bid you avoid the fruit of every tree in Paradise?" H evidently read *leave* as infinitive and replaced preposition by adverb at 210.

221–4   The serpent's words are significantly different from those in Genesis 3/4: *Nequaquam morte moriemini* (AV "Ye shall not surely die").

233-40, stanza 30   The stanza rhymes aaabcccc; 239 contains three strongly stressed syllables instead of the expected four, 240 four instead of the expected three. The arrangement of lines in H, whereby 240 precedes 237, is to be preferred, since it provides a potential b-rhyme for *false* and restores the three-stress 239 to final position. No manuscript has, however, the correct form, *als*, at 239. The destruction of the second b-rhyme and the re-arrangement of the lines are clearly interdependent.

240   *one apple* Although the fruit of the tree of knowledge is not specified in Genesis, it was traditionally apples. Since Eve evidently takes only one apple, of which Adam also eats some, 250, *morsell* 240 R gives sense. In *Ludus Coventriae* Eve takes one apple for herself and another for Adam, 2/191; in the *Cornish Ordinalia* she picks a handful. Compare 256, 291.

248 + SD   Compare 233, 240. The Serpent evidently picked the apple and offered it to Eve, in contradiction to Genesis 3/6, of Eve: *Tulit de fructu illius* (AV "She took of the fruit thereof"). The nearest equivalent appears to be the Cornish Ordinalia, where the serpent bends the branches down so that Eve may pick the apple. In R, however, the text may suggest that Eve takes the fruit herself from the tree, if *of* (3) rather than *of* (2) is taken as possessive: "Eve takes the fruit from the serpent's tree" (i.e. the tree in which the serpent has placed himself).

249-56   The dialogue is unbiblical, but a pretext for it may be found in Bede, *Hexaemeron*, Lib 1 (PL 91/54): *Atque ideo " Tulit de fructu illius, et comedit, deditque viro suo", fortassis etiam cum verbo suasorio, quod Scriptura tacens intelligendum reliquit*. Adam here appears to be unaware of the nature of the fruit and is therefore deceived, whereas in other plays he eats with full knowledge — compare York 5/83-8, *Ludus Coventriae* 2/234-7, Cornish Ordinalia, pp.8-9. The ignorance blurs the parallel with Christ's resistance to temptation, 12/169-216.

252 + SD H relates to the action following 256 and seems misplaced.

253   *Eve* See 149-52 note.

260   *be*, attested by AR and H, may be preferred to its omission in HmB in supplying a necessary auxiliary verb and producing a more regular sequence of strongly and weakly stressed syllables. But the omission in HmB may suggest that *shente* is considered parallel to *cursed* 259 and that *mote bee* is to be understood at 260: "Woman, may thou be cursed, for we may both now be destroyed".

266   *hir* The sex of the serpent is presumably determined for Eve by its possession of a maiden's face; compare *shee* 294 (*om* H).

269-72   Compare 149-53; Adam made no such prophecy. The etymology has the appearance of a commonplace, comically reversed by Chaucer's Nun's Priest:

> *Mulier est hominis confusio,*—
> Madame, the sentence of this Latyn is,
> 'Womman is mannes joye and al his blis'.
> (*Canterbury Tales* VII/3164-6)

275   *hillinge* is perhaps used in HmAB in the sense of "something that protects" (MED *hilinge* 1(d) — cf. "hiling of reasonable cloþis" cited as example); *hillinges* R is evidently an error in view of the article. But H seems to take it as "a garment, vestment, clothing" (MED 1(b)), deleting the article and substituting a plural noun.

280 + SD In Genesis 3/8, Adam and Eve hide only when they hear the voice of God. The SD seems to refer to Adam's comment at 278, but there the suggestion seems to be that Adam remains under the tree of knowledge; compare *sub arbore* H. The position of the SD in H perhaps suggests an attempt to match the sequence of actions to the Genesis account. On the other hand, Adam hides before God's arrival at York 5/135-7, Norwich B 68, Cornish Ordinalia p.9; so also *Cursor Mundi* 859-62.

284-8 The past tense, *hyd* 284 Hm, is required both by the sequence of verbs in the preceding lines and by the source, Genesis 3/8. *hyde* ARBH suggests that Adam is still hiding. But *forbade* 288 RBH is indicated by the general sense and by Genesis 3/11, in preference to *forbydd* Hm; A evidently also read *forbade* here.

290 *me* ARBH is to be preferred to its omission in Hm in reflecting Genesis 3/12: *Mulier quam dedisti mihi sociam* (AV "The woman whom thou gavest to be with me").

309 + SD H Presumably the serpent's exit follows 312 in H. In HmARB, however, the serpent remains, since she is included in Adam's reference to *you too* at 359. Since H has already removed the serpent, it reads *them* at 359 instead.

309-11 "There is no beast on earth, I promise you, that Man shall esteem so little, and you shall be trodden under foot." The meaning of Genesis 3/15 — a form of which is quoted beside the lines in H (see TNs) — is obscure: *Ipsa conteret caput tuum, et tu insidiaberis calcaneo eius* (AV "It shall bruise thy head and thou shalt bruise his heel"). It is broadly rendered by 305-8, and 309-10 has no biblical counterpart, but 311 may further reflect the Genesis account.

Rhyme supports *feete* 311 ARBH against *foote* Hm, but *his* ARB seems to overweight the line syllabically, a fault redressed by B's omission of *bee*. Despite *man* 310, the rest of the speech, and Genesis 3/15, suggests that the reference is to the woman.

327 *thee* ARBH is to be preferred for rhyme to its erroneous omission in Hm.

345-60 Without biblical counterpart. Laments, repentance and mutual recriminations are dramatised in York 6/24-168, *Ludus Coventriae* 2/378-416, AN *Adam* 519-590, *Mistère* 1561-1620. Compare 269-72.

363-6 Without biblical counterpart. See Comestor, *Historia Scholastica*, 'Liber Genesis' 24 (PL 198/1074). The incident is not dramatised in the other cycles.

369-70 The speech omits the difficult phrase, Genesis 3/22: *Ecce Adam quasi unus ex nobis factus est* (AV "Behold, the man is become as one of us").

375-6 "Therefore you must go hence, having satisfied your desire." HmARB regard the desire as fulfilled by the eating of the apple. But rhyme indicates that *fulfill* 376H is to be preferred to the erroneous *fullfilled* HmARB, meaning that Adam and Eve can satisfy their desire for the knowledge only in the world — "Therefore you must go hence and satisfy your desire." Deimling cites the H variant as evidence of H's superiority. The line has no biblical counterpart.

377 *covetteste* The line is without biblical counterpart and the exemplar was evidently obscure. The variations in verb-root suggest a confusion of *u* (for *v*) with a form of *n*, with some subsequent "emendation". No manuscript gives the verb an inflexional ending, although such an ending is used in this section, cf. *wouldeste* 373. *este* HmAR gives no sense unless as an inflexional ending, but Hm could also be the adverb *efte* (see TNs), while H reads *els* and gives the replacement-form *elswheare*. B alone recognises that a smoother rhythm will result from a disyllabic form and supplies the scribal replacement *anie*. The H-reading is erroneous since it destroys the rhyme. The reconstructed form given in the text is the most probable reading.

379   *this fruite* Compare Genesis 3/22: *Nunc ergo ne forte mittat manum suam, et sumat etiam de ligno vitae, et comedat et vivat in aeternum*. (AV "And now, lest he put forth his hand and take also of the tree of life, and eat, and live for ever"). The reference is therefore not to the fruit of the tree of knowledge but to the fruit of the tree of life. This tree is not mentioned specifically in the play, but the use of the demonstrative here suggests that it was on the stage; it would be possible to take *trees*, 280 + SD, as including only the two trees, of knowledge and of life, since both are said in Genesis 2/9 to grow together in the midst of the garden.

384 + SD   *angell* The reference is apparently to *Primus Angelus*, 392 + SH, the leader of the order of Cherubyn. *angelles* AR includes all four angels in God's address.

385–92, stanza 49   *hase* 388 H is to be preferred for rhyme to *hathe* HmARB.

389   *swordes* Compare Genesis 3/24: *Et collocavit ante paradisium voluptatis cherubim et flammeum gladium atque versatilem* (AV "And he placed at the east of the garden of Eden Cherubims and a flaming sword which turned every way"). *sworde* ARBH reflects the biblical singular form, but in the English construction the plural form seems more acceptable; compare 413, 422 where only H has the singular form.

391–2   "They [i.e. the order of angels called Cherubynn] are granted that special privilege, to keep this place..." The reference of *the* is not clear, but seems to give best sense in reference to *Cherubynn* 386; the H version, however, takes it to refer to *man* 391. By reading *forgright* at 392, H gives: ".. that no earthly man should ever go in - they are denied that grace"; compare 420 H. Compare 17/233–6.

393–424   The emphasis throughout the speeches is on the discord between Man and God and the justice of Man's expulsion from Eden. The key to the whole is the clear statement of Man's separation from God at 393–400.

399 seems to be a remote echo of Psalm 84/11: *Misericordia et veritas obviaverunt sibi; justicia et pax osculatae sunt* (AV 85/10: 'Mercy and truth are met together; righteousness and peace have kissed each other'). The debate of the Daughters of God was held to precede the reconciliation of God and Man and is dramatised in *Ludus Coventriae* 11/1–188 and *The Castell of Perseverance* 3229ff.

401   *chyce* Compare *chis* MED, (c) "solicitous". *choyce* RH suggests identification with *chois* adj, MED (a) "distinguished, excellent, noble". *coyse* A is a scribal error, but its *s* may indicate an exemplar long *s* which, in *chyffe* B, has been misread as *f*.

404   *wynynge* OED last records *winning* vbl. sb^2, "dwelling, habitation", in c1575. *woninge* ARB represents *wonning*, "place of habitation, dwelling-place", last recorded by OED in 1602 and hence, perhaps, slightly more familiar to the scribes. *woming* H is a scribal error resulting from the miscounting of minims.

PLAY II

410 The line seems to contain three strongly stressed syllables instead of the expected four. *freely* B or *sleelie* H would supply the deficiency and give acceptable sense; *sleelie* represents a form which could readily generate the other variants.

ever see HmB and *oversee* H seem equally possible; AR's unnecessary change of word-order, however, suggests that the scribe was confident of his reading.

420 H here repeats 392 H, thereby destroying syntactical continuity; there seems no reason for the change.

425 *highe* ARBH is to be preferred for meaning to the scribally erroneous *hight* Hm.

434 Unbiblical; compare Comestor, *Historia Scholastica*, 'Liber Genesis' 25 (PL 198/1076), reflected in ME *Genesis and Exodus*:
> For fiftene yer hadde Adam
> Ðan Caim of Eue cam.
> And oðer fiftene a swilc sel
> Quane Eue bar rigtwise Abel.
> (415-8)

No reference to these dates is made in the other cycles, but they are necessary in Chester to signal the passage of time between 424 and 425.

437-72 Adam reveals his vision, as promised at 137-40. Adam's "sleep", when God removed his rib to create Eve, was generally accepted as an ecstasy in which his soul, separated from his body and hence both incorporeal and yet sinless, was transported to Heaven where it received intimations of divine intention. See, for example, Augustine, *De Genesi ad Litteram* 9/19 (PL 34/408). On the immediate effects of this revelation, see 145-60 and note. The wider implications of the vision, now revealed, are described in Comestor, *Historia Scholastica*, 'Liber Genesis' 16 (PL 198/1070). The account refers to the immediate prophecy, withheld at 145-60, and its transmission to his sons, as here. The material is as set out by Comestor, although the union of Christ and his Church is more clearly presented as the introduction of *a new lawe* 455. It is, however, strange that Adam combines God's first and last destructions — *water or fyer* 457. The effect is to continue the sense of the unfolding of a pre-ordained plan, of which the Fall of Man was part, which began at 1/3. Adam is given wider knowledge than Lucifer at 1/254-65 (see note), and seems to have greater knowledge than the lesser angels, 20/104 ff.

445-8 "Son, I will speak before you in order to make you aware of dangerous circumstances and to keep your deeds from sin — but I will not tell everything." Hm's construction of possessive pronoun and gerund, *your doinge* 446, is not shared by the other manuscripts; H, however, seems worried by the construction in *you* and rephrases the remainder of the line to give an infinitive construction instead of the gerund.

Since Adam is addressing both his children, a plural form might be expected for *sonne* 447. *some* BH may be preferred for meaning: "I will recount some before you, but I will not tell all."

449-56, stanza 57   *yt finde* 456 H is to be preferred for rhyme and meaning to *them sure* HmARB; Deimling cites the variant as evidence of H's superiority. The

HmARB reading is an affirmation of faith, "And so men shall have certainty", and therefore perhaps represents an "emendation" on didactic grounds.

461 *that nye* is evidently intended to suggest the destruction of sinners. But in context it relates specifically to the destruction described in 457-60, which 465-8 seems to fix as a reference to the Flood. H, evidently uneasy at the suggestion that Cain and Abel may be thought to be involved in the Flood, reads *they* for *yee*, referring to *men* 459. The H interpretation has some point, if it is intended to suggest that the sinners destroyed in the Flood are the descendents of Cain; compare, for example, Augustine, *De Civitate Dei* 15/20 (PL 41/463-5). If Cain was not sinful, there would be no occasion for the Flood.

472 *I* ARBH is to be preferred to its omission in Hm for syntax, meaning and metre. Hm's omission is a scribal error.

473-88 Genesis 4 gives no reason for the religious devotions of Cain and Abel. With the ascription to Adam of the practice of offering, compare Bede, *Hexaemeron* 2 (PL 91/63) and Comestor, *Historia Scholastica*, 'Liber Genesis' 26 (PL 198/1077). Abel in Wakefield 2/72 attributes the practice to Adam's teaching, while *Ludus Coventriae* 3/32-44 dramatises Adam's words and Cornish Ordinalia pp.13-14 shows God enjoining the practice of tithing upon Adam. But in York 7/23-33 an angel informs the two brothers that God requires tithes; and in *Stanzaic Life*, following *Legenda Aurea*, there is no mention of Adam instituting the practice.

Chester follows Genesis 4 in enjoining only an offer of good corn from Cain and the first-born beast from Abel. In this, it seems to follow the concept of the three good deeds said in *Stanzaic Life* 2317-524 (following *Legenda Aurea*) to have been performed to please God before any law was ordained — offering, by Cain and Abel; tithing, by Abraham to Melchisedech; and sacrifice of beasts, by Noah. This account differs from that in the other cycles, where the offerings are said to be a tithe — compare Wakefield 2/73 etc., York 7/27-9, *Ludus Coventriae* 3/88-91 etc. (although Adam's injunctions there follow Genesis 4), Cornish Ordinalia p.13. In Chester tithing begins with Abraham (4/133-4) and Cain and Abel merely make offerings as tokens of appeasement, 461-2, 473-4, 485-8, indicative of a continuing latent enmity between God and Man.

477-8 Adam seems to have in mind grain-growing on well-drained, and probably furrowed land, with its roots out of the water of the lower land or ridges between the furrows. This view seems confirmed by Cain's use of the plough, 516+SD, following Josephus' claim that "he first contrived to plough the ground", *Antiquities of the Jews* 2; see note to 516+SD. Adam's comment may have had particular significance for a Chester audience, since the soil and climate of the county of Cheshire made the cultivation of wheat difficult and *corn* would there usually have the sense of barley or rye.

489-512 The division of occupation between Adam and Eve is unbiblical but follows a well-established tradition, whereby Adam "delved" and Eve "span". For further examples, see Carleton Brown and Rossell Hope Robbins, *Index of Middle English Verse* and Supplement (New York, 1943), nos. 3921 and 3922.

490 *without* ARBH is to be preferred to the scribally erroneous *withou* Hm.

PLAY II

491 *feele* The sense seems to require a past tense, *felt*, which *feelde* AR suggests. H substitutes *fell*, which may be preferable for meaning: "For since I fell — that cursed misfortune to eat of that fruit — I have dug — ".

500 The line in HmARB appears to contain four strongly stressed syllables instead of the expected three. *nowld* H may be preferred as producing the expected number of stressed syllables, although *ne would* would be metrically smoother.

511 The ARBH reading is preferable for sense and a more regular sequence of strongly and weakly stressed syllables. *please* Hm lacks the object supplied by *God*.

516 + SD Cain evidently leaves the stage to collect the plough, thereby signalling the passage of some time between 516 and 517. The plough was presumably a one-man shoulder-plough, made of wood; compare Wakefield 2, where a plough and team are required. Cain's plough marks a technological advance over Adam's spade — compare 3/52–80 and note — and may, by implication, suggest the cause of Cain's *great plentee* 517. H omits the SD and therefore this dramatic detail.

517–20 Cain is prosperous, and intends to offer in the hope of further gain, not to propitiate an angry God. Compare Vincent of Beauvais, *Speculum Historiale* 1/56: *Cayn, auarus agricola*; Comestor, *Historia Scholastica*, 'Liber Genesis' 26 (PL 198/1077): *Munera vero Cain, ex avaritia hominis nata, Deo non placuerunt*. No other cycle stresses Cain's prosperity; Wakefield emphasises his bad harvest, 2/122–3. See 560 + SD and note.

521–8, stanza 66   The b-rhymes, *choyse* 524 — *leese* 528, do not rhyme. Since no manuscript reads *chese* 521, *lose* 528 R may be preferred. But an original -*e*-rhyme is probable.

521 *with devotyon* Compare Hebrews 11/4: *Fide plurimam hostiam Abel quam Cain obtulit Deo* (AV "By faith Abel offered unto God a more excellent sacrifice than Cain").

529–52 There is no suggestion in the biblical account that Cain did not offer of the best. Compare Comestor, *Historia Scholastica*, 'Liber Genesis' 26 (PL 198/1077), and *Stanzaic Life*:

> But Caymes offering in that place
> forsaken was in Goddes sight,
> for fuylet corn bifore his face
> he brand, ther-fore hade they no light.
> (2337–40)

The order of offering is not specified in the Bible. Cain's concern with the priority which goes with age, 529–30, seems to derive from God's later assurance to Cain — see 589–90 and note, 599–600, 601–6 — and becomes an important element in his characterisation. The feature is absent in other plays — Abel offers first at Wakefield, and *Ludus Coventriae*, Cain in the Cornish Ordinalia and AN *Adam* (the equivalent section is missing from York). *Stanzaic Life* 2333–44 describes Cain's sacrifice first.

537–44, stanza 68   There is no obvious reason for A's large omission in the stanza; it is not shared by R. *penne* 537 H is required for perfect rhyme; but the -*a*- form was clearly a standard, capable of various pronunciations — compare 205.

552 + SD H   The action referred to in the SD is effected at 560. H has the plural, *animalia*; compare the singular *the best beaste* 557.

560 + SD   Compare Genesis 4/4–5: *Et respexit Dominus ad Abel, et ad munera eius, ad Cain vero, et ad munera illius, non respexit* (AV "And the Lord had respect unto Abel and to his offering: But unto Cain, and to his offering, he had not respect"). The form of approval is not indicated but can be found in, e.g. Bede, *In Pentateuchum Commentari* — Genesis 4 (PL 91/215) and Comestor, *Historia Scholastica*, 'Liber Genesis' 26 (PL 198/1077). The burning of Abel's tithe is the sign of acceptance in the other cycles (except York, where the passage is lost), but it is not clear whether the fire is ignited by Abel or by God. In *Ludus Coventriae* and Cornish Ordinalia, Cain's tithe is not ignited at all, but in Wakefield 2 it almost chokes Cain with the smoke as it smoulders and is extinguished.

Genesis gives no reason for God's preference for Abel's offering. Explanations have been prompted particularly by Epistle to the Hebrews 11/4: *Fide plurimam hostiam Abel quam Cain, obtulit Deo, per quam testimonium consecutus est esse iustus, testimonium perhibente muneribus eius Deo: et per illam defunctus adhunc loquitur* (AV "By faith Abel offered unto God a more excellent sacrifice than Cain, by which he obtained witness that he was righteous, God testifying of his gifts: and by it he being dead yet speaketh"). Thus Cain lacks the spiritual perspective necessary for the understanding of sacrifice. Augustine reviews the possible reasons in *De Civitate Dei* 15/7 (PL 41/443–5) and at 15/1 (PL 41/437). In all cycles sacrifice, to Cain's mind, is a waste of good grain.

574   *myne* ARBH is to be preferred for morphology to the scribally erroneous *my* Hm.

575–6   The text is more specific than Genesis 4/5: *Iratusque est Cain vehementer* (AV "And Cain was very wroth"); compare Augustine, *De Civitate Dei* 15/7 (PL 41/445).

580   *meede* HmAB seems required by context; compare Genesis 4/7, *recipies* (AV "shalt thou not be accepted" or "have the excellency") and Comestor, *Historia Scholastica*, 'Liber Genesis' 26 (PL 198/1077): *Recipies praemium*. *need* RH gives less satisfactory sense and may derive from confusion of *m* and *n* involving he miscounting of minims, or from a misunderstanding of the meaning; the error could readily arise independently in the two manuscripts.

589–92   "Your brother shall always be obedient and be wholly under your authority; the enjoyment of that belongs to you. Give thought to what you do." *shalbe* 589 must be understood at 590; on *luste* 591, see *lust* MED, 2(a). Neither *fulfill* 590 H nor *after this* 590 B gives sense; the former may represent an incomplete attempt to redraft 590 occasioned by the lack of a verb, but there seems no obvious reason for B's substitution. 591 H represents a substitution for 591 HmARB, but it is impossible to assign priority to either version; 591 HmARB is, however, semantically more obscure than H and might suggest the need for a clearer alternative.

The lines are based on Genesis 4/7, the source of Cain's primogenital concerns throughout the play; compare Chrysostom, *In Cap 4 Genesis Homil.* 18/6 (PG 53/157).

PLAY II

594–6 Baugh compares *Mistère*: "Il fault aller Ung peu aux champs et *entre nous* De noz necessitez parler."

596 *an* ARBH is to be preferred for syntax to the scribally erroneous *and* Hm.

612 + SD H The SD relates to the action completed at 616 + SD HmARB.

630 *shalbe* ARBH is to be preferred for meaning to *shalt bye* Hm, which is presumably merely a scribal error.

635–40 Genesis 4/14 does not mention Cain's fear of wild beasts; but compare Josephus, *Antiquities of the Jews* 2: "And when he was afraid that in wandering about he should fall among wild beasts, and by that means perish, God bid him not to entertain such a melancholy suspicion, and to go all over the earth without fear of what mischief he might suffer from wild beasts", seen also in Comestor, *Historia Scholastica*, 'Liber Genesis' 27 (PL 198/1077).

641–4 To his earlier sins of avarice and envy, Cain now adds despair, as in *Glossa Ordinaria*, 'Liber Genesis' 4/13 (PL 113/99).

649–64 Compare Genesis 4/15: *Dixitque ei Dominus: Nequaquam ita fiet: sed omnis qui occiderit Cain, septuplum punietur* (AV "And the Lord said unto him, Therefore whosoever slayeth Cain, vengeance shall be taken on him sevenfold"). The text is developed in two ways, in accordance with orthodox exegesis: (1) the slayer will be punished seven times more than Cain, 653–4; (2) Cain and seven generations of his family will be punished, 657–64 (compare Comestor, *Historia Scholastica*, 'Liber Genesis' 27 (PL 198/1078)). The third possibility, the slaying of Cain by Lamech, the seventh generation of his family, is not here included; see *Ludus Coventriae* 4/141–97.

657–60 "But because you were prepared to do this deed, you and your children may expect — into the seventh generation — punishment for all your sinful acts." *trust* is not recorded as "expect"; OED records it as "hope for, look for" (*trust* vb 3(b)), but the connotations are not appropriate and the usage is *obs.rare* and supported only by one quotation, of 1573. Two ideas seem to underlie the sentence here — that Cain may believe what God says, and that he may have confidence that punishment will follow. R, and probably the incomplete A, seek to supply a verb at 660 which resolves the sense in the direction of the second idea; H redrafts the line in favour of the second idea, but at the same time avoids the difficulty of *whole*.

673–80, stanza 85 H has alternative forms of 674 and 676. At 674 either version is possible, but 676 H supplies the required b-rhyme and gives good sense. HmARB does not rhyme and requires some straining of sense: "None of [my] sorrows may now cease".

675 *cursed Cayne* A stock collocation; compare *thou cursyd Cayme* York 7/82; *cursyd Caym Ludus Coventriae* 3/166. Since no reference is made to the mark of Cain, Genesis 4/15, it is not clear how men will recognise Cain's fault or his immunity.

678–704 Without biblical counterpart. There is a tradition of Cain's repentance which provided an example to Adam; see 'Cain', *Jewish Encyclopaedia* 5, p.22. English cycles do not dramatise the meeting, but a defiant Cain returns to his parents in Cornish Ordinalia, pp. 18-19; in *Mistère*, Cain reports his crime to his sisters, who tell their parents.

681–*Finis* B inexplicably omits the end of the play. The blank page-and-a-half following 680 suggests that the omission was not a result of a deficient exemplar or of mere scribal error; the scribe left space to complete the play.

688+SH H's omission has the effect of assigning 689-96 to Adam, who thus takes full responsibility for the Fall and its consequences. Compare *Mistère*, where Adam similarly assumes responsibility: "La mort d'Abel est mon trespas" 3003.

702 *thee* H is to be preferred for meaning to *three* HmARB. OED lists *thee* as archaic by the sixteenth century and places its latest recorded use, apart from imprecations, as 1573. *three* perhaps represents the substitution of a more familiar, though meaningless, form, perhaps influenced by *thryve* 701.

703-4 Compare Wakefield 2/443-8, York 7/134-8. H substitutes an alternative form of the lines, avoiding repetition of *all* 703 and perhaps metrically improving 704.

PLAY III

Dramatis Personae God, Noe, Sem, Cam, Jafett, Noes Wife, Semes Wyfe, Cames Wife, Jafetes Wife, The Good Gossips.

NOTE The number of gossips is unspecified; on *Gossip* H, see 225–36, stanzas 29–31 note.

Locations
some high place or in the clowdes if it may bee, *before* 1 SD
The arke *before* 1 SD, chiste 206, boote 245, 249, shippe 96; *with* one window 29, upon the syde a door 31; *hence* without the arke *Before* 1 SD, within the bordes 260 + SD.

NOTE 1. Some interior location seems indicated by *come in* 80.
2. If the rainbow is shown, *the fyrmamente* 310 may identify a separate location, although this may be identical with the *high place* of *Before* 1 SD.
3. For general dimensions and appearance of the ark, see 25–36 and notes, and for details of the rigging etc., see *Properties* below.

Properties
Construction-tools — axe 54; hatchett 57; pynne 61; hammer 62; hackestocke 69
Construction-materials — tymber 65, bordes 85; slytche 73; chippes 77 *for* a fyer 78
Rigging for the Ark — maste 89; gables 90, seale-yard 91; bowespreete 93; seale 197; cordes and roopes 94
a pottell full of malnesaye 233
beastes, fowles 267
bowe 309, 318.

NOTE 1. On the possible implications of *wrauge dead carryen*, see 290 and note.
2. *topcastle* 93 may be part of the ark from the start, or be constructed in the play.
3. The *bordes* may be those painted with *all the beastes and fowles hereafter reahersed* 160 + SD, or the latter may also have been part of the ark from the start; see 161–92 for the animals depicted.
4. The appearance of the rainbow may not have been staged but merely described.
5. Some items which may be regarded as properties are listed above under *Locations*.

Costume
None specified

Source: Genesis 6/1–9/17. The play also utilises a tradition of Noah's belligerent wife compatible with medieval anti-feminist literature; for documentation, see F. L. Utley, *The Crooked Rib* (Columbus, 1944). HmARB lack H's scene of the 'Raven and Dove'; see Appendix IA, which further supplements the staging-requirements listed above.

Play-heading The Flood is dramatised in Wakefield 3, York 8–9, *Ludus Coventriae* 4; a play of somewhat different content from that in the cycles survives from Newcastle. The episode is also dramatised in the Cornish Ordinalia, pp.26–35.

Before 1 SD   Genesis 6/5–6 and 12–13 does not indicate God's situation in relation to Noah. Genesis 6/13 mentions only Noah as addressed by God, although 52 suggests that all Noah's family hear God's words.

Noe Noah was from the line descending from Adam through Seth, and hence from the line of grace, and not from that descending through Cain, which provoked the corruption described by God; compare 55 note. As the tenth patriarch before the Flood, Noah also stands mid-way in the line of descent from Adam to Abraham, the subject of the following play.

1–4   Compare 1–2 with 2/425–6; 3–4 with 2/459–60.

5–8   Compare Genesis 6/3: *Non permanebit spiritus meus in homine in aeternum, quia caro est*(AV "My spirit shall not always strive with man, for that he also is flesh"). The Chester text echoes, but does not quite reflect, the sense of the passage. God's anger, which resulted in the Flood, was generally held to be inspired by the events of Genesis 6/1–4, in which the sons of God (*filii Dei*) married the daughters of men (*filias hominum*) and produced a giant race. These events were frequently interpreted as the mating of the male descendants of Adam's third son, Seth, with the female descendants of the evil Cain, so that the Flood is consequential upon the events of Play 2. 5–6 may represent a misunderstanding of the biblical text, or an attempt to underline lechery as a cause of sinful rebellion. The immediate cause of God's anger is seen in Genesis 6/5, *multa malitia hominum* (AV "the wickedness of man was great"); compare 14.

   mone 5 HmA is to be preferred to *man* RBH for rhyme.

   but tyll 7, "But I shall wait until"; the reference is to the time when the action announced at 5 will be carried out.

9–16, stanza 2   *mon* 16 Hm is to be preferred to *man* ARBH for perfect rhyme.

10   *fowle to flye* Compare Genesis 6/7, *volucres caeli* (AV "The fowls of the air"). *to flye* is an infinitive of purpose, requiring *that I made* 9 to be understood: "Bird [that I made] to fly".

20   *trees drye and light* AV "gopher wood" is the first recorded instance of the phrase in English; the dramatist was attempting to render Genesis 6/14: *de lignis levigatis*. No other play refers to the wood from which the ark was constructed, except the Cornish Ordinalia which specifies oak boards. A useful summary of various descriptions of the Ark may be found in D. C. Allen: *The Legend of Noah*, 71-2.

25-32, stanza 4   No manuscript has the form *shit* for *shutte* 31, required for perfect rhyme and a variant of *shut* (see OED); *sit* H represents an alternative, perhaps substituted because of the lack of rhyme—but compare *sutte* A; *shoote* B is a scribal error, destroying rhyme and sense.

27   *of height sixtye* Genesis 6/15 gives the height as thirty cubits. The A and H variants suggest fifty cubits. If the latter represent independent confusion with *fiftye* in the preceding line, the exemplar may have erroneously read *sixty*; but it seems more probable that the exemplar gave the height in barely legible arabic numerals, 30, which might be variously misread as 50 or 60.

the meete thou fonge "Take the measurement." The AR variant gives good sense: "The next measurement you should take is of the height, sixty." The H variant gives no obvious sense and may represent an attempt to render in more familiar form some word such as *meete*.

29-30   *one window* Neither Genesis nor the play indicates the position of the window, but some opinion held that if the window had been in the side of the Ark, the water would have entered: cf. *Polychronicon* 2/5, translated by Trevisa: "Here me may wondre how þe wyndowe was i-made byneþe in þe side of þe schippe for comynge [yn] of water." Hence a tradition grew up that the window was a skylight in the deck — compare Hugh of St. Victor, *De arca Noe morali* (PL 176/627), and *Cleanness* 318: "And a wyndow wyd uponande wroght upon lofte." The general stage-business of the play would be expedited if the window was in the roof of the ark, near the mast (compare Appendix IA/15 + SD).

33-40, stanza 5   The b-rhymes, *make* 36 — *face* 40, do not rhyme. Possibly *mase*, "confound" (MED *masen* 1(a)), was intended at 36, but its voiced fricative would give only imperfect rhyme and poor meaning; *sake* 40 H is to be preferred. See also 37-40 note.

33-4   Compare Genesis 6/16: *Deorsum, cenacula et tristega facies in ea* (AV "With lower, second, and third stories shalt thou make it"). Augustine's account of the Ark was retailed in standard compendia and some such account seems to have influenced the dramatist's description. He may have conjectured that the three upper rooms were *eatinge-places*; or used the phrase to distinguish the living-quarters from the other rooms; or associated Genesis' *cenaculum* with *cena*, "dinner, banquet". *rowfed*, 34 H, and the other variants seem to derive from a common, partially illegible form in the exemplar; OED has no word corresponding to *ronett* HmAB, but J. O. Halliwell, *A Dictionary of Archaic and Provincial Words, Proverbs and Ancient Customs from the Fourteenth Century* (London, 1865) II, p.691 lists *ronette* as "round, circular" and Thomas Wright, *Dictionary of Obsolete and Provincial English* (London, 1857), II, 868 lists *ronette* as "circular"; *rounde* R may then be a more familiar replacement for *ronette*. The various words may represent attempts to translate *camera*, "arched chamber". Deimling felt that *rowfed* H was "alone reasonable". The uncertainty of *one or too* 34 is seen in Wakefield 3/129, 133: "three chefe/chese chambres" and "parloures oone or two". This may be a formula for the sake of rhyme; or originate in a manuscript reading of *aut* for *et*; or, more probably, reflect an uncertainty about the number of storeys in the Ark since the lower rooms were variously considered to be disposed on one or two levels — see Hugh of St. Victor, *De arca Noe morali* 1/3 (PL 176/626–34) and the diagrams comparing the two dispositions in *Polychronicon*, Rolls Series, vol.2, p.236. By the latter interpretation, the *rowfed chambers* would refer to the levels rather than the rooms.

37–40 "All the world shall be destroyed, shall fall before your eyes — except you, your wife, your three sons and their wives also with you." Compare Genesis 6/18: *Ponamque foedus meum tecum: et ingredieris arcam, tu et filii tui, uxor tua et uxores filiorum tuorum tecum* (AV "But with thee will I establish my covenant: and thou shalt come into the ark, thou, and thy sons, and thy wife and thy sons' wives with thee"). Some corruption in the HmARB text may be suspected not only by the elliptical construction but also by the absence of a second b-rhyme in the stanza. The H-form gives an easier syntax and sense and supplies the necessary rhyme. Some formal connexion can be seen between 40 HmARB and 40 H; both have *shall* and *thy, before* HmARB seems related to *be for* H, and a simple confusion of *f* and long *s* goes some way towards explaining the relationship between *fall* and *saved* and between *face* and *sake*. Compare 43–4.

49–52 Noah addresses his family, who have been standing by him; see *Before* 1 SD. But the reference to *this water* and the use of *us* 52 suggest that they are thought to have heard God's address to Noah. 50 H weakens this sense, since the information is then relayed by Noah without reference to God's threats. With 49–50, compare 153–4.

54–80 Basic tools of the shipwright's trade are shown. These might have particular significance in Chester, a major port. Behind this simple realism may lie an echo of Noah's technological innovations; compare *Jewish Encyclopaedia* 12, 'Noah', col. 1194: "*In the Aggadeh*...Noah's first good deed was to 'introduce plows, sickles, axes, and all kinds of tools to his contemporaries'." The tools represent a continuing sign of Man's control over his hostile environment; compare 2/156 + SD. The men here are the craftsmen, using the tools while the women do the labouring jobs of gathering wood, preparing pitch, sweeping up and cooking.

55 *thys towne* Compare 60. The reference is most immediately to the surrounding town of Chester. The Bible does not suggest that Noah was a town-dweller. But Cain, in his exile, founded the city of Enoch (Genesis 4/17), the first city, which for Augustine symbolised the force of evil in the world; compare *De Civitate Dei* 15/5 (PL 41/441). It is the descendants of Cain who are destroyed in the Flood (*id.* 15/8 — PL 41/445–7), i.e. Noah's fellow citizens.

65–72, stanza 9   *fayle* 72 ARBH is to be preferred to *fable* Hm for rhyme and meaning.

74 *clam* HmB, "to smear, daub", does not seem to have been frequently used in this sense in ME; MED cites only one example, OED two (c1380 and 1584), together with *clamme* or *clam* from 1884 Cheshire Glossary, "to plaister over". The more common word and form seems to have been *cleam, cleme*, "to smear, anoint, bedaub", and it is tempting to speculate that some form such as *cleame* may underlie the scribally erroneous and semantically inappropriate *cleane* H. *caulke* AR is obviously a substitution, first recorded by OED (apart from here) in 1552.

PLAY III 37

75 *with stitche* HmA does not give good sense; *bout stitche* R seems to be an attempt to make sense of the construction, perhaps taking *stitche* to mean "pain", whence the rather inappropriate "without pain". *every stitche* H seems preferable; see OED *stitch*, 10, *every stitch*, "every inch". But this is the first example cited before 1817.

81–8, stanza 11   The b-rhyme at 84–8 is the same word, *fludd*, but it is appropriate to the context and no alternative suggests itself. *froude* 84 R is meaningless and evidently a scribal error.

85–95   Without biblical counterpart. Noah apparently works first on the hull 85–6, then raises the mast and sails, complete with the yard-arm from which the sail was suspended, and the bowsprit along which it was extended out over the bows. Possibly Noah also has oars or a steering oar — compare *rowe* 87. The absence of navigational devices on the ark was often stressed by commentators as evidence of Noah's submission to divine providance, as in Augustine, *De Civitate Dei* 15/27 (PL 41/475); or *Cleanness* 417–20:

> Withouten mast oþer myke oþer myry bawelyne,
> Kable oþer capstan to clyppe to her ankreȝ,
> Hurrok, oþer handehelme hasped on roþer,
> Oþer any sweande sayl to seche after hauen.

Compare the similarly elaborate ship of Wakefield 3/262–88, which has a *stere-tre* 433.

On the function of the mast in staging the flight of the birds, see Appendix IA/15 + SD and note.

89–96, stanza 12   *blaste* 91 ARBH is to be preferred for meaning to the scribally erroneous *baste* Hm.

96   Since the line can only mean that the Ark is complete, it makes little sense for Noah and all his family to continue working on it beyond this point, as suggested in 96 + SD H and 112 + SD HmARB. A form of the same SD appears in H after 80, where it seems most appropriate. The variations in position of the SDs and their appearance in inappropriate positions suggest a confusion arising from the exemplar. One possibility is that some provision was made for the insertion/deletion of 81–112 in the exemplar; alternatively, the exemplar scribe may have attempted to rectify an error of placing the SD after 112 instead of after 80 and his attempted correction was misunderstood. By this theory, 96 + SD would represent an idiosyncratic attempt by the H-scribe to find a more suitable position for 112 + SD, perhaps indicated by his use of *iterum* which shows a consciousness of the repetition of 80 + SD.

97–8   The Wife's rebellion may seem ill-motivated in view of her co-operation at 65–8 and her awareness of God's injunction. But Noah's words, 50 and 95, suggest that he does not know when the rains will come; he therefore suggests that they all enter the Ark before the rain begins. The Wife responds that she will enter only when need arises, 103.

100   "For all your Frenchified goings-on". The Wife sarcastically alludes to Noah's brusque instruction at 98 as if it were an elaborately polite invitation. The reference is not indicative of any particularly French influence in the cycle.

104   The line contains four strongly stressed syllables instead of the expected three; a regular line would result from the omission of *all daye*.

112 Compare 203.

129–36, stanza 17   *forgetten/foryeten* 131 B/H is to be preferred for rhyme to *forgotten* HmAR. *foryeten* H avoids repetition of the verb-root seen in *getten* 130.

143   *mightes* HmARB is to be preferred for rhyme to *mighte* H.

145–52   Compare 7–8. Noah here seems to suggest that he has caused God to delay the Flood by delaying the completion of the Ark; ironically, he has complied with God's avowed intention. Compare *Jewish Encyclopaedia* 12, 'Noah', col.1194: *"In the Aggadah* Finding it difficult to disregard God's command, yet dreading the destruction of the human species, he waited for 120 years in the hope that his contemporaries would depart from their evil ways."

153–4   Compare 49–50.

169   *cattes* The only animal to be mentioned twice in the list; compare 178. The repetition is probably the result of the use of *cat* in two common collocations — with *dog*, as here, and with *mouse*, as at 178.

171   *gayle* Hm is evidently the adverbial form represented by *gaylie* H; but the monosyllabic adjective *gaye* B produces a more regular sequence of strongly and weakly stressed syllables. The erroneous A and R variants seem to represent the substitution of familiar forms, probably indicating that *gayle* was the exemplar form which was not recognised in AR.

195   "In God's name, come; it's almost time." BH omit *name*, giving "For God's sake [On God's behalf], come; it's time." It is possible that *name* and *halfe* represent alternatives.

197   The rebellious Noah's Wife is a feature of the English cycles and Cornish Ordinalia (*Ludus Coventriae* is an exception), and the origins of the character have been much discussed. In Islamic legend she was an unbeliever and, in one account, died in the Flood; but folk-material and antifeminist literature have contributed to the picture. Various naturalistic and symbolic reasons have been proposed for her initial co-operation in the building of the Ark and her later rebellion.

206   Although metrically acceptable, the line is perhaps smoother if a syllable is omitted, a consideration perhaps underlying the omission of *wilte* in A and *to* in H.

chiste Although a common ME term for the Ark, and one reflecting the shape which emerges from the biblical account, the word here seems employed as a term of abuse against *shippe* and *boote*. It may be significant that Noah's ship is never called an *Ark* in the spoken text, although the term is used in SDs. *chest* B produces imperfect rhyme.

207   *thou* RBH is to be preferred for syntax and meaning to *thy* HmA, since *liste* is clearly a verb. *thy* may result from independent confusion in Hm and A with *thy* 206. *liste* is regarded as a personal verb by RBH, but an impersonal construction, *thee liste*, would be possible; one may speculate that an alteration from *thee* to *thou* in the exemplar could obscure the pronoun-form.

209–16, stanza 27   *wraowe* 209 HmB may be preferred for rhyme to *wrawe* AH, since the a-rhyme seems to require a rounded vowel. R may not have recognized the word, or been confused by the distribution of the stanza-lines between two speakers;

its substitutions of *ny* for *wraowe* 209 and *see* for *knowe* 210 destroy the stanza-rhymes but establish 209–10 as an independent rhyming couplet.

214 *shippe* ARBH makes explicit the reference of *yonder*, but the additional syllable thus introduced destroys the regular sequence of strongly and weakly stressed syllables in the Hm line; Hm's omission may therefore represent a metrical improvement. A regular line would be restored by reading *yon* for *yonder* in ARBH; Hm may be justified by reference to the visual context in which the speech is uttered.

217–24, stanza 28 *all daye* 220 AR represents the substitution of an a-rhyme for the required b-rhyme, *withowte*. The scribe may have been misled by the distribution of lines among different speakers.

224 + SH–36, stanzas 29–31 On the problems of identifying the sung section of the 'Gossips' Song' and on date and analogues, see Rastall, pp.156–7. 224 + SH HmARB indicates a plurality of gossips, but *Gossip* H suggests that only one gossip speaks; compare, however, *gossips* 201 in HmARB and also in H.

The rhyme-schemes of the three stanzas are: stanza 29, abac; stanza 30, abab; stanza 31 aaab. Stanza 29 may be regarded as abab if *farre* 226 is accepted as an imperfect rhyme for *nere* 228, or as a formal error for *ferre*; H substitutes an a-rhyme at 226 and further destroys the link of 226 and 228 by its substitution at 228, giving an aaab form. H also omits stanza 31, producing an eight-line speech, perhaps in imitation of the usual eight-line stanza; Deimling (p.xiv) comments that the (Hm)ARB lines "are not only unnecessary but are also out of all rhyme connection with *alyke*" (the AR form at 236), and cites the variant as evidence of H's superiority. As Deimling indicates, the absence of rhyme-link for 236 permits the AR substitution of *alike* for *atyte*, the latter perhaps being an unfamiliar form to the scribe.

H places the SH and song after 242, perhaps considering it to be logically motivated by *my gosseppes all* 242; in HmARB it has no connexion with the preceding text, other than the reference to fear of the Flood at 224 which the song takes up. But its position after 242 disrupts the pattern of stanza 32 and awkwardly separates the Wife's *that will I not* 241 from Sem's retort, *yett thow shall* 243. In terms of staging, either position is possible.

The song serves different functions in the two versions. In HmARB, the gossips attempt to entice the Wife to them with "You've time for a quick one": "Though Noah may think we've never taken so long, yet we will drink at once" 235–6; on the other side, Jafett distracts the Wife long enough for Sem to pounce. H's gossip appeals for entry to the Ark—see particularly *lett me come in* 228 H for *lett us drawe nere* 228 HmARB—on the pretext of having a parting drink inside.

On the function of the gossip(s), compare Matthew 24/38–9: *Sicut enim erant in diebus ante diluuium comedentes et bibentes, nubentes et nuptui tradentes, usque ad eum diem quo intrauit Noe in arcam, et non cognouerunt donec uenit diluuium et tulit omnes* (AV "For as in the days that were before the flood they were eating and drinking, marrying and giving in marriage, until the day that Noe entered into the ark, and knew not until the flood came, and took them all away").

246 "Take that for your reward"; see *note*, OED sb¹, 1, "use, usefulness, profit". But *note*, OED sb², 4, "a cry, call, or sound, esp. that made by a bird or fowl", and 5, "In transferred applications", is also possible: "Take that for your din". The pronoun reference is indicated in 246 + SD H and in the action on stage as Mrs. Noah strikes her husband.

252 *hee* (1) is redundant and seems to be an error in position of the subject of *will* which has not been cancelled. Its omission in ARBH may be preferred.

252 + SD Whereas HmARB indicate that the Noah family sings at this point, H omits the SD here and includes the singing of an antiphon at 260 + SD where HmARB's *hee shalbe scylent* excludes such a possibility. Whatever the reason for the change, the effect is that in HmARB the family can sing at the window, or even on deck, before the window is shut, whereas in H the singing comes from within the Ark.

258 *my chamber* No such room is specified in 33–6, but if the window is at the top of the Ark, so also, according to standard accounts, is the family's quarters.

260 + SD The opening of the window at Genesis 8/6 heralds the despatch of the birds, as in H. This episode is lacking in HmARB, but as Deimling admits, the (Hm)ARB form is "not absolutely unintelligible". In fact, the possibility of a savage production-cut at this point cannot be excluded. The difference between the stage-directions here and at 252 + suggests rather different concepts of action; the omission of the stage-business of sending out the birds also means that a mast is not required—see p. 96 note on the possible omission of the section relating to the erection of the mast, and Appendix IA/15 + SD on the use of the mast; while continuity is preserved from the H-version because stanza 35 reiterates the intention to sacrifice with which the H-addition concludes, Appendix IA/40–7. Although the sending of the birds is a standard feature of the account, its omission here would put greater emphasis upon God's covenant with Noah, which in Chester has a number of features not dramatised elsewhere. The SD covers a passage of 300 days, Genesis 8/3; the absence of actors and action in HmARB could create an awkward hiatus. Rastall, p.157–60, proposes an identification for *Save mee O God*.

262 *such grace* Deimling comments: "You are rather at a loss to know what the patriarch means by *such grace*." However, the phrase seems adequately explained by 263.

263 *borne* Some additional context must be understood for the word (e.g. "borne away by the Flood"), and it is tempting to propose that *borne* is an exemplar error for *lorne*; B erroneously began a word in *b* after *all*, which was then cancelled (see TNs), and it seems probable that this was *borne*, a further confirmation of the *b*-reading in all manuscripts.

salfe Hm, *saffe* RH reflect the same form; *false* AB shows scribal confusion of long *s* and *f*, while serving to confirm *salfe* as the exemplar reading.

264–8 A consequence of the lack of Appendix IA material in HmARB is that there is no counterpart in the play to God's injunction to Noah to leave the Ark, and no clear evidence of disembarkation. The idea that Noah left the Ark of his own decision is supported by Josephus, *Antiquities of the Jews* 3; see Wakefield 3/526–31. Neither York not *Ludus Coventriae* dramatises the disembarkation; Cornish Ordinalia is closest to Chester, dramatising not only God's injunction to leave, but also the family's sacrifice and its consequences.

PLAY III 41

277-84, stanza 37   *lett* 283 indicates that the c-rhyme requires short *e*. No manuscript has a form with short *e* at 281. *all that may fleete* 281 corresponds to Genesis 9/3: *Et omne quod movetur* (AV "Every moving thing that liveth"), and *fleete* HmB is therefore an error for the short-vowel *flette*, from *fletten*, MED 3, "to be in motion, to move or shift about"; *fleete* may indicate confusion with *fleten*, MED v¹, 1(b) "of fish, persons: to swim", influenced by the collocation at 281. *flitte* ARH gives the *i*-form of *fletten*, destroying rhyme; *behitte* 282 A, and *behite* 282 H, may represent further substitutions in an attempt to sustain an *i*-rhyme which must lapse with *lett* 283.

278   *to edifye*   The infinitive depends upon *shall* 277; on the use of the *to*-form, see Mustanoja, p.528. *you* H for *to* perhaps indicates unease at the construction.

279-82   279-81 correspond to Genesis 9/2; 281-2 correspond to Genesis 9/3. The punctuation adopted accepts *fleete* 281 as a form of *fleten* and *all* as comprehending only *fishe*; but *fleete* is erroneous—see 277-84, stanza 37 note. The text would correspond to the biblical arrangement by deleting the full-stop at 280 and replacing the comma at 281 after *saye* by a full-stop. The lines would then mean: "Every animal, and every bird that can fly, shall be afraid of you—and so shall the fish in the sea. Everything that can move shall nourish you, I promise you."

that may flye 279 qualifies only *fowle*; as translated above, *eache* is understood before *fowle*.

281-92   Compare 2/333-6 and 489-96. The dietary concessions are not dramatised in the other cycles; in Chester they typify the movement of reconciliation between God and Man as Man bows to God's power and God becomes reconciled to Man's sinful nature; they therefore show a change in the impositions upon Man and an advance in his material and spiritual well-being.

cleane 284, 287 stands in contrast to *wrauge deade carryen*; see 290 and note. The word is suggested by the biblical account and suggests "ceremonially clean" (see *clene* MED 1(d)); but in relation to *carryen* it may also suggest "free from (disease, infection, etc), healthy; of food, healthful, wholesome" (see *clene* MED 1(c)). Its reference would then depend less upon a knowledge of the Jewish dietary laws and more upon assessment of the character of the meat—"which you can recognise as wholesome" 284.

285-92, stanza 38   H's omission, 291, gives a more regular sequence of strongly and weakly stressed syllables and may be preferred.

let 292 H is to be preferred for rhyme to *leave* HmARB. *let* in the sense of "quit, abandon, forsake" is last recorded by OED in 1599. *leave* may suggest an exemplar-alteration of an obsolescent usage accepted by HmARB, while H has reverted to the original reading. Deimling cites the variant as evidence of H's superiority.

289   *blood and fleshe*   Compare Genesis 9/4: *Excepto quod carnem cum sanguine non comedetis* (AV "But the flesh with the life thereof, which is the blood thereof, shall ye not eat"); Josephus, *Antiquities of the Jews* 3: "Excepting their blood, for therein is the life". The text finds its meaning in conjunction with later biblical injunctions which make up the Jewish dietary laws. The sense is perhaps clearer in Comestor, *Historia Scholastica*, 'Liber Genesis' 35 (PL 198/1086): *Excepto quod carnem cum sanguine non comedetis, id est animal suffocatum*; compare *wrauge dead carryen* 290 and note. The injunction against consuming blood is seen also in Cornish Ordinalia, p.34: "I command you not to eat flesh with blood".

fishe H reflects a non-biblical distinction at this point, perhaps indicating failure to understand the text. Some justification may be found in the separation of *beast and fowle* 279 from *fishe in saye* 281. Jewish law permitted the consumption of any fish with scales and fins; see *Jewish Encyclopaedia* 6, 'Fish', pp.1326–7.

290 *wrauge deade carryen* The RBH forms, and the defective A form, of *wrauge* indicate that Hm has erroneously confused *u* and *n* here. *wronge deade* RBH suggests "those which have died other than by the permitted means"; see 289 and note.

that is here seems to suggest that the phrase refers to something present on stage. It is unlikely to refer to the animals that have been sacrificed. Probably it refers to the animals destroyed in the Flood—compare *carryen*, MED 3(a) "decaying corpses collectively"—in which case the existence of further carcasses has to be assumed.

293–300, stanza 39   No manuscript has the form *mankynne* at 296 which is required for perfect rhyme.

295–7   "Those who shed blood—man or woman—anywhere among mankind, that blood shall be [deemed to be] foully shed and shall have vengeance, men shall see." Compare Genesis 9/6: *Quicumque effuderit humanum sanguinem fundetur sanguis illius* (AV "Whoso sheddeth man's blood, by man shall his blood be shed"). Although 295–7 H seems closer to the Vulgate text, it destroys metre and repeats the opening phrase of 295 at 297.

299   The line appears to contain three strongly stressed syllables instead of the expected four. *now* H supplies the deficiency and is to be preferred.

314   *hath* Compare Mustanoja, p.503: "The auxiliary *have* may stand alone, without the participle, when the meaning is clear from the context." Of the attempts to remedy the supposed "omission", only R, which emends to a personal form, gives sense. A supplies a past participle, but both destroys sense, by adding *he*, and also gives a rough metre. *is* H offers no improvement.

321–2   The dramatist interprets the rainbow as an archery bow, with the string towards the earth, so that the arrow, i.e. the threat, points away from Man. This interpretation does not appear to be in the standard accounts.

328   The line contains four strongly stressed syllables instead of the three usual in the last line of a Chester quatrain.

darlinge This is the only play before play 8 which does not conclude with a direct address to the audience, and the B-variant actually supplies such an address. Throughout the rest of the speech a distinction has been made between what is pledged to Noah, where the singular address, *thou/thee*, is used—269–72, 282, 301, 305, 324—and the general address to mankind, including the audience, where the plural address, *you/yee*, is used. One might have expected, therefore, a double farewell in the final stanza, and suspect that the text is abridged, since it ends with a quatrain rhyming aaaa and repeats *thee* rather awkwardly at 325–6; or that *s* is omitted from *darlinge*. But all manuscripts are unanimous in their readings and clearly reflect the exemplar-form.

PLAY IV

Dramatis Personae Preco, Abraham, Loth, Melchysedech, Armiger, Expositor (Docter), Deus, Isaack, Angelus, Angelus Secundus, Messenger.

NOTE Preco may be doubled with *Messenger*, and perhaps also with *Armiger*; *Expositor* may be doubled with *Docter*.

Locations
Lot — in his owne place 16 + SD, home in this place 23
Melchizedek — to my cyttie 109 (cf. the cyttee 31, 40; here 33)
Sacrifice — that hyll there bysydes thee 214, 228, the hill 263, this hilles bryncke 288; yonder monte 250; the/this place 250 + SD, 279; *with* bryers 441.

Properties
Offerings etc.
Abraham — ryches with greate araye 28, ryches enough 54; an horse that is laden 88 + SD, the laden horse 112 + SD, horse, harnesse, and petrye 93 (*representing one tenth of the whole*)
Lot — my good 46; a goodly cuppe 96 + SD, this royall cuppe 103, the cuppe 104 + SD
Melchizedek — bread and wyne 61, 77, 112 + SD; pocola 64 + SH, a standinge-cuppe 64 + SD, a cuppe full of wynne 72 + SD; bred white and cleare 66, bread 64 + SD, 72 + SD
Sacrifice: wood 231, 239, fagott 243, 257, the bundell of stickes 236 + SD; sworde 233, 236 + SD, 278; fyer 233, 236 + SD alter 358 + SD, 420 + SD
carchaffe 386, 389 + SD
lambe 434, 443 + SD, an horned wether 440.

NOTE 1. Melchizedek, *Before* 1 SD, and Expositor, 112 + SH, enter *equitando*.
2. See 72 + SD BH: *calecem cum vino et pane super patenam*.
3. It may be that a sheath is implied by *that drawen sworde* 266.
4. Material for binding Isaac to the altar is implied in 358, 358 + SD, 420 + SD.
5. *tyed* 441 suggests that the lamb is tethered; but see note.

Costume
None specified.

Sources The biblical sources of the play are:
Abraham and Melchizedek — Genesis 14
God's covenant, and Circumcision — Genesis 15/1-2, 17/1-14
Abraham and Isaac — Genesis 22/1-13.

Critics have detected a connexion between the 'Abraham and Isaac' section of the play and the Brome play on the same subject; see works cited in Bibliography, and also *Non-cycle Plays and Fragments* (ed. Norman Davis), EETS ss 1, 1970, pp.lxiii–lxiv. For convenience, parallels listed by J. Burke Severs, 'The Relationship between the Brome and Chester Play of *Abraham and Isaac*', *MP* xlii (1945), pp.137-51, are cited in the notes below. A. C. Baugh, 'The Chester Plays and French Influence', (in *Schelling Anniversary Papers*, ed. A. H. Quinn (New York, 1923), pp.35-63), notes that 'Abraham and Melchizedek' is found in the *Mistère*, but regards this compatibility as "of less significance" than certain other episodes.

Play-heading For information about the characters named, see 16 + SD note and 32 note.

et dicat Abraham suggests an opening speech from Abraham which does not in fact follow in the text; compare *doth firste of all begine the play* 16 + SD. There are indications that 1-16 represent a change from a version in which Abraham did begin the play; B's side-heading, which adequately characterises the function of the opening speech, may derive from a note in the exemplar. H avoids the difficulty by its variant Play-heading and its variant 16 + SD.

In no manuscript does the play-heading indicate that the play consists of three episodes; all refer only to the first. No other English cycle contains Melchizedek and the Covenant and Circumcision, although these episodes occur in the comprehensive *Mistère*. The episode of 'Abraham and Isaac' is dramatised in Wakefield 4, York 10, *Ludus Coventriae* 5, and in the Cornish Ordinalia, pp.35-8, as well as the *Mistère*; there are also two independent plays of the episode — Brome and Northampton.

Before 1 SD *Preco* On the possibility of the opening and closing speeches by the same speaker, see 13-6 and note. *Nuntius* H would adequately render *Messenger* 483 + SD, rather than *Preco* HmARB, and some initial plan to identify the speakers of the opening and closing speeches may underlie the otherwise inexplicable change in H from *Preco Play-heading* to *Nuntius* SH.

1-16, an address directed to the audience from outside the historical action of the play, is balanced by the similar audience address in 484-90 with which the play concludes. The link is pointed in B, where the side-note to *Before* 1 SD complements 483 + SD. It is lost in H, which omits 475 + SD–*Finis*.

It may be noted that a number of English SDs in HmARB contain information of a non-dramatic nature, that they are often used instead of or as supplements to SHs, and that a number of them are therefore redundant. They may provide an uncertain guide to the actions as suggested in the spoken text. See particularly 48 + SD–112 + SD note.

1–8 Two functions for this prologue are implied by the text. First, the lines suggest that the removal of Noah's Ark, and its replacement by Abraham has been a complicated manoeuvre, so that the audience has now to be called to attention once more after some distraction or delay; such delay might be understandable if the Ark has to be dismasted, the rainbow removed and the bodies of sacrificial and other beasts stored away before the play can change. Secondly, the prologue identifies Abraham, who is apparently not distinguished by costume, and is not mentioned by name before 41—contrast the usual early identification of characters on entry at 1/5, 141; 2/1, 433; 3/1, 17. A third function is discussed in 9–12 note.

8 H's omission seems to be deliberate; a line-space is ruled but left empty after 12 (see TNs).

9–12 It is difficult to see any particular reason why the play should be in *worshippe of the Trynitie*, although reference beyond God the Father is made at 335 and 415. Some specific Trinitarian association betwen Abraham and the figures of the two angels and God who visited him on their way to Sodom (Genesis 18/2) was sometimes proposed, as by Augustine, *Sermones Suppositos* 3 (PL 39/1744). But this identification was not generally adopted, and its connexion with the play is remote. The reference may be less specific, building upon the frequent references to Abraham in the Bible—including his role as God's friend (Isaiah 40/8, 2 Corinthians 20/7, James 2/23) and Christ's statement in John 8/56 that Abraham had seen the day of Christ. But possibly the lines are to be taken as a disclaimer, in which *begynne shall hee* 9 refers only to the Melchizedek episode, with its connexion with the theologically difficult subject of the Eucharist. Reference was made to Melchizedek in the Canon of the Mass, and the Second Vespers and the Prose for Corpus Christi. On the Trinity and the link of the Chester Cycle with Trinity Sunday, see 1/4 and note. Here, the idea may be simply that, whatever the theological complications surrounding the Eucharist, the play is performed to the glory of God.

13 *Goobett-on-the-Greene* Under *gobet*, MED gives examples of its use as a surname under 5, and proposes two derivations—from *gobet*, "fragment", or *go bet*, "go quickly" (MED *gon* 4 (a)). The latter sense seems indicated here, both formally—if *oo* suggests the long vowel—and dramatically, in view of the character's speedy departure at 14–15; compare also the Messenger's speedy departure at 490–1, which would reinforce identification of the speaker of the opening and closing speeches. Although, as Richard Axton suggests (*European Drama of the Early Middle Ages* (London, 1974) p.185), the figure may owe something to folk-lore, it is possible that his name serves to mark him off from other characters in the historical action, and particularly to prevent possible identification of him with the Expositor/Doctor figure.

16 "So that I do not hold up your play". *your* ARBH is to be preferred to the scribally erroneous *you* Hm for syntax and meaning.

16+SD *Abraham* Son of Terah, whose importance as the recipient of God's covenant and as founder of the Israelite and other nations is indicated in the play. On the form of his name see 41 note.

his brother Loth Compare 21, 40+SD, 41. Lot was not Abraham's brother but his nephew, the son of Haran. The confusion here may result from the phrase *Lot fratrem suum* (AV "His brother") in Genesis 14/16; contrast the more accurate phrase *filium fratris Abram* (AV "Lot, Abram's brother's son") in Genesis 14/12.

his owne place Lot lived in the plain of Jordan, towards the city of Sodom, Genesis 13/12. But compare 22-3, where the reference appears to be to the place where Abraham and Melchizedek meet, the valley of Shaveh. See also 31 note.

doth firste of all begine the play: See *Play-heading* note.

Very little of the information in the SD is required for production; the information that Lot is first *restored* before Abraham speaks is conveyed in 22-4. H replaces the SD with a Latin SD, although its content can be inferred from 15-6.

17-24, stanza 3 The repeated rhyme-word *hase* in 18-9 HmH seems to have troubled the other scribes. A substitutes the syntactically inappropriate *hath* in both cases, destroying rhyme; the error perhaps resulted in part from the separation of the verb from its subject at 17, which obscured the fact that it is a second person singular form. The error is shared by B at 18; but the close collocation of *thou hase* 19 evidently prevented B from making a similar mistake and led R to 'correct' the A-reading; but the resulting *hast* RB also destroys the possibility of rhyme. R evidently understood the construction at 18-9, since it does not follow A, and its reading at 19 may therefore indicate only unwillingness to repeat the rhyme-word.

17-8 Compare 1/5-6, 2/1-2.

20 *geven* ARBH is to be preferred to the scribally erroneous *give* Hm for morphology.

The audience is given only a sketchy idea of the circumstances of the battle, as described in Genesis 14/1-16.

25-32, stanza 4 *wond* 25 H is to be preferred to *worne* Hm for rhyme, and to *wonne* AR, *woone* B for rhyme and sense. The AR form suggests an attempt to replace an unintelligible exemplar reading by a more familiar form—influenced either by *wone* 29, "won", or *won*, "dwell, remain", which destroys the sense. The variation between H and Hm probably arose in the simple confusion of *d* and *e*. For perfect rhyme, *wand* is required unless a rounded vowel is postulated for the succeeding rhyme-words.

lande 26 ARH is to be preferred to *landes* HmB for rhyme; the use of the plural form was perhaps influenced by *kinges* earlier in the line.

can wyn 29 H is to be preferred to *have wone* HmARB for rhyme. One construction has been replaced by the other; since HmARB's form has survived, the replacement of an archaic by a more current construction in HmARB seems probable.

26 *iiii kynges* Named in Genesis 14/9 as Chedorlaomer, King of Elam, Tidal, King of nations, Amraphel, King of Shinar, and Arioch, King of Ellasar.

30 Compare Genesis 14/20: *Et dedit ei decimas ex omnibus* (AV "And he gave him tithes of all"). Although the text does not make it clear who was offering tithes to whom, later commentators followed Hebrews 7/2: [*Melchizedek*] *cui et decimas omnium divisit Abraham* (AV "To whom also Abraham gave a tenth part"). In Genesis, Abram's offering follows his receipt of Melchizedek's offering, and no indication of prior intent is given.

31 *the cyttee* Compare 40, and see 16 + SD note. i.e. Salem, where Melchizedek met Abram in the valley of Shaveh, Genesis 14/17. Although Salem is mentioned in the play-heading and in 56 + SH (neither in H), no reference is made to it in the spoken text.

33–4 Genesis gives no biography of Melchizedek and offers no explanation for the exchange which follows. This lack of detail, and the mysterious character of the action and its main participant, Melchizedek, prompted a range of theories which are conveniently summarised in Jerome, *Epistola 73: Ad Evangelum Presbyterum* (PL 22/676–81). Two such theories are applicable to the place of the episode in the Chester Cycle. First, Melchizedek was identified with Noah's son, Shem. The currency of this theory may be judged by its appearance in Comestor, *Historia Scholastica*, 'Liber Genesis' 46 (PL 198/1094–5); Vincent of Beauvais, *Speculum Historiale* 1/104; *Glossa Ordinaria*, 'Liber Genesis' 14/18–19 (PL 113/120); and in vernacular works such as the ME *Genesis and Exodus* (ed. O. Arngart, Lund, 1968), 905–9 and *A Stanzaic Life of Christ*:

> And for Melchisedech aldest was
> of Noe sones, leue ȝe me,
> presthode he occupiet in þat plas,
> And that was gret autorite.
>
> (2493–4)

This theory, which explains Melchizedek's superior position to the patriarch Abram, would also suggest a link to the preceding play for a knowledgeable audience. Secondly, Hebrews 7/11–22 interprets the episode as indicative of two priesthoods— that of Aaron to be superseded in Christ by that of Melchizedek, marking the extension of God's favour to the Gentiles; compare Jerome, *Epistola* 73 (PL 22/678). See also 129–32, 139–44 and notes. With the establishment of the "gentile priesthood", compare the gentile prophecy of Balaam in the following play.

39 I(1) *my* BH is to be preferred to the erroneous *I* Hm and, for meaning, to *a* AR. Compare 32.

41 *Abraham* The patriarch was originally named Abram in Genesis 11/27, but God changed the name to Abraham at the second covenant, Genesis 17/5. All manuscripts have the form *Abraham* here, and strangely no reference is made to the change of name in the dramatisation of God's covenant, although one might have felt that the episode strengthened the link with baptism emphasised at 200.

45–8 Lot is not mentioned in the Genesis account of the meeting of Abram and Melchizedek, and no standard commentary refers to his tithing. His presence balances Melchizedek's *Armiger* and could perhaps also be regarded as representing an exemplary, as opposed to a typological, action of lay reverence for the priesthood; but possibly his function is to restore to Melchizedek a chalice to replace that given to Abraham.

of his sending 47, "from what God has sent". *his* has no immediate antecedent, but clearly refers to God. Lot distinguishes his usual income (45-6) from the spoils sent to him that day.

48 + SD–112 + SD The text at this point includes ten detailed SDs— 48 + SD, 56 + SD, 64 + SD, 68 + SD, 72 + SD, 80 + SD, 88 + SD, 96 + SD, 104 + SD, 112 + SD. Only HmB contain all these SDs; AR omit 112 + SD, and R additionally omits 68 + SD; H omits 64 + SD, 68 + SD, 80 + SD. 112 + SD, but has a further SD at 62 + SD which replaces the parenthetical Latin of 64 + SH.

All SDs are in English in HmARB, but in Latin in H. 48 + SD HmARB is in both English and Latin—R omits the Latin, H the English. B also has both English and Latin forms at 72 + SD and 88 + SD, where the Latin agrees with H's Latin SD.

The position of the SDs varies with each instance and from manuscript to manuscript. AR include all SDs in the body of the text. B places the Latin SDs at 48 + SD, 72 + SD, 88 + SD in the body of the text, but sets all the English SDs in the margin to the left of the text. Hm places 48 + SD Latin, 56 + SD, 64 + SD, 68 + SD, 72 + SD, 80 + SD, 96 + SD in the body of the text, but sets 48 + SD English, 88 + SD, 104 + SD, 112 + SD on the margin to the right or left of the text. H places 48 + SD, 72 + SD, 96 + SD, 104 + SD in the body of the text, but sets 56 + SD, 62 + SD, 88 + SD in the margin to the right of the text.

While any explanation of these variations must be speculative, it is possible that the exemplar contained a series of marginal SDs which B has retained in the margin but which HmARB have incorporated in all or in a number of cases into the body of the text. The exemplar also contained some Latin SDs, e.g. 48 + SD, 72 + SD, 88 + SD, which were glossed by the English SDs in the corresponding margin; HmAR substitute the English forms, but BH retain the Latin forms. H may have ignored the marginal SDs completely; but possibly it selected such aspects of the English SDs as seemed important for production and translated them into Latin, as in the curtailed 56 + SD, the more explicit and intelligible 96 + SD H, and 104 + SD H. 62 + SD replaces the Latin of 64 + SH.

If SDs are intended to indicate movements and the use of properties, 68 + SD, 80 + SD are unnecessary, and 64 + SH HmARB/62 + SD H makes 64 + SD redundant also. 112 + SD, omitted in ARH, merely confirms 109 and is also unnecessary.

dicat 48 + SH R, *et dicat* 56 + SD R may suggest an awareness of exemplar Latin SDs. RH's omission of 68 + SD reflects the SD's redundancy in view of 68 + SH ARBH.

52 *hee* The Armiger/Messenger seems to have been a follower of Abram; 55–6 suggest that he was with Abram during his speech at 17–40. *I* H therefore also gives sense. It would be possible to double this part with that of Preco and the concluding Messenger; the use of *Messenger* in the English SD may suggest that the latter doubling was intended at some production of the Cycle.

57 Compare 10, and 9–12 note; also 1/9–10 et seq. The origin of the line may lie in the phrase of Genesis 14/18: *Erat enim sacerdos Dei altissimi* (AV "And he was the priest of the most high God"). The general anachronism is continued at 60–2, since the Genesis account does not suggest Melchizedek's motives.

63 The line contains three strongly stressed syllables instead of the expected four; *fast* BH may be preferred to its omission in HmAR in producing a four-stress line.

70–2 "For he has certainly everything he prayed for, and he has a special grace from God." Difficulties in this passage arise first because the third person pronouns do not have the same reference—those at 70-1 refer to Abraham while that at 72 refers to God; and secondly, because the referent Abraham was last named at 58, some time previously. These problems are variously resolved by R's *power* 70, which transfers the Abraham-referent pronouns to God, and by H's *great* 72 which replaces the God-referent pronoun. The later change of *hys* to *here* made on the A-manuscript (see TNs) suggests an intention similar to H. The omission of *of* AR is probably the result of a failure to understand the partitive construction.

73–80, stanza 10   *beseeke* 80 A is to be preferred for rhyme to *beeseche* HmRBH. *beseeke* was current until the seventeenth century but, if in the exemplar, had been changed to *beeseche* there.

73–6   Compare 6/1–4; the phrase is reminiscent of the angelic salutation.

75   Either *thou bee* HmARB or *be he* H is acceptable for rhyme or meaning. H may, however, reflect Genesis 14/20: *Et benedictus Deus excelsus, quo protegente hostes in manibus tuis sunt* (AV "And blessed be the most high God, which hath delivered thine enemies into thy hand").

77–8   As here presented, *them* should be understood after *brought* 78. Alternatively, the semi-colon could be placed after *bred*, making *wyne* the object of *brought*. This difficulty does not arise in H, where the omission of *here is* and the reversal of lines makes *bred and wyne* the object of *brought*. The metre of 77 is rough, unless it is assumed that *here is* is elided as *here's*; H's omission gives a more regular sequence of strongly and weakly stressed syllables.

thou 78 Hm is to be preferred to *you* ARBH as continuing the singular form used elsewhere in the speech.

83–6   *ye* 85 picks up the subject *God* 83, separated from the main verb, and the sentence is therefore invocatory—"God, you shall have ... " By omitting the relative pronoun *that* 83, AR make 83–4 into a separate sentence, avoid the repetition of the subject, and change the reference of *ye* from God to Melchizedek. *he* 85 H changes the sentence from invocation to statement. *ye* would be an appropriate vocative form, *you*, the subject; but here one might expect *thou shalt* rather than *ye shall*. H may therefore reflect the original reading, of which *ye* is a corruption; or indicate unease at *ye* rather than *you*.

88 + SD   The form of Abram's tithe is not specified in the biblical account. It may be assumed that the form of tithe shown here was selected for dramatic purposes.

88 + SD–96   95 HmAB gives no sense unless spoken by Abram but the lines are assigned to Melchizedek in 88 + SH AB. R and H resolve the conflict in different ways. By its rewording of 95, R makes the speech appropriate to Melchizedek, while H assigns 93–6 to *Abraham*. BH also have a Latin SD associated with 88, which in B accompanies the English SD and in H replaces it. The Latin SD in B suggests that the following speech will be by Abram, although the English SD and the SH both assign it to Melchizedek; by omitting *dicens*, H avoids this suggestion, and assigns the speech to Melchizedek in the SH. Some preliminary confusion in H may be inferred by the omission of the usual ruling after 92 and the empty quatrain-space after 96 (see TNs).

Of the three possibilities in the manuscripts, that in H is to be preferred as requiring minimum change. At the same time, the possibility that the whole stanza, 12, was spoken by Abram cannot be entirely dismissed since the ascription of all or part of the stanza to Melchizedek seems to rest on the authority of the English SD; the English SDs here tend to have the force of SHs as well as SDs, and the SHs which follow them seem to be at the discretion of the individual scribe and do not appear consistently. In B, the Latin SD was evidently in the exemplar, since it appears also in H, and may reflect the situation before the writing of the English SD. H generally omits the English SDs and, in Latin forms shared with B, such as 72 + and 88 +, omits the part of the SD which acts as SH. Its practice at 88 + may represent an attempt to reconcile the conflicting information of the two SDs. At 96 + SD H has the Latin equivalent for the action described in the English SD after 88, a Latin SD perhaps omitted because it duplicated 88 + SD. If the action described in 88 + SD actually took place after 96, the ascription of 89–96 to Abram would give good sense. Before 88 Abram has reassured Melchizedek that his offering is acceptable and announced his intention to tithe. In 89–90 he accepts Melchizedek's gift, revealing that he understands its significance, and then explains his own offering.

96 + SD   See preceding note. The action described in HmARB at this point is indicated in H as occurring at 104 + SD.

101–4 + SD   Lot announced his intention of tithing with Abram at 47–8 and it may well be that the cup represents his tithe. 104 + SD H, however, seems to suggest either that Lot gives Melchizedek another cup with bread and wine, or that he returns to Melchizedek the cup and the unconsumed bread and wine just presented to Abram. *royall* 103 would then suggest that the cup belonged to Melchizedek rather than that it was appropriate to his rank. Presumably H implies either that Lot makes a different offering at 97–102 or that *will* 97, 102 represents futurity rather than intent. No reference is made to the cup in 112 + SD HmB, where Abram retains the bread and wine.

117–20   Compare Hebrews 7/21–2 (*Hic autem cum iureiurando, per eum qui dixit ad illum: Iuravit Dominus et non paenitebit eum: Tu es sacerdos in aeternum), in tantum melioris testamenti sponsor factus est Jesus* (AV "The Lord sware and will not repent, Thou art a priest for ever after the order of Melchisedec. By so much was Jesus made a surety of a better testament"); also Jerome, *Epistola* 73 (PL 22/678): *Melchisedech, autem, id est Christi et Ecclesiae.*

121–8   Compare Jerome, *Epistola* 73, 3 (PL 22/678) or *Glossa Ordinaria*, 'Liber Genesis' 14/18–19 (PL 113/120), the latter reflecting Isidore, *Quaestiones in Vetus Testamentum* 11 (PL 83/240). A similar idea is found in *Stanzaic Life*:

> The thrid remedy ordeynt was
> aȝeynus our forme-fader syn,
> was sacrifice to gete vs gras
> of bestaile, as I shal ou myn.
> (2509–12)

PLAY IV 51

125–8 "But since Christ died on the cross, we remember his death in bread and wine; and at his last supper, our own 'Last Supper' was commanded by him". 126 has five main stresses instead of the usual four; B reduces the number by omitting the object and destroying the sense, H by supplying a different object. The sense of *mandee* 127 is not clear; it may refer specifically to the ceremony of washing the feet on Maundy Thursday, or to the Last Supper, as in H's version—"And on Maundy Thursday in his Last Supper"—but the HmARB reference seems best taken to be to the Eucharist.

133–4 Compare Vincent of Beauvais, *Speculum Historiale* 1/104, Comestor, *Historia Scholastica*, 'Liber Genesis' 46 (PL 198/1094), and the ME *Genesis and Exodus*:

> Abel primices first bi-gan
> And decimas first abram.
> (921–2)

137–8 Compare 468–71: Abraham is more usually identified with God the Father in the interpretation of the Sacrifice of Isaac. Perhaps the sense here is "the name Abram", meaning *pater excelsus* (Jerome, *Liber de Nominibus Hebraicis* (PL 23/819)).

139–40 Compare Isidore, *Allegoriae Quaedam Scripturae Sacrae* (PL 83/104).

141 *the foresayde day* Presumably the reference is to 125–8, although only the H-version specifies a day.

143 H's omission destroys sense and seems to be a scribal error; a line space is blank after 144 (see TNs).

144 *his* HmB may represent the exemplar form; R, taking *presente* as adjective rather than noun, substitutes *here*, to the detriment of meaning. *Melchesadeckes* AH the inflected possessive, may perhaps be metrically preferable.

149 "O lord, O that you would have regard to one thing." The subject is expressed in *lord* and may be understood before *wouldest*. But *thou* ARBH is to be preferred for syntactical completeness, and in producing a more regular sequence of strongly and weakly stressed syllables. Hm's omission may originate in scribal confusion of the consecutive forms *that* and *thou* (or $þ^t$ and $þ^u$?), reflected also in A's omission of *that*; the A-line is, however, syntactically complete.

154–8 With *my nurrye* 154, compare Genesis 15/3: *Mihi autem non dedisti semen, et ecce vernaculus meus heres meus erit* (AV "Behold, to me thou hast given no seed; and lo, one born in my house is mine heir"). At this point in Genesis the reference is apparently to the son of Abram's steward, Eliezer of Damascus. But the Chester account combines two different covenants. 145–68 traces the first covenant, of Genesis 15/1–6, while 169–92 deals with the second, Genesis 17/1–14. Between these two accounts, in Genesis chapter 16, Abram has a son, Ishmael, by his wife's handmaiden, Hagar. Hence, although the biblical text underlying the line does not refer to Ishmael, such a reference might be understood from the telescoped chronology of the Chester account. However, the obliqueness of *nurrye*, and the lack of detail in the text to give it more precise meaning, may suggest that the term is used merely to suggest Abram's dilemma in lacking an heir and is not intended to evoke specific biblical reference.

162 *tell* Compare *numera* (AV "tell"), Genesis 15/5; the verb has the sense of "count", *tell* OED II.1, but was apparently taken by H to mean "communicate", OED I.3. H accordingly provides an indirect object, *me*, although the construction would remain syntactically incomplete.

165–7 *for noe neede* 165 has no biblical counterpart, but gives acceptable sense. *for thy meede* H may represent an anticipation of the reaffirmed covenant of Genesis 22/16–8, where the covenant is presented as a reward for Abraham's obedience in not sparing Isaac; compare 444–51.

withowten dreede 167 is also without biblical counterpart but is acceptable. *deede* B is a scribal error which destroys the sense. It may, however, reflect an exemplar error in view of the adoption of the same reading by H. H, however, redrafts 167 to accommodate *deede* and continue the idea of the covenant as a reward—apparently for Abraham's offering to Melchizedek, but see preceding paragraph.

173 Compare Genesis 17/4: *Erisque pater multarum gentium* (AV "And thou shalt be a father of many nations"). No manuscript gives good sense. Deimling accepts the A-reading, "you shall be advanced so much more", but the sense is rather strained and A is to be preferred only because B's "so much further shall you be advanced" and R's "so great shall you be" are even weaker, while Hm gives no meaning. Perhaps a corrupt exemplar, which could account for these versions, also explains the omission of 173–4 in H. For closer conformity to the biblical passage, read *to* for *soe* and *father* for *forther*, both simple scribal confusions which, if they existed, were present in the exemplar.

175–6 The Messianic prophecy is not explicit in Genesis as here; compare 205 and note; and 6/105–6, 439–42.

182 *mee* The BH omission is a shared and inexplicable error which destroys the sense of the line.

187-90 Compare *Glossa Ordinaria*, 'Liber Genesis' 17/10 (PL 113/123), and *Stanzaic Life*:

> Anoþer cause assignet is
> qvy circumcisioun ordeynt was,
> to know þat folk fully for his.
>
> (1441-3)

187 contains only three strongly stressed syllables where one would expect four; the variants to 187, however, seem rather to indicate unease at the pronoun-subject, perhaps from a feeling that it challenges the omniscience of God. None gives improved sense over Hm, and the variants have only limited textual interrelationship, seeming rather to represent different solutions of a semantic problem.

191 *owne* ARBH is to be preferred to *one* Hm; the latter is formally erroneous, although the meaning is clear in context.

193–200, stanza 25 The b-rhyme in HmARB is imperfect; 200 H, rhyming *tane—began*, is preferable. A better rhyme would be obtained from the more common ME form *bapteme*.

193 Hm is acceptable, but ARB or H give a more regular sequence of strongly and weakly stressed syllables.

PLAY IV 53

193–200 Compare Aquinas, *Summa Theologiae* 3a, 70, art. 1 (p.156).

211–6 God, and the dramatist, gives the audience no reason for the command, although some motive may readily be deduced from Genesis 22/1: *Tentavit Deus Abraham* (AV "God did tempt Abraham"). Explanations are offered to the audience in Wakefield 4/49–56, York 10/67–8, Northampton 1–34 and, perhaps significantly, Brome 32–46; no explanation is given in *Ludus Coventriae* 5 or the Cornish Ordinalia.

214 Compare 228: in Genesis 22/2–4 the hill is in *terram visionis* (AV "the land of Moriah"), three days' journey away. The journey was presented by some commentators as part of God's test—see Chrysostom, *In Cap. Gen. Homil.* 47 (PG 54/428–34), *Glossa Ordinaria*, 'Liber Genesis' 22/2 (PL 113/137). The journey is dramatised in Wakefield 4/113–20, York 10/108–50, and *Mistère*: there is a reference to it in Northampton 135 + SD, and Brome specifies the land at 63. *Ludus Coventriae* alone resembles Chester here—*3on hey hylle* 5/83, *3on hille* 5/87. The action is obviously abridged and concentrated by having the hill nearby.

224 The line has four strongly stressed syllables where one would expect three. 224 H offers a regular three-stress line. The fact that Hm, A, R, B, and H all have different readings at this point argues strongly for some obscurity in the exemplar, probably arising from either the erroneous transfer of *lorde* from the preceding line, or some difficulty in alignment whereby the status of *lorde done* was not clear.

225 Compare 154 and note. Abraham had only two children, Ishmael and Isaac, and the point of the sacrifice is its apparent nullification of God's earlier covenant with Abraham. Genesis 20/2 emphasises that Isaac is Abraham's only legitimate son, a point stressed also in the other cycles. Compare 317, where Isaac expressly states that Abraham has other sons, and Brome 198–9, the only play to make the same point.

227–8 + SD Since Chester does not dramatise the journey, it is perhaps not surprising that it makes no reference to the two servants who accompany Abraham and Isaac to the hill in Genesis 22/3. In this Chester resembles *Ludus Coventriae*, the Cornish Ordinalia and Brome.

The lines and SD indicate that Isaac is present on stage with Abraham at this point in the play.

228–48 The correspondence with Brome begins at 229.

The preparations for the journey seem to be duplicated at 229–40 and 241–8; Severs (p.141), contrasting this duplication with the single section in Brome 116–8, cited the duplication as evidence of Chester's inferiority to and dependence upon Brome: "The two passages involved go back to a common original eight lines and some scribe or compiler or author, confronted with alternate forms, unwisely or unconsciously included them both." Some confirmation of Severs' view may be seen in the different positions of the SD indicating that Isaac has picked up the wood—after 236 in HmARB and after 248 in H. If the passages do represent alternatives, the choice between them must follow 224, when one can continue to 225 or move directly to 241. In the second account, Abraham gives Isaac no explanation of what he is doing, and no reference is made to the sword.

237   The ARBH reading is to be preferred to Hm, which has erroneously omitted *am*.

257–64, stanza 33   257 ARBH is to be preferred to Hm for rhyme.

At 264 there are four strong stresses where one would expect three and, for a regular sequence of strongly and weakly stressed syllables, *in* ARBH is to be preferred to *upon* Hm, but a further syllable would still have to be lost. The omission of *here*, found in all manuscripts, would improve the line, though AR's omission of *this* would also 'regularise' the line. Hm's choice of *upon* rather than *in* is unusual, though not unintelligible since the site is a hillside; but some influence from *upon the hill* 263 may be suspected.

258–80   The reply to the absence of the sacrificial animal, and Isaac's fear of the drawn sword, are duplicated—261-8 and 269–80. Severs compares Brome 135-49; he argues that 263-4 originally belonged to Isaac's speech, to which Abraham replied at 269-72: but that later, Isaac's lines, 263-4, were re-allocated to Abraham. As a result of the re-allocation, motivation had to be supplied for Abraham's words at 269-72; so a new speech, 265-8, was created for Isaac, with resulting duplication. *sonne* 263 would not have appeared in the original, since Isaac would have been the speaker; its omission would improve the movement of line 263. Abraham's speech at 263-4 has no biblical counterpart, unlike his reply at 269-72 which is based on Genesis 22/8.

Two other possibilities exist. First, the text may be correct. Isaac's question takes Abraham by surprise, and as he is seeking to amplify his inadequate answer at 263-4, Isaac asks a second question. When Abraham has at last groped his way to an answer to Isaac's first question, Isaac points out that his second question is not answered. Second, the two accounts may represent alternatives in the manner proposed by Severs for 228–248 (one assumes that because Severs could postulate a process by which the text in Chester could have been derived from that of Brome, he felt it unnecessary to suggest that the text presented a conscious choice here). 263-8 gives Isaac grounds for growing suspicion as Abraham fails to answer either question satisfactorily; 269-80 initially lowers the tension by suggesting an answer to Isaac's first question, but then builds up Isaac's doubts once more.

If the text is not correct but is either corrupt or presenting alternatives, it should be noted that the two versions divide in the middle of stanza 34 and that it is impossible to move directly from 262 to 269 or from 268 to 281 without destroying the stanza-patterns.

Isaac's fear of the drawn sword is seen also in Wakefield 4/201-2. *drawen* 266 presumably indicates that the sword was previously sheathed, a fact which may explain Abraham's failure to refer to it in the second version of the preparations, at 241-5.

265–72, stanza 34   For perfect rhyme, some form such as *aferd* is required at 265. Although the form survived into the seventeenth century, and longer in dialect, it was replaced in standard usage by *afraid*, and the form here probably represents a modernisation in the exemplar. *aferd* would give a true rhyme with *sword* 266, and with the ME form *midelerd* 267, which has become corrupted in the various manuscripts.

stydd 271 H is to be preferred to *fyelde* HmARB for rhyme, and also for sense since the latter is hardly appropriate to the hilltop setting. *stead* in the sense of "place" is

PLAY IV 55

last recorded by OED in 1596 and was becoming obsolete at the time of the earliest extant manuscripts. Since it is unlikely that all scribes would independently substitute *fyelde*, the substitution of a current word for an archaic one in the exemplar may be suspected. In choosing *fyelde* the moderniser may have been influenced either by a desire to avoid the repetition of *stedde* 264, which has not been changed, or by a desire to indicate a rhyme with *wylde* 272. Deimling cites the variant as evidence of H's superiority.

274 *harme* The meaning seems to be "take harm","take hurt"; compare *harmen* MED 2. The unease of the scribes at this passage is indicated by AR's transformation of the construction into the passive and H's rephrasing, making *harme* a noun object.

282 A erroneously repeats 276.

286–92 Genesis does not indicate Isaac's age, but at 22/5 describes him as *puer* (AV "the lad"); Chester here follows the majority of plays in presenting Isaac as a young boy. An alternative tradition, that Isaac was twenty-five years old at this time, is given in Josephus, *Antiquities of the Jews* I, 13/2, and is relayed by some standard commentators—compare Comestor, *Historia Scholastica*, 'Liber Genesis' 18 (PL 198/1104); the tradition of the adult Isaac influenced the presentation at York.

297–302 Chester has the reverse of the sequence in Brome where Isaac's reference to his mother's prayers precedes Abraham's lament. Chester has no counterpart to Isaac's final plea (178–80), which would have to follow 300:

And sythyn that my moder ys not here
I prey 30w, fader, schonge 30wr chere,
And kyll me not wyth 30wyre knyffe.

Compare also 322–4. Genesis makes no reference to Sarah at this point, but commentators took up the fact that Abraham apparently did not tell his wife and interpreted it as evidence of the patriarch's stoicism and resolve; compare (Pseudo-) Chrysostom, *De Homilia in Beato Abraham*, Homilia 2 (PG 50/739). Sarah's farewell to her husband and son is dramatised in Northampton and the *Mistère*.

309–16 Severs notes that the pledge of obedience by Abraham corresponds to Isaac's pledge of obedience in Brome 187–97, and that the equivalent speech in York 10/191–6 is also assigned to Isaac; he finds the Brome arrangement smoother. Chester perhaps focuses more steadily upon Abraham and limits Isaac's role.

315–6 Isaac's willing participation in the sacrifice may be inferred from his continued silent waiting with his father at Genesis 22/8, but Jewish traditions made him a more active partner—compare Josephus, *Antiquities of the Jews* I, 13/4, and the convenient account under "Isaac" in the *Jewish Encyclopaedia*. Since such willing co-operation increased the exemplary and typological functions of Isaac, it was noted by commentators; compare Comestor, *Historia Scholastica*, 'Liber Genesis' 57 (PL 198/1105). In York 10/213–6 and Northampton 224–5 the binding is at Isaac's request.

316–7 Compare 154, 225 and notes.

329–42 Severs notes that these lines represent the reverse of the sequence in Brome 210–25 where the reference to Sarah follows Isaac's request for blessing.

333-40, stanza 43   the b-rhymes, *light* 336 — *gryll* 340, do not rhyme, No manuscript has the required form *gright* at 340, so the exemplar may be assumed to have had *gryll*. But scribes appear to have experienced some difficulty with the passage. B recasts 340, presumably with the sense "lest I, afraid, should turn away"; and AR omit 332 + SH and 333-6.

346-7   As presented in the text, 347 explains the *one thinge* of 345; the sentence is either exclamatory or elliptical, requiring a verb to be understood. Possibly the omission of 346 in H is not a mere scribal error but an attempt to clarify the construction by bringing 347 closer to the noun to which it is in apposition.

357-66   Severs compares Brome 242-7, where Abraham tells Isaac he must be bound so that he will not interfere with the sacrifice, and Isaac protests that he will not hinder Abraham's offering; he argues that in Chester the absence of Abraham's explanation, which is replaced by Isaac's abrupt statement that they will never meet again, leaves 366 without real meaning. Moreover, he notes that 359 refers to Abraham while Brome refers to Sarah, giving Brome a better integrated text; he concludes that in Chester the line "has, through garbling, been misplaced." The lack of objection by Isaac strengthens the notion of his voluntary co-operation and weakens the idea of paternal coercion.

358 + SD   The action, which conforms to Genesis 22/9, is complete only at 381; hence the H-version accurately indicates the immediate action of 357-8 only.

364   H here erroneously repeats its version of 356.

367-8   *I* 368 ARBH is to be preferred to *yee* Hm for meaning and syntax. 367 appears in two different forms. The Hm version includes *to*, indicating the dependence of *doe* on *wyll* 366—"but [will] always do what you request"; *vowe* here has the sense of "earnest wish or desire; prayer" recorded from 1563 by OED. If, however, Hm had not had *to*, it would be possible to retain *yee* 368—"but always do what you have vowed as long as you are able"; a similar result would be obtained by understanding *yee maye* or another auxiliary before *to doe*—"but [you are] always to carry out what you have vowed". The ARBH version gives more obvious and immediate sense—"but always obey you, as long as I am able"; *unto* 367 H is perhaps to be preferred to *to* ARB as giving a more regular sequence of strongly and weakly stressed syllables. The two versions are clearly alternatives and are not linked by any pattern of textual modification.

369   *brethen yonge brethren* ARBH is to be preferred to the scribally erroneous *brethen* Hm. On the use of *yonge* 369 in an *-i-* rhyme, compare 21/280.

374   The metre of the line is rough and the variants in B and H perhaps represent an attempt to produce a more regular sequence of strongly and weakly stressed syllables; neither attempt is completely satisfactory.

378   "You make me unhappy every time"—i.e. every time Isaac "moans". Severs compares Brome 270: "In all thy lyffe thow grevyd me neuer onys", and concludes that the Chester dramatist fails to appreciate that Isaac has never offended, hence the Chester Abraham does forgive his son at 380. Some such idea seems to underlie the variants in AR and H, which suggest that Isaac's sole offence is to cause Abraham

PLAY IV

anguish on this one occasion. But if a link with Brome is postulated, it might also involve a comparison with Brome 282–3, where Isaac cries:

> A, mercy, fader, morne 3e no more.
> 3owr wepyng make my hart sore.

By the interpretation suggested here, Abraham's forgiveness at 380 is a general act and has no connexion with his words at 378. Protests of Isaac's innocence are found in Wakefield 4/219 and Northampton 176; in York 10/265–6, forgiveness for the sins of the adult Isaac is implored.

385–9 Severs compares Brome 285–90, where the request for blindfolding is followed by a further request for a speedy despatch which motivates Abraham's farewell; he feels that 389 is an inappropriate response to 385–8. The blindfolding is dramatised also in York 10/288–9, where the reason is enigmatically given as "Thus may yowre offerand be parfite", and in *Ludus Coventriae* 5/179–82, where the intention is to spare Abraham distress. Possibly some echo of execution-ritual is involved here. See 389 + SD note.

389 + SD A is clearly wrong in suggesting that Isaac kneels; Abraham, who had placed Isaac on the altar at 381, now kneels to speak in his son's ear. Significantly, R does not share A's error. But the error seems to result partly from the lack of a subject in the SD, and hence of a reference for the pronouns; and partly because the speaker after the SD is Isaac and not Abraham. Since the first part of the action described fulfils 385–6, and since the SD is in the margin in Hm and B (the position in the latter perhaps being particularly significant, see TNs), it is likely that the SD should follow 388, and that 389, which Severs feels to be an inadequate response, is isolated from the preceding line by a series of actions. Abraham would then address 389 to Isaac while kneeling. H omits this important SD, perhaps because of the difficulties resulting from its misplacement.

420 + SD There is no justification in the spoken text for this further binding, nor does there seem to be any practical or dramatic necessity for it. This part of the SD is omitted in R and was not included in the H version. If the further binding is correct, we are presumably to distinguish between the binding of Isaac at 358 + SD and his binding to the altar here.

420 + SH The SD mentions only one angel; but compare *Angelus Secundus* 428 + SH. By adding *2* to 420 + SH and 422 + SH, H seems to reduce the number of speaking angels, since it lacks any *Angelus 1*. In Genesis 22/11 and other plays, the speaker is a single angel.

429–35, stanza 56 The stanza, unusually, contains only seven lines; it lacks an a-rhyme line in the second quatrain. H supplies an extra, and acceptable, line after 434.

434 Compare 443 + SD, but contrast *a horned wether* 440, reflecting Genesis 22/13: *Arietem inter vepres haerentem cornibus* (AV "A ram caught in a thicket by his horns"). The use of *lambe* may be designed to strengthen the link of the sacrificial beast with the Lamb of God; compare Isidore, *Quaestiones in Vet. Testam.* 18 (PL 83/251): *Sed illud, quod figuratum est in Isaac, translatum est ad arietem. Cur hoc, nisi quia Christus ovis? ipse enim filius, ipse agnus.* See also *Glossa Ordinaria*, 'Liber Genesis' 22/9–11 (PL 113/139).

441 *tyed* Compare Genesis 22/13, *haerentem* (AV "caught"). The form of 440–1 may suggest that the ram was physically tethered, rather than held by its horns.

442 B's omission is apparently a scribal error; the resulting text still gives sense.

450 *het* H is to be preferred for sense to the erroneous *highe* HmARB.

452–9, stanza 59   No manuscript has the form *bede* 455 required for rhyme. The use of the past tense *bade* is prompted by *haste beene* 454, but present tense is clearly indicated.

454–5   The B/H variant at the start of 454 seems to be an attempt to render the construction of Genesis 22/18: "*Quia obedisti voci meae*" (AV "Because thou hast obeyed my voice").

456   "And you shall be blessed by all nations". But compare Genesis 22/18: *Benedicentur .... omnes gentes terrae* (AV "Shall all the nations of the earth be blessed"). Possibly *of* should be taken to imply a preceding collective—"[Men] of all nations ... shall be blessed"; H's omission of *of* brings the text closer to the biblical text.

459+SD   The SD is in the margin of HmB (see TNs) and duplicates the information of 459+SH. It is omitted by ARH, and was evidently a further marginal addition to the exemplar. *Expositor* B is evidently a substitution influenced by 459+SH.

464–75   The exposition which equates Abraham with God the Father and Isaac with Jesus is commonplace. Compare Isidore, *Quaestiones in Vet. Test.* 'In Genesin' 18/6 (PL 83/250); also *Glossa Ordinaria*, 'Liber Genesis' 22/5–8 (PL 113/138).

468–75, stanza 61   The b-rhymes, *to* 471—*confounde* 475, do not rhyme. *underfonge* H equally does not rhyme, but indicates that the true rhyme may have been the original infinitive form, *underfo*. *Underfo* is last recorded by OED in 1513 (*vnderfonge* ppl.), *underfong* in 1614. The former was therefore obsolete by the time of the extant manuscripts; *underfang* was becoming so during the life of the plays and was presumably replaced by *confounde*. *confounde* destroys the rhyme, but shifts the emphasis from the typological parallel of the Crucifixion to the Resurrection, "to confound death". It is unlikely that H would substitute for *confounde* a form which was obsolete and still did not rhyme, and it seems possible that H endeavoured to restore the original form which was distinguishable in the exemplar but not clear. Since *underfonge* contains one syllable more than *confounde*, H's omission of *for* 475 is metrically justified; no similar justification exists for B's omission of *for*, but the BH agreement here may suggest that *for* had been inserted in the text when the rhyme-word was changed, and B misunderstood its status.

A's word-order at 472 destroys the aaabcccb rhyme-scheme, but substitutes an a-rhyme word.

471   The line seems to contain four strongly stressed syllables instead of the expected three. H's omission of *that* may be preferred in restoring a three-stress line.

475+SD–*Finis*   On H's omission of this section, compare *Before* 1 SD note.

476–83   Abraham was traditionally an example of human faith; compare Hebrews 11/17: *Fide obtulit Abraham Isaac, cum tentaretur; et unigenitum offerebat qui*

PLAY IV

susceperat repromissiones (AV "By faith Abraham, when he was tried, offered up Isaac: and he that had received the promises offered up his only begotten son"). The Doctor shifts emphasis from the typological level of the historical action to its exemplary function for a contemporary audience.

484–91, stanza 63   No manuscript has the required rhyme-form *abye* 491. This form, in the sense of "remain", is last recorded by OED in 1596. *abyde* may perhaps represent the replacement of an obsolescent form by its more current equivalent.

489   *he save* ARB is to be preferred for meaning to *the same* Hm. The Hm reading probably derives from a misreading of the exemplar-form underlying ARB.

PLAY V

Dramatis Personae Deus, Moyses, Doctor, Balaack, Miles, Balaham, Asina, Angelus.

NOTE It is assumed that *all my people that bine here* 2, *populo* 32 + SD, 80 + SD, refer to the audience.

Locations
monte(m) 32 + SD, 80 + SD, 95 + SD, this hill 265, *representing initially* the monte of Synaye 70.

Properties
tables 67 *and note*, 78, stonye tables 53, tables kerved owt 74, tabulas 80 + SD
Balaam's asse 197, 217, 225, asinam 215 + SD, 223 + SD, 271 + SD
Balak's equo 271 + SD
Angel's gladio extricto 216 + SD, evaginatum gladium 239 + SD
Balak's sworde 143 + SD.

NOTE 1. 272–9, 304–7 are not here regarded as reflecting a realised setting.
2. *kerve* 66, 74, *effoderet de monte* 80 + SD, may suggest a stone-cutting instrument, perhaps also required by *wryte* 67, 76, 77, *scribens* 80 + SD.
3. *extricto* 216 + SD, *evaginatum* 239 + SD may suggest a sheath.
4. *equitabunt* 199 + SD, 255 + SD confirms the obvious requirement of a horse for Miles.

Costumes
None specified.

Sources
Moses and the Law — giving of the first set of tables, Exodus 20/1–17, Deuteronomy 5; giving of the second set of tables, Exodus 34/1–35/6
Balaam and Balak — Numbers 22/1–24/25
Moabite Women and sequel — Numbers 25/1–18, 31/1–12.
A. C. Baugh, 'The Chester Plays and French Influence', notes that "Balaam and his Ass" is found also in *Mistère*, but regards this compatibility as "of less significance" than that in other episodes.

NOTE A different version of Play 5, that in H, is printed in Appendix IB of Volume I. The notes below relate only to the HmARB version, but they are applicable also to the corresponding passages in H where the two versions agree. Reference here is made to H to indicate major points of divergence between the two versions and wherever the H readings are helpful for the interpretation of HmARB. The notes to Appendix IB relate only to passages unique to H.

Play-heading HmARB refer only to the first part of the play, the giving of the Law; compare *Play-heading* H and Banns. The play contains three episodes — the giving of the Law, Balaam and Balak, and the seduction of the Israelite youth by the Moabite women. The giving of the Law is dramatised in *Ludus Coventriae* 6 and *Mistère* 25186–896; the commandments are recited by Moses in Wakefield 7/31–90, and by Christ in Wakefield 18/113–80 and York 20/145–92. The Balaam and Balak episode is found in no other English cycle, but is shown in *Mistère* 26651–7010 and was also a feature of liturgical drama. *Mistère* refers to the final decisive battle, but not to the seduction. The episode of Balaam and Balak is also recounted in *Stanzaic Life* 1593–728, although the account shows only general correspondences with the Chester version.

2 *here* i.e. Mount Sinai, on whose lower slopes the Israelites remained while Moses received the Law; compare the Exodus and Deuteronomy accounts. Here the unspecified nature of the place encompasses the Chester audience.

3–4 Compare 148–55. The episode of the exodus of the Israelites from Egypt is dramatised in Wakefield 8 and York 11; in neither cycle is the giving of the Laws presented.

5–6 Compare *x poynctes* 44. The biblical account nowhere specifies ten commandments; the division into ten was adopted by Jewish writers and followed by Christian commentators. Since Moses received the Law on two tables, Jewish writers held that there were five laws on each table, but Christian commentators accepted a division corresponding to Christ's account of the dual responsibility of Christians to God and to their fellow men, holding that the first table contained commandments relating to one's duty to God and the second commandments relating to one's duty to one's fellow men. The generally accepted division, following Augustine, was that there were three commandments on the first table and seven on the second; but an alternative tradition, from Origen, held that there were four on the first table and six on the second, although the content of the two tables was identical by either system and the main difference was in the division of the commandments into ten. Augustine regarded Exodus 20/3–6 as one commandment, Origen as two. Compare Vincent of Beauvais, *Speculum Historiale* 2/9: *In distinctione autem doctores dissentiunt, nam primum mandatum quod secundum Augu. vnum est: Origenes in duo diuidit.* The division has some importance since the Roman Catholic Church used the Augustine division while the Church of England used the Origen division. From 1552 the Anglican form was regularly disseminated by the introduction of the recital of the commandments in the Communion Service in place of the *kyrie*. HmARB seem to have the latter arrangement, although *nor* 6 B, *ne* H may suggest that 5 and 6 are to be regarded as separate injunctions. Compare 16–20 note.

9–11 "I will that you keep and also honour your holy day, [and keep and honour] father and mother in all possible ways." By this reading *hould* bears the MED senses 18(a) at 9–10 and 17(a) at 11; *worshippe* combines the senses of *sanctifices* and *honora* in Exodus 20/8: *Memento ut diem sabbati sanctifices* (AV "Remember the sabbath day, to keep it holy") and 20/12: *Honora patrem tuum et matrem tuam* (AV "Honour thy father and thy mother"). H omits *yt* 10, making *father and mother* the sole object of *worshippe*; the result is an ostensibly simpler syntax, but the suppression of *sanctifices*, which is presumably held to be comprehended in *hould*. Compare *Ludus Coventriae* 6/100, "halwe well þin haly day"; and *Cursor Mundi*:

  And hald þu wele þi haliday
  Fadir and moder ye worschip ay.
     (6473–4)

13 *fornication* Compare Exodus 20/14: *Non moechaberis* (AV "Thou shalt not commit adultery"). *fornication* may be used in the specific sense of adultery, but may also be used to comprehend other forms of lechery. Compare *Glossa Ordinaria*, 'Liber Exodus' 20/14 (PL 113/255), Comestor, *Historia Scholastica*, 'Liber Exodus' 40 (PL 198/1165), and Wyclif, *Ten Comandmentis* (ed. Thomas Arnold, *Select English Works of John Wyclif*, Vol. III, 87): "Þe sixte comaundement is þis: 'Þou schalt do no lecherie, bodili ne goostli'".

14 *meanes* Hm gives an erroneous form intermediate between R's singular and H's plural. R, AH, and B are all acceptable here. B is derivable from the HmARH forms only as a misreading of the final *s* of a singular form as an abbreviation for *-ner*; but it may well be an independent substitution—"no kind of goods".

15–6 Compare Exodus 20/16: *Non loqueris contra proximum tuum falsum testimonium* (AV "Thou shalt not bear false witness against thy neighbour"). *lenge* is last recorded by OED in 1586 and may therefore have been obsolete by the time of the extant manuscripts. It is interpreted as a present participle by A and B; compare *abyde* 15 H.

17–24 See 5–6 note. To compensate for the "amalgamation" of Exodus 20/3–6 as one commandment, commentators divided Exodus 20/17 into two commandments; compare Vincent of Beauvais, *Speculum Historiale* 2/9: *Et ultima quae secundum Augu. duo sunt, Origines in vnum colligit, cui etiam Iosephus consentit*. The Augustinian division is based on the version in Deuteronomy 5/21, where the injunction prohibiting the coveting of one's neighbour's wife precedes the other injunctions, as here; but Comestor, *Historia Scholastica*, 'Liber Exodus' 40, gives a division based upon Exodus 20/17, where the injunction prohibiting the coveting of one's neighbour's house precedes the other injunctions. This latter was widely disseminated through such works as John Gaytrigg's Sermon and Wyclif's exposition. In the Origen/Anglican version, such a subdivision was unnecessary. Wakefield 7/79–84, 18/169–76 and *Ludus Coventriae* 6/163–78 follow the Augustinian arrangement, while York 20/186–90 rather clumsily combines the Augustine and 'Comestor' versions in a complete ninth commandment. Chester seems to make no such division, combining the reference to wife and other prohibited possessions in a single construction. But, since 20 represents the end of

PLAY V 63

the commandment in the Bible, some trace of the 'Comestor' distinction between movable and immovable goods (*that hee hath bought* versus *his thinge*) may linger, though in reversed sequence. More probably, however, 21–2 represent a distinction between covert desire for the unattainable and continuing desire for the attainable which the neighbour has refused to bestow; compare *Mistère* 25319–21 and *Glossa Ordinaria*, 'Liber Exodus' 20/15 (PL 113/255).

25–32 Moses' speech to God has no biblical counterpart; H has instead a stanza corresponding to the Exodus continuation at 20/18–9. Moses' fast is mentioned in Deuteronomy 9/9; Exodus 24/18 refers to his forty-day sojourn, and 34/28 to his fast at the giving of the second tables. The stanza makes Moses an example of the obedience, and consequent divine favour, of which the ordinary human being is capable.

31 *tokenn* OED *token* 4, "an act serving to demonstrate divine power or authority". Here, not only are the tables themselves a *token*, but the commandments themselves are *tokens*, to be learned; and at 39, the *token* of the Law can also be performed (*doe yee*). Deimling regards *token* 39 as "meaningless", preferring *teachinge* H.

34 "God has contrived this as a means of testing you." HmH read *with*, and correspond in sense to Exodus 20/20, *probaret vos* (AV "to prove you"). A and R destroy this sense; B accurately reflects the biblical phrase, though at the expense of a rougher metre.

35–6 The lines differ significantly from 35–6 H, which are close to Exodus 20/20. The HmARB form may derive from Deuteronomy 4/10: *Congrega ad me populum, ut audiant sermones meos, et discant timere me omni tempore quo vivunt in terra, doceantque filios suos* (AV "Gather me the people together, and I will make them hear my words, that they may learn to fear me all the days that they shall live upon the earth, and that they may teach their children"). The import is that this is the first authoritative definition of good and evil for mankind; and the text seems to be amplified from Romans 3/20: *Quia ex operibus legis non iustificabitur omnis caro coram illo; per legem enim cognitio peccati* (AV "Therefore by the deeds of the law there shall no flesh be justified in his sight; for by the law is the knowledge of sin").

37 *this sight* i.e. the sight of God. In Exodus 20/18 the Israelites' fear is aroused by specific manifestations of God's presence rather than by his words; in H 26, the fear is aroused by the brightness of God.

41ff. After 40 H diverges from HmARB, having one speech without counterpart in HmARB, followed by a speech corresponding to 81–95 and an exposition corresponding to 41–64.

41–8 The Doctor distinguishes the most effectual of the many instructions given by God to Moses, i.e. the Decalogue, from the other items. The pronoun at 43 AR and B gives a more regular sequence of strongly and weakly stressed syllables than the omission in Hm.

49–57 The lines contain three temporal references which are best discussed together:

after 49, "later in the story"—after God had pronounced the Law, he gave the tables to Moses.

before 54, "at first"—in contrast to 57; "At first, when the Israelites worshipped idols, Moses broke the tables, but later ..." Alternatively, but less probably, the lines may suggest "earlier in time"—before they received the Law, men worshipped idols. The tables are mentioned at Exodus 31/18 and 32/15-6; between the references lies the account of the Israelites' secession from God to worship the golden calf and God's warning to Moses of their rebellion and his intended wrath. Hence, even before Moses delivered the law to his people, they worshipped idols. A further possibility is that true worship of one God was not prevalent among men before God showed his favour to Moses. Such a view is endorsed by Balaam's conduct—compare 248 H. *after* 57, "later in time"—after Moses had broken the tables.

58-9 The biblical accounts show some contradiction at this point. In Exodus 34/1 God says that he will write on the second set of tables supplied by Moses, but Exodus 34/27-8 indicates that they were written by Moses. Deuteronomy 10/4, however, states that God wrote the second set of tables. Although 58-9 do not indicate the writer, 78-9 HmARB follows the Exodus version: compare Comestor, *Historia Scholastica* 'Liber Exodus' (PL 198/1192): *Potest dici quod auctoritas scribendi fuit in Domino, ministerium in Moyse.* H, lacking the later passage, leaves the issue of authorship unresolved.

61-4 ARBH *shryned* 61, *shryne* 63 are to be preferred to the erroneous *shryved*, *shryve* Hm, which results from the confusion of *u* and *n*. Deuteronomy 10/1-5 combines the second giving of the Law with the building of an ark to house the tablets on which it was written, whereas Exodus 34/29 continues with the account of Moses' transfiguration.

64+SD The SD indicates that God has withdrawn from the scene unnoted at some point after 24. *appeared* AR is evidently a substitution resulting from the use of the past tense in 41-64.

75 *this boone boon* in the sense of "a prayer to God, Christ, etc." is last recorded by OED in 1513, but the form continues in other senses to the end of the century and beyond. The use here seems to have troubled AR, although possibly the word was not clear in the exemplar. A omits the two words; R substitutes *what bene*, destroying meaning and metre.

80+SD According to Exodus 34/4, Moses cut the stones in advance and carried them up the mountain. No suggestion of descent and re-ascent is made here, although 69 follows Exodus 34/1 in having God summon Moses to Sinai, a summons issued the previous day.

81-5 The metre of these lines would be smoother if a further syllable was added—81, with *people* A or *you* H; 85, as in 53 H; 83, where no manuscript has an additional syllable and the version in H is unduly extended. At 82, ARB read *unto* for *to* Hm, but only AB have the required compensatory loss of a syllable elsewhere in the line.

85-95 Compare Exodus 34/21-2, where these injunctions are given by God to Moses with the second giving of the Law, and Exodus 35/1-6, where Moses transmits them to his people. From Exodus 35/2 comes information omitted in the summary of the third commandment, 8-9.

bodely 85 HmARB is to be preferred to *boldelye* 53 H for meaning; compare Wakefield 18/145, "ffrom bodely wark ye take youre rest." The lines enjoin upon the Israelites an obedience comparable with that of Moses himself.

89–95, stanza 12   No manuscript has the required rhyme-form *bede* 92. Hm perhaps represents the present tense here; BH have past tense, destroying rhyme; R has a modernised, non-rhyming form; A does not give sense.

In HmARB the stanza has only seven lines, lacking a c-rhyming line; but the result still gives sense. H supplies a line which is acceptable, supplies a verb appropriate to 94, and corresponds to Exodus 35/5–6, from the second verse of which HmARB derives. Since the exemplar may have contained two versions of the play, the omission was made in the HmARB version but not in the H version.

90–2   The lines combine Exodus 34/22: *Solemnitatem hebdomadarum facies tibi in primitiis frugum messis tuae triticae* (AV "And thou shalt observe the feast of weeks, of the first fruits of wheat harvest"), and Exodus 35/3–5: *Non succendetis ignem in omnibus habitaculis vestris per diem sabbati ... Separate apud vos primitias Domino* (AV "Ye shall kindle no fire throughout your habitations upon the sabbath day ... Take ye from among you an offering unto the Lord"). The form at 58–60 H represents the biblical text and is to be preferred. That in Hm gives sense; *forever* may represent a scribal corruption of *fire* 58 H, or the suppression of an injunction which might have little meaning for the audience.

93   *byse* BH is to be preferred for meaning to the scribally erroneous *kyse* HmA, *gkyse* R. The order of listing here reverses that of Exodus 35/6: *Hyacinthum et purpuram* (AV "And blue and purple").

97   "If I had all Israel in my power". Hm gives good sense but no other manuscript has this reading. AR evidently regard *and* as a conjunction and substitute *hand* for *had*, giving an elliptical construction comparable with 96: "All Israel and I hand in hand", which suggests a mutual harmony that 98–99 destroys; but *hand in hand* in the sense of "well matched" is recorded by OED only from 1611. B replaces *and* by *land*: "I [once] had all the land of Israel in my power"—an intelligible, if inappropriate, reading. A similar idea seems to underlie the omission of *and* in 90 H, the metre being restored there by the addition of *it* after *had*.

98   *wrath*   In Numbers 22/2 the reaction of Moab is one of fear rather than anger, as in *ME Genesis and Exodus* (cf. 3919). But a tradition of the wrathful Balak, comparable with the wrathful Herod and similar tyrant figures, also existed, as in *Mistère* (cf. 26651–6), and *Stanzaic Life*:

> This kyng and al his reme al-so
> pursueden Goddes peple ay
> (1621–2)

where the Moabites are presented as aggressors.

110   *Balaham*   Balaam, a Midianite and hence a Gentile, was not a prophet in the Jewish sense but a soothsayer who became the vehicle for a Messianic prophecy. Two traditions relate to him. Insofar as he uttered a Messianic prophecy and was granted a meeting with God, he was held worthy of honour; some rabbinic traditions held him to be a greater prophet than Moses—see 'Balaam', *Jewish Encyclopaedia*; Josephus, *Antiquities of the Jews* 4/6, para. 6, shows him in a favourable light. But insofar as he incurred God's anger and was held to be responsible for the seduction of Israel by the Moabite women, he was esteemed corrupt; this view is endorsed by New Testament texts such as 2 Peter 2/15-6 and Apocalypse 2/14. H presents a picture of the virtuous Balaam, elevated to parity with the Jewish prophets, but HmARB present the picture of the corrupt Balaam, conspirer against the chosen people of God. The *Mistère* also suggests a corrupt Balaam; compare Pseudo-Augustine, Sermo 33, "De Balaam et Balac" (PL 39/1809-11).

111+SD   Here, as at 115+SD, 143+SD, 151+SD B, there are clear signs that in HmARB Balak carries and brandishes a sword. In H, where Balak seems more subdued, the SDs are absent.

117-9   Compare Numbers 22/4: *Ita delebit hic populus omnes qui in nostris finibus commorantur, quomodo solet bos herbas usque ad radices carpere* (AV "Now shall this company lick up all that are round about us, as the ox licketh up the grass of the field"). *commen* 117 may be an infinitive parallel to *anoye* 116 and dependent upon *doe*: "[do] come to destroy"; or it may be a past participle, requiring *have* to be understood: "[have] come to destroy". But BH seem to take it as a variant of the adjective *commune* in the frequent collocation *commune peple* and supply an auxiliary (*doe* B, *can* H) in place of *for to* to give the sense: "[They] do destroy/are able to destroy my common people". Possibly the removal of the verb of motion in BH brings the reading there closer to the biblical text. ARBH's omission of *for* Hm is arguably preferable metrically.

as 118 ARBH is to be preferred to the scribally erroneous *and* Hm, which may result from confusion with *and* 117; *gnawes* 111 H is to be preferred to the scribally erroneous and meaningless *graweth* HmB, and to *draweth* AR, although *gnaweth* would be metrically preferable and is suggested by the HmARB inflexions.

120-3, stanza 16   Compare 113-20 stanza 15 H, and 164-7 stanza 22. H does not have 124-63, and its stanza therefore consists of a combination of HmARB's stanzas 16 and 22. In addition to the completion of an eight-line Chester stanza and the provision of a b-rhyme, H also avoids the wide separation of *Balaham* 120 from its referent pronouns *hym* 164, *he* 165. See 124-63 note.

124-63   Unbiblical; the lines are not in H. The end of the biblical address to the envoys, Numbers 22/6, corresponds to 120-3 here. There seems no justification for *but* 124, and 124-31 seems to return to ideas raised in 104-9; *therefore* 164 does not seem to follow from 160-3; and *hym* 164, *he* 165 have no immediate referent. Posssibly 124-63 represent an alternative to 104-19 which, not being clearly located in the exemplar, became misplaced in HmARB to follow 123 instead of 119. Dramatically, the passage intensifies the image of Balak as a comically infuriated pagan ruler, recognising the power of God but not admitting God's supremacy.

124-5   "But yet I hope to be avenged either by warfare or by an act of cunning"; *pollicye* here seems to have the sense of *policy* OED 4. Compare 166-7 and note.

131+Latin   Based on Deuteronomy 32/37-8: *Et dicet: Ubi sunt dii eorum, in quibus habebant fiduciam, de quorum victimis comedebant adipes, et bibebant vinum libaminum? Surgant, et opitulentur vobis, et in necessitate vos protegant* (AV "And he shall say, Where are their gods, their rock in whom they trusted Which did eat the fat of their sacrifices, and drank the wine of their drink-offerings? Let them rise up and help you,

PLAY V 67

and be your protection"). The passage, ironically and anachronistically, comes from the Song of Moses. It represents an affirmation of God's power over that of other gods, hence its immediate irony; but it serves as a warning by Moses to the Israelites that when they turn to evil, as he forsees, God will forsake them—a suggestion relevant to the seduction of the Israelites by the Moabites and, more widely, to the mission of the Gentiles, which may be seen as beginning in Balaam.

132–4 Mars, Roman god of war, is appropriately invoked and set in an infernal pantheon. While the intention may be merely to invoke a familiar pagan god, it is possible that a parallel is intended between Balak's procedure and the Romans' practice of entering battle only after consulting an augur to determine the will of the gods. Compare 212–5.

136–9 The reference of *mediators* 137, "mediators, negotiators, messengers", is not clear. There is no indication in the play or the biblical text that the Israelites sent negotiators to Balak, although messengers were sent to the kings of Edom (Numbers 20/14) and Sihon (Numbers 21/21) in the passages preceding the Balaam-Balak episode. If messengers are assumed to have been sent to Balak, the passage would mean: "I am informed by true report how the negotiators are trying to win my land for the delight of those descended from the line of Jacob." The passage would be more readily intelligible if *mediators* could be regarded as a term of abuse for the Israelites generally, but it is difficult to see how such meaning is possible; perhaps Balak has in mind the intercession of Moses to God on behalf of the Israelites, as at 104–7—compare Galatians 3/19: *[Lex] ordinata per angelos in manu mediatoris* (AV "[The Law] was ordained by angels in the hand of a mediator"). *meditators* A is either an error or a Latinate substitution; OED does not record *meditator* until 1665.

147 *them* ARB is to be preferred to its omission in Hm for syntactical and semantic completeness.

148–51 Exodus 14/19–31; compare Joshua 24/5–10, where the Exodus and the Balaam episode are also linked, and 3–4 above.

156–63, stanza 21 *destroyed* 159 ARB is to be preferred for rhyme and meaning to the scribally erroneous *distroye* Hm.

158 The account of the defeat of these kings—Sihon, king of the Amorites, and Og, king of Bashan—in Numbers 21/21–35 precedes and prompts Balak's response in Numbers 22/2, where he witnesses what has happened to the Amorites.

164–5 In Numbers 22/7–15 Balak sends two embassies to Balaam. The first, consisting of the elders of Moab and Midian—*seniores Moab et maiores natu Madian*—is rejected, but the second, by the princes of Moab—*multo plures et nobiliores quam ante miserat*—is conditionally accepted, as here. The *Mistère*, like Chester, employs a single ambassador, *Le Chevallier*, but dramatises both embassies; *Stanzaic Life* 1634–44 also has only one embassy, like Chester, but "with dukes that for hym wer sent" 1646.

164–7, stanza 22 See 120–3, stanza 16 note.

166–7 Compare 124–7. Here also some limitation of *in no manere* must be understood since Balak's summons of Balaam would otherwise be futile. Compare Numbers 22/6.

168–75, stanza 23   *fonne* 170 ARB, 123 H, is to be preferred for rhyme to the scribally erroneous *fanne* Hm.

At 174 *conn*, found in no manuscript, is required for perfect rhyme.

172–3   An oblique reference to Balaam's avarice, a feature to be developed later—see 190–2, 202–3, 209, 268–9. The biblical basis appears to be Numbers 22/7: *Habentes divinationis pretium in manibus* (AV "With the rewards of divination in their hand"), and Balaam's reply to the second embassy, Numbers 22/18: *Si dederit mihi Balac plenam domum suam argenti et auri* (AV "If Balak would give me his house full of silver and gold"). This sense of greed motivates Balaam's later disobedience.

180–99   In conflating the two embassies the dramatist uses God's refusal of the first embassy, Numbers 22/12, for 184–7, and his conditional agreement, Numbers 22/20, for 193–5. Balaam's replies have no basis in the biblical account; with 182–3 compare *Stanzaic Life*:

> he sayd he durst not verrayment
> but God ȝaf leue with hom [to] dele.
> (1639–40)

183 + SD   In the biblical account, Balaam does not deliberately go to consult God but awaits God's coming; at Numbers 22/9 God asks Balaam who the ambassadors are. Compare Josephus, *Antiquities of the Jews* 4/6, para 2: "And when he had supped, he inquired what was God's will."

ARB append an English SD to the Latin SD, indicating that Balaam kneels in prayer. Hm may have omitted the English SD as an unnecessary "gloss"; H has no equivalent SD at this point. *Deum* B seems to represent a scribal misunderstanding of syntactical function resulting from the inverted word-order; but *et* B may also suggest that B misunderstood the second part of the Latin SD, regarding Balaam as addressing God while sitting, in which case *Deum* might be an error for *Deo* and represent the person addressed. The English SD clearly shows the error of such a reading by B.

199 + SD   No reference is made to the two servants who also accompany Balaam in Numbers 22/22.

200–7   Although no reason is given in the biblical account for God's sudden anger against Balaam, it was commonly ascribed to a change of intent by Balaam. Compare Comestor, *Historia Scholastica*, 'Liber Numerorum' 32 (PL 198/1237), and *Stanzaic Life*:

> for gret ȝiftis and fair hetyng
> sone he had turnet his entent,
> And kest as sone as he come ther
> to wary Goddes folk anone.
> (1647–50)

200   *my lawe* for Balaam is stated in 212–5; his *law* is in opposition to the Decalogue.

204   Compare 190. No offer has been made to Balaam at this point and he knows nothing of Balak's promises. In the biblical account, Balak's promises are reported by the second embassy to him, Numbers 22/16–7.

205 *hest* BH is to be preferred for meaning to *hoste* HmAR, although both give sense.

208–15 This stanza is not in H, perhaps because, like 132–64, it presents an unequivocally evil picture of Balaam. Compare Augustine, *Sermo* 33: *Hic Balaam famosissimus erat in arte magica, et in carminibus noxiis praepotens ... Daemones enim ad maledicendum invitantur, non ad benedicendum ... Deus ire Balaam atque invocare daemones ad maledicendum prohibet.*

208–15, stanza 28 No manuscript has *seeche* 215, required for the b-rhyme. OED notes that the form survives to the present day in the Cheshire dialect; but it was probably replaced by a "standard" form in the exemplar. The sense is: "There is no deception to look for."; i.e. "I will not deceive you". *will* RB, "desire", seems to be an error, but would yield sense: "There is no desire [on my part] to look further [for help]."

213 *Ruffyn and Reynell* The names of two devils, both well attested in Middle English. On the occurrence of the former, see 1/260 note; on the latter, J. J. Anderson, *Patience* (Manchester, 1969), p.59. Thomas D. Hill, 'Raguel and Ragnel: Notes on the Literary Genealogy of a Devil', *Names* xxii (1974), pp.145–9, suggests the possible origin and development of the latter. Compare especially Digby *Mary Magdalen* 1200–1:

> Ragnell and Roffyn, and other, in þe wavys,
> Gravntt yow grace to dye on þe galows.

Antichrist invokes Ragnell at 23/647. Hill seeks the origin of Ragnel in *Raguel*, the name given to one of the seven angels guarding the earth in the *Book of Enoch*. Raguel was one of the names of Moses' father-in-law, a priest of the Midianites, Numbers 10/29, which may give the reference here more point.

Ragnell B reflects the usual form of the name. *Reynall* may show vocalisation of ffigffi, while *Ranell* R seems to reflect either the vocalised form or some further development of it. But possibly the forms in ffiyffi result from a misreading of ffigffi.

215 + SD In Numbers, the angel confronts Balaam three times unseen — once when the ass is forced to turn aside into a field, once when it crushes Balaam's foot against a wall, and once when the ass, being unable to pass, falls down. Only the final incident is dramatised here.

216 *Burnell* On the etymology and development of the name, see *Nigel de Longchamps: Speculum Stultorum*, ed. J. H. Mozley and R. R. Raymo (Berkeley and Los Angeles, 1960), pp.148–9, note to 595. In the ass Nigel satirised clerical vanity and ambition. If the Chester dramatist had this usage in mind, *Burnell* here shows the traditionally vainglorious symbol rebuking Balaam, a vainglorious soothsayer.

218 *shee* Following *asina* in the biblical account and 215 + SD, the pronoun accurately indicates that Balaam rode upon a she-ass.

223 + SD Hm omits the English translation of the final Latin phrase in ARB; *asinam* B is an error resulting from the inversion of word-order.

226 *thrye* Compare Numbers 22/28: *Cur percutis me ecce iam tertio?* (AV "Thou hast smitten me these three times"). But in Numbers, the ass refers to the beatings that she has received on each of her three falls — see 215 + SD note; here it would seem that Balaam has struck three blows.

239 + SD   *adorans* RB is to be preferred for morphology and meaning to the scribally erroneous *adoramus* Hm and *a adoriens*A. All manuscripts include the English SD which explains the action of *adorans*; compare Numbers 22/31: *Adoravitque eum pronus in terram* (AV "And he bowed down his head and fell flat on his face").

245–7   Compare Numbers 22/32: *Ego veni ut adversarer tibi, quia perversa est via tua, mihique contraria* (AV "Behold, I went out to withstand thee, because thy way is perverse before me"). The lines here acquire meaning as a continuation of the greed and intent of 200–15.

248–55, stanza 33   *goe* 197 H is to be preferred to *gonne* 252 HmARB; the latter may represent an error in the exemplar, perhaps influenced by *gonne* 248 and the other a-rhymes of the stanza.

255 + SD   In Numbers 22/36, Balak goes out to meet Balaam at a city on the border of Arnon and they journey together to Kirjathhuzoth, Numbers 22/39. The "cursing" takes place the following morning.

262–3   "To redeem the later generations of my race", 262. Balaam here unbiblically anticipates his Messianic prophecy and ironically expresses his regret at the situation in 263. *forbidd* B destroys meaning and is an error.

268–9   Foster (p.379) notes that the H-equivalent of these lines, 213–4, has some resemblance to *Stanzaic Life* 1689–90. But the version in HmARB is significantly different and those manuscripts therefore lack "the only verbal parallel" between the play and *Stanzaic Life*.

279 + SD   The play makes no reference to the sacrifices which precede Balaam's words, or to the soothsayer's dialogue with God on the hilltop at Numbers 23/1–6. Since Balaam here occupies the hilltop position previously held by Moses, the danger of equating the two men rather than contrasting may have been a consideration in the omission of the dialogue. The biblical account does not specify the direction in which Balaam turns to "curse".

288–95   Balaam's "curse" in Numbers 23/8–10 stresses the exclusiveness of the Jews and their steady increase in population. Possibly the single "curse" in Josephus, *Antiquities of the Jews* 4, 6/4, influenced the wording here: "Happy is this people, on whom God bestows the possession of innumerable good things, and grants them his own providence to be their assistant and their guide; so that there is not any nation among mankind but you will be esteemed superior to them in virtue, and in the earnest prosecution of the best rules of life, and of such as are pure from wickedness." 294–5 is based on Numbers 23/10 and assumes deeper irony in HmARB than in H in view of the later account of the way in which Balaam really met his death.

293   "And they shall experience no other sort of censure." The line, which is without biblical counterpart, presents a number of problems:-
    (1) The antithesis implied by *other* is not clear. It may mean: "Other than the sort of censure that I am bestowing" — viz. a blessing; or it may mean: "No censure other than from God himself", who protects them.

(2) *reproffe* usually has the sense of "censure" in Middle English, but the number of variables in the context makes its exact meaning doubtful. R substitutes *hurte*; H, in a changed context, reads *repreve*.

(3) *they* clearly refers to the Israelites. H reads *I* and thus makes the line a defensive utterance by Balaam: "I may have no further censure" — possibly from Balak, but more probably from God who rebuked him through the angel earlier.

(4) *wave* HmB is not recorded by OED in any sense that seems appropriate here. ARH read *have*, which is semantically appropriate but repeats the rhyme-word of 294; R has merely reversed the rhymes of 293 and 294, suggesting that *wave* was the exemplar form and that *have* is a scribal substitution.

296–303 Only Numbers 24/10, the third "curse", indicates Balak's emotional state: *Iratusque Balac contra Balaam* (AV "And Balak's anger was kindled against Balaam"), which may suggest that only then did the king become enraged. At the first cursing Comestor, *Historia Scholastica*, 'Liber Numerorum' 33 (PL 198/1238), describes Balak as *contristatus*. Here the speech develops the opening picture of the irate Balak.

303 + SD At Numbers 23/14, as on other occasions, Balak leads Balaam to another place, but here they simply move to face a different direction on the hill.

304–11 Balaam's speech represents the third "curse", Numbers 24/5–9. HmARB lack the second "curse", Numbers 23/19–25, whereas 241–60 H has that curse in the expected position and the third "curse" at 265–72, delivered *ad occidentalem partem*. While the HmARB form may represent an error, it may also be indicative of the nature of the staging, where the actor could only face in three directions, or of unease at the specifically Messianic application given to the prophecy in H, which weakens the impact of the final, and distinctive, Messianic prophecy. The *ME Genesis and Exodus* 4035–42 combines the third cursing and the final prophecy; in *Mistère* the published text lacks the first "curse" because of a manuscript lacuna. See 316 note.

304–7 Compare Numbers 24/5–6: *Quam pulchra tabernacula tua, Jacob! et tentoria tua, Israel! Ut valles nemorosae ut horti iuxta fluvios irrigui...* (AV "How goodly are thy tents, O Jacob, and thy tabernacles, O Israel! As the valleys are they spread forth, as gardens by the river's side ..."). The sustained comparison in Numbers is here translated into a concrete vision; the temporary camp of the Israelites has here become a fixed settlement, perhaps appropriate to the urban surroundings of the performance.

valles 306 HmR seems confirmed as the exemplar reading for the Group by B's erroneous *walles*; *valleyes* A is evidently an independent substitution, and it is probably not significant that it is also the H reading.

yordes 307 corresponds to *horti*, "gardens", in the biblical account. *ryvere* is confirmed by rhyme, but *rivers* RH corresponds to biblical *fluvios*.

311 The line contains four strongly stressed syllables instead of the expected three. A regular line would result from the omission of *to God*.

316 *thrye* Compare 318 and Numbers 24/10: *Ad maledicendum inimicis meis vocavi te, quibus e contrario tertio benedixisti* (AV "I called thee to curse mine enemies, and, behold, thou hast altogether blessed them these three times"). As noted at 304–11 HmARB lack one "curse", and *thrye* is therefore inaccurate. The word either results from a slavish adherence to the Bible text or reflects the removal of a "curse" from the text without a corresponding adjustment here. H is accurate, both in this line and in *twye* at 318.

317   The line has no biblical counterpart; 278 H is different. In HmA it seems to mean "For [that is] the means to harm me"; R and B more plausibly treat the phrase as verbal and supply a subject — B is preferable: "For you intend to destroy me." Possibly *the* is an exemplar error for *thou*, with independent substitutions in R and B; *menen* is not recorded by MED in impersonal use.

319   After this reply, Numbers 24/11 has a speech of dismissal by Balak which is omitted from HmARB but partially represented in 281–8 H. But in H, Balak unbiblically offers Balaam a further opportunity to rectify his "disobedience", while HmARB, in moving without warning to Balaam's Messianic prophecy, are closer to the effect of Numbers 24/14, where Balaam acts on his own initiative.

319 + SD   *respiciens coelum spiritu prophetico* With Balaam's stance, compare Numbers 24/15–6. This is the only prophecy not preceded by an augury. In Chester, the gesture marks off the prophecy from Balaam's other pronouncements.

Orietur ff. The version of the prophecy given here and in H is somewhat different from that in Numbers 24/17: *Orietur stella ex Jacob, et consurget virga de Israel; et percutiet duces Moab vastabitque omnes filios Seth* (AV "There shall come a star out of Jacob, and a Sceptre shall rise out of Israel, and shall smite the corners of Moab, and destroy all the children of Sheth"). The Chester version excludes the application to the immediate situation of the Jews and makes it more clearly Messianic. No similar version of the prophecy is found in standard commentaries. The quotation is translated adequately in 320–5; see 323 note.

AR omit the SD, for no obvious reason. They also omit the following SH, no longer necessary since 318–27 is now a continuous speech.

323   *man* Compare *homo* 319 + SD, as against *virga*, Numbers 24/17 (AV "sceptre"). Comestor, *Historia Scholastica*, 'Liber Numerorum' 33 (PL 198/1239), notes the usual Marian application of the word here changed: '*virga*', *id est Maria*.

327 + SH   AR omit the SH, assigning 328–35, lines of resigned belief, to Balaam, perhaps because they were felt to be more appropriate to the Gentile soothsayer. R seems to seek to clarify the situation further by changing the reference of 329 from *this man*, i.e. Balaam, to *these men*, i.e. the Israelites.

328–35   After 327, the H-version continues with the procession of Jewish prophets, after which the Balaam-Balak episode concludes, 433–40, with a passage corresponding to 328–35. In Numbers 24/25 the episode ends with: *Balac quoque via qua venerat rediit*. (AV "And Balak also went his way"). Compare *Stanzaic Life*:

> Quen Kyng Balaak seȝe þis cas
> that Balaam propheciet oryght.
> he wist wele þat no bote was
> forto stryue with God al-myȝt.
> (1721–4)

328   *wee* i.e. Balak and Miles.

335ff. Balaam's responsibility for suggesting the seduction of Israel by the Moabites, an event narrated in Numbers 25/1–3, is noted briefly in Numbers 31/16, Apocalypse 2/14. A fuller account is to be found in Jewish traditions, is set out in Josephus, *Antiquities of the Jews* 4, 6/6, and is found in shortened form in Comestor, *Historia Scholastica*, 'Liber Numerorum' 34 and the *ME Genesis and Exodus* 4043–70. The incident is not in H. It completes the picture of the corrupt Balaam and of the vengeance of God upon the unrighteous through the mediation of Moses and the Israelites.

344–5 Compare Josephus, *Antiquities of the Jews*, 4 6/6: "For the providence of God is concerned to preserve them from such a misfortune."

348–9 Chester omits Balaam's grim warning, seen in Josephus, *Antiquities of the Jews* 4, 6/6: "But after that they will flourish again, to the terror of those that brought those mischiefs upon them."

353 Compare Josephus, *Antiquities of the Jews* 4, 6/6: "The handsomest of such of your daughters as are most eminent for beauty"; contrast Comestor, *Historia Scholastica*, 'Liber Numerorum' 34 (PL 198/1239): *Virgines quarum specie illudi posset castitas.* Compare 380–3.

364–7 No manuscript has the required form *leve*, "abandon", for *love* 364 Hm. Compare Josephus, *Antiquities of the Jews* 4, 6/6: "Till they have persuaded them to leave off their obedience to their own laws and the worship of that God who established them".

At 365 a more regular sequence of strongly and weakly stressed syllables would result from the omission of one syllable, e.g. *the*. AR erroneously substitute *their* and *trenetie* in the line.

With 366–7, compare Josephus, *Antiquities of the Jews* 4, 6/8: "Our gods are common to all men, and yours such as belong to nobody else but yourselves." The metre of 366 would be improved by the addition of a further syllable, as in A; at 367 a smoother metre results from the B-reading.

372–9, stanza 49 The b-rhymes, *performe* 375 — *destroye* 379, do not rhyme, but no manuscript has a rhyming form; some word such as *convey*, *convoy* is required at 375, but *destroye* was clearly the exemplar reading. *fulfill* 375 A represents the erroneous repetition of the 373 rhyme-word.

384 *hie me* B gives a more regular sequence of strongly and weakly stressed syllables than *hie* HmAR.

405–7 "They [the Moabite women] said it [their love] should be put to the test, [love] which they could not otherwise endure for fear of being deceived." Compare the women's words in Josephus, *Antiquities of the Jews* 4/6, para 8: "And if we may receive such assurance of your good-will as we think can alone be sufficient, we will be glad to lead our lives with you as your wives; but we are afraid that you will in time be weary of our company, and will then abuse us, and send us back to our parents, after an ignominious manner."

408–11 *those blynde people* i.e. the seduced Israelite youth, who remain as the referent of *they* 410; *them* 410, 411 refers to *those women* 404.

wrothe 410 is apparently a noun: "Would have anger towards them"; but the metre is rough and a more regular sequence of strongly and weakly stressed syllables results from the readings in R (where *wrath* is an adjective) or in B (where *wroth* is a verb). *the* A for *them* seems to be a scribal error.

412-9, stanza 54   *me* 416 ARB is to be preferred for rhyme to *now* Hm, which seems an inexplicable error.

416-35   Compare Numbers 25/4-15. Josephus, *Antiquities of the Jews* 4/6, paras 9-12, provides a more extended account which omits the reference to the execution of the ringleaders in Numbers 25/4. The two accounts are fused in Comestor, *Historia Scholastica*, 'Liber Numerorum' 34-5 (PL 198/1239-40).

416-7   See 412-9, stanza 54 note. B apparently dislikes the ellipsis in the construction and, by inserting *spake to* in 416, by omitting the equivalent *bade him* in 417, and by adding *thou* at 417, B turns 417 into direct speech. The resulting construction then breaks down at 418-9.

420-4   According to Josephus, Moses summoned a general assembly of all the people, "but then accused nobody by name": Comestor states *eos culparet, non nominatim tamen*. But Moses was publicly rebuked by Zimri, who had married a Moabite wife and whose speech commanded some support among the people. Moses himself had a wife, Zipporah, who was a Midianite, Exodus 2/21, hence his own difficult position. So the assembly dissolved. The aid from God here mentioned is the vengeance of Phineas, who slew Zimri and his wife, thereby setting an example which other young men followed. The Chester account here does not give a clear impression of the events.

427   The line contains four main stresses instead of the expected three; perhaps *upon* should be omitted, leaving *those wretches* as indirect object.

431   Compare Numbers 25/8-9: *Cessavitque plaga a filiis Israel. Et occisi sunt viginti quattuor millia hominum*. The Vulgate does not indicate how the 24,000 were slain, but implies it was by plague; compare AV "And those that died in the plague were twenty and four thousand." Josephus, *Antiquities of the Jews* 4, 6/12 states: "Accordingly many of those that had transgressed perished by the magnanimous valour of those young men, and the rest all perished by a plague, which distemper God himself inflicated upon them." Comestor, *Historia Scholastica*, 'Liber Numerorum' 35 (PL 198/1240), points the AV version: *Et occisi sicut tringinta quatuor millia, forte a Domino per plagam aliquam praecedentem, quae tunc cessavit*. Comestor claims 34,000 dead, Josephus 14,000, but Chester has the biblical total.

435 + SD   Psalms 105/30-31 but with the variation: *in generatione sua*] *in generationem et generationem et generationem usque in sempiternum*; AV 106/30-1: "Then stood up Phinehas and executed judgement; and so the plague was stayed. And that was counted unto him for righteousness unto all generations for evermore." The reference is found as an addition in Comestor, *Historia Scholastica*, 'Liber Numerorum' 35 (PL 198/1240). The Psalm refers to the comment in Numbers 25/13, especially: *Pactum sacerdotii sempiternum* (AV "The covenant of an everlasting priesthood"). The change in the Chester quotation may be significant since the text had also been compared with the reference to Melchizedek's everlasting priesthood in Psalm 109/4 (AV 110/4), and its removal takes away a possible link to play 4; the parallel was current — see *Glossa Ordinaria*, 'Liber Numerorum' 25/13 (PL 113/428).

436–55, stanzas 57–9   In stanza 57 the b-rhymes, *moe* 439 — *beforen* 443, do not rhyme; R's *more* — *before* are to be preferred for rhyme. In stanza 58 the b-rhymes *borne* 447 — *more* 451 do not rhyme; no manuscript has the form *bore* required for rhyme at 447. It may be noted that the final stanza in H, stanza 56, corresponds to 440–7 HmARB and therefore rhymes *beforne* (=443) — *borne* (=447) as the b-rhymes; the breakdown of b-rhymes in stanzas 57 and 58 may reflect uncertainty by the exemplar-scribe about the stanza-division at this point, and might even suggest adaptation from the H-version. It may also be noted that in terms of structure the lines fall into three sections:
436–9 The death of Balaam and conclusion of the narrative.
440–7 The significance of the story in God's wider plan for the Incarnation.
448–55 The announcement of the next day's performance.
and it is possible to argue that the stanza-division should follow this structural division, with stanza 57 a quatrain and stanza 58 a normal Chester stanza as in H.

The case for such a division is strengthened by the rhyme-patterns of the final eight lines of the play. The final quatrain of the present stanza 58 rhymes cbcb (accepting a rhyme *bore* — *more*) instead of the expected cccb; and its final line, 451, contains four strongly stressed syllables instead of the expected three. Stanza 59 is a quatrain rhyming aaab; and its final line also contains four strongly stressed syllables instead of the three expected of a normal Chester quatrain. In fact, although there is no rhyme-link between 448–51 and 452–5, the eight lines are linked structurally as the announcement of the next day's performance, and metrically in containing four strongly stressed syllables in each line. Arguably, therefore, stanza 59 could begin at 448 and take the form ababcccd.

436–9   Numbers 31/3–8. But with *gyants* 439, compare Numbers 31/8: *Quinque principes gentis* (AV "Five kings of Midian"). Standard commentaries do not have the Chester reading, which might derive from a misunderstanding of the biblical text.

440–1   The meaning of *then* 441 is "than", but AR apparently take it as a temporal adverb; they also erroneously and inexplicably substitute *free(y)* for *here* 441, destroying rhyme. The resulting lines in AR seem to mean: "Sirs, then, you have heard much more substance in this noble story." The AR reading seems to suggest that *then* was the exemplar form.

444–7   It was a commonplace that Balaam's prophecy, recorded here by Moses, was transmitted to the Gentiles. Compare 8/1–40; Origen, *Homilia in Numerorum* (PG 12/675) 13/7; and Comestor, *Historia Scholastica*, 'Liber Numerorum' 33 (PL 198/1239). *Stanzaic Life* recounts the Balaam story only to explain the original reason for the Magi's journey, 1593–6.

451–5   *tomorrowe nexte* 451 suggests that the HmARB version of play 5 ended a day's performance so that play 6 would begin the following day's performance. The lines have no counterpart in H, which might suggest that H did not envisage a break at this point. It must be a matter of conjecture how far these considerations account for differences between the two versions. H is essentially an Advent play which presents Balaam as a Gentile prophet who ushers in a series of Jewish prophets leading up to the following Nativity. HmARB dramatises the rewards of obedience and the futility of disobedience to God's commands, and is thus a more self-contained exemplum, despite its final references to the Nativity.

PLAY VI

Dramatis Personae Gabriell, Maria, Elizabeth, Joseph, Angelus, Nuntius, Octavianus, Preco, Primus Senatour, Secundus Senator, Sybbell, Tebell, Salome, Expositor.

NOTE: 1. Doubling of parts is possible for Gabriell and Angelus, Nuntius and Preco
2. An infant Jesus is required, 430–1, 439–52 et seq.

Locations
this towne (*Rome*) 275
this cyttye (*Bethlehem*) 456, 473
this stable 458, 463.

Properties
this hackney 283
ox 423, bovem 468 + SD
asinam 468 + SD (*compare* 461–4)
stella 508 + SD
the stare 693, *containing the vision of*
         a mayden bright
         a yonge childe in her armes clight,
         a bright crosse in his head
                (652–4)
this cratch 523, *with* haye 524
incense 659.

NOTE: 1. *in see* 5 is here regarded merely as a conventional phrase.
2. The star over the stable and that seen by Octavian may be the same.
3. Some device is needed for Salome's withered hand, 539 + SD.

Costume
None specified.

Sources
The angelic visitation and Mary's visit to Elizabeth — Luke 1/28–56
Joseph's jealousy — Matthew 1/20
Taxing — Luke 2/1–3
The birth — Luke 2/6–7.

Much of the content, however, derives from non-Biblical sources, especially: Joseph's jealousy, Mary's vision at 429–36, the midwives — The Book of James and the Gospel of Pseudo-Matthew.
Octavian's vision — *Mirabilia Romae* and its extended version, the *Graphia*.
A.C. Baugh, 'The Chester Plays and French Influence' p.47, sees major significance in the fact that "the Conversion of Octavian is a favorite in the Old French drama".

Play-heading
A number of plays in the other English cycles deal with the same material as parts of Chester. The angelic visitation is in Wakefield 10/1–54, York 12/1–96, *Ludus Coventriae* 11/217–340, Coventry Shearmen 47–99; the visit to Elizabeth in Wakefield 11, York 12/97–140, *Ludus Coventriae* 13/1–36; Joseph's jealousy in Wakefield 10/155–373, York 13, *Ludus Coventriae* 12, Coventry Shearman 100–67; Christ's nativity in York 14, *Ludus Coventriae* 15, Coventry Shearmen 278–96. Wakefield 9 shows the decree ordering the taxing of the world and presents a tyrannical Octavian, but Chester's Octavian material is not otherwise found in the cycles, although it has counterparts in the French drama (see above). The play has also been held to show strong direct influence from *A Stanzaic Life of Christ*.

1–4 These are not the words uttered by Gabriel to Mary in the Bible but an amalgamation of the addresses to Mary by Gabriel, Luke 1/28, and Elizabeth, Luke 1/42, known as the 'Ave Maria', 'Hail Mary' or 'The Angelic Salutation'. Although the other English cycles follow Luke 1/28 only, the form was in common liturgical use, is found in Pseudo-Matthew 9 and in *Stanzaic Life* 233–6, *Cursor Mundi* 10837–40. Hence the parallel with *Stanzaic Life*, noted by Foster, is regarded as inconclusive by Wilson. Only the liturgical form includes the word *Maria*, 'Mary', which provides a useful means of identifying the person addressed here. *mother* 1 is predictive, and no other cycle uses this address; Elizabeth, in *Stanzaic Life*, appropriately refers to *modir Mary* 233; *maiden* H is equally possible. *shalt* 3 B may represent an attempt to clarify the appellation by emphasising its future application.

10–11 Compare Luke 1/30: *Invenisti enim gratiam apud Deum* (AV "For thou hast found favour with God"). HmARB seem to reflect the biblical order; the reversal in H, while acceptable, may perhaps be a development of the syntactical inversion of *found thow hase* 10.

14–6 "His name shall be Jesus — none shall ever be as great as he — and he shall be called God's Son." Compare Luke 1/31; *Vocabis nomen eius Iesum* (AV "And shalt call his name Jesus"); 1/32: *Filius Altissimi vocabitur* (AV "shall be called the Son of the Highest"). Here the two constructions are combined elliptically, requiring the continuation of *shalbe* to 16 with a different subject understood.

19 *rayninge* Hm gives the more regular sequence of strongly and weakly stressed syllables, but *raigne* ARBH seems morphologically preferable in rendering Luke 1/33, *regnabit* (AV "he shall reign").

25 Mary does not seem to recognise Gabriel as an angel; compare Pseudo-Matthew, where the speaker is called *iuvenis*, and *Ludus Coventriae* 11/233 where Gabriel apparently assumes the form of Joseph. *beast* HmH has the sense of MED *beste* 1(a), "any living creature"; it has either been misunderstood in ARB or rejected because of its "animal" associations. *arte* AR suggests identification with the second sg. pres. of *be*, while *angell* B removes all ambiguity, the additional syllable being compensated for by the omission of *so*.

32 "He shall be called the Son." Compare Luke 1/35: *Vocabitur Filius Dei* (AV "Shall be called the Son of God"). *his* ARH may be preferred as referring to *Godes* 31 and expressing *Dei*; *Jesus* B, though possible, lacks biblical authority.

34 *as thow maye see* Compare 130–1, and Luke 1/36: *Et ecce* (AV "And behold"). The words prompt Mary's visit to Elizabeth, although the passage could be taken to mean that Elizabeth is already present on stage and that the Annunciation takes place in her house. Luke 1/39 makes it clear that after the Annunciation Mary journeyed to a city of Juda in the hills to meet Elizabeth; compare Comestor, *Historia Scholastica* 'In Evangelia' 3 (PL 198/1538) and *Stanzaic Life*: "The quich cite is four mile ffrom Ierusalem, as rede we" (213–4).

36 *bedill* BH is to be preferred to the scribally erroneous *kedyll* HmAR for meaning; compare *bidel* MED 3(a) and *Ormulum* 633, "Cristess bidell, Sannt Johan". The life of Elizabeth's son, John the Baptist, is not developed further in the Chester Cycle.

40 The line contains only two strongly stressed syllables instead of the expected three, but no manuscript supplies the necessary addition.

45 "Behold, the chosen of God [standing] meekly here." No verb is required in Luke 1/38; *Ecce ancilla Domini* (AV "Behold the handmaid of the Lord"), but the adverb *meekelye* here suggests some verb form should be understood. *cossen* A, *cozin* R, "kinsman", seems to be a scribal error or a substitution based on a misunderstanding; compare *feare* 76.

49 *nece* Elizabeth was Mary's cousin, Luke 1/36 *cognata* (AV "cousin"). The word seems to have the sense here of "female relative", last recorded by OED in 1508, although the word continued to be used in a variety of related senses long after. The relationship is specified by Mary here because it was not stated by Gabriel at 33 as it is in Luke 1/36 and the other English cycles. Although in the other cycles Gabriel calls Elizabeth Mary's cousin, *niece* is the term used also in such passages as *Cursor Mundi* 10891 (2 mss), *Stanzaic Life* 212.

51 *frute* ARBH is to be preferred to the scribally erroneous *fruites* Hm for meaning. Compare 4, 60, and Luke 1/42; *Fructus ventris tui* (AV "The fruit of thy womb").

55 *gree* H, in the sense of *degree* 4, "rank", is recorded by OED to 1590 and is possible here, although obsolescent by the date of the extant manuscripts; its adoption may give a more regular sequence of strongly and weakly stressed syllables. *degree* might be a "modernised form", present in the exemplar.

59–60 Compare Luke 1/44: *Exsultavit in gaudio infans in utero meo* (AV "The babe leaped in my womb for joy"); *Stanzaic Life* 226; "ffor ioy of Crist þer hoppet he".

64+SD The Magnificat, which takes its name from Mary's opening word in Luke 1/46–55, is sung at vespers in Roman Catholic and Anglican liturgies and is one of the few pieces of Marian poetry to survive the Reformation. The opening line, quoted in Latin at 69–70, is prefaced by a loose translation at 66–8. Wakefield 11/49–78 similarly translates the Magnificat; York 12 ends with its singing; *Ludus Coventriae* 13/81–104 shows Mary reciting the Latin and Elizabeth supplying a translation.

72+Latin Luke 1/47: AV "And my spirit hath rejoiced in God." The final words, *salutari meo*, are here omitted. The text is loosely translated in 73–4.

73–96 79–86, stanza 11 appears to be misplaced, since 87–88, which here erroneously begin stanza 12, are the last two lines of stanza 10. The similarity of 79 and 87 probably explains the confusion, and since all manuscripts contain the error, it may be assumed that the mistake was present in the exemplar. R's omission of 79–80 and 91–92 may represent some attempt to remove the repetition and adjust the stanza-forms.

The re-location of 79–86 presents some difficulty since the lines are without obvious biblical counterpart unless taken as a loose reflection of Luke 1/49. Possibly the stanza should precede or follow stanza 9.

75 *see* Compare Luke 1/48, *respexit* (AV "hath regarded"). In view of this, and of the following *was*, *saw* might have been expected here, although no manuscript has the form.

81 Wilson compares *Stanzaic Life* 262, "that prince is z of most power", as the only possible direct influence of the *Life* on this part of the play.

88 *hallowed* ABH is to be preferred to the scribally erroneous *hollowed* Hm; compare 84. R provides an alternative.

be aye AR suggests a misunderstanding of the structure of this "stanza" (see 73–95 note), an attempt to create a rhyme for *today* 87. A duplicates *aye*, but R has transposed *eye* from its position earlier in the line.

91–6 "Through his might he gave supremacy [to] all who truly fear him, to accomplish his power. [He] scatters the proud fearlessly whenever he wishes, speedily with the resolve of his heart." The passage does not fully correspond to the biblical account; compare Luke 1/50: *Et misericordia eius a progenie in progenies timentibus eum* (AV "And his mercy is on them that fear him from generation to generation"), a version which would be obtained by reading *on* for *and* 91. Compare Wakefield 11/62–3:

> tyll all tho
> that ar hym dredand

Ludus Coventriae 13/89, "ffor all þat hym drede"; *Stanzaic Life*:

PLAY VI   81

>   to all men that on hym han mynde,
>   ffrom progeny to progeny,
>   That dreden hym ɼ ben to hym kynde.
>   (266–8)

All the forms cited are possible renderings of *dispersit*, Luke 1/5 (AV "hath scattered"); *disparcles* 94 is recorded in use to 1661, despite its replacement in AR and B. But unless B's unbiblical present participle, *dispercing*, is adopted, a subject *he* must be understood at 94.

 with myght of his harte 95 Compare Luke 1/51: *Mente cordis sui* (AV "In the imagination of their hearts"); Wakefield 11/65–6:

>   And dystroed in his thoght
>   Prowde men and hygh berand

Ludus Coventriae 13/90–1

>   he hath mad so
>   þe prowde to dyspeyre · and þe thoght of here hertys only.

Stanzaic Life

>   Proude dispelet fer ɼ ner
>   with thoȝt of hert ouer al about
>   (271–2)

97–104, stanza 13 The b-rhyme, *fullfellede* 100 — *guylte* 104 Hm, seems to have presented diffiulties to AR, perhaps because perfect rhyme requires an unvoiced consonant at 100. *owine* 104 seems to represent an attempt to supply a further c-rhyme, while *store* 104 R seems to represent an attempt to supply a form fitting the a-rhyme of the following stanza.

 is wacken 103 ARBH is to be preferred for rhyme, syntax and meaning to the erroneous *his wakinge* Hm.

98 Either *mylde* Hm or *meeke* ARBH is possible as a rendering of *humiles*, Luke 1/52 (AV "them of low degree"), but *meek* is the term used in Wakefield 11/69, *Stanzaic Life* 274, and the Wiclif and Prayer Book versions of the Magnificat. *Ludus Coventriae* 13/93 refers to "þe lowly vpon heyth."

99–100 "He has filled full with good things the hungry, the needy, those lacking (or desiring) grace." Compare Luke 1/53: *Esurientes implevit bonis* (AV "He hath filled the hungry with good things"). With *wanting grace* 99, compare T. Arnold (ed.) *Select English Works of John Wyclif* (Oxford, 1869–71), vol. III, 'Magnificat', 50: "Þe hungrynge Oure Lady clepiþ hem þat greetli coveiten riȝtwisnes, wisdom of God, grace and cumfort of þe Holy Goost, þat evere stiriþ her desier to coveiten moore and moore, and contynuen þerinne; for siche good fulfilliþ of goostli goodis, profitable, delitable, and honest."

101 Although the sense here is clear, the construction can be considered in a number of ways: 1. "He has removed power from those who are rich", taking *that* as relative pronoun and supplying a verb. 2. "He has removed that power appropriate to the rich", taking *rych* as possessive. 3. "He has denied power to those who seek it", taking *rych* as a variant of *reach* and *that* as relative pronoun. 4. "He has taken power away from the rich", taking *that* as error for *the*, and *rych* as indirect object.

102 Compare Luke 1/54: *Suscepit Israel puerum suum, recordatus misericordiae suae*; Wiclif, *Magnificat*: "He resseyvede Israel his child, he þou3te of his mercy"; AV "He hath holpen his servant Israel, in rememberance of his mercy"; *Ludus Coventriae* 13/98–9:

> Israel ffor his childe · vp-toke he to cum
> On his mercy to thynk · ffor hese þat be.

106 *full yore*, "long ago". Compare Luke 1/55; *in saecula* (AV "for ever"). *for yore* AR may suggest an attempt to approximate more closely to the biblical text.

107–12 The doxology is found in liturgical usage and appears also at the end of the Magnificat in *Ludus Coventriae* 13/99 + Latin–104. Foster considers this a significant parallel to *Stanzaic Life* 287–8, but Wilson takes little account of it.

112 The line contains four strongly stressed syllables instead of the expected three. Although no manuscript contains the reduction necessary for regularity, the omission of *Amen* and the adoption of *mightes* RBH would produce a three-stress line.

113–20 This transition passage links the visit to Elizabeth, from Luke, with Joseph's jealousy, from Matthew. Although the order of events is not clear from the biblical accounts, Chester conforms to the pattern of standard harmonies, such as Tatian and Augustine, in presenting the visit before the jealousy. Wakefield 10–11, *Ludus Coventriae* 12–13 reverse this sequence. Since Chester is the only cycle to present the two episodes in a single play, only here is such a transition passage necessary. In *Ludus Coventriae* 13 Joseph accompanies Mary to Elizabeth.

114 *thy husband* The biblical accounts do not make it clear whether Mary was married to Joseph before the Annunciation or merely betrothed, and married later. The apocryphal gospels, however, describe Joseph's betrothal and marriage before the Annunciation, and that view was adopted by many commentators.

122 *brought* Only Hm presents *brought* as past tense; ARBH, by including the auxiliary *have*, present it as past participle. Possibly the rougher metre of BH's *here I have brought* led Hm and AR to reduce the line by a syllable, Hm omitting *have* and AR *here*.

123–8 The account of Joseph's jealousy, although authorised by Matthew 1/19, derives largely from the apocryphal Book of James and Gospel of Pseudo-Matthew, where his reluctant betrothal to Mary and his later jealousy are both fully described. With 124, compare Book of James 13/1; "Who is he that hath ensnared me? Who hath done this evil in mine house and hath defiled the virgin?"; with 125, Book of James 9/2: "I have sons, and I am an old man, but she is a girl: lest I become a laughing stock to the children of Israel." Adultery is specified as Joseph's suspicion by Comestor, *Historia Scholastica*, 'In Evangelia' 3 (PL 198/1539); compare particularly York 13.

127–8 Joseph's reference to previous sexual desire and activity here and at 135–6 relates to the fact that he was a widower with children by his previous marriage; see *Historia Iosephi Fabri Lignarii* 2. He had been a widower for a year when betrothed to Mary, who was fourteen at the time of the Annunciation. But the legends were

PLAY VI   83

strongly contested by commentators, and the developing picture of Joseph also owes much to the picture of the comic and aged cuckold.

129–132 Mary was usually held to have stayed with Elizabeth until the birth of John; see Comestor, *Historia Scholastica*, 'In Evangelia' 3 (PL 198/1538) and *Stanzaic Life* 292–4. But Luke 1/56–7 first relates Mary's return, then Elizabeth's delivery.

Naturalistically, a woman three months pregnant would not resemble one at term. The reference to Mary's distended abdomen may reflect the tradition that Christ was conceived as a fully formed baby rather than a developing embryo; compare Comestor, *Historia Scholastica*, 'In Evangelia' 2 (PL 198/1537), and *Ludus Coventriae* 11/297–8:

> Nott takynge ffyrst o membyr and sythe A-nother
> but parfyte childhod 3e haue A-non.

But the tradition would also help to resolve two difficulties, the first that Mary does not leave the stage and so must be visibly pregnant from an early point — perhaps from the start, with Mary standing with her back to the audience; the second that Elizabeth also does not leave the stage and so cannot be delivered before the visit to Joseph.

Although Luke 1/56 states that Mary stayed with Elizabeth three months, *Historia Iosephi Fabri Ligni* 5 states that Joseph returned to Mary, having been away working, three months after Christ's conception; Book of James 13/1 dates Joseph's return to his wife as "the sixth month"; Pseudo-Matthew 10 dates his return as the ninth month, as also Wakefield 10. These various accounts may also explain Joseph's response here, although Chester seems generally to support the version in Luke — compare 129.

141 *dyscreeve* Compare Matthew 1/19: *Cum...nollet eam traducere* (AV "Not willing to make her a publick example"). *descriven* has a range of meanings, of which MED 2, "to characterize or define", might seem most suitable, although it is never recorded as intransitive or with a personal object. More plausibly, the word has been confused with *descrien*, "to tell, reveal (a confidential matter)", "to denounce, rebuke, criticize".

her ARBH is to be preferred for meaning to its omission in Hm, the latter perhaps a scribal error.

143–4 Compare 139–40 and Matthew 1/19: *Voluit occulte dimittere eam* (AV "Was minded to put her away privily"). But this was also interpreted as indicating that Joseph decided to leave his wife, as in *Glossa Ordinaria*, 'Evangelium Secundum Matthaeum' 1/19 (PL 114/70–1). See also the accompanying note in H· "Voluit clauculum ab ea depertire" (133–4 TNs). Joseph's flight is in York 13/239–40, *Ludus Coventriae* 12/108–17, Coventry Shearmen 136–42.

153–6 "Therefore, when I have slept for a time, because I will go from my wife who has so deceived me — truly I am reluctant to take proceedings in this matter." As here interpreted, the construction is broken, and *fyle* is used as in OED 1b, "to place .... in a due manner among the records of a court or public office" 1511. But the text is obscure here and the scribes generally uneasy. At 153, AR unnecessarily replace the inverted construction with a temporal clause introduced by *when*; at 154, three

different and equally possible orders for the words are supplied; at 155, ARBH supply a more usual infinitive form, *goe*. The two major changes, however, are:
1. The removal of the ellipsis in Hm by placing *for* before *yt* in RH, which is preferable for syntax and meaning to Hm — "I will go from her because I am reluctant ... "; *for* is supported also by AB.
2. The replacement of *yt* by *her* AB, thus identifying *fyle* with *filen* (2), MED 3(a), "to revile, vilify, or disgrace (someone)", a possible and attractive reading.

158 *sleepe* Although Matthew 1/20 states that the angel appeared to Joseph *in somnis* (AV "in a dream"), no reason for the sleep is given; but in the Book of James "night came upon him". The prayer for God's mercy is unbiblical.

159 + SH *Angelus* It is possible for the angel to be shown as Gabriel. Although no such identification is made in the Bible, it is found in *Historia Iosephi Fabri Lignarii* (in *Evangelia Apocrypha*, ed. C. Tischendorf (Lipsiae, 1853)), and also in 7/528 of Chester.

166 Hm is acceptable. The rough metre results from the weak stress in the first two syllables; although AR and BH in different ways reduce the line length by one syllable, there seems little gain in metre, syntax or meaning.

168 The line seems to refer to the prophecy of Isaiah 7/14 which Matthew quotes immediately after the angel's words, 1/22–3. The biblical angel does not in fact refer to the fulfilment of prophecy. But compare 5/319 + Latin–27 and 5/444; also 174.

170 Compare 16/193–4. Since Joseph has not, in fact, been Mary's foe, H's reading is perhaps less probable than HmARB's.

177–84 Compare 4/484–91. The two passages are clearly related since the only differences from the other stanza here, apart from names, are:
    fayre maye]   can saye 4/486   he have]   the same 4/489
As here presented, *maye* is a noun; as the play develops, the beautiful virgin Mary and the aged Joseph are balanced by the beautiful Sibyl and the aged Octavian. But it could be construed as a verb — "that may very pleasingly tell you ..."; in view of the easy confusion of long *s* and *f*, the superscript *r* in *fayre* Hm (see TNs) and the A reading should be noted. *have* 182 has the sense of *haven* MED 5a (d), "preserve, protect", especially in the phrase *God have you*; but AB here repeat the phrase which they use at 4/489 — R significantly does not follow A.

The speech suggests a new entry, and perhaps directs the audience's attention in a new direction. The succeeding events originate in the brief allusion to the universal tax, Luke 2/1–5.

184 + SH *Octavianus* The first Roman emperor, Augustus Caesar. As the representative of the pagan Roman world and the man ultimately responsible for Herod's appointment (cf. Josephus, *Antiquities of the Jews* 15, 6/6), he was regarded as evil and is so characterised by Higden, *Polychronicon* 4. Hence, Christ was held to have been born into an evil and sinful world; compare Mirk, *De Nativitate Domini Christi*: "For, as Seynt Austeyne saythe: 'When Cryst schuld be borne, þe world was so full of derknes of synful lyuyng, and nomely of syn of lechery, and of synne aȝeyne kynde, þat had nye to haue laft to haue ben yborne of mankynd'." Octavian appears in an unfavourable light in Wakefield 9, and the picture of the evil world may be reflected in the Wakefield Shepherds' Plays. Traces of this evil picture may be detected in parts of the Chester play — compare the account in the Banns. But Chester generally follows the more favourable picture of Octavian. The ultimate source of the miracles is *Mirabilia Urbis Romae*, but a major influence is the account of the Nativity in *Legenda Aurea*.

185–240 This part of Octavian's opening speech falls into two sections, separated by the two French stanzas, 209–17. It is unusual to find French in the middle of a speech in Chester; passages of French or Latin are usually used at the start of a speech. Moreover, the two sections of the speech show some duplication, corresponding to the material in *Mirabilia Urbis Romae* 37. 185–88, 218–24 deal with Octavian's personal attributes; 193–204, 225–230 with his powerful and peaceful reign; 205–8, 229–32 with the general tribute paid to Rome. It is therefore tempting to suggest that 185–208 and 209–40 represent alternatives.

187–8 "The most beautiful person to fight, no man may shun my presence." The lines do not give good sense, and do not correspond to *Mirabilia: Videntes eum tante pulchritudinis, quod nemo in oculos eius intueri poterat*. The text could be made more meaningful and would conform more closely to *Mirabilia* by reading *see* for *flee* 188, and perhaps *in sight of sere* for *to fight in fere*, both originating in readings with long s. The resulting sense would be: "The most beautiful person in the sight of many; no man may behold my face." 187 in A and B does not give sense.

194 "All around me is part of my whole delight." *blys* has the senses of "happiness" and "source of happiness", as well as echoes of "heavenly bliss", "the kingdom of heaven".

209–17, stanzas 27–8 The text at this point is very corrupt. It seems to have made little sense to the scribes, although the corruption may lie in the exemplar or even in earlier forms still. Probably the lines were never intended to convey precise meaning to an audience, but only the flavour of an upper-class register. But a meaningful text seems to lie behind the corruptions and, with the help of others more expert than ourselves (see Preface, vol. i), we propose the following (any errors are our responsibility):

    Lords, all assembled here at my noble council,
    I can make [people] miserable or happy, and cast [them] into despondency.
    None of you should leave here intending to perform evil deeds,
    for I am the sovereign full of wisdom, and the lordly emperor.

    I am a person, none so capable; I know how to do so many praiseworthy deeds.
    [215 almost totally obscure — see note below]
    Discreet and wise I am in council, friend to lady and maiden.
    By the pure and holy mother — another such [ruler] does not live.

The corruptions seem too extensive to justify a detailed discussion of the many VRs, but the following notes serve to indicate some of the assumptions underlying the above version and some alternatives proposed to us: 209 Read *ici* for *si. proles* BH is also possible for *probes*, "noble, elevated".

    211–2 Probably stanza 27 originally had the same four-line form as stanza 28, rhyming abab. Deimling prints both as eight-line stanzas.

213 *demande* is here taken as *demaine*, "lordly"; but it may also be read as *du monde* — "emperor of the world".

214 Read *suis* for *si*; read *sais* for *sa*. But alternatively, translate "I know no person as capable as I am", taking *sais* for *si*; and "I know how to do so much and [to be] praiseworthy", taking *leable* as referring to Octavian.

215 *plerunt* seems to mean "they shall weep", but the rest of the line is obscure.

216 Read *descret* for *destret*; read *suis* for *sua*; read *au* for *ou*.

217 Prefer *vivant* B as rhyme for *plerunt*. If so, possibly consider the latter as *plerant*?

218–24, stanza 29 The stanza lacks one a-rhyme line in the last four lines; the absence of any such line in all manuscripts indicates that the omission was in the exemplar. An empty line space follows 223 in H (see TNs); as Deimling points out, H is the only manuscript to recognise the deficiency, but is unable to remedy it.

220 *preistes* RBH may be preferred for morphology to *pryest* Hm and to the scribally erroneous *prese* A; *princes* seems to require a complementary plural form to follow.

225–32, stanza 30 *is all thing* 229 BH is to be preferred for rhyme to the readings of Hm, A, R. These readings suggest a process of modification from the BH form, through *must all bee* Hm to *moste/must it be* AR, possibly indicating a later emendation in the exemplar influenced by the rhyme-word of the preceding line.

233–40, stanza 31 R's omission of 233–6 is a scribal error, perhaps resulting from confusion of *sythen* 233 and *syth* 237. For perfect rhyme, read *trist* for *trust* 240.

237–8 The establishment of the *pax Romana* was seen as Octavian's primary contribution to the coming of Christ; compare Orosius 1, 1 par.6, and 7, 2 par. 16, 3 par.9 etc, *Glossa Ordinaria*, 'Evang. Luc' 2/1 (PL 114/249); and *Legenda Aurea*, 'De Nativitate Domini Nostri Jesu Christi'.

241–4 The taxing is here presented as a manifestation of authority. Compare *Legenda Aurea*, 'De Nativitate'; Comestor, *Historia Scholastica*, 'In Evangelia' 4 (PL 198/1539); and *Stanzaic Life*, 313–6.

243–4 Compare *Stanzaic Life*:
    and iche hede, als leue ȝe me,
    that shulden tribute to hym bere.
        (323–4)

249 Compare 385–8 and note.

251–4 Compare Ezechiel 5/5: *Ista est Ierusalem, in medio gentium posui eam, et in circuitu eius terras* (AV "This is Jerusalem; I have set it in the midst of the nations and countries that are round about her"). Comestor, *Historia Scholastica*, 'In Evangelia' 4 (PL 198/1539): *Prima dicitur quantum ad Cyrinum Syriae praesidem, quia enim Judaea in umbilico Zonae habitabilis esse dicitur, provisum est ut in ea inchoaretur, et deinde per circumstantes regiones alii praesides prosequerentur*. Comestor is cited by *Legenda Aurea*. The detail is not in *Stanzaic Life*. Compare 265–8.

257 Perhaps an oblique reference to the governorship of Cyrenius in Syria, Luke 2/2.

265 *this* ARBH is to be preferred for meaning and style to *thus*(1) Hm. The confusion of *this* and *thus* in Hm is paralleled in reverse in A.

275 *tayles tupp*, "tail-less ram", perhaps a breeding ram whose tail has been docked. The phrase almost certainly contains sexual suggestion which prompts the comic exchange between Preco and Octavian.

277–96 A omits 276 + SH–92, perhaps a deliberate censoring of Preco's impertinence but more probably a result of an eye-slip, confusing *boye* 277 and *boye* 293; hence stanza 36 A consists of 273–6 and 293–6, destroying the rhyme-scheme but linking Octavian's offer more closely with the suggestiveness of 275–6. R follows A in omitting the dialogue but replaces 293–6 with 289–292 and omits Octavian's reply, thus removing Octavian's share in the repartee. The episode may be seen as a humanised presentation of a remote and terrifying emperor, or as a deliberate comic deflation of his pomposity

279 i.e. the gallows, which for the city of Chester were set up in the nearby Boughton Heath some two miles to the south-east. The gallows were for the public execution of the common criminal; noble "criminals" were usually beheaded, often at private executions. Hence 283–8 is insolently reductive of Octavian's noble rank.

297–372 The basis for accounts of Octavian's proposed deification is *Mirabilia Urbis Romae*, which is transmitted more widely by *Legenda Aurea* and thence into *Stanzaic Life*. In *Legenda* the deification follows the Nativity account, as in *Stanzaic Life*, but the chronology of the narrative indicates that the start of the action precedes the Nativity.

297–312 In *Mirabilia* the senators, of unspecified number, impute deity to Octavian; *si hoc non esset, non tibi omnia essent prospera*. The reasons for deification in Chester — the widespread love for the emperor, his concern with justice, the establishment of peace — are more substantial and constitute a picture of the ideal ruler.

313–36 In *Mirabilia* the emperor gives a similar reply, but on a different occasion, when *populus dominum illum vocare descrevisset*: *Cum sim mortalis dominum me dicere nolo*. Compare *Legenda Aurea*, 'De Nativitate': *Prudens autem imperator se mortalem intelligens, immortalitatis nomen sibi noluit usurpare*; *Stanzaic Life*:

> But the emperour was wys
> And thoȝt wel that he was dedly,
> sich honour shuld noȝt be hys
> (601–3)

Here, the reply takes up earlier references to immortality as the attribute of deity, 1/5–6, 2/1–2; compare 351–2. Such a reminder might be especially helpful if Play 6 began the second day; compare 5/448 55.

319 Wilson sees as the only certain parallel between the *Stanzaic Life* and this part of the play (297–372) this line and *Life* 602, "And thoȝt wel that he was dedly."

321–8, stanza 42 *I see* 328 ARBH is probably correct. *in mee* Hm repeats the rhyme-phrase of 324 and is probably an eye-slip.

322 The AR reading is an echo of Job 14/1: *Homo, natus de muliere, brevi vivens tempore repletur multis miseriis* (AV "Man that is born of a woman is of few days, and full of trouble"), used at the grave-side in the 1559 burial service.

329–36, stanza 43   The b-rhymes have *I* 332 — *unkynde* 336 do not rhyme; *unkindly* BH is to be preferred for rhyme to *unkynde* HmAR. Both adjectival forms were available, but HmAR may have misunderstood the *-ly* form as adverbial.

347–8   The question asked does not follow directly from the senators' request. *Mirabilia* and *Polychronicon* do not indicate the question asked. In *Legenda Aurea*, 'De Nativitate', Octavian summons the Sibyl but cites her earlier prophecy. But the question is asked elsewhere — compare *Speculum Humanae Salvationis*, cap.8:
> Of whilk thing he counseild / with Sibille the prophetess
> Where in this world shuld eure / man passe hym in gretenesse.

Stanzaic Life 605–8:
> And asket qveþer þat euer shuld be
> Any mon born in flesch ϡ blode
> So gret a lord as then was he,
> so gracious ϡ eke so gode.

Similar accounts are found in the French drama. Compare *Mistère du Vieil Testament*, 48937–40; *Mistère de la Passion*, 2903–4; and Le Verdier's *L'Incarnation et Nativité* p.427.

347   Deimling notes *there* RB as evidence that occasionally R leaves A in favour of 'the parent manuscript' of the Group. His deduction is called into question by the shared omission of *there* by HmAH.

349–52   In *Mirabilia* the Sibyl fasts for three days before replying, as in *Stanzaic Life* 609–12, *Polychronicon* 4 — a marked difference from the play. She then utters a Doomsday prophecy:
> Judicii signum tellus sudore madescet,
> E celo rex adveniet per secla futurus,
> Scilicet in carne presens, ut iudicet orbem, et cetera que sequuntur,

a prophecy not relevant to the situation in Chester 6. She then shows Octavian the vision. Here Octavian, receiving his answer, requests a *signe* 354 which, in view of the chronology of the play, presumably takes place on the same day; compare 371.

350   The various readings may suggest a desire to avoid the jingling *barne borne* of B — either by changing the subject-word, as Hm, or by moving the past participle, as ARH.

361–4, stanza 47   The ARBH quatrain is required to complete the stanza and has been erroneously omitted by Hm.

366   *not* ARBH is to be preferred to the scribally erroneous *non* Hm.

376   Deimling cites the erroneous substitution, *stronge* AR, as evidence of the close relationship of the two manuscripts.

381–8, stanza 50   No manuscript has the required rhyme-form *mankynne* 388.

385–6   Compare Comestor, *Historia Scholastica*, 'In Evangelia' 4 (PL 198/1539), seen also in *Polychronicon*, and *Stanzaic Life* 329–36:

of siluer shuld þat peny be,
ten comune penys hit was worthy,
And on hit writen was, leue 3e me,
hor knowlachyng apertely,
And by þat peny bounden wer thay
fforto be obedient
to þe emperour of Rome for ay,
be þat 3yft with gode entent.
(329-36)

Wilson regards this as the only detail shared by the *Life* and the play in the section 373-428. Luke 2/1-3 uses the terms *describeretur, descriptio*, and does not specify the reason for or manner of the "description".

Some influence may be suspected from the episode of Luke 20/21-6, to which the taxing was linked by commentators such as Bede. Jesus, asked about the legality of paying tribute to Caesar, asked to see a denarius and, pointing to the image and inscription on it, said: *Reddite ergo quae sunt Caesaris Caesari, et quae sunt Dei Deo* (AV "Render therefore unto Caesar the things which be Caesar's and unto God the things which be God's"). Compare Bede, *In Lucae Evangelium Expositio* 1/2 (PL 92/329). The method described is also reminiscent of the English poll-tax and sometimes seems so described; compare Mirk, *De Nativitate*, "Ley a peny apon his hed."

389-406 Joseph's complaint seems to reflect badly upon the emperor and may suggest the image of the "bad" Octavian; indeed, Le Verdier *L'Incarnation et Nativité* (pp. 5-6) takes steps to forestall such a reading. But the point may rather be a piece of contemporary satire since the play was the responsibility of the Chester Carpenters. Although Joseph was a carpenter, Matthew 13/55, the fact is not acknowledged in the English cycles apart from this clear instance where he carries the tools of his trade. The image then becomes one of the contemporary Cestrian complaining against bureaucratic interference.

398 *perscer* ARBH is to be preferred to the scribally erroneous *perces* Hm.

401-4 "I never had in my power castle, tower or rich manor, but being a simple carpenter I had only what I could get with these tools." Probably *thes* A, *these* RH is to be preferred to *those* 404 Hm, since Joseph holds the tools, 397-9; *this* B is less probable.

405 A more regular sequence of strongly and weakly stressed syllables results from the insertion of a weakly stressed syllable after *store*, as in ABH or R. *of* R is not necessary, and perhaps suggests an attempt to replace the ABH reading by a "more modern" construction. Hm corrected the line by inserting *newe* and later erasing it (see TNs); the inserted form is probably a misreading of *nowe*, later erased because *newe* does not give sense.

422 *sister* The word seems in contradistinction to the expected *wife*. Compare *sister* OED 2, "One who is reckoned as, or fills the place of, a sister"; 3b "A female fellow-member of the Christian Church as a whole." Compare also the Book of James 17/1: "How shall I record her? as my wife? nay, I am ashamed. Or as my daughter? but all the children of Israel know that she is not my daughter."

423–8 Compare Comestor, *Historia Scholastica*, 'In Evangelia' 5 (PL 198/1540), a detail also in *Legenda Aurea* and *Stanzaic Life*:

        And an ox with hym toke he
        to selle ʒ to lif þeropon
        quyl þai duellide in that cite,
        And also tribute forto pay
        of that he shuld take for that best
        (350–4)

426 *this* H continues the idea expressed in 425–8 + SD H, *cum ad stabulum pervenerit*, that Mary's vision occurs in Bethlehem rather than on the journey, as the other manuscripts indicate. *Stanzaic Life* 357 also locates the vision in Bethlehem; see 429–32 note.

429–32 Compare Book of James 17/1: "And Mary said unto Joseph: It is because I behold two peoples with mine eyes, the one weeping and lamenting and the other rejoicing and exulting"; so also Pseudo-Matthew 13/1. The order of people in *Legenda Aurea* is reversed, as also in *Stanzaic Life*:

        Qven þei to Bethleem comen wer,
        As frer Bertilmewe beris witnes,
        Sum of þe peple made gode cher,
        And sum mournyng ʒ tristes.
        (357–60)

429–68 Wilson compares *Stanzaic Life* 357–416, claiming that the play here "seems taken straight from the *Life*, although there are no verbal parallels."

431 The line has only three strongly stressed syllables instead of the expected four. No ms has the necessary addition.

433–6 Some corruption may be suspected here since *came* 433 is awkwardly duplicated by *is commen* 434, and 435 contains only three strongly stressed syllables instead of the usual four. The text, however, gives good sense as it stands. It would be improved by the omission of *came* 433 and the transference of *be* from the start of 436 to the end of the preceding line, as in B; but 436 B seems to read more easily with four strongly stressed syllables than with the expected three.

437–52 Compare Pseudo-Matthew 13/1, where the speaker is "puer quidam speciosus." There is no equivalent passage in the Book of James. Pseudo-Matthew is cited by Vincent of Beauvais, *Speculum Historiale* 6/73. In *Legenda Aurea* the speaker is an angel, addressing Mary. *Legenda* provides the basis of *Stanzaic Life* 361–84.

439 *commen peple* i.e. Gentiles: compare *Legenda Aurea*, *populus gentilis*, *Stanzaic Life* 365, *the folk*. *commen* is in contradistinction to *chosen*, i.e. to the Jews.

441 *blood* H is an uncancelled error resulting from the automatic writing of a common collocation.

447 "For they (the Jews) abandoned their innate moral feeling." Compare *kinde* MED 5(a). *it* H has no obvious reference. See texts cited under 437–52 note.

PLAY VI

455-6 Compare *Legenda Aurea*, Comestor, *Historia Scholastica*, 'In Evangelia' 5 (PL 198/1539-40), and *Stanzaic Life*:

> ffor thai wer pore ȝ al nedie,
> herber myȝt thai non com ner
> fforto leng in honestly,
> ffor taken was ich hous ȝ maner
> to lordes ȝ men that wer myȝty.
> (395-9)

458 *this stable* The apocryphal gospels locate the birth in a cave. In Pseudo-Matthew, the angel halts Mary's ass at the cave immediately after the explanation of the vision. Compare Comestor, *Historia Scholastica*, 'In Evangelia' 5 (PL 198/1540), as also *Legenda Aurea*, and *Stanzaic Life*:

> But a hous woghles þer was,
> that sett was negh þe heȝe-way,
> bitwene two houses hylyng it has,
> but side al opone, soth to say.
> (401-4)

459-60 Compare Mirk, 'De Nativitate': "Wherfor, þagh he hymselfe wer lord of all lordes, he was borne full porly, and of a pore mayden, and yn pore place, and yn a pore araye, ȝeuyng ensampull to all men forto set not by worldly ryches, noþer by pryde of þys world; for haue a man neuer so moche good ne so moch worschyp, here he fyndythe hit, and here he schall leue hit."

470 *too middwives* The episode of the midwives derives from the apocryphal gospels of James and of Pseudo-Matthew. In Book of James 18/1 Joseph goes out to look for one midwife, but the plural is indicated in Pseudo-Matthew 13/3: *Ioseph perexerit quaerire obstetrices*. In Mirk, 'De Nativitate,' it is at Mary's request that Joseph goes to look for the midwives, but Chester follows the standard account of *Legenda Aurea*: *Joseph licet Deum de virgine nasciturum non dubitaret, morem tamen gerens patriae obstetrices vocavit.* Compare *Ludus Coventriae* 15/133-4:

> It is not conuenyent a man to be
> þer women gon in travalynge.

484 + SH *Tebell* The names of the midwives in Pseudo-Matthew 13/3 and *Legenda Aurea* are Zelomi and Salome; Mirk, 'De Nativitate', anglicises as Zebell and Salome, as does *Ludus Coventriae* 15/137-48. *Tebel* is, however, the name of the believing midwife in *Stanzaic Life* 454 and Foster and Wilson accept the similarity of name with Chester as conclusive evidence of the connexion between the *Life* and the cycle. A. C. Baugh, 'The Chester Plays and French Influence', comments (p.49) "[Tebel] is found in the Golden Legend and occasionally elsewhere. But .. it is the form regularly found in French mysteries and nowhere else in the English drama." But compare South English Nativity:

> Þo þe child was ibore, Iosep þider brouhte
> Tuo wymmen þat coude on þe craft þat wel wyde he souhte.
> Here names were Tebel and Salome.
> (379-81)

— three of the nine manuscripts read *Zebel*. Although Foster, *Stanzaic Life* 454, treats this reference cursorily as being in a work "which has no other significant parallel with the *Stanzaic Life*, both works draw extensively upon some form of *Legenda Aurea* and may reflect a form of the name available in some versions of *Legenda*. Hemingway suggests that the name derives from the lost *Gospel of Bartholomew*.

493 The birth of Christ precedes the arrival of the midwives in Mirk, 'De Nativitate'. In *Stanzaic Life* the birth precedes the account of the midwives, although the chronology is not conclusive. In York 14/50–6 Jesus is born during Joseph's absence to seek for a light; in *Ludus Coventriae* 15/124 + SD, Jesus is born while Joseph seeks the midwives.

505 Compare Pseudo-Matthew 13/3: *Sed et nulla sanguinis pollutio facta est in nascente, nullus dolor in parturiente*.

508 *thow* is the usual pronoun of address between Joseph and Mary; compare, e.g., 492–5. *you* H perhaps extends the address to the midwives.

508 + SD Compare Book of James 19/2: "And they stood in the place of the cave; and behold, a bright cloud overshadowing the cave." Hence York 14/78–83. Compare also Innocent III, Sermo 2 (PL 217/457): *Novum fecit in signo; quia, Christo nascente, stella magis apparuit, secundum vaticinium Balaam: 'Orietur, inquit, stella ex Jacob, et exsurget virga ex Israel* (Num 24). Mirk, 'De Nativitate', also points the symbolic significance: "Wherfor Cryst was borne at mydnyght, and turnet þe darkenes of nyght ynto day-lyght." In York 14/78–83, Joseph described the sudden light; in *Ludus Coventriae* 15/161–4 the midwives comment on the light.

510 Compare 14.

511–2 "Now I believe the angel's word — that you are a pure virgin — is true." In Hm the lines suggest an earlier doubt about the truth of the angel's words; *wordes* ARBH may be preferred: "Now I am fully convinced of the angel's true words, that you are a pure virgin." The sense of *leeve* may be "fully believe, am convinced by", suggesting that Joseph now has concrete proof of what he earlier believed by faith.

One reason for Mary's marriage to Joseph was traditionally that he bore witness to her virginity: compare *Legenda Aurea*: *Tertio per custodiam: Joseph enim ex eo, quod ipsam custodivit, testis suae virginitatis exstitit*. See also 7/516–39 and note.

513–4 "For you are come to create man's bliss, are come for all who will observe your law." *shewe* is here taken as "display, exhibit". Alternative punctuations would link 514 to 515, or, less probably, present it as an independent sentence, with *that* as pronoun referring to *mans blys* — "your law will display that to everyone." This last version would most readily accommodate *saw* H, "saying, teaching".

516 *joye* AR represents a significant shared error which destroys the meaning of the line.

519 *preeve* HmH, "deprive", seems to have been somewhat obscured in the exemplar. *prive* A is correct; *reave* B is an acceptable substitution; but *prove* R is an error, perhaps based on a misunderstanding since *preve* is also a variant form of *prove*.

521 *diversorye* MED has only three other citations for this word in ME, two of which are in the Nativity context but referring to the stable itself. Here the sense is clearly "lodging house" as opposed to the "shelter" supplied by the stable, though literally the word means "a place to which one turns in by the way" OED. B erroneously attempts a formal division into two familiar words; A and R attempt to guess the meaning from the context, especially from *lapped*.

524   *be* must be understood. AR supply the form, at the expense of a rougher metre, while B replaces the conjunction with an adverb to remove the necessity for a verb-form at all.

525-32   In Pseudo-Matthew and *Legenda Aurea* Zebel touches Mary and satisfies herself about Mary's virginity. In Book of James, Zebel sees the light accompanying the birth. But in Chester Tebell seems convinced by the evidence of painless delivery; compare the rather ambiguous *Stanzaic Life*:

Tebel by signe sothlie con se
that Mary was a clene may
(457-8)

and the equally ambiguous Mirk, 'De Nativitate': "But when Zebell fonde well þat our lady was clene mayden..." The contrast between the believing and unbelieving midwives is to some degree obscured in the ultimate sources since Salome merely does what Zebel has done, albeit in a different, more sceptical spirit; compare *Legenda Aurea*: *Salome autem dum non crederet, sed hoc probare similiter vellet.*

533-9, stanza 69   The stanza contains seven lines instead of the usual eight, an error shared by all manuscripts and therefore present in the exemplar.

536   *and had* BH is to be preferred to *and* HmAR in supplying the verb required for sense. The HmAR reading, however, gives a more regular sequence of strongly and weakly stressed syllables. Perhaps *had* should be substituted for *and*, in which case *withoutten* H would improve the metre.

542   *handes manus* 539 + SD is similarly plural. But at 719 the Expositor refers only to *hyr hand* and gynaecologically this is more probable. Compare *my hand*, Book of James 20/1; *aruit manus eius*, Pseudo-Matthew 13/4 and *Legenda Aurea*; *my hand*, *Ludus Coventriae* 15/255.

547 + SD   *dicens* ARBH is to be preferred for meaning to its omission in Hm. On the latter, see further 547 + SH note. No reference is made to the star's disappearance after it first appears at 508 + SD.

547 + SH   *Angelus* Compare Book of James 20/3: "an angel of the lord"; Pseudo-Matthew 13/5: *iuvenis*; *Legenda Aurea*: *jussu angeli*, as also Mirk, "De Nativitate", and *Ludus Coventriae* 15/275 | SII.

The speech ascription is also carried by the preceding SD, hence perhaps the omission of a 'redundant' SH in B. Hm's ascription of the following speech to Tebel is not impossible in itself, but has no sanction in analogues and seems precluded by the SD — where Hm significantly omits *dicens*. Hm would have the effect of limiting the angel's role at this point to accompanying the star. Compare 8/84 + SD.

548-9   The request for forgiveness seems here sufficient, but in other accounts it is accompanied by physical contact with Christ. Salome is commanded to touch Christ in Book of James 20/3, Pseudo-Matthew 13/5, *Legenda Aurea*; Compare *Stanzaic Life* 478, "And touchide Ihesu that born was". In Mirk, 'De Nativitate': "And bade hyr towch þe chylde, and be hole", the touching alone is sufficient. In *Ludus Coventriae* 15/281-9, *Salomee* asks forgiveness of Jesus and is told by Mary to touch his clothes. The absence of this feature is the more striking in Chester because the shepherds later insist on physical contact — see 7/490-1.

548 *wemen* AB suggests that the angel is addressing both midwives. The manner of the ensuing speech and the use of the second singular pronoun indicate that the plural form here is an error.

555 HmAR seem correct. *here* H gives less satisfactory meaning and metre, but may indicate some change made in the exemplar which is further suggested by the erroneous *liere* B. Compare Mirk, 'De Nativitate': "Þus, good men, ȝe mou vndyrstonde how God ȝeueth pes to hom þat ben men and wymen of good wyll, and callyth hom his chyldren."

565 *freere Bartholemewe* Apparently directly taken from the *Legenda Aurea* ascription: *Ut in compilatione Bartholomaei habetur et de libro Infantiae salvatoris sumptum fuisse videtur.* In *Stanzaic Life* this appears as *Frater Bartholomaeus in sua compilacione de infancia Christi.* Hemingway notes: "Probably referring to the (now lost) Apocryphal *Gospel of St. Bartholomew* which is mentioned by Jerome (Migne P. L. 26.17) and Gelasius (Migne P. L. 59.162)." But see also Kevin J. Harty's suggestion (*American Notes and Queries* xvi (1977), pp.18-9) that the lost Gospel of Bartholomew may be Pseudo-Matthew.

564-7, stanza 73   *beforne* 567 HmAH is to be preferred for rhyme to *before* RB.

568–*Finis*   Wilson and Foster agree that influence from *Stanzaic Life* continues for the remainder of the play.

568   Since the Expositor lists three miracles, *and other myracles* HmAH is to be preferred to *another mirackle* ARB here.

Wilson notes that, although Chester does not include the marvels of the well of oil (*Stanzaic Life* 565-80) and the statue of Romulus (*Stanzaic Life* 645-84), it does have four miracles in the same order as in the *Life* — the midwives, *Salvatio Romae* (Temple of Peace), three suns, ox and ass — which are used to separate the Octavian episodes.

573-635   The account of the Temple of Peace (*Salvatio Romae*) was widely known. Compare the account by Innocent III, Sermo 2, and *Legenda Aurea*, and Comestor's brief note, *Historia Scholastica*, 'In Evangelia' 5, Additio 1 (PL 198/1540): *Romae templum pacis corruit.* Hemingway, 575-60 note, reviews the development of the story, citing as the earliest extant form that by the Greek Cosmas in the eighth century. It also appears in *Polychronicon*, and in *Stanzaic Life* 481-536.

578-9   Compare *Stanzaic Life* 486, "thrid part þe world hit was worthy," a detail in *Polychronicon*.

580-3   Compare *Stanzaic Life*:
>   Vchone hade written on his brest
>   his nome, the londes name also
>   (493-4)

— a detail in *Polychronicon*.

586 The line is metrically rough and would be improved by the omission of a syllable. AR omit *was*, which must then be understood; BH, more acceptably, read *als* for *alsoe*.

587 *god of Rome* It is not clear who is here intended. Candidates include Janus, the doors of whose temple were closed in time of peace, and Romulus — compare *Legenda Aurea*: *Et ibi statuam Romuli posuerunt*. But Le Verdier's *L'Incarnation et Nativité* (p.428) suggests Apollo.

588–95 Compare Neckham (*De Naturis Rerum*, ed. T. Wright (London, 1863), Bk.II, chap. clxxiv): *Miles vero aeneus, equo insidiens aeneo, in summitate fastigii praedicti palatii hastam vibrans, in illam se vertit partem quae regionem illam respiciebat*. Also *Polychronicon* (Bk.I, chap. xxiv): *Erat etiam in tecto domus illius eques quidem aeneus concordans mobiliter motui illius imaginis, lanceamque contra gentem illam sic insurgentem dirigebat*, which *Stanzaic Life* 501-4, 513-28, follows closely.

588–9 is not clear. As here presented, it means "Also there, moving round the house [was] a man on a horse — men stood to look at it"; *was sett* 586 is understood. Alternatively, *stoode* may be regarded as past participle — "A man on a horse was set up to guide (steer) men"; or even "[He] stopped (stood still, ceased moving) to direct men". *feare* 589 B also gives sense — "he was set up to terrify men".

At this point the text does not make it completely clear that the horseman is outside the temple, on its roof. Compare 604, and the more explicit *Stanzaic Life* 501: "Aboue þat temple al with-out". 604 H, however, reads *about* for *above*, perhaps because of the 588 phrase; but possibly *abowt* should be regarded as an error for *above* here.

Some contrast seems intended between the general public, *men* 589, who saw the horseman, and *certayne preystes* 594 who saw the idols inside the temple.

598 *image* BH is to be preferred to the erroneous readings of Hm, AR, which seem to represent attempts to give familiar form to a difficult exemplar reading. Deimling cites the AR form as evidence of the close relationship of the two manuscripts, but Hm represents a potential corruption of *image* and supplies a verb form which points towards the AR reading. The Hm form is followed by a cancelled eye-slip error (see TNs).

600 Compare *Stanzaic Life* 511, "And turnet his bak ful deignously." Only in Chester does the rebellious image look challengingly towards Rome. The more common account is obtained by reading *from* for *to* 601.

610 Compare *Stanzaic Life*:
        thai senden onon bout tarying
        legiouns þat londe to destrie.
        (523–4)
and all standard accounts refer to invasion of the rebellious province. Only Chester seems to suggest a defensive measure.

612–9, stanza 79 Each line in 612-4 has three strongly stressed syllables instead of the expected four. The omission of 616-9 R may reflect an intention to isolate the "irregular quatrain". 619 Hm contains four strongly stressed syllables, and the ABH version is therefore to be preferred in eliminating unnecessary repetition and conforming to normal metrical expectations. See also 616 note.

616   *in that*, presumably "on account of that" — see MED *in* 22. *that* is taken up and explained in 618–19. But the definite article or a demonstrative must then be understood before *temple* — the line is metrically regular and no omission can be assumed. H avoids the problem by omitting *in* and making *that* demonstrative.

620   *that* H is to be preferred for meaning *to* to HmARB since *hee* has no obvious reference without a defining relative clause.

cuninglye AR may suggest an awareness of the word's special sense, "possessing magical knowledge or skill", OED *cunning* 3.

621   *the devyll* Compare similar pejorative references at 595, 613, 624, 635. The diabolical associations perhaps derive from the identification of pagan gods with demons; compare Peter Damian, Sermo 61 (PL 144/848). But the Temple of Peace seems to represent the explanation of the *pax Romana* for which Octavian was praised, and the attribution of the peace to diabolical art seems to weaken Octavian's claims to reverence. Innocent III, Sermo 2, links the temple's construction to Octavian's supremacy, but presents it as commemorative rather than causative and shows its fall as an example of the limitations of human wisdom and earthly peace (PL 217/457). Compare 614; also 195–6, 230–1, 237–8.

A distinction seems intended between the architect of the temple and his master; compare *Legenda Aurea*: *Consulentes autem Apollinem, quantum duraret*. A tradition quoted by Hemingway ascribed the temple to Virgil.

626   *wemmostlye* No manuscript has the expected form, *wemlesly*, "sinlessly", and the exemplar reading may well have been obscure. AR and B have formally familiar but meaningless readings; Hm seems to have been influenced by *most*.

632–5   Compare *Legenda Aurea*: *Ibi est modo ecclesia Sanctae Mariae Novae*; but also Damian, Sermo 61 (PL 144/848–9): *Ita cecidit, et confractum est illud murale et columnatum opus, ut vix appareant vestigia ruinarum*. The reference to contemporary fears here has no counterpart in standard accounts. It is not in *Stanzaic Life*.

636–9   Compare *Stanzaic Life* 581–4 et seq., a detail also in *Legenda Aurea*.

640–1   Compare Pseudo-Matthew 14: *Ingressa stabulum posuit puerum suum in praesepio, quem bos et asinus adoraverunt ... Ipsa ergo animalia, bos et asinus, in medio eum habentes incessanter adorabant eum*. *Stanzaic Life*, following *Legenda Aurea*, is more specific:

> the ox ʒ asse doun knelyng
> honouret God þer hom biforn.
> (686–7)

But Chester is less specific about the form of adoration. Compare York 14/122–32.

642–3   Compare *Stanzaic Life*:

> ʒet wer miracles mony mo
> showet in diuerse place,
> As I shal showe ʒou er I go
> After this pagyn a little space.
> (693–6)

Wilson calls this "the extreme of abject copying from the manuscript of the *Life*" (p.428). Compare IB/409–10.

PLAY VI

643 + SD The star here, described at 651-4, 691-8, is clearly that which appeared at Christ's birth, 508 + SD, 547 + SD, and it therefore forms a link between the Nativity and Octavian episodes.
   In *Mirabilia* (*Mirabilia Romae*, ed. Gustáve Parthey, Berlin, 1869) the vision follows immediately upon the Sibyl's prophecy; in *Legenda Aurea* Sibyl sees the vision alone in her chamber and shows it to the emperor.

644-50, stanza 83   All manuscripts originally had the seven-line stanza of Hm. In HmRB the lines rhyme aaaaaab; in A, aaaaaaa; in H aabaaab. But in H a later, non-scribal hand has created a regular Chester stanza by:
1. Re-arranging 644-7 in the sequence 644, 647, 645, 646 by means of letters in the margin (see TNs), giving a rhyme-sequence aaab, with the three-stress line now in the expected position.
2. Supplying an extra a-rhyme line to follow 648 (see VRs and TNs).
3. Changing the construction of 648 by reading *so* for *that* (see TNs) to permit syntactical continuity to the new line which is to follow.
The status of the H-alteration is not clear. Deimling speculated that it was either conjecture or the result of a check against another copy of the plays. We have accepted *power* as the H-scribe's reading here.
   It should be noted, however, that the A version is equally, if not more, probable, and that if all lines contained an a-rhyme, the confusion whereby one line might be lost would be more readily understandable. It also seems unlikely that the rather archaic *postee* should replace *power*, rather than vice-versa.

651-4   The form of the vision varies in different accounts. Compare *Mirabilia*: *Ilico apertum est celum, et nimius splendor irruit super eum. vidit in celo quandam pulcherrimam virginem stantem super altare, puerum tenentem in brachiis*; *Legenda Aurea*: *In die media circulus aureus apparuit circa solem et in medio circuli virgo pulcherrima, puerum gestans in gremio*; *Stanzaic Life*:

>   A sercle obuf þe sonne was
>   And in þe sonne a swete wiȝt,
>   A maiden clene al ful of gras,
>   A child hade in hir armes clyght
>   (614-7)

— Wilson sees a close verbal parallel of 653 and *Life* 617; Mirk, 'De Nativitate': "Sygh at mydday a cercule of gold aboute þe sonne, and yn þe myddyll of þe cerkyll a wondyr fayre mayden, and a chyld yn hyr barme." The Chester account seems to have much in common with the description of the Magi's star — compare 8/69-72, 79-80; and *Legenda Aurea*, 'De Epiphania Domini', reflected in *Stanzaic Life*:

>   The quich shapen was
>   like a childe, non fairer myȝt be,
>   And opon his hede he has
>   a shynyng croys as they conen se.
>   (1757-60)

French drama generally accords with the *Legenda* account; compare *Mistère du Vieil Testament*, 49053 + SD and 49099+101; and Le Verdier's *L'Incarnation et Nativité*, (*Mystère de l'Incarnation et Nativité de notre Sauveur ... Jésus-Christ*, ed. P. le Verdier (Rouen, 1884-6), p.437)

Naturalistically in Chester, the Octavian-vision seems to follow directly the birth of Christ, in the middle of the night, and the dramatist may have felt that the sun-emblem would be inappropriate, as well as dramatically uneconomical and confusing. Possibly also, however, he was conscious of the potential for a continuing link through the star-image of plays 5–9.

655–6 Compare *Mirabilia*: *Statim in terram procidens adoravit Christum venturum*; more specifically, *Legenda Aurea*: *Ei thura obtulit*, and *Stanzaic Life*:

> The emperour honouret then knelyng
> that child ĩ to hym made praiere,
> and with encens als vp-steyng,
> comaundet also both fer ĩ nere.
> (625–8)

Mirk, 'De Nativitate': "Þen þe Emperour toke sens, and dyd hym sacryfyce."

throughout 656 Hm gives the most acceptable sequence of strongly and weakly stressed syllables. AR and B revise the expected stress-pattern, while H removes a required syllable.

666 + SD Some variation occurs in analogues in the speaker and the words uttered. Compare *Mirabilia*: *Vocem de celo audivit dicentem*: '*Hec virgo concepta est salvatorem mundi*'. *Rursumque aliam vocem de celo audivit*: '*Hec cara filia dei est*'. But Nichols's translation, presumably of the *Graphia* version, reads 'This is the altar of the Son of God', while *Legenda Aurea* gives two versions: *Audivit vocem dicentem sibi*: '*Haec est ara coeli*', and, in the version attributed to Timotheus: *Audivit vocem sibi dicentem*: '*Puer aethereus ex Deo vivente, sine tempore genitus, non multum post ex intemerata virgine Deus homo nasciturus sine macula*'. *Hoc audito ibi aram aedificavit, cui hunc titulum inscripsit*: '*Haec est ara filii Dei viventis*'. *Stanzaic Life* offers also two slightly different versions: '*Verba Angeli*: '*Hec est ara dei celi*'. (620 Latin) and:

> A voice from heuen sone herde was:
> 'her is Goddes auter dight,
> As thou may se bifore þi fas.'
> (618–20)

Mirk does not mention the voice. In *Mistère du Vieil Testament* the speaker is called "La Voix" and says:

> En ce lieu
> Est le filz de Dieu
> (49070–1)

Hence only *Stanzaic Life* specifies the speaker as an angel, although the fact that an angel accompanies the star at the Nativity in Chester would undoubtedly also direct the dramatist to use him as speaker. The original form of the prophecy, in *Mirabilia*, was strongly Marian, but the change from *cara filia* to *ara filii* and thence to *ara coeli* weakened this connexion. It is not clear whether the Chester text implies the existence of an altar on the stage; the fact that the vision is apparently depicted on a star makes such a device less necessary than perhaps the *Mirabilia* account would indicate.

Only *Stanzaic Life* suggests that the words are sung. No text is recorded in liturgies and the words in Chester, *Fiat notam secundum arbitrium agentis*, probably suggests a free form, perhaps a chant at the discretion of the performer.

PLAY VI

667–74, stanza 86   The omission of 671–4 B is an error; no reason for the omission is obvious, although the recurring b-rhyme of 670–4 may have contributed to an eye-slip.

677   The line may be read as the object of either *leeve* 675 or, as here punctuated, *shewe* 678. The former reading requires a comma at the end of 676 and a semi-colon at the end of 677; Octavian is to believe by faith in Christ's birth (675) and also in his purpose (676), and the vision is a demonstration of the necessity for this belief. The second reading, here preferred, suggests that the vision, in addition to signalling Christ's birth, also suggests his purpose; but nothing in the vision itself indicates that Christ has come "for mans blys". The statement of purpose is supplied by the Sibyl from the prophetic knowledge evidenced in 350.

681–2   *but* represents the alternative to *otherwise* — "he who thinks other than to recognise him as Christ does wrong". ARBH supply *he* 681 — AR before the relative pronoun, BH after the relative clause — but the pronoun is not required for sense, and its varying position perhaps argues for its absence from the exemplar. Arguably, however, a smoother metre results from its inclusion.

683–90, stanza 88   *mone* 687 R is to be preferred for rhyme to *man* ABH, since an -*o*- form is required. *maye* Hm does not rhyme and is clearly an erroneous substitution. *can* 688 ARBH is required for rhyme and has been erroneously omitted in Hm; but for perfect rhyme here, it would take the form *con*.

687–90   The anachronistic injunction to worship Christ is not in *Mirabilia*, but is suggested in *Legenda Aurea*, and more clearly and specifically in *Stanzaic Life*:

> comaundet also both fer ʒ nere
> That alle men suld do hym honour
>   (628–9)

and Mirk, 'De Nativitate': "Dyd hym sacryfyce; and charget all men þat þay schulden do also, and call þat chyld God, and not hym."

690 + SH   The SH seems to have been missing from the exemplar. H supplies it at this point; A, noting that 691–4 could be uttered by Octavian, inserts it before the direct question of 695 which unambiguously indicates a change of speaker; R removes A's SH and also the direct question which prompted it.

691–8, stanza 89   The b-rhymes of Hm, *maye* 694 — *binne* 698, do not rhyme. It is tempting to speculate that the original reading of 694 was *queen*, for which *maye* was later substituted to remove associations with *quean*, "prostitute". But an alternative possibility is suggested by the forms in 698, where ABH add *non* in rhyme-position, R *borne*. For sense, *borne* is preferable, and its adoption might suggest the substitution of *barne* for *maye* 694; if *non* is preferred, *baron* would give rhyme at 694 (compare 648). *barne* 694 might give stronger force to *this child* 695, where this gives sense only in relation to the vision and has no counterpart in the speech.

699–714   Compare *Mirabilia*: *Hec visio fuit in camera Octaviani imperatoris, ubi nunc est ecclesia Sancta Marie in Capitolio, ubi sunt fratres minores. Idcirco dicta est sancta Maria in ara celi.* Similarly *Stanzaic Life*, following *Legenda Aurea*:

> That ilke chirch now calde is
> Sancta Maria, as hyt wel may,

in ara celi, no thing omys.
(641–3)

Mirk does not mention the later church. *in* ARB indicates the form of the name in the standard accounts, although *is* HmH is equally possible in this context; but since 712 contains only three stressed syllables instead of the usual four, a reading *is in* would be most acceptable. The church was certainly familiar to the sixteenth century, the more so since it was the church at which a special feast of Our Lady was instituted in honour of the Christian victory over the Turks at Lepanto in 1571.

700   *signes true* B may reflect a reluctance to repeat *verey* 699, but removes a syllable required for smooth metre.

715–9   Wilson compares the résumé of the Salome story in *Stanzaic Life* 765–80, which he thinks may have influenced the Chester recapitulation here.

722   The line has four strongly stressed syllables instead of the expected three. Possibly some form such as *today* should appear in rhyme-position instead of *within this playe* although all manuscripts have a form of what must have been the exemplar phrase. *place* AR destroys the rhyme, and is cited by Deimling in evidence of the close relationship between the manuscripts.

PLAY VII

Dramatis Personae Primus Pastor (Hannkeynn), Secundus Pastor (Harvy), Tertius Pastor (Tudd), Garcius (Trowle), Angelus, Maria, Joseph, The First Boye, The Second Boye, The Thyrd Boye, The iiii[th] Boye.

NOTE An infant Christ is also required.

Locations
Shepherds' high place — lowe 46, on height 94, on high here 343; *perhaps with* wall 257
Garcius' high place — lowe 163, this hill 206
Bethlem 448, 454, 468, *with* that holy stable 453.

Properties (See also *Costume*)
First Shepherd — henbane, horehounde, tybbe, radishe, egermonde, fynter, fanter, fetterfowe, penyewrytte 21–8; tarre 33; a pott 33
Second Shepherd — the fether of a crowe 51, plumam cornicis 48 + SD; gravell and greete 75; an ould panne 76; horne 151, 155, 160
Garcius — tarboyste 175; tarboll 175; nettle 177, hemlocke 177; butter 177; pott 189
Items of Food — bredd 113; onyons, garlycke, leekes 114, 156, 157; butter 115; greene cheese 116; ale 117; whot meate 118, 130; a puddinge 119, with a pricke in the ende 132; a jannock 120; a sheepes heade sowsed in ale 121; a grayne to laye on the greene 122; sowre milke 123; a pigges foote from puddinges purye 128; gambonns 131; tonge 135; sowse 213; curye 282; cake 282
Containers — flackett 144 (*see also* 571); bottell 145; bowles 146 (*but see note*)
starre 316, 318, 325, stella 299 + SD, *with* all this light 300 ff.
Stable — haye 483, the cratch 491
Gifts — bell 559; flackett 571 (*see also* 144); spoone 572; cappe 582; bottle 614; hood 623; pipe 627; nuthooke 640.

NOTE 1. *drinke* 44, *potat* 44 + SD suggest that the First Shepherd has drink in a container.
2. *blowe* 47, *flabit* 48 + SD indicate that the First Shepherd has a horn.
3. Garcius has a *dogge* 178.

4. Sheep may be represented — compare *drive thy sheepe to the lowe* 46, *my flocke here* 166.

5. The variants occasionally suggest different items of food from those listed in Hm. In its additional lines after 124, H also adds: *a piggs foote, a panch-cloute, a womb-clout, a lyveras, a chitterling.*

Costume (See also *Properties*)
First Shepherd —cloacke 125, this clowt 282; poacke 127, sotchell 133
Second Shepherd — cum vestis parte veteris 48 + SD H, ould ragges 263
Third Shepherd — black beard 302
Garcius — soe ragged is myne araye 223
Joseph — his head ys whore 497; his beard is like a buske of bryers with a pound of heare about his mouth and more 498–9.

NOTE H also includes for the Third Shepherd *my sacke* 124 + 2 and *this burden I beare on my backe* 124 + 8.

Sources
The visit of the shepherds is in Luke 2/8–20. But much of the material seems to have been invented, with elements from folk-drama, conventions of the comic rustic, and occasional touches of "realism". Some suggestion of the shepherds' feast may be found in Joseph's vision of the feasting workmen in the Apocryphal Book of James 18/2.

Play-heading The visit of the shepherds is found in all the extant English cycles — Wakefield 12 and 13; York 15; *Ludus Coventriae* 16; Coventry Shearmen 204–77, 297–331; Shrewsbury Fragment A.

Before **1 SH** *Primus* Luke gives no indication of the number of shepherds involved. Wakefield 12 has three shepherds and a boy; Wakefield 13 has three shepherds, but the third is servant to the other two. The other cycles have three shepherds, a number perhaps influenced by the traditional number of three Magi (see 8/*Play-heading* note), with whose visit the Shepherds' visit was often compared. Chester has three shepherds, their boy, and, in HmARB four other boys.

1–4 Compare Luke 2/8: *Et pastores erant in regione eadem, vigilantes et custodientes vigilias noctis super gregem suum* (AV "And there were in the same country shepherds abiding in the field, keeping watch over their flock by night"). The account does not suggest the idea of the wandering shepherd, weary with seeking and protecting his flock, as here. The picture in Chester may be influenced by the image of the Good Shepherd and by the later conversion of the shepherds to spiritual pastoralism; see further, 660 note.

PLAY VII 103

Cheshire is noted for dairy farming, sheep farming being found sporadically on the poorer farming areas in the east of the county; but the hills of Wales, to the west, support a major sheep farming industry. Moreover, the possible upland suggestion of *wouldes* 1 — perhaps not understood by B — would not be applicable to the Cheshire plain in which Chester stands. The world of the shepherds may perhaps be considered to be slightly alien to Cestrians. See also 5 note.

5 *Conwaye* Name of a Welsh river, and of the town which stands at its estuary. The town, some 45 miles west of Chester, was a major town on the Holyhead road and the site of one of Edward I's castles.

Clyde Two identifications are possible. The first, proposed by Hemingway, is the Welsh river Clwyd, on which stand the towns of Ruthin and Denbigh. Ruthin, about 15 miles west of Chester, was the site of another Edwardian castle (1281) and was finally made a free borough, in confirmation of Edward I's charter, by Henry VII. Denbigh, 20 miles west of Chester, was the centre of the lordship of Denbigh bestowed on the third Earl of Lincoln (d.1311), who built a castle there that was completed in 1322 by Thomas of Lancaster. River and towns were therefore probably familiar to Cestrians, and this identification therefore seems the more likely. If it is adopted, the shepherds become characteristically Welsh shepherds.

Alternatively, the reference may be to the Scottish river Clyde, on which Glasgow stands. Adopting this location, the line means little more than "everywhere"; compare 685.

6 *tyldes* This is the latest example of the word cited by OED; it is not recorded in EDD. It was apparently unfamiliar to B, which substitutes *hilles*, presumably with the idea of "below (in the lee of) hills". H seems to misunderstand the phrase, inappropriately reading *on the* for *under*.

10 *the suche* Hemingway postulates a reference to the river Sychnant, two miles west of Conway. But *such* means "swampy place" (see Glossary), with related senses such as "brook, ditch; gutter, ravine" (EDD *sich(e)*), which give good sense in context. *sluch* H, apparently a scribal substitution, is also possible. ARB do not seem to understand the phrase; *all suche* B changes the meaning of the phrase and leaves *suche*, "such", without obvious reference; if *thee* AR represents the second person singular pronoun, that reading also destroys meaning.

11 *taytfull* Hm, *tytefull* H, "nimble", does not seem to have been understood by AR and B. *talefull* AR seems to represent merely the substitution of a familiar form for the first element of the compound; its meaning is obscure. *toylefull* B, "hard working", is an acceptable, if not obviously appropriate, substitution; the word is recorded by OED only from 1596.

tuppes "rams". The breeding rams are particularly important in guaranteeing the continuity of the flock, hence the shepherd's particular concern. The rams are usually released to the ewes at "tupping-time", normally December for Spring lambing. The reference here may therefore be seasonally appropriate, and may also suggest that the nimble rams have led the flock far from their usual pastures.

13–6 Some technical knowledge of the specific vulnerability of sheep is suggested by this passage; viz.:

(i) *the schrewde scabb yt sought* The phrase gives no sense in context. Possibly *yt sought* should be regarded as a parenthetical and elliptical construction: "the pernicious scab — [when I have] sought [and found] it"; compare also the phrase "to search a wound". With *scabbe*, compare *scab* OED 2, "A cutaneous disease in animals, esp. sheep, resembling the itch and the mange". Sheep are particularly vulnerable to a range of diseases from infected wounds, of which tetanus is the most familiar to the layman; lambs are vulnerable to infections from the unhealed navel. Treatment is by the application of some sterilising substance.

(ii) *the rotte* Compare *rot*, OED 2: "A virulent disease affecting the liver of sheep which are fed on moist pasture-lands; inflammation of the liver caused by the flukeworm, liver-rot."

(iii) *the cough* Perhaps pseudotuberculosis or caseous lymphaderitis, another common sheep disease; the ailment is, however, rarely fatal; the shepherd could plausibly claim to heal sufferers from it.

19–20 "They would cause a healthy man to fall down in a very short time"; i.e. they would be fatal for a man to ingest. The shepherd points out that the herbs are *saffe and sownde* only because he knows how to use them safely.

21–2 *henbane* Hyoscyamus niger, a common and poisonous plant which is a source of narcotics today, but also, in purified extract, a remedy for muscular spasms and hysteria. *Liber de Diversis Medicinis* recommends its roasted root as remedy against toothache and mouth worms, as well as a constituent of other remedies.

horehounde Marubium vulgare, a popular domestic remedy for coughs.

22 *tybbe radishe* No such herb as *tybbe* Hm *tibbie* B is recorded. *bybbey* A is the only example of the form given in OED, where it is vaguely defined as '*obs*. Some kind of herb'; *bybbe* R is not listed. *rib* occurs as an abbreviated form of ribwort, the narrow leaved plantain, plantago lanceolata, an ingredient of a number of domestic remedies, and on this basis *ribbie* H may be preferred. The radish is a member of the cruciferae or brassicaceae family, which comprises many common hedgerow plants — *Liber de Diversis Medicinis* prescribes "rute of radik" as a remedy for worm-holes in man. Possibly *tybbe-radishe* or one of its variants suggest a common weed, such as watercress.

egermonde Agrimony, cited as an ingredient in a number of domestic remedies; specifically, it is a herb yielding a yellow dye, but the term is applied loosely to a whole range of different common plants.

24 On the additional line in R, see TNs.

27 *fynter* Probably an error for *fymter*, Fumitory; Fumaria officinalis, the common fumitory, is a garden weed noted for its medicinal properties.

fanter Doubtful, but perhaps the fan weed or field penny grass (compare 28). MED questions, and hyphenates *fynter-fanter* as a single word.

fetterfowe Feverfew, chrysanthemum parthenium, recommended by *Liber de Diversis Medicinis* as a remedy against "evyll at þe hert".

28 *penywrytte* Pennywort or navelwort, cotyledon, a member of the crassulaceae family. The form *pennywort* is required for rhyme, but no manuscript contains the form, which suggests that *pennywrytte* was the exemplar reading.

30 *wether* Technically, a castrated ram, in contrast to *tup*, a breeding ram.

PLAY VII

31 *them* ARBH is to be preferred for meaning to *then* Hm.
  thraw H, "instant", seems to be a scribal subsitution which weakens rhyme, but was perhaps felt to be semantically preferable.

33 *tarre* i.e. wood tar, an antiseptic dressing against worms, here carried by the shepherd in a small pot.

34 The line contains only three strongly stressed syllables instead of the expected four.

35–6 "I am very skilful and very knowledgeable in extracting the tallow from them (i.e. the sheep)." Tallow here is unlikely to represent the result of rendering the sheeps' fatty tissues, since the sheep evidently survived the process, but probably means "sheep wax, lanolin" extracted from the wool and used as the basis of various salves. *talgh* seems to have puzzled A, which supplies a different word that gives sense in context but cannot be used for *talgh* 38; the difficulty may underlie the omission of 37–40 in A, followed in R. *talch* H is an acceptable variant of *talgh*; *taylinge* B gives smoother metre but little sense.

37–40 "And even if the devil had sworn it (should be otherwise), nevertheless the tallow shall be in my wallet and the sheep none the worse for running on the pasture." On AR's omission of these lines, cited by Deimling as evidence of their close relationship, see 35–6 note. Hemingway suggests that the lines imply that the devil had the sheep, or that the sheep was bewitched.

45 The additional *how* in H produces a line of the expected four stresses, as opposed to the three-stress line of HmARB, and may be preferred.

49–52 Hemingway compares 'making bricks without straw', but possibly the allusion is more specifically one to extreme poverty — compare the saying "down at heel", i.e. "in decayed circumstances, like a beggar whose boots are worn out at the heels" (Brewer, *Dictionary of Phrase and Fable*). The crow's feather is presumably a quill needle.
  Deimling erroneously cites as variant *sow*] *loe* 50 AH. After *sowe* Hm erroneously repeats the first two words of 51.

53–60, stanzas 8–9 The two stanzas, of abab form, are linked by the b-rhyme and could be regarded as an eight-line form ababcbcb. *needes* 54 must be disyllabic, a fact stressed by B. At 58 AR replace a b-rhyme by an a-rhyme appropriate to stanza 9, giving an aaab form. 60, which is unusually long and metrically rough, would be improved by the omission of *well*.

61–8 *for thy fathers kyn* 61, "for the sake of your father's kin", is a common phrase — see *fader* MED 1(a); but it is given added force when the first shepherd urges appellation by *his damys name* 68. Metronymics were not uncommon in surnames and various reasons have been proposed for them — including cases of widowhood and second marriage; but it has also been suggested that they were used in households where the wife was a dominant partner — compare 85–90 — and also where the child was illegitimate — the suggestion here perhaps being that Tudd did not know his father's kin. See P. H. Reaney, *The Origins of English Surnames*, pp.76–80.

Tybb 65 A pet form of Isabel, itself a Provençal form of Elizabeth, popular as the name of the wives of John, of Edward II and of the second wife of Richard II, and sustaining its popularity for centuries afterwards; see further E. G. Withycombe, *The Oxford Dictionary of English Christian Names*, 3rd. edn. (London, 1977), p.164. An added comic undertone here may lie in its extension in northern England as a word of general reference meaning "cat". Although the surname Tibson is recorded, in many cases it will derive from a pet form of Theobald.

The third shepherd is also somewhat deaf, 60, and the eldest of the three, 380.

69–76, stanza 11   The stress-pattern of the stanza is highly debatable, although 75 clearly contains only three strongly stressed syllables. Some corruption may be suspected.

done 72 Hm is to be preferred for rhyme to *doe* ARBH. The extra syllable provided here by the BH reading, however, produces a more regular sequence of strongly and weakly stressed syllables.

sheepe 73, although attested by all manuscripts, is an imperfect rhyme.

74–6   The shepherd has borrowed one of his wife's pans to render tallow for ointment. Although he is scouring it to remove all trace before she discovers, his salve does contain noxious ingredients and his concern with hygiene has additional point.

76   *an* ARBH is to be preferred to the scribally erroneous *and* Hm for meaning.

77–80   "Hemlock and goosegrass — take heed — must be completely mixed with tar-ointment, pennywort and butter for fat sheep" i.e. if the sheep are to grow to be fat.

hemlocke 77 Name of various plants of the parsley family, umbelliferae — especially poison hemlock, water hemlock and fool's parsley, all of which are poisonous; water-hemlock is especially virulent and a particular threat to cattle.

hayriffe 77 Cleavers or goose-grass, Galium aparine, a common hedgerow plant.

penyegrasse 79 Perhaps pennywort; see 28 note.

butter 79 In the sense of MED 1(b), "ingredient in medicines; cure for diseases, venom, etc."

78 H destroys the rhyme and perhaps reflects some problems of interpretation by the H-scribe.

81–8, stanzas 13–14   As here presented, stanza 14 rhymes abcb. 87 ARBH is to be preferred to Hm in providing a second a-rhyme, *unknowen — bowne*, to produce an abab form. If, however, the readings *unknowe — bowe* — the latter the Hm form — were adopted, stanzas 13–14 could be presented as a single stanza, ababacac.

lafte 84 HmBH is to be preferred to *lefte* AR for rhyme.

89–96, stanzas 15–6   Alternatively, these lines could be presented as a single stanza, ababaaaa.

91   *I* ARBH is to be preferred to Hm's scribally erroneous omission for meaning and metre.

92   *Hankeynn* i.e. Johan-kin, "son of John", a diminutive form which spread from the Low Countries. Bardsley, *Dictionary of English and Welsh Surnames* (London, 1901), notes "Hankin Booby was a common name for a clown", although his example

PLAY VII   107

is 17th century. Reaney, *Surnames*, comments of the surnames that it was "among the artisans of the towns and the labourers of the countryside that names in *-kin* and *-cock* were popular."

93   "Hankin, stretch out your hand and grasp me" — i.e. give me a helping hand up. The shepherds meet on a hill — cf. *the lowe* 46, *on height* 94.

95   The line is metrically rough. *ban* H for *bee by* HmARB may represent an attempt to improve the metre; but for meaning *ban* would have to be understood in the sense of "command", and it is so recorded only in the context of a formal summons to arms — cf. *bannen* MED 1(a) "to summon (troops) by proclamation; assemble (a fighting force)."

97–104, stanzas 17–8   Alternatively, these lines could be presented as a single stanza, ababcaca.
   wene 103 AR would provide a closer rhyme for *seene* 101 than *deeme* HmBH.

99   *wel fayre wedder* A jocular address to the third shepherd, "you gorgeous wether", perhaps comparable with our "my old beauty"; although since a wether is a castrated ram, the appellation may perhaps be rather more insulting.

101–2   Similar feasting is shown in Wakefield 12/188–286, Coventry Shearmen 238–241 + SD. Some precedent may exist in the feasting workmen, seen by Joseph in the Book of James 18/2, whose eating momentarily stops when Christ is born; but folk-influence on such scenes is strong.

105–12, stanzas 19–20   Alternatively, these lines may be presented as a single stanza, ababcbcb.

113–20, stanzas 21–2   Although it would be possible to propose the alternative of a single stanza, ababacac, here by reading *han* for *have* 117 and *deprave noe man* for *noe man deprave* 119, the possibility is not strong. From this point onwards, alternatives to the quatrain stanza abab become difficult or impossible to sustain, hence our preference for such a form in earlier cases.

115   *Blacon* A village approximately 1¼ miles north-west of Chester. The name is used probably more for local colour and for alliteration than for any special fame of Blacon's butter.

116   *greene cheese* Fresh cheese, not thoroughly dried and hence unripened, with a high fat content — hence perhaps the reference to greasing the cheeks.
   A more regular sequence of strongly and weakly stressed syllables results from the adoption of the ARBH reading.

117   *Halton* Village and manor approximately ten miles north-east of Chester. Hemingway is certainly mistaken in locating it in Lancashire. Again, the name is probably used more for local colour and for alliteration than for any superiority of Halton ale.

118   *to my hyer* i.e. it is part of the shepherd's wage that he is supplied with hot (cooked?) meat. At 123 the supper is said to come from his wife. Possibly the suggestion is that his wife in his "boss"; alternatively, stanzas 22 and 23 may be alternatives — compare *After* 124 note.

120   *jannock*, "an oaten cake or loaf", is claimed by OED to be found especially in Lancashire, and Hemingway — perhaps following this authority — claims positively (p.235) that "The dish and the name 'jannock' seem to have originated there [i.e. in Lancashire]". But EDD indicates that the word is current in much of northern England.

121–4, stanza 23   *on sale* H is to be preferred for rhyme to *ordayned* HmARB, a variant cited by Deimling in support of H's superiority. Adopting H requires repunctuation of 123–4 — removal of the full stop to link *sowre milke* to *on sale*, and a dash after *sale* to indicate that 124 is an exclamation.

122   *grayne* HmAR The sense is here obscure. Possibly *groyne* BH is to be preferred as reflecting *groin* sb. EDD 1. "The snout of a pig; the mouth or nozzle of any animal". Perhaps synecdoche is intended, the shepherds producing a pig's head.

123   *sowre milke* i.e. curds, here eaten as food, but also forming the basis of cheese. Compare the green cheese of 116 and Langland's "Twey grene cheese, and a fewe cruddes and crayme" (*Piers Plowman* A 7/269).

After 124 H   Although no other manuscript has this additional stanza, B has a space of 12 (Deimling estimates 8) lines after 124 (see TNs) which indicates its presence in the exemplar. The sequence of speakers after 124 — first shepherd followed by third — supports the ascription of 125–8 to the second shepherd in BH and indicates that the additional stanza belongs to the first shepherd. Its omission is understandable since it duplicates the *pigges foote* of 128 in the *piggs foote* of 4 H; if it was additionally ascribed to the third shepherd, the quantity of food which he would be required to bear would be excessive. Some further confusion might result from the fact that its b-rhyme also forms the a-rhyme of stanza 24. In saying that the lines "contain nothing recommending or condemning them", Deimling seems to have overlooked their importance in the sequence of speakers. But B's evident awareness of their existence and its omission of them notwithstanding suggests that their absence from HmARB results not from error but from a doubt about their status in the exemplar.

128   *and* has no clear conjunctive force here and seems to represent a colloquialism — compare *after* 124 + 2H. The sense seems to be "and a pig's foot left over from a sausage mixture", with *puddinge* in its earlier sense.

129–32, stanza 25   The stanza rhymes aaab instead of the expected abab. *hend* 130 H is to be preferred for rhyme to *here* HmARB; it seems to be a verb, presumably *henden*, MED (a) "to seize". But *here* may also be an exemplar error for *hende* adv., MED (b) "quickly, skillfully, diligently, well".

The parenthetical construction of 130 seems to have troubled A and R, which rephrase the line to remove the construction; R is not syntactically acceptable unless *what* is taken as a variant of *hott*.

129–30   Possibly this, like earlier addresses, is directed as much to the audience as to the company on stage. From guild accounts, Clopper has postulated that the shepherds actually dispensed items of food to the audience. There is an echo of the salesman's pitch in HmB which is lost in ARH — the H form gives a stanza abab at the expense of sense.

133 The line contains only three strongly stressed syllables instead of the expected four. H increases the number to the equally unusual five.

137–40 + SH A erroneously and inexplicably omits this passage.

144 *flackett* is well attested in OED from 1320 to 1753; *flaggen* H, "a metal bottle with a screw top such as was carried by pilgrims", is also possible, but it may be noted that a *flackett* is the second shepherd's gift to the infant Christ at 571. The form is there attested by rhyme — *flackett* — *take yt* 575 (with short vowel for *take*), while significantly H avoids the form and weakens the rhyme by *flasket*.

145–8, stanza 29 No manuscript has the form *libbe* for *live* 147, needed for perfect rhyme. *fele* 145 H destroys all possibility of rhyme.

leste 148 HmAR is required for rhyme; *lost* BH is erroneous. The resulting stanza in H therefore lacks a rhyme-scheme.

145–6 "And now I will drink of the contents of this bottle, for here are the finest bowls." The shepherd evidently poured out drinks from the bottle into the bowls. But on first glance, 145 could be taken to suggest that the shepherd drinks directly from the bottle, a sense strengthened by *but* 146 ARBH.

150 Garcius/Trowle is employed by the three shepherds as herdsman — presumably an apprentice shepherd who is learning the skills of the craft of which his masters have spoken. Below him are other boys; see further 607 note. Possibly some tradition of the lazy and negligent shepherd's boy existed — compare Wakefield 13/177–9:

>wher ar oure shepe, boy, we skorne?
>Sir, this same day at morne
>I thaym left in the corne

and the nursery rhyme, *Little Boy Blue*:

>Little Boy Blue, come, blow up thy horn.
>The sheep's in the meadow, the cow's in the corn.
>But where is the boy that looks after the sheep?
>He's under a haystack, fast asleep.

sheepe H is an erroneous replacement which destroys rhyme.

151 *Trowle* Unrecorded as a Christian name; as a surname, it may be compared with Trowell, based on a Nottinghamshire place-name. But probably it is a coined name (compare Goobett 4/13), perhaps influenced by the special use of *trowel* in the idiom "to lay it on with a trowel", "to express a thing coarsely or bluntly", in keeping with Trowle's usual conduct here.

152 *some* ARBH may be preferred for meaning to the rather familiar *sonne* Hm. The variation results from a miscounting of minims.

153–6, stanza 31 The a-rhymes, *soothe* 153 — *lesse* 155, do not rhyme. Since there are no obvious alternatives which would produce perfect rhyme, it is possible that the original rhyme was imperfect and has become further modified. *lesse* probably represents MED *lesen* (4), 6a(a) "to fail to accomplish (sth.), fail (to do sth.)", but perhaps in the exemplar formally identified with *losen* (2) from the same OE stem. Such identification would explain the change in vowel from *o* to *e*; *lose* would be an acceptable imperfect rhyme with *soothe*. *leese* 155 BH accurately indicates the long vowel, whereas *lesse* HmR suggests confusion with *lessen*, MED 2a(a) "to lessen (sth.) in quantity, size, number, or duration", semantically possible but further reducing the possibility of rhyme; *lette* A, "hinder, stop", is a scribal substitution.

Although the order *us seekes* 154 Hm seems appropriate for the rhyme with *leekes* 156, ARBH all have the order *seekes/seke us*, and this may represent the original reading — compare *heddes* 142 — *reade us* 144. *leckes* 156 A destroys rhyme and meaning, apparently by scribal confusion of *e* and *c*.

155 *lille* Probably an error for *lilt*, although EDD records *lill* as a nCy variant of *lilt* sb, "hole of a wind instrument". *lilt* may underlie *tilt* H; A substitutes; *bill* R is the only example cited by MED of *bilen* v.(1), (b) "to 'mouth' or blow (a horn)".

159 *mote* ARBH, "note of a horn", is acceptable, and perhaps preferable to the somewhat technical and flattering *note* Hm, "a written character or sign, a strain of music, melody".

mittinge A, *mytinge* RB, *mytting* H seem to be variant forms of *miting*, MED (a) "an infant, a young child; youth". OED records the word 1440–1585. Hm does not seem to have understood the word, and substitutes *meetinge*.

161–4, stanza 33   *howe* 161 ARH gives a closer formal rhyme than *hooe* Hm; *howte* B destroys the rhyme.

164   The additional syllable supplied by the BH reading produces a more regular sequence of strongly and weakly stressed syllables.

164 + SD   *cantabit* The subject of the verb in HmARB may be either Primus Pastor or Garcius. *cantant* H indicates that all the shepherds are to sing before Garcius arrives (*venit*); but compare 205.

165–97, stanzas 34–41   These lines seem to manifest considerable corruption; viz.

(i) At 165–72, where the Hm form suggests a link only through the a-rhyme, abacadab, H creates a regular stanza with *have* as a recurring b-rhyme, abababab. Deimling notes the significant agreement of RB (and Hm) against A at 168.

(ii) At 173–9 it is possible that we have an originally similar eight-line stanza, much corrupted, and now lacking a line. A reconstruction would read:

> Wotte I not day or night
> necessaryes that to mee bee [needing],
> [nettle], tarboyste and tarboll —   175
> small hannes that to me [be needing],
> hemlockes and butter abydinge,
> and my good dogge Dottynolle
> that is nothing choyse of his chydinge.

with a c-rhyme omitted between 176 and 177. The arguments for such reconstruction, other than rhyme-scheme, are:

(a) at 174 ARBH have a form of *need*, which strongly supports it as a root form, but the regular metre requires an additional syllable such as is supplied by *beelongen* Hm. If *bee* is accepted as the syllable, then syntax, meaning and rhyme indicate a present participle form.

(b) at 173 the HmARB form has clearly suffered loss. H supplies the loss by adding *nettle* in rhyme-position from 177 (where the rough metre is improved by the transfer); but rhyme supports *tarboll* in final position. The transfer of *nettle* is

PLAY VII   111

better understood if it moves from initial position in one line to initial position in another.
  (c) 176 is the most questionable of the changes. If it is retained in the H-position, as is possible, the omitted line would follow 174. But the line in the position above gives better sense in context; smoother metre results from the omission of *of*.
  (d) adopting this arrangement, stanza-form, syntax and sense coincide in all the following stanzas, as they do not in the present Hm arrangement.
  (iii) 180–7 represents a single stanza, abababab, providing that *were* 185 H is accepted as rhyme-form. *best* 185 H does not give good sense, since Trowle clearly grudges his activity in rising for any man; but a form *lest*, "lost", although not found in any manuscript, could underlie *lost* HmARB and *best* H, and would give rhyme. The a-rhymes are imperfect.
  (iv) 188–93 — the two lines after 191 H constitute a further stanza, abababab, somewhat corrupted. 188 A/R destroys rhyme; A omits 189–91 while the R arrangement produces an abbc pattern. 192 H is to be preferred to Hm, AB, R for rhyme.
  (v) 194–7 represent a final quatrain. No manuscript has the form *lit* 194 required for rhyme instead of *little*, clearly the exemplar form.

173–6 "I do not know, day or night, what necessities may be needful to me — nettle, tar-ointment, balls of tar — little equipment that I need!" This translation takes *hannes* as an error for *harneis* MED 3(a), "personal apparel", 3(b) "furniture", 3(c) "provision or ware for traveling".

178 *Dottynolle* Compare *dotipol* MED (a) "simpleton's head or brain", (b) a term of abuse "fool, simpleton, blockhead". *knoll* survives in dialect as a term for "head".

179 "who isn't choosy about whom he barks at". *choyse* ARH, *chysse* B are to be preferred to the scribally erroneous *cheeffe* Hm, where long *s* has been confused with *f*; Hm would mean that the dog is not the best of watchdogs.

189 The meaning of *pippe* (*at*) is obscure. Since Garcius is about to drink, 192–3, some sense such as "drink (from)" seems appropriate. A suggestion of such a sense may perhaps be found in OED *pipe* v² 1. "*trans* ?To draw through pipes or taps; to drink. *Obs rare*", for which a single example of 1575 is cited.

After **191** H "All men can learn from me how to handle this 'Golgotha' resolutely". Although the exact meaning is obscure, the reference seems to be to Garcius' action in seizing the *pott* 189. *Golgotha* may be a comic allusion to the pot, which perhaps was skull-shaped; although OED records *Golgotha* as "place of interment; 2 graveyard, charnel house", and that only from 1593, the gospels all state the etymology of the name of the Crucifixion-place as "place of a skull", and an extended sense may have been current. The self-conscious distinction of *at me all men learne mon* seems echoed in *noe man..save myself*, 192–3.

194 *this lottes* Compare *lot(e)* n. MED 3, "noise, din; the cry of a bird or animal", or 1, "gesture, expression"; Garcius is unmoved by the horn, and perhaps the summoning gestures, of the shepherds — cf. the derogatory *yee lades* 195. The lack of concord between demonstrative and noun, coupled with the fact that B and H have plural nouns, perhaps gives credence to *thie* B; the reference then, as in 197, would be specifically to the first shepherd, while at 195–6 the reference widens to all three and the pronoun form becomes plural. *lathes* H "hostilities", is possible; *bottill* AR is evidently a replacement for a difficult word, but gives good sense: "I set little store by the whole bottle", i.e. I can drink it all easily.

195 *sett I not by yee* "I have no opinion of you". *kepe not* [*nett* B] *to lye thee* ARB, "I don't care if I deceive you", would be quite characteristic, but would not follow so obviously from the preceding lines; since it occurs in AR and B, however, the reading may represent an alternative in the exemplar. *thee* ARBH is difficult to reconcile with the plural *yee lades*, and the Hm reading is preferable.

203 *liverastes* The word is not recorded in OED or MED. Possibly it is an error for *levenath*, variant of *liveneth* n. MED, "provision of food, subsistence, victuals". *lyveras* H may suggest identification with *liverais*, another form of *liverye* 202.

208 *my fellowes* Since his fellows seem to be distinct from the three shepherds, the reference is presumably to his companions, the other boys, who in HmARB appear to give gifts to the infant Christ. Their presence on stage is perhaps suggested by 447 + SD H; *sitt* A carries the same suggestion here.

218–25, stanza 46   *wage* 221 H is to be preferred for rhyme to *wages* HmARB, a variant noted by Deimling as evidence of H's superiority. Although it would be possible to postulate *pages* at 225, as comprehending the boys, such a postulate is made improbable by the fact that one would expect a final stressed monosyllable in this form.

224 *pinches is* A disyllabic form only is required here. Syntactically and metrically *pinchinge* B is possible, but one must suspect a misdivision of *pinchis* into *pinches is* in the exemplar.

226 The anachronistic reference to *Godes tree* Hm seems to have troubled the scribes, who offer various alternatives — from the theologically unacceptable *three* B, through the unlikely *fee* AR, to the possible *pitty* H.

229 *greene* AR is an error, perhaps influenced by *greene* 122, which destroys the rhyme; Deimling (p.xv) suggests *greene* was "better known" than *wold*.

233 Although no additional word is here required, ARBH supply one. *wager* H is preferable for meaning to *wages* ARB at this point, although Garcius clearly intends to win his due wages from his masters.

240–1 The lines show minor but significant variations among the manuscripts. In 240 ARBH read *spare I will* for *spare* Hm; the mock delicacy of "I will refrain" — compared with Hm's imperative, "Don't bother!" — is offset comically by the coarse continuation. R seems to miss the point by substituting *non* for *naye* — "I will spare no-one."

thy heade 241 ARB suggests that Garcius' vomit will be directed exclusively towards the first shepherd; *your heades* HmH suggests a wider distribution over all three shepherds. The omission of *yt* in ARB produces a more regular sequence of strongly and weakly stressed syllables, leaving *all* as the object of *light*, "the whole lot"; the retention of *yt* in HmH suggests that *all* is there an adverb, "entirely".

249 A more regular sequence of strongly and weakly stressed syllables would result from the omission of the two definite articles. *myddest* is, however, a noun, meaning "middle" (OED *midst* A1) and seems to require an article, as in HmBH; it may be used in the prepositional phrase *in midst*, but would then have the somewhat inappropriate sense of "among, amid, surrounded by (a number of things or persons)" (OED 2). If it is prepositional phrase, *of* may be omitted, as in AR; but as noun, it seems to require *of*.

Dee RBH, the name of the river on which Chester stands, is to be preferred for meaning to *daye* Hm; *dde* A is a scribal error, based on the confusion of *d* and *e* . However, it is unusual to find the definite article used with a river-name (T. Mustanoja, *op. cit.*, pp.242-3) and the omission of *the* (2) seems required by the adoption of *Dee*; its inclusion by Hm seems to be a scribal insertion accompanying the substitution of *daye* for *Dee*. Possibly Hm experienced difficulties with the exemplar form; *drent*, which seems to confirm *Dee*, appears in Hm as *d* with *rent* inserted above the line.

262-5 "Howl on, you, with grimaces and groans! It would be a good idea for you to save your old rags at once. Hateful cur, there's small fear from such idlers as you on the evidence of what you've done in the past."

The passage presents a number of problems:

gole is here taken as ME *goulen*. It might equally, however, be regarded as ME *golle*, "gull, stupid fellow", of which *gloe* AR would be an acceptable variant. Since *goulen* is not recorded as a reflexive verb, *thee* is here taken as direct address; *that so* H evades the problem of *thee* and indicates clearly that for H *gole* represents *golle*.

groyns can take any of the variant forms here listed.

drownes HmARB is here regarded as a variant of *drones* H. OED attests *drone*, in the figurative sense of "non-worker; idler, sluggard," from 1529.

The extra syllable provided in 265 ARBH is preferable to the Hm reading for meaning and metre.

263 + SD H H is probably correct in including an SD relating to the second shepherd's fall; compare 257 + SD and 279 + SD.

266-74, stanza 52   *lendes*, found in no manuscript, is required for rhyme at 266 and 272 instead of *loynes*. OED last records *lend* in 1550, so that the word may have been obsolescent about the time of the extant manuscripts; *loynes* was clearly the exemplar reading.

Some of rhyme-variants at 268 and 270 may reflect unease at the resulting lack of rhyme — in particular, *shenes* 268 B, *shyndes, sheindes* 268 AR, and *byndes* 270 H suggest a determination to rhyme on -*i*-, perhaps influenced by the *y* in *loynes*; *byndes* H does not give sense.

owt shad 269, "isolated", is an application of *shed* OED 1(b), "to part company, to separate", but may also echo an original transitive sense, now found only in dialect, OED 1 "to separate [lambs] from the ewes; to separate [sheep] from the flock". *shutt* B destroys rhyme and sense.

273 "Then I expect to have the same luck as I have had already". H's omission destroys the sense. The repetition of *have* seems to have troubled A, B, H, which offer unnecessary alternatives.

274-9 "The better [result] against the fool, even as I had before of this braggart — yes, even more so, I hope. Keep your mark well, for fear of breaking wind."

bore is obscure. As here translated, it is identified with *boor*, "fool", although a by-form of *bere*, "outcry", would be possible. The probability of an indecency as a primary or a secondary sense must also be admitted, perhaps looking to *bore* OED sb[1], "a hole made by boring". With 278, compare "come up to scratch"; the *score* was presumably the mark on the ground where the contestants met. The shepherd is presumably to avoid being thrown in case he should break wind on impact with the ground. ARB, however, read *store*, referring perhaps to the store of food which Garcius seizes at 282; again, given the context, the possibility of an indecency must be admitted. The variation results from the easy confusion of *c* and *t* and the scribe's sense of what was appropriate to the context.

280–7, stanza 54   *wake* 286 H is to be preferred for rhyme to *walke* HmARB. With HmARB, compare 1; the line is semantically appropriate. But H suggests that Trowle watches over the wold, presumably guarding the sheep as before.

282   *curye* Perhaps a term of contempt — "the portions of slain animals given to the hounds", a sense current from 1500. The meaning "cooked dish of meat, fish, fruit or vegetables used as a relish" is also recorded by OED from 1598. *cup* H seems unlikely, the more so in that manuscript in view of its reading at 146.

287   "Let all the world marvel at the watchman." *wache* is here regarded as a form of *watch*. The line perhaps reinforces 286 H; Trowle watches over the world, and the world looks back at him in wonderment.

287 + SD   *recedat* Garcius is nowhere said to re-enter; but 318–23 seems to suggest that he withdraws only as far as his own mound, from where he sees and comments on the star. The absence of an indication of re-entry may have been a factor in H's omission of the SD.

290   "Entirely against our wishes he has what is his"; i.e. Garcius has won his due wages. Some noun must be understood with *his*; here it has been expanded to emphasise the possessive force, but possibly *will* should be understood — "He has his desire, totally against our desire."

291   *harmes* Hm, "injuries", has concrete force; ARBH all have a singular form, ARH suggesting "hurt, suffering", while *horne* B is a scribal error.

294–5   The second shepherd says that because he is bruised and weary, he will not leave but will stay on the wold to watch the sheep, or to await what the weather will do; the latter is perhaps supported by the singular *wedder* 295, by the R form, *weather*, and by the bad weather mentioned in 3.

H repeats the last phrase of 294 at the start of 295.

297   *wakinge* HmH, "watching", is to be preferred to *walkinge* ARB for rhyme and meaning.

298   The line has a proverbial ring, suggesting that "Every dog has his day" — "We are often on top, although on this occasion we are beaten." *over though* H is to be preferred to the erroneous *in thought* HmARB for meaning. H has, however, also erroneously substituted the rhyme-phrase of 296 for *now under* which is needed after *over though*. *in* seems to have here an antithetical sense to *under*, although such sense is not recorded in MED; and possibly *bee in*, "be on top" was misunderstood later as a prepositional construction and *t* was added to *though* to provide a noun for the preposition.

301 *blasses* Hm, "to shine like flame", gives good sense, as does *shynes* H, a replacement. But *blackes* A, "to make black", *blakes* R, "to become pale", and *blak is* B, "is black, is pale", all reflect scribal confusion.

309–10 AR omit 310; possibly A's omission is the result of an eye-slip, confusing *nowe* in 309 and 310. R followed A and, lacking 310, substituted *light* for *nowe* 309 as "more appropriate" for rhyme and meaning than the A-form.

316 Compare Luke 2/9: *Claritas Dei circumfulsit illos* (AV "The glory of the Lord shone round about them"). No reference is made to the appearance of a star to the shepherds, and indeed commentators frequently commented on the distinction between shepherds and Magi; compare *Glossa Ordinaria*, 'Evang. Matth' 2/2 (PL 114/73). But with the exception of *Ludus Coventriae*, where the light-source is not specified, the English cycles all indicate a star appearing to the shepherds — Wakefield 12/321–5, 13/654–5, York 15/53, Coventry Shearmen 271; York 15/13–24 even has a shepherd invoke Balaam's prophecy in the manner of the Magi. Doubtless it was necessary to indicate a light source, and the parallel of the Magi, which influenced other aspects of the shepherd's play, would suggest the star. Here the shepherds seem to derive information from it without the help of the angel — 338–9, 450–1 — so that it may perhaps have carried an image in the manner of the star of play 6. Like the Magi's star, it serves to guide the shepherds, 450–1.

On the shepherds' response, compare Luke 2/9: *Timuerunt timore magno* (AV "They were sore afraid"). Although fear is suggested here, it rapidly gives way to wonder and to a robust spirit of inquiry.

318–23, stanza 61   *stonde* 318 RH is to be preferred for perfect rhyme to *stande* HmAB. *land* 321 BH and *stand* 322 H similarly affect a rhyme in -*a*-.

ARBH are probably correct in omitting *mee* 320, 323, since in preceding and succeeding stanzas the last syllable of the third and sixth lines is strongly stressed.

324–7, stanza 62   Two lines, of ba-rhyme, are required after 324 to produce the six-line stanza expected in this section of the play, although no manuscript has these lines and they were clearly absent from the exemplar.

330   H erroneously omits this line, perhaps confused in attempts to accommodate the stanza as a three-line unit in the manner of 334–9; see TNs.

333 + SH   *Secundus* ARBH is to be preferred to the erroneously repeated *Primus* Hm in giving point to the SH, which in IIm is unnecessary, and establishing the usual "1–2–3–Garcius" sequence of speakers.

336–9   Here and elsewhere the shepherds seem to recognise the meaning of the star without angelic assistance.

338   A more regular sequence of strongly and weakly stressed syllables would result from the omission of both instances of *for*. *for* (2) is omitted in ARBH, suggesting that its occurrence in Hm is influenced by *for* (1); but *for* (1) is in all manuscripts and was clearly the exemplar reading.

348 *fayre* H is a substitution which destroys rhyme. Although the reason for the substitution is not clear, it may be noted that H rearranges the line-divisions of stanzas 65 and 66, and that *fayre* might constitute a suitable form for the a-rhyme of stanza 65.

352 The unanimity of ARBH in reading *I* as the second word perhaps suggests an exemplar form such as H in which the reading has become obscured. Hm, AR, B do not give good sense, although none is impossible.

357 + SD Luke 2/14: AV "Glory to God in the highest, and on earth peace, good will toward men." The form here has *excelsis* for Vulgate *altissimis*; the phrase *Gloria in excelsis* is in Luke 19/38.

In Luke, these words follow the angel's explanation to the shepherds and are sung by *multitudo militiae caelestis* (AV "a multitude of the heavenly host"). Here a single angel, identified as Gabriel 401, sings, and no prior explanation is given to the shepherds, who seem to work out the meaning for themselves. But see 448–51 note. Wakefield 12, 13 exclude the *Gloria*; York 15 does not specify the nature of the angel's song or message; *Ludus Coventriae* 16/1–13 combines the message and the *Gloria*; but the Coventry Shearmen shows the *Gloria* (263 + SD), and later the message (297–306).

360 *heighte* ARBH is to be preferred for rhyme to *highe* Hm.

360 + SH Erroneously omitted by H.

361–435 In Wakefield 13/656–664 and York 15/58–64 + SD the shepherds try to imitate the angel's song. In *Ludus Coventriae* 16/78–89, the shepherds debate the words. In Coventry Shearmen 272–7 the first shepherd accurately reports the words.

367–9 "From this strange account such entertainment is hilarious; I would have a part of it." Garcius, hearing the debate of his masters, is amused and decides to return to share the fun. *more I* 368 ARBH is possible, but requires a verb to be understood: "I (would have) more of such entertainment from this strange account." A omits *I* 369, perhaps to avoid repeating the final word of 368.

372 *sange* A may suggest that A sees in 372 an imperfect continuation of the b-rhyme from stanza 69.

384–7 + SH H's omission of these lines and SH probably results from an eye-slip, since 384 and 388 both begin with *nay*.

392–9, stanza 73 *dafte* 397 AR is to be preferred for rhyme to *defte* HmBH. The line, however, involves a play on the two words — *deft*, "apt, skilful, dexterous, clever", with a sense of "neat, trim, handsome" especially appropriate here but recorded only from 1579; and *daft*, "silly, wanting in intelligence, stupid".

lafte 398 H is to be preferred to *lefte* HmAR for rhyme; *loste* B is a scribal error involving the confusion of *f* and long *s*.

398–9 "No, he came by night — when all's said and done — to mark our rams with tar." Garcius mockingly adds to the debate by suggesting that the "intruder" might have been a sheep-stealer, seeking to change the markings of the sheep. *teale*, or *tayle* H, represents *tail* OED 7, "to make a mark on, to mark"; *tell* ARB, "to count", suggests formal confusion.

PLAY VII 117

401 *Gabryell* There is no reason why the shepherds should know the angel's name; compare Joseph's similar identification, 528.

gurd is presumably a form of *greden*, MED 4 "to proclaim, announce". Perhaps because of confusion with *gurd*, "rail, jeer", BH prefer *good*, which destroys syntax.

404–7, stanza 75   A feminine b-rhyme is usual. Possibly *beganne* 405 ARB represents an original form, rhyming with a *han* at 407, replaced by the *have* found in all manuscripts and therefore probably in the exemplar. *sayde* Hm and *sang* H would then represent later replacements. For rhyme, *have* 406 should be pronounced *ha*. H attempts to improve rhyme by reading *have I*.

408   *ye* AB, *you* RH is to be preferred for reference to *hee* Hm. The latter suggests confusion with *hee* (2).

410   *sang* H may be preferred to *singes* HmAR and *sing* B for tense.

sar suggests a form of Sara, seen in the surname Sarr; although Sara is found in England from the twelfth century, it only becomes common as a name after the Reformation.

cis suggests the abbreviated form of Cecilia, Cecily or Cicily, a popular medieval name.

The suggestion of ladies' names gives point to 411. Compare also *Castle of Perseverance* 1576–7:

> Goo ageyn, þe deuelys mat,
> And pleye þe a whyle wyth Sare and Sysse.

M. Eccles, in his note on these lines (*The Macro Plays*), also cites Skelton's *Elinor Rumming* i.99:

> Thyther cometh Kate, Cysly, and Sare

411   Probably a line of a popular and seemingly bawdy song. *Pax*, the kiss of peace from the Mass, is used here with unmistakable sexual connotation. *Mawd* is a French form of Matilda, popular in the Middle Ages and later.

412   *tarre* is required for rhyme, and for the required play on *terra* and *tar*. *terre* AR misses rhyme and pun. Compare 399.

415   H substitutes the 422 rhyme-form, destroying rhyme.

418   *loden* MED does not record an *-o-* form; the form here may suggest the rounded vowel more conventionally indicated by B, or may be an error for the more regular *-e-* form of H. Some suggestion of the basic sense, "the Latin language", may also be intended in the choice of word.

422   *quoked* Hm A double past form, unrecorded by OED; *quocke* ARBH is to be preferred.

425   "For some word is worthy of a further comment", or "For some word is worth a great deal"; for the latter, compare *fother* MED 1, 3(b), the form required for rhyme. The variants here may suggest an obscure or corrupt exemplar form, probably containing *-d-*. *forder* Hm, *foder* RB suggest such a form; *founder* H seems to represent the substitution of a familiar form, to the detriment of meaning. *wordes* RB may reflect the fact that two words are involved, 426. A erroneously substitutes 429 for the line.

427   "That is a thing that exceeds all others"; see *cropp* MED 4(b).

437   *unbrace* BH is to be preferred to the scribally erroneous *umbrace* Hm and semantically inappropriate *imbrace* A, *ymbrace* R.

441   Hm is alone in treating this line as the main clause of a sentence, 440–1. ARBH subordinate it to the main clause of 442 by reading *for* at the start of the line, making stanza 84 a single sentence.
  hase ARB destroys the meaning, having no clear subject or object; it seems to be a scribal error based upon an obscure exemplar form.

447 + SD   *cantabunt* The plural form confirms *singe we* 444, and 446; *cantabit* B apparently takes up *will I assaye* 445.
  H's *hilare carmen* indicates the nature of the song. Rastall, p.161, proposes an identification for it. H also indicates the presence of others apart from the shepherds — perhaps the boys of the later presentation scene. If so, the absence of the scene in H would suggest a deliberate omission on the part of the scribe.

448–51   Compare 467–70, 471–2. The decision to go to Bethlehem is apparently made twice — first as an independently reached conclusion, and then under the angel's guidance. This awkward duplication suggests that the two decisions reflect alternative versions, perhaps having their different origins in the preceding debate about the meaning of the song. Thus, after 375, having reached *excelsis*, there is a break in stanza-form, a line which seems to inaugurate a debate, and a further discussion which again reaches *excelsis* at 411. Possibly, after 357 a choice exists between continuing 376–463, or 358–75 and 464–95.
  It may be noted that the usual speaking order of *Primus — Secundus — Tertius — Garcius* changes at 443 + SH, where *Garcius* precedes *Tertius Pastor*.

452–5, stanza 87   *lynes* 454 H, a plural form of *lende*, is required for rhyme. It is, however, equivalent in meaning to *limb*, which has replaced it in HmARB.

460–3, stanza 89   *stonde* 461 A is to be preferred for perfect rhyme to *stand* HmRBH.
  fonde 463 Hm is to be preferred to *founde* ARBH for perfect rhyme, although it represents the same word, "discovered". H's rewording of 463 is unnecessary and gives a rough metre.

465   Compare Luke 2/10–12, where the angel's words precede the angelic chorus. Here, the context suggests that the angel is indicating the stable, the sight of which the shepherds may fear; but in Luke it is the glory, and the sight of the angel, which the shepherds fear. Something of this sense would be recaptured by the arrangement proposed at 448–51 above, whereas the sense in context here is somewhat puzzling.

471   *cover* Hm, *kever* AH are both possible. *ken* RB suggests that the scribes did not recognise an abbreviated form and confused the final -*u* of *keu* with *n*.

476–7   The shepherds at York 15/82–85 + SD, Coventry Shearmen 274–77 + SD also proceed to Bethlehem singing.

478   H's omission of *it* may be preferred to its retention in HmARB in producing a more regular sequence of strongly and weakly stressed syllables.

479   *kinges* ARBH is to be preferred to *kinge* Hm for syntax.

480   *sym* Perhaps onomatopoeic; compare *sum*, "to hum softly".

502–3   "Listless he is now, for he looks all the time down at his heels." 503 H represents an unnecessary "clarification" which weakens rhyme and metre.

504–7, stanza 97   *be rough* 504 HmH gives good sense and, if *rough* is pronounced *rowe*, perfect rhyme. ARB substitute *hydes*, perhaps influenced by the 505 rhyme-word, destroying rhyme and meaning. *heedes* 505 AR, *heedis* H are to be preferred to *hydes* HmB for rhyme and sense.

Some obscurity has evidently arisen in the final phrases of 506–7, *wee nowe* 506 and *in weedes* 507, in the exemplar, resulting in their erroneous omission in ARB. The omissions may reflect confusion resulting from the '*hydes*' forms in 504 and 505 ARB.

507–39   Compare Luke 2/19: *Maria autem conservabat omnia verba haec, conferens in corde suo* (AV "But Mary kept all these things, and pondered them in her heart"). This is the only indication of the response of any member of the holy family to the shepherds. But here the occasion is used to underline Mary's virginity by developing the necessity for her marriage through the witness of Joseph. The reasons given — to safeguard Mary's virginity (514), to observe the laws governing marriage and procreation (516–25) and hence to prevent scandal (525–6), and to deceive the devil (527) — are commonplace; compare Bede, *In Lucae Evangelium Expositio* 1, cap 1 (PL 92/316), and Vincent of Beauvais, *Speculum Historiale* Bk.VI, Cp. 73.

521   B's omission is an unexplained scribal error.

528   Compare 6/161–8

530   All versions of the line have an irregular sequence of strongly and weakly stressed syllables. A regular sequence is obtained by adopting the H-reading and also by omitting *have* (1), found in all manuscripts, and reading *flee* for *fled*. One suspects that present infinitives have at some time been transformed to past forms, thus allowing for the possibility of the Hm word-order.

536–7   Compare Luke 2/17: *Videntes autem cognoverunt de verbo quod dictum erat illis de puero hoc* (AV "And when they had seen it, they made known abroad the saying which was told them concerning this child"). The function of the shepherds as witnesses is frequently mentioned — compare *Legenda Aurea*, 'De Nativitate'. But nowhere in Bible or standard commentaries is this task expressly enjoined upon them. Joseph's words prepare for 641–96, where, contrary to his advice here, the shepherds part company. Compare Wakefield, 12/491, 13/744 where Mary asks the shepherds to report what they have seen.

539   *an ... to myne* RB gives acceptable sense but a slightly rougher metre, as opposed to *mynne* HmH; *and* A is clearly an error for *an* R, itself clearly a variant of *one* B. It is possible that the *-on* ending of *common* has influenced the RB readings or even derives itself from a phrase *come on*.

544–7   The bestowal of gifts by the shepherds is unbiblical and absent also from standard authorities, but seems to have developed as an effective piece of stage business, probably influenced by the bestowal of gifts by the Magi. The gifts vary — in Wakefield 12 a spruce coffer 466, a ball 471, a bottle 480; in Wakefield 13 a bob of cherries 718, a bird 722, a ball 734; in York 15 a brooch with a bell 103, two cob-nuts

112, a horn spoon 124; in Coventry Shearmen a pipe 310, a hat 317, mittens 323; no gifts are offered in *Ludus Coventriae*. Here the shepherds offer a bell 559, a flask and spoon 571-2, a cap 582, a pair of old hose belonging to Garcius' wife 591; their boys offer a bottle without a stopper 614, a hood 623, a pipe 630, a nuthook 640. In view of the shepherds' condition and the nature of their gifts, 546 must be read as a semi-humorous recognition of the kind of gifts that would be appropriate — compare 609-12, as well as the debate on precedence at 548-51 and the unusually formal *homage* 548.

550 *father* The noun "father" is possible, but perhaps *forther*, "more advanced", is intended. H contrasts the three older shepherds with Garcius, hence the plural form.

556-62, stanza 105   Unusually, a seven-line stanza, aabcccb; the loss of an a-rhyme must be suspected. H further modifies the stanza, omitting 560, so that the gift of the bell is presented as if it is a means of obtaining favour. The intention seems to be to remove all premonition of redeeming grace in the speech, since H also substitutes *farewell* for *serve thee* 562.

563-6, stanza 106   *als* 564 H is to be preferred for rhyme to *alsoe* HmARB. However, *fell* 565 HmARB is to be preferred for rhyme to *fall* H.

567-75, stanza 107   *barne* 569 ARBH is to be preferred for rhyme to *baronne* Hm. No manuscript has the form *starne* at 567 required for rhyme, suggesting that *stare* was the exemplar form.

    570, omitted in ARB, is required for rhyme and meaning. Its omission may reflect an unease at the nine-line stanza, ababcdddc.

573   *porage* R is not recorded by OED before 1532, but it represents a formal development of *pottage* and shares the latter's meaning to 1805.

580-83, stanza 109   *happe* 580 AR is to be preferred to *hope* HmB for rhyme; *happes* H weakens the rhyme. *hope* is perhaps possible, but would require *cope* for *cappe* 582, a less probable reading.

584   H is syntactically awkward and metrically unacceptable; it is not clear why H should have this version.

596 + SH-640   No other account or play mentions the shepherds' boys. Here they may well have been previously comprehended in 208 and in 447 + SD H (see note). The SD is a reason for believing that H may have had an exemplar containing the scene and intended to include it, but later decided to omit it.

604   *him* RB is to be preferred to *her* Hm for meaning. The Hm form is probably influenced by the preceding *her*. *bene* A reflects a misunderstanding, erroneously suggesting that Jesus is the subject.

604 + SH   *Thirde* R expresses the logical expectation that the next speaker after the second boy will be the third boy. But the speaking sequence runs 1-2; 1-2-3; 1-2-3-4.

607   The third boy is not the last to present, since a fourth boy makes the last presentation, 633-40. There seems no way in which a fourth boy could be included in this stanza, and one must conclude that he represents a later addition, perhaps to balance the fact that three shepherds and Garcius make the first presentation; but the

PLAY VII

fourth boy would then have to be Garcius' own servant, ignoring the fact that Garcius is not himself a shepherd but the chief herdsman of the three shepherds.

617-20, stanza 116   No manuscript has the form *barne* 620, required for rhyme; *child* was clearly the exemplar reading.

625-32, stanza 117   ARB seem to have found difficulty in reading the concluding phrases of 625-30. B also omits the rhyme-word of 631, while ARB change the ending of 632.

632   *quiver* ARB is recorded by OED from 1490; *quaver* Hm, "to vibrate, tremble", is gradually replaced in this sense by *quiver*.

633-40, stanza 118   No manuscript has the form *hommes* 638, "ham; back of knee or thigh", required for rhyme. AR and B seem to recognise the resulting loss of rhyme, seen in *handes* HmH; B supplies a rounded vowel, while *thombes* AR gives rhyme and an acceptable meaning.

647   *thou* ARBH is to be preferred as continuing the address to Mary, followed by *thy* 649 ARBH, *thee* 650. *hee* Hm probably reflects influence from *his* 649 rather than any anti-Marian bias. *memoriall*, "an example", would give best sense in reference to Mary, but would perhaps also stress her exemplary function more appropriate to Protestant thinking than her elect position in Catholic teaching.

The expansion of *for* Hm in ARBH is unnecessary and destroys metre, but must have its origin in an exemplar reading.

650   The line has no place in the rhyme-scheme of the stanza, though it picks up the a-rhyme of the following stanza.

651-6, stanza 121   *homwardlye* 652 Hm is to be preferred to *whomwardes* ARBH for rhyme. The Hm form is not, however, recorded by MED or OED.

crye 654 ARBH is to be preferred to *knowe* Hm for rhyme; the latter seems to have been the mechanical reproduction of a common phrase.

657-60, stanza 122   The word-order of 658 ARBH is to be preferred to that of Hm in giving a more regular sequence of strongly and weakly stressed syllables. Adopting the ARBH order gives a rhyme-phrase *goe nowe*; feminine rhyme would suggest a corresponding phrase *moe nowe* 660, although H reads *more nowe*. Such a reading would make the repeated *nowe* redundant and might suggest that it was included only when the original rhyme was obscured by the adoption of *more*; its existence makes the Hm word-order possible. *non* 660 ARB is a substitution which weakens metre but would be readily derived from *moe*.

660   The literal "pastorate" as the image of the spiritual pastorate which underlies this vocational change is seen also in 13/15-28. Compare Bede, *Homelia* (PL 94/37) and also *In Lucae Evangelia* 1/2 (PL 92/331-2).

665   *ever* ARBH adjusts the stress-pattern of the line so that a main stress falls on the first syllable of *sickerlie/securely* instead of the final syllable, as in Hm. But the Hm pattern here matches that of 663, and it seems more probable that *ever* has replaced *aye* than vice-versa.

666   Either ARH or B is to be preferred to Hm in supplying an extra syllable which produces a more regular sequence of strongly and weakly stressed syllables.

669–76, stanza 124   Scribes seem to have tried to remove some of the repetition in the stanza — witness *paie* 670 AH, avoiding the repeated *praye* 670, 674; *wake* 671 H, avoiding the repeated *walke* 671, 672; *ever* 672 A, avoiding the repeated *aye* 672, 676.

677–80, stanza 125   *ones* 677 AR, *onys* B are to be preferred to the erroneously substituted *alwayse* Hm, *honestie* H — the latter incorporating *ones* in its form and suggesting an attempt to remodel the line. *and* 677 is required for metre and is erroneously omitted by AR. B perfectly rhymes *onys* — *monys*, AR *ones* — *mones*. The imperfect rhyme *refuse* — *kys* may have been a factor in H's omission of 680, but the presentation of the lines in H (see TNs) may have contributed to the error.

681–8, stanza 126   The rhyme-forms in this stanza, evidently correct in Hm, seem to have presented difficulties to the other scribes.

mouthes 683 H is a plural form following the plural possessive *your*, but the singular form is required for rhyme.

At 685–6 H has erroneously transposed the first word of 686 to final position in 685, destroying rhyme.

686 is a metrically unwieldy line. Possibly the metre would be improved by reading *not where is*, "do not know where [such a shepherd] is", and the HmH form may represent an expansion of such a phrase based on a misunderstanding of *not*. AB support the verb reading, but, like R, they lack the final *is* which is required for rhyme. An alteration on the exemplar might well have obscured the rhyme-word.

cought 687 H also destroys rhyme, see 687 note.

At 688 ARB destroy rhyme by substituting *amen* for *all his blys* HmH. Possibly the word existed in the exemplar as an extra-metrical conclusion to the prayer — compare 20/192 — but has been treated as an alternative to the final phrase by ARB. Since ARB also lack the corresponding b-rhyme at 686, the mistake was the more likely to pass unnoted.

685   *Lowth*   Louth, a market town 26 miles east-north-east of Lincoln by a road on the River Lud where it flows out of the Wolds.

687   *frend and cowth*   The original phrase was probably *fremed and kouth*, "unknown and familiar" (see MED *fremed* adj. (a)); it is simply a phrase meaning "everybody" and, as here punctuated, represents an address to the audience. The phrase is perhaps best represented in AR, where *framed* seems an acceptable variant of the form *framde*, recorded by MED as a variant of *fremed*; although H correctly reads *fremd*, it does not appear to have understood the second word and erroneously presents it as if it were a participle, *cought*; *tremed* B seems to be a mechanical and slightly erroneous transcription of the exemplar form, suggesting that the scribe did not recognise it. The Hm reading, however, does give sense, suggesting phrases such as *sibbe and couth*, "kinsmen and acquaintances" (MED *couth* adj., 2); it would mean "friends and acquaintances".

689–92, stanza 127   The rhyme-pattern abab is destroyed by a number of scribal alterations in different manuscripts. At 692 A omits *yee*, a syntactically redundant word, but required for rhyme. R also omits *yee*, but additionally reads *wee* for *you* 691, presumably feeling that the action refers to the shepherds and perhaps also wishing to avoid repeating the 690 rhyme-word and to substitute a b-rhyme for an a-rhyme. B's changed word-order in 692 also destroys rhyme.

The most radical changes are made by H. These seem designed to achieve two effects. First, H seems unhappy with the pronoun-changes, whereby a collective address to the audience, *you* 689 and 691, is combined with an appeal to God, *thy* 690. It therefore changes *you* 689 to *us*, turning the reference to the shepherds, and rephrases 691 so that 690–91 become a single sentence: "May great God bring us to that bliss. If it be your will, set to right all things that may be amiss." Second, it attempts to make line division conform with syntactical structure by transferring *great God* from the start of 690 to the end of 689. The changes destroy rhyme at 689 and bring the rhyme of 691 into conformity with the b-rhymes of stanza 126.

The omission of *that* 690 A and addition of *now* 692 H seem designed to smooth the metre, but the metre in this section is too rough for such attempts to be justifiable. *God graunt* 690 B seems to be a substitution designed to achieve the correlation of line- and sentence-units, as in the H alteration; but it has the effect of destroying the syntax unless *bringe* is taken as infinitive: "To bring you to that bliss, God grant."

PLAY VIII

Dramatis Personae Primus Rex, Secundus Rex, Tertius Rex, Angelus, The Messinger/Explorator, Herodes, Doctor.

NOTE   1. A *fellowe* 41 holds the horse of Tertius Rex — H reads *fellowes*.
            2. *Minstrells* are required at 144+SD.
            3. A *boye* is required at 381+SD.

Locations
this mounte 14, the Mounte Victoryall 30, that hill 34 *Herod's* pallace 140.

NOTE   An open area seems implied by *ryde abowt* 112+SD.

Properties
this coursere 41, equis 48+SD; dromodaryes 102, 105, beasts 103, 108, 112+SD; stella 64+SD, esteile 67, the starre 79, 129, 213, our light 114, une semblant de une virgin portant, come le semble de une enfant em brace apportement 69–72, in the starre a chyld 79; bookes of prophecye 234, bookes 351, *with leaves* 241; a pigge 381+SD, *with* wyne 416, *and* cuppes 418 (sg. H).

NOTE   1. The Messinger *rydes* 123.
            2. For Herod's equipment, see *Costume*.
            3. Herod sits *on hye* 146.
            4. H requires *nefrens* 381+SD — see note.

Costume
Herod crowned in gould 146; sword 200+SD, 288+SD B, 289; bill 282+SD, my bright brond so keene 336; staffe 156+SD, 196+SD, 389+SD.

NOTE   another gowne (implying the existence of an earlier one) is required by 209+SD ARB, *toga alia* 209+SD H, and by 365+SD B.

Sources   Matthew 2/1–9.

Play-heading Trium Regum Orientalium — compare Matthew 2/1, *Magi ab oriente* (AV "wise men from the east"). The traditional number of three appears first in Origen, *Contra Celsum* I, and was probably based on the number of gifts mentioned, but wider significances accrued to the number — compare *Glossa Ordinaria*, 'Evang. Matt.' 2/1 (PL 114/73). The idea that they were kings is latent in Tertullian, *Adversus Judaeos* 9/12 (PL 2/659), but originates in prophecies such as that at 338 + Latin. Compare the account of the well-established tradition in *Legenda Aurea*, 'De Epiphania Domini'. An extensive series of legends accumulated round these figures, influentially retailed in John of Hildesheim's *Historia SS Trium Regum*, of which a number of English versions survive; their bodies were preserved and translated from Milan to Cologne in 1164, where their tomb became a place of pilgrimage, and they are therefore referred to also as the three kings of Cologne (see Chester play-lists). Their visit to the stable is commemorated in the Feast of the Epiphany on 6th January. The visit of the Magi to Herod is found in all the extant English cycles — Wakefield 14/1-492, York 17/1-216, *Ludus Coventriae* 18/1-229, Coventry Shearmen 475-688.

1-16 See also Play 5. Compare Comestor, *Historia Scholastica*, 'In Evangelia' 7 (PL 198/1541), so also *Legenda Aurea*, 'De Epiphania Domini', and *Three Kings of Cologne*: "Wherfore in þat tyme þat Balaam so gloriouslich prophecied of þe incarnacioun of oure lord Ihesu and of þe sterre ... than all þe grete lordys and all þe oþer peple of ynde and in þe eest desired gretlich to see þat sterre, and byhotten 3iftes to þe kepers of þis hille of Vaws." Also see *Stanzaic Life* 1729-52. The kings represent the Gentiles, as opposed to the *people of Judee* 2 and the all-inclusive *man* 3; compare Augustine, Sermo 199 (PL 38/1026). See also the link with Balaam in Wakefield 14/205-28, York 17/1-12, 157-60, *Ludus Coventriae* 18/159-66.

The Chester Magi meet by prior arrangement to watch for the star, as also in *Stanzaic Life* 1753-56; Foster (*Life*) and Wilson ('The *Stanzaic Life* of Christ and the Chester Plays') discern a general similarity of Chester 1-112 and *Life* 1729-84. Elsewhere, in *Three Kings* and in the other English cycles, the kings see the star independently and meet in the course of their journey.

11 Either HmB or H is possible. AR, having an extra syllable, offer a less regular sequence of strongly and weakly stressed syllables, but perhaps suggest that both readings existed as alternatives in the exemplar.

15 *once in the yeare* Chrysostom, reported in *Three Kings*, described a permanent watch of twelve men, on whose report the people selected the three magi to bear gifts and worship Christ, a tradition followed by *Cursor Mundi*. *Stanzaic Life* 1741 follows *Legenda Aurea*: "iche moneth ones thay went". Mirk, 'De Epiphania', more vaguely mentions "oft-tyme, on nyghtys". Only here among standard accounts is an annual vigil mentioned.

17 *Balahams bloode* Compare *Legenda Aurea, successores Balaam*; Mirk: "of þe lynage of Balaam þat prophysyet, how þat a sterre shuld spryng of Jacob." Compare also the wording of *Stanzaic Life*:

> And casuelie thes kynges thre
> that weren of Balaams blode.
> (1749-50)

AR surprisingly fail to understand the reference.

22 *hym* ARBH is to be preferred for meaning and metre to the Hm reading.

30 *the Mounte Victoryall* Compare *Legenda Aurea, super montem victorialem; Stanzaic Life, Mount Victorial* (1743). Compare also *Three Kings* (Cambridge MS): "Þan was there a hille þat was cleped Vaws, þe wich hille also was cleped þe hill of Victory: and on þis hill þe warde and þe kepyng of hem of ynde was ordeyned and keped by diuers aspyes by nyȝt and by daye, ffor þe childryn of israel and afterwarde for þe Romayns; so þat, ȝif any pepil in any time purposed with stronge hande to entre in to þe countreye of þe kyngdom of ynde, anoon aspyes of othir hillys aboute thorwe tokeyns schewed and warned þe kepers þat wer in þe hill of Vaws, as by nyȝt þey made a grete fyre and by daye þey made a grete smoke. ffor þat hill Vaws passeth of heithe all othir hills in þat countreye of ynde and in all þe eest."

45 + SH H has misplaced by four lines 48 + SH, an uncancelled error resulting from a miscounting of quatrains.

56 *kinges* ARH is perhaps more expected than *knightes* HmB, although the latter may appropriately evoke associations of vassalage and of the *miles Christi*.

57–64, stanza 8 The a-rhymes here appear to be a mixture of long and short vowels. Hm forms suggest that the rhymes of 61–3 all have short vowels, and the readings give sense; but *weale* 61 AH, *deale* 63 ARBH are possible if the mixture of vowel-length is accepted — compare *Israell* 57, where metre supports a trisyllabic pronounciation with short vowel in final syllable, while 58 and 59 suggest long vowels. *counsaile* 59 H should be compared with the cancelled *consealle* B (see TNs), although the forms may suggest some influence from *counselour* 61 as well as influence from a particular exemplar-form; for perfect rhyme, read *counselere* 61.

62 *Emanuell* Compare Isaiah 7/14: *Ecce, virgo concipiet et pariet filium, et vocabitur nomen eius Emmanuel* (AV "Behold, a virgin shall conceive, and bear a son, and shall call his name Immanuel"), the first Messianic prophecy of the Pseudo-Augustinian *Sermo beati Augustini Episcopi de Natale Domini* (Arles text in Karl Young: *The Drama of the Medieval Church*, 2/126–131, but see also *Contra Judaeos, Paganos et Arian, Sermo de Symbolo*, PL 42/1177–30). But the reference seems here to derive not directly from Isaiah, but from its citation by Matthew 1/23, just before the Magi episode; 63 seems to echo Matthew's interpretation of the name: *Ecce virgo in utero habebit et pariet filium; et vocabunt nomen eius Emmanuel, quod est interpretatum nobiscum Deus* (AV "Behold, a virgin shall be with child, and shall bring forth a son, and they shall call his name Emmanuel; which, being interpreted is, God with us"). Since it was generally held that the Magi were more meritorious than the Jews in having only one prophecy, which they believed, instead of the multiplicity of prophecies which the Jews refused to believe, this echo of Isaiah may seem incongruous; see further, *Legenda Aurea*: 'De Epiphania Domini'.

64 + SH H presumably omits the SH since the speaker does not change and in H no SD interrupts the text.

65–72, stanzas 9–10 French:
PRIMUS REX   A, sir king, if it please you, / Look up above your head.
SECUNDUS REX   There is a star there / which shines upon you.

PLAY VIII 127

TERTIUS REX   Behold, there is there an image / of a virgin, bearing, / as it
                   seems, a child, / carrying it in her arms.
plaist 65 H is to be preferred for rhyme to *ploitt* HmARB.

68 + SH, 72 + SH   These SHs seem to have caused some problem for the scribes, since H erroneously omits 68 + SH and HmA 72 + SH. Hm leaves a line-space after 72, presumably for the omitted SH (see TNs), which suggests confusion rather than mere scribal carelessness. H may have been misled by its own combination of 69–70 and 70–71 into believing that there was a single quatrain of 67–71.

69–80   Compare *Legenda Aurea*, 'De Epiphania Domini', which is followed by *Stanzaic Life*:

>   The quich shapen was
>   like a childe, non fairer my3t be,
>   And opon his hede he has
>   A shynyng croys as thay conen se.
>   (1757–60)

similarly, *Cursor Mundi* 11418–9, *Three Kings* and Mirk ("undyr his hed a bryght[t] crosse of golde"). A somewhat different version appears in the *South English Nativity* of Mary and Christ:

>   Amydde þe sterre þei seye a child al blody on a rode
>   (480)

and the Magi are then guided by a different star from the one containing the vision. Chester's star, exceptionally, seems to require a Virgin and Child image and makes no reference to the cross. Although the vision recalls the star of Play 6, it is surprising that reference is there made to the cross, 6/654, which is not found in any account of Octavian's vision and suggests derivation from the Magi's vision, but that no reference to the cross occurs here, where the main tradition requires it.

78   *well* ARBH is to be preferred for meaning, syntax and metre to *well well* Hm, where the repetition seems to be erroneous.

89–96   In *Legenda Aurea*, *South English Nativity*, *Stanzaic Life* 1761–4, Mirk, the speaker is the Christ in the star; in *Three Kings* "a vois was herde in þe sterre". The choice of the angel as speaker here seems to arise from the practical demands of staging, since the star presumably bore a picture and the angel was required to carry the star, 84 + SD.

101–8   Compare Isaiah 60/6: *Inundatio camelorum operiet te, dromedarii Madian et Epha; omnes de Saba venient, aurum et thus deferentes, et laudem Domino annuntiantes* (AV "The multitude of camels shall cover thee, the dromedaries of Midian and Ephah; all they from Sheba shall come: they shall bring gold and incense; and they shall shew forth the praises of the Lord"). Behind the discussion of the dromedary's powers lies a serious issue — that if the star appeared to the Magi only when Christ was born, they would not have had time to journey to Bethlehem before the Holy Family left; see Chrysostom, *In Matthaeum Homilia* 7 (PG 57/76). The speed of the dromedary offered an alternative solution, as *Legenda Aurea* 'De Epiphania Domini', indicates.

105–8   It was usual to establish the speed of the dromedary by comparison with a horse, as in *Legenda Aurea*, 'De Epiphania Domini', Mirk "þay woll renne on a day ifur þen any oþer hors yn þre dayes", or *South English Nativity*, 489–90. Comestor, *Historia Scholastica*, 'In Evangelia' 7 (PL 198/1541), is less precise. But, as Foster and Wilson note, only *Stanzaic Life* establishes the comparison with equivalent precision to Chester:

> Ierom also berys witnes
> dromedarys thay riden opon,
> that is a best of gret swiftnes
> a hundredth myle one day to gone.
> (1777–80)

The dromedary, the one-humped Arabian camel, can sustain a speed of 8–10 m.p.h. for a period of up to eighteen hours.

109–10 "Lords — and [this] I may well believe — that child, who is greatest in hierarchy, wishes to reduce the journey considerably for us who are bringing presents for his delight." Compare the other reason for the Magi's speed given in *Legenda Aurea*, 'De epiphania domini', reflected in *Stanzaic Life*:

> But, as Remyge berys recorde,
> sithen þai soȝten God almyȝt,
> No wonder thaȝe sich a lord,
> thagh way wer long, made hit but liȝt.
> (1773–6)

For easier syntax, *that* 112 B has been preferred in the above translation, and "are" has been understood in 111; *bringinge* is probably an error for *bringen*. Alternatively, following HmARB, 112 may be regarded as exclamatory.

112+SD *beastes Promptorum Parvulorum* characterises the dromedary as *beest*; H prefers *eques* (*e*(2) error for *o*), despite the text, and the preference may underlie *corsers* 108 H.

The SD covers a journey of thirteen days, the arrival at Bethlehem being on the thirteenth day.

113–20 The star's disappearance, though not expressly mentioned by Matthew, may be inferred from the Magi's need to ask directions in Jerusalem, and from the emphasis given to the guiding star and the Magi's rejoicing as they leave Herod's court in Matthew 2/9–10. Compare *Legenda Aurea*, 'De Epiphania Domini', and *South English Nativity*:

> Þo þei comen to Ierusalem furst þe sterre [hem] was yhud,
> [For þat] þei scholden after vr lord esche þat is burþtyme were ykud;
> Þat þe Iewes schole nout forsake þat he was among hem ybore.
> (537–9)

Wilson notes that the disappearance of the star is not a feature of other plays of the Magi but is found in *Stanzaic Life* 1909 ff., a further point of similarity.

121–32 Compare Matthew 2/2: *Ubi est qui natus est rex Judaeorum? Vidimus enim stellam eius in Oriente, et venimus adorare eum* (AV "Where is he that is born King of the Jews? for we have seen his star in the east, and are come to worship him").

121–8, stanza 17 *tydinge* 124 HmR is to be preferred for rhyme to *tydinges* ABH.

123 *belamye* ABH is to be preferred to the scribally erroneous *bellany* Hm, where minims have been miscounted, and *ballamy* R. MED notes the word "in direct

PLAY VIII 129

address [often to enemies or inferiors as an expression of contempt]". HmARB identify the man as a messenger (124+SH), an identification continued in H's *Nuntius* of 144+SD, H's only use of the term here, which may suggest that the HmARB description was elsewhere changed by H. H's *Explorator*, "a prying person; a spy" (Latin), recorded in OED from 1450 as "one who is employed to collect information, esp. with regard to an enemy or an enemy's country; a scout, a spy", seems paralleled by *Ludus Coventriae* 18/95–110, where Herod's *stywarde* is employed as spy, seeking news of "Any thynge shuld greve þe kynge" (99–100). The messenger appears also in Wakefield, where he is also termed *bellamy*, 14/343.

129 *see* Hm, though an acceptable past tense form, has been replaced by *sawe* in ARBH as a rendering of Vulgate *vidimus*.

his H renders Vulgate *eius*; but compare 213, where, despite the quotation from the Vulgate text at 212+Latin, all manuscripts read *the*.

136 OED has no example before 1584 of "out of one's skin", "denoting excessive exertion, or more usually (with *jump* etc.) extreme delight, excitement, high spirits, or surprise."

137–44 The sequence of events here is unbiblical. Matthew 2/1–7 indicates that Herod, having heard what the kings were asking, had the scriptures consulted on his own behalf and then summoned the Magi to a secret meeting; whereas here the Magi seek out Herod, who is then led to commission the search of the scriptures. The biblical sequence is found in *Legenda Aurea*; *Stanzaic Life* is more ambiguous. But sanction for the Chester sequence can be found in Comestor, *Historia Scholastica*, 'In Evangelia' 7 (PL 198/1541), and Mirk. In Wakefield, Herod hears of the kings, but summons them before he consults the doctors.

145–52, stanza 20 Deimling regards this stanza, of unusual metre and abababab rhyme-scheme, as possibly spurious and hence omitted by H. He points to the second sentence of the preceding SD; to the apostrophe of *Mahound* 147; to the recurrence of *tidings-tell* 149 after 144; and to the pointlessness of 151–2. Against this, he notes H's Latin equivalent to the first sentence of the preceding SD, which then fails to introduce a further speech, arguing that no speech is in fact necessary. It seems, however, safest to conclude that the Latin SD indicates that H shared the exemplar of HmARB but omitted the speech because of its unusual stanza-form.

150 *kinges* ARB is to be preferred to *kinge* Hm for concord and meaning.

153–60, stanza 21 French:
PRIMUS REX   Sir King, royal and revered, / May God preserve you, all powerful one.
SECUNDUS REX   We have come together / to seek tidings.
HERODES   Welcome, noble kings. / Tell me all that you intend.
TERTIUS REX   We seek a child of high parentage / and king of heaven and earth.

154 *Deu* The king invokes God, whereas the messenger had invoked the "pagan god" *Mahound*, "Mahomet", 147. Tyrant figures such as Herod are usually considered pagans, and Herod was not a Jew by birth — see 278–9. But the historical Herod was a Jew by faith and, in Chester, shows interest in and knowledge of the Jewish scriptures.

156+SD The marginal SDs which punctuate Herod's speeches read like production notes which indicate significant actions involving Herod's two symbols — his wand of office, indicating his power of government, and his sword, indicating his bellicose nature. The occasional variations in the occurrence and wording of these SDs, and in their exact positioning in the text, may indicate some doubt about their status in the minds of the scribes. They suggest a particular attention to the visual presentation of Herod, and perhaps also indicate that the exemplar had served as a practical acting-text, bearing a producer's annotations.

161-212 Matthew does not at this point suggest Herod as a wrathful tyrant, commenting at 2/3 only *Audiens autem .... turbatus est* (AV "He was troubled"). Indeed, he commissions a scholarly inquiry, and then sends for the Magi and closely questions them about the exact time of the star's appearance as he does not here. Only when the Magi fail to return is Herod *iratus .... valde*, Matthew 2/16 (AV "Exceeding wroth"). But the picture here and elsewhere derives from a long tradition of the comically irate Herod, going back into liturgical drama.

Among the reasons commonly cited for Herod's consternation was the fact that an earthly king's power was confounded by that of a spiritual king; see *Legenda Aurea*, 'De Epiphania Domini'. Some historical basis for the picture may be found in Josephus' account of Herod, which suggests that he was politically ambitious, ruthlessly vengeful and contemptuous of public opinion. Some element of worldly-mindedness may also have been suggested by his common title, *Magnus Herodes* or *Herod the Great*.

The speech reapplies, with telling irony, a number of divine attributes, — Herod's claims to be king of kings 169 (cf, e.g. Apocalypse 17/14, 19/16); to rule the world 173 (cf e.g. Job 34/13, Psalm 50/12); to cast down devils 175 (e.g. Luke 12/15 — compare Play I); to have the divinely bestowed Petrine power to loose and bind 178 (Matthew 16/19, 18/18); to be above all hierarchy (e.g. Exodus 18/11, Job 33/12 — compare Chester 2/1) and for all time (compare 1/3-4 note and 181-2 note below). Some similar effect can be seen in Coventry Shearmen 486-528. These claims, reinforced by absurd hyperbolic assertions of power over planets and elements, are further undercut by threats of physical violence, a confession of physical inadequacy, and a clear indication of his insecurity as king. Herod therefore stands in marked contrast to the Octavian of Play 6.

165-8 The historical Herod does appear to have attempted to ally the Jewish faith to his political concept of an independent Jewish kingdom. There was, moreover, a section of Jewish belief which looked to the Messiah as a king of territorial power. It is difficult to assess how far these considerations affected the presentation of Herod, to what extent he should be considered as attempting to assume for himself a Messianic role; compare Origen, *Contra Celsum* I (PG 11/771).

171 *tyrant* Latin *tyrannus* occurs in the neutral sense of "ruler" and the pejorative sense of "despot", and the ME word similarly has these two applications. Herod thus terms himself "king", unconscious of the pejorative sense which his own description emphasises. The "neutral" sense is last recorded by OED in 1737.

175-6 Compare Wakefield 14/23-4, *Ludus Coventriae* 18/7-8.

176-80, stanza 24   The omission of a quatrain from the exemplar may be suspected here.

PLAY VIII

181–2 Compare 1/4 and Apocalypse 1/4.

189–90 *nye* is reported as rhyme word in HmAB; R and H substitute to avoid repetition. *wrye* 190 R, OED *wry* v.2, II *trans* 1 "to deflect or divert (a person or thing) from some course or in some direction". 2. "to twist or turn (the body, neck, etc.) round or about; to contort, wring, wrench", is possible; but *destroy* 190 H seems semantically more probable.

198–200 *hee and you all three* 198 seems to refer to the Messenger and the three Magi, but possibly *hee* refers to Jesus — compare *he* 200 where the reference to Jesus seems clear. If the pronouns do refer to Jesus, they take up 159–60.

199 *kinge of Gallilee* Herod was formerly tetrarch of Judaea, being expelled but in 37 B.C. reconquering Jerusalem. He was confirmed in his kingship by Octavian in 31 B.C. Judaea, Galilee and Samaria constituted the three provinces of Palestine.

201–12 Compare 382–9, Wakefield 14/469–80.

205–12, stanza 28 Neither *give* 206 Hm nor *geve* ARBH gives rhyme. Probably *gie*, from *gien*, MED intr. 3(b) "to govern", was intended. *guy* v. is recorded to 1600 in OED as the equivalent of *guide* v¹.

210 "That I have totted up my royal prerogatives"; on *rialtye*, compare *royalty* OED 5 — B does not seem to have understood this usage.

212 + SD Matthew 2/2: AV "For we have seen his star in the east and are come to worship him." Chester differs from the Vulgate in:
vidimus] vidimus enim Vulg.   cum muneribus] *om* Vulg.

221 *prophecye* HmARB is used generically, but *prophesies* H seems inapplicable since it suggests the range of Judaic prophecy which the Magi do not know; they have only Balaam's prophecy. Contrast York 17/161–8, where the kings know Jewish prophets, and Chester 9/140–3, where the Magi seem to have acquired further knowledge.

232 *my clarke* Compare Matthew 2/4: *Et congregans omnes principes sacerdotum et scribas populi* (AV "And when he had gathered all the chief priests and scribes of the people"). Demands of production may well have determined the restriction to a single informant, here identified as the Chief Priest, 233. The historical Herod played a considerable part in the appointment and dismissal of priests, and the evident dependence of the Doctor upon Herod's favour, a major comic element in the scene, has therefore some basis in reality.

234 *thy bookes of prophecye* In Matthew 2/2–4 Herod seeks an answer to the question (posed here by the Magi at 126–8, although in Matthew the Magi never directly ask it of him) where is Jesus born. Herod directs the Doctor's inquiries to that point at 309–10 and is there answered by the same prophecy cited by Matthew. All the other prophets cited here seem designed to confirm the blindness of the Jews in general and of Herod in particular; they also provide a wealth of confirmatory evidence for Balaam's prophecy, the Magi's sole authority, and may therefore be compared with the prophecies of Play 5 H.

The list of prophets given by Herod at 235 and 261–8 does not follow any obvious order. It contains the three major Jewish prophets and eleven of the twelve minor

Jewish prophets of the Hagiographa, omitting the minor prophet Jonah but including Isaiah twice, 235 and 261 (both in rhyme position, hence not in error). Herod also includes David, not a Jewish prophet but included among the prophetic books in the English Bibles, and Daniel, also not a prophetic book but containing a number of texts of prophetic import — compare 289 + Latin and note. The forms of the names seem to have caused problems for the scribes. The listing suggests knowledge, but imperfect understanding, of the prophets, as might befit Herod.

235 Deimling comments: "The original of H either had no proper names whatever, or those it offered to James Miller disagreed with those of another manuscript, so that he, irresolute, left the space blank, perhaps in order that the names might be inserted in strict accordance with the actual performance." A less elaborate explanation might be that the gaps indicate an intention to rubricate the names which was never carried out.

268 + SH *Doctor* is erroneously omitted by Hm here and after 310. The emended form here follows B, the only manuscript with the SH before the Latin.

Wakefield 14 cites Isaiah 7/14 and Micah 5/2 (both in Matthew); York 17 (where the kings cite the prophecies) Isaiah 7/14 and Hosea 14/5; *Ludus Coventriae* 18 has only the Balaam prophecy.

268 + Latin Genesis 49/10: AV "The sceptre shall not depart from Judah, nor a law giver from between his feet, until Shiloh come; and unto him shall the gathering of the people be." The AV version of Jacob's words to his sons differs somewhat from the Vulgate version, here accurately reported. Compare its interpretation in *Glossa Ordinaria*, 'Lib. Gen.' 49/9 (PL 113/178). The same prophecy is cited in *Stanzaic Life* 1833–44 + Latin.

277–82 As the descendant of an Idumaean, Herod was not a Jew by birth and nationality; but his family had adopted the Jewish faith and he himself was a practising Jew. Compare *Three Kings*: "Herodes was but an alyen but was made kynge by þe emperour and by þe Romayns"; *Stanzaic Life*:

> So fel hit, neȝe er Crist was born,
> Þat kyng of Iewes wer past out
> And al þe world to Rome sworn
> And thider wer buxum al about.
> So was Heroude þider sent
> fro Rome to be kyng of Iude.
>
> (1853–8)

284 *villard* Jacob lived 147 years, Genesis 47/28, and the words cited were uttered by him to his sons on his death-bed. Herod is therefore accurate in characterising the speaker as aged and here, as elsewhere, reveals a detailed knowledge of the context of scripture.

287 *parage* ARBH may be preferred to *parentage* Hm. Either gives sense — *parage* is the usual ME term, last recorded by OED in 1652, but *parentage* in the sense of "derivation or descent from parents, esp. in relation to inherited rank or character" is recorded by OED from 1490.

289 + Latin The form of prophecy here quoted is that of the second prophecy of *Sermo Beati Augustini de Natale Domini*, ascribed to Daniel and finding its way into

PLAY VIII

liturgical drama and into such plays as the AN *Adam* 826+, the Beauvais *Daniel* 274-5, the Benediktbeuern Christmas Play 11-26 and Wakefield 7/216+ Latin. There is no exact Biblical correspondence, but reference is usually made by critics to Daniel 9/24: *Septuaginta hebdomades abbreviatae sunt super populum tuum et super urbem sanctam tuam, ut consummetur praevaricatio, et finem accipiat peccatum, et deleatur iniquitas, et adducatur iustitia sempiterna, et impleatur visio et prophetia, et ungatur Sanctus sanctorum.* (AV "Seventy weeks are determined upon thy people and upon thy holy city, to finish the transgression, and to make an end of sins, and to make reconciliation for iniquity, and to bring in everlasting righteousness, and to seal up the vision and prophecy, and to anoint the most Holy").

297-303   Compare 15/65-80.

304   *that dreame-reader* God gave to Daniel "understanding in all visions and dreams", Daniel 1/17; from chap. 7, the emphasis shifts towards the visions which Daniel himself was granted, hence the reference to *noe sleepie sluggard* 305.

307   *godlinge*, "a little god, an inferior deity", seems to be a late sixteenth century form — compare 326, cited by OED as first occurrence but dated by OED as 1500; the next example is 1570-6. In both instances it is probable that the later form, either by intention or by error, has replaced an older *gedling* H, a variant of *gadling*, whose OED sense 2, "base, low-born person", seems most appropriate in these contexts.

310+SH   The inclusion of *Doctor* ARBH is to be preferred to its erroneous omission in Hm.

310+Latin   Matthew 2/6: AV "And thou Bethlehem, in the land of Juda, art not the least among the princes of Juda: for out of thee shall come a Governor, that shall rule my people Israel." The text differs from the Vulgate as follows (cycle text given first):
quidem] om   Judae] Juda   regret] regat
Matthew 2/6 is quoting Micah 5/2 but it is not an exact quotation and the text is here cited in New Testament form. The same text is cited in Appendix IB/392+Latin.

311-7, stanza 42   *livinge was* 317 ARBH is to be preferred for rhyme to *were livinge* Hm. The Hm order suggests an attempt to produce a b-rhyme through misunderstanding of the rhyme-scheme; but the change also involves the use of a plural pronoun and verb morphology, suggested by the plural subject of 315. *the* AR seems also to be a plural pronoun, but without the corresponding verb-form; *ther* BH is therefore syntactically preferable, accepting the BH word-order. 317 BH would then mean: "[Isaiah and Jeremiah] prophesied of Christ's coming while [each] was living there [i.e. in Israel, 314]."

Either *lyving* 315 BH or *beinge* HmAR is possible; some confusion in BH with *livinge* 317 may be suspected, but equally, in Hm, where *livinge* is the 317 rhyme-word, the substitution of *beinge* at 315 when 317 was erroneously altered to avoid repetition of the rhyme-word is also possible. AR's agreement with Hm at 315 and in the pronoun form of 317 may suggest that the Hm reading was available to AR, but that they preserved the 317 rhyme at the expense of syntax.

315   *Esaye and Jheremye* e.g. Isaiah 2 and 40-66; Jeremiah 23/5-6. Compare 317+Latin.

317 + SH   In all other passages there is a regular alternation of speeches by Herod and by the Doctor. The break in sequence here, the omission of the SH in ARB, and the apparent lack of connexion between the text and Herod's initial question, all suggest an omission transmitted by the exemplar.

317 + Latin   Isaiah 60/3: AV "And the Gentiles shall come to thy light, and kings to the brightness of thy rising." The passage was familiar as part of the third lectio, *In primo Nocturno*, on the Feast of the Epiphany in the Sarum usage.

318–24, stanza 43   *coste* 321 ARH is to be preferred for rhyme to *coasts* HmB. *nacion* AB represents a parallel usage. *folcke* AR is a similar collective, but perhaps may be considered less probable in view of the form *gentes* which it renders.

322   *birth* ARBH renders Vulgate *ortus* and is to be preferred for meaning to the erroneous *death* Hm, the latter an apparently mechanical substitution of a related concept.

324 + Latin   The quotation is made up from two separate passages in Jeremiah. On *Effundam..juvenum*, compare Jeremiah 6/11: *Effunde super parvulum foris, et super consilium iuvenum simul; vir enim cum muliere capietur, senex cum pleno dierum* (AV "I will pour it [the fury of the Lord] out upon the children abroad, and upon the assembly of young men together: for even the husband with the wife shall be taken, the aged with him that is full of days"): on *disperdam..meo*, compare Jeremiah 9/20–21: *Audite ergo, mulieres, verbum Domini, et assumant aures vestrae sermonem oris eius, et docete filias vestras lamentum, et unaquaeque proximam suam planctum; quia ascendit mors per fenestras nostras, ingressa est domos nostras, disperdere parvulos de foris, iuvenes de plateis* (AV "Yet hear the word of the Lord, O ye women, and let your ear receive the word of his mouth, and teach your daughters wailing, and every one her neighbour lamentation. For death is come up into our windows, and is entered into our palaces, to cut off the children from without, and the young men from the streets"). Both passages refer to God's punishment of sinful Israel but are reapplied by Herod to his proposed Massacre of the Innocents. Standard commentaries do not appear to make this application.

327–30   Matthew 2/16 indicates that Herod's anger was kindled when the Magi failed to return, and that the Massacre of the Innocents followed. There is no suggestion of prior intent, although Herod's response is partially foreseen by the angel in 2/13. See further, 9/224–31 note.

328   *congion* AH is to be preferred to the erroneous *conge* B and to *coninge* Hm, the latter suggesting formal confusion; *connyon* R is apparently only a formal variant. OED has no examples, other than glosses, of *congeon* after the fifteenth century. The word rhymes with *crowne* and *downe* here.

332–8, stanza 45   *beforne* 332 H and *were borne* 334 H are to be preferred to *before* and *were* HmARB for the a-rhyme. HmARB suggest an attempt to rhyme *were*, with a pronunciation *wore*, with *before*, suggesting that the change from *beforne* may have preceded the change in 334.

333   *Athalia* Athaliah, daughter of Jezebel and Ahab, who after her marriage to Jehoram introduced the worship of Baal into the southern kingdom of Israel. The murder of the remnant of the royal children at her command to secure her power is

PLAY VIII 135

recorded in 2 Kings 11/1, and her subsequent death at the hands of Jehoiada's men in 2 Chronicles 23/12–5. On Athaliah as figure of Herod, see *Biblia Pauperum*, fol. 7.

335 *her soone* i.e. Ahaziah, killed by Jehu (2 Kings 9/27).

338+Latin Psalm 72/10 AV "The kings of Tarshish and of the isles shall bring presents; the kings of Sheba and Seba shall offer gifts." The ascription to Psalm 71 reflects the Vulgate numbering. With the interpretation, compare *Glossa Ordinaria*, 'Lib. Psalm' 71/10 (PL 113/954). The anthem occurs in *Secundo Nocturno* on the Feast of the Epiphany in the Sarum Usage. 70 B is an error.

341 *misticall* Compare Origen, *Contra Celsum* I (PG 11/771). See also Play 9 for symbolic interpretations.

343 *Abrahams seede* The linear descent of Christ from Abraham is set out in the genealogy of Matthew 1/1–17. Compare Chester 4/173–6, 6/105–6.

345 AR's omission is an inexplicable but significantly shared error.

351 "These books should be torn and ripped up." *those* HmB and *these* ARH are equally possible; *all totorne* H is similarly acceptable.

354 *David that sheppard with his slinge* Alleged author of the book of Psalms, from which the last prophecy is taken, and included in Herod's list of prophets, 235 — see also 235 note. David is said to be keeping his father's sheep in 1 Samuel 16/11, 17/15; his sling is the weapon with which he defeats Goliath at 17/40. Again Herod shows a knowledge of Jewish scriptures, but fails to appreciate the ironic implications of the reference for his own situation.

354–7, stanza 48 It seems probable that a quatrain required for a regular Chester stanza was omitted in the exemplar. Some confusion may have arisen because the b-rhyme here is identical to that for the preceding stanza. *gett* 356 has no obvious subject.

366–73 Herod seems to express an unbiblical doubt about the truth of the prophecies — contrast Matthew 2/8: *Et cum inveneritis* (AV "And when ye have found him"). While in Matthew the kings will return when they have found Christ, here the kings will return either because they have found Christ or because they wish to accept Herod's offer of hospitality at 368–9.

370–3 As Wilson notes, *Stanzaic Life* does not make explicit the intention of Herod to worship the infant Christ himself, as does Chester following Matthew 2/8.

374–81, stanza 51 The rhyme-scheme aaaaabab, instead of the expected aaabaaab, is found in all manuscripts and was presumably the exemplar reading. It perhaps arises from a transposition of the speeches of the second and third kings, which would produce the expected aaabaabb form and give as b-rhyme *layne—agayne*.

381+SD *pigge* i.e. "earthenware pot, pitcher", OED sb² 1, used presumably to contain the wine which Herod demands. *nefrens* H "that cannot bite, has no teeth", hence in Rider's *Bibliotheca Scholastica* of 1589 as "a weined [weaned] pigge", suggests that H's Latin derives from the English SD, not vice-versa, and that H wrongly envisaged a "circus-type" performance by a boy with a pet animal.

390–7, stanza 53   HmARB repeat the rhyme-word *hee* 395 at 396; H seeks to avoid the repetition by reading *he and they* 396 for *they and hee* HmARB. But *they* gives imperfect rhyme. H may have been misled by the form *contrey* 394 for *contree*.

394–401   No such threats are voiced by the biblical Herod, but they have their basis in Matthew 2/12–3. Compare Origen, *Contra Celsum* I, *Legenda Aurea*, 'De epiphania domini', *Glossa Ordinaria*, 'Evang. Matth', 2/8 (PL 114/74). This hidden intent is not in *Stanzaic Life*.

402   "God's grace shall not avail them". The construction seems to have troubled AR; they substitute *the* "they", nominative, for *them*, indirect object/dative: "They shall not gain God's grace".

413   Hm is preferable to BH in supplying an additional syllable which produces a more regular sequence of strongly and weakly stressed syllables. AR erroneously repeat the 409 rhyme-word.

419   A's omission is an inexplicable error.

PLAY IX

Dramatis Personae Primus Rex, Secundus Rex, Tertius Rex, Maria, Josephe, Angelus.

NOTE   1. A non-speaking Infant Christ is required.
   2. After 183 in AR God — presumably the Infant Christ — speaks.

Locations
the stable 25, an oxe stall 35, howsinge 20, this simple house 30 — *situated* yonder 25.

Properties
the starre 3, 16, 25
Magi's gifts — gould 40, 45, 51, *in* sciatuum 135 + SD; incense 53, myrre 56.

Costume
None specified.

Sources
Matthew 2/9-12, apparently directly supplemented from the interpretation of the gifts in *Legenda Aurea*, 'De Epiphania Domini'.

Play-heading Compare 8/*Play-heading* note. The play includes not only the Magi's offering but also the angel's warning and the Magi's return to their own lands.

The offering of the Magi occurs also in Wakefield 14/493-642, York 17/217-336, *Ludus Coventriae* 18/230-334, Coventry Shearmen 689-767.

21-4 The exemplary paradox of the humble circumstances of the birth of the King of kings was a commonplace; see Bede, *In Lucae Evangelium Expositio* 1/2 (PL 92/331).

33-6 The symbolic interpretation of the Magi's gifts was known to Bede, *In Matthaei Evangelium Expositio* 1/2 (PL 92/13); but was developed and elaborated. The account in Chester, as the passages cited below clearly suggest, derived from the full and readily available interpretation in *Legenda Aurea*, an interpretation followed also by *Stanzaic Life*. No other cycle has such an extended account, although justifications for the gifts do occur briefly, generally in terms of their appropriateness to Christ's triple role of secular ruler, spiritual leader and Saviour — compare Wakefield 14/541-52, York 17/253-88, *Ludus Coventriae* 18/235-58, Coventry

Shearmen 699–716. In all other plays, however, the explanation is given at the time of presentation; only Chester has a preliminary exposition.

33–40, stanza 5   No manuscript has the form *lasse* for *lesse* 36, required for perfect rhyme.

41–7, stanza 6   No scribe seems to have recognised that the stanza lacks an a-rhyme line in the second quatrain, although the indentation of 47 in Hm may be significant. H contains a line between 46 and 47 but it is in a different — questionably scribal — hand (see TNs) and its appropriateness in context is not immediately clear; possibly it was supplied to meet the metrical deficiency. The line was evidently missing in the exemplar.

41–4   "For it is the custom in our land not to approach any king except with gifts choice, precious and costly, as befit his dignity." Compare *Legenda Aurea* 'De Epiphania Domini': *Prima, quoniam traditio antiquorum fuit, ut dicit Remigius, ut nullus ad Deum vel ad regem vacuus introiret.*

45–6   Compare Remigius, Homilia 7 (PL 131/906): *Aurum enim solet esse pretiosius in regalibus donis.*

48–59   Compare *Legenda Aurea* 'De Epiphania Domini': *Secunda quae est Bernardi, quoniam beatae virgini aurum obtulerunt propter inopiae sublevationem, thus propter stabuli foetorem, myrrham propter membrorum pueri consolidationem et malorum vermium expulsionem.* The final phrase has no counterpart at this point — contrast *Stanzaic Life* 2061: "And wormus wayues eke also."

54   *stynke of the stable* Compare *Stanzaic Life* 2054: "stenche of stabul forto qvace" and the B and H variants.

56–9   The suggestion is that Jesus was bathed in myrrh to strengthen his limbs, although the account makes this less clear as a development of *Legenda consolidationem* than the equivalent passage in *Stanzaic Life*:

        And myrre also nothyng amys
        for childes membres ȝyuen was,
        To anoynt hom fote ʒ kne.
        for the kynde of myrre is this,
        hit strengthes, þat men may oft se,
        senowes ʒ ioyntes þat faren amys.
        (2055–60)

64–87   Compare *Legenda Aurea* 'De Epiphania Domini': *Tertia, quoniam aurum ad tributum thus ad sacrificium, myrrha ad sepulturam pertinet mortuorum.*

67   *temporalitye* H's *temporaltye* may be preferred for metre. AR do not seem to recognise the word; or perhaps feel its meaning, "the laity" to have primacy over its sense of "temporal authority"; *parcialitie* R corrects A's scribally erroneous *pacialitie*, but the appropriate meaning, "fondness for someone", is recorded by OED only from 1581.

72–9   Compare *Stanzaic Life*:

        And als sithen he shuld bischop be
        And hede of holi chirche also,

PLAY IX 139

>encense was gode for that degre
>to sacrifise imong mo
>(2069-72)

where the correspondence is significantly close.

78 *giftes* The context would suggest a singular form, although all manuscripts have plural.

80-7 Compare 168-83. In ascribing exegetical interpretations to the third king, Chester elevates him to prophetic status.

84-5 "Myrrh that puts corruption away from man and preserves him from harmful decay." *sinne* is not recorded by OED with concrete application, but can hardly bear moral import in this context. *him* may refer to Christ but, since this is a general definition, it seems preferable to assume that it refers to *man* 82, to be picked up in *man* 85. *rowtinge* HmB may be taken as a form of *rout, root*, "to root up, dig up", usually used of pigs but also applied to the activities of worms, but is perhaps better taken as a form of *rottinge* ARH, which conveys the same idea of decay.

88-95 Chester seems marginally closer to *Legenda Aurea*, 'De Epiphania Domini', than to *Stanzaic Life* 2077-80; compare with *Legenda, kinges powere — Life: kynges realte*; *godhead — Life: Goddes my3t* (and see 92 note); *bodely death — Life: deth that tholet he*.

92 *lasteth* ARBH is to be preferred to the erroneous *lastlye* Hm — this is not the last item, and in Hm *aye* has no function. ARBH emphasise the recurring attribute of godhead in Chester, timelessness, and hence take *Legenda*'s *divina majestas* into a more technical and appropriate sense for the cycle than *Life*'s *Goddes my3t*.

96-103 Compare *Legenda Aurea* 'De Epiphania Domini': *Quarta, quoniam aurum significat dilectionem, thus orationem, myrrha carnis mortificationem*. This cryptic comment receives fuller development in *Stanzaic Life*, to which Chester may owe something; see 96-9 note and 102-3 note.

96-9 Compare *Stanzaic Life*:

>Gold als luf may signifie,
>for it is 3yuen in no place
>but þer mon loues hertfully,
>As thay diden Ihesu ful of grace.
>(2081-4)

98 *ther* BH is to be preferred to the scribally erroneous *these* Hm and to the marginally better *thoes* AR which would have to be taken as dative, "to those". With BH compare *Stanzaic Life*'s "þer mon loues hertfully" (2083).

102-3 102 does not appropriately correspond to *Legenda*'s *carnis mortificationem*, more suitably rendered as "ouercomyng of our fleschlie wille" in *Stanzaic Life* 2090. Some influence from the previous triad, *humana mortalitas*, may be suspected — compare 94-5. The effect is to remove the coherence of the interpretation in 96-103 suggested in *Stanzaic Life*:

>And alle þes vertuse rekenet her
>offre we most to God almy3t,

luf, deuocioun, flesch enter
(2093-5)

— contrast 104-11 where the triad is more accurately interpreted. Hence 103, "And all these shall be appropriate to him", must refer to the three gifts, not to the obligations which they symbolise for the Christian nor to their manifestation by Christ himself.

104-11 Compare *Legenda Aurea* 'De Epiphania Domini': *Per aurum ergo, quod est pretiosus omnibus metallis, intelligitur divinitas pretiosissima, per thus anima devotissima, quia thus significat devotionem et orationem.* Psalm: *dirigatur oratio mea, etc. Per myrrham, quae conservat a corruptione, caro incorrupta.* This passage has been moved in Chester from its position in the *Legenda*, where it concludes the exposition of the Magi's gifts, to precede the fifth triad — compare 112-9 note. The passage has no counterpart in *Stanzaic Life* and seems to show influence from the wording in *Legenda*.

104-11, stanza 14   *sayd* 108 gives a b-rhyme where an a-rhyme is required; some word such as *known* may have been erroneously replaced in the exemplar. The change has also interrupted the recurring prepositional construction, *by gould* 104 and *by myrre* 110, depending upon *understand wee mon* 106; the construction corresponds to a repeated *per* construction in *Legenda Aurea* — hence the sense of alteration at this point is strengthened.

108-9   "And incense may well be said to be a source of great devotion." See *root* OED II.1; the word has no counterpart in *Legenda*'s *devotionem et orationem*.

112-8   Compare *Legenda Aurea* 'De Epiphania Domini': *Quinta, quoniam per haec tria significantur tria, quae erant in Christo, scilicet divinitas pretiosissima, anima devotiosima et caro integra et incorrupta.* Compare also *Stanzaic Life* 2097-120, where, however, the idea of divine love is developed for gold and of virgin birth for myrrh.

After **127**   B The additional line appears to be an uncancelled and erroneous version of 128.

128-35, stanza 17   *arne* 131 H and *barne* 135 H are to be preferred to *are, baron* HmARB for rhyme.

128-31   Compare Matthew 2/11: *Invenerunt puerum cum Maria matre eius* (AV "They saw the young child with Mary his mother"), followed by *Legenda Aurea* and hence by *Stanzaic Life*: "And founden the child, his moder eke" (2030); and no part is played by Joseph in the scene in Wakefield, *Ludus Coventriae* and Coventry Shearmen. Joseph is, however, specifically included in York 17/230-1. Compare *South English Nativity*:

>Þei come in and founde þat swete bern myd is moder Marie,
>Ac Iosep ne founde þei nout leste þei þouhten folye
>—[þat þe] child hadde is sone ybe, and þat þe moder vnclene were.
>(555-7)

Joseph's presence in Chester parallels his presence at 7/496-507, and his role as witness at 7/516-39 is repeated here at 200-23, perhaps with some comment such as that of the *South English Nativity* in mind.

PLAY IX 141

133 *from* ARBH is to be preferred for meaning to *in* Hm. The additional syllable supplied by *farre* Hm, *our* BH produces a more regular sequence of strongly and weakly stressed syllables.

135 + SD *sciatuum, sciathum* No such word is recorded. It may be an error for *cyathum*, "chalice", perhaps influenced by *scapium*, glossed by Cooper's *Thesaurus Linguae Romanae et Britannicae* of 1565 as, *inter alia*, "a drinkynge potte" and "a vessell used in maner of a vialle". Although the containers for the gifts are not usually specified in the plays, in Coventry Shearmen the gifts are offered by the *cupefull*, 703, 707.

140–3 Moses is not generally considered to be a Messianic prophet, but his inclusion here may recall Deuteronomy 18/15: *Prophetam de gente tua et de fratribus tuis sicut me suscitabit tibi Dominus Deus tuus* (AV "The Lord thy God will raise up unto thee a Prophet from the midst of thee, of thy brethren, like unto me"), quoted in Pseudo-Athanasius, 'Homilia in Occursu Domini' 8 (PG 28/983) in the context of prophecies of Abraham, Jacob and Balaam; on David and Isaiah, see 8/235, 317 + Latin, 338 + Latin and notes; on Balaam, see 8/1–16, 17 and notes. Realistically, as Gentiles the Magi could not be expected to know the Jewish Messianic prophets, although it might be argued that they would know of Moses from Balaam's contact with the Israelites, and that they had heard the prophecies of Daniel and Isaiah at Herod's court.

144–83 *Stanzaic Life* merely reports the offering, 2029–33, following it with the explanations, in the manner of *Legenda Aurea*, whereas, as Wilson notes, Chester includes a brief recapitulation of their significance at this point. In other cycles, these comments by the kings at their offering constitute the only explanations of the audience.

152–9, stanza 20 *saye* 156 HmAR supplies a b-rhyme where an a-rhyme is required, duplicating the b-rhyme of 159. *said* B adjusts the tense but does not restore rhyme and seems to be an alternative based on the HmAR reading. Deimling cites *fayle* H, which does supply rhyme, as evidence of H's superiority, but it is difficult to see what meaning the word conveys. Probably *tell* has been replaced by *saye* in the exemplar as a result of mindless association with *saye* 159 or in error to rhyme with *awaye* 155.

157 On Isaiah and Ezechiel, see 8/235, 317 + Latin and notes. Like Herod, the Magi twice refer to Isaiah. Herod mentioned Ezechiel, but no prophecy by him was cited to the Magi. See 140–3 note above.

158–9 "And Abraham was not able to keep the truth about you from being told." Although Abraham was the patriarch with whom God first made the covenant establishing the elect position of the Jews, it is possible here that the allusion is to the Melchizedek episode; see 4/33–4 note. If so, the idea may be that Abraham was not able to prevent a Gentile from revealing the truth about Christ's sacrifice. Otherwise, there seems no reason to believe that Abraham would wish to conceal the truth about Christ. The construction here is, however, unusual and elliptical, and the possibility of error cannot be ignored.

166 The line has only three strongly stressed syllables instead of the expected four.

172-5 Deimling (p.xxiii) characterises B's omission of this necessary quatrain as "a mere mistake".

After **183** AR Deimling (p.xxiii) comments that A and R "insert .. a half-stanza which remains incomplete, and which is unjustified by the very situation." In fact, a physical response from the infant Christ is requested at 183 and perhaps also at 149, and an infant of some maturity — such as often appears in pictorial representations of the scene — is suggested. However, the lines do not appear in the other manuscripts, although it is difficult to credit Bellin with their invention. It may be noted that 4 contains four strongly stressed syllables where a regular Chester quatrain would required three.

184 No response from any member of the Holy Family is indicated by Matthew, but Mary usually replies in the plays — Wakefield 14/559-76. York 17/289-300, *Ludus Coventriae* 18/259-64, Coventry Shearmen 713-6.

192 *leve lorde* A may indicate that *hath* 194 has suggested a singular subject, although the context clearly requires plural.

196 In HmARB the line appears to have only three strongly-stressed syllables; the extra syllable supplied by H gives a more regular form.

200 *all* is strongly stressed and must therefore be regarded as adjectival rather than adverbial; reduction of stress would produce an irregular three-stress line.

202 *menskie* Hm is not otherwise recorded and seems to be an error for *menske* H, MED 1(c) "Honor shown to someone or something; respect, reverence". Since OED last records *mensk* in 1509, unfamiliarity with the word may underlie the replacements in AR and B.

204-7 R's apparently erroneous omission of this quatrain is noted by Deimling as an unusual divergence of A and R.

205 *leefe of kynde*, "consent of nature". The phrase is unusual, and some confusion with *leeves* 204 may be suspected; H's *lynde* suggests a common, but here totally inappropriate, alliterative phrase.

208-11 Compare 6/127-8 and note.

223 + SH Matthew 2/12, the account of the warning, follows without preamble from the offering, as here; but in Matthew the warning is *in somnis* (AV "in a dream"), indicating that the Magi were asleep. All other plays indicate that the Magi had left the stable and were resting on their way back to Herod when the warning was delivered — Wakefield 14/557-94, York 17/301-11, *Ludus Coventriae* 18/265-90, Coventry Shearmen 717-24. Chester, however, does not even indicate the idea of dream.

Matthew 2/12 also does not specify how the Magi were warned, or what form the warning took. But the idea of an angel-advisor, perhaps influenced by the angel who warns Joseph, Matthew 2/13, was well established — Wakefield 14/595-606, York 17/313-24, *Ludus Coventriae* 18/291-304, Coventry Shearmen 725-32. Compare also *South English Nativity:* "an angel hem het" (561) and *Stanzaic Life:*
in slepe an aungel, leue ȝe me,
warnet hom lest thay wer shent.
(2123-4)

PLAY IX

Finally, Matthew 2/12 does not explain why the Magi were not to return to Herod's court. Coventry Shearmen is similarly unspecific — "for drede of Eyrode" (729); but other cycles specify Herod's desire to *sheynd* (Wakefield 14/600, York 17/318) or *kyll* (*Ludus Coventriae* 18/293) the kings. Compare 7/398-9.

240-7, stanza 31   The stanza takes the irregular form ababcccb. It bears a striking resemblance to two passages in Coventry Shearmen:

II REX   Now farewell, Sir Jaspar, brothur, to yoeu,
                    Kyng of Tawrus the most worthe;
                Sir Balthasar, also to you I bow;
                And I thanke you bothe of youre good cumpany.
                            (750-3)
III REX   ...Now he thatt made vs to mete on playne
                And offur to Mare in hir jeseyne,
                He geve vs grace in heyvin a-gayne
                    All to-geyder to mete.
                            (764-7)

Two factors might suggest direct influence from Coventry. First, the rhyme-scheme of 240-4 is that of Coventry, not Chester; second, the names of all three kings are given by the angel in Coventry 725-7, whereas in Chester this is the only passage in which the kings are named — hence the audience never learns the name of the first king and the address seems out of place. It is difficult to see, however, why such influence should occur at this point.

240-4   See also 240-7 note. The names of the three Magi are recorded by Bede, *Collectanea et Flores* (PL 94) — see also *Legenda Aurea*, citing Comestor: *Latine, Caspar, Balthasar, Melchior*. The kingdoms of the three were established by reference to the quotation from Psalms, see 8/338 + Latin; compare *Three Kings of Cologne*: "As Melchior, kyng of Nubye and of Arabum, þe which was leest of stature of body, took out of hys tresory a rounde appil of gold ... Balthasar, kyng of Saba, þat offrid encense to god, he was of a mene stature in his persone. And Iaspar, that was kyng of Thaars and of þe yle of Egriswill, þat offrid Mirre, he was moost of persone; and he was a blak Ethiope." Wakefield 14 has the same ascription; Coventry Shearmen 723-7 makes Balthasar king of Arraby, Melchior king of Aginare; the other cycles do not give names, nor does *Stanzaic Life*. Wakefield presents them in the sequence Jaspar (gold), Melchior (frankincense), Balthasar (myrrh); the Coventry angel lists them in the sequence Jaspar, Balthasar, Melchior. If the Chester sequence reflects the order of presentation, Jaspar offers frankincense, Balthasar myrrh and Melchior gold. Although the audience does not hear the first king named, B gives his name in a margin note (see TNs).

Since the kings had met at the Mount Victoriall and journeyed to Jerusalem together in play 8, there is no reason for them to separate for their return journey — compare *all in fere* 238. Where the kings meet only on the outskirts of Jerusalem, such a separation may be appropriate, as in Wakefield 14 and Coventry Shearmen; but even in York 17 and *Ludus Coventriae* 18 they do not finally separate. Wilson, noting that *Stanzaic Life* does not refer to their separation but traces their subsequent joint fortunes, 1729-84, argues that the parting represents part of an older dramatic level subsumed elsewhere by the *Stanzaic Life*'s influence. If, however, there is influence on the start of the parting-scene from Coventry and if 238 does point to a version without separation, it would be as plausible to argue that the separation is a later rather than an earlier feature. It may be compared both with the meeting of the kings at play 8 and also with the similar separation of the shepherds in play 7, where likewise the separation runs contrary to an earlier suggestion of unity — compare 7/536–7 note.

244–7 H's omission of *to* 244 is to be preferred in producing a more regular sequence of strongly and weakly stressed syllables.

offer 245 H is to be preferred to *offered* HmARB; the latter is an erroneous substitution, perhaps influenced by *made* 244, which suggests that *hee* is subject and so destroys meaning. It is, however, significant that Sharp's transcript of the Coventry Shearmen reads *offurde* for *offur* in this position.

249 *us* ARBH is to be preferred for meaning to *you* Hm, in view of *wee* 250. Hm may reflect confusion with *you* (2) 248.

253 *land* Compare Matthew 2/12: *in regionem suam* (AV "into their own country") and *land* 261, fixed by rhyme. *landes* BH suggests an idea of different nations and territories, aided by the idea of separation.

254 Deimling cites *talke* AR as evidence of the close connexion between these two manuscripts.

256–63, stanza 33   No manuscript has the form *tray* for *trayne* 259 required for rhyme — compare *tray* 1/209. *trame* B is evidently an error for *traine*.

258 *is* ARBH is to be preferred for syntax and meaning to its erroneous omission by Hm.

PLAY X

Dramatis Personae Herodes, Preco, Primus Miles, Secundus Miles, Doctor, Angelus, Josephe, Maria, Primus Mulier, Secundus Mulier, Demon.

NOTE 1. Compare 289, 350 and note on the possible number of non-speaking soldiers required.
2. An infant Christ is required.
3. Infants are carried by both women.

Locations
to Bethlem 150, 178, 188, 194, 233
into Egipte 258, 275.

Properties
For the Flight — asse 274, 478; mahometes 285, aliqua statua sive imago 288 + SD
Women — distaffe 303; this bote 355 *and note*
Soldiers — speare 195, 324, 362, 406
Demon — this crocked crambocke 438.

Costume
Herod — crowned in gould 89
Joseph — mantell 479
Soldiers — bassnetts bygge and broade 319
Infant Herod — in gould harnesse paynted wonders gaye 403-4, in silke araye 409, in gould and pyrrie that was so gaye 410.

NOTE Herod gives to Preco *a gaye garmente* 80.

Source
Matthew 2/13-8.

Play-heading The play contains four episodes — Flight into Egypt, Slaughter of Innocents, Death of Herod, Return from Egypt, although so much of the play is concerned with the summoning and commissioning of the soldiers (1-255) that this could be considered an episode in its own right. The Flight is dramatised in Wakefield 15, York 18 as a separate play before the Massacre; and in *Ludus Coventriae* 20/73-88, Coventry Shearmen 818-29, Digby *Killing of the Children* 233-80 as an episode within the account of the Massacre. The Massacre is dramatised in Wakefield 16, York 19,

Ludus Coventriae 20, Coventry Shearmen 768–900, Digby 1–380. Herod's death concludes *Ludus Coventriae* 20/168–284, Digby 381–8. No other cycle shows the Return.

Chester, like Wakefield, presents the Flight and Massacre before the Purification of the Virgin Mary. *Ludus Coventriae*, like the lost Beverley cycle, adopts the more traditional order, established by gospel harmonies such as Tatian and Augustine, in which the Purification preceded the Adoration of the Magi, the Flight and the Massacre — the order of Vincent of Beauvais, of *South English Nativity*, of *Cursor Mundi*, for example. Comestor reverses the positions of certain events, to give an order 'Adoration — Purification — Flight — Massacre', but essentially adopts the same logic, whereby the Purification must take place in Israel and hence precede the Flight. York does not show the Purification.

1–8, stanza 1   A stanza consisting entirely of three-stress lines.

1   *plelates* A Compare the cancelled *pl* B (see TNs).

2   *blamner* HmRH An error for *blaunner* resulting from miscounted minims. OED dates the last occurrence of the word as 1460, and MED's last example is a1450–1509. The word might therefore be unfamiliar not only to the scribes of the extant manuscripts but also to the scribes of the exemplar. *balmer* A is the only example of the word cited by OED; OED quotes Halliwell: "Apparently some kind of coloured cloth." *baunner* B suggests confusion with *banner* in the appropriate sense of "the distinctive banner of a lord", MED *baner(e)* n.1(a).

7   *under me* BH should be supplied for meaning and metre. The BH agreement here may be significant, since there is no obvious reason for the HmAR omission.

11   *you is lett*, "there will be restraint for you", an apparent euphemism for "you will be imprisoned". AR evidently did not understand the phrase, or wished to avoid repetition of *lett* as rhyme-word at 11 and 12.

15   *mar(e)* BH is to be preferred for meaning to *marye* HmAR.

16–24   Compare Matthew 2/16: *Tunc Herodes, videns quoniam illusus esset a Magis, iratus est valde; et mittens occidit omnes pueros...* (AV "Then Herod, when he saw that he was mocked of the wise men, was exceeding wroth, and sent forth, and slew all the children..."). Here Herod deduces that he has been deceived because the Magi have not returned; *this same nighte* 18 suggests that he expected their immediate return, although no such limit was previously stipulated. In other plays he is informed that the Magi have left his realm — Wakefield 16/145–7, York 19/107–13 (where he is also told that they found Christ), *Ludus Coventriae* 20/1–8, Coventry Shearmen 768–76, Digby *Killing* leaf 147, 16–21. Comestor, *Historia Scholastica*, 'In Evangelia' 10 (PL 198/1543), gives the standard account, found also in *Legenda Aurea*, *Stanzaic Life*, *South English Nativity*, etc.

PLAY X

though it be agaynst the right 23   This moral consciousness and deliberate defiance of moral law by Herod is unusual but prepares for the death of Herod at the end of the play. Compare 122 and 416–33.

a thousand 24   Compare 171. The number, by association with Apocalypse 7/4, is often said to be 144,000, as in *South English Nativity* (661), *Cursor Mundi* 11, 577–80, Wakefield 15/487–8.

22   *in your sight*   The pronoun comprehends those mentioned at 1–2 and 9–10, and presumably the audience. *in height* R is a substitution perhaps intended to remove the audience-reference.

31   *recked*   HmR is unlikely to be a form of *reck*, "to take care, heed"; probably a form of *wretched*, OED 3, "contemptible", is intended, with an exemplar misinterpretation of -*cc*- as a plosive form. *ricked* A suggests confusion with *rick*, "to twist"; *rocked* BH perhaps suggests "to move gently to and fro in a cradle", of the infant Christ.

35–8   Apparently by an eye-slip, R has jumped from the third line of the first quatrain to the fourth of the second, producing an erroneous omission which Deimling notes as one of the few examples of divergence between A and R.

39–40   No such justification is stated in Matthew, but it was commonly assumed, as in Comestor, *Historia Scholastica*, 'In Evangelia' 10 (PL 198/1543), and similarly in *Legenda Aurea*.

41   *prettye Pratte Pratt* is a common surname, probably from *prat* OED A "trick, piece of treachery or fraud", B "cunning, astute". *prettye* perhaps reinforces this sense with the meaning "clever, astute", OED II 2a. Possibly the summoning of the knights is merely a useful piece of stage-business, although the force of *mittens*, Matthew 2/10, is not clear. Compare the summoning in Wakefield 15/276 ff.

48 + SH   H erroneously ascribes the speech to *Doctor*. The text distinguishes *my messingere* (41) from *counselour* (125), and *Preco* and *Doctor* are clearly different characters.

54–6   R has replaced 54 by 56, with consequent loss of meaning and metre, and has supplied a new, non-rhyming 56. The change must be deliberate. Possibly R misunderstood 56 as meaning "And remain always in fear of you", and hence appropriate to Preco rather than Herod; whereas Herod hopes that Mahound will be with Preco and always remain in his company.

After 56 there is break in time and location, unspecified by SD.

58   *Grymball*   ARH supply the more usual form, *Grymbalde*, "helmet-bold", a common surname and etymologically appropriate to a knight.

Lancherdeepe   No such word or compound is recorded. OED cites *lancer* as a variant of *lancet*, "?small lance, dart"; the word may suggest therefore "one who drives a lance home deeply", perhaps even with sexual connotations. A and R supply forms with an additional *l*.

The fact that Preco mentions two names, each prefaced with *syr*, suggests that there are only two knights — both of whom have speeches. *Grymball* is evidently the name of the first knight — see 85. But later in the play, some variation occurs in the names and in the probable number of knights — see 226 and note.

61 *sowne* Hm, "to swoon", gives perfect rhyme and may be preferred to *swone* H; see further, OED *swoon*, v. *stonne* B, "be astounded", destroys rhyme; *swaine* AR destroys rhyme, and also meaning (unless taken as an infinitive of *sway*, OED v. I.1.b. "to fall or sink into a swoon", last exemplified in 1533). Deimling cites the variant as evidence of H's superiority.

64 + SH *Primus* York 19, *Ludus Coventriae* 20 and Coventry Shearmen have, like Chester, two soldiers; Wakefield 16 has three and Digby *Killing* four. But Chester seems to employ more soldiers at a later stage — compare 289, 350.

73–80, stanza 10   *in see* 73 ARBH is the better attested reading, but *on hye* Hm is possible for meaning and rhyme and has been used before in address to Herod — compare 8/146.

81–96, stanzas 11–4   The sequence of "Chester" stanzas is interrupted. Stanza 11 has the appearance of a regular Chester quatrain, but 81 contains three strongly stressed syllables instead of the expected four. Stanza 12, aabb, is defined as a single unit only by the following and preceding stanzas. Stanza 13, abab, is of the pattern of the address of 8/145–52 — compare particularly 89 with 8/146. Stanza 14, aaab, is of the same three-stress form as stanza 1.

81–4   "Thank you, my lord king; I am well pleased to my delight. Mighty Mahound, whom I have kept in my thoughts, preserve you in this place." *regent* is here taken as substantive, OED 1B, "one who rules or governs", attested from 1480; as adjective, "reigning", the word is attested only from 1555.

84 + SH   B's ascription of the speech to *Herode* is deliberate, since the required SH has been cancelled (see TNs), but 86 clearly shows the ascription to be impossible and it is difficult to see why this erroneous change has been made. It is tempting to speculate that B may have restored a SH cancelled in the exemplar to accommodate some textual changes which resulted in the break in stanza-form at 81–96.

90   *kesar* H is to be preferred to the erroneous HmR, A and B forms, all of which have final -*n* — perhaps from an exemplar confusion with the *n* of *kennes* following. The word was common, and it seems more probable that H corrected an exemplar error than that the H and HmARB forms originate in different exemplars. The word has a primary sense of "Roman emperor", and more generally "emperor, ruler", and is therefore a particularly hyperbolic reference for a tributary king.

   your bett, "any better than you". A, partially followed by R, substitutes *bendes at your beck*, "bows at your command", destroying rhyme; *lett* B, presumably "permission", gives no sense. *bet*, comparative of *good*, is last recorded by OED in 1586, which may explain the difficulties experienced by ARB.

91   *your grace* HmAR is apparently a flattering courtesy-title; OED records *grace* in such usage from 1500. *worship* B is recorded as a courtesy-title by OED from 1548 and could therefore be a later replacement, perhaps indicative of a shift in the reference of *grace* towards its modern use; but its meaning "a position of dignity", recorded by OED to 1606 is possible and might then suggest a substitution by *grace* after 1548. H has modified the word-order of B.

97–104, stanza 15   The stanza has the unusual rhyme-scheme aaabbbba in HmARH; *good* 97 B destroys rhyme by the substitution of a common collocation. No

PLAY X

alternative arrangement seems obvious from the text, but some corruption may be suspected.

125–32 Matthew does not suggest any such prompting. The suggestion of the Sanhedrin's support may derive from the idea that the Flight into Egypt symbolically suggested God's desertion of the Jews; see *Glossa Ordinaria* 'Evan. Matth.' 2/14,15 (PL 114/76). Hence the advice given to Herod suggests a collective responsibility on the part of the Jews. The idea of the massacre originates with the Jews in Wakefield 16/253–9 and York 19/139–59, but it is Herod's alone in *Ludus Coventriae* 20/9–21, Coventry Shearmen 789–92. Herod is also urged to retribution in the liturgical drama by figures such as the Malmedy Gladiator, the Freising Armiger, the Laon Archelaus.

131–2 Compare Matthew 2/16: *In Bethlehem, et in omnibus finibus eius* (AV "In Bethlehem, and in all the coasts thereof").

141 "Ascertain, in manly fashion, what sex they are" — compare 305–6, 363–4. 139–40, however, would lead one to expect the pronoun *you*, and *they* has no obvious antecedent. The statement gives sense only in conjunction with Herod's previous speech.

144 *they* RBH is to be preferred for meaning to *there* Hm; *the* A is presumably a formal variant of *they*.

145 *congeon* R is to be preferred to the scribally erroneous *commen* Hm and the variant forms in A, B and H, all evidently arising from an obscure exemplar reading.

153–68 Similar scruples are shown by the soldiers in Coventry Shearmen 793–800, until threatened with execution by Herod; a comic judgement on the unknightly nature of the deed is provided by the cowardly Watkin of the Digby *Killing*.

165 All manuscripts read *them*, presumably the exemplar reading, although the context would suggest *him*.

179–80 "All male children between the ages of one day old and two years old". Matthew 2/16 states *A bimatu et infra* (AV "From two years old and under"), but this more precise formulation is common — compare Comestor, *Historia Scholastica*, 'In Evangelia' 11 (PL 198/1543), *Legenda Aurea* 'De Innocentibus', and *Stanzaic Life*:

> from childer that weren of one night
> to tow 3er ful.
> (3402–3)

According to the chronology of the play, the action continues through the night of the Magi's visit (see 16–24 note), and the Massacre is ordained for *this nighte* 152. Hence there seems little point in the age-limits stipulated by Herod here. Chrysostom, cited by *Legenda Aurea* and hence by *Stanzaic Life*, argued that the star appeared a year before Christ's birth and that a further period of a year passed between Herod's intention and its execution because of the family feuds which compelled Herod to visit the Emperor in Rome, as Josephus records. By this account, the child was at least two years old — compare Comestor, *Historia Scholastica*, 'In Evangelia' 11 (PL 198/1544), and *Stanzaic Life*:

> Therfore knaue childer two 3er olde
> he sl[o]gh, but noght 3unger then thay.
> (3433–4)

Compare *Evangelium Thomae Latina* 1/1 (Tischendorf, p. 1649): *Erat autem Iesus annorum II cum ingressus est in Egyptum*. An alternative explanation of the age-limit is seen in Comestor, *Historia Scholastica*, 'In Evangelia' 11 (PL 198/1543), *Legenda Aurea*, and Mirk, 'De Innocentibus': "He was aferd, lest Crist þat made þe sterre brynge þe kynges so ferre, couþe haue turnet hym ynto dyuerse ages, and made hymselfe oldyr or 3ongyr, at his one lyst."

180 seems to contain only two strongly stressed syllables.

192   "And contain him in the rabble", i.e. ensure that Christ is among the children killed. *kill* A makes the sense clearer.

192 + SD   Compare 256 + SD. Since both SDs require the departure of the soldiers, either one of the SDs has been misplaced or erroneously duplicated in the exemplar; or the duplication suggests that the text contains two alternative developments — to move directly from 192 to 257 or to include 193–256. It may be significant that the latter section contains a new introduction for the soldiers containing names different from those given previously.

193–216, stanzas 27–30   These stanzas break the sequence of "Chester" stanzas. Stanza 27 is one of the abababab form; stanza 28 is apparently a regular Chester quatrain; stanza 29 reverts to the abababab form; stanza 30 is a further regular Chester quatrain. The change in stanza form should perhaps be considered in conjunction with other difficulties in this and the following speech — see notes below.

197–208   AR's omission of these lines is cited by Deimling as evidence of the close relationship of the two manuscripts. There is no obvious reason for the omission, which seems to be deliberate, although one may speculate that it might reflect some uncertainty about the status of the lines in the exemplar, unease at the metrical change (see 193–216 note) or at the inconsistencies (see 202 note, 225–9 note) or dissatisfaction with the comic belligerence of the speech (compare 308 + SH–20, 349–60 and notes).

197   *blab* BH may be preferred for meaning to *blacke* Hm. *blab-lipped*, "having swollen or protruding lips", may suggest the characteristic configuration of the lips of a suckling baby, but some association with *blabber*, "to babble", must be suspected.

202   *Syr Waradrake* No such name or compound is recorded elsewhere. It may represent a coined name, "War-drake", i.e. "War-dragon." But from 85 one might have deduced that the knight's name was *Lancherdeepe* — compare 226 and note.

209–12   212 has four main stresses; the other lines of the stanza have only three.

212   "All babes shall full sorely pay the penalty for that brat." ARB omit the syntactically redundant *they* HmH. B substitutes *die* for *bye* HmAH, apparently a semantic preference; *rew* R gives meaning but destroys rhyme.

216   *not* ARBH is to be preferred to *non* Hm for meaning.
   scathe BH is to be preferred to the scribally erroneous *scatche* Hm and the subsituted *searche* AR for meaning.

217–24   AR's omission of these lines has no obvious reason but has the effect of removing reference to the war with Scotland.

No specific battle with the Scots is indicated or necessarily intended by the passage, but it is probable that a sixteenth-century Chester audience would associate such a reference with the English victory over the Scots at Flodden Field in 1513 when some 10,000 Scots, including leading nobles and churchmen, were killed. The battle had particular local connexions, in that the action of a company of archers under Sir Edward Stanley, Earl of Derby (Lancashire), was decisive in the victory. The battle is celebrated in the last extant poem of the alliterative long line, *Scottish Feilde*, written by a gentleman of Bagulay, Cheshire, seat of the Legh family.

219   *sett by* HmAR is evidently a phrasal verb, "set aside, disregard"; but BH regard *by* as preposition and require *not*, "I set no store by their vaunts."

225–8   The quatrain is isolated in A as a result of A's previous and subsequent omission. This isolation may have influenced Bellin to omit it from R, or perhaps he was conscious of the inconsistency resulting from 126 — a previous omission in AR removes the inconsistency of name at 202 (see note).

226   *Syr Grymbald Lancherdeepe* Compare 58, 85 and 202 and notes. What had previously represented the names of two knights now appears as the name of a single knight. The inconsistency could be removed only by omitting either this identification or the former one, presumably the whole scene of 57–72.

229–32   AR's omission removes the final reference to the Scottish war.

233–40, stanza 33   The last four lines of the stanza contain three strongly stressed syllables each, in the manner of stanza 1.

237   *gedlinge* H may be preferred to *geldinge* HmARB as a variant of *gadling*, "low-born, base fellow". Compare 8/307 and 8/326 notes.

243–52   Deimling notes R's omission of 245–52 as one of the few slight differences between A and R. The omission was apparently deliberate, since R supplies a concluding statement at 243–4. The first soldier duplicates a reference to Samson made at 164 by the second soldier, although it is debatable how far such duplication may have affected R's omission.

252   *yet* H may be preferred to *yett yett* HmAB in avoiding repetition and producing a more regular sequence of strongly and weakly stressed syllables, but HmAB is dramatically effective.

254   *losingere* HmB does not seem to have been familiar to AR and H, although it was a word in current use. *lossayne* H gives no sense, although *losaniour* is a recorded variant of *losengere*. *solingere* AR seems to be a mindless transposition of the letters of *losenger*.

257–63   Chester gives no indication that the angel appears to Joseph *in somnis*, Matthew 2/13 (AV "in a dream"); compare 9/223 note and contrast Wakefield 15/1, York 18/37, *Ludus Coventriae* 20/73, Digby *Killing* 232, all of which indicate Joseph's sleep. Coventry Shearmen 817–22 does not specify the sleep — the angel there addresses both Joseph and Mary; but sleep may be inferred from Joseph's *Aryse up Mare* 823.

In Wakefield 15, York 18 the warning and flight precede Herod's decision. *Ludus Coventriae* 20, Coventry Shearmen and Digby *Killing*, like Chester, do not indicate the time which elapses between Herod's decision and the angel's warning, or between the flight and the massacre; the Gospel of Pseudo-Matthew 17 claims that the angel appeared *ante unum vero diem* before the massacre.

259 With the B-reading, compare Matthew 2/13: *Accipe puerum et matrem eius* (AV "Take the young child and his mother"). B may well be correct, since HmARH have no counterpart to the angel's specific and primary injunction to take Jesus. A confusion of long *s* and *f* could underlie the HmARH form, which was clearly that of the exemplar.

264 + SD R has introduced here the first part of 288 + SD, omitting *et* (1) and erroneously reading *ingradientur* for *ingrediatur*. The SD is, however, appropriate only at 288. Since AR omit 288 + SD, it must be assumed that in writing A Bellin was uncertain about the position or correctness of the SD, but in writing R he decided to include it and erroneously inserted it after the first speech of the angel instead of after the second. Such an error might perhaps support the view that in R Bellin was working primarily from A but simultaneously checking against the exemplar.

267-74 Compare 281-2, 492-3. No reference is made to either the ass or the accompanying angel in Matthew, or in Wakefield 15, *Ludus Coventriae* 20, Coventry Shearmen. The ass, but not the accompanying angel, appears in York 18/204-6, where Mary is said to ride, and in Digby *Killing* 280. Parallels should be sought in visual representations of the Flight.

274-5 "You must sit on my ass, so that we may come to Egypt." On *hit to*, see *hitten*, MED 4(a). As here rendered, *hitt* is subjunctive; but if *tell* A, *till* BH is accepted, *hitt* may be taken as indicative.

279-80 *yt* 279 is slightly ambiguous, referring either to the journey to Egypt or to the necessity of obeying Joseph. See also 474-81 note.

285-8 + SD Compare Gospel of Pseudo-Matthew 23: *Factum est autem cum beatissima Maria cum infantulo templum fuisset ingressa, universa idola prostrata sunt in terram, ita ut omnia convulsa iacerent penitus et confracta in faciem suam; et sic se nihil esse evidenter docuerunt.* So Comestor, *Historia Scholastica*, 'In Evangelia' 10 (PL 198/1544), citing the same biblical quotation as Chester and followed by *Legenda Aurea* and *Stanzaic Life* 3317-24.

The text cited is Isaiah 19/1: AV "[The burden of Egypt]. Behold, the Lord rideth upon a swift cloud, and shall come into Egypt; and the idols of Egypt shall be moved at his presence." The Chester version differs from the Vulgate:
 movebuntur] Vulg. commovebuntur   domini exercituum] Vulg. eius
while *ingredietur* H is to be preferred to *ingrediatur* Hm, *ingredetur* B as reflecting the Vulgate reading.
 cadet H is to be preferred to the scribally erroneous *caldet* Hm and *cadat* B.
 On AR's omission of the SD, see 264 + SD note.
 The only other English play to mention the fall of the images is Digby *Killing* 243-4 and 280 + SD.

289-96, stanza 40   291 has a rough metre and does not rhyme in HmARB. *all to thrast* H gives a more regular sequence of strongly and weakly stressed syllables and perfect rhyme; *in haste* AR gives rhyme at the expense of meaning.

PLAY X

clowetes 292 — *about us* 296, the b-rhyme, requires the former to be disyllabic. *awaie* AR destroys rhyme, suggesting that the women are afraid of the soldiers in advance, although they clearly are not; possibly AR were not conscious of the rhyme.

289 *fellowes* HmRBH suggests more soldiers than the two speakers — compare *all thy fellowes with thee* 350. *fellowe* A limits address to the second soldier only.

haste downe ARB may be preferred to *have/hase don(n)e* HmH; the latter suggests some unspecified delaying action by the second soldier.

hie B is to be preferred to *hyses* HmH, which is not an acceptable imperative form. As it stands, however, the line seems to lack a weakly stressed syllable, and *hastes downe* A is metrically preferable to HmBH here. It seems strange that *hast downe* occurs three times in R, twice in A, once in B and not at all in HmH in this line.

296+SH, 301+SH, 312+SH   Hm erroneously uses a masculine adjectival form; B additionally erroneously supplies *Miles* at 296+SH and 301+SH, but has corrected both adjective and noun errors by 312+SH. H is correct in all instances. AR agree with H at 296+SH and 301+SH, but then begin masculine reference for all SHs in *Mulier* which they contain. At 321+SH, H uses a feminine adjectival form with *Miles*. The confusion probably results from the mechanical continuation of an adjectival form in a context of changing masculine and feminine reference. Such continuation would be particularly understandable if the exemplar contained an abbreviated form. The SHs provide an interesting indication of the different degrees of intelligent attention paid by the scribes to their exemplar.

297-304, stanza 41   *biche* 297 ARBH is to be preferred for rhyme to *dogge* Hm. Hm may have felt that masculine reference was semantically more appropriate to the soldiers.

syche 298 ARBH is to be preferred for rhyme to *stike* Hm.

stiche 299 Hm is formally preferable for rhyme to *suche* ARBH

298-9   The first woman plays upon the two words, *quen* — "queen" and "prostitute", for as knight to the king the soldier's *dame* is the queen.

daystard 298 seems to be a form of *dastard*, MED n. "worthless fellow, wretch ..... coward". The word is recorded in OED from 1440 onwards and was current at the time of the extant manuscripts, but it does not seem to have been recognised by the scribes — although possibly the absence of final -*d* in ARBH represents the common transmission of an exemplar error. The word then would seem more readily applicable to the soldier and *thou*, rather than the *thy* of all manuscripts, would be required; if so, scribal confusion is the more understandable. *daster* AR is apparently a scribal error; *deighter* B is a replacement by a familiar form which destroys meaning; *drister* H is apparently a nonce-word.

299   "She burned a kiln, every bit." The expression is clearly one of abuse. Probably a malt-kiln, where malt was dried in brewing, is intended, the suggestion being that the soldier's mistress (the queen?) is a common ale-wife. Compare the attacks on false brewers at 450-3 and 17/277-336; also the term *ale-knight*, "votary of an ale-house", which may give added point to the jibe here. *knave* AR is a substitution which suggests infanticide.

It may be noted that an added dimension to this exchange between soldier and citizen is given by the fact that Chester was a garrison city.

303 A distaff is the weapon also of the women in Digby *Killing* 329–30, 334, 347. In Coventry Shearmen, one woman wields a pot-ladle 864. Blows are struck by the second woman at Coventry and by all the women at Wakefield.

305–12, stanza 42   The b-rhyme, *areste* 308—*peace* 312 (pronounced *pesse*), is imperfect. *areste* seems fixed by its repetition at 309, and is used for its ironically legalistic overtones; if the imperfect rhyme is not acceptable, some alternative to *peace* (e.g. *rest*) must be postulated.

309 and 310 have three strongly stressed syllables instead of the expected four.

308 + SH–20   A has omitted 312 + SH–20 in moving from fol.71^r to fol.71^v. The effect is to remove the women's comic belligerence. Compare 369–72 note. R has not corrected the omission, but further omits the preceding quatrain; A's speech-sequence: *Primus Miles—Primus Mulier—Secundus Miles, Prima Mulier—Secundus Mulier* has been 'balanced' by R's omission of the second speech. Deimling notes the omission of 312 + SH–20 as evidence of the close relationship of AR.

313–4   *rotten* Some play is apparently intended on *rotten*, "morally, socially or politically corrupt", and *rotten*, a variant form of *ratton*, "a rat" — compare 3/179. The woman sees the soldier as a rat-catcher with a stick. Compare also *styck-tode* 314, "toad-stabber".

stallon 314 is a variant of *stallion*, OED 1, a horse "kept for the purpose of serving mares" and, from 1533, 2b "a man of lascivious life." *stytton* is not other-wise recorded; *stibbon* H is perhaps intended as a variant of *stubborn*.

325–36   According to the SDs, the first child (of the first woman) is killed by the first soldier after 344 and the second child (of the second woman) is killed by the second soldier after 376. Therefore, the pattern of events in this section is not clear. It would seem that at 305–12, the first soldier takes, inspects and kills the first child, and at 313–24 the second soldier takes, inspects and kills the second child, while at 325–36 the women lament together. 330–2 can only be motivated by the child's death. This scene is apparently then repeated — 337–44 corresponding to 305–12, 361–76 to 313–24 — even to verbal echoes in 323–4/362 and 313–5/369–70. But on the second occasion the response is one of defiant belligerence to the last; contrast the instruction of the second woman at 335–6 to the soldier to convey her blow to the king with the revelation at 384 that her child is Herod's son. There seem to be two possible explanations. The simplest is to assume that there are four women with children accosted by the soldiers, with similar actions but very different outcomes; hence the continuing SHs, *Prima* and *Secunda Mulier*, conceal a change of character. The existence of four women might explain references which suggest that there were also more than two knights. The more tenuous alternative is to assume that 305–36 and 337–76 represent different versions of the massacre, giving different effects.

The laments of the women are suggested by Matthew 2/17–18, and were a feature of the liturgical drama. Here, however, the sense of sorrow is subsumed under the vindictiveness and comic belligerence of the women.

326   *abyd* Hm must represent a past tense, more conventionally represented by *abode* BH. A and R attempt in different ways to make sense of the form.

335–6   "Take this to the king from me, and take that — I sent it to him." *sennd* must be past tense for perfect rhyme with *torment* 332; cf. *sente* RB: *saye it I* B avoids the

PLAY X   155

problem of the reference of *yt*. The injunction to go to the king is superfluous when the woman is in the king's employ — see 325–36 note and compare 381–4.

336   *Parnell*   A contracted form of *Petronella*; compare E. G. Withycombe (*Christian Names* p.233): "*Pernel* or *Parnel*, for some reason, came to be used as a generic term for a priest's concubine, and is so used as early as 1362 in *Piers Plowman*. Later it meant any loose woman, and survived in dialectal use until the 18th century."

344 + SD   *transfodiet* RBH is to be preferred to the scribally erroneous *trasfodiet* Hm.
   Compare 325–36 note; A's omission of the SD removes a problem of consistency.

349–60   R's omission seems to be a deliberate attempt to limit the violence and vindictiveness of the speech.
   With 349–50, compare 378, 387.

350   *all thy fellowes*   See also 289 note, 326–36 note. The woman evidently strikes five blows — compare *thou* at 353, 354, 356, 357 (twice). Although this may suggest five knights, it would be possible to argue that the pronouns and number of blows are no guide to number since the woman merely lays about her. If, as suggested at 325–36 note, four knights were envisaged, the distinction between the *fowle harlott* 353 and the *knight* 354 might suggest that the four knights were accompanied by the Doctor — see 390 and note.

354   *to make a knott*   Perhaps playing on the senses "to make an end of the matter" (compare *knotte* MED 2(b), and (c)), and "to cause a lump" (compare *knotte* MED 7(b)).

355   *bote* has two possible meanings — "boot", in which case the woman either kicks the soldier or removes her shoe and hits him with it; or "bundle, bolt of cloth", in which the baby was wrapped (compare *bolt* MED 4), producing a more poignantly ineffectual response.

367   i.e. the orifices of anus and penis only, lacking the third "hole", the female pudendum; see *hole* MED 2. *under the tayle* is used generally, "in the pelvic area".

369–76, stanza 50   A omits the first quatrain, for no apparent reason, while R omits the whole stanza, perhaps to lessen the impression of violence — compare 349–60 note. Deimling notes the common omission of AR as evidence of their close connexion.

370   *bid* BH is to be preferred for meaning to *byde* Hm.

378–9   *all* 378 BH may be preferred in producing a more regular sequence of strongly and weakly stressed syllables, and also perhaps for meaning — "the whole pack of you" being perhaps more forceful. The fact that in B *all* is a later scribal insertion (see TNs) indicates that it was probably in the exemplar but that its status was not immediately obvious — hence its absence from HmAR. Compare 350.
   theffe 379 AB suggests that the speech is addressed to the second soldier, an idea continued in *thou* 379 B; but *you* 378, 379, 380 suggests plural address, and *rowte* is collective.

381–92 Compare Macrobius, *Saturnalia* 2/4: *Cum audisset inter pueros, quos in Syria Herodes rex Iudaeorum intra bimatum iussit interfici, filium quoque eius occisum, ait: 'Mallem est Herodis porcus esse quam filius'* — a misapplication of a comment made elsewhere of Herod's treatment of his sons. The story is taken up and developed in *Legenda Aurea* 'De Innocentibus', whence *Stanzaic Life*:

> For one sone of his there was slayn
> that was 3iuen to keping.
> (3453–4)

Herod recognises the death as punishment at 399–400.

381 The line contains only three strongly stressed syllables instead of the expected four. B supplies the necessary additional syllables, but at the expense of rhyme.

390 *Syr John* Compare OED *John* 3: 'Sir John': "familiar or contemptuous appellation for a priest: from *Sir* as rendering *dominus* at the Universities." The implication may be that the Doctor has accompanied the soldiers. Compare 350 note.

393–6 393–6 have three strongly stressed syllables instead of the expected four; at 393 H has an exclamatory four-stress line in the manner of 377. At 394 *to* ABH may be preferred as producing a regular four-stress line; the word is not syntactically necessary — hence its omission from HmA — compare its omission by B at 381.

meanye 395 ARBH is to be preferred for meaning to *contreye* Hm which implies a non-existent distinction (unless Herod's non-Jewish ancestry is treated literally, or he is to be considered a Roman with Roman soldiers).

be 396 H destroys the b-rhyme, substituting an a-rhyme; the scribe perhaps mistook the stanza-structure because of the metre of the preceding lines.

403–4 Compare 409–14. Evidently the child was costumed as a miniature Herod, with kingly and knightly accoutrements, a worldly infant-king to balance the spiritual infant-king, Christ. Such delicate gold-work might well demonstrate the skill of the goldsmiths, the performing guild.

406 *theire speares* Only one spear is mentioned at 362 and 376+SD.

411 *by this daye* Only Hm has this phrase; *by his araye* ARBH gives excellent meaning, but repeats the rhyme-word of 409 in a stanza already containing the repeated rhyme-word *sonne* at 412, 416.

417–33 Accounts of the death of Herod originate in Josephus. The death, in 3 B.C., occurred some time after the Massacre, compare Comestor, *Historia Scholastica*, 'In Evangelia' 23 (PL 198/1549): [Joseph] *qui rediens ab Aegypto post annos septem*. In Chester, *Ludus Coventriae* and Digby *Killing*, the death follows immediately on the Massacre, Chester alone showing the death of Herod's son.

The main details of Herod's last illness, described by Josephus, are summarised in *Legenda Aurea* 'De Innocentibus': *Ipse autem Herodes cum jam annos lxx haberet, in gravissimam aegritudinem cecidit, nam febre valida, prurigine corporis, continuis tormentis, pedum inflammatione, vermescentibus testiculis, intolerabili foetore, crebro anhelitu et interruptis suspiriis torquebatur*. This illness had for long been regarded as punishment for the Massacre; see *Historia Iosephi Fabrii Lignarii* (Tischendorf) 9. The illness was not the final cause of Herod's death — Mirk reports that he killed himself with a knife. Some trace of his sin of despair can be seen in 420–1.

PLAY X 157

York 19 shows Herod finally tormented by the fear that Christ may have escaped, while Coventry Shearmen 888–91 has Nuncios confirm Jesus' escape to the king — both looking to the apocryphal infancy gospels rather than to Josephus.

417–25, stanza 56   The stanza contains nine lines, abbbcdddc. 417 does not fit the rhyme-scheme and is superfluous; A attempts to create a rhyme-form *mone* which destroys meaning. The line, which must have been present in the exemplar, separates the potential a-rhyme of stanza 56 from the b-rhyme of stanza 55.

419 contains three stressed syllables instead of the expected four, except in B, where additional syllables are appropriately supplied; but there can be no suggestion that 419 is the misplaced fourth line of the quatrain. Its omission would not impair the sense of the stanza.

420 is omitted in H, apparently to give the eight line stanza, but its omission leaves 421 as a weak continuation from 419.

423 and 424 are reversed in H, thereby avoiding the broken construction of HmARB.

423   The Demon is both an appropriate judgment upon Herod and a convenient way of removing the body from the stage. Compare *Ludus Coventriae* 20/233–45 where Diabolus similarly removes the body.

430–1   Rosemary Woolf (*The English Mystery Plays* (London, 1972), p.210 and p.393, fn.83) notes these lines as a travesty of the medieval testament form, seen also in *Piers Plowman* B, Passus 6, 88–9. She suggests possible influence from Comestor, *Historia Scholastica*, 'In Evangelia' 14 (PL 198/1545); chapter heading: *De priori testamento Herodis, et odio ipsius, et Antipatre*.

433 + SD   In the margin beside 441 H has a form of the SD similar to that in HmARB but cancelled (see TNs). Possibly a different SD was composed for H and inserted, but the exemplar SD was then added, on the mistaken belief that it had been omitted in error, and that change in turn subsequently cancelled.

434   The line has, unusually, six alliterating stressed syllables.

438   *camrocke* AR or *cambroke* BH are to be preferred to the scribally erroneous *crambocke* Hm, where *r* has been misplaced, perhaps by influence from the preceding word.

439–41   By decree of the fourth Lateran Council (1215), rulers who failed to rid their lands of heresy were threatened with deposition and loss of realms. In consequence, many rulers imposed a death penalty for heresy which they imposed on heretics convicted under canon law and delivered to the civil authority for punishment. Although no single method of execution for heresy was invoked, the devil's threat of eternal damnation for the heretic, such as Herod — himself a ruler now deposed — would inevitably suggest to a later sixteenth-century audience the civil execution of heretics by burning, a form of execution applied particularly during the reign of Mary, although practised by others before.

444   The omission of *there* (1) ARB may be preferred in removing a repeated word and producing a more regular sequence of strongly and weakly stressed syllables. A less regular version results from H's omission of two syllables.

449   "So that his body will never go away"; *to* is here purposive.

450–7, stanza 60   *grace* 453 ARBH is to be preferred to *grave* Hm for rhyme and meaning.

No manuscript has the form *dayes* for *daye* 457 required for rhyme; *daye* was clearly an exemplar error.

450–2   "No more shall you do wrong. By my troth, whoever fills their measures [of ale] dishonestly shall keep this lord company." *you* 450 refers to the dead Herod. R and BH seek to make *you* an audience address, BH by supplying *tapstars* and thus giving a specific reference for *that*, and R by requiring some verb such as *commit* to be understood.

456   *ever* BH may be preferred as supplying the additional syllable for a line which, in HmAR, contains only three stressed syllables instead of the expected four.

457 + SH   Compare Matthew 2/19: *Ecce angelus Domini apparuit in somnis Ioseph in Aegypto* (AV "Behold, an angel of the Lord appeareth in a dream to Joseph in Egypt"). *aryse* 458 represents the Vulgate *surge* and Chester again gives no suggestion of a state of sleep.

The period of sojourn in Egypt varies among commentators. Compare, for example, Comestor, cited under 417–33 note: see also R. E. Witt's summary ('The Flight into Egypt', *Studia Patristica* II (1972) p.94): "For Hippolytus the Holy Family stayed in Egypt three and a half years, a period which is almost the same as the three years and seven months of the Ethiopic version. The apocryphal *Gospel of St. Thomas* represents Jesus as being three years old when he was taken into Egypt and as having remained there for twelve months in the house of a certain widow ... Later patristic authors, when they mention the Anachoresis can stretch the length of time: thus St. Antonine and St. Thomas state that the total period in Egypt came to seven years." Here, since retribution followed immediately upon the massacre, the implication is that the sojourn was short.

460   With B's omission of *Ihesu*, compare Matthew 2/20: *Accipe puerum et matrem eius* (AV "Take the young child and his mother").

461   *Judye* Matthew 2/20 refers to *terram Israel* (AV "the land of Israel), and at 2/22 expressly states that the Holy Family did not go to Judea because they were warned in a dream of the hostile intent of Herod's successor, but went to Nazareth in Galilee, as Comestor also reports, *Historia Scholastica*, 'In Evangelia' 23 (PL 198/1549). But compare *Stanzaic Life*:
>This ʒer at aungeles forwarning
>come Ihesu aʒayn to Iude.
>(3613–4)

470–1   *a whome* 470 Hm and *agayne* 471 Hm are reversed in ARBH. Deimling cites the erroneous *be againe* 470 AR as evidence of the close relationship between the two manuscripts. The metre of both lines is somewhat rough.

474–81   The episode provides a final example of Joseph's function; compare 7/507–39 note and Pseudo-Chrysostom, *In Matthaeum*, Homilia 2 (PG 56/645): *Vides quia Joseph non ad conjugium Mariae erat electus, sed ad ministerium eius? Eunte autem illa in Aegyptum et redeunte, nisi desponsata illi fuisset, quis ministerium ei tantae necessitatis impleret.*

PLAY X

488 *soonne* Hm is to be preferred to the omission in ARBH in supplying an additional syllable producing the expected four-stress line.

489+SH has been misplaced by one quatrain in H.

497 Compare *Stanzaic Life*, introducing the quotation from Isaiah cited at 288+SD:

> that spak þe prophete Ysaye
> a twousand ʒere befor in faye.
> (3319–20)

thousande ARB is to be preferred to the scribally erroneous *thousands* Hm; *hundreth* H is apparently a substitution, of improbable underestimation.

497+Latin The statement of Hoseah 11/1 here appears in the form in which it is quoted by Matthew 2/15; AV "Out of Egypt have I called my son." To the Vulgate quotation, Chester adds *ut salvum faciet populum meum* — compare Matthew 1/21: *Ipse enim salvum faciet populum suum a peccatis eorum* (AV "For he shall save his people from their sins").

PLAY XI

Dramatis Personae Symeon, Anna Vidua, Angelus, Maria, Josephe, Primus Doctor, Deus, Secundus Doctor, Tertius Doctor.

> *NOTE* Unless *Deus* 231–334 is identified with the infant Christ, an infant Christ is also required.

Locations
the temple 131 *in* Jerusalem, 4, 212, the cittye 218
alio loco procull a templo 118 + SD.

Properties
Temple — booke 19, 53, librum 24 + SD, 40 + SD; altare 40 + SD
Mary's offering — dove-byrdes two 132, or a turtle 133, *or* bryddes three 140
Joseph's offering — virgin waxe 144.

> *NOTE* *write* 39, 63, *scriberet* 40 + SD suggest that writing materials are needed, while *scrape* 37, 62, *fabricabit* 40 + SD suggest that a means of erasure is needed.

Costume
The doctors — so gaye in furres fine 314.

Sources
Purification — Luke 2/22–39
Doctors — Luke 2/41–51; but sharing significant features with the Doctors episodes in Wakefield, York and Coventry Weavers.

Play-heading Reference is made only to the first section of the play, the Purification of the Virgin Mary, 1–206; the remainder of the play presents Christ Before the Doctors. On the place of the former in the chronology of the Nativity, see 10/*Play-heading* note. The Feast of the Purification is 2 February and is celebrated not only by Roman Catholics but also by the Anglican Church, in which it is a red-letter festival. It is also known as Candlemas.

The two episodes are consecutive in Luke, but Chester omits reference to the twelve year gap between them. Both require the same temple-set.

The Purification is also dramatised in Wakefield 17 (incomplete), *Ludus Coventriae* 19, Coventry Weavers 367–721 (incomplete),

PLAY XI 161

Digby *Killing of the Children* 389–566. Christ Before the Doctors is also dramatised in Wakefield 18 (incomplete), York 18, *Ludus Coventriae* 21, Coventry Weavers 722–1192. The Chester, Wakefield, York and Coventry versions of the Doctors play derive from a common version; see Greg and Salter, *Chester Play Studies*, pp.101–20, '"Christ and the Doctors" and the York Play'.

3 Although Luke does not mention Simeon's age, the sense that his life has been divinely prolonged past the normal span that he might see Christ has led commentators to assume that he was old. Compare Comestor, *Historia Scholastica*, 'In Evangelia' 9 (PL 198/1542): *Simeon senex*, Stanzaic Life 2678 "þat old mon". His age was more precisely defined by tradition; compare *Cursor Mundi*:

Þer was a good holy mon
In þe temple wonyng þon
Of six score ȝeere, and symeon hiȝt.
(11, 313–6)

South English Nativity: "An hundred and twelue ȝer he was old" (582). Augustine, Sermo 163 (PL 38/891), sees him preserved from death by piety. His age was held to be a factor in his election as witness; compare *Glossa Ordinaria*, 'Evang. Luc.' 2/25 (PL 114/250) and Ambrose, *Expositio in Lucam* 2/58 (PL 15/1655). As such, he was a traditional witness to Christ's divinity.

4 *preist* Luke does not say that Simeon was a priest; the occupational ascription derives from Gospel of Nicodemus 16 (trans. M. R. James): "For we all know the blessed Simeon, the high priest, which received Jesus in his hands in the temple." The reporters of the Gospel of Nicodemus, Charinus and Lenthius, are allegedly Simeon's sons. Similar identification is provided in *Ludus Coventriae* 19/1: "prest in jherusalem"; in Coventry Weavers Joseph calls him *bysschope* 650, and he is in charge of the temple; in Digby *Killing*, where he receives Jesus, Jesus is delivered into a "prestes handes" 417.

This line is the only key to Simeon's identity until 41. Compare 124, 135, 142.

5–8 A conventional lament on the discomforts of old age. Contrast *South English Nativity*:

Þulke byheste be abod so longe þat he was in feblesse ybrouht,
And naþeles for hope him to se is elde greuede him nouht.
(591–2)

More extended laments by Simeon about his aged infirmity are in Wakefield 17/1–48 and *Ludus Coventriae* 19/1–20.

11–2 Compare Luke 16/22, where the dead Lazarus *portaretur ab angelis in sinum Abrahae* (AV "was carried by the angels into Abraham's bosom"). Abraham's bosom was traditionally regarded as the limbo of the patriarchs, where the saints of the Old Covenant remained until the coming of Christ. Simeon is shown there in 17/41–56.

13 *but* is attested by all manuscripts and was clearly the exemplar reading. Although here treated as conjunction, it should more properly be regarded as a variant of *bout*, "without" and the line taken as a continuation of 12.

19   The singular *booke* Hm is seen also in 53, 86, and in 117 AR; but *bokes* ARBH is here better attested and probably more appropriately suggests a collection of books, from which Simeon selects one. Compare 50.

23   *deed* Hm is apparently a variant of *dyed* H, past tense; but AR and B take it as past participle and, by supplying an additional syllable, produce a more regular sequence of strongly and weakly stressed syllables.

24 + SD   Isaiah 7/14: AV "Behold, a virgin shall conceive, and bear a son" etc.

25ff.   The miracle of Simeon's book seems to be found in English only here and in *Stanzaic Life* and constitutes a further significant similarity between the two works. Foster compares Nicephorus Callistus, *Ecclesiasticae Historiae* 1/12 (PG 145/670).

40 + SD   *Stanzaic Life* 2761–4 states that on the first occasion Simeon merely laid the book down, and on neither occasion does it indicate how the alteration was effected; compare Nicephorus Callistus, *loc.cit. Stanzaic Life*:

>   then leuet he þat fullily
>   ther hade þe holy gost ben tho
>   (2798–9)

provides a vague explanation.

In *Stanzaic Life* a day elapses before Simeon's discovery — cf. *anoþer day* 2765, *the day bifore* 2770. Here, the action is apparently continuous.

40 + SH–210   The H omission represents a loss between the end of the present fol.58^v and the start of fol.59^r. 59^r bears the number *Fol:lxi* (vol.I, xxvi); fols. 57–8 are by Scribe C, while 59–62 are by scribe A (vol.I, xxiv). The omission represents the contents of two folios, perhaps lost when the manuscript was transferred to guards. The book-miracle is thereby excised from H.

40 + SH   Anna, a widow of 84 years of age (80 in Mirk, 82 in *Ludus Coventriae* 19/151; compare 194), and a prophetess (*prophetissa*) first appears in Luke 2/36–8 after the Nunc Dimittis and takes no part in the book-miracle in *Stanzaic Life*; see also Ambrose, *Expositio in Lucam* 2/62 (PL 15/1656–7), Bede, *In Lucae Evangelium Expositio*, 1/2 (PL 92/347), and *Glossa Ordinaria*, 'Evang. Luc.' 2/36 (PL 114/251).

49–55, stanza 7   All manuscripts lack an a-rhyme line in the second quatrain. the line has perhaps been omitted before 53, where *to* has no obvious antecedent. The placing of 49–52 after 53–5 in B may suggest some confusion in the exemplar arrangement, or a conscious scribal re-arrangement to clarify in advance the reference to *this writing* 51.

51–2   "But it seems to me that he wrote this passage wonderfully and it seems to me a marvel." B's omission of *that* improves meaning and metre. *this writinge* presumably refers to the contents of the book on the altar.

58   *red letters Stanzaic Life* 2769–80 makes no reference to the colour of ink.

71 + SD   Compare *Stanzaic Life*:

>   And hud his boke fro las ⁊ more
>   vnder lok for any cas.
>   (2787–8)

The difference is probably a response to the requirements of staging.

PLAY XI 163

100 The line corresponds to Luke 2/26: *Non visurum se mortem* (AV "That he should not see death"), where it refers to the promise of the Holy Ghost and is not part of a prayer by Simeon. The line here contains five strongly stressed syllables instead of the expected four.

104–10, stanza 14   The additional line, supplied after 110 by ARB, is necessary for a regular stanza-form and is to be preferred to Hm, where it has been omitted in error; the omission was perhaps facilitated by the fact that the stanza contains only a-rhymes and that the additional line is not necessary for syntactical and semantic completeness.

105   Compare Luke 2/25-6: *Et Spiritus Sanctus erat in eo. Et responsum acceperat a Spiritu Sancto...* (AV "And the Holy Ghost was upon him. And it was revealed unto him by the Holy Ghost...") On the use of the angel messenger here, compare Nicephorus, cited at 25 ff note; an angel is similarly used in Wakefield 17/73-8, *Ludus Coventriae* 19/41-50, and Coventry Weavers 293-9. In Wakefield and Coventry, a second angel is also used to announce Christ's arrival.

117   *Essayes* RB is to be preferred to the erroneous *Esaues* HmA.
boke AR is here preferable to *bookes* HmB; compare 19 note.

118 + SD   Compare Luke 2/25: *Exspectans consolationem Israel* (AV "Waiting for the consolation of Israel").

119–26   Compare Coventry Weavers 367-92, where the instructions are given to Mary by an angel and she relays them to Joseph.

121–4   So Luke 2/22, citing Leviticus chap. 12, from which details of the offering are taken.

127–30   Compare *Legenda Aurea*, 'De Purificatione Beatae Mariae Virginis': *Beata igitur virgo huic legi purificationis non tenebatur, quia non peperit suscepto semine, sed mistico spiramine*. *Legenda*, followed by *Stanzaic Life*, then rehearses the four reasons justifying the purification; compare Mirk, likewise citing the traditional justifications — to show humility, fulfil the law, prevent scandal and serve as an example to all Christian women to be similarly purified.

132–3   The offering is that for the poor. Compare Leviticus 12/8: *Sumet duos turtures vel duos pullos columbarum* (AV "She shall bring two turtles or two young pigeons"), cited by Luke 2/24.
The number of birds here involved is not clear. At 133 Joseph departs from the law in suggesting an alternative of only one turtle-dove. At 140 Mary claims to present *bryddes three*. Foster and Wilson have drawn attention to similar confusion in *Stanzaic Life*:

A turtur bridde or pigones two (2573)
A turture-brid and pygones two (2302)

a similarity which they hold shows the dependence of Chester upon *Stanzaic Life*. 2302 refers to the actual offering, 2573 to the requirements of the law.
Possibly the passages in *Stanzaic Life* are too widely separated to influence independently a confusion occupying only ten lines in Chester, particularly where Luke offers a clear statement. The wording in the *Life* differs otherwise from that in Chester. It is possible that the confusion in number at 133 results from a separation

of *two* from its noun — that originally *a turtle* read *turtles*, but that *two* was then misunderstood as an adverb (compare the AR variant), with corresponding alteration: G. McN. Rushforth, *Medieval Christian Imagery* (Oxford, 1936, p.282) comments: "Though Luke 2/24 (cf. Lev. 12/6–8) definitely speaks of two birds being offered, three are sometimes represented .... in later medieval art"; his footnote 4 comments that in Chester the alternative in Luke 2/24 was misunderstood, and cites B. Zeitblom's altar-piece (1497) in Stuttgart Museum where "Joseph's basket contains four birds, i.e. both alternatives."

With 140, compare Coventry Weavers:
> Unto the tempull thatt thou schuldist goo,
> And to whyt turtuls with the also
> And present the chyld and them to,
> All iij of them in offeryng
> (375–8)

an idea similarly indicated in Digby *Killing*, 436 + SD: "Her shall symeon receyve of maria, Iesu and ij dowis", the whole termed *myn oblacion* 436. A dash after *bryddes* 140 would indicate that the offering consisted of two birds and one child, three items in all.

In *Ludus Coventriae* 19/116 the number of birds is not specified but Joseph takes *dowys and turtelys*; in Wakefield 17/125, Joseph refers to *turtels two*.

141–2 "As is fitting, sir, for your rank and for your office [of priest] also." No symbolic overtones seem indicated, although the appropriateness of the offering is developed in *Legenda Aurea* and *Stanzaic Life*.

143–4 Joseph's offering derives not from the Bible but from the ceremonial of Candlemas, the alternative name for the Feast of the Purification, where a procession of lighted candles which have been blessed forms an important part of the service. On the symbolic significance of the wax, see Fulbert, *Sermones ad Populum* 3 (PL 141/319), 'De Purificatione Beatae Mariae'. *Legenda Aurea*, 'De Purificatione', gives, as second reason for the candles: *Propter ostendendam virginis puritatem*, followed by *Stanzaic Life* 2873–940. The other reasons given by *Legenda Aurea*, relating to the origins of the celebration and its meaning for worshippers, would be inappropriate to the context of the historical event itself. In *Ludus Coventriae* 19/163–6, Joseph gives candles to Mary, Anna and Simeon, but without explanation; but in Digby *Killing*, Anna summons the virgins to worship Jesus with *tapers of wex* 462, and they process round the temple singing the Nunc Dimittis, after which Simeon explains the symbolism of the taper.

151–8, stanza 20   The b-rhymes, *harte* 154—*blys* 158, do not rhyme, although the words are attested by all manuscripts and seem to have been the exemplar reading. Corruption may be suspected.

Lines 151, 156, 157 seem to contain only three strongly stressed syllables, perhaps deliberately contributing to a lyric effect. *my* 151 ARB produces the more usual four stressed syllables for that line.

159–62   Compare *Legenda Aurea*, 'De Purificatione': *Senex puerum portabat, puer autem senem regebat*; cited also in *Stanzaic Life* 2712 + Latin.

166 + SD   The *Nunc Dimittis* or Song of Simeon derives from Luke 2/29–32. A rendering of the Latin follows at 167–74; there is no translation in *Stanzaic Life*.

PLAY XI

167-74   There are two minor discrepancies between the version here and the Vulgate.

bee 167 removes the sense that Simeon can now die peacefully contained in Vulgate *dimittis* (AV "depart"); but compare Wiclif (ed. Arnold; vol.III, p.61): "Þou levest now þi servaunt in pees."

lightninge 173, "enlightenment" — compare Vulgate *lumen ad revelationem Gentium* (AV "a light to lighten the Gentiles") and *Stanzaic Life* 2719: "Hele, liȝt, ioy of Israele." Chester excludes the specifically non-Judaic reference of the line.

175-82   Compare Luke 2/34: *In ruinam et in resurrectionem multorum in Israel* (AV "For the fall and rising again of many in Israel"); also Bede, *In Lucae Evangelium Expositio* 1/2 (PL 92/346): *Bene in resurrectionem quia lumen est, quia gloria plebis Israel ... ruiniae his qui offendunt verbum, nec credunt.*

183-4   The lines do not reflect closely Luke 2/34: *Et in signum cui contradicetur* (AV "And for a sign which shall be spoken against").

185-90   "For a sword of sorrow shall pass through your heart which men shall understand to mean the thoughts (that rise) in your heart — in sequence — from (seeing) men who shall act against you and try to create anguish for you." Compare the somewhat obscure passage in Luke 2/35: *Et tuam ipsius animam pertransibit gladius, ut revelentur ex multis cordibus cogitationes* (AV "Yea, a sword shall pierce through thy own soul also, that the thoughts of many hearts may be revealed"). Commentators generally regarded the passage as a reference to Mary's anguish at Christ's Passion; see Bede, *In Lucae Evangelium Expositio* 1/2 (PL 92/346), cited by *Glossa Ordinaria*, 'Evang. Luc.' 2/35 (PL 114/251), and Comestor, *Historia Scholastica*, 'In Evangelia' 9 (PL 198/1542). Similarly, *South English Nativity*:

>   For þat swerd was vr lordes deþ þat þoruout oure leuedies herte wende
>   Þo heo stod vndir þe rode and ysey þat þe Iewes him so schende.
>   (613-4)

Here *men* 187 is taken to mean "later generations", and *men* 189 "the Jews".

In *Ludus Coventriae* 19/87-90 Simeon utters these words to Anna as part of his prophecies before he sees Christ.

191-8, stanza 25   *yeaire* 193 AR is to be preferred for rhyme to *yeares* HmB.
No manuscript has *hase* 198 for *hast*, required for perfect rhyme.

197-8   198 does not seem to give good sense. Possibly the relative pronoun or *it* is to be understood; *it* B, referring to *godhead*, produces a rougher metre. Alternatively, *in* 197 has been erroneously substituted for some word such as *for* or *syth*, influenced by *in* at 195 and 198.

206 + SH-26   The episode of Christ before the Doctors here begins as if it follows immediately on the return from the Purification, although according to Luke 2/42 it occurred when Jesus was twelve years old, at the time of the feast of the Passover. Luke 2/43-4 indicates that Joseph and Mary had travelled a day's journey from Jerusalem before becoming anxious about Jesus, *existimantes autem illum esse in comitatu* (AV "supposing him to have been in the company"). They then first sought him among their kinsmen — compare 210 — and then returned to Jerusalem.

The episode is substantially that of the equivalent episode in Wakefield, York and Coventry Weavers. The analogues are cited in that order of cycle, but York is generally held to be the most appropriate base.

Carrie A. Harper comments ('A comparison between the Brome and Chester Plays of *Abraham and Isaac*, *Radcliffe College Monographs* 15 (1910), p.53): "Chester XI, which agrees with York XX and Towneley XVIII, has preserved in its quatrains the alternate rhymes which characterize the York stanza, ababababcdcd." Rhymes are certainly alternate, but the stanza-form varies considerably.

With this opening section, compare York 20/1–12:

JOS	Marie, of mirthis we may vs mene
	And trewly telle be-twixte vs twoo
	Of solempne sightis þat we haue sene
	In þat cite were we come froo.
MAR	Certis, Joseph, 3e will no3t wene
	What myrthis with in my harte I maie
	Sen þat oure sone with vs has bene
	And sene ther solempne sightis alswae.
JOS	Hamward I rede we hye
	In all þe myght we maye
	Be-cause of company
	Þat will wende in oure waye.

Also Coventry Weavers 815–26:

JOSOFF	Mare, my spretis be ravisschid cleyne,
	And clerely cast owt off all woo
	With these solam syghtys thatt we have seyne
	In yonder tempull that we cam froo
MARE	Now, serten, Josoff, you wold not wene
	Whatt myrthe I make withowt woo
	Thatt my chylde with hus hathe bene
	And those solam syghtis seyne alsoo.
JOSOFF	Then whomwarde, Mare, lett us goo
	Whyle thatt we haue the lyght off the day;
	For you have eyver lovid cumpany
	For yt dothe schorttun well youre wey.

In Chester, as in York, the whole dialogue occurs on the journey home, rather than on leaving the temple, as in Coventry. Chester develops the notion of "company" as "evil company" — a possibility latent in the York section cited, though immediately excluded by the following two lines in York which are not quoted, but excluded from the start in Coventry.

That Chester's version is corrupt is indicated by:

1. The breakdown of the ababbab rhyme-scheme of the remainder of the episode in stanza 27 (ababbcbc), stanza 28 (quatrain), stanza 29 (abcbdcdc).
2. The breakdown of syntax at 213, 221, 224–5, with corresponding lack of connexion in meaning. 213 is particularly difficult to understand in context.
3. The omission of 214+SH HmAR and of 218+SH HmARH; both SHs are needed, and are indicated in the text by changes of address at 215 and 219. They are supplied from BH for 214+ and B for 218+.
4. The inconsequentiality of the dialogue, whereby 215–8 is not a response to 207–14, and 219–26 not a response to 215–8.

The other versions may indicate the origins of Chester's corruptions; viz:

PLAY XI

1. 207–14 has no counterpart in York or Coventry and seems to be left over from a different play when the common original version was adopted from 215, since 215–8 begins York and has a counterpart in Coventry. It is improbable that the recognition of Jesus' absence, which follows the dialogue of Joseph and Mary in York and Coventry, should precede it in Chester; 215–8 corresponds in content, but not in wording, to York 20/15–24 and would give much better sense if it followed 226. Syntactic and semantic difficulties occur in 213–4, perhaps marking the point at which a different version was inserted.

2. 219–20 corresponds to the start of Mary's reply in York and Coventry, but in those cycles Mary continues by rejoicing that Christ has shared their experience, an idea absent from Chester. The break in the Chester rhyme-scheme perhaps marks an omission at this point. Nothing in Chester corresponds to York 6/Coventry 820 or York 8/Coventry 822. Since *weene* 219 continues the a-rhyme of stanza 28, it is tempting to speculate that a line was originally lost between 219 and 220; that further omission would be aided by the echo of 217 which, on the evidence of York and Coventry, would be expected to follow 220; and that, by an inversion of *binne* and *with* 220, a new rhyme-form to stanza 29 was produced.

3. Logically, and on the evidence also of York and Coventry, there should be an SH, *Joseph*, after 220, corresponding to the change of rhyme and to the interruption of syntax.

4. 226 has no counterpart in York or Coventry, repeats 221 and is both weak and redundant. It has the appearance of having been supplied to make up the requisite eight lines of a defective stanza.

The errors in the Chester manuscripts here must derive from a confused exemplar. Possibly the exemplar itself derived from a version in which the bridge-passage, necessary to cover the time-interval between the two episodes of the play, had been altered, leaving some elements of a different version, some lines of difficult legibility or uncertain status, and two SHs which were probably omitted in the exemplar.

215 *myrthes* HmAR may be compared with *mirthis* Yk; contrast *mirth* BH which Greg regards as a modernisation.

216 *betwene* ARBH is well attested, but with Hm compare *betwixte* Yk.

217 *fearly* Compare *solempne sightes* Yk, Cov.

219 *wende* AR, while destroying the link with stanza 28, gives better meaning in context then *weene*.

221 ARBH reflect York 20/8, but the repeated *I read* Hm is required for a regular sequence of strongly and weakly stressed syllables and is therefore to be preferred.

221–2 H's reversal of these lines is to be preferred for meaning to the HmARB version since it restores the meaningful connexion of 221 and 223, as in York 20/9–10, and eliminates the broken construction.

227–38 have no close counterpart in York or Coventry. With 227, however, compare York 20/49–50:

I^{us} MAG   Maistirs, takes to me in tente,
         And rede youre resouns right on rawes

and Coventry 857–8:

I DOCTOR   Now, lordyngis, lystun to me a whyle
              Wyche hathe the lawis vndur honde.

Both introduce a series of speeches proclaiming the need to obey the law, into which Christ intervenes. In Wakefield 18 they discuss Messianic prophecies. Some abridgement of such a dialogue here may be suspected from the quatrain form of stanza 30 and from the apparent non-sequitur of 228–9.

In all versions, Christ is invited to stay and learn, but rejects information because he has nothing to learn from the doctors.

225   Greg notes *aye* H as an obvious error.

230   Deimling cites *heede* AR, "the commoner and younger (synonymous)" equivalent of (Hm) BH's *tent*, as evidence of the close relationship of these two manuscripts.

235–6   Compare 13/7–11.

237   Compare 1/23–31 — *trynitie* B would be an acceptable reading.

239–46, stanza 32   With 239–42, compare Wakefield 18/63–6, York 20/89–92; with 243–6, compare Wakefield 18/93–6, York 20/121–4. The Chester b-rhymes are here all imperfect in all manuscripts. No manuscript has *knawes* for *knowes* 240, the form required for rhyme and found in York and Wakefield. Similarly, no manuscript has *drawes* for *drawe* 244, or *knawes* for *knowe* 246; Wakefield and York's equivalent is in a later passage and rhymes *law—knaw*, so that 246 may possibly suggest an unthinking borrowing in Chester. Wakefield and York have the required rhyme-form *yinge* where Chester has *yonge* 241.

240   *hee knowes* Wakefield 18/64 similarly has singular, but York 20/90 reads *we knawes*.

241–2   Jesus was at this time twelve years old and, as Rosemary Woolf points out, (*The English Mystery Plays*, p.213), a recital of the Decalogue was well within the competence of a child of that age in the period of the cycle's supposed and recorded productions. In York and Wakefield, therefore, Christ's assurances that he knows the law give rise to excessive amazement by the Doctors. In Chester, however, the doctor's response is prompted, more appropriately, by Christ's Messianic claims, which ran counter to all Pharisaical belief — compare 13/189–209 — and are here excused on account of his age.

246   Greg accepts *may* H as correct, since it is supported by York, and takes *might* as indicative of the Group-exemplar postulated for HmARB.

251–4   Compare Wakefield 18/73–6, York 20/101–4, where Christ claims possession by the Holy Ghost. *kingdome of heaven* 251 does not give good sense and may well represent an erroneous anticipation of the phrase at 254.

255–64   Compare Wakefield 18/181–90, York 20/193–202, Coventry Weavers 1001–8. The lines in these plays follow Christ's recital of the Decalogue and are thus adequately motivated. Here there seems no reason for the doctors' response, especially at 255. Although the speakers in Wakefield and York are as Chester, in Coventry the speech, which lacks counterpart to 263–4, is divided between the first and second doctor. It may be indicative of a cut that no speech is assigned in Chester to the third doctor before 299, whereas the second doctor speaks twice in sequence — before Christ's words, 247–50, and after, 255–8 — where a change of speaker might have been expected.

255   With *learned* HmARB, *lead* H, compare *lege* Wakefield 18/181, *alleggis* York 20/193. *lead* H, representing *layd*, "established", may seem stylistically preferable, since *learned* recurs at 256. Greg (p.119) suggests an exemplar *a lege*, amended in H to give a form which, though "nonsense", "preserves a reading closer to the original" than HmARB.

260   Greg notes that *withouten* HmARB agrees with York and is to be preferred to *without* H for metre.

261   In a somewhat tenuous argument, Greg urges the acceptance of *will full sone* H, which agrees with York. He suggests that the postulated Group-exemplar contained the HmB reading; and that, having omitted *full*, AR were compelled to revert to the H word-order by considerations of metre.

263–70, stanza 36   For perfect rhyme, northern forms *mare* 268, *sare* 270 are required, but are not found in any manuscript. Lines 267–8 have no counterpart in the other cycles, but equivalents to 269–70 occur in Wakefield 18/107–8 (second doctor), York 20/135–6 (second doctor), Coventry Weavers 955–6 (third doctor). While Coventry rhymes *before—sore*, Wakefield and York rhyme *mare—sare*.

265–6   Compare Wakefield 18/105–6, York 20/133–4, Coventry Weavers 953, where the words relate to Christ's opening assertion of authority. In Wakefield the speaker is the second doctor, in York the first, in Coventry the third. In Wakefield and York, the pronoun is *we*; in Coventry it is *I*, although Coventry does not correspond closely to 266.

farrely 266 is an acceptable variant of *ferli* but does not seem to have been understood by AR.

267–8   The exact reference of *matters* 267 is not clear, although it may refer to Jesus' Messianic claims; if so, they are accepted at this stage with surprising speed. The lines have no counterpart in the other cycles.

271–8, stanzas 37–8   *lawe* occurs three times in rhyme-position. *lawe* 278 has little meaning and Greg says "the group is certainly in error" (p.117); *sawe* H is slightly preferable but rather weak — Greg proposes a meaning "wisedom" (*sic*) but concedes that "this is not a proper use of the word, and it may be only a clumsy attempt at emendation". The correspondence with the other versions of the play is not here close enough to permit further assessment of the rhymes.

shewe 273 does not rhyme; it would be possible to postulate *say*, with perhaps *lay* 276.

thinge 277 HmARB is to be preferred for rhyme to *thinges* H, as Greg notes.

271–4   Similar challenges, but without close verbal parallels, occur in Wakefield 18/113–6, York 20/141–4, Coventry Weavers 961–4. Luke 2/46 states that Joseph and Mary found Christ *audientem illos et interrogantem eos* (AV "both hearing them, and asking them questions"). Exegetes usually cited Christ's conduct on this occasion as an example of humility; see *Glossa Ordinaria*, 'Evang. Luc.' 2/46 (PL

114/251). But Christ's conduct here seems to have something in common with the attitude of the Scribe addressing Christ in Mark 12/28: *Interrogavit eum quod esset primum omnium mandatum* (AV "Asked him, 'Which is the first commandment of all?'"). This episode seems to have influenced the rest of the scene — see further, 275-8 note.

275-98 Luke does not indicate the nature of Christ's discourses with the doctors, but with the exception of *Ludus Coventriae*, the cycles in their common play rehearse the Decalogue. Cawley ('Middle English Metrical Versions of the Decalogue with reference to the English Corpus Christi Cycles', *LSE* VIII (1975), p.136) suggests that a hint of this development may be found in the apocryphal Gospel of Thomas 19/2: "And after the third day they found him in the temple sitting in the midst of the doctors and hearing and asking them questions. And all men paid heed to him and marvelled how that being a young child he put to silence the elders and teachers of the people, expounding the heads of the law and the parables of the prophets." Compare also Nicephorus Callistus, *Ecclesiasticae Historiae* 1/14 (PG 145/675): *Exhibuit in templo sedens, et cum doctoribus legis disputans*, and the similar description of the doctors as *maystres of þe lawe* in *South English Nativity* 780.

York contains no previous recital of the commandments, but they are dramatised in Wakefield 7/31-90 and in Chester 5/1-20, Appendix IB/1-24; compare notes to 5/1-20. The recital here contains some slight modifications in conformity with Christ's general teaching concerning obedience to the spirit as well as to the letter of the law.

275-8 The first doctor does not cite the first commandment (Exodus 20/3: *Non habebis deos alienos coram me*, AV "Thou shalt have no other gods before me"), but the first part of Christ's statement in Mark 12/29-30: *Quia primum omnium mandatum est: Audi, Israel, Dominus Deus tuus Deus unus est; et diliges Dominum Deum tuum ex toto corde tuo, et ex tota anima tua, et ex tota mente tua, et ex tota virtute tua: hoc est primum mandatum* (AV "The first of all the commandments is, Hear, o Israel; The Lord our God is one Lord: And thou shalt love the Lord thy God with all thy heart, and with all thy soul, and with all thy mind, and with all thy strength: this is the first commandment"). This injunction was held to comprehend the first table. It is cited by the first doctor in Wakefield 18/117-22, York 20/145-50, where Christ adds a summary of the second table from Mark 12/31. In Coventry Weavers 965-70 the second doctor gives the full summary. Nowhere else is the summary of the first table regarded as the first commandment, to be followed by the recital of the second, although Wakefield, York and Coventry treat the summary as comprehending two commandments and recite the remaining eight.

It is notable that Christ's summary in Mark is addressed to a Scribe who concurs with Christ's comments and repeats them, Mark 12/32-3. It is possible that the dramatists recast the doctors in the role of the enlightened Scribe.

284 *save almes-deedes*, "except for acts of charity"; the phrase has wider significance than "giving alms" — compare 24/135, 154, Christ's criteria for salvation. See also Matthew 12/12: *Licet sabbatis benefacere* (AV "It is lawful to do well on the sabbath days"), and compare Mark 2/27, 3/4. This qualification is not made in any other version.

283-6 Compare 5/5-6 note.

287-98 The prohibitions of the second table in Exodus 20/12-7 are, in order — honour thy parents, do not kill, do not commit adultery, do not steal, do not slander, do not covet (compare 5/5-6 note). Chester's sequence here is a little arbitrary, with an apparent double prohibition against theft, 288, 295-6 (but see note) and a somewhat vague formulation of the prohibition against covetousness. Other versions, with some slight differences, follow the biblical sequence. Chester cannot here be easily defended against charges of confusion and error.

291-8, stanza 41 No manuscript has *non* for *not* 293, required for rhyme. The resulting stanza-form, ababbcbc (compare the ababacac of stanza 40), may suggest textual corruption at this point.

291-4 Compare Wakefield 18/169-70: "Not desyre thi neghburs wyfe ne his women"; York 20/188-9: "Take noȝt be stresse His wiffe nor his women"; Coventry has a different tenet here. Chester's version may link prohibitions against adultery and covetousness in the manner of the division of the tenth commandment — see 5/5-6 note; but possibly it also looks to Matthew 5/27-8: *Audistis quia dictum est antiquis: Non moechaberis. Ego autem dico vobis, quia omnis qui viderit mulierem ad concupiscendum eam, iam moechatus est eam in corde suo* (AV "Ye have heard that it was said by them of old time, Thou shalt not commit adultery: But I say unto you, That whosoever looketh on a woman to lust after her hath committed adultery with her already in his heart").

295-6 The repetition of the injunction against stealing may reflect influence from Mark 10/19, in which Christ says to an enquirer after eternal life: *Praecepta nosti: ne adulteres, ne occidas, ne fureris, ne falsum testimonium dixeris, ne fraudem feceris, Honora patrem tuum et matrem* (AV "Thou knowest the commandments, Do not commit adultery, Do not kill, Do not steal, Do not bear false witness, Defraud not, Honour thy father and mother"). Here the intention may be to distinguish fraud — theft of "what is lent" — from theft.

299 *syr* The address is presumably to the first doctor; *sires* AR comprehends the second also.

303-14, stanzas 43-4 Compare Wakefield 18/207-20, York 20/219-32, Coventry Weavers 1027-40. This passage is preceded there by the search of the temple, corresponding to Luke 2/45-6: *Regressi sunt in Ierusalem requirentes eum. Et factum est, post triduum invenerunt illum in templo* (AV "They turned back again to Jerusalem, seeking him. And it came to pass that after three days they found him in the temple"). Chester excludes this sense of time.

304 contains three strongly stressed syllables instead of the expected four; *there* H is to be preferred, and Greg notes that H alone is metrical. The other cycles have forms of: "In warld was neuer so semely a sight" (Wk.208).

In 305 Greg notes the variants, arguing on the basis of the York form — where *that* is demonstrative, with a relative pronoun understood — that *which* was probably the form in the postulated Group-exemplar, emended independently to *thatt* in HmR; and that its suppression in H is original.

yonder 306 agrees with Coventry 1030, but the line would be improved metrically by reading *yond* Wakefield 210, York 222.

309-10 lack exact counterpart in the other versions, all of which stress the need for speedy return; see 315-8 note.

No manuscript has *tyne* for *teene* 312, required for perfect rhyme and the form in Wakefield and York; Coventry has a different phrasing.

315–8   Compare Luke 2/48: *Fili, quid fecisti nobis sic? Ecce pater tuus et ego dolentes quaerebamus te* (AV "Son, why hast thou thus dealt with us? behold, thy father and I have sought thee sorrowing"). Although the other cycles follow this passage, Chester expresses Mary's concern only at 309–10 and never to Christ himself. The divergence from the biblical account weakens the point of Jesus' reply; one explanation for deliberate change here might be to suppress Mary's implied rebuke to her son.

315   A disyllabic form is preferable to *deareworthy* HmH for metre, and *worthy* ARB may therefore be preferred. The HmH form may result from the use of *deare* in rhyme-position; but it seems unlikely that both manuscripts would independently produce this form and it seems more probable that a form *dearewoth* was changed to *deareworthy* in the exemplar. *dearewoth* is last recorded by OED in 1557 and might well have been changed to *worthy* by the addition of *y* and the cancellation of the first element, the latter unnoted by HmH.

319–26   Compare Wakefield 18/245–52, York 20/257–64, Coventry Weavers 1065–72. These versions all begin with a line equivalent to Luke 2/49: *Quid est quod me quaerebatis?* (AV "How is it that ye sought me?"), lacking in Chester.

With 323–6, compare *Glossa Ordinaria*, 'Evang. Luc.' 2/51 (PL 114/251): *Omnia quae de Domino, vel a Domino facta cognovit, sive quae intellexit, sive quae nondum intelligere potuit, omnia in memoria recondebat, ut, quando tempus praedicandae seu scribendae incarnationis ejus adveniret, sufficientur universa prout essent gesta posset explicare quaerentibus.*

323–4   *thy* 323 ARBH is to be preferred for meaning to the scribally erroneous *they* Hm — compare *thise* Wakefield 249, *there* Yk 261.

With *heale* 323 HmARB, compare *seale* H, *cele* Yk. Either form is here possible, but H's agreement with York is notable.

I 324 is supplied from A here — the pronoun has been erroneously omitted in HmR. On the order in A as compared with BH, compare *I can* Wakefield 200, Coventry 1070, but *can I* Yk 262.

326   Compare Wakefield 252: "To fownd what is folowand"; likewise York 264. *the* Hm is apparently a formal variant of *they* BH but seems to reflect the exemplar form underlying the A and R readings.

327–34, stanza 48   The play concludes with a regular Chester stanza. The reference to the Purification in 327–30 is clear; probably 332 may be taken as an oblique reference to the Doctors' episode.

329   *Esay* RBH is to be preferred to the scribally erroneous *Esau* HmA; compare 117.

334   *leene* The AR and B forms, which destroy the rhyme, seem to result from a confusion of *n* and *u*, giving *leeue*. AR omit *to*, syntactically redundant but metrically necessary.

PLAY XII

Dramatis Personae Diabolus, Deus, Doctour, Primus Pharaseus, Secundus Pharaseus, Mulier Adulteria.

Locations
in desertum *Play-heading, containing* these stones 59; super pinnaculum templi 112 + SD, de pinnaculo 124 + SD, so high 113 (cf. come downe 115), *in* this holy cittie 107; super montem 128 + SD, a hill 130.

Properties
None specified.

Costume
None specified.

Sources
1. Temptation   The Temptation is briefly alluded to in Mark 1/12–3. There is an extended account in Luke 4/1–13, but the order of temptations differs from that in the other extended account, Matthew 4/1–11, the source of the episode here. The theology of the Temptation has been the subject of a number of studies, of which may be noted:
   Elizabeth Mary Pope: *Paradise Regained: The Tradition and The Poem* (New York, 1962).
   Alan H. Nelson: 'The Temptation of Christ, or, The Temptation of Satan', in *Medieval English Drama: essays critical and contextual* (ed. Jerome Taylor and Alan H. Nelson: Chicago and London 1972), pp.218–29.
David L. Wee: 'The Temptation of Christ and the Motif of Divine Duplicity in the Corpus Christi Cycle Drama', *MP* lxxii (1974), pp.1–16.
The reader is referred to these studies for detailed analogues and discussion.
   At 170 the Doctor bases his exposition expressly on St. Gregory the Great, *In Evangelia*: Homilia 16.
2. The Woman Taken in Adultery: John 8/1–11.
   At 285–7 the Doctor bases his exposition expressly upon St. Augustine, *Tractatus in Iohannem*, 33 (PL 35/1647–51).

Play-heading All other cycles include the play of Christ's baptism by John the Baptist — Wakefield 19, York 21, *Ludus Coventriae* 22 — which precedes the Temptation and was held to mark the start of Christ's ministry, as well as instituting the sacrament of baptism to which Chester refers at 4/199–200. Chester omits this important episode and moves directly from the Doctors' play to the Temptation.

The Temptation is dramatised in York 22, *Ludus Coventriae* 23. The Woman Taken in Adultery is dramatised in York 24/1–98 (incomplete), where it is linked to the Raising of Lazarus and follows the Transfiguration; and in *Ludus Coventriae* 24, where it follows the Temptation.

The two episodes are unrelated in the Bible itself and in gospel harmonies, being well separated in time and contained in different gospels. Both are here presented as evidence of Christ's resistance to different temptations and his awareness of both justice and compassion.

7–16 The devil's doubts about Christ's parentage were based on the phrase, Matthew 4/3, Luke 4/3 *Si Filius Dei es* (AV "If thou be the Son of God"). The birth of Christ to a married couple, Joseph and Mary, had deceived the devil into believing that Christ was an ordinary man, tainted with original sin — compare 7/527 and Mirk, 'De Circumcisione Domini Nostri': "This was also þe cause why oure lady was wedded to Ioseph, for to deseyue þe fende, þat he schuld wene, þat he was his fadyr, and not conseyuet of þe Holy Ghost." But the devil's doubts are usually held to spring from the events of Christ's baptism: see Chrysostom, *In Matthaeum*, Homilia 13 (PG 57/210) and Comestor, *Historia Scholastica* 'In Evangelia' 35 (PL 198/1556). In Chester, where the Baptism is not shown, the devil argues from first principles, assessing the virtue shown by Christ. Strangely, he seems to recognise that Mary is a virgin, 11–2 and 17, and that Joseph is not Christ's true father, 7–8 and 13–4. In York 22, the devil similarly undertakes to test Christ's divinity, but dismisses scornfully tales of a Messiah, 19–24, and makes no reference to the preceding Baptism; compare Sathan, *Ludus Coventriae* 23/20: "Ffayn wold I knowe who were ffadyr his".

9 "What sort of teacher can this ever be?" The line seems to lack a monosyllable for metrical smoothness.

13 *father* H is required for meaning and metre. It omission seems to reflect the exemplar. Of the Group, only R recognises a semantic difficulty and supplies a pronoun subject for the unattached possessive. Deimling cites the H reading as evidence of H's superiority.

15 H's version, perhaps metrically preferable, convincingly shifts the emphasis from the devil's ascription of heaven to Christ to the idea of Christ's own presumption.

PLAY XII 175

17-24, stanza 3   24 H is preferable for meaning to the syntactically corrupt and semantically obscure version in HmAR. B supplies a line inappropriate in context which destroys the rhyme. The reference appears to be to the homage paid to the Infant Christ in plays 6–11 in the absence of a play of the Baptism to which the line would more immediately refer.

never 20 ARBH is well attested but would produce a four-stress line; R avoids this by omitting *before*, destroying rhyme. Hm is to be preferred.

28   Unless given emphatic stress, the line contains two strongly stressed syllables instead of the expected three. H is semantically and metrically acceptable, but Hm becomes semantically acceptable if *wemles* BH is supplied for *wembles* HmAR, the latter scribally erroneous. The HmARB readings are consistent with an obscure exemplar reading, with *hee* misread as *how* and *yet* as *yt*. Since the speech focuses upon Christ and the second word of HmARB begins with *h*, masculine reference may be preferred.

33-40   The devil exonerates Christ from the deadly sins of envy, covetousness (36), pride, gluttony and lechery; he completes the list with avarice and slander rather than the more usual anger and sloth. The sequence here seems arbitrary, perhaps governed by considerations of metre and rhyme. Compare Gregory, *In Evangelia*, Homilia 16: *Certe iniquorum omnium caput diabolus est, et huius capitis membra sunt omnes iniqui*.

42   Compare 16/291-2.

47   *honge he hasse* Hm would represent a possible reading if *honge* is regarded as an error for *honger*. *hongarye* is found in ARBH, but support for Hm is given by B, where *he hasse* is inappropriate to the construction and is better explained as the retention of an earlier form than as an error for *he is*. AR gives sense and corresponds to the HmB word-sequence; H inverts the construction. For an accepted interpretation of this temptation, see Bede, *In Lucae Evangelium Expositio*, 1/4 (PL 92/367).

55-6   Chester does not indicate that Christ's fast which he has undergone in the desert before the Temptation has lasted forty days, Matthew 4/1-2; contrast York 22/44: "Fourty dayes with-owten foode", *Ludus Coventriae* 23/66-7: "xl^{ti} days and xl^{ti} nyght now haue I fastyd for mannys sake."

fast ARH give a more modern form, *fasted*; only H recognises that this increases the number of syllables by one and compensates by the omission of *nowe*.

The period of Christ's fast is commemorated in Lent. Some notion of a fasting season may underlie 56, and may also have suggested *meat* (in the sense "meat of animals") H rather than *bread* HmARB. With H, compare 67 and also York 22/62: "I wolde now som mete wer sene".

56+SD   No change of speaker, or new action, is indicated by the SD, and it is probably for this reason that it is omitted by RBH. *abyde* 57, however, suggests that the devil stops Jesus; possibly the SD concludes a break in the speech during which Jesus enters and the devil moves to intercept him.

61-4   So Matthew 4/4, quoting Deuteronomy 8/3. 63-4 corresponds to Matthew 4/4: *Sed in omni verbo quod procedit de ore Dei* (AV "But by every word that proceedeth out of the mouth of God") — contrast Luke 4/4: *In omni verbo Dei* (AV "By every word of God").

65–72   Compare 177–80 and 169–208 note.

79–80   Compare 295.

84   *kindlye be* ARBH is to be preferred to *kindlye* Hm as producing a more regular sequence of strongly and weakly stressed syllables while improving syntax and meaning.

89–92   See Bede, *In Lucae Evangelium Expositio* 1/4 (PL 92/369), and compare *Glossa Ordinaria*, 'Evang. Matth.' 4/5 (PL 114/85): *Qui ex responsione Christi victus et incertus remansit: post primam ad secundam accessit tentationem.*

91   Compare 5/106

94   *doscibeirde* AR, *dosaberd* H seem more probable than *disobedient* HmB; compare 5.

96   *unhappelye* ARBH is to be preferred for meaning to the nonce-form *unhappingely* Hm.

98   *deceate* ARBH is to be preferred for meaning to the scribally erroneous *discent* Hm; compare 13/176. The Hm form may suggest *descent*, a conceptual confusion with Satan's fall.

107   The line has three strongly stressed syllables instead of the expected four.

105–12   The second temptation in Matthew, as here, but the third in Luke. Compare *Glossa Ordinaria*, 'Evang. Matth.' 4/5 (PL 114/85): *Prima et ultima tentatio in deserto, media quoque historialiter, ultima fuit postquam regressus est Jerusalem. Quia Matthaeus non secundum ordinem historiae sed secundum tentationem Adae prosequitur: Lucas vero ut res gesta est.*

Luke 4/9 locates the temptation in Jerusalem, but Matthew 4/5 *in sanctam civitatem* (AV "into the holy city") — compare 107. The location on a pinnacle of the temple is not mentioned in the spoken text but is indicated in 112 + SD and was presumably evident from the set.

113–20, stanza 15   *high* 113 does not rhyme with *sleight* 114 HmA, *sight* 115 HmARB. *sleigh* 114 R restores rhyme but at the expense of meaning; B and H attempt to produce a meaningful phrase, treating *sleigh, slye* as adjective. At 115, only H attempts to restore rhyme. The simplest explanation of the confusion is an exemplar error whereby *so high* 113 has been substituted for *on hight*.

118–9   Matthew 4/6, Luke 4/10–11 make it clear that at this point the devil is citing a scripture, Psalm 91/10–11 AV — which Christ can fulfill. This quotation is answered by Christ with another scriptural quotation, but the point of the conflict of authority here is lost because Chester does not indicate the scriptural base for the devil's demand but suggests that the comment is the devil's own. Bede, *In Lucae Evangelium Expositio* 1/4 (PL 92/369) emphasises the devil's misinterpretation of scripture. York 22/103 and *Ludus Coventriae* 23/122 make it clear that the devil is quoting here.

PLAY XII

120 The line has four strongly stressed syllables instead of the expected three. Perhaps *therbye* was added to avoid repetition of the rhyme-word of 116, a repetition further avoided in H.

121–8, stanza 16 *mooved* 124 H is to be preferred for rhyme to *ment* HmARB. H alone has the required rhyme-form *reproved* 128. *deprived* AR seems to be an attempt to give familiar shape to an unfamiliar form, at the expense of meaning, and is cited by Deimling as evidence of the close relationship between the two manuscripts. Possibly the original read *meved — repreved*. 121-4 reflects Matthew 4/7, Luke 4/12, quoting Deuteronomy 6/16. Compare Bede, *In Lucae Evangelium Expositio* 1/4 (PL 92/369): *Falsas de Scripturis diaboli sagittas, veris Scripturarum frangit clypeis.*

128 + SD H's omission may reflect the fact that 129-32 state the substance of the SD. But the SD may have been carelessly omitted in moving from fol.61^v to fol. 62^r. Compare 130 note.

129 *fellowe* The third temptation is the only one in Matthew not prefixed by *Si Filius Dei es*. *fellowe* perhaps marks the growing irritation of the devil at Jesus' responses and perhaps suggests a desire to evoke an equivalent retort in word or deed.

130 "Let us go to a hill to disport ourselves." The line combines the two constructions *Goe we playe us* and *Goe we to a hill*. *upon this* H may reflect unease at the construction or a translation of *adducet super montem* 128 + SD.

134 Compare Matthew 4/8: *Omnia regna mundi et gloriam eorum* (AV "All the kingdoms of the world, and the glory of them"). *these realmes* H may represent an attempt to convey the plurality in the bible text — compare *londes* 207. *this realme* HmARB must be most immediately "the world", although in context it refers to the realm of England.

139–40 Compare Matthew 4/10: *Scriptum est enim: Dominum Deum tuum adorabis, et illi soli servies* (AV "Thou shalt worship the Lord thy God, and him only shalt thou serve"), citing Deuteronomy 10/20 in slightly modified form. The last clause of Matthew has no counterpart in Chester. *though thee nye* Hm seems addressed to the devil, and may not be intended to form part of the quotation.

140 Hm requires a pronoun subject to be understood. Such a subject is supplied by BH but at the expense of a regular metrical pattern. It would be more usual for the phrase to take the form *though it nye*, "though it causes annoyance", last recorded by OED in 1555. AR provide an absurd, if ingenious, alternative to a phrase which they clearly did not understand.

145–52, stanza 19 *lafte* 152 BH is to be preferred for meaning and rhyme to the scribally erroneous *laste* HmAR, where *f* has been confused with long *s*.

153–60, stanza 20 H supplies an alternative final quatrain. To accommodate the rhyme-word *shitte* 160, H replaces *fyre* 156 with *dyrt*, although the result is a very imperfect rhyme.

156–68 The switch from self-pity to sudden joyful defiance perhaps reflects the position at the end of play 17 where we move from despair, 221-8, to the gleeful repopulation of Hell, 277-336. H's replacement for 157-60 and omission of the following stanza removes this change of tone and may be compared with the omission of 17/277-336 by H.

168   York 22 and *Ludus Coventriae* 23/195 + SD conclude the episode with the coming of the angels to Christ, as indicated in Matthew 4/11.

169-208   The content of the speech derives from Gregory's Homilia 16. See particularly:

173-4: *In tribus se tentationibus erexit: quia hunc videlicet gule, vana gloria, et avaritia tentavit.*

177-88: *Ex gula quippe tentavit, cum cibium ligne vetitum ostendit, atque ad comedendum suasit. Ex vana autem gloria tentavit, cum diceret 'Eritis sicut dii'. Et ex provectu avaritiae tentavit, cum diceret 'Scientis bonum et malum'.*

189-92: *Avaritia enim non solum pecuniae est, sed etiam altitudinis.*

193-208: *Sed quibus modis primum hominem stravit, eisdem modis secundo homini tentatio succubuit. Per gulam quippe tentat, cum dicit 'Dic ut lapides isti panes fiant'. Per vanam gloriam tentat, cum dicit 'Si Filius Dei es, mittate deorsum'. Per sublimitatis avaritiam tentat cum regna omnia mundi ostendit, dicens 'Haec omnia tibi dabo si procedens adoraveris me'.*

209-16: *Sed eisdem modis a secundo homine vincitur quibus primum hominem se vicisse gloriabitur.*

The homily exerted a formative influence on exposition of the Temptation and underlies all cycle representations. Its three heads are listed by the devil in York 22 and by Belsabub in *Ludus Coventriae* 23/49-52. But *Ludus Coventriae* 23/196-221 concludes by stressing also the exemplary nature of the action for contemporary man resisting temptation. The interpretation in the play differs significantly from *Stanzaic Life* 6241-6300.

190-2   *onlye* 190 ARBH is to be preferred for meaning to *greatly* Hm and corresponds to Gregory's *avaritia non solum pecuniae est*.

in willinge of highnes and state 191-2 — compare Gregory's *avaritia .... altitudinis*.

unskylfullye 192, "foolishly" — compare Gregory: *Recte enim avaritia dicitur, cum supra modum sublimitas ambiter*.

196   *sleightely* HmR, "cunningly", is recorded by OED but was clearly not common. Some exemplar change seems to underlie the *yea/yee/you* forms of ABH, all of which destroy metre and, with the exception of H, yield limited sense. The measure of agreement among the different manuscripts, the retention of *sleilye* A balanced by the reversion to an Hm form in R all suggest divergence from a common but altered exemplar.

199-200   "And so to instigate the display of his divinity which he doubted." *prove* H is equally acceptable, avoiding the repetition of *move(d)* 196.

208   "And [promised him] that through his own great position". Compare 135-6. The line requires *height him* 207 to be understood; the *estate* is the devil's, not that to be granted by the devil to Christ.

209   "So the devil was overcome three times in this matter, as was performed in this place". *overcome* is past participle, requiring *was* to be understood — the auxiliary is expressed in 210 and 211. H treats the verbs as past tense and supplies a subject. *thus*

PLAY XII

BH is to be preferred for meaning to *this* HmAR; it is difficult to determine how far the latter form is, like the H reading, an attempt to treat *overcome* as an active verb and supply a subject.

215–6 "For truth from his godhead was at that time completely overcome by guile." In HmARB the lines apparently justify Christ's action because Adam was deceived by the devil at the time of the Fall and so Christ legitimately practises deception upon the devil. H, however, reading *Sathanas* for *soothnes* 215, gives a meaning: "For Satan was at that time completely deceived about his divinity". Although this may seem acceptable, it is difficult to reconcile with Satan's comments at 149–60, although these in turn do not accord with Satan's defiance in play 17.

216 + SD No location for the action is specified. In John 1/1–3, the episode takes place in the temple while Jesus is teaching the people — compare 230–1. The number of Pharisees (and Scribes) is unspecified by John; York 24 requires at least four. The use of *Judaeorum* by H here, and a similar usage in SHs, perhaps suggests a desire to comprehend both Pharisees and Scribes; York 24 terms each *Judeus*.

217 *maister* HmRBH represents an address to the second Pharisee; *maysters* A suggests more than one other.

220 *advowtrye* Hm suggests a partial spelling modernisation of ME *avoutrie*, the representative of the OF form was later remodelled, on the pattern of Latin *adulterium*, to give a form such as *addulterye* RH, dated as 15th or 16th century by the *Oxford Dictionary of English Etymology*. Since all manuscripts have a form with *d*, it seems probable that the exemplar also contained a form with *d*, but the HmAR forms may indicate a form without *d*, underlying the exemplar. All are acceptable for rhyme. Compare 293.

222–32 Compare 216 + SD H, and 289–96; also Bede, *In S. Joannis Evangelio Expositio* 8 (PL 92/735), cited substantially by *Glossa Ordinaria*, 'Evang. Joan' 8/1 (PL 114/389), and Comestor, *Historia Scholastica*, 'In Evang.' 98 (PL 198/1587).

232 + SH H's omission, with 232 + SD relegated to the margin (see TNs), ascribes 233–40 to Secundus Pharaseus.

233–40, stanza 30 *stone* 237 gives imperfect rhyme with *uncleane, meane*, although attested by all manuscripts and corresponding to *lapidare* in John 8/5: *In lege autem Moyses mandavit nobis huiusmodi lapidare* (AV "Now Moses in the law commanded us that such should be stoned"). Compare 289–96, stanza 37, and note.

238 contains only three strongly stressed syllables instead of the expected four. H supplies *women*, an extra stressed syllable, which may be preferred; HmARB suggest the unspecified *huiusmodi* of John.

234–6 Compare John 8/4: *Magister, haec mulier modo deprehensa est in adulterio* (AV "Master, this woman was taken in adultery, in the very act"). The circumstantial detail of *to yeare* 234 has no biblical counterpart and the whole passage may be intended as a form of gloss to make clear the meaning of adultery. H removes the detail at 234, while A and R, perhaps with confusion from *another* 235, change the meaning improbably. *was* and *here* 236 H represent an attempt to reproduce the passive construction in John.

237-8 The law requiring the deaths of both adulterer and adulteress is stated in Leviticus 20/10, Deuteronomy 22/22, although no mention is made here of the guilt of the woman's partner; *Ludus Coventriae* 24/124 + SD–144 dramatises his escape. Stoning is not specified there as the means of death, as it is in John 8/5.

240 + SD–9 In John 8/6, Jesus does not immediately reply but *inclinans se deorsum, digito scribebat in terra* (AV "stooped down, and with his finger wrote on the ground, *as though he heard them not*" — italics not in Vulgate). It is only after further questioning that he replies. Here the writing and reply are simultaneous, but the first Pharisee continues to question after Jesus' reply, while the comments of the second at 249 suggest that Jesus has made no response — as in the AV addition. H reverses the biblical sequence in showing Jesus as writing after his reply, at 244. *Ludus Coventriae* 24 preserves the biblical sequence of events.

243 Compare John 8/7: *Primus in illam lapidem mittat* (AV "Let him first cast a stone at her"). The biblical wording is seen at 300, as compared with the wording here, which anticipates a common modern misquotation.

247 *here today* H seems to be an attempt to remove the dramatically ironic suggestion in the Pharisee's words that Christ does have the power to remit sins.

249–64 Compare 301–4 and note, and John 8/9 AV: "They which heard it, being convicted by their own conscience" — the passage has no Vulgate equivalent. In addition to the explanation from Augustine, other possibilities exist; see *Glossa Ordinaria*, 'Evang. Joan', 8/6 (PL 114/389), and Comestor, *Historia Scholastica* 'In Evangelia' 98 (PL 198/1587). An echo of the idea that Christ wrote out his spoken words is in 251–2.

249–56, stanza 32 The stanza in H contains nine lines instead of the usual eight, with an additional line after 255. It should be noted:

  1. that 253 is a partial echo of 250 and in HmB has a rough metre. The omission of *me* ARH improves the metre.

  2. that the omission of 253 would permit the adoption of H's additional line, but that the line cannot otherwise be incorporated into a regular stanza since no other line can be omitted.

  3. that 255 H gives a more regular sequence of strongly and weakly stressed syllables than 255 HmAR or B. HmARB contain an additional syllable, lost by H's omission of *for. for* is used to connect 255 to the exclamation of 254, which it explains. The explanatory link is implicit in H, but the removal of the syntactical connexion of 254–5 permits the insertion of the additional line in H after 254 (where it gives sense). No such insertion is possible in the HmARB form.

Perhaps 253 represents an additional line, on the model of 250; and to accommodate it, the original 254 was omitted and a new syntactical link created at the expense of metrical regularity, to link the present 254–5. H found both versions in the exemplar, having 253, the original 254 and the original version of 255; H included all the lines, and misplaced the original 254.

256 + SD Compare John 8/9: *Audientes autem unus post unum exibant, incipientes a senioribus* (AV "And they which heard it .... went out one by one, beginning at the eldest, even unto the last"). This might suggest that the second Pharisee is the senior in years or rank, although this is not the impression given by the dominant role of the

PLAY XII

first Pharisee up to this point. The departure of the Pharisees is indicated in the text, hence the SDs after 256 and 264, omitted by H, are redundant.

259–60 The reference to France has sometimes been taken with other evidence of alleged French influence in the cycle, although it seems a conventional phrase. Presumably the direction is to be seen as being from England overseas, rather than from Palestine in the direction of England; but compare Wakefield 13/353 where the first shepherd dreams they are near England.

259 HmARB contains four stressed syllables only by distortion of normal lexical and sentential stress — "álās thát Í ẃeare āẃay" — but this version seems syntactically preferable to H, which is metrically regular.

beyonde 260 HmB is to be preferred for meaning to *behynde* ARH.

261 *Sybble* The term is clearly used as a general term of abuse, although OED records the name as a word, meaning "a prophetess, a fortune-teller, a witch" only from 1589.

263 *againste* ARBH is to be preferred to the scribally erroneous *agayst* Hm.

265–8 *those* 265 H and *putt* 266 H seem to reflect the construction of John 8/10: *Qui te accusabant* (AV "Those thine accusers"). Compare *tho* 268 Hm, *thoes* 268 ARBH and the changed verb tense in that line. *these* and *putten* 265 HmARB are, however, equally acceptable.

condempne 267 B reflects John 8/10 *condemnavit* (AV "condemned").

The equivalent to 267–8 in John 8/10: *Nemo te condemnavit* (AV "Hath no man condemned thee") is treated in modern texts as a question to which the woman supplies an answer. While 267–8 could be regarded also as a question, the questioning would be by intonation only; as here indicated, Jesus answers his own question, and the woman echoes him.

271 *neyther* BH reflects *nec* in John 8/11 (AV "neither"). Its adoption requires alterations in word-order to restore metre.

condempne B reflects *condemnabo* in John 8/11 (AV "Do I condemn").

273–80 No response from the woman is indicated in John, but here she becomes a witness for Christ, accepting his divinity with certainty, in contrast to the devil of the preceding episode. The woman voices praise of Christ also in York 24/70–4 and *Ludus Coventriae* 24/281–4.

278 "Who knows the deeds we do". *worke* Hm is collective; the plural form is attested by ARBH. Perhaps influenced by Jesus' awareness of the Pharisees' deeds, AR read *done* for *doe*, and H makes the form clearly past by reading *done be*. *all* H may be preferred as producing a more regular sequence of strongly and weakly stressed syllables.

The woman in HmARB has no way of knowing why the Pharisees fled, unless she is assumed to have read what Jesus wrote, though such a possibility would seem to run counter to 305–8. The additional line at 155 H might account for her knowledge of the content of Jesus' writing here.

281–8, stanza 36   *take hede* 281 H is to be preferred for rhyme to *marke here* HmARB. Deimling cites the H reading as evidence of that manuscript's superiority.

was 284 ARBH is to be preferred for rhyme to *were* Hm. The Hm form represents concord with *these thinges*. Concord is lost in ARB, but re-established by *this thing* H, which is also therefore to be preferred to *these thinges* HmARB.

It seems unlikely that the change at 281 would precede that at 284, since the intention seems to have been to provide a rhyme *here—were* and a quatrain-stanza abba.

At 282 AR attempt to supply a further rhyme for *here—were*, namely *deere*; meaning is lost in consequence.

285–312   See *Sources* above.

289–96, stanza 37   The c-rhyme, *stone* 292 — *cleane* 296, is imperfect. Compare 233–40, stanza 30 and note.

289–96   Compare Augustine (PL 35/1649): *Cum ergo de duobus istis, id est de veritate et mansuetudine ejus, inimici livore et invidia torquerentur; in tertio, id est justitia, scandalum posuerunt. Quare? Quis Lex jusserat adulteros lapidari ... Offeramus ei mulierem in adulterio deprehensam, dicamus quid de illa in Lege praeceptum sit: si eam jusserit lapidari, mansuetudinem non habebit; si eam dimitti censuerit, justitiam non tenebit.*

291–4   *comaunded* 291 ARBH is to be preferred to *commandeth* Hm both for meaning and as a reflexion of *iusserat* — see quotation, 289–96 note. H also adjusts the tense of *trespassen* 293 to *trespassed*, although this is not a necessary change. A also unnecessarily changes *hoped* 294 to present tense.

On *advowtrye* 293, compare 220 and note.

296   "Or [they hoped that he would] set the law aside completely." *blenquyshe* HmB is not otherwise recorded. It may reflect an AN law term, or some regional variation related to the rare OE *blencan*, "deceive", ON *blekkja*, "delude" — compare ME *blenchen* 4(a), "to mislead"; or it may be a nonce-form, confusing *vanquish* with *blemyshe* ARH.

297–312, stanzas 38–9   H has erroneously reversed the quatrains 301–4, 305–8, destroying rhyme and meaning. There is no obvious explanation for the error.

H also has an alternative form of 304, with *omd* as error for *ond, and*.

299–310   These lines rather tortuously convey the sense of Augustine (PL 35/1649–50): *Quid vobis aliud significat, cum digito scribit in terra? Digito enim Dei Lex scripta est; sed propter duros in lapide scripta est. Nunc jam Dominus in terra scribebat, quia fructum quaerebat. Audistis ergo, Impleatur Lex, lapidetur adultera: sed numquid in illa punienda, Lex implenda est a puniendis? Consideret se unusquisque vestrum, intret in semetipsum, ascendat tribunal mentis suae, constituat se ante conscientiam suam cogat se confiteri. Scit enim qui sit: quia nemo scit hominum quae sunt hominis, nisi spiritus hominis, qui in ipso est. Unusquisque in se intendens, peccatorem se invenit .... Puniatur peccatrix, sed non a peccatoribus; impleatur Lex, sed non a praevaricatoribus Legis. Haec vox omnino justitiae est: qua justitia illi tanquam trabali telo percussi, sese inspicientes et reos invenientes, unus post unum omnes recesserunt.* York 24/55–6 and Ludus Coventriae 24/233–56 also indicate that Christ wrote out the Pharisees' sins.

H's *other* 307, *owne* 308 changes the meaning from Hm's "Yet none of them was any the wiser, but [i.e. even though] each man knew his [own] sins" to "Yet none was any the wiser about the other, but [i.e. since] each man knew [only] his own [sins]".

311 Either *helped* ARB or *holpe* H is to be preferred for meaning to the scribally erroneous but potentially intermediate form *helpe* Hm.

PLAY XIII

Dramatis Personae Jesu, Puer, Caecus, Petrus, John, Primus Vicinus, Secundus Vicinus, Primus Pharaseus, Secundus Pharaseus, Nuntius, Mater, Pater, Primus Judeus, Secundus Judeus, Maria, Martha, Thomas, Lazarus.

Locations
the water of Siloe, 68, 72, aquam 70 + SD
Bethenye that standeth herebye 16, Judye 333
sepulchrum 332 + SD, *with* lapidem 441 + SD.

Properties
super terram spuit et lutum faciat 66 + SD, claye 127
water 109
lapides 260 + SD, 284 + SD, stones 257, 298.

Costume
Jesus — tabret 300 (*see note*).

Sources
Healing of the Blind Man — John 9/1–38
Raising of Lazarus — John 11/1–46.

Play-heading Chelidonio H alone uses this name for SHs in the play, the other manuscripts less specifically referring to *Caecus*; the name is never used in the spoken text and would not therefore be suggested to the audience. See further *Acta Sanctorum* 23rd August, *De S. Cedonio vel Sidonio*, esp *Sanctus Cedonius vel Chelidonius, discipulus, cooperator et successor sancti Maximini episcopi primi Aquensis ... Fertur hic fuisse caecigenus ille quem Christus lux vera gratiae et sol justitiae illuminavit*. So *Legenda Aurea* 'De Sancta Mary Magdalena': *Beatus Cedonius qui caecus a nativitate exstiterat, sed a domino fuerat liberatus.*

The healing of the blind man is not shown in any other cycle. The Raising of Lazarus is also dramatised in York 24/147–209 (incomplete) where it follows the Woman Taken in Adultery; and in *Ludus Coventriae* 25. The episode forms part of the Digby *Mary Magdalen* 776–924.

PLAY XIII

Before 1   John 8/12: AV "I am the light of the world; he that followeth me shall not walk in darkness, but shall have the light of life." The text follows upon the account of the Woman Taken in Adultery, but its repetition at John 9/4 suggests its appropriateness also as a preamble to the healing of the blind man; compare 63–6 and note, 353–6 and note. 1–3 provide a translation for the audience.

1–35   These opening five seven-line stanzas, ababbcc, represent a compilation of various passages from St. John's gospel and are framed by Latin quotations from John before 1 and after 35, producing the effect of a distinct prologue to the play. The compilation picks up major themes from John's gospel which are given more specific illustration by the episodes in the play, while providing also an example of Christ's teaching to his disciples, with which compare 15/193–256.

3   *scriptures* There is no clear Old Testament parallel to the opening text; in fact, John 8/13–9 is taken up with Jesus' answer to the Pharisees' immediate objection that his words are untrue since he alone says them — the answer being that two testimonies are sufficient for proof and he has those of himself and his Father. The intention here, however, may merely be to indicate that the words are, for the audience, to be found in the Bible.

4–5   On Abraham, see 9/158 and note; on Abraham and Isaac, see Play 4; on Jacob, see 8/268 + Latin–89 and note. The reference to Abraham may also be prompted by Jesus' comment to the Pharisees at John 8/56: *Abraham pater vester exsultavit ut videret diem meum; vidit, et gavisus est.* (AV "Your father Abraham rejoiced to see my day: and he saw it, and was glad"). Something of the latter text may have prompted 6–7; compare 8/58: *Amen, amen dico vobis antequam Abraham fieret, ego sum* (AV "Verily, verily I say unto you, Before Abraham was, I am"). See also 2/449–56.

8   John 10/30: AV "I and my Father are one." The text follows the image of the Good Shepherd and its development. Compare 251–6, stanza 35 note, and 281–4.

9–12   Compare John 3/16: *Sic enim Deus dilexit mundum, ut Filium suum unigenitum daret, ut omnis qui credit in eum, non pereat, sed habeat vitam aeternam* (AV "For God so loved the world, that he gave his only begotten Son, that whosoever believeth in him should not perish, but have everlasting life"). *loved* 11 R may reflect the tense in such a text, or be influenced by *hath sent* 9.

16   Bethany, the home of Martha, Mary and Lazarus, was a village about two miles from Jerusalem. There is nothing in John's account to suggest that Christ had already decided to go to Bethany when he encountered the blind man; the episode of his healing follows Jesus' departure from the temple to escape stoning at John 8/59.

18–21   The text at 21 is John 10/11: AV "I am the good shepherd: the good shepherd giveth his life for the sheep", cited by Christ in his discussion with the Pharisees after the healing of the blind man.

ovibus 21 BH is to be preferred to the substituted *omnibus* HmAR for meaning and as reflecting the Vulgate wording: the latter perhaps originates in confusion of *u* and *n* and 'emendation' of the resulting form.

22–5   An echo of John 9/4; compare 59–62 and note.

26–8 A rendering of John 10/16: *Et alias oves habeo, quae non sunt ex hoc ovili, et illas oportet me adducere, et vocem meam audient, et fiet unum ovile, et unus pastor* (AV "And other sheep I have, which are not of this fold; them also I must bring, and they shall hear my voice; and there shall be one fold and one shepherd").

29–30 Compare Epistle to the Hebrews 8/10: *Quia hoc est testamentum quod disponam domui Israel post dies illos, dicit Dominus, dando leges meas in mentem eorum et in corde eorum superscribam eas; et ero eis in Deum, et ipsi erunt mihi in populum* (AV "For this is the covenant that I will make with the house of Israel after those days, saith the Lord; I will put my laws into their mind, and write them in their hearts: and I will be to them a God, and they shall be to me a people").

The text refers to the New Covenant, written in the hearts of men, to replace the Old Covenant of the Jews, representing a movement away from the old legalism.

31–5 + Latin The Latin after 35 is John 8/31–2: AV "If ye continue in my word, then are ye my disciples indeed; and ye shall know the truth, and the truth shall make you free." The text is freely rendered in the preceding lines. It forms part of the teachings of Jesus after the episode of the Woman Taken in Adultery.

36–9, stanza 6 The quatrain has the metrical shape and the abab rhyme-scheme of the previous stanzas, but is followed by the usual stanza-form, the Chester stanza, of the rest of the play.

36–43 Compare 83, dramatised in this section. The neighbours' comments there derive from John 9/8, although there it is said that the blind man *sedebat et mendicabat* (AV "sat and begged"). Possibly the emphasis on *neighbour* 39, 42, indicates that the neighbours are thought of as present at this part of the action; but the speech is addressed to Jesus and the disciples and no other characters are necessarily involved. The sight of the blind beggar is a further example to the audience of alms-giving; it also, in the context of the play, establishes a symbolic identity between the blind man and the seeing audience (compare *of youre owne kynd* 39) which permits symbolic development in terms of spiritual blindness.

43 + SH, 47 + SH John 9/2 does not specify individual speakers but assigns the remarks generally to Jesus' disciples.

44–50 The disciples assume that the man's blindness is a punishment. Peter's words reflect John 9/2, where the cause is sought in the sins committed by the sufferer, or in the transmitted consequences of parental sin. But John's words in the play unbiblically seek a further answer in the consequences of original sin, reflecting again the identity of the blind man with the common human condition. Compare Augustine, Tractatus 44, 1/1 (PL 35/1713).

48–50, stanza 8 In HmAR the stanza rhymes aaa. If the BH line after 50 is added, as seems preferable, a rhyme-word equivalent to the c-rhymes of stanza 7 is established, and it becomes possible to postulate alternative stanza-divisions, taking 44–50 + 1 as a single stanza and regarding 39–42 as a separate stanza, if desired. 44–50 + 1 are linked semantically; it might then be postulated that 40–3 represents the second part of a Chester stanza, the first part having been replaced by 36–9 in continuation of the form of 1–35. Deimling, lacking Hm, cites the absence of the additional line in AR as evidence of the close relationship between those two manuscripts; its absence also from Hm perhaps suggests that its status in the

PLAY XIII

exemplar was not clear — it unbiblically repeats the sense of 47 and may have been rejected stylistically.

51–66 Jesus' reply is basically that in John 9/3–6, but the action assumes a symbolic import also. See Augustine, Tractatus 44 (PL 35/1713–4), a text which endows the boy-guide with special significance since he will be rendered unnecessary by the spiritual guide, Jesus, and also *Glossa Ordinaria*, 'Evang. Joan.' 9/3 (PL 114/394).

51–8, stanza 9   *borne* 54 — *reforme* 58 gives an imperfect b-rhyme. *restore* 58 R destroys this rhyme, but might represent an original exemplar-reading indicating that the rhyme word at 54 was correspondingly *bore*. Compare 124, 192.

67–76, stanza 11   The stanza contains ten lines instead of the expected eight, rhyming aaabaacccb. A regular stanza would result from the omission of 71–2, which Deimling (p.xv) considers "an interpolation, which spoils the stanza, but whose origin is easily to be explained from the situation".
alwayes 76 H is to be preferred for rhyme to *alwaye* HmARB. Deimling cites the H reading as evidence of H's superiority.

68   *Siloe* The form is that of the Vulgate, trisyllabic with two strongly stressed syllables. AV, following the Septuagint, calls the pool *Siloam*. Compare *Siloei* 105 H.

70   No such instruction is given by Christ — it is the instruction given by the Pharisee in John 9/24; compare 189. The instructions have rather different meanings and the similarity is thematic. The Pharisee wishes to distinguish between God and the fallible, sinful human prophet who has acted as his agent; compare *Glossa Ordinaria*, 'Evang. Joan.' 9/18 (PL 114/395). But Jesus has already established the identity of God and himself at 8, hence the injunction involves the glorification of Christ as God. The blind man complies with the instruction fully, 73–80.
The praise is seen also as part of the blind man's spiritual rebirth; compare Augustine, Tractatus 44/2 (PL 35/1714), who regards the washing as a sign of baptism, and *Glossa Ordinaria*, 'Evang. Joan.' 9/6 (PL 114/395).

73   *omnipotente* ARBH is to be preferred to the scribally erroneous *omipotent* Hm.

80 + SH, 84 + SH   John does not specify the number of neighbours and other involved. *neightboures* AR 81, 85, suggests more than the two speakers. At 80 + SH, A has erroneously replaced *Vicinus* by *Pharaseus* — compare 130 + SH.

82   *yesterdaye* No temporal indication is given in the comments of the neighbours in John 9/8: *Qui viderant eum prius quia mendicus erat* (AV "They which before had seen him that he was blind"). The implication may be that a day has elapsed between 80 and 81.

101–3   The praise of Jesus here has no counterpart in John at this point. Since no healing miracles have hitherto been dramatised in the cycle, the effect may be to suggest the episode as typical of a pattern of healing which has already been established. *gratiouse* 103 perhaps also points back to Christ's attitude towards the penitent adulteress, and clearly contrasts with the legalistic demands for justice by the Pharisees.

109–18, stanza 16   The stanza contains ten lines, rhyming aaabcccccb, instead of the expected eight. It is difficult to regard the extended stanza as other than a deliberate creation, since 109–12 seem required to complete 101–8, while 113–4 exactly correspond to John 9/12 and 115–6 to John 9/13, but the omission of 113–4 would restore a Chester stanza. Compare also 135–44, stanza 19, and note.

It is not clear why R substitutes *as was I* at 112, destroying rhyme.

109–10 Compare 16A/388–91.

135–44, stanza 19   The stanza contains ten lines, rhyming aaabccdddb, instead of the expected eight. All the lines have a counterpart in John 9/16–18, and it is difficult to regard the extended stanza as other than a deliberate creation. The two c-rhymes, 139–40 are particularly close to the biblical text.

135–40   The second Pharisee, who here represents those who believe, seems unconvincingly to become aligned with those who disbelieve at 193–6, 205–8.

135   *it* ARBH is to be preferred to the scribally erroneous *I* Hm.

145–76   The proceedings of the Pharisees suggest the activities of the ecclesiastical courts. Nuntius appears in the role of Summoner. The parents fear excommunication and heavy fines, 168, the latter unbiblical. Such courts were the object of satiric attack in medieval literature, particularly stressing the plight of the poor and helpless, as the blind man's parents are presented as being.

153–60, stanza 21   The b-rhymes, *out* 156 — *waye* 160, do not rhyme. No alternatives are immediately obvious, although it may be significant that 156 repeats the final b-rhyme of the preceding stanza. The readings seem to be those of the exemplar.

161–8   The parents' response is explained in John 9/22: *Quoniam timebant Judaeos; iam enim conspiraverant Iudaei, ut si quis eum confiteretur esse Christum, extra synogogam fieret* (AV "Because they feared the Jews; for the Jews had agreed already that if any man did confess that he was Christ, he should be put out of the synagogue"). *course us* 168 presumably conveys this sense of expulsion, suggesting also the contemporary excommunication.

164   Compare 6/389–406, 439. The parents' impoverished state is presumably inferred from the fact that their son was a beggar, although such a fact would not necessarily suggest parental poverty.

170   No indication of the parents' age is given in John. Presumably they are held to be aged because their son is an adult — see 185.

174   *you* ARBH is to be preferred for meaning to *wee* Hm, the latter perhaps influenced by *us* 173, 174. The line is metrically improved by A's omission of *ere*; R, however, does not follow A but replaces *ere* by *ever*; *that* BH represents an acceptable alternative. It is impossible to give priority to one reading, though the variants suggest an alternative in the exemplar.

176   *deceate* ARBH is to be preferred to *descent* Hm for meaning. Hm may suggest "dissent, rebellion", the suppressed response of the parents.

The Pharisee does not ask the whole question in John 9/19: *Hic est filius vester, quem vos dicitis quia caecus natus est? quomodo ergo nunc videt?* (AV "Is this your son, who ye say was born blind? How then doth he now see?"). But at 177–84 the father replies as if asked the full question. See 177–80, stanza 24, note.

PLAY XIII

177–80, stanza 24   The stanza is a single quatrain. Since the Pharisee asks only part of the biblical question at 173–6, whereas the father replies as if the full question had been asked, a quatrain omission in the exemplar may be suspected — perhaps following 175.

187   *bye nor sell* Although apparently a fill-in phrase, the words take up the previous references to begging, 36–43, and to poverty, 164. They also perhaps assume added significance when uttered by a guildsman in a medieval town who was authorised to trade by virtue of his guild-status.

197–204, stanzas 27–8   The two quatrains are not linked by a b-rhyme. 204 is the only line in the stanza to lack biblical equivalent; speculatively, if 204 read *to be free* for *to have remission*, a regular stanza-form would result.

H's omission of 201 + SH is erroneous. It may reflect uncertainty at the distribution of the eight lines among the speakers.

203   *you* ARH is to be preferred for meaning to *hee* Hm, and also in reflecting *vos* (AV "ye") in John 9/27. The Hm form is perhaps a result of confusion from the preceding *his*. *yea* B is apparently a formal variant of *you*.

205–34, stanzas 29–32   The stanza-division here is somewhat arbitrary. It would be possible to arrange the stanzas as three ten-line stanzas, viz: 205–14 (aaabccddde); 215–24 (aaabccddee); 225–34 (aaabccccc).

224 contains four strongly stressed syllables instead of the expected three; the omission of *as this* would produce a more regular form, but at the expense of the present rhyme-scheme.

eyee 231 Hm is presumably intended to suggest the rhyme-form *ee*, less clear in *eye* BH and lost in *eyne* AR.

234 contains four strongly stressed syllables instead of the expected three.

229   *Godes* ARBH is to be preferred to the erroneous *God* Hm for meaning and as reflecting John 9/35, *Filium Dei* (AV "The Son of God").

restored B does not seem intended as part of the line (see TNs). Its reference is not clear, but it seems to suggest the re-instatement of a word, line or sequence of lines in the text, and may well be an exemplar margin-note. Its presence suggests perhaps that the exemplar had been subjected to editing or censorship.

230   Compare John 9/36: *Quis est, Domine, ut credam in eum?* (AV "Who is he, Lord, that I might believe on him?"). *yea* here suggests the willingness expressed in the final clause of the Vulgate.

233   The omission of *I*(1) ARBH is to be preferred for syntax and meaning to its inclusion in Hm, the latter perhaps an anticipation of *I*(2)

234 + SH–300   Instead of continuing with the dialogue of Christ and the Pharisees which follows Christ's words to the blind man in John 9/39–10/21, the play moves to John 10/22–39, which is also set in the temple at Jerusalem but in wintertime at the feast of the dedication, John 10/22. In this account the questioners are called *Judaei*, John 10/24, 31, and there is no reference to the Pharisees. The shift of reference is suggested in the use of *Judaeus* in SHs here, although since the play's action is continuous these speakers must be either assumed to have been present as silent onlookers up to this point or identified with the *Vicini* or *Pharasaei*. The reasons for the change can only be a matter of speculation. The change may be to avoid a repetition of the image of spiritual blindness and sight in John 9/39–41, already used, or a preference for the more explicit nature of the later account in John. The image of the good shepherd from the omitted discourse has already been used in the prologue to the play, but it is taken up by the later discourse here used. But perhaps the naked hostility of the Jews on the later occasion was felt to provide a more effective conclusion to the episode.

235–6 Compare John 10/24: *Quousque animam nostram tollis?* (AV "How long dost thou make us to doubt?").

237 *appertly* For a regular four-stress line, the word must be tetrasyllabic, with two strongly stressed syllables.

249 *in my owne* It seems necessary to supply a further word (e.g. *realm, right*), unless the phrase is to be understood as "alone, unaided". *name* AR gives a clear meaning at the expense of rhyme; the variant is noted by Deimling as evidence of the close relationship between the two manuscripts.

251–6, stanza 35 The stanza has the irregular form aaabcb. Possibly two c-rhymes have been omitted. No reply from the Jews is quoted by John, but possibly a two-line speech by the first Pharisee has been lost. It may, however, be noted that the play lacks Christ's final words from John 10/30, having quoted them and explained them in the prologue to the play, 8–14; and that the key word of that explanation, *one*, would satisfy the requirement of the c-rhyme here. If the loss is from that part of Christ's reply, some deliberate intention to avoid duplication may be suspected and it might follow that the prologue should be considered to be later than the body of the play.

A has resolved the difficulties of stanzaic structure by forming a single line from elements of 255–6, producing an aaabb form by eliminating the 'irregular' c-rhyme line.

258 Although there is no obvious reason for A's omission of this line, which is restored in R, it is possible that the anachronistic *for cockes bones* may have worried the scribe if mere carelessness was not the cause.

265–76, stanzas 37–9 The BH arrangement is to be preferred in producing two regular eight-line Chester stanzas instead of three quatrains; viz.

JESUS	Wretches, manye a good deede
	I have donne, yea in great neede;
	now quite you fowle my meede
	to stone me on this manere.
PRIMUS JUDEUS	For thy good deede that thou hast wrought
	at this time stone we thee nought
	but for thie leasinge falsely wrought
	thou shewest apartelie here.
	Thou, that art man as well as I,
	makes thieself God here openly.
	There thou lyes fowle and falslye
	both in word and thought.

PLAY XIII

JESUS   But I doe well and truely
                              my Fathers biddinge by and by,
                              ells may you hope well I lye
                              and then leeves you me nought.

The AR reading suggests that the exemplar contained the whole passage, but that the additional BH lines had been cancelled. AR copied the resulting non-rhyming form. Hm adapted this version to produce the more usual rhyme-pattern aaab in stanza 38, a change possible because the a-rhymes of the first stanza were identical with the b-rhymes of the original second stanza; but the b-rhyme line contained three strongly stressed syllables instead of the four required for its new position at 271. Hm did not increase this line, but was able to reduce the four-stress a-rhyme line to three stresses to meet its new position as 272 by omitting *fowle and*. It is therefore difficult to explain the Hm-reading unless it represents a modification of the reading represented by AR and hence the exemplar-reading. Although it is possible that HmAR and BH derive from separate exemplars, it seems simpler to assume that BH merely recognised the resulting metrical irregularity and restored the cancelled lines. The cancellation may result from a feeling that the rebuke to Christ, deriving from John 10/33 and reflecting a characteristic objection to Christ's claims, was inappropriate, or even unnecessarily blasphemous, for the audience. It may be noted that John 10/34-6, Christ's rebuke in response, has no counterpart in the play.

266   *you* ARBH is to be preferred to the scribally erroneous *yea* Hm in reflecting John 10/32: *Ostendi vobis* (AV "Have I shewed you"). Hm may have been influenced by the emphatic *yea* of 261.

269   Compare John 10/33: *De bono opere* (AV "For a good work"). *deedes* ARB may be preferable to *deede* HmH in view of the specific *thy* HmBH, *the* AR; HmH suggest specific reference to the healing of the blind man.

278–80   "But since you will not believe me, address yourselves in a spirit of belief to my deeds that you can see, for nothing can be more true." Compare John 10/38: *Si autem facio, et si mihi non vultis credere, operibus credite* (AV "But if I do, though ye believe not me, believe the works"). *nor* 278 destroys the meaning of the passage and seems to be an error — perhaps for *believe*, which would be the equivalent of Vulgate *credite*, or for some preposition (e.g. *to, on*). If it is an error, it was present in the exemplar. It could have arisen as a result of the broken construction in which *deedes* was taken as object of *leeve* 277 instead of the object of *to* 279, *them* referring to *deedes*.

284 + SD   Although the direction and the following reaction seem to suggest that Jesus almost miraculously disappeared (compare *quyntly* 286), no such suggestion is present in John 10/39: *Et exivit de manibus eorum* (AV "But he escaped out of their hand").

288   *to-frapped* The word is not recorded by OED; but compare MED *frappen* (a) "to strike, beat", well attested into ME by OED. OED does, however, record *to-flap*, "to knock to pieces" (OED *to-*, prefix 2), a word of rare occurrence, attested by an example of 1382. The word seems to have been unfamiliar to AR and B. *to-clapped* AR is not recorded by OED but evidently derives from MED *clappen* 3 (a) "to strike (sb), beat", exemplified by OED to 1670; B takes *to* as an infinitive marker and in its substitution also replaces *all*. *wrapped* B gives no sense in this form, but may perhaps be regarded as a variant of *rap*, "to strike". The variants perhaps indicate that the participle-form was obscured or altered in the exemplar; the possibility that the exemplar contained a reading other than those attested by the manuscripts (e.g. *to-flapped*) cannot be excluded.

293–6 Compare 14/328–76 and 16/29–36. No such threat is issued after the present discourse in John, but in the raising of Lazarus, John 12/46–53, some Jews go to report Jesus's deeds to the Pharisees whereupon a meeting is summoned, as dramatised in play 14. Possibly it was felt that such an action should be anticipated in this play, but that it should not be allowed to disturb the effect of the raising of Lazarus.

300 *taberte* AR may be preferred to *tabret* HmBH as a form of *tabard*, "a garment of coarse material, a loose upper garment without sleeves" (OED). In this sense it is last recorded in 1568 by OED but it continued in related senses and should have been familiar to the scribes. *feare*, attested by all manuscripts, seems inappropriate and may represent an exemplar error for *tear*.

301–*Finis* On Mary, see further 14/1–136 and notes. Mary and Martha are presented also in Luke 10/38–42, where Mary sits attentively at Christ's feet and is rebuked by Martha, busy about household chores. This may be the episode indicated in 303, although no previous encounter of Christ and the sisters is dramatised in the cycle. The earlier characterisation of the sisters in Luke may be suggested also by John 11/20: *Martha ergo, ut audivit quia Iesus venit, occurrit illi; Maria autem domi sedebat* (AV "Then Martha, as soon as she heard that Jesus was coming, went and met him; but Mary sat still in the house"). The legendary history of the three characters is briefly indicated by *Legenda Aurea*, 'De Sancta Maria Magdalena'.

305–6 Compare John 11/3: *Miserunt ergo sorores eius ad eum* (AV "Therefore his sisters sent unto him"). John does not suggest that one of the sisters went herself to Christ to give him the news. In *Ludus Coventriae* 25/97–100, a *nuncius* goes to Jesus, his arrival being shown after the dramatic presentation of Lazarus' death and burial; in Digby *Mary Magdalen* both sisters go to Jesus and a similar idea may underlie *we* 305 AR, although 313 and 316+SD make it clear that only Martha meets Jesus, while Mary remains behind.

316 *by him* ARBH is to be preferred to *loe I am him* Hm for metre, and in reflecting the form and sense of John 11/4: *Pro gloria Dei, ut glorificetur Filius Dei per eam* (AV "For the glory of God, that the Son of God might be glorified thereby [i.e. by the sickness]"). The Hm reading gives four stressed syllables instead of the expected three.

317–24, stanza 45   *this plase* 319 ARBH is to be preferred to *this* Hm for rhyme and meaning, Hm having erroneously omitted the rhyme-word.

317–28 These early protestations of faith, anticipating 394–401, are unbiblical, but point at this early stage to the balance of human misery, faith in Christ and bewilderment at Christ's apparent indifference which constitute a major element in the dramatic effect of the play.

328 *leeche* Deimling comments: "Both [A] and [R] replace in 13/332 (Deimling's numbering) the verb *leech*, which occurs also in 11/159 and 13/332, according to H's reading, by the better known *ease."*

331   AR read *payne* for *pennance* HmBH, to the detriment of metre. Possibly Bellin felt that the sense of "penitential suffering", or even the theological overtones of the word, outweighed the general sense of "suffering, misery".

332 + SD   *sepulchrum* John 11/17, 38 uses the term *monumentum*. It is described in John 11/38 as: *Spelunca, et lapis superpositus erat ei* (AV "A cave, and a stone lay upon it"). The parallel with Christ's sepulchre is clear; but just as illustrations of the resurrection of Christ often showed him rising from a medieval tomb-chest, so illustrations of the raising of Lazarus often show him stepping out of a similar chest. John 11/21, 30–1 seems positively to exclude any possibility that the sisters kept vigil at the tomb, as here, but the play creates an effective tableau, with — if a table-tomb is envisaged — the sisters serving as weepers in the manner of sixteenth-century memorials. In *Ludus Coventriae* 25/165 the grave is called a *cave*, but at 149 it is a *pytt* and at 161: "This coors we burry here in þis pytte"; while at 165–72 the sisters also sit by the grave weeping, though only for a short time. Compare Digby *Mary Magdalen* 835: "With wepers to þe erth yow hym bryng".

procul   The play telescopes distance and time. Jesus was at Bethabara, beyond the Jordan, John 10/40. After receiving the news of Lazarus' illness, he delayed two days before setting out, John 11/6; and on reaching Bethany, he learned that Lazarus had been entombed four days, John 11/17, Chester 411–2. So, realistically, 301–8 takes place at least five days before 373; 318–32 four days or less before 373; and 333–72 two days after the dialogue at 309–16.

333 + SH   John 11/8 does not ascribe the warning to any specific speaker.

334–6   Compare 255–300.

340   *trespasseth* Compare *tresspasseth* 343, and John 11/9–10, *offendit* (AV "stumbleth"). *Ludus Coventriae* 25/225–8 makes a less awkward combination of concrete and abstract:

> But if men walke whan it is nyght
> Sone they offende in þat dyrknes;
> be-cawse they may haue no cler syght
> they hurte there ffete ofte in such myrkenes.

345–56   The exposition has no biblical counterpart but has authoritative precedent in commentaries such as Augustine, *Tractatus in Evangelium Ioannis* 49 11/8 (PL 35/1750–1).

353–6   Compare *Before* 1 and note.

thester 355 H may be preferred to *Chester* HmARD in continuing the day night imagery — compare *thesternes* 1/12, 2/12, which seems to have caused no difficulties for HmARH. This is the last occurrence of *thester* recorded by OED, dated a1500, the previous occurrence being 1400; the word does not seem to have been in general use. *Chester* HmARB may derive from confusion of *c* and *t*. Such confusion might be helped by the city-name, giving a slightly comic implication. It might also be helped by association with *chest* OED 3, MED 2, "coffin", *chesten* MED, *chest* EDD, "to put into the coffin"; *chesting*, "the ceremony of putting a corpse into the coffin"; and *chester*, "one who puts a corpse into a coffin", recorded once in 1552 by OED. Some sense of underlying symbolic journeying might underlie the reference. The meaning would then be "Whoever follows me, truth to say, can go no mortal way (i.e. to the coffin or grave) for light is established in him" — suggesting the life-death antithesis rather than day-night.

356 + Latin   John 9/4–5: AV "I must work the works of him that sent me, while it is day; the night cometh, when no man can work. As long as I am in the world, I am the light of the world." The text occurs as part of Jesus' reply to his disciples' questions about the cause of the man's blindness — see 59–64. It is used in this position presumably to suggest a continuing thematic link, pointed by the day-night symbolism continued from the first episode, and particularly by the echo of the Latin with which the play began.

357–64, stanza 50   *tydinge* 357 H is to be preferred for rhyme to *tidinges* HmARB. The variation is not an indication of earlier and later forms, but *tidinges* may have been felt to be the more frequent form. The singular, "a piece of news", is semantically appropriate here. H may simply have substituted the singular form in recognition of rhyme.

358   *my* John 11/11 reads *noster* (AV "our").

361 + SH   No speaker is specified by John 11/12.

361–64 + SH   In an inexplicable omission, B has also re-ascribed 365–9.

367–8   "I am happy, I know, that I was not there, as you can see." The passage diverges so markedly from the biblical text as to suggest corruption; compare John 11/15: *Et gaudeo propter vos, ut credatis, quoniam non eram ibi; sed eamus ad eum* (AV "And I am glad for your sakes that I was not there, to the intent ye may believe; nevertheless let us go unto him"). *propter vos* has no counterpart in the text, leaving the nature of Jesus' joy unspecified; and the purpose clause, *ut credatis* seems to have been rendered as *as you may see* 368 — the object of *see* being apparently Jesus' joy. Other possible indications of textual corruption are the repeated rhyme on *I* 366 and 367; the apparent four-stress line at 368 instead of the expected three-stress line; and the inconsequential *I wott* 367 Hm. This last is rendered *you wott* in ARBH, perhaps suggesting the awareness stated in *as you may see* 368; but A and R negate the verb, perhaps attempting to suggest that, though the disciples might see Jesus' joy, they could not know how or why it existed.

It seems probable that *as* 368 represents an exemplar substitution for *that*; the substitution could arise if *that*, introducing the result-clause of the biblical text, was misunderstood as a pronoun and replaced to avoid a supposed syntactical ellipsis. It is possible that the much varied words *I wott that* 367 Hm represent a confusion of some counterpart to biblical *propter vos; you* 367 ARBH would then correspond to the biblical pronoun, and *I* Hm would be a scribal substitution resulting from the presence of *I*(1) and (3) in the same line.

The mistranslated phrases are central to the understanding of the miracle as a sign; compare *Glossa Ordinaria*, 'Evang. Joan.' 11/15 (PL 114/399): *Non quod modo inciperent credere, sed ut robustius crederent. Semper enim fides eorum miraculis augebatur*; and Comestor, *Historia Scholastica*, 'In Evangelia' 108 (PL 198/1593) claims that Jesus added the words: *Quia dum eis longe posita indicat, roboratur fides eorum.* The lines should thus be a counterpart to 55–8.

PLAY XIII   195

389–93, stanza 54   The stanza consists of five lines, rhyming aaabc; three lines have been lost in the second quatrain. 389–92 correspond to John 11/25. 393 corresponds to Jesus' final *Credis hoc?*, John 11/26 (AV "Believest thou this?"). But the passage has nothing corresponding to John 11/26: *Et omnis qui vivit et credit in me, non morietur in aeternum* (AV "And whosoever liveth and believeth in me shall never die"). Possibly this section of John made up the part of stanza 54 which seems to have been lost.

393 is a four-stress a-rhyme here; *be* ARBH seems required for rhyme and meaning.

402–9, stanza 56   The b-rhymes, *to* 405 — *donne* 409, do not rhyme, although the forms are attested by all manuscripts. Rhyme would be restored by reading *do* 409.

422–9   Compare John 11/35: *Et lacrimatus est Iesus* (AV "Jesus wept"); Jesus' sorrow at Mary's words is also stressed in John 11/33. But John also indicates that the Jews were present in the house of Mary and Martha to comfort them — they grieve also, John 11/33, and they marvel at Christ's grief, John 11/34. There is no sense there that they are hostile or cynical bystanders, as here. In *Ludus Coventriae* 25 the neighbours are four *consolatores* who help the sisters; in Digby *Mary Magdalen* they are presumably suggested by the *wepars arayyd in blak* 841 + SD.

422   *donne* Compare John 11/34: *Ubi posuistis eum?* (AV "Where have ye laid him?"). The H rendering is acceptable and is perhaps a better reflection of the Vulgate.

427   *reeme* Apart from an occurrence of 1674, specifically defined as Lancashire usage, this is the last instance of the verb recorded by OED. But it is listed by EDD for Lancashire and Cheshire and seems to have continued in local use. For other occurrences in the cycle, see *Glossary*.

440   *grace*, John 11/40: *Gloriam Dei* (AV "The glory of God"); *graces* H seems an unnecessary change to plural.

shalt HmARB reflects *videbis*, John 11/40; but *shouldst* H provides the form expected after the past tense *leeved* 439 (John 11/40 *credideris*), and AV similarly reads *shouldest*.

441   The line contains four strongly stressed syllables instead of the expected three. The omission of *thee* would give the more usual final line.

441 + SD   Compare John 11/41: *Elevatis sursum oculis* (AV "Jesus lifted up his eyes"). The more detailed instructions here are presumably for dramatic emphasis. Compare 5/319 + SD.

451–7   No speech is attributed to Lazarus by John. Here the incident is more clearly linked to the Harrowing of Hell; compare 17/137–8 ff. Compare the comment of *infernus* in the apocryphal Gospel of Nicodemus (Tischendorf, *op.cit.*), Pars II, 'Descensus Christi ad Inferos', 4/3 (20/3): *Ego enim tunc quando audivi imperium verbi eius, contremui perterritus pavore, et omnia officia mea simul mecum conturbata sunt. Nec ipsum Lazarum tenere potuimus, sed excutiens se ut aquila per omnem agilitatem et celeritatem salivit exiens a nobis, et ipsa terra quae tenebat Lazari corpus mortuum statim reddidit vivum. I* 454 would seem to be a re-ascription of *ego* in the above passage from reference to Hell to reference to Lazarus.

458–65, stanza 63   The b-rhymes, *beforne* 461 — *kneene* 465, do not rhyme. Some corruption may be suspected in view of the similarity of 465 to the last line of the following stanza, 473. *kneey* RBH, and the formal variant *knye* A, lacking *n*, increase the sense of the absence of rhyme, but may reflect an exemplar form to which Hm has added *n*.

458   *loose*   Compare John 11/44: *Ligatus pedes et manus institis, et facies illius sudario erat ligata* (AV "Bound hand and foot with grave-cloths, and his face was bound about with a napkin"). Compare also *Ludus Coventriae* 25/145–6: "Now he is wounde in a chete"; Digby *Mary Magdalen* 910 + SD: "Here xall lazer a-ryse, trossyd with towelles, In a shete."

466–73, stanza 64   The Hm b-rhymes, *men* 469 — *knees* 473, do not rhyme. Two possible solutions exist. One is provided by H, reading *meny* 469 and *knee* 473, although such a reading breaches the convention of ending the three-stress line on a stressed syllable. The alternative is to read *knen* at 473 — compare *kneene* 465, and 458–65, stanza 63 note. However, only Hm has a plural form at 473, ARBH being singular.

473 + SH   It is not clear why H ascribes the penultimate stanza of the play to *Martha* unless following a mechanical pattern of ascribing individual stanzas to different speakers. While there are no major indicators of speaker in the stanza, the extended emotional statement and the vow of constant devotion seem more appropriate to Mary, the more emotional of the two sisters, and prepare us to some extent for her important roles in plays 14 and 18.

482–5, stanza 66   The last stanza is, unusually, a quatrain, although it seems complete in itself and appropriately concludes the play.

482   The plural forms, *daughters* AR, *deghter* H, are to be preferred for meaning to the singular *doughter* HmB which implies a specific address to Mary alone.

485   *to Jerusalem*   These words are found in other plays — compare York 24/204: "And to Jerusalem will I wende", *Ludus Coventriae* 25/451: "To-ward my passyon I wyl me dyght". But in those plays, the raising of Lazarus is followed by Christ's entry to Jerusalem and the start of the Passion sequence. In John 11/5, Jesus went into Ephraim after the raising of Lazarus, and in Chester 14/1 he is shown returning to Bethany again before setting out for Jerusalem. There is no obvious reason for this precise but misleading statement in the play; it would, however, allow a producer to move directly to 14/137, omitting Jesus' anointing by Mary.

PLAY XIV

Dramatis Personae Jesus, Petrus, Philippus, Simon, Lazarus, Martha, Maria Magdalena, Judas Iscarioth, Janitor, Primus Civis, Secundus Civis, Tertius Civis, Quartus Civis, Quintus Civis, Sextus Civis, Primus Puer, Secundus Puer, Primus Mercator, Secundus Mercator, Cayphas, Annas, Primus Pharaseus, Secundus Pharaseus.

Locations
The house of Simon the Leper — his/my/thy house 6, 22, 101, *in* Bethanye 1
a castle 138 *in the* holye cittie 209, towne 150, 188, cittie 158, 163, civitatem 152 + SD
this/the temple 244, 253, 261, 366, templum 224 + SD.

Properties
Anointing — oyntment 49, 67, 271, 286, *in* pixidem 56 + SD, boyst 69
Entry — an asse and a foale 140, 165, asellam 208 + SD, asine 224 + SD; branches 204, branches of the palme tree 189, ramis palmarum 208 + SD; clothes 195, vestimenta 208 + SD, pannos 224 + SD
Cleansing of Temple — flagello 224 + SD, 260 + SD; all our warre 230, my table with my money 234
Betrayal — sylver 388, thirtie penyes 399, thy moneye 395, 404.

Costumes
Judas — pursse 284.

Sources
Anointing — Matthew 26/6 14, Mark 14/3–9, Luke 7/36–50, John 12/1–9
Entry to Jerusalem — Matthew 21/1–11, Mark 11/1–10, Luke 19/29–44, John 12/12–9
Cleansing of the temple — Matthew 21/12–16, Mark 11/15–9, Luke 19/45–6, John 2/12–6
Judas' intent to betray Jesus — Matthew 26/14–6, Mark 14/10–2, Luke 22/2–6

The Council — Matthew 26/3-5, 14-6, Mark 14/1-2, 10-11, Luke 22/1-6, John 11/47-53.

Play-heading The play consists of a number of episodes, each attested by three or four gospel accounts, which carry the action from the raising of Lazarus to the eve of the Passover. Of these, *Ludus Coventriae* 26/462-525 presents the anointing in the context of the Last Supper, and Digby *Mary Magdalen* 615-721 presents the anointing, preceded by details of Mary Magdalen's sinful life and the origins of her repentance. York 25 shows the entry into Jerusalem, as does *Ludus Coventriae* 26/179-337. The cleansing of the temple is not elsewhere dramatised. The conspiracy and bargain appear in Wakefield 20/1-313, York 26, and the remainder of *Ludus Coventriae* 26 to line 668.

1   *Bethenye* Compare 13/485 and note. Jesus was in the wilderness of Ephraim, but came to Bethany six days before the Passover, John 21/1 — Matthew 26/6, Mark 14/3 merely state that he was in Bethany. No account suggests a particular purpose in the visit, as here.

2-6   The account here represents a conflation of two different biblical narratives. Matthew 26, Mark 14, John 12 describe the supper with Martha, Mary and Lazarus; Luke 7/36-50 describes an earlier occasion where Christ was dining at the house of Simon the Pharisee. The events on these two occasions were comparable, in that Christ was anointed on both occasions but also differed in some important details. Augustine, *Harmony* II, 79/154, regards the incidents as separate occasions but involving the same woman, a view taken also by Bede, *In Lucae Evangelia* 3/28 (PL 92/423-4) and transmitted in *Glossa Ordinaria*, 'Evang. Luc.' 7/38 (PL 114/271). Conflation of the accounts, in the manner of Chester, was aided by the fact that the hosts on both occasions were called Simon — the Pharisee in Luke, the Leper in Matthew 26/6, Mark 14/3. John 12/2 does not specify the location, but his statement that Lazarus sat at meat and Martha served perhaps suggests rather the house of Martha, Mary and Lazarus.

Ludus Coventriae 26/357 sets the anointing in the context of the Last Supper, identifying Symon Leprous as the man bearing the pitcher of water who provided the room for the Last Supper.

12   *there place* Contrast *his house* 6. The change in pronoun may reflect the ambiguity in location between Matthew-Mark and John, noted under 2-6 note above. But it was also inferred that Simon was related to Martha, Mary and Lazarus, an idea which might remove the inconsistency here — see Nicephorus Callistus, *Ecclesiasticae Historiae* 1/27 (PG 145/711); but contrast 13/301–*Finis* note.

14-20   There is no biblical authority for the healing of Simon by Jesus. But compare Jerome, *Commentar. in Evangelium Matthaei* 4/26 (PL 26/198), reflected in Comestor, *Historia Scholastica*, 'In Evangelia' 116 (PL 198/1597): *Simon fuerat*

PLAY XIV

leprosus, et a Domino sanatus, sed tamen adhuc pristinum nomen manebat, sicut et adhuc dicitur Matthaeus publicanus.

27-32   Compare 13/450-7.

33   "Welcome, my lovely and beautiful lord." *and* conjoins *lovely* and *leere*, indicating that the latter is an adjective. *of* H suggests that *leere* is there a noun, "countenance".

39-40   The reference is presumably to Luke 10/38-42: *Martha autem satagebat circa frequens ministerium* (AV "But Martha was cumbered about much serving"). If *other place* 40 refers to location, it might suggest a distinction between the previous occasion at Martha's house and this occasion at Simon's. It is difficult to determine what the lines would convey to the audience.

40 + SD   *Maria Magdalena*   See 13/301-*Finis* note. Of the gospels, only John 12/3 names the woman as *Maria*, and nowhere is there any biblical identification of her with the Mary Magdalen of a separate episode, Luke 8/2. But the fact that the redemption of Mary Magdalen is mentioned in Luke as the episode following the anointing led to the identification of her with the woman in Luke's account of the anointing. The similarity of name with the woman of John's account encouraged the idea that the same "Mary" was involved on both occasions. John does not expressly identify the woman with Martha's sister, but the inference is reasonable, and hence it followed that Mary Magdalen was identified as the sister of Martha and Mary. This identification was influentially stated by Gregory — compare *In Evangelia*, lib 2, Homilia 53 and Homilia 25 — and is seen also in Bede, *In Lucae Evangelia Expositio* 3/28 (PL 92/423-9) and in *Glossa Ordinaria*, 'Evang. Marc.' 14/3 (PL 114/229). Similar identifications are made in *Stanzaic Life* 7014, Digby *Mary Magdalen*, *Ludus Coventriae* 25.

The woman in Chester is never spoken of by name; compare the unspecific *woman* 121 of Jesus' address. The audience might argue, from Jesus' reference to Martha and Mary (2) and the fact that one sister — also not identified by name in the spoken text — has already appeared, that this is Mary; and a knowledge of the account in Luke combined with 133 would suggest Mary Magdalen. On the absence of name, compare *Legenda Aurea*, 'De Sancta Maria Magdalena': *Cum igitur Magdalena divitiis abundaret, quia rerum affluentiam voluptas comes sequitur, quanto divitiis et pulchritudine splenduit, tanto corpus suum voluptati substravit, unde jam proprio nomine perdito peccatrix consueverat appellari.* The gospel accounts give no real indication of Mary's age, social standing, or sin; but compare her presentation as youthful courtesan in the Digby *Mary Magdalen*.

ulublustro unguenti alabastro BH is to be preferred to the scribally erroneous *alablastro* Hm, *albastro* AR. The phrase *alabastro unguenti* occurs only in Luke 7/37; compare Matthew 26/7: *alabastrum unguenti pretiosi* (AV "an alabaster box of very precious ointment"), Mark 14/3: *alabastrum unguenti nardi spicati pretiosi* (AV "an alabaster box of ointment of spikenard very precious"), John 12/3: *libram unguenti nardi pistici pretiosi* (AV "a pound of ointment of spikenard, very costly").

55   *great* H may be preferred in producing the expected four-stress line instead of the unusual three-stress line of HmARB.

57–64 The dialogue with Simon is from Luke 7/39–47. But at Luke 7/39: *Phariseus ... ait intra se* (AV "The Pharisee ... he spake within himself"), and Jesus read his thoughts, whereas here Simon speaks in an aside to Judas, prompting the following speech and identifying the disciple to the audience. In Digby *Mary Magdalen* Christ's words to Simon are unprompted, the intention apparently being to suggest secret doubts in Simon.

59–60 The lines have been inexplicably and erroneously reversed by A, but the error is corrected in R. The reversal does not affect the syntax or meaning.

61 Simon's disbelief stands in contrast to Mary's faith, a point emphasised by Gregory, Homilia in Evangelia II, 33/4 and found also in *Glossa Ordinaria*, 'Evang. Luc.' 7/47 (PL 114/272).

64 + SH Only John 12/4 specifies the speaker as Judas. Immediately after the identification, John 12/5, Judas' true reasons for concern are stated, but here they remain concealed from the audience until 281–8.

65 *brother* An ironic claim of fellowship with the Pharisee made by Jesus' betrayer which effectively points to the collusion of Judas with the Pharisees later.

70 *three hundreth penyes* Compare 289–96 and note.

75 *your* ARBH is to be preferred for meaning to *you* Hm. The Hm reading assumes some meaning: "Whatever you desire may be so", a fact contributing to the error.

76 + SH–80 The lines are required to complete stanza 10 but are erroneously omitted by H. They have no biblical counterpart. H's omission coincides with the movement from fol. 73^v to 74^r.

85 *the* ARBH is to be preferred for meaning to the scribally erroneous *they* Hm, the latter perhaps influenced by *they* 86.

95 "That the one to whom Jesus forgave the greater portion". ARH remove *hee* (2), with corresponding loss of meaning; B omits *that hee* (1), supplementing the line with an additional syllable to give an acceptable reading.

104 Compare 56 + SD. Luke 7/38 mentions Mary wiping tears from Jesus' feet with her hair. John 12/3 suggests that Mary wiped the ointment from his feet.

110 Matthew 26/7, Mark 14/3 refer only to the anointing of Jesus' head; Luke 7/46 — on which this part of the play is mainly based — and John 12/3 refer only to the anointing of his feet. Compare 56 + SD and 270. Augustine, Harmony II, 79/155 argues that both head and feet were anointed, as also Comestor, *Historia Scholastica*, 'In Evangelia' 116 (PL 198/1597). But Bede, *In Lucae Evangelium Expositio* 3/28 (PL 92/423–4) and *Glossa Ordinaria*, 'Evang. Matth.' 26/7 (PL 114/167) argue that Mary anointed the feet as a sinner and, on a later occasion, anointed the head when chaste.

112 Compare Luke 7/47: *Remittuntur ei peccata multa* (AV "Her sins, which are many, are forgiven"). *her* HmARB is to be preferred to *here* H in reflecting *ei (her)* in the Vulgate account.

113–7 One might have expected some use to be made of the comments in John 12/7–8 that Mary was anointing Jesus' body for burial, an idea reflected also in Jesus'

PLAY XIV   201

final words in Matthew 26/12, Mark 14/8. Instead, the text derives from Matthew 26/10, Mark 14/6.

thou 114 BH may be preferred for syntax, meaning and metre to its omission in HmAR, an omission perhaps influenced by its juxtaposition with *thee*. 114–5 do not accurately reflect Matthew 26/10: *Quid molesti estis huic mulieri?* (AV "Why trouble ye the woman?"). The singular pronoun here indicates that Jesus' comment is fittingly directed only to Judas, as opposed to the more general statement at 118–9.

121–8   The lines combine Jesus' comments in Luke 7/47, 48, 50, in 121–4 with his final words in Matthew 26/13, Mark 14/9 in 125–8.

133–4   The expulsion of seven devils from Mary Magdalen is mentioned in Luke 8/2, immediately following the account of the anointing in that gospel. It is recalled in Mark 16/9. It took place during Christ's tour of Galilee and is quite distinct from the anointing, which seems to have occurred at Capernaum.

With *dryven* HmARB, compare Mark 16/9 *eiecerat* (AV "he had cast"); with *removed* H, compare Luke 8/2: *De qua septem daemonia exierant* (AV "Out of whom went seven devils").

In *Ludus Coventriae* 26/495 Jesus expels the devils after the anointing; in Digby *Mary Magdalen* 691 + SD the devils are seen to leave her after the anointing.

136 + SD   It is only in John that the entry into Jerusalem follows the anointing immediately, although the entry takes place on the following day. Jesus requested the animals near Bethphage and Bethany, at the Mount of Olives. The episode of commandeering the animals is not in John, and the account here is a composite of the other gospels.

137   The gospels do not specify the two disciples, although Peter and Philip also go in York 25. In *Ludus Coventriae* 26 they are named as Philip and Jacobus Minor. Here the reference to *Phillippe* 147 serves to distinguish the two for the audience.

138   *a castle* Compare Matthew 21/2: *Ite in castellum quod contra vos est* (AV "Go into the village over against you"), as also Mark 10/2, Luke 19/30. Compare *civitatem* 152 + SD, *this cittie* 158, 163, where the sense is clearly that Jesus sent the disciples ahead into Jerusalem to find the animals. Compare Comestor, *Historia Scholastica*, 'In Evangelia' 117 (PL 198/1598): *Castellum ... id est in Jerusalem.* York 25/14 and *Ludus Coventriae* 26/183 similarly used the term "castle".

140   Matthew 21/2 specifies the two animals, *asinum ... et pullum cum ea* (AV "an ass ... and a colt with her") —' compare Mark 11/2 *pullum*, Luke 19/30 *pullum asinae. a* Hm suggests the Vulgate reading, but *her* ARBH may be inferred from Matthew and Luke.

143   Compare 157–60. In neither case in the gospel accounts is Jesus' purpose specified in advance.

153–60, stanza 20   No manuscript has *gone* for *goe*, required for rhyme at 156. The error was apparently in the exemplar.

154–6   Matthew does not record any objection. Mark 11/5 refers to objections from *quidem de illic stantibus* (AV "certain of them that stood there"). The account here presupposes an "owner" (Janitor) and also bystanders (168 + SD). Janitor is also spokesman in York 25 and spreads tidings to the burgesses, as here; in *Ludus Coventriae* 26 he is *Burgensis* but seems to play no part in heralding Christ's coming.

161–8 The basis of the stanza is two statements in John:

164–5 — John 12/12, of the people in Jerusalem for the feast: *Cum audissent quia venit Iesus Ierosolymam* (AV "When they heard that Jesus was coming to Jerusalem").

167–8 — John 12/17–8: *Testimonium ergo perhibebat turba, quae erat cum eo quando Lazarum vocavit de monumento, et suscitavit eum a mortuis. Propterea et obviam venit ei turba, quia audierunt eum fecisse hoc signum* (AV "The people therefore that was with him when he called Lazarus out of his grave, and raised him from the dead, bare record. For this cause the people also met him, for that they heard that he had done this miracle"). See also 185–8.

170 Compare Matthew 21/11: *Populi autem dicebant: 'Hic est Iesus, propheta Nazareth Galilaeae'* (AV "And the multitude said, This is Jesus the prophet of Nazareth of Galilee").

175–6 *worlde* 175 ARB is to be preferred for meaning to its omission in HmH. The omission of the word in HmH is strange and may reflect some obscurity in the exemplar. Even including it, however, a rough metre results and a disyllabic form might be preferable.

it 176 BH may be preferred to its omission in HmAR in producing a more regular sequence of strongly and weakly stressed syllables, but H's addition of *great* destroys the resulting regularity. The variants here further strengthen the probability of obscurity in the exemplar.

189–96 John 12/13 mentions only the palm-branches, Luke 19/36 only the clothes. Matthew 21/8, Mark 11/8 refer to both, but in the reverse order to Chester, mentioning clothes first and branches second; they do not specify *palm*-branches. But whereas Matthew and Mark mention the strewing of the branches on the ground, John 12/13 says only that the people were carrying branches, as here.

197 *preeven* Hm is to be preferred to *approven* AR, *appreven* BH which seem to have been influenced to the detriment of metre by *appertlye*. It is possible that Hm has restored an altered exemplar form.

200 + SH The gospels do not mention the boys in the account of the entry itself, but there is reference in Matthew 21/15, the cleansing of the temple: *Videntes autem principes sacerdotum et scribae mirabilia quae fecit, et pueros clamantes in templo et dicentes 'Hosanna filio David', indignati sunt* (AV "And when the chief priests and scribes saw the wonderful things that he did, and the children crying in the temple and saying 'Hosanna to the Son of David'; they were sore displeased"). Compare Comestor, *Historia Scholastica*, 'In Evangelia' 118 (PL 198/1599) and *Legenda Aurea*, 'De Dominica Ramis Palmarum'. The entry is commemorated in Palm Sunday, the Sunday before Easter Day.

201–8, stanza 26 No manuscript has *hond* for *hand* 204, required to rhyme with *fonde* 208 H; and no manuscript has *fande* 208, required to rhyme with *hand* 204. *handes* 204 AR and *founde* 208 HmARB remove the possibility of rhyme.

PLAY XIV

201 See 170. Presumably the boy is the Janitor's son and fulfills an informing and organising role similar to that of his father.

208 + SD The quotation concluding paragraph 1 is from Matthew 21/9: AV "Hosanna to the son of David. Blessed is he that cometh in the name of the Lord; Hosanna in the highest." The wording is slightly different in the other gospel accounts. It derives from Psalm 118/26 AV, itself Messianic, referring to the entry of the Messiah into his kingdom.

No reference is here made to the mounting by Jesus, with the apostles setting garments on the ass's back — Matthew 21/7, Mark 11/7, Luke 19/35; contrast York 25/267–87, *Ludus Coventriae* 26/211–2.

209–24 The lament is found only in Luke 19/41–4.

210–2 "You do not know today what peace you have — you cannot see it — but you shall endure misery." Compare Luke 19/42: '*Quia si cognovisses et tu, et quidem in hac die tua, quae ad pacem tibi. Nunc autem abscondita sunt ab oculis tuis*' (AV "If thou hadst known, even thou, at least in this thy day, the things which belong unto thy peace! but now they are hid from thine eyes").

214 *syde* H represents an uncancelled error, resulting originally either from the automatic writing of a common collocation or from confusion with *syde* 216. But A omits *waye*, perhaps suggesting some confusion about the rhyme-word in the exemplar.

217–24, stanza 28 *come* 220 H is to be preferred for rhyme and meaning to the past participle *commen* Hm, which suggests an attempt at imperfect rhyme. *coming* B destroys rhyme; AR substitute *commaundmente(s)*, destroying rhyme. The H form is cited by Deimling as evidence of H's superiority. *come* sb, OED "arrival, coming", is last exemplified by OED in c1470. *coming* B may represent a substitution of the more familiar form, perhaps even a basis for Hm's modification. AR change the meaning of the passage.

217–24 Compare Bede, *In Lucae Evangelium Expositio* 5/19 (PL 92/570) and Comestor, *Historia Scholastica*, 'In Evangelia' 118 (PL 198/1600): *Merito autem eam perituram dixit Dominus, quia, cum milvus et hirundo cognoscant tempus suum, ipsa non cognovit tempus visitationis suae.* Both cite Jeremiah 8/7. It was commonplace to contrast the ecstatic welcome given to Jesus as he rode from the Mount of Olives with the jeering audience for his ascent of Calvary, as in *Legenda Aurea*, 'De Dominica in Ramis Palmarum'.

224 + SD The cleansing of the temple is described in all gospels, but in John 2/12–6 the account is from an early stage of Christ's ministry and seems to be a separate occasion. *Glossa Ordinaria*, 'Evang. Joan.' 2/13 (PL 114/365), suggests two separate occasions; but Tatian conflates the accounts, including the detail from John 2/15: *Quasi flagellum de funiculis* (AV "A scourge of small cords"), as here. Mark 11/11–2 indicates that the cleansing took place on the day after Jesus' first entry into Jerusalem; i.e. Monday.

225–32, stanza 29 The b-rhymes do not here rhyme. One may read either *marchandie* for *marchandize* 228, or *anyes* for *anoye* 232. OED regards *merchandy* as an earlier form of late ME *merchandry*. The error seems to have been present in the exemplar since no manuscript has an acceptable form.

227-8   The lines render John 2/16: *Nolite facere domum Patris mei domum negotiationis* (AV "Make not my father's house an house of merchandise").

228 + SH   The number of traders here specified may be influenced by Matthew 26/60, where two false witnesses appear before the High Priests, corresponding to the third and fourth Jews of Play 16.

234   The line contains three strongly stressed syllables instead of the expected four.

234-5   The detail of the overthrow of the tables derives from Matthew 21/12.

237-48   The idea that Christ's action suggests regal pretension has no explicit counterpart in the biblical accounts, but anticipates charges levelled against Christ at his trial. The dialogue of Christ and the merchants is taken from John 2/18-20.

241-8, stanza 31   *thinge* 242 ARBH is to be preferred for rhyme to *thinges* Hm.

249   *signe* AR may be preferred to *signes* HmBH in reflecting John 2/18, *signum*. Compare *tokeninge* 246.

250   *thou* BH and *of* B may be preferred for meaning and metre to HmAR, which contain only two strongly stressed syllables.

253-6   Compare John 2/19: *Solvite templum hoc, et in tribus diebus excitabo illud* (AV "Destroy this temple, and in three days I will raise it up"). Jesus does not suggest that he will destroy the temple but challenges the Jews to destroy it; but compare the report to the High Priests in Matthew 26/61: *Hic dixit: 'Possum destruere templum Dei'* (AV "This fellow said: 'I am able to destroy the temple of God'") — similarly Mark 14/58 — seen also in 16/21-8. John 2/21 claims that Christ was referring to the temple of his own body, but it is doubtful if such a sense is conveyed by these lines in the context of the play. The reply is not found in other gospel accounts, but instead, a debate on Christ's authority takes place on the following day — Matthew 21/23, Mark 11/27-33.

257-64, stanza 33   *moe* 262 ARBH is to be preferred for rhyme to *more* Hm.

265-88   The characterisation of Judas is found in John 12/6, immediately following his complaint about Mary's extravagance. But the betrayal is not in John but in the other gospels. Matthew 26/8 notes that the disciples *indignati sunt* (AV "had indignation"), Mark 14/4: *Erant autem quidam indigne ferentes intra semetipsos* (AV "And there were some that had indignation within themselves"), and both gospels then pass immediately from the anointing to Judas' betrayal, suggesting a causative link thereby. Commentators were at pains to stress that Judas' action at this point did not contradict John 13/27 where Satan enters Judas when Christ gives him the sop of bread: compare Bede, *In Lucae Evangelium Expositio* 6/22 (PL 92/593).

270   See 110 and note.

276   *too*, "also". *twoo* B suggests that the scribe understood the word to represent the number *two*, being perhaps misled by *thrye* 275; *towe* A may show similar confusion, but the form is more ambiguous.

PLAY XIV

289–96 It was commonplace that the sum for which Judas sold Christ bore some relationship to the cost of the ointment. See Comestor, *Historia Scholastica*, 'In Evangelia' 148 (PL 198/1614), and also *Stanzaic Life* 7013–36, especially 7029–36:

> ȝ ffor he vset had by-fore
> Of Cristes gode the tethe to stele
> ther-fore hym greuet wonder sore
> that he with hy[t] might not dele
>
> And euen for als muche mony
> as teithe of hit wold come to
> Ihesu Crist to hom sold he
> for hym thoght hyt was forto do.

Similarly Wakefield 20/270–81, especially 278–9:

> And if thre hundreth be right told
> the tent parte is euen thryty

and York 26/127–54.

John 12/5 gives the value of the ointment as *trecentis denariis* (AV "three hundred pence") and the covenanted sum for Christ's betrayal, Matthew 26/15 is *triginta argenteos* (AV "thirty pieces of silver"). Since the argurion was equivalent to three denarii, the mathematics of the computation were confused. The illogicality of *hundrethfould* 296 is indicative of Judas' state of mind.

289 *hundreth* ARBH is to be preferred to the scribally erroneous *hundeth* Hm.

305–20 305–12 are the words of priests and Pharisees at John 11/48, to which Caiaphas' retort, John 11/50, is here added to give a single speech. The text, however, rephrases John 11/50: *Nec cogitatis quia expedit vobis ut unus moriatur homo pro populo, et non tota gens pereat* (AV "Nor consider that it is expedient for us, that one man should die for the people, and that the whole nation perish not"), expressly stated to be prophetic in John 11/51. In Matthew and Mark the meeting follows the anointing; in John it follows the raising of Lazarus. In Wakefield and York, Pilate is a member of the assembly.

308 "And have delight in him". *likinge* is used in the sense of OED *liking* 4, "the condition of being fond of or not averse to". B does not seem to have understood the construction and, in substituting *haste* for *hase*, destroys rhyme.

320 + SH Annas is not mentioned in any of the preliminary meetings of the Sanhedrin, but in Luke 3/2 Annas and Caiaphas are said to be high priests for the year, and at John 18/13 Annas is said to be Caiaphas' father-in-law. It is to Annas that Jesus is first taken after capture. Here, although subordinate to Caiaphas, the main mover for Christ's death according to John, he is given an early and prominent role in the conspiracy. And to him is ascribed first the advice to act discreetly deriving from Matthew 26/5, Mark 14/2, and preceding there the anointing — see 321–8, 353–60.

322 *needesly* Hm represents OED *needsly*, "necessarily, of necessity", but seems to be a scribal substitution in view of *nedelye* ARBH.

327 Compare 12/91.

328 "So that no method may succeed". AR take *noe waye* as adverbial and supply a subject, to the detriment of metre.

329–52 The summary of grievances at this point is not biblical but serves as a useful résumé of material already presented, placing it in a wider context of the sayings and deeds of Christ as indicated in the gospel narratives:-

329–36 With 329–33, compare the adulteress, play 12 and the unsuccessful attempt at stoning, play 13, as well as other attempts to destroy Christ, Luke 20/47–8, anticipating Christ's rebuke to the soldiers at Gethsemane, Mark 14/49, Luke 22/53.

337–44 Compare the raising of Lazarus, Play 13, which may identify the speaker as that play's Secundus Judeus. There is a report to the Pharisees after the episode, John 11/46, and after the anointing a meeting of the chief priests to consult to put Lazarus to death, John 12/10.

345–52 Compare the healing of the blind man, play 13, and the Pharisees' dismay at Jesus' triumphal reception on entering the city, John 12/19, as well as the miracles which followed the cleansing of the temple, Matthew 21/14. York 25/288–391 and *Ludus Coventriae* 26/306–21 show healing miracles during Christ's entry.

337 Deimling (p.xi) cites *againe* AR as evidence of the close relationship of the two manuscripts, regarding their reading as "absolutely unintelligible". But AR seem to mean: "Yea, lords, one matter may serve again", as opposed to HmBH: "Yea, lords, one matter may produce advantage". AR, however, repeat the 339 rhyme-word.

349–52 B's omission of these lines, noted by Deimling, constitutes an unexplained error. Perhaps the scribe was misled into an eye-slip by the similarity of the b-rhyme of stanza 44 to the a-rhyme of stanza 45.

354 *this great solempnitie* i.e. The Feast of the Passover. This is the first clear indication given to the audience of the specific occasion of Christ's visit to Jerusalem. The meeting of the Sanhedrin seems to have taken place on the Wednesday of Holy Week.

357–8 The verb-tenses in these lines seem to have troubled the scribes. *come* 357 A, *came* RBH is to be preferred for meaning and tense to *comes* Hm; *come* A is an acceptable past-tense form, and may even have been the exemplar form, misinterpreted as present by Hm and inflected accordingly. H seems unconsciously to have suspected this possibility, since it originally wrote *cames* and then cancelled *s* (see TNs).

The possibility of present tense at 357 may also be reflected in the inappropriate *maie* ARH for *might* 358 Hm B. The meaning required is "as you may have seen", with the past tense being conveyed by the modal auxiliary rather than a perfect infinitive.

359–60 Compare 208 + SD. There is no previous indication that the citizens knelt in reverence on Jesus' entry.

361–76 See 224 + SD–60.

381–4 Based on Matthew 26/15.

383 The line contains three strongly stressed syllables instead of the expected four. B's reading may be preferred in restoring the expected number of syllables. It is tempting, however, to postulate an exemplar loss of *shall* before *bee* resulting from a sense of its redundancy after *shall* 382.

PLAY XIV

393–400, stanza 50 *lasse* 396 HmH is to be preferred for rhyme to *lesse* ARB.
393 contains only three strongly stressed syllables instead of the expected four. Possibly *to* has been omitted in the exemplar before *thee*.
There seems no obvious reason for or against the reversal of 398 and 399 in H.

405–16 The references in Matthew 26/16, Mark 14/11, Luke 22/6 indicate that Judas did not at this stage have a specific plan. The details here derive from the events of the capture itself; compare Matthew 26/48: *Quemcumque osculatus fuero, ipse est: tenete eum* (AV "Whomsoever I shall kiss, that same is he; hold him fast"), and Mark 14/44: *Quemcumque osculatus fuero, ipse est: tenete eum et ducite caute* (AV "Whomsoever I shall kiss, that same is he; take him and lead him away safely"). 414 looks to Matthew, 415 to Mark.

406 "Before Friday, when it is night". Jesus' capture took place on Thursday or in the early hours of Friday, and the sense of "Before it is night on Friday" is therefore improbable. This is the first clear reference to a day in the Holy Week sequence. 425 seems to suggest that Judas plans the capture for the early hours of Friday morning.

421–4 Judas suggests that his loyalty is of a kind that the King of France might wish from the people of England — i.e. that they would betray their true lord. The lines would perhaps have particular force for the period during which England was attempting to retain its French possessions, the last of which, Calais, was lost in the reign of Mary, 1558; *his* 423 H shifts the reference from England to France. AR's omission of 421–4 may be the deliberate removal of a contemporary reference — compare 10/215–32 and notes — and Deimling notes the omission as evidence of the close relationship between the two manuscripts; but R reverses A's substitution of *eskape* 420. Baugh mentions the passage as having possible implications for the question of French influence in the cycle.

430 The omission of *to* (2) is well supported, ARH, and may be preferred in producing a more regular sequence of strongly and weakly stressed syllables. Its retention in HmB may perhaps indicate influence from *to* 429.

PLAY XV

Dramatis Personae Jesus, Petrus, Servus, Pater Familius, Johannis, Andreas, Jacobus, Judas, Thomas, Phillipp, Malchus, Primus Judeus.

NOTE 1. Twelve disciples attend the Last Supper 115.
2. Judas comes *cum militum cohorte* 304 + SD.

Locations
Last Supper — *in* a fayre parlour 29, a parloure all readye dight, with paved flores and windowes bright 53-4, *in* a house 21, 22, 38, 42, domum 44 + SD, *in* the cittie which yee doe see 17, the fayre cittie 35.

NOTE Movement to another location is indicated at 264 + SD.

Properties
Preparation — a water pott 19, vas aquae 36 + SD
Last Supper — mensam 60 + SD; the pascall lambe 7, 62, 66; panem 88 + SD, bread 89, 122; this meate 137; calicem 96 + SD; patina 104 + SD, 120 + SD, my cuppe 122
Washing — linteolo 144 + SD, lintheo 160 + SD
Capture — laternis facibus et armis 304 + SD, sword and staves and armerye 352; *Peter's* gladium 332 + SD, sword 339.

NOTE 1. It is not clear what action is required by *adornent mensam* 60 + SD.
2. *drinke* 102, *bibit* 104 + SD confirm that the chalice contains an unspecified liquid.
3. The washing, 139 ff, requires an unspecified water and container, possibly that carried by Servus.
4. *extrahet gladium* 332 + SD suggests a sword in a sheath.
5. It is not clear what is involved in *abscindet auriculam Malchi* 332 + SD or *my eare hee hase* 336.

Costumes
None specified.

Sources
The Last Supper — Matthew 26/17-9; Mark 14/12-6; Luke 22/7-13
Institution of the Eucharist — Matthew 26/26-9; Mark 14/22-5; Luke 22/14-20

PLAY XV

Judas Unmasked — Matthew 26/21-5; Mark 14/18-9; Luke 22/21; John 13/21-30
Washing the Feet — John 13/1-17
Dialogues — John 13/33-14/19
Peter's Denial Foretold — Matthew 26/34, Mark 14/30; Luke 22/34; John 13/36-8
Gethsemane — Matthew 26/36-57; Mark 14/26-50; Luke 22/39-51; John 17/1-18/12.

Play-heading The Play gathers together in a particular order a number of events narrated in connection with the Last Supper and Betrayal in the four gospels. Comparable events occur in the other cycles, and the following list also indicates the sequence:
Wakefield 20 — Preparing the room (314-51), Judas unmasked (352-77), Peter's denial foretold (378-81), Washing of the feet (382-415) [followed by a second foretelling of Peter's denial, 416-31], Discourses (432-87), Gethsemane (488-709).
York 27 (incomplete) — Washing the feet (37-72), Judas Unmasked (90-115), Peter's denial foretold (116-42);
York 28 (incomplete) — Gethsemane.
Ludus Coventriae 27 Preparing the room (338-97) [followed by Mary Magdalen], Judas unmasked (526-88) [followed by the conspiracy], Institution of Eucharist (670-832, but containing a second unmasking of Judas), Washing the feet (833-56) Peter's denial foretold (857-92), Gethsemane (893-1040).
Cornish Ordinalia, Christ's Passion — Preparing the room (pp.98-101), Judas Unmasked (p.102), Institution of the Eucharist (pp.103-4), Peter's denial foretold (pp.106-7) [followed by the conspiracy], Gethsemane (pp.110-5).

1-12 The opening derives from Luke's account, since that gospel is the only one to suggest that Jesus rather than his disciples first raised the question of the celebration of the feast, and is the only one to name the two disciples sent by Jesus into the city as Peter and John. This pattern is followed by the Cornish Ordinalia, but Wakefield 20/314-5 and *Ludus Coventriae* 27/338-45, like Comestor, *Historia Scholastica*, 'In Evangelia' 149 (PL 198/1615), give the disciples the initiative. York does not dramatise the preparation.

3 *Easter* The English term for the Christian feast which is substituted here for the Feast of the Passover. The Passover's institution during the Israelites' exile in Egypt is described in Exodus 12/1-51; its institution is not dramatised here, but an echo of its rules may be seen in 5/89-92 and note. In York 27/1-16 the origins of the feast are narrated, and in *Ludus Coventriae* 27 not only are the origins indicated, but an elaborate correspondence of the paschal lamb and Christ is worked out.

7–8 The sacrifice of a male yearling lamb, to be eaten roasted and all that remained to be burnt by morning, is enjoined in Exodus 12/3–10. Cornish Ordinalia p.100 suggests that the lamb was there roasted over a fire by Peter and John.

The lamb was to be selected on the tenth day of the month and killed on the fourteenth day. This, together with some contradiction in the gospel references to the day, has led to some debate about the time when the Last Supper was held and the appropriateness of it in Jewish law. The play gives very limited information about time at this point however.

19 The man is not otherwise identified in the gospels. *Ludus Coventriae* 27/347 calls him "A pore man in sympyl A-ray", and at 357 + SD identifies him as Simon Leprous. It would be dramatically economical to utilise the water for the washing of the disciples' feet, and it was frequently explained in a way similar to the use of water in the later ceremony; see Bede, *In Marci Evangelium Expositio*, 4/14 (PL 92/270).

25–8 Compare Luke 22/11: *Et dicetis patrifamilias domus: Dicit tibi Magister: Ubi est diversorium, ubi Pascha cum discipulis meis manducem?* (AV "And ye shall say unto the goodman of the house, The Master saith unto thee, Where is the guestchamber, where I shall eat the passover with my disciples?"). Mark 14 uses *refectio* rather than *diversorium*. It is possible here that 27–8 are to continue Christ's reported words; 27 would then begin a separate sentence, to end at 28.

29 *a fayre parlour* Luke 22/12 terms it *coenaculum magnum, stratum* (AV "a large upper room furnished"). This point is stressed by commentators; compare Comestor, *Historia Scholastica*, 'In Evangelia' 149 (PL 198/1615): *In superiori parte domus faciebant Palaestini coenacula, inferius autem cubicula*. Here, presumably for the requirements of staging, the express sense of "upper room" has been removed, and a term recalling contemporary English house-design used. The description is elaborated at 53–4. Compare Cornish Ordinalia, p.100: "A really nice room, spacious as a barn, plenty of straw on the floor".

For reasons not immediately obvious, Deimling regards *shew you* H as superior to *you shewe* HmARB.

32 + SH *John* A is evidently a scribal substitution, perhaps resulting from unease at the fact that John remains silent during the dialogue with Jesus. R restores the ascription to Peter.

50 ARBH have a different, active, construction from Hm's passive construction. Although one form is not obviously superior to the other, it is tempting to accept the majority reading as that of the exemplar and to regard Hm's as an alteration. If so, perhaps Hm's reading was influenced by *all readye dight* 53, perhaps suggesting that the preparation was not entirely the work of the two disciples. But ARBH may look to the active form, Matthew 26/19, Mark 14/16, Luke 22/13: *Paraverunt Pascha* (AV "And they made ready the passover").

52 + SH *Familias* H is to be preferred to the erroneous *Familius* HmARB

59 The line in Hm appears to have five strongly stressed syllables instead of the expected four. ARH and B, in different ways, correct this excess. B is preferable, in producing a more regular sequence of strongly and weakly stressed syllables. It is possible that B represents an original reading, changed in ARH because a rhyme with *I* was felt to be preferable to one with *wee*; the change in wording in ARH compensates for the additional syllables in *you and I*. Hm would then have copied the original order, but with the new rhyme-phrase.

63 Here, as in Wakefield 20/345-6, *Ludus Coventriae* 27/381-97, the action is continuous, Jesus coming as soon as preparations are complete. But, as Mark 14/7 notes, the meal was in the evening, and the preparations therefore took place earlier in the day; Cornish Ordinalia, p. 100 specifies an evening meal. No sense of the time of day is suggested, although the reference to *windowes bright* 54 might indicate daylight during the preparations.

65–80 The opening instruction, 65, derives from Luke 22/14: *Discubuit et duodecim apostoli cum eo* (AV "He sat down, and the twelve apostles with him"). The rest of the passage has no counterpart in the gospel narratives at this point.

66–8 relate to the celebration of the passover, and may be compared with York 27/25–32, where Jesus abolishes its observance henceforth. 67–8 seem to mean: "And then we shall concern ourselves with other things which have greater effectiveness"; see *entreten* MED 2. *greater* HmH suggests direct comparison between the "effective" sacrament to be instituted and the "commemorative" feast of the passover, a comparison stressed by commentators and inherent in the development of the passage (see below). *greate* ARB may represent an attempt to avoid the comparison on the grounds that the two feasts are not comparable — the passover is not "effective", as the comparison might suggest. *effecte* probably carries also overtones of its philosophical use — compare MED 4a, "the embodiment or manifestation of 'being' or 'substance' in individual acts or things; the action of embodying 'forms' in 'real things'"; and 4c, "A property or attribute (of something) regarded as the observable manifestation of its essential nature" — hence prompting the following reference to *sygnes and shadowes*.

68–80, if they derive from any point in the narrative of the Last Supper, may relate to John 16/25: *Haec in proverbiis locutus sum vobis; venit hora, cum iam non in proverbiis loquar vobis, sed palam de Patre annuntiabo vobis* (AV "These things have I spoken unto you in proverbs: but the time cometh, when I shall no more speak unto you in proverbs but I shall show you plainly of the Father"), a passage forming part of the discourses after supper. Compare *Glossa Ordinaria* on the passage (PL 114/414): *Quaecunque dicuntur de incorporea et immutabili substantia, habet quasi proverbia*; also on Luke 22/15 (PL 114/337): *Desiderat primo typicum Pascha manducare, et sic passionis suae mysteria mundo declarare, ut et antiqui Paschae probator existat, et hoc ad suae dispensationis figuram pertinuisse demonstrans, jam adveniente veritate umbra cessare debeat*. But closer parallels in spirit lie in the comparison of the old and new testaments in the Epistle to the Hebrews, chaps 9–10. See especially Hebrews 10/1: *Umbram enim habens lex futurorum bonorum, non ipsam imaginem rerum; per singulos annos eisdem ipsis hostiis quas offerunt indesinenter numquam potest accedentes perfectos facere* (AV "For the law having a shadow of good things to come, and not the very image of the things, can never with those sacrifices which they offered year by year continually make the comers thereunto perfect"); and Hebrews 9/15: *Et ideo novi testamenti mediator est; ut morte intercedente, in redemptionem earum praevaricationum, quae erant sub priori testamento repromissionem accipiant qui vocati sunt aeternae hereditatis* (AV "And for this cause he is the mediator of the new testament, that by means of death, for the redemption of transgressions that were under the first testament, they which are called might receive the promise of eternal inheritance"). See also *Ludus Coventriae* 27/682: "þis fygure xal sesse A-nothyr xal folwe þer-by".

73–80, stanza 10   No manuscript has *moste* for *muste* 80, required for perfect rhyme.

80 + SD   The detail is here derived in part from John 13/23, 25, where, although the disciple is identified only as *unus ... quem diligebat Iesus* (AV "One whom Jesus loved"), the reference is accepted to be to the author of the gospel. A reclining posture perhaps indicates the use of benches (cf. *seate* 65) and some attempt to realise in living tableau the common pictorial representations of the Last Supper. It may be noted that the account of the unmasking of Judas in John from which the detail is taken is not the version followed by the play. On John's sleep and its significance, see 22/173–6 and note; the detail is unbiblical.

81–104   The sequence of events during the Last Supper is a matter for Gospel harmonies. Augustine begins from the consecration of the bread, passes to the washing of the feet, the giving of the sop to Judas, the committing of body and blood, and the unmasking of Judas according to John. Comestor, *Historia Scholastica*, 'In Evangelia' 149–52 (PL 198/1615–8), has the sequence — washing of feet, unmasking of Judas, institution of the Eucharist. Chester here looks mainly to Luke 22/15–20, which alone mentions the institution of the Eucharist as the first main event of the meal, in contrast to Matthew and Mark, which begin with the unmasking of Judas. 81–4 derive from Luke 22/15 and 95–6 from Luke 22/19. 89–96, the consecration of the bread, is a composite of Matthew 26/26: *Accipite et comedite: hoc est corpus meum* (AV "Take, eat; this is my body") and Luke 22/19: *Hoc est corpus meum, quod pro vobis datur: hoc facite in meam commemorationem* (AV "This is my body which is given for you; this do in remembrance of me"). 97–104, the consecration of the wine, derives from the account in Matthew 26/27–9. Although the institution of the sacrament is central to the theme of the cycle and to Christian teaching, its presentation here does not seem indicative of any particular theology.

85–8   The quatrain has no counterpart in the gospel narratives at this point, but seems to anticipate Christ's vow of obedience, 294–6. 86 and 87 each seems to contain only three strongly stressed syllables instead of the expected four.

89–96, stanza 12   No manuscript has *mankynne* for *mankynde* 93, and *mynne* for *mynde* 95, required for perfect rhyme.

A has inexplicably and erroneously omitted 95, but the omission is corrected in R.

The b-rhymes, *bodye* 93 — *evermore* 96, do not rhyme. No alternatives are immediately obvious, but 93 reflects the gospel wording (see 81–104 note), while the tautology of *aye evermore* 96 seems odd — A removes it acceptably. Possibly some fill-in phrase such as *upon hye* has been replaced at 96.

97–8   The lines apparently derive from Matthew 26/27: *Et accipiens calicem, gratias egit* (AV "And he took the cup and gave thanks"). The nature of his thanks is not indicated, but see further, Bede, *In Matthaei Evangelium Expositio* 4/26 (PL 92/113).

99–100   *this* 99 reflects *hic*, Matthew 26/28 (AV "this"); *that* 100 is relative. But A and R seem to have regarded *that* as demonstrative and changed the syntax to resolve

PLAY XV

the reference under *this/yt*.

The passage does not fully render *sanguis meus novi testamenti* (AV "my blood of the new testament"). It is surprising that the passage contains no explicit reference to the fact that wine is the consecrated element, despite the reference to *hoc genimine vitis* (AV "this fruit of the vine") in Matthew 26/29.

102–4   So Matthew 26/29. Compare *Glossa Ordinaria* on the passage (PL 114/169): *Non delectabor caeremoniis hujus populi, in quibus sacra paschalis agni praecipua sunt. Post passionem non assumam carnem, donec assumam eam novam quae modo mortalis est*; and *id*, 'Evang. Luc.' 22/16 (PL 114/337): *Non ultra Mosaicum Pascha celebrabo, donec in Ecclesia quod est regnum Dei spiritualiter intellectum compleatur. In hoc regno usque hodie manducat Christus, cum ea quae Moyses rudi populo carnaliter observanda praecepit, in membris suis spiritualiter exercet.*

These lines constitute a promise to the disciples, including — in this sequence of events — Judas. The objection is met by *Glossa Ordinaria*, 'Evang. Joann.' 13/26 (PL 114/406) and by *Ludus Coventriae* 27/772–7, 787–98, where Judas accepts the elements to his own damnation. No such overt connexion is made here, but possibly some significant link is to be seen with the unmasking of Judas which follows. Compare 23/565–84.

104+SD–36   The order remains that of Luke, where the unmasking of Judas follows the institution of the Eucharist. The passage is, however, a composite; viz: 105–8 Mark 14/18, which alone has *Qui manducat mecum* (AV "Which eateth with me"), corresponding to 107.

109–20 The disciples' questionings are related in Matthew 26/72, Mark 14/19, Luke 22/22; but the account is independent of John 13/22–5, where Peter prompts John to ask Jesus the identity of his betrayer — see 80+SD note. 109, 117 suggest the general sorrow of Matthew 26/22, Mark 14/19, not found in Luke. 110–2 may owe something to Luke 22/23: *Et ipse coeperunt quaerere inter se* (AV "And they began to inquire among themselves"). The questioning of Jesus, 116, 120, derives from Matthew 26/22, Mark 14/9. No individual speakers are specified in the synoptic gospels.

121–8 Matthew 26/23–4, Mark 14/20–1.

129–36 129–32 derive from Matthew 26/25; 133 from John 13/27; 134–6 from John 13/29.

120+SD   Judas completes the action which he began at 104+SD. No such coincidence of act and prophecy is suggested by the gospels. In Matthew and Mark Jesus seems merely to reassert his earlier comment that his betrayer will be a disciple. But in John 13/26, Jesus identifies Judas as his betrayer himself by giving him the sop.

122   *cuppe* Matthew 26/23 *in paropside*, Mark 14/20 *in catino* (AV "in the dish"). *dishe* R seems to be a substitution for closer reflection of the biblical text. But it may be that the *cuppe* is the chalice circulating among the disciples.

125–8   "It would be well for him if he had not been born, for he is utterly lost, body and soul, who has acted so falsely before, and still he is of that mind." *will* here has the sense of "desire, wilful intent" — compare the defiance of 136; *witt* B suggests "And he is still in his right mind". 127–8 have no biblical counterpart; they suggest Jesus' awareness of Judas' bargain with the Jews, and perhaps also of his previous malpractices.

126 *bouth* AH represents an unusual agreement of these two manuscripts, the word supplying the syllabic deficiency caused by the omission of *hee* ABH which B does not compensate. The change is reversed in R, which agrees with Hm. Either reading is possible; the plural subject may be regarded as collective, hence *is*, and the AH reading avoids the repetition of *hee* 125, but *hee* HmR removes the problem of syntax formally posed by the conjoined subject and avoids an awkward change of subject between 126 and 127.

128 "And he is still of that mind." *witt* suggests "And he is still in his right mind."

134–6 A contrast may be intended between a private exchange between Judas and Jesus at 129–33 and Judas' public farewell. Without the preceding dialogue, these lines suggest a specific mission and feed the sort of assumptions among the disciples mentioned by John 13/28–9, where they assume that Jesus has given his purse-bearer an instruction possibly about a charitable act.

137 The line presumably indicates the clearing and removal of the table and its contents, thus removing specific suggestions of setting in preparation for 257 ff.

138–68 + SD The washing of the disciples' feet was an incident ceremonially commemorated on Maundy Thursday. John 13/4–12, which alone describes it, says that it occurred before the giving of the sop but after supper itself was ended. There Judas was present and the ceremony may also be read as indicative of the presence of a corrupt member in an otherwise clean body — see 139–44 note. That possibility is here removed.

139–44 Jesus sets an example, 141, 160 + SD, which is followed by the other disciples, 167–8 + SD. The incident is capable of triple significance — as an example of humility, as a sign of the washing away of sins, and as an indication of the presence of the corrupt Judas among the disciples. See *Glossa Ordinaria*, 'Evang. Joann.' 13/10 (PL 114/405); Comestor, *Historia Scholastica*, 'In Evangelium' 150 (PL 198/1616); and Augustine, *In Joannis Evangelium*, Tractatus LV (PL 35/1787). The act is regarded in the cycles as an example of humility — Wakefield 20/403–15, York 27/61–72, *Ludus Coventriae* 27/855–6, Cornish Ordinalia p. 105. But York develops the idea of the washing as a spiritual cleansing in preparation for the sacrament, thus strengthening the link with baptism and providing a further justification for its position before the institution of the Eucharist:

> In þat stede schall be sette
> A newe lawe vs by-twene
> But who þerof schall ette,
> Behoues to be wasshed clene.
> For þat new lawe whoso schall lere,
> In harte þam bus be clene and chaste
> (27/31–8)

A similar idea is found in Cornish Ordinalia, p. 105: "If by my grace you are not made clean, heaven will never become your home . . . He whose spiritual body has been cleansed by baptism has no need of further washing, except his feet"; and it goes on to point the comparison with the disciples, one of whom remains defiled. Here, the

PLAY XV 215

wider symbolic implications are lost, partly by the order of events adopted but partly also by the failure to develop explicitly the grounds for Jesus' insistence at 151–2. The exemplary aspect of humility alone is stressed.

144 + SD   The girding with the towel is preceded in John 13/4 by *ponit vestimenta sua* (AV "laid aside his garments"), omitted here. It is followed, John 13/5, by *mittit aquam in pelvim* (AV "he poureth water into a bason"), which is perhaps to be understood here.

145–52, stanza 19   The stanza contains a number of imperfect rhymes; B's *beheat* 146, *weete* 147 are formally preferable. For perfect rhyme, *d* must be unvoiced in *afterwarde* 148.

145   *shalt* Compare John 13/6 *lavas* (AV "dost thou wash"). John indicates that Jesus has already washed the feet of a number of disciples when he reaches Peter and, since he apparently continues with the action for Peter without question, the present tense is there appropriate. Here, Jesus seems to begin with Peter, and Peter's future tense suggests an attempt to stop him beginning the process, hence the change of tense. Possibly also some idea of necessity — "Must you wash" — is involved.

146–8   As here punctuated, *that* 146 is demonstrative and the opening phrase an assertion — "That is what I am doing". But compare John 13/7: *Quod ego facio, tu nescis modo* (AV "What I do, thou knowest not now"). It might be both possible and preferable here to regard *that* as relative, "that which" and, by substituting a comma for the full-stop 146, to regard 146–8 as a single sentence.

152   *of joye* replaces *mecum* John 13/8 (AV "with me") to give a more explicit sense.

153   Peter, in John 13/9, does not suggest the washing of hands and head as an alternative but as an addition to the washing of the feet.

155   "All the rest of your body is clean." Compare John 13/10: *Qui lotus est, non indiget nisi ut pedes lavet, sed est mundus totus* (AV "He that is washed needeth not save to wash his feet, but is clean every whit"). Lacking the detailed exposition, *therfore* 155 does not follow easily from the opening statement.

157   Compare John 13/11: *Sciebat enim quisnam esset qui traderet eum, propterea dixit: Non estis mundi omnes* (AV "For he knew who should betray him: therefore said he, Ye are not all clean"). The change of pronoun from singular *thy* 156 to *you*, plural, 157, should indicate a similar change of address, from Peter to all the disciples. But in John, Judas, his traitorous intent formed, is still present at this point and presumably has his feet washed. In Chester, where Judas has left, this application is excluded, and moreover Peter's reply, 158–60, suggests that he may regard 157 as meaning "And you, Peter, shall be clean — but not completely."

159   *do* H may be preferred for syntax and in producing a more regular sequence of strongly and weakly stressed syllables.

163   A subject for *should bee*, such as *I* B or *it* H, seems preferable for meaning and to produce a more regular sequence of strongly and weakly stressed syllables. Since HmAR lack any subject, while B and H supply different subjects, it seems probable that the subject was omitted in the exemplar and independently supplied by B and H.

166   *your* AR is without Vulgate equivalent but could be inferred from the text, as it is in AV.

As an alternative punctuation, the parenthesis could end after *maister* and *in meeke manere* be read with either 165 or 167.

167   *so* ARBH is not metrically, syntactically or semantically necessary and lacks Vulgate equivalent, although it is difficult to regard the Hm reading as other than an omission from the exemplar.

168 + SD   The literalism of the communal action pehaps detracts from the symbolic and dramatic effect of Jesus' action and is without parallel elsewhere.

169–256   The discourses, and the prophecy of Peter's denial, are drawn from John 13/33–14/19, where they follow Judas' departure. Peter's denial is in the other gospels, but the details here given are found together only in John. Luke and John describe the prophecy before Jesus leaves the house, Matthew and Mark after his departure.

169   John 13/33 contains only one vocative, *filioli* (AV "little children"). *litle* HmAR seems to reflect the sense of the biblical word but its omission in BH arguably contributes to a smoother metre. Deimling, lacking Hm, noted the variants as indicative of the close relationship of A and R. Although the two terms, *children* and *brethren*, may serve only to fill out the line, the second phrase may be read as an explanatory gloss on the first, or a distinction may be intended between *children* (audience) and *brethren* (disciples).

184   ARB suggest confusion resulting from the fact that the end of stanza 23 does not correspond to the end of Jesus' speech; they substitute an additional c-rhyme for the final b-rhyme. The resulting phrase is sufficiently common to have been supplied independently by the scribes.

186   In Hm, metrical stress runs counter to sentential stress, requiring *whye* and *yt* to be strongly stressed. This requirement is removed by BH, producing a more 'regular' line, and by AR, which reduce the number of strongly stressed syllables to an 'irregular' three. It is possible that BH and AR represent responses to a metrically rough exemplar line such as Hm contains.

190   *thrye* No gospel refers to three cock-crows; Matthew 26/34, Luke 22/34, John 13/38 say that Peter will deny Christ before the cock crows, while Mark 14/30, the only specific reference to the number of crows, says that the denials will occur before the cock has crowed twice. But Matthew 26/34, Mark 14/30, Luke 22/34 and John 13/38 all agree in specifying the number of Peter's denials as three, whereas Chester does not mention the number here. The denial is dramatised in 16/379–94 and alluded to in 18/401–20, but neither passage indicates the number of cock crows, if any; three denials are shown in 16/379–94 and Peter uses *thrye* at 18/408 of his denials. Here, either *thrye* should be read with 191 by placing a comma after *crowen*, leaving the number of crows unspecified; or it should be regarded as an error for *twye*, reflecting Mark's version. Other cycles follow either Mark (Wakefield 20/428–9, *Ludus Coventriae* 27/883–4) or the less specific version in other gospels: (York 27/134–5, Cornish Ordinalia, p.106); but since all specify the number of denials, they perhaps lend support for repunctuation of 190 rather than emendation.

193-264 York 27/142-89 contains Luke 22/35-9 and Cornish Ordinalia contains both Luke 35-9 and Luke 22/24-30. Neither passage has counterpart in the dialogues in Chester.

197 *Fathers* ARBH is to be preferred for syntax and meaning to *Father* Hm. H erroneously omits *house*.

197-8 Compare John 14/2: *Mansiones multae sunt* (AV "Are many mansions"). Rhyme requires *is* 197; and possibly *wonnynge* 198, not found in any manuscript, would therefore be preferable to *wonnynges* on the grounds that number is expressed by *manye* and that "many a mansion" would morphologically suggest the use of a singular verb.

210 *waye* is attested by John 14/6; *very* H is either a scribal error or a substitution. But in John, Jesus' use of *via* is prompted by Jesus' earlier use of *via* in John 14/4, which has no counterpart here, and by Thomas' use of *viam* in John 14/5, which is here rendered by *gate* 206, 208, perhaps to avoid the jingling effect of *waye* with the c-rhymes of stanza 26. Hence, although there is a semantic link between Thomas' and Jesus' words in HmARB, the formal link is lost and H has more scope to substitute *very*.

213-6 The plural address, *you* 213, is to be preferred to H's singular *thou* as reflecting John 14/7. H, having embarked on singular reference, perhaps because of *thee* 209, reverts to plural in 215, presumably because the plural address, *yee* 216, is fixed by rhyme; it may, however, be significant that AR omit *you* 215.

221-32 Based on John 14/9-11, but reflecting a recurring idea in the cycle; compare especially 13/8-14, 229-34, 273-84.

243 See play 21 — since the Chester cycle was performed at Whitsuntide, the coming of the Holy Ghost had particular point. John variously uses the terms *Paraclitum* 14/16 and *Spiritum veritatis* 14/17 here.

253-6 B's omission of this quatrain is an inexplicable error.

257-60 257-8 suggests a change of location, corresponding to Jesus' transition to the Garden of Gethsemane, Matthew 26/36, Mark 14/26, on the Mount of Olives, Luke 22/39, at this point. In John 18/1, Jesus, having remained in the house for prayer, moves into the Garden later. *Ludus Coventriae* 27/888 indicates that Jesus walks to Bethany; the Cornish Ordinalia lacks this section; Wakefield does not name the new location. Chester also does not name a new location, and 259 may even suggest that the disciples do not move at all.

If a translation is suggested, 259-60 represent Jesus' words on reaching the new location, in which he separates himself from his disciples for private prayer. But *everychwonne* 259 suggests that all the disciples remain together, whereas Matthew 36/26, Mark 14/32 indicate that Jesus first withdrew with Peter, James and John and then left them to watch; his words of reproach to the sleeping disciples are then directed to those three. This small group accompanying Jesus is suggested in Wakefield 20/492, York 28, Cornish Ordinalia; but *Ludus Coventriae* does not suggest it, although retaining the specific address by Jesus to Peter which Chester also lacks.

261–4 The injunction against temptation is from Luke 22/40, but the dangers specified in 263–4 echo Matthew 26/41, Mark 14/38 at the end of the first prayer — compare 285–8.

With 263, compare Matthew 26/41, Mark 14/38: *Spiritus quidem promptus est* (AV "The spirit indeed is willing/The spirit truly is ready"). The text was usually understood to contrast the spiritual aspirations of man with his carnal weakness, with particular application not only to the disciples but also to Christ, who both wished to fulfil God's will and also feared death; see Bede, *In Matthaei Evangelium Expositio*, 4/26 (PL 92/115). But the meaning here seems conditioned by the juxtaposition with 262, where the spirit also is seen to be in peril; see Bede, *In Marci Evangelium Expositio* 4/14 (PL 92/277). Thus 269 translates *promptus* "yielding to temptation" rather than "inclining towards virtue".

263 *speritte* ARBH is to be preferred to the scribally erroneous *sprite* Hm.

265–80 In John 17 Jesus prays for his disciples before he leaves for the Garden. In Matthew 26/39–44, Mark 14/36–9, Luke 22/42 he utters the same petition to God in the Garden three times, the "Thrice repeated prayer", returning after each petition to find his disciples asleep. Luke 22/43–4 relates that Jesus sweated blood and was comforted by an angel.

Here Jesus utters two petitions in the Garden, returning after each to his sleeping disciples. The first represents the prayer before departure, taken from John: 265–70, John 17/1–2; 271–2, John 17/4; 273, John 17/6; 274–8, John 17/8–9. No other cycle shows this prayer; York 28 lacks the first prayer, but the second and third prayers suggest it resembled Wakefield 20, which does not use John.

287 Compare 263 and see 261–4 note. The meaning seems to be "And the spirit is preoccupied always"; see *occupy* OED 4. B evidently did not understand the construction and, by reading *so is* for *ghooste*, changes the reference to the flesh: "And is always so preoccupied"; it thus unbiblically removes all reference to the spirit by Jesus here.

289–96 The second prayer here is the "Thrice repeated prayer"; see 265–80 note. 289–90 represent Matthew 26/38, Mark 14/34, where the words are not part of Jesus' prayer but are addressed to Peter, James and John; they reflect a human, instinctive fear of death and are specifically taken up by the devil in 17/105–6 — see note. 291–6 derive principally from Mark 14/36, which alone has *Omnia tibi possibilia sunt* (AV "All things are possible unto thee"), corresponding to 293.

In Luke, the prayer is followed by the sweat of blood and the appearance of a comforting angel. The coming of the angel is shown in York 28, and *Ludus Coventriae* 27/944 + SD, where the angel bears a chalice; in the Cornish Ordinalia, which shows the thrice repeated prayer, Gabriel is sent to give comfort after the first prayer, while in Wakefield 20/500–55 the prayer is followed by an exposition of God's purpose by *Trinitas*. Chester is thus unusual in omitting this episode.

292 *this* Compare *calix iste* (AV "this cup"), Matthew 26/39, and similar expressions in Mark 14/36, Luke 22/42. The concreteness of reference seems to have troubled all the cycle-writers — Wakefield 20 reads *payn* 500, 514, and *passyon* 521; York 28 *payne* 58, *turnement* 90; *Ludus Coventriae* 27 *passyon* 918, *peyn* 939. The reference of *this* here is not immediately obvious, deriving as it does from the biblical demonstratives but lacking a following noun, and it may be taken as a vague referene to the impending death of 290; *it* BH substitutes a more specific pronoun reference, referring to *death* 290.

293 *thinge* seems to have confused the scribes by its singular form. Hm substitutes *eych* for *all*, while RB read *thinges* for *thinge*. But the singular is confirmed by *is*. *all* ARBH probably represents MED 3 (a), "every, each and every". *all thinge* therefore seems to have been the exemplar form.

297–301 The words are addressed in Matthew 26/45–6, Mark 14/41–2, to the disciples after the prayer has been repeated three times and Christ finally returns.

302–4 *this night* The phrase perhaps suggests specifically the night to Maundy Thursday and may indicate for the audience the presence of darkness, perhaps also suggested by the soldiers at 304 + SD. York 29/227–8 specifies the time of capture as "The tyme aftir tenne." On 303–4, compare 125–8.

304 + SD Compare John 18/3: *Iudas ergo, cum accepisset cohortem et a pontificibus et pharisaeis ministros, venit illuc cum laternis, et facibus et armis* (AV "Judas, then, having received a band of men and officers from the chief priests and Pharisees, cometh thither with lanterns and torches and weapons"). Bede, *In S. Joannis Evangelium Expositio*, 18 distinguishes soldiers from Jews (PL 92/896). In Wakefield 20 they are evidently called knights, but some serve the high priests and are termed *Judeus* in SHs. Here they seem unambiguously to be armed Jews — compare *Primus Judeus* 313 + SH.

305–18 The repeated question and reply derive from John 18/4–8, the two questions being separated by an incident in which the Jews move back and fall to the ground. Here that incident is replaced by Judas' kiss of betrayal, 309–12, from Matthew 26/49, Mark 14/45, Luke 22/47–8. The arrangement of events in Chester has the ironic effect of making Judas' intervention unnecessary and allows Jesus tellingly to disregard him completely; Judas' explanation of his action is without biblical counterpart. The kiss of betrayal precedes the repeated question in Wakefield 20, York 28 and Cornish Ordinalia, but follows it in *Ludus Coventriae* 27. In York 28, a brilliant light terrifies the soldiers and in *Ludus Coventriae* 27 they are cast down after the first question and rise only at Jesus' command.

305 + SH The gospel accounts suggest a communal response. Malchus, named only in John 18/10, has no obviously prominent part to play in the capture but is identified as *pontificis servum*. He is not named for the audience here; contrast Wakefield 20 where he is identified by Pilate, 598, given command of the troop, 598, and called *Malcus Miles* 599 + SH, in distinction to *Primus Miles*. Some equivalence of status is perhaps suggested by the fact that on the second occasion, 314, the question is answered by *Primus Judeus*, perhaps to be identified with the *tribunus* (AV "captain") of John 18/12, (see also 313 + SH note). The effect may also be to suggest an equivalence of 'civilian' and 'military' members of the company.

306 + SH Erroneously omitted by H.

313–8, stanza 40 The stanza contains only six lines, aabbbc, instead of the expected eight, the third and fourth lines of the first quatrain being omitted, presumably in the exemplar; Deimling postulates a loss of two lines after 314. But all lines in the stanza have biblical equivalents, without omission, and it is impossible to suggest what may have been lost.

313 + SH *Primus* There is, in fact, no *Secundus Judeus* among the speakers in the play from whom *Primus Judeus* is to be distinguished. *Primus* therefore merely identifies the speaker as the foremost in the company of soldiers. See also 305 + SH note.

315 *said* B may be preferred for meaning to *saye* (1) HmARH as conveying the sense of *yore* and reflecting John 18/8, *dixi vobis* (AV "I have told you"); Deimling, identifying the line as 315, although it is by his numbering 317, also accepts B's superiority. It seems probable that B, guided by the adverb, corrected an exemplar error transmitted by the other manuscripts and resulting from confusion with *saye* (2).

319–22 The gospel accounts do not suggest special hostility on the part of Malchus, but his action here accords with his prominent position at 306 and serves to motivate Peter's action. See also 343–6 note. *Ludus Coventriae* 27 does not identify Malchus for the audience and gives no reason for Peter's attack.

320 See 359 note.

322 + SH Peter is specified as the assailant only by John.

326 "And take that as an advance payment". *onward*, in the sense of "provisionally, on account, in advance", OED 2, is last recorded by OED in 1555. *this* AR destroys the rhyme.

333–4 "Now go and make a formal complaint to Caiaphas and beg him to give you justice." The sense of what is just, underlying the lines, emphasises Jesus' act of charity; compare 343–6 note.

339–42 Based on Matthew 26/52; but the rest of the rebuke, in which Jesus asserts the power of God to help him, has no counterpart here.

342 + SD The healing of the servant's ear is described only in Luke 22/51. It represents the last healing miracle performed by Jesus.

342 + SH B has erroneously and inexplicably omitted the SH.

343–6 With Malchus' conversion, compare his continuing defiant obduracy in Wakefield 20/692–5, York 28/287–9, Cornish Ordinalia, p.115. The two views correspond to different interpretations of the event. Compare the accounts in *Glossa Ordinaria*, 'Evang. Luc.' 22/50 (PL 114/341); and in Augustine, *In Joannis Evangelium*, Tractatus 112 (PL 35/1931). Jesus' act of healing love balances the act of justice by Peter, expressed in legalistic language; compare 333–4 and note.

343–50, stanza 44 *gone* 350 AR is to be preferred to *goe* HmH for rhyme.

346 + SH–*Finis* B's omission is hard to understand. As indicated in vol. I p.275, fol. 109^r contains only the SD and a single quatrain, while, as indicated in vol I, p.576, the *Finis* formula is also omitted, indicating that Bedford recognised that he had not completed the play. No other scribe seems to have experienced difficulty in transcribing the concluding lines.

351-8, stanza 45   *armere* 352 R, *armyre* H are to be preferred for rhyme to Hm's substituted *armerye* (MED *armurie* (a), "arms and weapons collectively") and to A's inappropriate agent-noun *armerer*. OED records *-er* forms of the noun only to the fifteenth century, hence perhaps Hm and A's confusion. Hm may derive from an exemplar form similar to the H reading.

351   *come* ARH is to be preferred to *came* Hm in reflecting *existis*, Mark 14/48, Luke 22/52 (AV "are you come").

352   *swordes* RH is to be preferred to *sword* HmA in reflecting *gladiis* (AV "swords"), Mark 14/48, Luke 22/52.

358   The flight of the disciples, which follows these words, is not dramatised here.

359   *to Cayphas* So Matthew 26/57, Mark 14/53 (to the high priest), Luke 22/54 (to the high priest's house), followed by York 28, *Ludus Coventriae* 27, Cornish Ordinalia p.115. In John 18/13 Jesus is taken first to Annas. In Wakefield 20 he is taken first to Pilate, who had ordered his capture.

365-6   The detail of the binding is taken from John 18/12. *handes* 365 ARH is to be preferred for meaning to *hand* Hm.

PLAY XVI

Dramatis Personae Primus Judeus, Secundus Judeus, Annas, Cayphas, Tertius Judeus, Quartus Judeus, Jesus, Pilatus, Herodes, The Damsell, Peter, The Jewe.

Locations
None specified; all indications of location take the form:
ad Annam et Caypham, *Before* 1
ad Pilatum, 117 + SD, 210 + SD
ad Herodem, 162 + SD.

Properties
cathedram 69 + SD, 322 + SD
a cloth 91
columnam 314 + SD
coronam spineam 326 + SD, of thornes 329
a reede 332, *for* a scepter 333
?yron 343
crucem 374 + SD.

NOTE Bonds are implied in *ligabunt* 314 + SD, *bounden* 315.

Costume
Herod's cloak given to Christ — cloth him in white 195, veste alba 202 + SD, 210 + SD, a worshipfull weede 204
Christ's dress — all thy clothes 312
The robe given to Christ by the scourgers — purpurea 322 + SD, whyte his clothinge ys 324 *and note.*

Sources
As the notes indicate, the play is made up of material taken from a number of different places in the gospels. The list here indicates only in general terms the location in the gospels of the episodes treated.
Jesus Before the Priests — Matthew 26/59–66, Mark 14/55–64, Luke 22/54, John 18/13–14, 19–23
The Buffeting — Matthew 26/67–8, Mark 14/65, Luke 22/63–5
Jesus Before Pilate — Matthew 27/1–2, Mark 15/1–5, Luke 23/1–7, John 18/28
Jesus Before Herod — Luke 23/6–12

PLAY XVI

Jesus Before Pilate — Luke 23/13–23
The Offer to Exchange Barabbas — Matthew 27/15–18, 20–23, Mark 15/6–14, Luke 23/17–23, John 18/39–40
Pilate Washing Hands — Matthew 27/24
Dialogue of Pilate and Jesus — John 18/33–38
Scourging — Matthew 27/26–30, Mark 15/15–20 John 19/1–5
Peter's Denial — Matthew 26/69–75, Mark 14/66–72, Luke 22/54–62, John 18/15–18, 25–27.

Guild-ascription
The four crafts named as responsible for the play in HmARC are increased to five in B by the addition of the Ironmongers, and reduced to three in H by the replacement of the Coopers and Stringers by the Ironmongers. Compare *Guild-ascription* 16A, where HmARB assign the play to the Ironmongers whereas H omits all indication of division and presents 16–16A as a single play. Greg held that H represented the earlier form of the play, which had been subsequently divided into two parts; Salter held that 16 and 16A represented two distinct plays which had been "thrown together" in 1575. See 379–*Finis* and *Finis* notes. Salter, developing his thesis, suggested that the exemplar contained a corrected heading which was copied by H correctly in view of the amalgamated form of 16–16A in H, and was ignored by HmAR correctly, since the plays 16 and 16A are there presented as separate plays. B, he held, had adopted the HmAR division but erroneously included the corrected heading, appropriate to the H arrangement. C, for which he postulated an intermediate exemplar, *k*, contains the uncorrected form because *k* was copied before the emendation was made.

Play heading
The play survives not only in the five cyclic manuscripts, but also in the Coopers' manuscript, C, printed as Appendix IIC, to which reference is made in discussion of the readings of the cyclic manuscripts.

The material in the play is treated also in other cycles, although in different order; the list of episodes following indicates the order of material in the cycles but should not be treated as a detailed indication of the content of each episode since each cycle employs a different combination of the material in the four gospels:
Wakefield 21 — Jesus before the Priests, Buffeting; 22 — Second

Wakefield 21 — Jesus before the Priests, Buffeting; 22 — Second Trial before Pilate, Offer of Barabbas, Scourging, Washing Pilate's hands, Delivery for Crucifixion.
York 29 — Peter's Denial, 89–171, Jesus before the Priests 172–354, Buffeting 355–82; 30 — First Appearance Before Pilate 290–546; 31 — Jesus Before Herod; 33 (incomplete) — Second Trial Before Pilate 1–348, Scourging 349–439, Washing Pilate's Hands 442–3, Release of Barabbas and Delivery for Crucifixion 444–485.
Ludus Coventriae 29 — Jesus Before the Priests 70–160, Buffeting 161–172, Peter's Denial 173–204; 30 — First Appearance Before Pilate 205–356, Jesus Before Herod 357–465 + SD, Second Trial Before Pilate 541–635 (including Offer of Barabbas, Dialogue with Jesus, Washing of Pilate's Hands), Release of Barabbas and Delivery for Crucifixion 636–58, Scourging 659–77 + SD.
Cornish Ordinalia pp. 116ff — Trial Before Priests, Buffeting, with Peter's denial included within the two episodes; First Appearance before Pilate, Jesus before Herod, Second Trial before Pilate (Dialogue with Jesus, Offer of Barabbas), Scourging, Second Offer of Barabbas, Release of Barabbas and Delivery for Crucifixion, Washing Pilate's Hands. The plays of "the appearance before Pilate" and "Jesus before Herod" once existed at Wakefield, on internal evidence of the cycle, but have been lost from the extant manuscript.
ad Annam et Caypham Compare 15/359 note. Some attempt to harmonise the account of John with that of the other gospels may be seen in *Glossa Ordinaria*, 'Evang. Joan.' 18/13 (PL 114/418): *Erant eo tempore duo sacerdotum principes (ut Lucas ait), Annas et Caiphas, qui vicissim annos suos agebant. Sed tunc erat annus Caiphae, et voluntate ejus primum ductus est Jesus ad Annam, non quia collega, sed quia socer ejus erat. Vel domus sic erant positae, ut non deberet Annas a transeuntibus praeteriri.* Annas does not otherwise have a major role to play in the trials of Jesus in the gospel narratives, although his role is comparable in the play-cycles.

4 A subject is required for syntax and meaning. ARBHC all supply *he*, a reading which is to be preferred. ARBC adopt a prepositional construction, with C showing a slightly different word-order from ARB; the result gives acceptable meaning but rough metre. *spurn at*, in a figurative sense, "to kick against or at something disliked or despised", is recorded by OED only from 1526. H offers an alternative form of the line which is acceptable for meaning, uses the older application of *spurn*, from 1000 onwards, in a transitive and figurative sense, and is to be preferred in producing a more regular sequence of strongly and weakly stressed syllables. H cannot be derived textually from HmARBC. The addition of *he* to Hm would give a most acceptable line.

10   *postie powere* The two words have identical areas of meaning, although it is possible that the retention of both by HmARBC may indicate that the scribes understood the line to mean "Now you can prove your *postie* to be *powere*"; alternatively, the two words may have been taken for a compound, although no such compound is recorded. *powere* is attested by rhyme, and it seems probable that the exemplar erroneously recorded *postie* and left the error uncancelled, correcting it by placing *powere* in the margin beside it. H alone recognised the error and deleted *postie* — Greg compares the cancellation of *power* at 6/646 H (see TNs).

13–16   "It seems to me that it would be a notable deed, either for money or entreaty, to free himself from his peril and show such cleverness." With *maistrye*, compare OED *mastery*, 5 "An exercise or work of skill or power", which is last recorded in 1586; H rephrases, using *maister* MED 4 (a), to read: "If he were a man of spiritual authority". With *pennye or prayere*, compare OED *penny or paternoster*, instanced in a single example of 1566: "Neither love nor money". *shutt* is used in the sense, OED 11, of "to set (a person) free *from*, relieve *of* (something troublesome)"; *shunt* is not recorded in an appropriate use. *his* HmARC and *this* BH are equally possible.

sleight had acquired the derogatory sense of "a cunning trick", "artifice, ruse, stratagem, or wile", OED 6, described as "common in the 16th and 17th cent". If A's omission of the word is regarded as more than scribal error, possibly the decorum of the word in application to Christ might be held to be a factor. The reference seems to be to the suggested *maistrye* 13, hence the singular form, although B's plural is possible. The inclusion of the article in H seems intended to provide an additional syllable to "improve" what seems to be an acceptable metre.

17–20, stanza 3   The additional lines in RHBC are to be preferred since they produce a regular Chester stanza instead of the quatrain in HmA and correctly reassign 17–20 to Caiaphas instead of Annas, as in John 11/50, 18/14. This is one of three major omissions in the play shared by HmA on the basis of which Salter suggested that for this play A was a copy of Hm.

18 H is acceptable for meaning and metre, but it does not closely reflect John 11/50: *unus moriatur homo* (AV "one man should die"); it may reflect an exemplar *mon* taken as noun by HmARBC but as verb by H.

nought 20 HmARBC is to be preferred for rhyme to *not* H.

17–20   Compare John 11/50, where Caiaphas says this at the meeting of the Sanhedrin after the raising of Lazarus. The words are repeated in John 18/14 at the start of Christ's trial before Caiaphas as a means of identifying the high priest; they there have an effect comparable with that here of suggesting a pre-formed judgment. *yt is needfull* is perhaps slightly more emphatic than John's *expedit* (AV "It is expedient").

20   *and* H corresponds to *et* in John 11/50. C reverses *so* and *that*.

21–30   Compare 14/253–6 and note. The charge is based on Matthew 26/60–1, Mark 14/57–8, where no such kingly aspirations are imputed. Similarly no kingly aspiration is suggested in the equivalent passages in other cycles — Wakefield

21/73–81, York 29/268–71, *Ludus Coventriae* 29/130–4, although in Wakefield 21/130–1, 199 Caiaphas does raise such a charge independently of this accusation. Here, the passage picks up the imputations at 14/237–48 and anticipates 118–32 and other passages in this play.

22 The ARB order is attested also by C; all versions—Hm, ARBC and the alternative form of H—are equally possible. Salter notes *or* AR as evidence of the agreement of these two manuscripts against the others; in B the word is abbreviated, however, and it is doubtful whether much importance should be attached to the AR agreement — we do not think that B or HmC constitute a notable difference from AR in this reading.

babelavaunt, babliant are the only instances of these forms recorded by MED; and A provides the only example of *babelavaunte* for OED.

29–36 The gospels do not contain such an accusation at this point. It could echo 13/239–54 or 14/227–8, although the preceding reference to the temple favours the latter. The charges anticipate 16/251–82, 299–304.

34 *fortye* The number is not verifiable from gospel accounts and seems arbitrary; *twenty* H is equally possible. Some reference to the audience may be intended. Deimling wrongly states that A shares the H reading here.

37–109 Based on Matthew 26/62–8, Mark 14/60–5.

37–44, stanza 6   The b-rhymes, *preven* 40 — *meven* 44 HmBC and *proven* — *moven* A, are equally possible, but R's *preven* — *moven* is not acceptable. *sayne* 40 H destroys rhyme and perhaps reflects some unease at the inappropriateness to Christ's situation — though not to Caiaphas' attitude — of *prove*, OED II.5, "demonstrate the truth of".

42–4   Compare Matthew 26/63: *Adiuro te per Deum vivum, ut dicas nobis si tu es Christus filius Dei* (AV "I adjure thee by the living God, that thou tell us whether thou be the Christ, the Son of God"). *conjure*, OED II, "to constrain by oath", reflects *adiuro* and is the word used in *Ludus Coventriae* 29/147, where Caiaphas 'conjures' Jesus 'be þe sonne and þe mone,' obscuring the point, and in York 29/292; Mark 14/61 does not have the adjuration, and is followed by Wakefield 21/249–50. That Matthew is primary here is also indicated by the absence of an equivalent to *benedicti*, Mark 14/61.

Unlike the gospel account, Caiaphas demands that Jesus answer the charges already laid, 43, and 44 does not constitute the high priest's charge. But as the passage is here worded, Jesus' silence would perhaps be interpreted as evidence that he was not the Son of God. Despite Caiaphas' words, Jesus does not address himself to the charges of Tertius Judeus but only to those of Quartus Judeus and to Caiaphas' premise. It may be noted that the capital charge is that of claiming to be Son of God, not of calling himself Christ, and Chester accurately reflects the Bible on this point.

45–53, stanza 7   The stanza, exceptionally, contains nine lines, rhyming aaaaaaaaa, instead of the usual eight.

Caiaphas, 50 + SH, echoes in anger the unscriptural *justefye* 50 before proceeding with his speech; 51 HmARBC may suggest a dramatisation of Matthew 26/65: *Tunc*

PLAY XVI

princeps sacerdotum scidit vestimenta sua (AV "Then the high priest rent his clothes"), suggesting a display of uncontrollable anger, as in *Glossa Ordinaria*, 'Evang. Matth.' 26/65 (PL 114/171). But *Glossa Ordinaria*, id, also claims that the action is the usual Jewish reponse to blasphemy and without 51 the sense of uncontrolled anger is muted.

H, perhaps recognising the overlaps of 52–3 and 56–7, and perhaps also noting that 51–3 are without biblical counterpart, assigns only 54–8 to Caiaphas, corresponding to Matthew 26/65, and gives the preceding lines to the collective Jews, omitting the line of echoing disbelief, 51. H also omits *of* 52, changing the meaning of the line to "All this company bears witness that he lies falsely", which prompts Caiaphas' response at 54–8. H thus produces the expected eight-line stanza.

Of 51, Salter (p.37), regarding the H version of the passage as "less confused", comments that "as a hypermetrical insertion, assigned to bystanders, [51] would belong to a flourishing period in the history of the play; but it would seem to have been scored out again later for reasons of economy, leaving at this point in the official register a mess of alteration which caused the variance between BC[Hm]R[A] and H." The line is metrically and semantically redundant. In HmC and R it contains five strongly stressed syllables instead of the expected four, an excess corrected in AB. Its omission would not, however, necessarily require the further changes in H.

50   *in clowdes* HmARBC is to be preferred to *in clowd* H as corresponding to Matthew 26/64 *in nubibus caeli* (AV "in the clouds of heaven").

to justefye No purpose is ascribed in the gospels at this point to Christ's coming, although it was frequently understood as a reference to Christ's second coming to judge the world; see 24/*Before* 1, and Bede, *In Matthaei Evangelium Expositio*, 4/26 (PL 92/118) and *Glossa Ordinaria*, 'Evang. Marc.' 14/62 (PL 114/234). The contrast of divine and human judgment is made explicit here, and seems to provoke Caiaphas' wrath at 51, rather obscuring the blasphemy which is the point of the charge and the biblical source of the high priest's anger.

59–61   *Reus est mortis*, Matthew 26/66 (AV "He is guilty of death") is surprisingly without counterpart here.

In the gospels the buffeting seems to be a spontaneous response to Jesus' "Presumption" and is given no formal ratification by the high priests. Here, as elsewhere in the play, the priests emerge as the official presenters of the popular feeling, 64–9.

60   HmARBC and H are equally possible; H echoes 15/73. Salter (p.37) considered H correct because it has "a line with better alliteration".

62–109, stanzas 9–15   The speeches of the Buffeting are in a form of the Chester stanza with a predominantly two-stress line throughout, a form used also at 306–54 for the Scourging.

62–109   The Buffeting draws details from all gospel accounts; viz:
76ff, spitting — Matthew 26/27, Mark 14/65
80, in Jesus' face — Matthew 26/67
77ff, striking — Matthew 26/67, Mark 14/65, Luke 22/63
90–1, blindfolding — Mark 14/65, Luke 22/64
96 "who struck you?" — Matthew 26/68, Mark 14/65, Luke 22/64; Luke is the only

account to specify blows to the face after the blindfolding; Mark 14/65 attributes the blows to the servants.
Luke records a further interview with the priests after the buffeting.

69 + SD   *in cathedram* The gospels do not mention that Jesus sits for the Buffeting. The SD here is the only indication of a sedentary position, but imposes the sense of "stoop with head and shoulders" on *stowpe* 87 (see note). Jesus also sits in Wakefield 21 on a *stoyll* 345, in York 29 on a *stole* 359, in *Ludus Coventriae* 29/160 + SD *on a stol*, but apparently not in the Cornish Ordinalia.

70–7, stanza 10   Deimling cites *elles* 77 AR as a shared inferior reading evidencing the close relationship of the two manuscripts; C reads *else. all* B is a scribal error for *alls* HmH, required for rhyme.

82   The sense is obscure; possibly it means "He shall go through his paces now", i.e. shall show what he can do, or "He shall pass quickly from one of us to another".

87   Salter prefers *stowpe* HmARBC to *carpe* H for meaning. Possibly the H substitution resulted from unease at the possible association of *stoop* with a standing position rather than the sitting position of 69 + SD (see note).

nowe ARBHC is to be preferred to *nowe nowe* Hm in producing a more regular sequence of strongly and weakly stressed syllables and a two-stress line.

90   *steake* HmAR, in the sense of "enclose", OED *steek* v[1] 1, is last recorded in 1450 by OED in current use but clearly survived in northern dialects. B and H supply inappropriate alternatives, perhaps not recognising the word; A perhaps suggests an inappropriate short vowel.

94–7, stanza 13   The additional lines in RBHC are to be preferred to HmA in producing a regular eight-line stanza instead of the HmA quatrain and restoring the 1–2–3–4 sequence of speakers destroyed in HmA. This is the second shared omission of HmA cited by Salter as evidence that in this play A was copied from Hm; see lines Before 102 and note.

97 + 2   *thrye* Christ has not identified the strikers of the three blows since 85 + SH, as requested at 96.

97 + 3–4   "Although my fist bruises him, nevertheless he gets a blow." With *flye* compare *flen* MED v(2), sense 3. The rhyme with *Christ* 97 excludes *feast* B, but some word-play with *fest* MED 4(a), "any enjoyable occasion or event", may be suspected.

98–101, stanza 14   *beshitt* 98 H, though with long vowel for perfect rhyme, is to be preferred to *skricke* ARBC for rhyme and to the semantically inappropriate *stryke* Hm for rhyme and meaning. The Hm form seems to derive from the ARBC form as a scribal error or misunderstanding. Possibly the H form was changed in the exemplar from some sense of decorum. Salter (p.37) comments that "H has the less elegant but better rhyming line" and speculates: "As the original line was here offensive, it was probably scored through in the exemplar and written over. The scribe of H could then, being of antiquarian disposition and intent upon preserving older forms, read the original while other scribes accepted the emendation."

The additional lines before 102 in RHBC are to be preferred to HmA in giving an eight-line stanza instead of the HmA quatrain and restoring the order of speakers as

PLAY XVI

1-2-3-4. Salter cites the shared omission of HmA as evidence that for this play A was copied from Hm; compare 17-20 stanza 3 note and 94-7 stanza 13 note.

100 *me* ARBHC is to be preferred to the erroneous *myne* Hm for meaning; Hm presumably means "No man can blame mine (i.e. my blow)".

101-2 *despitte* A variant form of *disputen*, MED 3(b) "to object to something, dispute"; a long vowel is required for rhyme. *despice* B is apparently a replacement which destroys rhyme, although the possibility of confusion of *t* and *c* exists.

109–109 + SD The Buffeting occupied the time between the trial and morning, when Jesus was taken before Pilate, Matthew 27/1, Mark 15/1. No indication of time is given here, despite the reference to *to late* 109; contrast York 29/348-9:

> My lorde, it is nowe in þe nyght
> I rede 3e abide tille þe mornyng

and *Ludus Coventriae* 30/237:

> Now serys þe nyth is passyd þe day is come

110-7 A distinction is here involved between Jewish law — *oure lawe* 113 — and Roman law — *the lawe* 117; see *Glossa Ordinaria*, 'Evang. Lucae' 23/1 (PL 114/343) and also Wakefield 21/277-9, 293. The Sanhedrin could pronounce Jesus guilty of an offence for which death was the punishment 111, but they had not power to execute the sentence; compare 16/249-50 and note.

116 *Syr Pilate* Pontius Pilate, the sixth Roman procurator of Judaea. *Syr* accurately reflects his status as a Roman knight appointed to act under the governor of a province to collect revenues and judge causes; compare York 29/343: "He is domysman nere and nexte to þe king." Pilate is not usually presented in a favourable light in commentaries or in the plays, but here, in his close attention to Jesus' words and repeated efforts to save him, emerges more creditably and may be compared with the other representative of Roman law in the cycle, Octavian in Play 6.

117 + SD John 18/28 indicates that the Jews took Jesus only to the hall of judgment; they did not enter the hall because it was the residence of a Gentile and by entering they would become defiled and unable to eat the Passover. Pilate therefore came out to them, and the public hearing presumably took place in the courtyard of the governor's residence, the palace of Herod the Great in Jerusalem. But Augustine postulates that the hearings before priests and before Pilate may have taken place in the same building; see Augustine, *In Johannis Evangelium*, Tractatus 114 (PL 35/1936) and *Harmony* lib. 3, 7/27. York 29 makes much of the journey from the priests' palace to Pilate; *Ludus Coventriae* 29/209, 218, 225 locates the hearing *at þe mothalle*. No location is here specified, but Pilate's *come up* 136 suggests an address from a higher level.

The hearing takes place in the morning of Good Friday, although no indication of time is given here — compare *Ludus Coventriae* 30/221, from Pilate: "Be þe oure of prime I xal comyn hem to". Peter's Denial, dramatised at the end of the play in HmARBC, precedes the hearing by Pilate, taking place at the priests' residence before cockcrow.

118-33 The priests put forward two accusations against Jesus:

(1) that he is a disturber of the peace and opponent of Jewish law, 118–9, 126–8, anticipating Luke 23/5 which forms the basis of 145–50;
(2) that he seeks to set himself up in place of Caesar and remove Caesar's privileges, 120–3, 128–31, from Luke 23/2.
Both follow from the accusations of kingly aspiration and Jesus' claim to *justefye* in the trial before the priests, neither of which had on that occasion biblical precedent. The capital offence for the Sanhedrin was Jesus' blasphemy, to which no reference is made here (the claim to be Christ, 128, was not itself blasphemous).

It was customary to contrast the accusation indicated here in 119–20 with Jesus' injunction to observe civil law; see *Glossa Ordinaria*, 'Evang. Lucae' 23/3 (PL 114/344). Here no such link is possible, unless made obliquely through association with the tribute of Play 6. However, the Jews' fear of the encroachment of Roman authority upon them at the support won by Jesus is shown at 14/311–2 and perhaps gives substance to their charge and cause for Pilate's careful, and perhaps sceptical, inquiry; resentment of Roman authority was hardly likely to be treated as a capital offence by the Jews.

122   *felowes* ARBHC is to be preferred for meaning to the scribally erroneous *fellowe* Hm.

124   *dome* ARBHC is to be preferred for meaning to *donne* Hm, the latter a scribal error resulting from miscounted minims.

125   *thee that* ARBC is to be preferred for meaning to *that he* Hm, correctly indicating that Pilate has the authority to pass sentence of death. H erroneously substitutes 133.

128   *Christ and kinge* The order in HmARBC reflects that of Luke 23/2: *Dicentem se Christum regem esse* (AV "Saying that he himself is Christ a King"). The H order perhaps suggests the emphasis appropriate to the political charge suggested to Pilate.

134–8, stanza 19   The stanza is of unusual form, containing two lines in French which do not rhyme, followed by two four-stress lines and one three-stress line, rhyming aab. The French occurs also at 18/1–4 in a longer opening address in French by Pilate, where the two lines are set out as four, rhyming aaab and forming part of an aaabcccb stanza form; here only A sets out the lines as four, misdividing 135 (see TNs).

A comparison with the equivalent passage in Play 18 suggests that *desepte* should read *disciple* and *vel atres in* read *que la tresin*. The general sense seems to be "Welcome, Sir Caiaphas; God save you Sir Annas; and his disciple Judas who effected the act of treason." There is, however, nothing to indicate the presence of Judas Iscariot here; indeed, Judas' remorseful restoration of the money to the priests and his subsequent suicide are recorded in Matthew 27/3–10 between the departure of Jesus from the priests' residence and his appearance before Pilate, although the episode is not dramatised in Chester as it is in York 32/127–389 (between the Trial before Herod and the Second Trial before Pilate), *Ludus Coventriae* 30/229–36+SD, Cornish Ordinalia (after the Buffeting) and Wakefield 32 — an incomplete play entitled *Suspencio Judi* and out of sequence. Judas' death is reported in 21/25–32+Latin.

The French is not appropriate here and seems removed, in much corrupted form, from play 18 to provide the sort of "foreign-sounding" introduction which often characterises kingly figures on their first appearance in Chester. It could replace five lines of a regular Chester stanza, of which 136–8 represent the remainder; or serve to introduce 136–8 as a later addition. 136–8 suggest both a raised area (*come up* 136) for the nobles (*lordinges* 136), and also perhaps an entourage for Pilate (*this fellowshippe here* 138), although the reference may be merely to the Jews attending. H omits the stanza entirely, without detriment to the rest of the play.

139–58 The exchanges with Pilate derive from Luke 23/3–7, but are parallel to John 18/33–34 which is represented by 252–5.

139 Deimling reads *mystarye* R, as we do; Salter, however, reads *myscarie* RC and places considerable emphasis upon this shared reading as indicating a common origin for RC not shared by A. Here HmABH have what may be formal variants or reflections of a confusion of "misery" with "mis-array" i.e. "dis-array"; *miscarye* C might be an error or an attempt to find a more meaningful word, based on the common verb "to miscarry", i.e. "to come to harm or misfortune", although no equivalent noun exists (*miscarriage* is dated from 1614 by OED) and the result is a nonce-word; *mystarye* R would represent a different, and semantically inappropriate, alternative. However, it may be noted that even if Salter's reading is not accepted, a scribal confusion of *c* and *t* would be easily made and neither could readily derive from *s*; hence a case for the connexion of RC can still be postulated, although it would then be weakened by the fact that Bellin may have made three different suggestions for a word which he found problematic.

148 *them* H is inappropriate. Compare 146, where H reads *perverted them* for HmARB's *converted to him*; since the construction here is comparable, *them* may suggest influence from H's previous substitution.

149 *dome* ARBHC is to be preferred for meaning to *downe* Hm, the latter perhaps influenced by *downe* 150.

151 Here no-one has told Pilate that Jesus was born in Galilee, whereas in Luke 23/6–7 Pilate asks if Jesus is a Galilean when he hears the name Galilee mentioned.

sayen RC, *sayn* H would seem semantically preferable to *steyne* HmA, *seene* B. But possibly *steyne* HmA represents *stay* v¹, OED 2b, "to cease speaking", recorded from 1551, which would fit the context. The agreement of HmA could be cited in support of Salter's thesis that in this play A derives from Hm; but probably all forms, including the inappropriate *seene* B, originate in an obscure exemplar reading.

152 *Herode* i.e. Herod Antipas, son of Herod the Great, appointed under the terms of his father's will as tetrarch of Galilee and Persaea and responsible for the death of John the Baptist. The account of Jesus' appearance before him is found only in Luke, who notes, 23/7, that Herod was in Jerusalem at that time, presumably for the Passover. As 157 indicates, Pilate seems to have sent Jesus to him in deference to his jurisdiction.

Although Herod Antipas was apparently confused on occasion with Herod the Great and given the same irascible manner (compare York), Chester dramatises the death of Herod the Great and such confusion is not possible. However, Herod Antipas was tetrarch, not king; ironically, the courtesy-title of king was granted to Herod's nephew Herod Agrippa, by Herod the Great, and it was after petitioning Rome for the right to that title that Herod Antipas was eventually banished. But

Chester bestows the rank of king upon Herod Antipas — Pilate refers to *his royaltie* 153, although this could refer only to his royal ancestry, and he is referred to as *kinge* at 162, 163, 209, 211. In this Chester is like other cycles — York 30/515, *Ludus Coventriae* 30/345, Cornish *Ordinalia* p.128. But the ascription of kingly rank strangely contradicts the later protestations of loyalty to Caesar, 299-304, a contradiction not in the Bible.

154 *blemished* HmAC is to be preferred for meaning to *blemyshe* RBH. HmAC treat the form as parallel to the past subjunctive *rafte* 153, whereas RBH may suggest the continuing future consequences of a past action viz: "I would have deprived him of his royal position and would thereby damage his reputation for ever."

159 *you* ARC suggests that Bellin consistently understood the line to refer to Pilate, perhaps in the sense "You shall have him [back again] very quickly". *he* HmBH is clearly correct; Pilate obviously hoped that he would not have to deal with the case further.

166 The line contains four strongly stressed syllables instead of the expected three. The omission of one of the tautologous adverbs *hens awaye*, found in all manuscripts, would produce the expected three-stress line.

169–70 Thus Luke 23/8, but looking back to Luke 9/9, when Herod first heard of Jesus' deeds; in Matthew 14/1-2, Mark 6/14 Herod then suggested that Jesus might be the resurrected John the Baptist. *Ludus Coventriae* 29/36-69 dramatises Herod's earlier eagerness.

173–4 In Luke, Herod does not require evidence of Jesus' divine origins but approaches the matter more in a spirit of speculative enquiry.

178 + SD Luke 23/10-11 indicates that during Jesus' silence the chief priests and scribes continued to accuse him and that Herod and his soldiers mocked him. Here there is no indication that the chief priests are present or that Herod has such an entourage. Contrast York 31, where Herod is seen with attendants and sons; *Ludus Coventriae* 30/356 + SD, where Herod is *in astat* and the priests and Jews accompany Jesus to accuse him; and Cornish *Ordinalia*, where Annas, Caiaphas, soldiers and learned doctors go with Jesus to Herod and his counsellor.

179–86 Luke does not suggest that Herod became angry; the passage may be a further reflection of the influence of the irate Herod of the Nativity.

181 *scalward* Of the three terms supplied by the manuscripts, only *stalwarde* RBC has an OED counterpart, *stalwart*, recorded from 1470 as "a strong and valiant man"; but the word seems to have a favourable sense, despite the pejorative overtones of sense 3 of the adjective — compare *stowte and sterne* 182. Both the nonce-forms, *scalwarde* HmA and *stanold* H, could derive from *stalwarde* by error or in unease at the connotations of the word. But it is equally possible that HmA or H transmit an exemplar error and that RBC represent the independent attempts by two scribes to find a formal, meaningful alternative. H's substitution of *and* for *so* 182 seems to suggest that *stowt and sterne* 182 are not necessarily implied by *stanold*. See also 314.

185 H omits *non*, a word redundant after *not* 184, but to the detriment of metre. A more regular sequence of strongly and weakly stressed syllables would result from

PLAY XVI

the omission of *but* 185.

192–4 "I forgive the enmity which was between us two, so that I will no longer be his foe after today." H supplies an indirect object which is syntactically unnecessary. A erroneously anticipates *to be* 193, perhaps troubled by the failure of line- and syntax-units to correspond; this error is consolidated by R. The source of this enmity is not specified in the biblical account, although Pilate's concern about areas of authority may suggest a felt insult arising from such a matter. The legendary account of the origins of the enmity is to be found in *Legenda Aurea* 'De Passione Domini', and in *Stanzaic Life* 6537–56.

195–202+SD   Compare Luke 23/11: *indutum veste alba* (AV "arrayed him in a gorgeous robe"). The robe is perhaps that for which the soldiers diced at the foot of the cross, 16A/96–148. Hence, although York 31/324 merely states "clothe hym in white", *Ludus Coventriae* 30/465+SD states "Þei xal don on jhesus clothis, and ouerest A whyte clothe", and Cornish *Ordinalia* p.133 calls it "a satin surcoat". See also 322+SD-26 note.

On Herod's reasons for the gift, compare Comestor, *Historia Scholastica*, 'In Evangelia' 164 (PL 198/1627): *Et in signum illusionis induit eum veste alba*; *Legenda Aurea*, 'De Passione Domini': *Pro derisione eum veste alba induit*; *Stanzaic Life*

> The secunde hokur þat Ihesu hade
> was in Herodes house þo kyng,
> þat as a fole ɀ madde hym made
> to clethe hym so in quite clethyng
> (5905–8)

The same idea is seen in York 31/329–30:

Dux   Mi lorde, fooles þat are fonde þei falle such a fee.
Rex   What! in a white garmente to goo ...

and 346–7:

Dux   He schall be rayed like a Roye
       And schall be fonne a Roye in his folie

which reflects the duality of 195–202 and 204–8 here. *Ludus Coventriae* offers no explanation. The Christian symbolism of the gift was otherwise developed. Compare Ambrose, *Expositiones in Lucam*, lib. 10 Par. 103 (PL 15/1922); Bede, *In Lucae Evangelium Expositio* (PL 92/611); and *Glossa Ordinaria*, 'Evang. Luc.' 23/14 (PL 114/344).

196   "It may be a source of amusement to Pilate" — the line makes explicit the sense of scorn and mockery.

198   HmARBC give a regular sequence of strongly and weakly stressed syllables. *so* H is arguably preferable semantically and syntactically in making the link with 195 clear.

R has interchanged *wood* 198 and *madd* 199, destroying rhyme at 198.

199   The somewhat rough metre of the line seems to have troubled A, R, H and C. A and H arguably improve the metre; R reduces the number of syllables by one and hence the number of strongly stressed syllables to an irregular three.

203–10, stanza 28   *guyfte* 210 ABHC is to be preferred for meaning to the erroneous *guyste* Hm and its rationalised equivalent *guyse* R, both originating in a confusion of exemplar *f* with long *s*.

The resulting b-rhymes, *light* 206 — *guyfte* 210, do not give perfect rhyme in ABC. In H, a change of word-order in 206 accompanies a change of rhyme-word to *lifte*, which is to be preferred for rhyme. Deimling argues that rhyme proves the correctness of the H reading; Salter (p.37) takes *light* as "an attempt at correction when *lifte* failed to be understood". But H's "that now is lifted over you" does not closely reflect any use of *liften* in MED, and *light* seems preferable for meaning. The evaluation of the readings is complicated by the awkward syntax of 209-10 — see note.

209-10 *beleave on thee* 209 H and C treat *beleave* as verb, "believe"; *will* H, *well* C are formally similar — "will you believe" H, "believe truly" C. But neither seems appropriate to the context. *of thee* ARB suggests that *beleave* is to be read as *be leave*, "by leave", "with your permission". If so, the reference is not clear — either the line is to be related to the act of departure and is thus elliptical; or Jesus in his royal garb is so arrayed at Herod's consent.

By either meaning *and* 210 ARB cannot be read as a true conjunction but only as introducing a tardily recalled courtesy — the suggestion being that the Jews are so preoccupied with Jesus that they almost forget their obligations to Herod. The readings of H and C, however, treat *and* as a true conjunction, linking the two verbs, *beleave* and *grauntmercye*.

215-34 Based on Luke 23/13-23, but omitting the reference to the reassembly of the people with priests and rulers at Luke 23/14 and Pilate's intention to chastise Jesus at Luke 23/16, the latter relating to the later scourging. The offer of Barabbas, which in Luke 23/18-19 is an unprompted request from the people, draws here on other gospel accounts; viz: 221-6, John 18/39; 227-30, Matthew 27/21, Mark 15/11; 231-4, Matthew 27/22, Mark 15/12-13. 227 lacks biblical equivalent. 232 combines Matthew's *qui dicitur Christus* (AV "which is called Christ") and Mark's *Quid ergo vultis faciam regi Iudaeorum*(AV "What will ye then that I shall do unto him whom ye call the king of the Jews?").

Here the four Jews represent the multitude, to whom Pilate attempts to appeal, as in the gospels, over the heads of the high priests. But then in Chester the public acts give place to "behind the scenes" diplomacy.

Chester omits the warning to Pilate by his wife which precedes the offer of Barabbas in Matthew 27/19 and which is dramatised in York, *Ludus Coventriae* and Cornish Ordinalia.

The offer of Barabbas is repeated at 363-4; see note.

219-20 The wording and metre of these lines varies among the manuscripts. 219 Hm contains five strongly stressed syllables instead of the expected four, an excess corrected in H and also in B (where *all* (2) is removed). *ney* ARB is rhetorically preferable for emphatic repetition to *all* Hm. 220 A contains only three strongly stressed syllables instead of the expected four.

221 *naye* B destroys rhyme; it echoes the opening of 219, and may suggest confusion resulting from the following b-rhyme, *saye* 222, and the distribution of the stanza between two speakers; B evidently regarded Pilate's speech as a stanza and accordingly substituted a b-rhyme.

PLAY XVI

230 *Barabas* The form *Baraban* is attested by rhyme at 364 HmH, where ARBC offer the erroneous variant *Barabam*, the Vulgate accusative form of Matthew 27/20–1. *Barabbas* is the nominative form of Matthew 27/16, and syntactically it is correct here since *Barabas* is the subject of an understood *worthye is* 228 — "Barabbas deserves to be spared". The HmH reading is therefore to be preferred.

Pilate does not here offer the Jews a choice between Barabbas and Jesus, as he does in Matthew 27/21 and in the second offer of 363–4; rather as in Mark 15/11, Luke 23/18, John 18/40, the Jews supply the prisoner's name — indeed, in Mark 15/8, the Jews also claim the custom unprompted.

Barabbas is not otherwise identified for the audience, nor is his release later shown, as elsewhere (see *Sources* above). In the gospels he is further described as a notable prisoner (Matthew 27/16), a leader of an insurrection in Jerusalem who had committed murder (Mark 15/7, Luke 23/19), and a robber (John 18/40). The irony of the exchange of a convicted criminal and rebel leader for Jesus, falsely arraigned for sedition, is here lost.

235–42 The washing of the hands is found only in Matthew 27/24, where it follows the offer of Barabbas and marks the end of the judgment. Jesus is then delivered for scourging. The biblical action echoes the practice enjoined upon the Jews in Deuteronomy 21/6–7. Its significance is suggested in *Glossa Ordinaria*, 'Evang. Matth.' 27/24 (PL 114/174): *Gentilem populum ab impietate Judaeorum alienum designans*.

There is no counterpart in the Chester account to Matthew 27/25, where the Jews accept responsibility for Christ's death upon themselves and future generations, a response lost from Wakefield and York, but shown in *Ludus Coventriae* and Cornish Ordinalia.

237 *present* in the sense of "presence" is recorded in OED only to 1470 although this seems to be the sense here required. Only H shows unease and provides an absolute phrase, "you all being present".

241 *in no intent*, "in no mind", is dependent upon *I am* 240, and parallel to *cleane and innocent* 240, to which it is linked by *and*. H, perhaps misunderstanding the syntax here, replaces *and* by *not*, making *for to sheede* dependent on *cleane and innocent* and making *in no intent* adverbial, "by no means".

242 + SD Compare 135 note. The priests and Pilate seem to be apart from the other Jews. *recedent* seems to imply withdrawal out of earshot. Presumably the interrogation by Pilate of Jesus, based on John, takes place in the priests' absence, since John 18/33 indicates the priests could not enter for the dialogue beginning here at 252. The dialogue ends at 290; then, in John 18/39 40, Pilate goes outside to offer Barabbas in exchange for Jesus, whom he leaves inside the hall, whereas here Pilate, if he ever leaves the priests, returns to them at 291 with Jesus, and then delivers Jesus for scourging to the Jews below at 305.

Ludus Coventriae 31 presents the dialogue also after the offer of Barabbas, but makes the separation of Pilate and Jesus from the priests clear:

> Jhesus A wyle with me xal go.
> I wole hym examyne betwyx us tweyn
> (581–2)

Ludus Coventriae 30/582 + SD indicates that Pilate then leads Jesus into the council-house and at 605 + SD he leaves Jesus alone to go to the Jews. Cornish *Ordinalia* p.139 shows the interview taking place in prison.

243-6   Based on Mark 15/12-13, which represents the question in that gospel following the popular demand that Pilate retain Jesus and release Barabbas. Here, what was originally a question addressed to the multitude becomes one addressed privately to *yee prelates*, so that the question and answer, echoing 217, 219-20, are given more authoritative status and Caiaphas again emerges as official spokesman for the popular viewpoint already expressed.

246 + SH-50   247-50 are based on Pilate's initial response to the priests' demands in John 18/31. H has erroneously and inexplicably omitted 246 + SH-8.

251-92   Based on John 18/33-8, with some link to Luke 23/3-4. John states that Pilate did not wait for a reply to his question concerning truth; his departure before Jesus replied was variously seen in his favour as indicating that he had suddenly realised that the offer of Barabbas was a means of freeing Jesus; or as indicating that he regarded the question as speculative, unanswerable or requiring an extended debate; or, against him, that he was not worthy to receive the answer, being corrupt. All the views are expressed in *Legenda Aurea*, 'De Passione Domini'. Here, however, Pilate receives and debates his answer in a passage deriving from the Apocryphal Acts of Pilate 3/2, also reported in *Legenda Aurea*, 'De Passione Domini'. Only Chester uses this passage, which increases the image of the rationally enquiring Pilate and avoids the hints of corruption and cynicism adhering to his biblical departure.

255-6   *hopes*, "think". Compare *dicis* John 18/34 (AV "Sayest thou"), paralleling *dixerunt* (AV "Did [others] tell") which corresponds to *tould* 256. It is odd that Chester misses the opportunity for telling verbal parallel.

256 H is closer than HmARBC to John 18/34: *An alii dixerunt tibi de me?* (AV "Or did others tell it thee of me?").

259-66, stanza 35   *han* 262 H is to be preferred for rhyme with *tayne* 266 to *have* HmARBC, the latter a "modernisation".

263   HmARHC seem to have five strongly stressed syllables. B's omission of *say* produces a four-stress line of more regular metrical pattern. The line, repeating 253-4, has no biblical equivalent — compare John 18/35: *Quid fecisti?* (AV "What hast thou done?"). *Glossa Ordinaria*, 'Evang. Joan.' 18/35 (PL 114/419): *Quasi: Si haec culpa non est, quod te regem dixeris, quid aliud fecisti?*

264-74   The passage represents an extensive elaboration of John 18/36: *Ministri mei utique decertarent ut non traderer Judaeis; nunc autem regnum meum non est hinc* (AV "Then would my servants fight that I should not be delivered to the Jews; but now is my kingdom not from hence"). The elaboration removes all notion that Jesus seeks to challenge the Roman authority in setting himself up as royal leader of the Jewish nation. This idea was the common interpretation of the passage; it is found, for example, in Bede, *In S. Joannis Evangelium Expositio* 18 (PL 92/903) and in *Glossa Ordinaria*, 'Evang. Joan.' 18/36 (PL 114/420).

265 *not* ARBHC is to be preferred, for meaning and as reflecting Vulgate *non*, to the erroneous *nowe* Hm.

were it ARBC is to be preferred for meaning, syntax and metre to *were* Hm. H's rewording, corresponding to John 18/36: *Si ex hoc mundo esset regnum meum* (AV "If my kingdom were of this world") gives good sense but rough metre.

274+SH–82 H erroneously omits the stanza required both by the biblical text and the continuity of dialogue here. Deimling (p.xxiii) comments: "The writer of H may have erroneously omitted this stanza because it contains, in its fourth and eighth lines, rhymes in *-aye* like the preceding one."

275 Pilate's statement here corresponds to John 18/37: *Ergo, rex es tu*? (AV "Art thou a king then?"). *or was* has no biblical counterpart, possibly indicating that the Chester Pilate does not understand fully Jesus' point.

287 *truth* ARBHC is to be preferred, for meaning and as reflecting *veritas* in Nicodemus 3/2, to the erroneous omission in Hm. *in* BH is supported by C against HmAR.

289 H's omission of *non* is to be preferred for meaning; the word has no counterpart in the apocryphal text — see 252–92 note. Possibly HmARBC confused 289–90 with a passage in the second dialogue of Pilate and Jesus, John 19/11: *Non haberes potestatem adversum me ullam, nisi tibi datum esset desuper* (AV "Thou couldest have no power at all against me, except it were given thee from above"). Alternatively they may simply reflect a misunderstanding of the meaning here. *non* was presumably the exemplar reading.

293–304 The Jews' charges are drawn from two separate passages in John. 293–8 derive from John 19/7, where they represent the Jews' response to the attempt by Pilate to deliver to them the newly scourged Christ. 299–304 derive from John 19/12, which is preceded by the second private interrogation of Jesus by Pilate, not here dramatised. John in both passages indicates that the speakers were the Jews collectively.

295–6 *Moyses lawe* viz. Leviticus 24/16.

299–306, stanza 40 The b-rhymes *him* 301 — *lythe* 306 do not rhyme. The choice lies between reversing *with him* 302 to give *him with* — compare C's omission of *him*; and reversing the phrase at 306, as in A. Deimling, holding that A and R share a common reading at 206, regarded that reading as superior to BH (correctly transcribed in his text but wrongly cited as *lim and like* (p.xvi)). Salter postulates the erroneous omission of *him* in the Register, at which stage the C-exemplar was copied and the omission transmitted to C, but suggested that *him* was supplied as a line-end correction with caret before *with*; hence, he held, B[Hm]H copied *him* in rhyme position, ignoring the caret, and A copied Hm but changed the word-order at 206, while R did not here follow A.

299–306 Compare 118–33, based on Luke 23/1, the equivalent of this section but used earlier to open the trial.

299 *appere* Apparently an error for "a peer, an equal", compare *a pere* C. Possibly the lack of division represents a confusion with "appear" — "whoever presents himself before ..."

301 *withsayth* corresponds to *contradicit* John 19/12 (AV "speaketh against"). A seems to misunderstand the word, but R corrects A's error; *wich* B may be a scribal error, or may reflect a misunderstanding comparable to that of A.

302-4 "And so *we* have proceeded with the case of this man. But whoever calls him a king here takes Caesar's power away from him." This rendering follows H, in which *himselfe a* 303 is replaced by a non-reflexive *him*. By this reading, the Jews argue that Jesus is at fault in setting himself up as equal to the king, 299-301, but Pilate, by accepting Jesus' claims, also commits an act of rebellion, for Pilate, perhaps in the priests' hearing, has called Jesus a king, 275-6, and condoned his claims, 291-2; the question of "heavenly or earthly king" forms no part of the law. The criticism of Pilate corresponds to John 19/12: *Si hunc dimittis, non es amicus Caesaris* (AV "If thou let this man go, thou art not Caesar's friend"). This charge is found in the other plays; compare Wakefield 22/213-4; *Ludus Coventriae* 30/291-2 and 617; and Cornish Ordinalia p.146. York has a gap in the play at this point. One would therefore expect a development of the text here, such as H provides.

In HmARBC there is no close counterpart to the biblical text since the manuscripts contain a reflexive which makes *whoso* refer to Jesus rather than to Pilate. This version also awkwardly duplicates 299-301, presumably the source of the confusion, with virtual identity of wording at 301 and 304, and a rough metre at 303 resulting from the reflexive form and accompanying article. The oblique accusation in H would motivate Pilate's unbiblical anger at 305-6.

307-54 The scourging and subsequent mockery draws upon the accounts in Matthew, Mark and John; in John it precedes Pilate's final attempt to win mercy for Jesus, an arrangement which influences the ordering of material here, but in Matthew and Mark it is carried out after sentence, the scourging being done "by" Pilate (i.e. presumably at his orders) and the mocking following before Christ goes to crucifixion. The details derive as follows:

311-14, stripping — Matthew 27/28
323-6, purple robe — Matthew 27/28, Mark 15/17, John 19/2
326 + SD, crown of thorns — Matthew 27/29, Mark 15/17, John 19/2
331-4, reed as sceptre — Matthew 27/29
336-9, bowing — Matthew 27/29, Mark 15/19
336, "Hail, King of Jews" — Matthew 27/29, Mark 15/18, John 19/3
343-50, spitting — Matthew 27/30, Mark 15/19
322 + SD, beating — with a reed, Matthew 27/30, Mark 15/19; with hands, John 19/3.

307-54, stanzas 41-6 The speeches of the Scourging are in a form of the Chester stanza with a predominantly two-stress line throughout, a form used also at 62-109 for the Buffeting.

314 + SD The SD distinguishes the Scourging from the following mockery. The binding to a column is unbiblical but was well established; compare Comestor, *Historia Scholastica* 'In Evangelia' 167 (PL 198/1628): *Adhuc columna cui alligatus fuit Jesus, vestigia cruoris ostendit*; ME *Harrowing of Hell*, Sion MS:

> Þe knyghtes þan his clothes of hente
> And band hym tille a piler faste
> (601-2)

PLAY XVI

a reference not in the other three manuscripts of the poem; Roman Breviary, Liturgy on Shrove Tuesday: "The column, or pillar, fastened to which our Blessed Lord was so cruelly scourged, is now venerated in the Church of St. Praxedes in Rome." The binding to the pillar is seen also in Wakefield 22/130, *Ludus Coventriae* 31/675 + SD, Cornish Ordinalia p.141.

315-22, stanza 42   *wounden* 316 ARH, "trussed up", is to be preferred for rhyme and meaning to *wandon* Hm, presumably a scribal error, to the substituted *wendon* B, which does not give appropriate sense, and to *wonden* C, presumably a formal variant of *wounden*.

320   *grounden* is past participle of *grinden*, MED v (1), "to grind"; *grane, granes* AH may be preferred, in that order, given a colloquial "his grain is ground", i.e. "his fate is sealed".

grave HmRBC suggests "his grave is prepared"; but such a reading requires *grounden* to be past participle of *grounden* MED 1(b), "to create (something)", a verb recorded only with weak past participle.

321   i.e. "No fellow in all the land between here and London."

322 + SD   *in cathedram* No gospel account suggests that Jesus sat during this mockery. A similar detail occurs in York 33/398, *Ludus Coventriae* 31/677 + SD.

324   *whyte* Jesus was dressed in a white robe by Herod, 195-202, and it is presumably to this that the line refers. Presumably, however, Jesus is divested of his clothes at 314 + SD, and the reference would have to be to the pile of clothes taken from him. As 322 + SD indicates, the robe brought by the Primus Judeus is purple — compare Matthew 27/28, *chlamydem coccineam* (AV "a scarlet robe"), Mark 15/17 *purpura* (AV "with purple") John 19/2 *veste purpurea* (AV "purple robe"). Thus, if *whyte* HmA — an agreement cited by Salter in support of his view that A here derives from Hm — is not accepted, *quoynt* H must be preferred as reconciling 322 + SD and 324. *whante* R, *whainte* B, *whaynte* C perhaps point to an altered exemplar, in which the older *quoynt* had been replaced as its meaning seemed less appropriate.

No reference is made to the removal of the purple robe, as in Matthew 27/31, Mark 15/20. But since the Jews who carry out the scourging are presumably also those who carry out the crucifixion, it would be strange if they quarrelled about the possession of a robe of their own bestowal and the re-investment of Jesus with his Herodian clothes may perhaps be assumed. Alternatively, the Jews may be thought of as carrying Jesus' clothes with them to Calvary.

326   H's substituted line avoids the repetition at 326, 330. But the repetition suggests a word-play of *weure* as "wear" and "harm" which seems justified. Salter (p.38) claims that "H may be, and probably is, emending on his own."

326 + SD   The SD is found only in HmBC. The SD at 328 H seems to suggest that the crowning takes place at that point in H. Possibly the exemplar had both the 326 + SD and the side-note at 328. Only H preferred the latter; AR omit both.

caput BC is to be preferred for syntax to the erroneous *capite* Hm. C alone omits *eius*.

326 + SH   B's omission may have been prompted by the specification of the speaker in the preceding SD.

331–8, stanza 44   *bede*, "offer", 333 HmH is required for meaning and rhyme; AR and B, apparently not understanding the word, substitute forms which destroy meaning and rhyme. *bed* IIC/345 C is formally unique and, if a reflection of the exemplar, may partly explain the failure of ARB to recognise the word.

335–8   *Hervye* 335 The speech is presumably addressed to one of the other Jews; *hevie* B is evidently a scribal error. But H, reading *harlott* 335 and *thy* 337, presents the speech as an address to Jesus.

340–1   "Now you regret what so many men demonstrate, villain." *shewes* 340 HmRB seems to have been obscure either in its exemplar-form or in its meaning for some scribes. *rewes* A does not give sense. *shrews* H is acceptable, but requires *it* to be understood at 341 and the lines to be repunctuated to allow *that*, as relative pronoun, to refer to *kinge of Jewes* 339: "Hail, king of the Jews, whom so many men curse. Villain, now you are made to repent." *sues* C, "follow", is also acceptable, but it is recorded by OED in the sense of "to follow as an attendant, companion or adherent" only to 1522 and in the sense of "to follow as a disciple or imitator" only to 1509; possibly the sense of "to take legal proceedings against", current from late ME, is intended: "Hail, king of the Jews, whom so many men accuse" — with the same repunctuation as H.

342   *thy reverence* "the reverence shown to you"; compare Mark 15/19: *Adorabant eum* (AV "[They] worshipped him").

343–6   "Hack on him with iron, and cut his side. An ointment (i.e. sputum) will revive you for your injury." But no gospel suggests the use of any metal implement here; Matthew 27/30, Mark 15/19 indicate that Jesus was beaten with a reed. H removes the reference, anticipating the 'spitting' by its substitutions of *spould*, *spues* at 343; this reading is preferred by Salter as "probably correct" on the basis of meaning, alliteration and the avoidance of the repetition of the 344 rhyme-word. *thyne offence* 346 ambiguously comprehends "the offence you have committed" and "the offence committed upon you".

347   Salter says: "I do not understand this line" and argues that [Hm] [A]RB[C] preserve a bad exemplar reading which H attempts to amend. Possibly *wryte* is used as OED 2b, "to form by painting", used here of nasal mucus discharged upon Christ. *to* would then be purposive, "in order to".

355–62, stanza 47   The b-rhymes, *pardee* 358 — *tyme* 362 do not rhyme. The omission of *pardee* by HC, and *tome* 362 H are to be preferred in restoring a normal Chester stanza. *pardee* seems to have been added, presumably in the exemplar, to create a four-stress line instead of the required three-stress line, with a-rhyme instead of b-rhyme. It is impossible to tell if the change was aided by, or if it prompted, the replacement of *tome* by the more usual *tyme*. The distribution of the stanza among three speakers may have obscured its structure. Bellin corrects the 358 error in C, though not in AR, but did not there also rectify the form at 362.

355–62   John 19/14–5 indicates that these events took place after the Scourging and also after the ensuing rejection of Pilate's plea to the chief priests, which forms the basis of 293–304, and after a further interview with Jesus. Pilate sat in the judgment seat at a place called the Pavement at about the sixth hour of the preparation of the Passover, probably 6 a.m. No change of location or indication of time is here given.

PLAY XVI

363-70, stanza 48 No manuscript has the form *hane* for *have* 363, required for rhyme: *have* was presumably the exemplar reading.

Baraban 364 HmH is required for rhyme; *Barabam* ARBC is the syntactically correct Latin accusative form.

364-5 There is no biblical equivalent to this late second attempt to replace Jesus by Barabbas. In Mark 15/12, Pilate offers the replacement again immediately after his first offer; in Luke 23/16 Pilate offers to replace Jesus by Barabbas and free Jesus after scourging, and in 23/20 makes an immediate second offer, a sequence which may suggest the arrangement here. But the direct choice of Jesus or Barabbas made by Pilate at 365 is found only in Matthew 27/21.

368-70 Pilate here delivers Jesus to the Jews for crucifixion. In Mark 15/16, John 19/1-3, those responsible for the mocking after the scourging are described as the governor's soldiers, i.e. Romans. Moreover the mocking took place in the *praetorium*, Matthew 27/27, Mark 15/16. In Matthew and Mark the scourging and mocking follow the commitment for crucifixion and the Roman soldiers also carry out the crucifixion. In Luke 23/25, John 19/16, the wording makes it possible to assume that the Jews assumed responsibility, although the reason for the trial by Pilate, the fact that he gave sentence and that crucifixion is the method of execution all support the view that there also the executioners are the Roman soldiers. Compare *Glossa Ordinaria*, 'Evang. Matth.' 27/26 (PL 114/174) and 'Evang. Joan.' 19/1 (PL 114/420): *Hoc fecit Pilatus, id est, milites facere permisit, vel etiam iussit ut Judaei satiati de poenis a morte desisterent*; Comestor, *Historia Scholastica*, 'In Evangelia' 169 (PL 198/1629): *Et licet hoc facerent gentiles, quia Judaeis auctoribus fiebant, ideo in parasceve cum oratur pro perfidis Judaeis, genua non flectimus. Tamen forte Judaei cum militibus hoc agebant*. But compare *Legenda Aurea*, 'De passione Domine': *Cum autem Pylatus dominum Judaeis crucifigendum tradidisset*. In Wakefield 21-23 the Buffeting, Scourging and Crucifixion are carried out by four torturers (*tortores*) who are evidently knights in the high priests' service; in York 29-35 they are carried out by four knights (*milites*), similarly in the priests' service; in *Ludus Coventriae* 29-32 Buffeting, Scourging and Crucifixion are carried out by up to four Jews (*Judaei*), although they are replaced at the cross by soldiers (*milites*) to guard: in Cornish Ordinalia they are carried out by four (Jewish) torturers. This continuity, which has the dramatic advantage of limiting the numbers required and avoiding awkward transfers of authority, also has the thematic effect of stressing the Jews' essential responsibility for Christ's death. It is possible, particularly at Wakefield, where Pilate is in league with the priests, and York that the servants of the priests are in fact Roman soldiers.

At 368 R and H substitute the second person plural pronoun for *I* HmAB. Either reading is possible, but *ye* R may have been suggested by the preceding *you; forth then* H removes the preceding pronoun. *ye, you* places responsibility firmly upon the Jews.

369 seems to have three strongly stressed syllables instead of the expected four: *for sáve him Í ne máye*; the addition of *I see* H restores the required number of syllables, although regularity would be restored more simply by inserting *to* before *save: fór to sáve him Í ne máye*.

371-8, stanza 49 *be hende* 376 BH is to be preferred for rhyme and meaning to *behind* HmARC — A with the required word-division.

379—Finis   Peter's denial is omitted in H, although the incident is apparently required to fulfil the prophecy at 15/186–92 and give meaning to 18/401–20. The omission has to be related to the fact that H presents 16–16A as one play and that the episode in its present position interferes with the continuity of action from the Scourging and Mocking to the Crucifixion in H.

Peter's denial is clearly misplaced, in location and time, here. In Matthew 26/69–75, Mark 14/66–72 it is recounted after the Buffeting; in Luke 22/54–62 it precedes the Buffeting; in John 18/17–18, 25–27, it is narrated in two parts, beginning at the house of Annas and ending after the hearing by Caiaphas. Hence Matthew, Mark and Luke place the episode outside Caiaphas' palace, John beginning outside Annas' residence and concluding outside Caiaphas' residence. The nature of the action places it before cock-crow, hence during the night; and Jesus was taken before Pilate in the morning. This misplacement in Chester strongly argues for textual corruption, a fact which must be seen in conjunction with the stanzaic irregularities of the episode — see 379–94, stanzas 50–2 note. Perhaps this corruption also explains the absence of any reference to the cockcrows and the abrupt termination of the episode here. The use of English SHs in a context of otherwise Latin SHs is also notable. It is difficult also to see how the episode could be accommodated in the present play at 109ff.

Whatever the arguments concerning the division of 16–16A, it is difficult to defend the inclusion of Peter's denial in HmARBC and one can only speculate that it represents a section of a Trial play which has been removed and rendered unnecessary within the context of Play 16, although it seems necessary within the cycle as a whole to give point to earlier and later passages. Compare Appendix ID, where a passage giving further scope to Peter's role and connected with the Denial is found only in two manuscripts. Further speculation might include some unease in Reformation England at the importance of Peter's role for the notion of papal authority, which might have led to such deletions.

379–94, stanzas 50–2   The stanzas do not conform to the usual Chester pattern.

Stanza 50 consists of six lines, rhyming in B aabbbc. *saith* 380 B is to be preferred, as rhyming with *Nazareth* 379, to *saies* ARC, *sayest* Hm, although it is not the expected form of the second person singular present of the verb. *playne—them— garden* are here regarded as three imperfect rhymes, although arguably the correspondence between them is not close. Only 384 contains three strongly stressed syllables, except in C, where the omission of *syckerlye* 381 reduces 381 also to three strongly stressed syllables — Salter (p.38) commenting on 379–80, remarks rather oddly, "somewhere here a line is missing". It seems probable that if there ever was a regular Chester stanza here, two lines, an a- and a c-rhyme, the latter of three stresses, have been lost after 380. The gospels offer no indication of additional material for such lines.

Stanza 51 consists of six lines, rhyming aaaaab, of which 390 contains three strongly stressed syllables. If a regular Chester stanza was ever intended, two lines, rhyming ab, the latter a three-stress line, have been lost after 386. Matthew 26/72 refers to Peter's denial as occurring with an oath and Mark 14/71 says that Peter began to curse and swear; both offer scope for development — compare 391–2.

Stanza 52 consists of four lines, aaab, representing the quatrain of half a regular Chester stanza. Matthew 26/75, Mark 14/72, Luke 22/62 refer to Peter's subsequent

PLAY XVI   243

departure and weeping, which are not shown here but are mentioned at 18/410, 413–5, 420. Possibly this represents the content of the missing quatrain and perhaps of further stanzas also lost.

378 + SH *The Damsell* Mark 14/66 says that she was one of the high priest's maids, and John 18/17 that she kept the door to the palace.

379 Only John 18/17 puts this as a question; in all other gospels, it is an accusing statement. Only Mark 14/67 uses the phrase "Jesus of Nazareth" here.

380 From Mark 14/68, which indicates that Peter then went out into the porch and the cock crowed for the first time.

380 + SH All gospels except Mark indicate that the second accusation was made by a different person from the first. Matthew 26/71 identifies the speaker as another maid, but John 18/25 presents the speakers as collective, and Luke 22/58 indicates that the speaker was a man. York 29 identifies her as *mulier* and indicates no change of speaker from the first accusation; but *Ludus Coventriae* distinguished $\mathit{1}^a$ *ancilla* from ij^a *ancilla*; Cornish *Ordinalia* describes her as *Portress*, following John, and ascribes the first two accusations to her.

381–4 Apparently from the third accusation in John 18/26, where — it being the final denial — the cock crows.

383 *the garden* i.e. Gethsemane — but the place of capture was not described or identified for the audience in play 15.

385–6 386 derives from Matthew 26/72, Luke 22/57. 385 perhaps reflects the oaths mentioned by Matthew 26/72, Mark 14/71; but see 379–94, stanzas 50–2 note.

386 + SH The third accuser is not specified in Matthew 26/73 and is collective in Mark 14/70. Luke 22/60 says he is a man, and John 18/26 says that he is a servant of the high priest and a kinsman of Malchus. York 29/132 + SH identifies him as *Malchus; Ludus Coventriae* 29/184 presents him as *cosyn* of Malchus, and also $\mathit{1}^{us}$ *Judeus*, who is one of Christ's tormentors; in Cornish *Ordinalia* the accuser is the Fourth Torturer, identified earlier as Malchus.

387–90 387 and 389–90 are based on Matthew 26/73 and less closely on Mark 14/70, which, however, has a counterpart in 388. 388 also reflects Luke 22/59.

391–4 *not* 391 ARBC is to be preferred for syntax to the scribally erroneous *no* Hm.
Both Matthew 26/74 and Mark 14/71 indicate that Peter cursed and swore after his denial. The plain denial of 391 is not the third denial in any gospel, most closely resembling the more direct *Non sum* (AV "I am not") of the second denial in Luke 22/58, John 18/25.
After the third denial, the cock again crowed. Luke 22/61 shows Jesus looking at Peter, as in York 29/164–71, *Ludus Coventriae* 29/192 + SD–204; and all gospels indicate Peter's recollection of the prophecy and his remorse at this point.

394 *keepe* HmRBC is parallel to *knowe* 393, but has been misunderstood as parallel to *did knowe* and hence replaced in A by past form.

Finis In HmARB, the *Finis*-formula includes a note to the effect that the story is concluded in the pages that follow (see TNs). Salter mentions the existence of such a note only for HmB; he concludes, probably correctly, that it derives from a note in the Register (exemplar) — he thinks written as a guide when 16 and 16A were combined. He holds that it was disregarded by H, and absent when the intermediate manuscript between C and the register, which he postulates, was written — hence its absence from C. Such a note would, however, be equally justifiable if the plays were originally one and had been separated, as Greg maintained.

PLAY XVIA

Dramatis Personae Cayphas, Annas, Symon, Primus Judeus, Prima Maria, Secunda Maria, Jesus, Secundus Judeus, Tertius Judeus, Quartus Judeus, Pilatus, Marye, Maria Magdalena, Maria Jacobi, Maria Salomee, Primus Latro, Secundus Latro, John, Centurio, Longyus, Josephe, Nycodemus.

> *NOTE* 1. *Prima* and *Secunda Maria* may be identified with two of the Maries, although this seems unlikely.
> 2. *Marye* is also called *Mary the First* 332 + SH; she is, however, to be distinguished from *Prima Maria*.

Locations
locum Calvariae *Play-heading*, the mount of Calverye 19, super montem 439 + SD.

Properties
this crosse 15, 18, 31 — *also termed* the mast 166, a tree 454 — crucem 176 + SD H; this whippecorde 46
For the sharing of the clothes — this coate bowt seame 97, *also termed* this coate 71, 73, 123, thys weede 84; kyrtle 109; *another* kyrtle 113; pawlle 110; dyce thrèe 90
For the crucifixion — a hommer 154; nayles good wonne 158, *including* this nayle 172, this iron pynne 195; a rope 165, 189, roopes 187
Pilate's superscription — thys table 218, tabulam 216 + SD
Piercing the side — speare 372, 376, 386, lancia 383 + SD; water 387
Burial — a hundreth poundes of spicerye, Myr, alloes, and many more therebye 473-4.

> *NOTE* 1. Probably *drynke* 353-4 indicates that Christ is given drink at this point.
> 2. It is not certain that the *tombe* 413 is represented on stage in this play.

Costume
(*see also Properties: sharing of the clothes*)
crowne of thorne 253.

Sources
The events of the journey to Calvary, the Crucifixion, Death, Deposition and Burial are treated in Matthew 27/31-61, Mark 15/20-47, Luke 23/26-56, John 19/16-42. See notes below for further details.

Guild ascription See 16/*Guild ascription* note.

Play heading H presents 16–16A as a single play — see 16/*Guild-ascription* note.

The events treated in this play are dramatised in the other cycles as follows:

Wakefield 22/242–*Finis* — beginning of the journey to Calvary; 23 — completion of journey, Crucifixion, deposition and burial; 24 — dicing for Christ's cloak.

York 24 — journey to Calvary; 25 — Crucifixion; 26 — death, deposition and burial.

Ludus Coventriae 32/678–34/1175 — events from journey to Calvary through deposition and burial.

Cornish Ordinalia pp.155–75 — as *Ludus Coventriae*.

Calvariae The place of execution, identified for the audience at 19, is so named by Luke 23/33; in the other accounts it is called Golgotha.

4 *fiste* It seems unlikely that the high priest should strike Jesus at this point, and more probable that he should continue to gloat over Jesus' inevitable fate, as he does in the rest of the stanza. *flyte* 3 H seems to recognise this, but the substitution seems influenced by a desire for alliteration. *fitte* would be more appropriate in context. But *fiste* was evidently the exemplar form. For a similar collocation, see 179.

9–16, stanza 2   *weare* 12 H, "protect", is to be preferred for rhyme to *warne* HmARB. The latter was evidently a substituted form, apparently felt to be more familiar or semantically appropriate.

15   *this crosse* Compare 16/374 + SD. In the Group this is the first indication in 16A that Jesus is carrying the cross.

16   *Symon of Surrey* An anglicisation of Simon of Cyrene, named in Matthew 27/32, Mark 15/21, Luke 23/26. Mark describes Simon as father of Alexander and Rufinus, as if these would be familiar figures to members of the early church. This is the only indication that Simon was a supporter of Christ, and no other cycle so presents him. In fact, any subsequent Christian persuasion by Simon might more readily be seen as a consequence of his experiences at the time of the Crucifixion. All accounts say that he was compelled to carry the cross, and Luke says that he was coming out of the country — a point taken up in 33–40 where Simon is seen as journeying to Rome. He was a passer-by, and hence not personally known to the soldiers. In the other cycles, he is abused as a *carll* Wakefield 22/359, *ladde* York 34/242, *harlot Ludus Coventriae* 32/710 (where, however, he is first more politely addressed as *sere* 698), but evidently an unknown. The fact that both Annas and Caiaphas know him here may be connected with his support of Jesus' cause, 21–8. On the carrying of the cross by a foreigner, compare Ambrose, *Expositionis in Lucam* 10/107 (PL 15/1923): *Non Judeus est qui crucem portat, sed alienigena, atque peregrinus.*

PLAY XVIA   247

Chester follows the gospels in suggesting that Simon assumes the cross at an early point in the journey — compare *bringe forth* 41, which seems to support the gospel suggestion that Simon's help was enlisted as soon as Jesus left Pilate's hall. Wakefield 22, York 34, *Ludus Coventriae* 32 set the episode after the laments of the women and Jesus' reply, here seen at 49–64.

22 The line contains three strongly stressed syllables instead of the expected four.

28 + SH *Cayphas* ARBH is to be preferred to the scribally erroneous *Caypas* Hm.

29–30 With Caiaphas' judicial coercion, compare the threats of physical violence in Wakefield 22, York 34, and the intimidating attitude adopted by the Jews in *Ludus Coventriae* 32.

37–40 37 appears to contain only three strongly stressed syllables instead of the expected four.

all 39 may suggest that Simon believes that Christ's death will bring about universal destruction — "Through your wickedness, truly, I believe that everything that exists will be destroyed". But H's *Jewes* for *iwys* would remove any ambiguity of reference and give an acceptable meaning; assuming an original *Jwes*, both H and HmARB forms could readily be generated.

H's reading should be read in conjunction with H's reversal of 38–9, which Deimling "corrects". As the lines stand in H, they do not give sense, but if *this* is taken as *thus*, H could mean: "But I take God as my witness, all Jews, through this wicked act that I thus carry out through compulsion, will, I believe, be destroyed."

44 + SH By omitting the SH, H quite appropriately assigns 45–8 to *Annas*; the priests are necessarily concerned with the pressure of time — compare 149–52. The HmARB reading means that *Primus* speaks twice in succession, 45–8 and 67–72, thus breaking the usual *Primus* — *Secundus* sequence. But either HmARB or H is acceptable. That H's omission is deliberate is suggested by the substitution of *you* for *we* 48.

45–6 *them* 45 HmARB refers to the two thieves, brought out by the first Jew in response to Annas' demand. *him* H seems to envisage a binding of Jesus when Simon takes the cross from him.

bounden 45 H, *here will* 46 H produce a more regular sequence of strongly and weakly stressed syllables than *bound, may* HmARB.

47 *the pryme of the daye* i.e. 6 a.m.; the sixth hour is mentioned in John 19/14 as the time of Pilate's judgment — see 16/355–62 note. Compare 216 and note.

48 + SH *Prima Maria* The laments at 49–56 are prompted by the reference in Luke 23/27 to women lamenting, but there no individuals are specified and the form of the lament is not indicated. In Wakefield 22 the women are shown as the Virgin Mary, Mary Magdalen and Mary Jacobi; and in York 34, where the passage is interrupted by a manuscript gap, the women are the Virgin Mary and the three Maries. But in *Ludus Coventriae* 32/678–85 they are merely first and second *mulieres*. Here there is nothing to identify the women more specifically, but 53 excludes the possibility of either being the Virgin Mary. However, although the speakers could be identified with two of the three Maries of 265–88, it would seem strange that they should lament twice and that their comments here — "He has healed so many" and

"How sad his mother will be" — should be so detached compared with the more emotional and personal character of the later laments. Probably *Mulier* 48 + SH, 52 + SH H should be preferred to *Maria* HmARB and the latter regarded as an exemplar error. H's correction could readily be deduced from Luke's account and the later laments in the play. See also 48 + SD H.

51 H's omission of *sycke* reduces the number of strongly stressed syllables from the expected four to three and must be considered an error. If deliberate, it may result from a desire to give spiritual significance to *saved*. On the sentiment here expressed, compare 293-4.

54 *thy* The pronoun is the only instance of direct address in the stanza. *his* R seems preferable, in view of *his* 53, *he* 56. If *thy* HmA reflects an exemplar form, that form may have been *thie* to account for B's scribally erroneous *thee* and H's stylistically odd *the* which seems an attempt to avoid the possessive form. *flecke* A is an inexplicable scribal error.

57-64, stanza 8   *swem* 58 is to be preferred for rhyme and meaning to the scribally erroneous and meaningless *swene* HmAR; *mone* B is apparently an attempt to provide a more meaningful form, which destroys the rhyme.

teame 59 ABH is to be preferred for rhyme to the scribally erroneous *teane* HmR.

57-64   Based on Luke 23/28-9, the start of Jesus' response; Chester omits the remainder of the response in Luke 23/28-31 which is used in Wakefield 22/344-5, York 34/171-80, *Ludus Coventriae* 32/694-7. There seems no obvious reason for Chester's abridgement of the speech.

65-72, stanza 9   *shyte* 67 H is to be preferred for rhyme to *skricke* AR, *skrike* B, the ARB forms being semantically possible but weakening rhyme and probably to be regarded as euphemistic substitutions in the exemplar. With this substitution, compare *pisse* 67 H and *growne* HmARB, and the forms at 16/90. *stryke* Hm is semantically inappropriate as well as destroying rhyme; it is the Hm form at 16/98.

65-6   *have donne*, i.e. "Halt!" The procession has apparently reached Calvary, as at Luke 23/33, although only H, in 64 + SD, specifies the new location here.

The division of Jesus' clothes and the episode of Christ's seamless cloak which follows at 67-148 is based on Matthew 27/35, Mark 15/24, Luke 23/34, John 19/23-4. Only John has the episode of the seamless cloak and indicates that Jesus' other garments were divided among the soldiers. Other accounts suggest that the clothes were divided by lot. All the gospel accounts suggest that the division was effected after the crucifying of Christ, not before as here — Luke places it after "Father forgive", here 297-300; it occupies a position after the crucifixion in York 35/288-300, *Ludus Coventriae* 32/769 + SD, Cornish Ordinalia p.164, while in Wakefield it appears in two parts — the division of the clothes follows "I thirst" in play 23, and in play 24, after the burial, the cloak is taken to Pilate who participates in the dicing and wins, thereby obtaining the cloak as indicated in *Legenda Aurea*, 'De Passione Domini'.

John 19/23 indicates that the garments were divided into four parts so that each soldier had a portion, thereby establishing the number of soldiers as four, as here. On the use of Jews rather than soldiers throughout the Passion sequence in Chester,

PLAY XVIA 249

compare 16/368 note; also compare Ambrose, *Expositionis in Lucam* 10 (PL 15/1923-4) and Augustine, *In Joannis Evangelium*, Tractatus 118/1 (PL 35/1947).

73–216, stanzas 10–27   The stanza-form for the dicing and crucifixion is a form of the Chester stanza with a predominantly two-stress line throughout, used also at 16/62–109 and 16/306–54.

73–80, stanza 10   *inclyne* 79 ARB, *enclyne* H is to be preferred for rhyme to *inclind* Hm, the latter reflecting confusion of *e* and *d*. ARBH represent *enclin* MED 2, Hm the past participle of *enclinen*.

73–6   Compare 16/322 + SD note and see Ambrose, *Expositionis in Lucam* 10 (PL 15/1926–7).

82   *the dyce* The method of division in the gospels is by lot. In York 34/293 and Cornish Ordinalia pp.164–5 the cloak is allotted by the drawing of lots, but dicing is held to be the method used in Wakefield 24/303 and *Ludus Coventriae* 32/769 + SD. Here three dice are used, 90.

88   *on boord*, "on the floor". *bord* means "anything made of wood", which may suggest a wooden floor — compare also 111 and note.

93   The despoiling process began at 71 with the coat but was delayed by the argument about its possession until 87 (88 + SD H), when presumably the rest of Jesus' clothes are removed. The second Jew then seeks to put all the clothes to the game of dice, but the third — who suspected his motives earlier at 77–80 — insists that all but the cloak be divided equally. The dispute may reflect the conflict in the gospel accounts where in Matthew, Mark and Luke all the clothes are divided by lot, whereas in John only the cloak is so bestowed, the remainder being divided in advance.

it H may suggest merely that *this ware* 92 is treated as a collective singular, whereas *they* HmARB treats it as plural. But possibly it is intended to imply that the third Jew is arguing that the cloak should be cut up and divided among the tormentors. Such an interpretation would suitably motivate the fourth Jew's angry intervention at 97–100, which in HmARB seems unprompted.

94   *egallye*, "in equal proportion". John 19/23 does not in fact say that the portions are equal. *equitye* H seems to be the substitution of a more familiar word, although *egally* is attested by OED to the later seventeenth century.

95–6   As here presented, the construction is interrupted by the following speech and is therefore incomplete. *in fowr parts* 95 H produces syntactic completeness by making 95–6 dependent upon 93. See also 93 note.

97–104, stanza 13   *shame* 98 HmARB gives imperfect rhyme with *seame* 97, *Jerusalem* 99; *sweme* H is to be preferred.

The b-rhyme word, *garment*, is repeated at 100 and 104. This repetition is avoided by H's substitution of *verament* 100; *one other* 104 R may result from similar unease but it destroys rhyme.

101–2   "His mother may speculate vainly on behalf of her own family"; with *dreame*, compare *dremen* MED v (2), 2(b) "to speculate". The meaning here seems determined by 103-4, which suggests a concern about who in the family of Jesus might have inherited the coat, which will now pass to the Jews.

109 *kyrtle* The same word occurs at 113. Although *kirtle* was on occasion used to refer to Christ's seamless robe (see MED), it is here distinct from the *coate* 97 and is presumably a garment under the seamless top coat. Although the kirtle was usually worn as an outer garment, it may here suggest either that the seamless robe had been placed over Jesus' outdoor clothes or simply refer to a tunic worn under an outer garment. Compare *pawlle* 110, "cloak", presumably also an outer garment. *kirtle* seems to have no very precise meaning and it might be possible to postulate two slightly different senses to account for its uses for what must have been distinct garments at 109 and 113; or possibly one could argue that the Jew did not use the word very specifically. But H's substitution of *corsett* 113 removes the duplication and is stylistically preferable to the HmARB reading. If H represents an original form, it may be that the sense of "bodice", applicable when the word was used of a woman's rather than a man's undergarment, had given rise to a feeling that the word was not appropriate.

111 *in this halle* The phrase seems inappropriate to the setting on Calvary and seems rather to be part of an appeal to the audience. It might be used as evidence of indoor performance, in a hall. Alternatively, the noun may represent *hale* n (2), MED "a temporary structure for housing, entertaining, eating meals, etc.; an open pavilion, a tent", of which *halle* is a recorded variant.

130 *dubletts* i.e. three two's, immediately to be beaten by the third Jew's three four's 133. H seems not to understand the term.

137-44, stanza 18 *swem* 144 H is to be preferred for rhyme to *sweene* HmAR — compare 97-104, stanza 13 note. *wine* B is semantically acceptable but destroys rhyme. AR erroneously and inexplicably omit 142.

138 The line contains four strongly stressed syllables instead of the expected two, an excess corrected by H.

143 *synnce* i.e. *cinques*, three fives to beat the previous three fours. No manuscript seems to recognise the word — see *synke* 147 and variants.

150 *pewee-ars*, "pissy-arse", an indecent allusion to the naked Christ. The indecency is either unfamiliar to or deliberately suppressed in ARBH. B perhaps suggests the origin of the variants as lying in a confusion of *e* (2) and *d*, a confusion reflected in all other forms.

153 Compare 23/653 — "All in good time".

157-8 H rhymes *by my bones — very good ones*. It is impossible to tell whether H is more concerned by *pon* or *wonne* in these lines, but its commitment to a plural form cannot be sustained at 159 and the H readings are clearly erroneous substitutions.

pon 157 is a form of *pan* sb¹, attested by OED to the fifteenth century; its sense of "the skull, especially its upper part" (OED 6) is evidenced into the nineteenth century, although it may have represented here a deliberate dialectal or colloquial usage. *wone* sb³, OED II.3, "Phr. great wone .... a great quantity", is last illustrated by OED from 1570; but H is untroubled by it at 1B/125, as it is by *ponn* at 16A/173.

PLAY XVIA   251

160   *and*, "if", but with the force of "even if" which is captured explicitly in *though* H.

161–2   "Let us work as quickly (as the second and third Jews). I have untied this wretch." *too* 161 may represent an adverb, "also", or a number, "two" (since *we* involves the fourth and first Jews). In ARH it is taken as part of the phrasal verb, *go to*, "Get down to it". On the unbinding of Jesus, compare 45–6 note; *cast* could suggest "cast down", however, in preparation for carrying him to the horizontal cross, 169.

169–76, stanza 22   No manuscript has the form *mon* required for perfect rhyme at 170. *can* 174 ARH, *wan* B further destroys rhyme, as does *head* 172 B which seems to result from a desire for semantic improvement.

181–212   B's omission occurs between the end of 119^r and the top of 119^v(see TNs). Since 181 and 213 are both preceded by the same SH, it seems probable that the omission resulted from an eye-slip following a loss of concentration in turning the leaf.

183–4   "The arm will not easily stretch to the point on the crosspiece where the hole is bored." The hole was presumably a shallow one to take the point of the nail, which could then be driven home. But presumably in actual crucifixion, and certainly in dramatic reconstruction, the symmetrical positioning of the body was essential to the balance of the cross for erection, and the boring would serve as guide for the positioning of the body. *shorte-armed* 182 indicates that Jesus did not fit the standard size. The H version, "It will not take long to bring [him] to this piece of wood", with its substitution of *longe* for *well* 184, may suggest unease at the idea of a pre-bored hole.

Although nails were certainly used in the crucifixion (see, e.g. John 20/25, 27), terms such as *ligare*, *deligare* are also used, suggesting the possibility of the use of ropes to support the crucified body until death. Some such idea may underlie the idea of stretching Jesus, which is a feature of all cycles — Wakefield 23/119–21, York 35/113–44, *Ludus Coventriae* 32/740–54, Cornish Ordinalia p.162.

185–92, stanza 24   *beheight* 189, in all manuscripts and therefore presumably the exemplar form, does not rhyme; moreover, the third Jew does not promise a rope. It is possible that *beheight* is a substitution for *bethought* — suggesting that the Jew had foreseen this eventuality.

200 + SD   Deimling (wrongly citing [204 + SD] as reference) mistakenly held that B shared the H reading here and that AR shared a common omission of the SD which attested the close relationship of the two manuscripts. B omits 181–212 and so has no reading here; H alone has the SD, against HmAR.

202   Although the text is not clear, it seems probable that a three-nail crucifixion is here envisaged, with a nail through each hand and a single nail through the two feet. *knee* 210 should perhaps be considered collective, "knees", the fourth Jew pulling down both Jesus' legs so that they reach the mark above the small platform built out to take the feet. The platform was designed to take the weight of the body so that the full weight should not be borne by the nails, which might have resulted in a body tearing away from the nails. In Jesus' case, the full body-weight here is envisaged as supported only by the nails.

213–6 The cross is evidently raised into vertical position at this point, an operation of some risk on stage. The raising is given considerable prominence in Wakefield 23/155–266, York 35/153–248 as an important piece of stage business.

216 *noone* Compare 47 and note, 16/355–62 note. *noon* is recorded by OED as indicating the ninth hour after sunrise, i.e. 3 p.m., until 1420; and the hour of the service of *Nones*, similarly 3 p.m., until 1561; but from ME it also had the modern sense of 12.00 mid-day.

Mark 15/25 states that Jesus was crucified at the third hour and goes on to say that darkness fell at the sixth hour until the ninth, when Jesus died. John, however, says that Pilate gave his judgment at the sixth hour. Commentators and harmonists attempted to reconcile these accounts. Augustine, *Harmony* 3/14 (PL 34/1183–90), makes two proposals — that Mark distinguishes the hour of the Jews' demand that Christ be crucified from the hour at which the Roman soldiers actually carried out the crucifixion; and that since John refers to the sixth hour of the preparation of the passover, he takes his starting point not from the Jewish passover but from the Christian "Passover" and that the sixth hour of John and third of Mark are in fact the same. He presents the same argument in *In Joannis Evangelium*, Tractatus 117 (PL 35/1044–5). It is today generally held that Mark's time-scale follows Jewish reckoning, by which Jesus was crucified at 9 a.m., darkness fell at 12.00 and Jesus dies at 3.00 p.m.

The time-scale in Chester is less clear. If the journey to Calvary began at 6.00 a.m., it might be reasonable to suppose that Jesus was crucified at 9.00 a.m., but the latter would not be a normal use of *noone*. Alternatively, the suggestion may be that it has taken six hours to reach Calvary and that Jesus is crucified at mid-day, the time of the darkness by modern reckoning. But *noon* may simply reflect *horam nonam*, Mark 15/33 (AV "the ninth hour") with no specific sense, or with the intention of suggesting the final hour of Jesus' life before his death. Some support for the last meaning derives from 18/41, where *noone* is used to define the time of the portents which accompanied Christ's death. If the latter, a significantly archaic use of *noon* may be involved, but also a puzzling curtailment of the period of Christ's crucifixion, since his suffering would then, despite the gospel account, have lasted minutes rather than hours.

217–40 The superscription is mentioned in Matthew 27/37, Mark 15/26, Luke 23/38, but the account of Pilate's personal intervention, as here, is in John 19/19–22. The inscription was in Hebrew, Greek and Latin, and is said by John to have been affixed to the cross by Pilate himself — contrast 217–8 and Pilate's provocative aside at 222. In John the affixing of the superscription occurs between the crucifixion and the lottery for the cloak, whereas in the other gospels it follows the sharing of the clothes, as here and in Wakefield 23/516ff.

224 + SH John 19/21 assigns the reply to the chief priests, as in York 36/105–13, *Ludus Coventriae* 32/854–7, and it is strange that the priests, who are present here, do not raise objections rather than the tormentors. In Wakefield 23 it is the torturers who complain to Pilate.

225 *beede* The sense seems to be "speak to us", i.e. "Let's discuss the matter". *byde* AR suggests *biden*, MED 6, "wait for"; but the verb is not recorded with the *-e-* form required for rhyme. *take hede* H is acceptable.

PLAY XVIA

228 The line contains four strongly stressed syllables instead of the expected three. A regular line would result from the omission of *a mon*; but *one* H gives acceptable metre.

234 HmARB repeat the 233 rhyme-word; H avoids repetition, employing a cruder expression of a sort which might have invited censorship in the manner of 67.

237 "What the devil sort of king is he, fellow?" *non* ARBH is strongly attested and may be preferred for meaning to *mon* Hm, in which case the line would mean "What the devil! He's no king!"

239 *to* RBH is well attested but produces a rough metre; in H, the effect is offset to some extent by the omission of *hee hasse*. HmA gives acceptable meaning and metre — "He has told many a lie", rather than RBH's "He has told lies to many a one".

240 + SD H is the only manuscript to indicate the raising of the cross. The H SD suggests that the raising follows the affixing of the superscription. But Matthew 27/37 suggests that the superscription was attached only after the cross was raised; other accounts are not clear. Possibly the raising of the cross in HmARB is to be inferred from 213-6, so that the superscription was added later.

240 + SH B and H include an identifying phrase, absent from HmARB; the phrase is perhaps an equivalent of the identifying second word in 264 + SH, 272 + SH, 280 + SH. Possibly the fact that the phrase is in the margin of B suggests that it was also in the exemplar margin and was therefore ignored by HmAR; H includes it in Latin form in the SH.

241-88 The laments of the Maries at the cross are unbiblical but a common feature of medieval literature, especially lyric. The gospels refer only to the presence of the Maries at the cross — the Virgin Mary (John); Mary Magdalen (Matthew, Mark, John); Mary Cleophas (John); Mary Jacobi, the mother of James and Joses (Matthew, Mark); Mary Salome (Mark); the mother of the children of Zebedee (Matthew).

On Mary Magdalen, see further 14/40 + SD note. Mary Cleophas was the wife of Clephas, perhaps to be identified with one of the two disciples who encountered Jesus on the road to Emmaus; see play 19, Luke 24/18. Mary Jacobi may be another name for Mary Cleophas, since the name is an abbreviation of the phrase in Mark 15/40 *Maria Iacobi minoris et Ioseph mater* (AV "Mary, the mother of James the less and of Joses"); she was a witness to the empty tomb, see play 18, Mark 16/1. Mary Salome is not, in fact, called Mary by Mark and, together with the other women mentioned by Mark, is said to have ministered to Christ in Galilee; she also was a witness of the empty tomb, see play 18, Mark 16/1. The children of Zebedee were James and John.

241-8, stanza 31 *lee* 241 BH, "peace, tranquillity" (MED *le* n (1) (c)), is to be preferred for rhyme to *leere* HmAR, ?"loss" (MED *lire* n (1) 2 (a)). That *leere* was an exemplar alteration or obscurely cancelled error may be inferred from B's cancelled *dere* (see TNs).

knee 246 H is to be preferred for rhyme to *brest* HmARB, the latter a substituted common collocation with *sucke*. Deimling (erroneously citing [242] as reference) cites the H reading as evidence of H's superiority.

242 "Alas, now mourning and woe befall me!" *mourninge* is to be regarded as syntactically parallel to *woe*. AR and H, however, perhaps uneasy at this construction, substitute verb-forms; AR's *woes* is based on the HmB forms; *madds* H gives good sense.

248 *thou feyles* "You lack". H's impersonal construction with *thee*, "No power fails you", is possibly preferable. AR substitute an inappropriate verb-form.

249 *nyll* HmARB require *be* to be understood; H supplies the verb *to be* instead, but at the expense of metre.

254 *made* HmB is acceptable if regarded as a formal variant of *madd* H, but formally it looks like an error, with confusion of *d* and *e*, involving the past tense of *make*. Some such confusion may underlie AR's substituted *mone*.

After **256** The additional H stanzas seem to emphasise the special role of the Virgin Mary as the elect of God, 5, entitled to special favour, 7-8, and express a claim to share Christ's suffering and death which might be held to suggest equality of Christ and the Virgin. Their removal leaves the focus of the speech as Christ and his tormentors, and preserves an unbroken sequence of *Alas* apostrophes; Mary's three stanzas then equal the lament stanzas of the other three Maries put together. Her requests are later answered — see 325–8.

The rhymes *chose* 5 — *was* 6 — *wemlesse* 7 are imperfect, the forms *chese* — *wes* — *wemlesse* being required.

260 The construction depends upon *when wyll thou* 257. *why wilt thou not* H 257 weakens metre and confers a rather less imperative force to 260.

262 The line is metrically rough. The omissions by A, R and to a lesser extent H improve the metre, but all seem to represent responses to the type of exemplar-form probably preserved in HmB. The substitution of *him* for *my sonne* would produce a more acceptable line.

281–8, stanza 36   The a-rhymes of 281–3 are imperfect. *wond* occurs in rhyme-position in 5/56 thus supporting *wondes* 283, and it seems likely therefore that the forms *bondes* 281, *hondes* 282 are required. All the manuscripts have different forms for the rhyme-word at 283, with variations in the pronoun according to the syntactic function of the final word. B and H yield limited sense, but A and R may suggest influence of *won*, "dwelling place". All forms could readily derive from an exemplar *wonnds* (= *wondes*) with confusion of *n*(1) and *u*, and of *d* and *e* in AR.

mon is required for perfect rhyme instead of *man* 284. All rhyme-forms seem to arise from exemplar-errors.

286 *unpeace* H, "absence of peace, dissension, strife", is evidenced by OED to 1470 and is revived in the late nineteenth century. It is possible, but not particularly appropriate here, and may be a scribal substitution under the formal influence of *seace* 287.

289–96, stanza 37   HmARB erroneously substitute 304, the last line of the following stanza, for 296, the last line of this stanza, thereby destroying the b-rhyme — cf. *flee* 292 — *ys* 296. The result gives sense, because the jeers of the two priests at 293–6, 301–4, deriving from the same passages in Matthew and Mark, are similar in

PLAY XVIA

content and allow parallel syntactical constructions in the final line. H is to be preferred in providing a line at 296 which gives acceptable meaning, metre and rhyme.

There is no direct equivalent for 296 in the gospels. If H is original, there seems no reason to have changed it. HmARB presumably result from an alteration in the exemplar whereby *be* was changed to *ys*. H may represent an independent 'emendation'.

289–96 289–92 have no direct equivalent in the gospels, but compare Luke 23/37: *Si tu es rex Iudaeorum, salvum te fac* (AV "If thou be the king of the Jews, save thyself"), uttered by the soldiers as they offer vinegar; but in Luke, these words follow "Father, forgive", and precede the reference to the superscription.

hoven 289 is past tense of *heave*, "raised up", and in Hm requires an auxiliary verb to be understood. AR delete *ye*, giving sense and syntax but a rough metre; H plausibly reads *is* (from *ys*?) for *ye*, supplying the missing auxiliary; B, unnecessarily changing the pronoun, reads *haven*, evidently a substitution.

to flee 292 depends on *can* and is parallel to *feight* 291. H supplies *fownd*, perhaps to explain the infinitive form.

293–6 derive from Matthew 27/42, Mark 15/31–2, where it follows the superscription and represents the mockery of the chief priests.

healed 293 represents the gospel *Alios salvos fecit* (AV "He saved others"), with less obviously physical associations.

294 *yf* ARBH may be preferred for meaning to the apparently erroneous *give* Hm; the latter is evidently a scribal variant of *gif*, "if", but *give* is not a variant recorded by MED.

297–300 Based on Luke 23/34, where it follows the act of crucifixion and precedes the parting of Jesus' clothes.

of heaven 297, omitted by H, lacks biblical counterpart but seems required metrically.

301–4 The text returns to the rebukes of the high priests from Matthew 27/2, Mark 15/32; but the ascription of divinity in *Godes Sonne* 302 replaces the purely secular reference in *Si rex Israel est*, Matthew 27/42 (AV "If he be the King of Israel") and *Christus, rex Israel*, Mark 15/32 (AV "Christ the King of Israel"). The phrase may have been suggested by Matthew 27/43: *Confidit in Deo; liberet nunc, si vult eum: dixit enim: "Quia Filius Dei sum"*. (AV "He trusted in God; let him deliver him now, if he will have him; for he said, I am the Son of God").

305–24 The episode of the two thieves is in Luke 23/39–43; there is a brief reference in Matthew 27/14. Compare 17/255–72.

The two thieves were to be crucified *on eyther halfe* 42 of Christ. Further details are given in *Legenda Aurea*, 'De Passione Domini'. The Gospel of Nicodemus supplies only the name of the penitent thief, not his situation.

315 Compare Luke 23/41: *Hic vero nihil mali gessit* (AV "But this man hath done nothing amiss"). H's *but this man* and omission of *so mych* are to be preferred in reflecting the Vulgate and producing a more regular sequence of strongly and weakly stressed syllables.

325-44   The commitment of Mary to John's care is in John 19/26-7, where it follows directly from the preceding reference to the Maries at the cross, John 19/25. The presence of the Maries here is established at 241-8 and this represents a response to Mary's lament. The disciple to whom Mary is committed is not specified by name, but only as *Discipulum ... quem diligebat* (AV "The disciple ... whom he loved"), but it is generally assumed that John is intended.

The references to Mary's virginity and Christ's resurrection are not in the gospel narrative; John offer similar consolation to Mary in Wakefield 23/373-81.

329   The line appears to have five strongly stressed syllables instead of the expected four. The metre is somewhat improved by the H word-order.

332   Compare John 19/27: *Et ex illa hora accepit eam discipulus in sua* (AV "And from that hour that disciple took her unto his own home"). John 19/25 states that the Maries stood by the cross, while the other gospels refer to them as standing afar off. John alone specifies the Virgin Mary's presence, and she may be assumed either to approach the cross in company with the other Maries, who leave her before Jesus' response, or to approach the cross alone. She presumably departs after 344, although she could appropriately remain until Jesus' deposition and burial, since her exit is not specified.

330-6+SH   R's omission occurs between the end of 137^v and the top of 138^r in that manuscript and presumably resulted from an eye-slip in which 332+SH was confused with 336+SH.

332+SH   Compare 240+SH, where only Hm has an anglicised form. Here *The First* does not stand in distinction to any other numerical reference.

345-59+Latin   The play groups together Jesus' remaining words from the cross; viz:

1   345-51 — Matthew 27/46-7, 49, Mark 15/34-5; Mark employs the form *Eloi*, as opposed to Matthew's *Eli*.
2   352 — John 19/28, *Sitio* (AV "I thirst".)
3   356-9 — Luke 23/46.
4   359+Latin — John 19/30.

The order here is not the usual order — compare Augustine, *Harmony* 3/18 (PL 34/1192); Comestor, *Historia Scholastica* 'In Evangelia' 177 (PL 198/1632-3) where (4) precedes (3). The "standard" order is also seen in Wakefield 23/590-2, York 36/257-60, but *Ludus Coventriae* 32/891-8 agrees with the Chester sequence.

345-59, stanzas 44-46   Stanza 44 contains seven lines, rhyming aaaaaab, each with four stresses with the exception of 345, 348 which each contain five. H replaces 345 by two lines, each of four stresses, giving an aaaaaaab form. A and H reduce the number of stresses in 348 to four.

Stanza 45 is a regular Chester quatrain, aaab, if *or noe* 351, present in all manuscripts, is omitted to reduce the number of strongly stressed syllables in that line from four to three, as required in the final line of a regular Chester quatrain. The words are unnecessary — compare Matthew 27/49: *An veniat Elias liberans eum* (AV "Whether Elias will come to save him"). If this change is adopted, it would be possible to regard 348-55 as a regular Chester stanza, aaabcccb, with b-rhymes *here* 351 — *yeare* 355.

PLAY XVIA

Stanza 46 is a quatrain, four four-stress lines rhyming abab. *handes* 359 HmARB corresponds to *manus tuas*, Luke 23/46 (AV "thy hands") which may have prompted a change from the original reading; *hand* H may be an attempt to provide a rhyme for 357, where *wonde* BH is to be preferred to the scribally erroneous and semantically inappropriate *wend* HmAR — for rhyme, *hond* would be required at 359. In ARB the Latin after 359 is written as if part of the stanza.

Accepting stanzas 44 and 46 in H and the proposed change at 351, the passage would consist of two quatrains enclosing a regular Chester stanza. Possibly the metrical irregularities result from an attempt to include in the briefest space all Jesus' words from the cross.

345–7 Compare Mark 15/34: AV *"Eloi, Eloi, lama sabachthani?* which is, being interpreted, My God, my God, why hast thou forsaken me?"

347 *thys* The word has no equivalent in the gospel account and can be omitted, as in H, without detriment to metre.

348 *Elye* i.e. Elias; compare 23/284+SH and note.

On the speakers, compare Bede, *In Matthaei Evangelium Expositionis* 4 (PL 92/125) whose view is reflected in *Glossa Ordinaria*, 'Evang. Matth.' 27/47 (PL 114/175): *Non omnes, forsitan Romani, Hebraei sermonis ignorantes proprietatem. Vel aliqui Judaei Christum minorem Elia reputantes, ut eius auxilium deprecetur.*

352 The repetition in HmARB is metrically necessary, but without biblical counterpart — hence perhaps the H form.

353–5 In John 19/29 Jesus' words are countered by the sponge of vinegar and hyssop offered to him. Matthew 27/34 and Mark 15/23 record the offer to him of a drink of vinegar and gall before the crucifixion began, and Matthew in addition records at 27/48 the offer of a sponge of vinegar in mockery during the Jews' response, here 345-51. Although there is here no direction, perhaps the offer of the sponge is to be understood, the mockery being influenced partly by Matthew's account. Comestor, *Historia Scholastica* 'In Evangelia' 177 (PL 198/1632) and *Legenda Aurea*, 'De Passione Domini', suggest that the intention may have been to hasten Christ's death. But Augustine *In Joannis Evangelium*, Tractatus 119 (PL 35/1952), followed by Bede, *In Matthaei Evangelium Expositio* 4 (PL 92/125), sees the gesture as symbolic of the Jews' degeneracy. Compare 17/131–2, where Satan boasts that the Jews acted under his will in offering the drink to Jesus.

358 *spiritte* ARBH is to be preferred for meaning to the scribally erroneous *speete* Hm.

359+Latin John 19/30: AV "It is finished"; the Latin phrase is similarly used in *Ludus Coventriae* 32/898. H omits the text.

359+SH–*Finis* H has a different version of the end of the play — see Appendix IC. The content and arrangement of material is, however, substantially that of HmARB and the two versions seem to be alternatives. The H form is used here wherever comparison with the Hm form is possible and helpful in an evaluation of the Hm reading.

360–7, stanza 47 The b-rhymes, *be* 363 — *knowe* 367, do not rhyme. A regular rhyme would result from readng *see* for *knowe; see* is the rhyme word in the very different stanza in H IC/8.

360–7 The episode of the centurion's witness is recorded in Matthew 27/54, where the earthquake and other portents attending Christ's death lead him and his colleagues to attest Jesus' divinity; and in Mark 15/39, where the centurion, hearing Jesus' cry, alone attests his divinity; and Luke 23/47, where, after Jesus' death-cry, the centurion, seeing what had happened, claims he was *homo iustus* (AV "a righteous man"). 364 HmARB indicates that the Group follows Mark, whereas *this noyce and this crye* H IC/6 indicates that H follows Matthew.

The centurion is evidently a Roman soldier, and hence another Gentile, and Roman, believer; see further Bede, *In Matthaei Evangelium Expositio* 4 (PL 92/126). The centurion's witness is part of the Resurrection play in Wakefield 26 and York 38; in *Ludus Coventriae* 33/1018–34/1034 the soldiers and centurion all attest Jesus' divinity; in *Cornish Ordinalia* p.168, the centurion already sympathises with Jesus before his death.

the prophecye 365 has no counterpart in H and is obscure in reference. The centurion would presumably, as a Roman, be ignorant of Jewish prophecies. The words of Jesus' cry, 356–9, echo Psalm 31/5 AV and John 19/28 indicates that 352–5 represent the fulfilment of scripture — Psalm 69/21.

368–407 The piercing of Jesus' side by a soldier is recounted in John 19/34, where it follows the breaking of the legs of the two thieves, at the Jews' request, to accomplish their deaths so that they could be buried before the sabbath; in Chester there is no counterpart to that episode and no reference to the deposition of the thieves. The Gospel of Nicodemus 16/7 names the soldier as Longinus. A full account of the development of the Longinus legend may be found in Rose Jeffries Peebles, *The Legend of Longinus in Ecclesiastical Tradition and in English Literature, and its connection with the Grail* (Baltimore, 1911). One version is in *Legenda Aurea*, 'De Sancto Longino', where Longinus is identified with the centurion. Another version, however, follows the Gospel of Nicodemus in distinguishing the two; see Comestor, *Historia Scholastica* 'In Evangelia' 179 (PL 198/1633–4). The act has symbolic as well as miraculous implications — see 398–9 and note.

369–75, stanza 48   No manuscript has the form *hond* for hand, required for perfect rhyme at 372. H IC/13–5 rhymes *hand—wand—land*.

370   John 19/34 merely says: *Latus eius aperuit* (AV "Pierced his side"), as indicated in 383 + SD. But possibly underlying the reference here is the Catholic cult of the sacred heart of Jesus, whereby the spear was held to have pierced Jesus' heart, and moreover to have struck through the left side as the side nearest the heart. The reference is made more explicit in IC/13–4. See further 24/421–8 + SD note.

376–83, stanza 49   *bede* 377 A is to be preferred for rhyme to *bade* HmB, *badd* H IC/18, evidently the exemplar reading and a past tense presumably because Caiaphas has issued the order already. *byde* R destroys rhyme and sense, but compare *byd* 380 and variants.

376–83   With the recruitment of Longinus, a later but frequent feature in the legend, compare ME *Harrowing of Hell*, Sion MS, 625–6, and *Cursor Mundi* 16837–9. Peebles compares with this section particularly *Northern Passion*:

PLAY XVIA   259

>   They made hym under Jhesus stond
>   And pute a spere in his hond
>   They leyd þe spere to Jhesus syde
>   Pute up þei seyd what so betyde

The responsibility is laid upon the Jews — see 398-9 and note. Similar responsibility is indicated in Wakefield 23/603-4, and *Ludus Coventriae* 34/1129.

377   *thou* ARB is to be preferred for meaning to the scribally erroneous *tho* Hm.

386-7   Compare *Cursor Mundi*:

>   Muchel þo þere ran
>   Of þat blood ran to his hond
>   (16843-4)

and *Northern Passion*:

>   Longeus stode welle styll þan
>   By his fyngerys þe blod ranne
>   With þat blode he wyped his face.

throwe 387 presumably suggests that the blood and water ran down the spear and over Longinus' arm.

398-9   Compare 296-300, where the image of blindness, here given concrete form, suggests spiritual blindness, an unbiblical addition in the earlier passage. 399 here closely reflects Luke 23/34: *Non enim sciunt quid faciunt* (AV "For they know not what they do"). Peebles compares the *Northern Passion*:

>   On his kneys he gane doune falle
>   And of Jhesu mercy calle
>   He sey "I wyst not what I dede
>   Bot as oþer hade me bede"

also *Cursor Mundi*, Trinity MS, 16839-40 and the Cotton interpolation, 33-4, and uses these as evidence that "the story had assumed stereotyped form and was used in much the same way by narrative and dramatic writers."

402   *this cittie* i.e. Jerusalem.

408-*Finis* The account of the deposition and burial draws on various gospels for its details. Only John mentions Nicodemus.

408-15, Joseph's intention — Matthew 27/57, Mark 15/43, Luke 23/50, John 19/38.
424-7, Joseph's request — Matthew 27/58, Mark 15/43, Luke 23/52, John 19/38.
428-35, Pilate's question — Mark 15/44-5.
436-9, Pilate's consent — Matthew 27/58, Mark 15/45, John 19/38.
440-3, Burial in Joseph's new tomb — Matthew 27/60.
472-8, Nicodemus' spices — John 19/39-40.

The marvels attending Christ's death are taken from the description of Christ's death in Matthew 27/45 (the darkness) and 51-4 (earthquake, rocks, open graves, and the significance), the signs which convince the centurion. Compare Pilate's rehearsal of these events, 18/27-40. Neither account mentions the rending of the temple veil, Matthew 27/51, Mark 15/38, Luke 23/45.

The account of the burial does not mention either the linen cloth supplied by Joseph, Matthew 27/59 (compare play 18/387-90), or the stone across the mouth of the tomb, Matthew 27/60, Mark 15/46 (compare play 18/334–6). The wrapping of the body is specified in all other cycles at this point — Wakefield 23/656, York 36/387–9, *Ludus Coventriae* 34/1156–7, Cornish Ordinalia, p.174; and the stone is mentioned at this point in *Ludus Coventriae* 34/1164–5 Cornish Ordinalia p.175.

407 + SH *Josephe* Described as Jesus' disciple, Matthew 27/57, John 19/38; as one awaiting the coming of the kingdom of God, Mark 15/43; a Jew, a good and just man, and evidently one of the Sanhedrin who had not agreed to the course of action pursued, Luke 23/51. All gospels say that he came from Arimathaea, as here indicated at 423 + SD but not in the spoken text.

413–4 The tomb is said by Matthew 27/60 to be *in monumento suo novo* (AV "his own new tomb"). Luke and John merely say it was a tomb in which no man had before been laid. Compare 422. John 19/41 locates it in a garden in the place where Jesus was crucified.

415 + SH *Nycodemus* Identified in John 19/29 with a Pharisee of that name who came to Jesus at night, professing to believe in his divine mission, and was given instruction, John 3/1–21; he later supported Jesus against his fellow Pharisees, John 7/50–1.

422–3 Joseph is said in John 19/29 to have approached Pilate secretly at night for fear of the Jews, and Nicodemus had already incurred unpopularity from his colleagues by supporting Jesus in defiance of them, John 7/52. The retribution of the Jews against Joseph, and Nicodemus' friendship for him, form a substantial part of the Gospel of Nicodemus, caps 12–16.

429–36 Based on Mark 15/44–5.

444–7 "You would never have such power as you have displayed since I knew you, unless your deeds should demonstrate divinity, as you have said before." *deedes* 446 B may be preferred for meaning to *deede* HmAR. *have had* 444 B is a tense change which would be appropriate but is unnecessary and destroys metre.

448 At this point Jesus' body is evidently removed from the cross.

464–71, stanza 60 No manuscript has the form *clight* for *clyft* 466 required for perfect rhyme. *clight* would be past participle of *clicchen; clyft* or *cleft* H that of *cleven* (2) MED. The latter has the sense here required, hence the substitution; the former does not have an appropriate sense, and *clight* is not recorded by MED as a past participle form for *cleven*. *clyst* R suggests scribal confusion of *f* and long *s*.

464 In Matthew 27/45, Mark 15/33, Luke 23/44 darkness lasted from the sixth to ninth hours and was not in itself a portent at the time of Jesus' death. But Luke 23/45 also mentions a darkening of the sun at the time of Jesus' death. Compare 18/38, which suggests that the darkness was only at *noone*.

468–9 The rising of the dead men in Matthew 27/52–3 is said to occur after Jesus' resurrection. The dead involved were saints (*multa corpora sanctorum*) and walked in Jerusalem. They were held to be those liberated by the Harrowing of Hell and included Karinus and Luceus, alleged authors of the account of the Harrowing in the Gospel of Nicodemus. The reference here is out of chronological sequence. It has no place in the marvels of *Stanzaic Life* 5393–404. It is, however, mentioned among the marvels listed by the centurion in the resurrection plays, Wakefield 26/122, York 38/97; and by the tormentors at the moment of Christ's death, Cornish Ordinalia p.169.

470-1 The lines seem to have been composed to echo the centurion's words at 360–1, thereby enhancing the force of the scene. Compare Matthew 27/54: *Vere Filius Dei erat iste* (AV "Truly this was the Son of God").

477 The line contains three strongly stressed syllables instead of the expected four.

PLAY XVII

Dramatis Personae Adam, Esayus, Simeon Justus, Johannes Baptista, Seethe, David, Sathan, Secundus Daemon, Tertius Daemon, Jesus, Mychaell, Enocke, Helias Propheta, Latro, Mulier.

Locations
in inferno, *before* 1, hell 93, 135, 163 ff., *with* hell-gates 153, 191, 193 this place 234, 238; ? paradice 267.

NOTE this holye cittye 250 has no obvious reference — see note.

Properties
lux materialis aliqua subtilitate machinata, *before* 1, this light 3 ff.
cathedra 96 + SD, sede 176 + SD, this see 171
sonitus magnus materialis 152 + SD
this crosse 270
my cuppes and kannes 298.

NOTE Bonds are implied in *stretlye tyed* 224.

Costume
None specified.

Sources
The biblical authority for Christ's visit to Hell to release those saints held by Satan and lead them to Paradise lies in Jesus' words to the penitent thief, Luke 23/43 (16A/321–4), and the resurrection of the saints at the time of Jesus' resurrection, Matthew 27/52–3 (16A/468–9, 18/28). I Peter 3/18–20 mentions Christ preaching to the spirits in prison, often interpreted as the preaching of his gospel after his death to those who had not been alive during his ministry. The main source, however, is the Descent into Hell which forms the second part of the Gospel of Nicodemus (Acts of Pilate), an apocryphal work; in continuous numbering from the start of that gospel, the Descent into Hell occupies caps. 17ff. Tischendorf prints Greek and Latin texts; James translates Greek and Latin A and Latin B versions. The gospel was widely known and rendered into English in a number of versions, of different forms and dates; for an account, see introduction to the *Middle English Harrowing of*

PLAY XVII   263

Hell and Gospel of Nicodemus, ed. W. H. Hulme. EETS, ES 100 (1907), which poem provides a useful vernacular base for comparison with Chester. The Descent into Hell forms part of *Legenda Aurea*, Cap. liv, 'De Resurrectione Domini' (ed. Graesse, pp.242-4) and hence of *Stanzaic Life* 7801-8108, which Wilson held to be the source of the Chester version.

The Descent into Hell was introduced into the creeds by the fourth synod of Sirmium and thus entered the standard western creeds, the Apostles' Creed and the Athanasian Creed (compare 21/326 + Latin-30). It was thus a familiar part of the professed faith of every Christian, being held by both Roman Catholic and Anglican churches — it is the subject of Article 3 of the Thirty-nine Articles of Faith of the Church of England. See also Rufinus, *Commentarius in Symbol. Apostol.* 28 (PL 21/363).

Play-heading The Harrowing of Hell is in all the cycles — Wakefield 25, York 37, *Ludus Coventriae* 33/971-1016 and 35/1344-1415, Cornish Ordinalia pp.182-7. Of these, only Cornish Ordinalia, like Chester, records the events on the ascent to Paradise.

ad Inferna Strictly, Jesus went to that part of Satan's realm in which the souls of those who lived before his coming awaited his message, the *limbus patrum*, or "limbo of the fathers" (as opposed to *limbo infantium*, "the limbo of the unbaptised infants"); compare *Legenda Aurea*, 'De Resurrectione Domini'; *sanctos patres qui erant in limbo*; Wakefield 25/96, York 37/102 "Þes lurdans þat in lymbo dwelle" and Wakefield 25/104, York 37/110 "they ar sperde in speciall space". No such precision is shown in Chester — compare 222 note — although the part of hell intended is evidently close to the gates, as in the other plays. The attribute of darkness, into which Christ's coming introduces light with physical and symbolic force, derives from Nicodemus 18/1.

Before 1 SH   In Wakefield, York, *Ludus Coventriae* and Cornish Ordinalia Adam is accompanied by Eve who speaks at this introductory stage and/or is taken out with him to Paradise; compare *Northern Passion* 3043: "With him he toke Adam and Eue". *Ludus Coventriae* and Cornish Ordinalia dispense with the introductory comments of patriarchs and prophets.

3   The line is omitted erroneously and inexplicably in B.

6   *lyven* HmB should be pronounced as a monosyllable for a regular sequence of strongly and weakly stressed syllables. A and H substitute more obviously monosyllabic forms; arguably, R represents an attempt to accommodate the A form in the inflexion of HmB.

8   *yore* H is to be preferred for meaning and metre. *yere* Hm may represent scribal confusion of *o* and *e*, or reflect a form resembling AR; *eyer* AR may be Bellin's reading of a form which could also generate Hm, or suggest that the exemplar contained a form of *ere* or even a correction of *yore* to *euer*. *earst* B is a replacement, but it may be significant that, like AR, this form also has initial *e*. For regular metre, a monosyllable is required.

9–13   Compare 2/1–424; the Harrowing fulfils Adam's dream, 2/449–56.

17–20   Compare 8/3–4, and *Stanzaic Life* 7893–6:
> Thenne said Adam, "this ilk light
> comes fro Gode whit-outen ende,
> that light euer-lesting vs bihight,
> when he to wynne vs dovn wold wende."

thou 19 ARBH is to be preferred to its omission in Hm for syntax and meaning, since no second person singular subject has earlier been expressed; but since a more regular sequence of strongly and weakly stressed syllables results from the Hm reading, it might be argued that the subject is to be understood from *thee* 18, *thy* 19.

18   *comon* ARH may be preferred to *come* HmB in producing a more regular sequence of strongly and weakly stressed syllables.

31   *to myght*, "to the best of my ability". The Hm version produces a regular sequence of strongly and weakly stressed syllables but requires the possessive pronoun to be understood. Since the pronoun is expressed in ARB, it is possible that the line was metrically rough in the exemplar and that the Hm omission is either an improvement or an error — either having its basis in the repeated sequence *my*. H supplies a different phrase, emphasising divine inspiration.

32 + Latin   Isaiah 9/2 — see 8/317 + Latin–324. Nicodemus 18/1, ME *Harrowing* 1189–1200 give the full continuation of the prophecy, but Chester here resembles *Legenda Aurea* and *Stanzaic Life* 7900 + Latin in giving only the first sentence.

39–40   Compare 48–9 and 24/677–708 for similar appeals.
With *booke* 39 HmARB, compare *booke* 48, confirmed by rhyme. With *books* 39 H, compare ME *Harrowing*, Sion and Additional manuscripts, 1187–8:
> lyfande yhow þus sayde I
> in my bokes fulle euen

The line has no parallel in Nicodemus, *Legenda Aurea* or *Stanzaic Life*.

40 + SH   Compare 11/1–206; B evidently did not recognise the speaker, perhaps confusing him with Simon, 16A/17.

42   Erroneously and inexplicably omitted by AR. The line corresponds to Nicodemus 18/2: *Glorificate dominum Iesum Christum filium dei*. *Stanzaic Life* alone here, 7905–6, refers to the fact that the presentation occurred thirty-three years before.

48 + Latin   Compare 11/166 + Latin; Luke 2/29: AV "Lord, now lettest thou thy servant depart in peace, according to thy word." The line is not in Nicodemus or *Legenda Aurea*, which begin with the second, and more relevant, line of the *Nunc dimittis*; but it is in ME *Harrowing* 1214–5; it appears in abbreviated form in *Stanzaic Life* 7908 + Latin.

PLAY XVII 265

50 *be* Compare 11/167–74 note. In the earlier version, *bee* is fixed by rhyme, but here H can replace it by *dye*, perhaps more accurately reflecting the Vulgate meaning. Compare Wakefield 25/58, York 37/66: "Pas in peasse to lyf lastande".

51–3 "For I had both touched and seen [that] he who was come is Christ whom he [God] had ordained for Man's salvation"; compare 11/169–72. *commen was* 51 perhaps suggests that *he was* would be preferable to *he is* 51; H's *swet* removes the difficulty.

56 + SH–72 + Latin The passage combines the account of the ministry of John the Baptist in the wilderness in Matthew 3/1–6, Mark 1/1–8, Luke 3/1–6, John 1/6–8, with the description of John's baptism of Jesus in Matthew 3/13–7, Mark 1/9–11, Luke 3/21–2. Nicodemus includes the full account of the descent of the dove and the voice of God after the baptism, but Chester here resembles *Legenda Aurea* and *Stanzaic Life* in omitting the continuation. The continuation is in Wakefield 25/69–76, York 37/77–84. Chester is the only extant English cycle which does not dramatise Jesus' baptism by John; see 12/*Play-heading* note.

57 Nicodemus 18/3 indicates that John spoke in response to a general demand by his fellows for identification: *Et posthaec supervenit quasi heremicola, et interrogatur ab omnibus: Quis es tu? Quibus respondens dixit: Ego sum Johannes*; similarly *Legenda Aurea*: *Et interrogatus a nobis, quis esset, dixit: ego sum Johannes*. But this interrogation is not in *Stanzaic Life*.

prophett corresponds to Nicodemus *Vox et propheta altissimi*, not in *Legenda Aurea* or *Stanzaic Life*. *ilk* H seems an unnecessary substitution.

57–72, stanzas 8–9 In H these stanzas become one by the omission of 61–4; by the replacement of 66–8 to give a b-rhyme, *commynge* 60 — *bringe* 68; and by the omission of 69–72. In the resulting Chester stanza, rhyming aaabcccb, 66 would seem to contain only three strongly stressed syllables instead of the expected four, and *was* 67 should be read as *wes* for perfect rhyme. With the omission of 61–4, H also omits 64 + Latin, cited in HmARB in support of those lines.

A omits 66–9, destroying the structure of stanza 9. This omission, corrected in R, may indicate some uncertainty about the status of the lines in the exemplar, perhaps suggesting that the HmRB and the H versions coexisted there as alternatives.

61–4 originate in John's teaching as reported in Nicodemus 18/3: *Ad dandam scientiam salutis plebi eius in remissionem peccatorum illorum*, which in turn derives from Mark 1/4, Luke 3/3: *Praedicans baptismum paenitentiae in remissionem peccatorum* (AV "Preaching the baptism of repentance for the remission of sins"). The precise reference to the Passion has no counterpart in scriptural account. The passage is not in the version in *Legenda Aurea*. Its inclusion or omission might reflect response to its possible theological implications.

The omission or inclusion of 61–4 might be sufficient explanation for the corresponding omission or inclusion of 69–72. 69–70 has no counterpart in Nicodemus. It may derive more remotely from John the Baptist's words in John 1/16–7: *Et de plenitudine eius nos omnes accepimus, et gratiam pro gratia. Quia lex per Moysen data est, gratia et veritas per Iesum Christum facta est* (AV "And of his fulness have we all received, and grace for grace. For the law was given by Moses, but grace and truth came by Jesus Christ"). The line, however, also recalls Psalm 84/11 (AV

85/10), which is also echoed at 2/399 — see 2/393-424 note. The passage may also have theological implications.

It may be significant that the HmRB version shares with the previous speeches the concluding reference to *these wordes* (compare 31, 47) which introduces the supporting Latin quotation with which the speech ends.

58 *followed* H represents the past tense of *fol(e)wen*, a form of *fulwen*, MED (a) "to baptize". OED last records the verb *full*[1] in 1483, from a de Worde text of 1515. Deimling cites H's use of the older word in support of his view that H contains the earlier form of 57-72.

65 Nicodemus 18/3 merely says: *Videns eum venientem*. The line here derives from *Legenda Aurea*: *Et ipsum ostendi digito*; compare *Stanzaic Life*:

> And with his fynger, in gode fay,
> he showet
> (7915-6)

70 *concluded* Compare OED *conclude* v[1] I.4: "To overcome in argument; to confute, 'shut up', convince"; similarly MED *concluden* 2(a), but see also MED 1 (b) "to restrain or debar"; and 2/398-400.

72+ Latin John 1/29: AV "Behold the Lamb of God, which taketh away the sin of the world."

73-88 Seth was the third son of Adam and Eve, born after Abel's murder, Genesis 4/2; but in the genealogy of 1 Chronicles 1/1 he is listed immediately after Adam, Cain and Abel being there omitted. His death at the age of 912 years is recorded in Genesis 5/8. His visit to Eden to request a drop of the oil of mercy to anoint the dying Adam and relieve his pains, in Nicodemus 19, is in *Vita Adae et Evae* and the *Apocalypsis Moyses* and formed an important part of the current medieval legends of the cross, being retailed in works such as the *Northern Passion* 1749-2074. In Wakefield 25/77-88, York 37/85-96 Moses occupies the place taken here by Seth; compare the list of patriarchs taken from Limbo in *Northern Passion*:

> And other þat war to him leue
> Iohn þe Baptist, Moyses alswa,
> Abraham aend other ma
> (3044-6)

— *Ludus Coventriae* 1376-83 includes a speech by Abraham, but makes no mention of Seth. Cornish *Ordinalia* dramatises Seth's quest in its Creation play, but does not mention him in the Harrowing.

In Nicodemus 19, Seth speaks at Adam's request, Adam being prompted by John's reference to baptism, but no such connexion is suggested in *Legenda Aurea* or *Stanzaic Life*.

83 Compare Nicodemus 19: *Noli laborare lacrimis orando et deprecando*, also in *Legenda Aurea*. *nyf* Hm, seen also at 85, is not recorded by OED in the required sense of "nor", and *nor* ARH is to be preferred. But *nys* B, also inappropriate, seems to suggest that Hm and B reflect a confusion of *f* and long *s* which could arise only through the intermediary of an exemplar form. See 85 note.

remynge Hm is the last recorded example of the verbal noun in OED, the previous example being 1400. But compare 13/427 note.

PLAY XVII

85 *nyf* Compare 83 variants and note. B again has the inappropriate *nys*. *ner* A evidently reflects confusion of *e* and *o*, however, which suggests an exemplar form; *nor* R would indicate a correction of the A form, while *nay* H is apparently a formal variant of *ne*, "nor". Possibly *nyf/nys* had been corrected by some form — *nor* or *ne* — here. If so, a similar argument may be extended to 83.

of that Hm corresponds exactly to *ex eo*, Nicodemus 19, and *de illo*, *Legenda Aurea*, and the Hm line gives acceptable meaning and sense. *of that oyle* ARBH is strongly attested and acceptable.

87–8 *Legenda Aurea*, *Stanzaic Life* and Chester lack the connection made by Seth with the preceding speech of John the Baptist (Nicodemus 19): *Cum autem egressus fuerit de aqua Iordanis, tunc de oleo misericordiae suae unget omnes credentes in se, et erit oleum illud misericordiae in generationem eorum qui nascendi sunt ex aqua et spiritu sancto in vitam aeternam.*

89–96 David's summarising speech has no counterpart in Nicodemus or *Legenda Aurea*. Some hint may perhaps be found in the comments of David and Isaiah in Nicodemus 21/2, but the connexion is weak.

89–96, stanza 12 The b-rhyme, *languor* 92 — *here* 96, is imperfect; MED does not record any form of *langour* which would suggest a rhyme with *here*, although sense (b) of the word suits the context. The H version of 92, with *danger* as rhyme-word, is therefore to be preferred.

102 Compare Nicodemus 20/1, *Legenda Aurea: Jesum qui se gloriatur Christum filium dei esse*; ME *Harrowing* 1291: "Sen he him god sun maked has"; *Stanzaic Life* 7949–50:

> He makes his bost and has grete blis
> Goddes sone to callet be.

The form of expression here suggests that Satan recognised Jesus as God's Son, whereas 105 suggests that Satan there sees him as an ordinary man. He had previously tried vainly to discover the truth about Jesus — see play 12. If H's omission of 105 is not mere error, it may suggest the scribe's recognition of the conflict between 102 and 105.

105 See 102 note; H omits a necessary line deliberately or carelessly.

108 Compare the text from Matthew 26/38, Mark 14/34, found also in Nicodemus 20/1 and quoted here after 108 in B: AV: "My soul is exceeding sorrowful, even unto death." The words were uttered by Jesus to his three disciples in Gethsemane before he went to pray alone, and have no counterpart in Play 15 at that point. Since the words were uttered in Gethsemane, it is debatable whether they were, in fact, spoken *todaye* 106, i.e. Friday. Moreover, the English line does not render the Latin; compare *Stanzaic Life*:

> My soule is sorowful, wel se,
> for bodile deth that comyng is
> (7953–4)

threst Hm, *thirste* ARBH bears formal resemblance to *tristis* and may suggest an incorrect equation or interpretation. Alternatively, *thirste* may represent an attempt to suggest reference to 16A/352.

109–12   The lines derive, not from the extended passage in Nicodemus 20/1: *Et multos quos ego caecos claudos surdos leprosos et vexatos feci, ipse verbo sanavit; et quos ad te mortuos perduxi, hos ipse a te abstraxit*; but from the abbreviated form in *Legenda Aurea*: *Et multos, quos feci surdos, sanavit et claudos erexit*, and particularly *Stanzaic Life*:

>   That I haue made bothe halte ʒ blind
>   he has heled thurgh his might
>   (7957–8)

112 + SH   The speaker is identified as *Secundus* presumably in opposition to Satan, who may be considered *Primus* but is not so identified here. The respondents to Satan in Nicodemus are comprehended under *inferus*, *Stanzaic Life Helle* 7961. In ME *Harrowing* Satan at this point addresses the porter of Hell, 1287, who responds. Possibly the second devil is to be considered here as porter since it is he rather than Satan who first responds to Jesus' challenge, 157–60.

117–20   Chester seems here closer to Nicodemus than to *Legenda Aurea*. Compare Nicodemus 20/2: *Si ergo potens es tu, qualis est homo ille Iesus, qui timens mortem potentiae tuae adversatur? Si ita potens est in humanitate, vere dico tibi, omnipotens est in divinitate et potentiae eius nemo potest resistere. Et cum dicit se timere mortem, capere te vult, et vae tibi erit in sempiterna secula*; and *Legenda Aurea*, which lacks the second sentence, on which 117–20 seems based, and contains the idea of deception in the third sentence which is not taken up here. *Stanzaic Life* is similar to Chester:

>   But ʒit [i]f deth were dred with him
>   Take þe [he] wol now in þis tyde
>   And greue þe, synne he ys so grym
>   Þat his sorwe shalt þou abyde
>   (7969–72)

a passage lacking in the base manuscript of the EETS edition.

121–8   The lines are without parallel in the texts consulted. The warning at 127–8 HmARB is syntactically incomplete — "But on you, Satan, before long, if his will prevails at all ....."; H provides syntactical completeness with *it is* 127 — "If his will prevails in any way, the consequence for you is far-reaching."

129–36   Compare Nicodemus 20/2, and *Legenda Aurea*: *In proximo est eius mors, ut perducam eum ad te subiectum tibi et mihi*; *Stanzaic Life*:

>   I haue temptet hym tenderly
>   and peple excitet whit A braide
>   to do hym harme and vilany,
>   Scharpenet to hym I haue a sper
>   Aysel and galle menget haue I,
>   purueit A croys hym on to der,
>   and bring him heder I wol in hye.
>   (7974–80)

The implication appears to be that Jesus was at this time approaching death, but had not actually died, a sense lost in 134. Jesus was held to have gone immediately to Hell on his death; compare *Speculum Humanae Salvationis*, cap.31 and *Northern Passion* 3031–2. See also 152 + SH note.

PLAY XVII 269

Chester omits the *Stanzaic Life* references to the temptation, the spear, the cross and the nails, which derive from Nicodemus 20/2, *Legenda Aurea*.

130 Compare Nicodemus 20/2, *Legenda Aurea*: *Ego* enim *tentavi illum, et populum meum antiquum Iudaicum excitavi* zelo et ira *adversus eum* (roman words not in *Legenda*), *Stanzaic Life* 7974-5:
> I haue temptet hym tenderly
> and peple excitet whit A braide ....

The references seem here to be to the temptation and to the animosity of the Jews. Chester, however, seems to combine the two, changing *tentavi illum* to *tentavi populum*. In view of the general antisemitic tenor of the cycle, the absence of an equivalent for the specific *meum antiquum Iudaicum* further indicates the absence of direct influence from Nicodemus in the play.

132-3 Compare 16A/353-5, and Nicodemus 20/2, *Legenda Aurea*: *Lanceam exacui* ad percussionem eius, *fel et acetum miscui* dare ei potum, *et lignum praeparavi* ad crucifigendum eum, et aculeos ad configendum (roman words not in *Legenda*). The reference there is to the various items assembled in preparation for Christ's crucifixion. Here, the emphasis is upon the verbs, and the reduction of items to two and the use of *sythen* 133 might seem to suggest that the passage proposes that Jesus was first given drink and then crucified, which is the order in Matthew and Mark — see 16A/353-5 note. H's omission of *sythen*, which still leaves an acceptable metre, may to some extent weaken this suggestion, which is counter to the sequence of 16A.

137-52 *Legenda Aurea* abridges Nicodemus 20/3 at this point, since in the gospel the starting-point for the debate lies in Satan's earlier criticism of Jesus for having raised the dead, a criticism without counterpart in *Legenda Aurea* and Chester. Hell's reply in Nicodemus ends with an affirmation of Jesus' divinity similarly lacking in *Legenda Aurea* and Chester. 145-52 is without counterpart in the gospel or the *Legenda*.

140 + SH H erroneously omits the SH, perhaps as a consequence of fitting 141-4 into a two-line space because of misruling (see TN.)

148 The line has no counterpart in *Legenda Aurea*, but compare Nicodemus 20/3: *Ad vitam divinitatis suae perducet in aeternum*, and ME *Harrowing*, Galba manuscript, 1315: "All þat him likes heþin will he lede".

152 Compare ME *Harrowing*, Galba manuscript, 1316-20:
> he es a strenkithi swayn,
> when we all might noght hald
> a wofull sawl ogayne,
> when he did noght bot cald

and 13/451-7.

152 + SD The quotation is Psalm 23/7,9 (AV 24/7,9): AV "Lift up you heads, O ye gates, and be ye lift up, ye everlasting doors; and the King of glory shall come in."

portae H, of which *porte* ARB is a formal variant, is to be preferred to the erroneous *portas* (2) Hm, the latter resulting from confusion with *portas* (1).

152 + SH In all other plays, a distinction is made between the human Jesus and the divine spirit which harrows Hell; see Wakefield 25/23-4; York 27/23-4; *Ludus*

Coventriae 33/979–82, where also *Anima Christi* is shown at the gates of Hell before the deposition, burial and setting the guard at the sepulchre; Cornish Ordinalia refers to the speaker as *Spirit of Christ*.

B omits the SH, perhaps relying upon *et dicat Jesus* in the preceding SD.

160   *mis* BH is to be preferred for meaning to *amys* Hm, which does not give sense, and to *anyse* AR, a nonce-word apparently deriving from a form similar to Hm.

162   *seghe* Hm is a variant of *see* H, past tense, "saw". Hm perhaps represents the exemplar form, since AR substitute *seinge*, accommodating *g*, while *sith* B seems an 'emendation' based on *seghe* and including *h*; neither AR nor B is syntactically acceptable.

169–76 + SD   This passage has no counterpart in *Legenda Aurea* but derives from Nicodemus 21/1: *Haec audiens inferus dixit ad Satan principem: Recede a me et exi de meis sedibus foras; si potens es praeliator, pugna adversum regem gloriae. Sed quid tibi cum illo? Et eiecit inferus Satan foras de sedibus suis.* The passage has no equivalent in ME *Harrowing* or *Stanzaic Life* at this point. The ejection of Satan from his seat does not necessarily follow from 169–76 and is not found in the Greek Nicodemus; H specifies it in *jaceant* 176 + SD, but it is not explicit in HmARB, where Satan perhaps rises only to confront Jesus.

This is the only passage in 157–84 with counterpart in Nicodemus.

184 + SH–92 + Latin   The ultimate source of the passage is Nicodemus 21/2, where it follows the account of the barricading of Hell's gates, an act which leads the inmate-prisoners to taunt Satan; the speech is there specifically addressed to Satan. Compare *Legenda Aurea*: "*Ad hanc vocem concurrerunt daemones et ostia aenea [sic] cum vectibus ferreis clauserunt. Tunc dixit David: nonne ego prophetavi dicens: confiteantur domino etc., quia contrivit porta aeneas [sic] etc.*" The text is developed in *Stanzaic Life* 8009–20, and David similarly replies in Wakefield and York.

H's omission of this section may be compared with its re-ascription of 198–204, having the effect of removing David from the play. Such changes may well spring from some sense of dramatic effectiveness, but are unwarranted by comparison with ultimate sources and analogues. Deimling (p.xxvi) comments: "The archfiend despairs already of his might to bar Hell's gates against Jesus' victorious march into them, and indulges in vain complaints. At this very moment David wants to bore him with his then certainly superannuated prophecy."

Unlike Wakefield 25/120–7, York 37/139–44 Chester does not emphasise the barricading of Hell, and David's words seem less a taunt to Satan, more a statement of a divine purpose inevitably fulfilled.

189   *my lyefe-daye* Compare Nicodemus 21/2: *Cum essem vivus*.

192   *wine* B is to be preferred, as an infinitive form dependent upon *should*, to *wonn* Hm and the formal variants of A and R.

192 + Latin   Psalm 106/14–6 (AV 107/15–6): AV "Oh that man would praise the Lord for his goodness, and for his wonderful works to the children of men! For he hath broken the gates of brass, and cut the bars of iron in sunder."

No manuscript has the form *filiis* for *filius*, the latter evidently an exemplar error.

193–6, stanza 25   The stanza consists of four four-stress lines, rhyming abab.

194 *peace* H represents the unthinking transcription of a common collocation inappropriate in this context.

197 Compare Psalm 23/8, 10 (AV 24/8, 10),: *Quis est iste rex gloriae?* (AV "Who is this King of glory?"). The line here contains five strongly stressed syllables instead of the expected four. The biblical text gives authority for the omission of one *what* by ARH and of *hee* by H; the BH reading *saye* for HmAR *staye* further modifies the stress-pattern of the line. Combining the variants into a line of regular metre might yield: "Saye what ys hee, that kinge of blys?" But the line has clearly been subjected to rhetorical elaboration for emphasis.

197 + SH Both Nicodemus 21/3 and *Legenda Aurea* confirm the speaker as David (Graesse erroneously has *Daniel*). H reassigns the speech to *Jhesus*, perhaps from a sense of dramatic propriety, and therefore has no change of speaker between 204 and 205. Deimling (p.xxvi) comments: "In the group it is the royal psalmist who answers Satan's question who it is that wants to come in; in H, Jesus himself reveals his true nature and character and acts in Hell — I think in an effective and forcible manner — as that which he is, the universal king and ruler. The man who was able to write and invent the preceding animated and dramatic Scene, was not Philistine enough to weaken Jesus' powerful speech to the academic explanation of a mere bystander, as is done in the group's text."

198–204 Compare Psalms 23/8 (AV 24/8): *Dominus fortis et potens, Dominus potens in proelio* (AV "The Lord strong and mighty, the Lord mighty in battle"). Nicodemus 21/3 continues: *Et ipse dominus de caelo in terris prospexit ut audiret gemitus compeditorum et ut solveret filios interemptorem*; *Legenda Aurea* merely echoes the end of the Psalm: *ipse est rex gloriae*. Neither has counterpart here.

204 + SD Chester does not mention the actual fall of the gates of Hell, which occurs at this point in Nicodemus 21/3 and was clearly a striking dramatic feature elsewhere. It is emphasised in appropriately violent terms in ME *Harrowing*, Galba manuscript, 1402–4, Wakefield 25/207–8, York 37/195–6, and Cornish Ordinalia, p.182. No such physical force is suggested by the Latin A version of Nicodemus, and the fall of the gates is not mentioned in *Legenda Aurea* or *Stanzaic Life*.

In Nicodemus, immediately on entering Hell Jesus delivers Satan to the powers of Hell (Latin A) or Satan is cast down and bound (Latin B, Greek). Then Jesus draws Adam to his brightness and, after Hell has reproached Satan for claiming Jesus without cause, extends his hand to his saints and his right hand to Adam, Nicodemus 23/1. The binding of Satan, here 221–8, is not mentioned by *Legenda Aurea* or *Stanzaic Life*. *Legenda Aurea* also somewhat cryptically comments: *Extendens dominus manum et tenens dextram Adae*; *Stanzaic Life* 8035–6, 8039–40:

> ʒ takes Adams hond in his
> ʒ toke him owt of hell in hye
> then aftur him saintes all connen sewe
> owt of helle, as wele was sene.

The SD here evidently combines the Nicodemus and *Legenda* ideas; Jesus apparently stretches out his hands down into the mouth of Hell and helps out Adam first, followed by the other saints who assemble at Hell-mouth and are then led off to Paradise by Michael. It is not clear, as it is in the other accounts, whether Jesus speaks to Adam before helping the other saints to emerge, or speaks after all have emerged. Other accounts indicate the former, but here 209–12 might be held to support the latter.

H separates the two actions, suggesting that the removal of Adam and the words addressed to him precede the emergence of the other saints at 220 + SD.

206 *ofspringe* ARBH is to be preferred to the erroneous *osspringe* Hm, the latter resulting from a confusion of *f* and long *s*.

211 *Mychaell* Michael is described as one of the chief princes, Daniel 10/13, and the prince of Israel, Daniel 10/21. He led the angels against the dragon in the war in Heaven, Apocalypse 12/7–10, and, as the defender of Israel against the powers of evil, is seen as the champion of the righteous against the devil. It is he who slays Antichrist — see 23/624 + SD note.

singinge Nicodemus 24/2 ff. has an extensive series of texts and responses at this point. In Wakefield 25, York 37, Cornish Ordinalia, Psalm 16/10 is cited — in the two former by David and in the latter by Eve. Compare 276 + SD and note.

213–28 Without counterpart in Nicodemus or *Legenda Aurea*.

221–8, stanza 29 The HmARB b-rhyme, *tyed* 224 — *afrayd* 228, is imperfect; H supplies a perfect rhyme — *dight*—*afright* — which is cited by Deimling as evidence of H's superiority.

221–2 Satan's despair here is in contrast to his defiant attitude in Wakefield 25/225–353, York 37/213–334, where he disputes with Christ. Wakefield 25/323–42, York 37/301–24, Cornish Ordinalia p.183 make it clear that Satan will continue to hold and have power over evil-doers.

224 Satan's words could be interpreted to mean that he is bound only while the saints leave limbo, whereas Nicodemus indicates that Jesus bound Satan on entering Hell with iron bonds round feet, hands and (Greek) neck and that Satan was cast into the depths of the bottomless pit. *Legenda Aurea* has no counterpart. Compare Wakefield 25/360, York 37/348: "I synk into hell pyt" — in York 37/339–40 Jesus summons Michael to bind the devil, but Michael does not appear in Wakefield's *Harrowing*. *Ludus Coventriae* 35/1400–7 presents Beliall bound, alone in Hell, with fiends as his foe.

227–8 See 1/292–3 note. H's omission at 227 damages the syntax.

229–76 The encounters on the journey to Paradise, in Nicodemus 25–6 and *Legenda Aurea*, are found in Cornish Ordinalia but not in the other English cycles. Adam here acts as spokesman where in Nicodemus the saints collectively speak.

236 + SH Enoch was father of Methuselah. His bodily translation into Paradise is based on Genesis 5/24; when Enoch was 365 years old, *Ambulavitque cum Deo, et non apparuit, quia tulit eum Deus* (AV "And Enoch walked with God: and he was not; for God took him"); compare Hebrews 11/5: *Fide Henoch translatus est ne videret mortem; et non inveniebatur, quia transtulit illum Deus. Ante translationem enim testimonium habuit placuisse Deo* (AV "By faith Enoch was translated that he should not see death; and was not found, because God had translated him: for before his translation he had this testimony, that he pleased God"). See 242 note.

PLAY XVII

242   Elijah the Tishbite, opponent of Jezebel and of those who tolerated her worship of Baal, whose priests he defeated in a confrontation on Mount Carmel. *Elias*, 244 + SH, is the Greek form of the name. His bodily assumption in a whirlwind *in caelum* is described in 4 Kings 2/11 (AV 2 Kings 2/11); the chariot of fire which transported him there is mentioned in Nicodemus and *Legenda Aurea*, whence *Stanzaic Life* 8059, but the mode of translation is not indicated here.

Nicodemus and *Legenda Aurea* describe the two men as *viri vetusti dierum*; compare ME *Harrowing* 1551: "Two graihared men with face ful klere"; *Stanzaic Life* 8048 "Two old men of ful gret price".

243   *in this araye* Compare 4 Kings (AV 2 Kings) 1/8: *At illi dixerunt: Vir pilosus, et zona pellicea accinctus renibus. Qui ait: Elias thesbites est* (AV "And they answered him, He was an hairy man, and girt with a girdle of leather about his loins. And he said, It is Elijah the Tishbite"). This was evidently Elijah's characteristic guise.

245-52   The basis for this statement in Nicodemus 25 is Malachi 4/5-6: *Ecce ego mittam vobis Eliam prophetam antequam veniat dies Domini magnus et horribilis; et convertet cor patrum ad filios, et cor filiorum ad patres eorum; ne forte veniam, et percutiam terram anathemate* (AV "Behold I will send you Elijah the prophet before the coming of the great and dreadful day of the Lord: And he shall turn the heart of the fathers to the children, and the heart of the children to their fathers, lest I come and smite the earth with a curse"). The coming of Antichrist is the subject of play 23.

248   *with hise*, "with his own"; the reference of the pronoun is not clear, but could include "kingdom", "followers" or "deeds" — see MED *his* pron. (2), 1. AR did not understand the phrase; A omits, while R substitutes *in haste*, destroying rhyme.

250   *the* H is to be preferred for meaning to *this* HmARB. The reference of *this* could be only to Paradise in the context of the play — perhaps a confusion between the earthly and heavenly Jerusalems underlies the HmARB form. More tenuously, the reference could be to Chester itself, a surrogate Jerusalem.

252 + SH   The SH has been erroneously and inexplicably omitted by H.

254   The existence in B of both HmAR and H versions of 254 strongly suggests that both versions existed in the exemplar. Possibly the B reading indicates that *that lives with you* was written above *with crose on shoulder*.

254 H corresponds to Nicodemus 26, *Legenda Aurea: Ecce supervenit alius vir miserrimus, portans humeris* suis *signum crucis* (roman words not in *Legenda*). HmAR specifies that the thief is already in paradise in fulfilment of the prophecy of Jesus from the start; compare 16A/313-24. Such specification might be particularly necessary if paradise was not scenically realised.

Chester suggests that the thief bore a cross — cf. *hanginge* 270; compare *Stanzaic Life* 8071: "A croys apon his bak bering". But Nicodemus above refers to *signum crucis*, perhaps less concretely presented — compare ME *Harrowing* Galba manuscript, 1581: "His takin he made on me".

261-8, stanza 34   *come* 264 HmH is subjunctive, "should come"; but formally it could be past tense and is replaced by the form *came* in ARB, to the destruction of rhyme. AR do not seem to have understood *nome* 268 HmBH and rephrase, using *anon*. Although *nome* means "went" (OED *nim* 2, last exemplified in c.1430), H supplies an object, using it in the sense of "took" (OED 1).

261 Compare Nicodemus 26: *Creaturarum mirabilia quae facta sunt per crucem Iesu crucifixi*, less explicitly rendered in *Legenda Aurea* as *credidi ipsum esse creatorem*.

signes ARH and *sines* B — the latter evidently a formal variant — are to be preferred to *synnys* Hm for meaning and as reflecting Nicodemus. The line has no counterpart in *Stanzaic Life*.

264 *realme* H is to be preferred for meaning to *regyon* HmARB; it reflects *in regnum tuum*, Nicodemus 26, *Legenda Aurea* — compare *Stanzaic Life* 8080: "When he is reme wer withynne". The disyllabic HmARB form produces a line most naturally read as a four-stress line, whereas H produces a three-stress line here required.

Possibly underlying HmARB is a distinction between the earthly and heavenly paradises which is obscured in H.

267 H reflects Nicodemus 26: *Hodie mecum eris in paradiso*, but HmARB gives sense and a smoother metre.

269–76, stanza 35 In HmB the stanza rhymes aaabcdad. At 272 R destroys rhyme by substituting *entrance*. No manuscript has *yinge* for *yonge* 273 required for perfect rhyme. Both A and H forms would restore a-rhyme to 274, and either would give sense; A, with the implication "he who wills all things", could suggest a base for the adverb in HmRB, where *willinge* seems to have been understood in a weaker sense of "anxious to please, obliging"; *weldinge* H would appropriately suggest a divine attribute and could be held to correspond to a phrase in the collective praise by the saints at this point in Nicodemus 26: *Benedictus dominus omnipotens*. A and H suggest a regular Chester stanza, aaabaaab.

271 Nicodemus 26, *Legenda Aurea* merely define the angel as *angelus custos paradiso*, whence *Stanzaic Life* 8089: "The angel wardeyn her". There is no indication that the archangel Michael was considered the custodian of paradise. Possibly this has been inferred from Seth's comment at 81; alternatively, some indication of the source of the confusion can be found in ME *Harrowing*, Galba manuscript, where the thief is told:

> when michaell sall þe se
> he sall noght say þe nay
> (1583-4)

and later, of his appearance at paradise:

> if þat the angel be noght glad
> þat þou cumes in þat stede
> (1587-8)

But possibly the identification is intended for simplification. It could, however, be argued that, since Jesus is not yet in Paradise (having gone directly to Hell), the thief is seen here just arriving. Such an interpretation would be possible only if 254 H were adopted, and is not warranted by ultimate sources.

276 + SD *Te Deum Laudamus* The composition of this Latin hymn was traditionally assigned to saints Ambrose and Augustine. It is the hymn of the saints similarly in Wakefield 25/404; York 37/408 read: *Laus tibi in gloria*.

276 + SH–*Finis* The ale-wife scene is omitted by H, perhaps because it was felt to be unwarranted or inappropriate, or perhaps because it was indicated as an optional continuation. Deimling believes the scene to be "a later appendix", added because

PLAY XVII 275

the play was short. Lumiansky, *Tulane Studies* X, discusses its relationship to the theme of the play.

It may be noted that H, which omits the scene, alone includes the *inkepers* as a performing company for the play — see *Guild-ascription*. Legislation for the control of alcohol was passed in Chester in 1503-4, but a new, tougher code of practice was introduced by the mayor, Henry Gee, in 1533, covering many of the abuses here revealed.

With the association of illicit alcohol trading with the work of the devil, compare 10/451.

276 + SH Brewers and inn-keepers were often women and *tapster* 286 here evidently continues its sixteenth century sense of feminine reference. By the 1533 regulations, no woman in Chester under the age of forty was allowed to keep an alehouse or tavern; see R. H. Morris, *Chester in the Plantagenet and Tudor Reigns* (privately published, 1893), p.425, fn.12.

289 The cans in which the beer and wine were sold did not contain as much as the statutory measure.

294-6 Hops were introduced into brewing in northern Europe only in the sixteenth century; the reference may have some significance for dating.

Hops are not essential to the brewing process, being used to impart a characteristic aroma and a bitter taste to the beer, to disperse cloudiness, and to act as a preservative. Morris, *op. cit.*, p.431, notes: "A statute of Henry VIII forbade hops to be used. 25 Hen.VIII Elizabeth Coke and Johanna Dudson are fined each 6d for putting *"les hopes in servisia"* contrary to the statute." Here, hops are listed with the other additives, *esshes* and *hearbes*, evidently used to give the illusion of strength by affecting the flavour of a normal-strength — or perhaps under-strength — brew.

301-8, stanza 39 No manuscript has *commonweale* for *commonwealth*, required for rhyme at 304.

306 Compare 294-6 note. *bruynge so thinne* may refer to an inadequate mash, a diluted mixture (see 315) or an unusually limited period of fermentation (see 317-8).

309-16, stanza 40 *combe* 314 ARB is to be preferred for rhyme to *combes* Hm.

314 *combes*, i.e. brewing tubs or vats (OED *coomb*); the word is recorded only from 1559 by OED, excluding this reference which is dated ?a1400.

316 "And little out of the sack." Compare *sack* sb¹, OED 2 "A sack with its contents; also, the amount usually taken as a unit of measure or weight for corn, flour, fruit, wool, coal, etc." The sense here is that the brew was all water, with very little added from the bag of malt.

317-20 A distinction is implied between *màshers*, who carry out the first process in brewing, *mashing*, in which the grist (malt flour and husk) is mixed with hot water, and the *mengers of wyne*, or wine-blenders. The implication seems to be that the lack of adequate fermentation in these processes has unfortunate consequences for drinkers.

claret is the traditional name for the wine from the Bordeaux region. In the twelfth century and later the word was applied to a pale wine made in that region by mixing reds and whites, hence its use here for a blended wine, though sarcastically. The reference is probably to bad vinification.

325-8, stanza 42   The stanza consists of a regular Chester quatrain. Each devil here utters a quatrain. The effect may be deliberate, or possibly Satan was allotted a full stanza originally and there has been a deliberate or erroneous omission in the exemplar.

325   *daughter* AR repeat the phrase in 333 HmB; at 333, A substitutes *daughter*.

330-2   Compare 23/683-6.

334-5   The sins of the tavern — see G. R. Owst, *Literature and Pulpit in Medieval England*, pp.434-42. Under the 1533 Chester regulations, taverners had to give surety against permitting unlawful games in their establishments.

336   *a feaste* Compare *feste* MED 4(d), *Luciferes feste* — a reference perhaps here evoked by *Lucifere* 278, the only instance of that appellation in the play — "the torments of hell, destruction"; and the cited example:

> Flateres and foles ....
> Leden þo þat louen hem to luciferes feste
> With turpiloquio, a lay of sorwe and luciferes fithele
>   (*Piers Plowman* B (Ld) 13/456).

PLAY XVIII

Dramatis Personae Pilatus, Cayphas, Annas, Primus Miles, Secundus Miles, Tertius Miles, Duo Angeli (Angelus Primus, Angelus Secundus), Jesus, Maria Magdalena, Maria Jacobi, Maria Salome, Petrus, Johannes Evangelist.

Locations
a tombe of stonne 45, the tombe here att our hand 142, the sepulchre 204, sepulchro 185 + SD, sepulchrum 344 + SD; *with* this great stonne that lyeth my sweet lord upon 334–5, the stonne 340, 343, 379; *the angels are disposed* alter ad caput, alter ad pedes 185 + SD.

Properties
thys great light 210; pecuniam 308 + SD; boyst 332; his sudarye 387 *and* all other clothes 390.

Costume
Knights — well armed 68
Angels — bright 214, *in clothing* all of whyte 342.

Sources
Setting the Watch — Matthew 27/62–66, Apocryphal Gospel of Nicodemus 11/2, 13/1–3
Resurrection — Matthew 28/2–4, Apocryphal Gospel of Nicodemus 13/1
Visit of Maries — Matthew 28/1, 5–8, Mark 16/1–8, Luke 24/1–11
Race to the Tomb — Luke 24/12, John 20/2–10
Appearance to Mary Magdalen — John 20/11–18.

Play-heading
The play ends abruptly at different points in HmA and B; RH share a common continuation — see Appendix ID.
 The events in the play occur also in Wakefield 26 (which lacks the race to the tomb); York 38 (Setting the Watch, Resurrection, Visit of Maries) and 39 (Appearance to Mary Magdalen); *Ludus Coventriae* 34–5/1176–1343 (Setting the Watch), 1416–1647 (Appearance to the Virgin Mary, Watch's discomfiture), 36/1–166 (Visit of Maries, Race to Tomb), 37/1–101 (Appearance to Mary Magdalen); Cornish Ordinalia pp.188–203 (Setting the Watch, Appearance to the Virgin Mary, Appearance to Mary Magdalen);

Digby *Mary Magdalen* 993–1132 (Visit of Maries, Race to Tomb, Appearance to Mary Magdalen and the other women); Shrewsbury Fragment B (Visit of Maries).

1–8   See 16/134–5 and note. The French here seems to mean:
> By you, sir Cayphas,
> and you and you, sir Annas,
> and his disciple Judas
> who committed treason,
> and the great light of brilliance
> to me perfectly revealed;
> our lady was judge
> to praise the noble king.

The exact references of the lines and their appropriateness in context are obscure. It has been suggested to us that *estreite/escrete* might be a distortion of *eslite*, "chosen, elected, selected", or the past participle of *estraire*, of similar meaning; 8 would then mean "chosen to praise the king".

9–16, stanza 2   The stanza rhymes ababcddc. Lines 9, 11, 12 consist of eleven syllables with four main stresses — x/xx/xx/xx/: line 10 consists of eight syllables with three main stresses — x/xx/xx/ (taking *kemps* as an error for a disyllabic *kempes* and *knightes of* as two syllables rather than three); line 13 consists of nine syllables with three main stresses — xx/xx/xx/; line 14 consists of twelve syllables with four main stresses — arguably x/xx/xx/xx/x. 15 and 16 have the more flexible Chester form, 16 with three strongly stressed syllables. The form of the stanza is unusual and suggests a revision of the first six lines of a regular Chester stanza.

B's omission of *man* 14 reduces the number of syllables in that line to eleven, as in 9, 11, 12, and removes the elision of *royall man*, whereby *royall* is taken as monosyllabic, to give a smoother alliterative phrase, *royall of ryches*, which may be preferred. *lordinges* 9 H suggests a determination to ensure the required disyllabic form here; as scanned above, *lordes* is taken as disyllabic.

17–20   Pilate was appointed by Tiberius, emperor at the time of Jesus' death — compare 250. But Tiberius did not deliver Jesus to Pilate, and some corruption in the text must be suspected here. Possibly *he* 19 should read *they*, referring forward, like *the* 21, to *the Jewes* 22, in which case 17–8 would be a single sentence, indicating the source of Pilate's authority, and 19–22 a further sentence, referring to the demands of the Jews. A pronoun-change at 19 is readily intelligible since *they* would have no antecedent; *he* was evidently the exemplar-form.

The recapitulation of events from 16 may suggest a need to remind the audience of events from the second day of performance, since the play of the Resurrection was normally the first play of the third day.

22   *piteous* BH produces a more regular sequence of strongly and weakly stressed syllables than *great* HmAR, but may have been felt to have inappropriate connotations for application to the Jews.

25–40   Based on Nicodemus 11/2: *Centurio autem retulit praesidi quae facta sunt. Audiens autem praeses et mulier eius, contristati sunt valde, et non manducaverunt neque*

PLAY XVIII

biberunt in die illa. Convocans autem Pilatus Iudaeos dixit eis: 'Vidistis quae facta sunt?'
But there is no suggestion that Pilate himself saw the marvels, 25-6, or was present at the end of the crucifixion, 35-6 — on the latter, compare 16A/428-31. On the marvels attending Jesus' death, see 16A/408-*Finis*, 464, 468-9 and notes; as there indicated, the reference to the resurrected saints is out of sequence.

29-32 Compare Nicodemus 17/6 on the reactions of the five men sent to investigate the crowd of about 12,000 resurrected saints on Mount Amalech; Latin B (James trans): "And though the men recognised many in that place, they were not able to speak a word unto them because of their fear, and the vision of angels.... Then they that had been sent were amazed and fell down upon the earth for fear", a passage not in Latin A or Greek.

32 *agryse*, "shudder with terror", is recorded by OED to 1598 (and to 1613 in the sense "to be horrified"). *agrie* B may be a scribal error or indicate that B did not understand the form. A rephrases the line, with consequent destruction of rhyme.

39 Matthew 27/51-3 does not include thunder and lightning among the marvels attending Jesus' death.

41-9, stanza 6 The stanza contains nine lines instead of the expected eight, having an extra a-rhyme line in the first quatrain. No line in the stanza can be omitted; it is, however tempting to speculate that the stanza may have lacked 42 and been totally ascribed to Pilate, with 41 as a statement. The change to the present text would then occur when 41 was considered to be a question, requiring a questioner and a response. See 42 note.

41 *yesterdaye about noone* The interview with the priests here takes place on the Saturday following Good Friday and the watch is set immediately afterwards. Matthew 27/62 confirms that the chief priests and Pharisees came to Pilate to request a watch on the day after the preparation for the Passover, as Nicodemus 13/1 notes, although Nicodemus 11/2 gives no indication of the time of the discussion here recorded. See further, Comestor, *Historia Scholastica*, 'In Evangelia' 182 (PL 198/1635). On the time of day of the portents, see 16A/216 note and compare *afternoone* 52.

Ludus Coventriae 34 follows Matthew, but Wakefield 26 and York 38 follow the suggestion of Nicodemus in making the setting of the watch a response to the centurion's testimony to Pilate.

42 *this ys one* It is not clear what this phrase means. Although some meaning such as "this is the very same" is appropriate (compare modern "that's the one"), such a usage does not seem to be recorded. See also 41-9 stanza 6 note.

45 Compare Matthew 27/60, echoed by Mark 15/46, Luke 23/53: *Quod exciderat in petra* (AV "Which he had hewn out in the rock").

50-7 The reply has no biblical or apocryphal warrant.

58-66 Without biblical counterpart. Compare 102-3, where Pilate states the reason attributed to the Jews in Matthew 27/63. In Matthew 27/64 the priests go on to express the fear — echoed here in 64 — that the disciples may steal Jesus' body away, as also in Nicodemus 13/1. In Cornish Ordinalia, where the priests have no part in this episode, the suggestion for the watch comes from the soldiers.

76–7 Matthew 27/65–6 and Nicodemus 13/1 indicates that Pilate merely gave the Jews permission to secure the sepulchre and set the watch, rather than that he supplied and commissioned a guard himself, as Comestor, *Historia Scholastica*, 'In Evangelia' 182 (PL 198/1635) indicates. But Pilate similarly commissions the guard himself in Wakefield 26/184–201, York 38, *Ludus Coventriae* 34–5/1200–15 and *Northern Passion* 3273–8.

77–80 The lines have, as Deimling notes, been erroneously omitted by A. Deimling suggests that, since the passage contains the names of the knights, it might sometimes have been appropriate to change the names, thus implying some doubt about the status of the lines. But it is simpler to explain A's omission as an eye-slip which confused *anonne* in 77 and 81. R corrects the error.

79–80 The subsequent development of the play, as well as the use of the title *syr* here, indicates that there are only three knights in the watch at Chester; *syr Jeragas Aroysiat* must be a single name. H's omission of *syr* 79 may suggest that H envisages four knights, which seems to have been the usual arrangement. Compare *Northern Passion* 3279: "Þan þai ordaind knyghts foure" and *Southern Passion* 1715: "Pilatus het þat body to wytie ·ffoure kniȝtes þer wende". Wakefield, York, *Ludus Coventriae* and Cornish Ordinalia have four soldiers.

We have found no obvious origins for the names of the knights. In *Ludus Coventriae* 34–5/1199–1203 the knights are named as *ser Amorawnt, ser Arphixat, ser Cosdram* and *ser Affraunt*.

82–105, stanza 11–3 The problems of rhyme in these stanzas may be considered together.

stanza 11 *short* 84 gives imperfect but acceptable a-rhyme. The b-rhymes, *donne* 85 — *stand* 89, do not rhyme; Deimling comments: "The tradition is bad in this place: 82–85 is a single half-stanza, *done* of which finds nowhere a corresponding rhyme." A slightly closer correspondence would result from reading *stond* 89.

stanza 12 The b-rhymes, *found* 93 — *lacke* 97, do not rhyme; possibly *lacke* is a replacement for some form such as *wand/wond*. *wond* 94 H is to be preferred for rhyme and meaning; *wend* Hm may be a replacement, suggesting "And [we swear] that we will not go away because of any fear", or it may be a simple error resulting from the confusion of *o* and *e*; *wonne* AR and *wounde* B are apparently replacements, inappropriate for rhyme and meaning, based on *wond*, although AR could represent an error, confusion of *e* and *d*.

stanza 13 H's a-rhymes, *draw—law—awe*, are to be preferred for meaning to HmARB's *drawes—lawes—awes*. A past-participle form *drawes* 98 is not possible; reference to the Jewish law is elsewhere singular, unlike 99; and there seems no justification for the plural form *awes* 100. H presumably rectifies an exemplar error which could arise after one *-s* form was introduced into the series. The b-rhymes, *spake* 101 — *tatch* 105, do not rhyme; acceptable rhyme would result from adopting *tack* at 105 — OED sb.IV, "as a quality. Hold; holding quality, adherence, endurance, stability, strength, substance, solidity", recorded from late ME and surviving also in dialect. The formal change here suggests *touch* — OED sb. III, *fig* 6 "a distinguishing quality, characteristic, trait", recorded only from 1539.

It is notable that *stand/stond* 89 would provide an acceptable rhyme for *fand/fond* 93, and that *lacke* 97 would provide an acceptable rhyme for *spake* 101. Possibly the origins of the b-rhyme problems in these stanzas lie in a pre-exemplar uncertainty about stanza-division.

99 *your* After *you* 96, 97, the reference would logically be to the soldiers, but they are Pilate's own guard. It is unlikely that the guard is to be considered Jewish, in view of 238, where the first soldier distinguishes himself and his fellows from *they Jewes*. *our* B is syntactically and semantically preferable; but possibly Pilate should be thought of as turning to the priests at this point. Compare 110 note.

102-3 Compare 58-66 note.

106 *he* BH is to be preferred for syntax and meaning to *him* (2) HmAR, the latter evidently arising from confusion with *him*(1) and with *him* 107.

107 Although *maye* ARBH is well attested, its inclusion produces a less regular sequence of strongly and weakly stressed syllables than its omission by Hm, and the word is syntactically redundant. B adds a further syllable, *yf*, suggesting a misunderstanding of *and* and further impairing the metre. H rephrases the line, but its replacement of *awarre* by *warr* is metrically detrimental to the line; H suggests dissatisfaction with the exemplar form, which may imply that Hm independently "emended" an unsatisfactory line which originally contained *maye*.

110 *ere* ARH is to be preferred for meaning to *yerre* Hm ("yore"?) and the replacement *her* B.

Apart from the centurion, the tormentors in 16-16A are termed *Judeus* and there is no evidence of other Roman soldiers in attendance. Possibly the soldiers are to be understood as silent bystanders with the centurion; but some confusion exists throughout the play — see 99 note, 124-9 note.

114 *hardelie* BH may be preferred to *hardlye* HmAR in producing a more regular sequence of strongly and weakly stressed syllables.

124-9 126 is not appropriate to Pilate, who was a Roman and fiercely denied any Jewish connexion in 16/257-8. H attempts to resolve the difficulty by removing the connective *and* 125 and assigning 125-9 to Caiaphas, so that Pilate supplies the guards, but the Jews commission them. But although H is the only manuscript to attempt to resolve the difficulty, its solution is not wholly satisfactory. *prynce* 131 is not appropriate to Caiaphas but only to Pilate, and echoes 14; it also seems inappropriate that soldiers under Pilate should be threatened with death by the Jews, who had no such authority. The simplest solution in the present text is to read *Roman trewe* for *trewe Jewe* 126, which not only restores meaning but also improves metre. But possibly something has been lost between 125 and 126, allowing for the completion of Pilate's instructions to the soldiers and the start of a final warning by Caiaphas; it may be noted that despite the request at 123, the soldiers are never told exactly what they must do.

128-9 Pilate similarly threatens the soldiers with death at Wakefield 23/200-1, York 38/173-4, and *Northern Passion*, 3275-8. Only *Ludus Coventriae* 34-5/1260-74 shows the sealing of the tomb by Pilate and the priests.

132–3 "Disregarding any prophecy or any other deed". *withowt* 132 is here taken as an extension of *without* OED 10c, "with no possibility of". *encharre* 133 is not in OED and is recorded by MED only from this occurrence, from which a sense "magic, miracle" is deduced; here *chare* OED sb¹, 4 "a turn or stroke of work; an action, deed; a piece of work or business" has been substituted from R and R's preposition disregarded. 133 is metrically improved by the omission of the syllable. *en-* or *in* clearly corresponded to an exemplar form, but A and B did not understand the word(s), or could not read it, and their substitution destroy rhyme.

138–45, stanza 18 No manuscript has *fand* for *found* 144, required for perfect rhyme.

150–1 The four soldiers were usually disposed on all sides — compare Wakefield 26/210, York 38/183, *Ludus Coventriae* 34–5 where they stand at feet, head, and left and right sides, and Cornish Ordinalia. Here Jesus evidently stood on the first soldier 274–7, who was in the middle, as he rose — see 153+SD.

152–3 R omits two lines between the bottom of fol.149ʳ and the top of fol.149ᵛ, evidently forgetting in the transition that stanza 19 was incomplete.

153+SD Two angels are mentioned by Luke 24/4, John 20/12; Matthew 28/2 and Mark 16/5 mention only one. The angels similarly sing *Christus resurgens* in Cornish Ordinalia. The text echoes Romans 6/4 and especially 1 Corinthians 15/20–1: *Nunc autem Christus resurrexit a mortuis, primitiae dormientium; quoniam quidem per hominem mors, et per hominem resurrectio mortuorum* (AV "But now is Christ risen from the dead, and become the first-fruits of them that slept. For since by man came death, by man came also the resurrection of the dead").

Only the first soldier mentions Jesus treading on him, 274–5.

154–85 Compare the resurrection address in Wakefield 26/226–333. York has no corresponding passage, and in *Ludus Coventriae* 34–5/1416–31 Jesus rehearses what he has achieved. Here the speech stresses the Harrowing of Hell as a symbolic act of the redemption available to all. It urges repentance, 164–6, as a preliminary to spiritual contentment, 167, and to the eucharistic bread, the token of and preserver of that contentment. Jesus promises eternal life to those who receive the consecrated bread in a state of spiritual grace, 172–3, but eternal damnation to those who receive it without repentance and spiritual grace, 178–85. The eucharistic passage is paralleled in Wakefield 26/322–33. But Wakefield emphasises the act of consecration, whereby the words of the priest effect transubstantiation, and that section of the speech has been excised in the manuscript, presumably a post-Reformation censorship. In Chester the equivalent lines, 176–7, are difficult and perhaps wilfully obscure; they appear to suggest that an act of faith on the part of the recipient effects transubstantiation, a view partially but not wholly fulfilling Roman Catholic and Anglican criteria. While *your beleeffe* is sufficiently vague to imply the faith of the Catholic Church, it can also accommodate the sentiments of the 1549 Prayer Book at the administration of the sacrament: "The body of our Lord Jesus Christ, which was given for thee, preserve thy body and soul unto everlasting life." It is difficult to know what weight to put upon the fact that reference is made to communion in one kind only, a practice proscribed by the Articles of Faith of the Church of England.

PLAY XVIII   283

The warning of the need for a proper spiritual condition in which to receive the Eucharist is standard doctrine in Roman Catholic and Anglican Churches; compare the 1549 Prayer Book, Exhortation in the Order of Communion: "For as the benefit is great, if with a truly penitent heart and lively faith, we receive that holy Sacrament; (for then we spiritually eat the flesh of Christ and drink his blood, then we dwell in Christ and Christ in us, we be made one with Christ, and Christ with us); so is the danger great, if we receive the same unworthily; for then we become guilty of the body and blood of Christ our Saviour, we eat and drink our own damnation, not considering the Lord's body." The exhortation in the Book of Common Prayer warns: "Lest after the taking of that holy Sacrament, the devil enter into you, as he entered into Judas, and fill you full of all iniquities, and bring you to destruction both of body and soul", a point made when Judas receives the sop in *Ludus Coventriae* 27/772-98 but not possible in Chester's order of events in play 15.

With *prynce of peace* 162, compare *princeps pacis*, Isaiah 9/6; with *verey bread of liffe* 170, compare John 6/35: *Dixit autem eis Iesus: Ego sum panis vitae; qui venit ad me non esuriet, et qui credit in me non sitiet unquam* (AV "And Jesus said unto them, I am the bread of life: he that cometh to me shall never hunger; and he that believeth on me shall never thirst"), and John 6/48.

154-85, stanzas 20-23   The stanzas are of eight lines each, rhyming abababab and of alternate four and three strong stresses. The effect is formally to isolate Jesus' address, perhaps rhetorically.

In stanza 22, no manuscript has the form *bend*, MED "fetter, shackle, chain" for *band* 177, required for perfect rhyme; 177 contains four strongly stressed syllables instead of the expected three — a regular line would result from the omission of *synfull*.

185 contains four strongly stressed syllables instead of the expected three — a regular line would result from the omission of *payne and*.

182-5   182-3 are obscure; possibly they mean "[In this case] the aforesaid bread must be regarded as being in place of the joy [which] is ever fully abundant"; or, adopting *their* 183 ARBH, "there, where", "The which shall be regarded only as bread in the place where joy is ever fully abundant." In either case, the basic idea is that the bread lacks the properties which it possesses when correctly received, 174-7, as 184-5 makes clear. *through fooles read* 184 seems to suggest that there are those who do not hold such belief.

185 + SD   Compare 214, 341-2, and John 20/12, of Mary Magdalen: *Vidit duos angelos in albis sedentes, unum ad caput et unum ad pedes, ubi positum fuerat corpus Iesu* (AV "Seeth two angels in white sitting, the one at the head, and the other at the feet, where the body of Jesus had lain"). The brightness, 214, seems to derive from Luke 24/4: *Ecce duo viri stetcrunt secus illas in veste fulgenti* (AV "Two men stood by them in shining garments"), although Luke does not suggest that they were at that time inside the tomb. The reference to children, 341-2, may reflect Mark 16/5: *Viderunt iuuenem sedentem in dextris, coopertum stola candida* (AV "They saw a young man sitting on the right side, clothed in a long white garment") — compare York 38/225, "a 3onge child". In Matthew 28/2-7, where the coming of the angel is attended by an earthquake, the angel of the Lord sits on the stone which he has rolled away and addresses the Maries while the guards swoon, as also in Nicodemus 13/1, where the guards hear the angel speak to the Maries, and describe the angel's appearance: *Adspectus eius sicut fulgur et vestimenta sicut nix*. Only in Chester does the flight of the guards follow the resurrection immediately; in Wakefield 26 and York 38 the visit of the Maries occurs before the guards recover, while in *Ludus Coventriae* 35 and Cornish Ordinalia Christ meets his mother before they awake.

186-241 The reactions of the guards dramatise Matthew 28/4: *Prae timore autem eius exterriti sunt custodes, et facti sunt velut mortui* (AV "And for fear of him the keepers did shake and became as dead men"), reflected also in Nicodemus 13/1. But both passages refer to the guards' reaction to the angel and there is no suggestion that they are aware of Jesus himself leaving the tomb.

The arrangement of material in H, whereby 201+SH-9 follows 217, is to be preferred to that in HmARB. It restores the regular "Primus—Secundus—Tertius" sequence of speakers. It sets 210-7 after 201+SD, to which it relates — the first soldier is already awake and the SD is therefore not applicable to him. And it groups together all the expressions of terror and immobility (186-201, 210-7) and, in a second series, all the witnesses of the soldiers of Jesus' divinity (202-9, 218-33). While the source of the error in HmARB will always be a matter for speculation, some clue may lie in the note to the left of 212-5 B, which may reflect a margin note in the exemplar, and suggests some problems about the speaker. It apparently implies that two verses are to be ascribed to the third soldier; since no manuscript contains an eight-line stanza division, the two "verses" possibly indicate two quatrains, presumably stanza 27. *com in at the right hand* may be a SD; but alternatively it may imply that stanza 27 had been misplaced and the note was to correct the misplacement. B would give substance to a suspicion that the exemplar contained an emendation at this point which was not understood by HmARB but was correctly interpreted — perhaps from first principles — by H.

194 The line contains four strongly stressed syllables instead of the expected three.

218-25, stanza 28 The b-rhymes, *stonne* 221 — *agayne* 225, do not rhyme. 225 H restores perfect b-rhyme and is to be preferred to HmARB. The wording at 225 may be influenced by the words of the priests to Pilate, Matthew 27/63: *Domine, recordati sumus quia seductor ille dixit adhuc vivens: Post tres dies resurgam* (AV "Sir, we remember that that deceiver said, while he was yet alive, After three days I will rise again"). Deimling cites 225 as evidence of H's superiority.

230 The third soldier says that he will go to Caiaphas, but the first says they will go to Pilate, 235, before whom they all meet, 241+SD. As soldiers commissioned by Pilate, they should presumably report to him; but in Matthew 28/11, Nicodemus 13/1, where they are apparently the servants of the priests, they report only to the chief priests and the Sanhedrin. Possibly the third soldier is here thought of as summoning the priests to meet Pilate, so that the priests may perhaps enter only at 282 and in any case may be considered to have debated and decided on a course of action to recommend to Pilate before they meet him. Since the events are on the day after the meeting with which the play opens, there is no reason why the priests should be with Pilate unless specifically summoned. In *Ludus Coventriae* 35/1578-9 Pilate does summon the priests, but in Wakefield and York the priests are inexplicably present when the soldiers report.

234 *we* The indirect object, *us*, might be expected, but *we* was evidently the exemplar form the nominative perhaps being used because of the position of the pronoun at the start of the sentence. Its relationship to the infinitive (cf. Mustanoja, pp. 541–2, 'Absolute Infinitive') may also have influenced the form RBH supply a subject, *it*, for the impersonal verb. AR have subjunctive for indicative.

236–40 Compare Matthew 27/64: *Et erit novissimus error peior priore* (AV "So the last error shall be worse than the first"). But in Matthew the words express the priests' fear that the disciples will remove Jesus' body and proclaim his resurrection; the error of his teachings will be surpassed by the error of his supposed resurrection. Here that sense is impossible, but the effect is rather the ironic reverse of Matthew, that the Jews will compound the error of the crucifixion, whose portents they have ignored, by falsifying the truth of the resurrection.

the 238 ARBH is to be preferred to the erroneous *they* Hm. The rhyme *wist* 237 — *firste* 241 is imperfect but seems acceptable.

241 + SH Since *Primus Miles* received the commission and set the watch, it seems strange that, as leader, he does not make the initial report to Pilate.

250–7, stanza 32 In HmRB, the stanza contains eight lines, 250 with five stresses and 251 and 252 each with two, rhyming abcdeeed. A combines 251–2 as a single line, producing a seven-line stanza. But H's version is to be preferred in restoring the regular rhyme-scheme, aaabcccb, with regular metre — excluding the overlengthy 250. If H reflects the exemplar, the last 13 letters of 251 and 252 were apparently illegible to the other scribes; since HmRB has two "half-lines" at this point, it would seem that they reflect the exemplar layout and that A has independently combined the two halves. But there is no obvious explanation for the loss in the Group.

250 may be reduced to four main stresses by omitting *syr* as in ARH and also omitting *nowe*, found in all manuscripts and hence in the exemplar.

253 "If the responsibility belongs to you"; compare *longen* MED v (3), 4(a). R prefers the equally appropriate *bilongen*, MED v,2; B evidently did not understand the line.

254–7 See 286–304 note.

258–65, stanza 33 No manuscript has the form *swow*, OED 1 "a swoon", 2 "a state of sleep, a trance", for *swoone* 264, required for rhyme. In sense 1, *swow* is last exemplified in c.1460, and in sense 2 in 1513. *swoone* evidently represents the exemplar reading.

259 The time is presumably taken from Matthew 28/1: *Vespere autem sabbati, quae lucescit in prima sabbati* (AV " In the end of the sabbath, as it began to dawn toward the first day of the week"). But Matthew gives this as the time of the visit of the Maries and the removal of the stone at the entrance to the tomb, when the guards swooned. Here, the guards swooned when Christ arose. But the time of resurrection may have been earlier — see Comestor, *Historia Scholastica*, 'In Evangelia' 185 (*PL* 198/1636–8), '*Opiniones de hora resurrectionis*,' and Nicodemus 13/1: *Dicunt Iudaei: Qua hora fuit? Dicunt custodes: Media nocte*. That Chester was not alone in its inference, compare *Southern Passion* 1719–20:

      In þe daweny[n]ge þe soneday ·as þe day gan springe
      As me wakeþ oure lord aros.

266–9, stanza 34   The stanza is a quatrain of irregular metre, rhyming abab. Its language is uncharacteristic of Pilate's manner elsewhere in the cycle. Compare 278–81, and 278–85, stanzas 36 and 37 note.

278–85, stanzas 36 and 37   Stanza 36 is a quatrain of irregular metre, rhyming abab; its expression is uncharacteristic of Pilate's manner elsewhere in the cycle but may be compared with 266–9. Stanza 37 is a Chester quatrain. Pilate may have originally uttered a single-stanza response at 278, and at a later stage it was decided to introduce separate responses to the soldiers' speeches; hence 266–9 was introduced, and the opening quatrain of Pilate's speech at 278 changed to give a parallel to his earlier reaction.

281   *on the rogge*   This is one of only two examples of *rog* sb cited by OED, which gives the meaning as "obscure" and indicates that the two words may not be the same; indeed, editors of the *Alliterative Morte Arthur*, which contains the other example, have tended to emend to *roo*. We cannot positively identify the word. Possibly it is an unrecorded variant of *ridge*, "back"; compare the recorded *rug*. But one would then expect the possessive pronoun *thy* — compare *upon my backe* 274. Alternatively, it may be a short vowel form of *rogue*, as perhaps indicated by the forms *rog, rogge* of fifteenth–seventeenth centuries (see *rogue* OED), in which case *thee* H is formally preferable to *the* HmARB and a comma should be supplied after *the* — "And let that villain so walk upon you, rogue."

286–308 + SD   The spoken text indicates that Pilate appeals to the loyalty of the soldiers to keep the matter quiet until a full inquiry can be held, an action wholly consistent with the earlier image of Pilate; he acts diplomatically, but is not thereby involved in a conspiracy with the Jews to conceal the truth indefinitely. Even 301–4 is ambiguous, perhaps allowing the view that the woe is for the miscarriage of justice evidenced by the resurrection. But the SD suggests that the soldiers are bribed, as they are bribed by the priests in Matthew 28/12, Nicodemus 13/3, where they are urged to spread the rumour abroad that the disciples stole Jesus' body, as the soldiers in Wakefield, York and *Ludus Coventriae* are bribed to do (in Cornish Ordinalia, where the priests have no part in this action, Pilate alone decides to buy the soldiers' silence). In both Matthew and Nicodemus, the priests assure the guards that they will protect them should the governor hear of the matter, perhaps implying some inquiry on Pilate's part. The only possible echo here is Pilate's assumption, 254–7, that the soldiers may have made a compact with the disciples for personal gain, a point on which he seems eventually satisfied. The only explanation of the resurrection offered is *witchcrafte* 297.

294–300, stanza 39   The stanza consists of seven lines, rhyming aaabccc. The rhymes at 297–300 are somewhat imperfect, and ARBH unnecessarily extend the line by adding *hereafter*, producing five strong stresses instead of the expected four. All other lines, except the three-stress 297, have four stresses. Possibly a line has been lost after 300.

298   *our counsell*   In Matthew 28/11–2, on hearing the soldiers' report, the priests call a council at which the soldiers are bribed. If 308 + SD is disregarded, this may be the reference of the line. 307 distinguishes the Jewish council from the Roman governor (*wee*); *our* 307 is less appropriate, but may simply suggest a body under the office of governor.

308 The H version suggests an inquiry simply into how the escape was contrived, perhaps with the implication still of conspiracy.

308 + SD The Maries here are named in Mark 16/1. Matthew 28/1 mentions Mary Magdalen and the other Mary; Luke 24/10 Mary Magdalen, Joanna, Mary the mother of James, and other women; John 20/1 Mary Magdalen alone. See also 185 + SD note.

309–32 The introductory laments are unbiblical, but seem to derive from the Latin planctus of the liturgical Resurrection plays, and from the corresponding tradition in vernacular lyric. Compare Wakefield 26/333–57, York 38/187–220, Cornish Ordinalia pp.197–200.

316 *luxonne* OED does not record the word, and MED exemplifies it only from Chester. All manuscripts attest the *-nn-* form here, but in other instances (see English word-list) only Hm has an *n*-form, the other manuscripts having *m*; it is therefore possible that *-nn-* here represents an exemplar error for *m*. The forms might represent *lovesome*, perhaps as a semi-phonetic spelling, or by a sequence of error — *lufsome—lussome—luxome*, whereby *f* has been confused with long *s* and the whole subsequently remodelled on analogy with words such as *buxom*.

325 *all* ARBH is to be preferred to the Hm omission in producing a more regular sequence of strongly and weakly stressed syllables.

331–2 The women are said to bring spices in Mark 16/1, Luke 24/1, but only Mark specifies that they are to anoint the body of Jesus. The restriction of the spices here to Mary Salome may reflect the fact that Mark mentions her last in the list of women before proceeding to mention the spices.

333–6 Compare Mark 16/3: *Quis revolvet nobis lapidem ab ostio monumenti?* (AV "Who shall roll us away the stone from the door of the sepulchre?"). There is no suggestion, as in 333–4, that one of the women should do it; but compare Wakefield 26/368–9:

> And which shall of vs systers thre
> remefe the stone?

and York 38/221–2:

> And who schall nowe here of vs thre
> remove þe stone?

this 334 seems inappropriate. If the stone is visible, it would be evident that it did not block the entrance, as is noted at 339–40. *the* would be preferable for meaning and as a reflection of the biblical text, although *this* was evidently the exemplar reading.

335 seems to suggest that the stone lies above Jesus — *upon* 335. Similar suggestions are to be found in the other cycles — compare *Ludus Coventriae* 36/157–8:

> A ston ful hevy lay hym up on
> Ffrom vndyr þat ston how xulde he breke

and Cornish Ordinalia p.190: "I've checked on the tomb. There's a big stone on top of it" and, after the resurrection (p.193), "As of now I see the big stone sitting mighty high on the edge of the tomb." *Southern Passion* 1795–6 states: "[oure lordes aungel] ouer-turnde þe ston þat was þe lyd", but at 1819–26 it seems rather to suggest the kind of tomb described by Comestor, *Historia Scholastica*, 'In Evangelia' 181 (PL 198/1634): *De monumento Domini dicit Beda super Marcum, quod domus fuit rotunda de subjacente rupe excisa tantae altitudinis, ut vix homo manu extenta culmen posset attingere, introitum habens ab oriente, cui magnus lapis appositus erat pro ostio* etc. Probably Chester envisages a table-tomb or tomb-chest cut down into the rock, as shown in some illustrations of the resurrection — see M. D. Anderson, *History and Imagery in British Churches* (London, 1971), pp. 123-4, who suggests influence from the Easter sepulchre in churches. Hence four soldiers are used in most cycles, one to guard each side. In Chester, where only three sides were guarded, the lid of such a tomb-chest would slide back to the unguarded side and Jesus would climb out on the opposite side, treading on the first soldier who was stationed there. See also 13/332 + SD note.

339   Compare 341 and 153 + SD note. Here, as in Augustine, *Harmony* 3/24 (PL 34/1199-1200), the accounts of Matthew, who refers to an angel sitting outside on the stone, and of Mark, who refers to an angel sitting inside the sepulchre on the right-hand side, seem to have been conflated.

341-4, stanza 45   The stanza is a regular Chester quatrain. It may be noted that each Mary speaks four lines, and also that the b-rhyme of this stanza is also that of stanza 46. There is no evidence of omitted lines from the gospel texts.

345-68   The angels' instructions derive from Matthew 28/6-7, Mark 16/6-7, although in each case they are given by one angel. But 345-6 has no biblical counterpart, perhaps rather recalling the liturgical *Quem Quaeritis*. The specific injunction to tell Peter is found only in Mark 16/7. No gospel specifies the women's consent to this request — in Mark they are terrified and leave quickly, saying nothing, and in Matthew they go in fear and great joy. Luke 24/9, however, presents them talking to the apostles, whereupon Peter visits the tomb; and in John 20/2 Mary Magdalen goes directly to the disciples.

346   *and with* RH represents an unusual agreement of the two manuscripts; the additional syllable, however, impairs metre and may represent independent repetitions of *with* in the two manuscripts.

353   A more regular sequence of strongly and weakly stressed syllables results by the reduction of the line by one syllable as in AR and H.

360   "That you may find him [Jesus] there [in Galilee]"; compare Mark 16/7: *Sed ite, dicite discipulis eius et Petro, quia praecedit vos in Galilaeam; ibi eum videbitis, sicut dixit vobis* (AV "But go your way, tell his disciples and Peter that he goeth before you into Galilee; there shall ye see him, as he said unto you"). No such specific reference occurs in Wakefield 26/398-9, York 38/251-2; but it does occur in *Ludus Coventriae* 36/72-3, Cornish *Ordinalia* p.203 (by Jesus to Mary Magdalen), and the Digby *Mary Magdalen* 1026.

Despite the injunction and Mary's comment here, the message is not in fact delivered to Peter, 369-76. He is therefore left in ignorance of Jesus' resurrection and of the angel's specific reference to him, and it seems almost coincidental that he is found, goes to the tomb and realises the truth. See further 401-20 note.

365   *suster* i.e. Mary Magdalen, who is thus separated from the other two women and, after her meeting with Peter and John, left in isolation. *obvient* 368 + SD, in all manuscripts (though in erroneous form in B), seems inappropriate in the circumstances; possibly it is an error for a singular form on the analogy of the

PLAY XVIII 289

preceding plural verbs, with the subject, *Maria Magdalena*, supplied by a continuation such as is found in the A SD.

369–96 The race to the tomb is described in John 20/2–8; Luke 24/12 briefly mentions a visit by Peter alone.

Augustine, *Harmony*, 3/24 (PL 34/1201–3) suggested that Mary Magdalen went to the tomb with the other women, but on seeing the stone removed, went immediately to the disciples without further investigation, hence her misunderstanding. But here no such explanation for her confusion is possible, and the conflict between the message given by the angels, which Mary seems to understand at 361–4, and her words at 371–2 seems to rest only on the hint of uncertainty at 364. Comestor, *Historia Scholastica*, 'In Evangelia' 187 (PL 198/1638) ascribes Mary's confusion to emotional intensity or distress. No attempt is made to remove the contradiction in *Ludus Coventriae* 36–7, where at 36/95–102 Mary announces Jesus' resurrection but is seen lamenting at 371–8. Similar contradictions occur in liturgical plays. In Cornish Ordinalia pp.201–2 Mary will not leave the tomb until she sees Jesus. The contradiction is also ignored in *Southern Passion*.

Johanni 368 + SD is described as *alium discipulum quem amabat Iesus* (AV "the other disciple, whom Jesus loved") in John 20/2.

385–96 According to John 20/5–8, John did not enter the sepulchre but looked in and saw the linen clothes; but Peter entered and saw that the napkin that had been round Jesus' head was wrapped up and separate from the other clothes. Peter's discovery is here attributed to John, and no reference is made to any observation by Peter about the clothes. The address at 385 and the fact that the second speaker enters the tomb, as Peter did, indicates that the two speeches must be correctly attributed to the speakers. Possibly the tomb is to be thought of as so disposed that John cannot naturalistically look in without seeing the clothes; or the *sudarye* was left outside the tomb by Jesus. Either thesis would tend to support the use of a table tomb, as would the fact that John is convinced without entering the tomb, whereas in John 20/8 he follows Peter in. The display of the grave clothes was a feature of liturgical plays of the Resurrection.

391–2 On the disbelief of all the disciples at the news of Jesus' resurrection, see Mark 16/11, Luke 24/11. The need for concrete proof here reflects a general tendency in the cycle, and anticipates particularly the doubt of Thomas in play 19, a comparison drawn by Bede, *In Marci Evangelium Expositio* 4/16 (PL 92/298).

397–400 The lines directly contradict John 20/9: *Nondum enim sciebant Scripturam, quia oportebat eum a mortuis resurgere* (AV "For as yet they knew not the scripture, that he must rise again from the dead"), and Peter's bewilderment at Luke 24/12: *Secum mirans quod factum fuerat* (AV "Wondering in himself at that which was come to pass") which Bede, *In S Jounnis Evangelium Expositio* 20 (PL 92/918) interprets: *Vidit scilicet inane monumentum, et credidit quod dixerat mulier, eum de monumento esse sublatum*, as also Augustine, *In Johannis Evangelium*, Tractatus 120 (PL 35/1955). A distinction seems here implied between John's belief in Mary's words and Peter's recall of Jesus' promise. John and Peter similarly attest Jesus' resurrection in *Ludus Coventriae* 36/135–50, although later, 159–66, Peter seems to have doubts; in the Digby *Mary Magdalen* 1051–4 John recalls the prophecy of the resurrection at this point. See 401–20 note.

401-20   Compare 16/379-94 and notes, and Digby *Mary Magdalen* 1043-6. Expressions of remorse by Peter occur also at Wakefield 28/65-79 and in Cornish *Ordinalia* p.209, where they precede the appearance of Jesus to the eleven. The meeting of Peter and Jesus is shown in the continuation of the play, Appendix ID/72-95.

Peter's previous denials of Christ were held to be the reason for the specific reference to him by the angel at the tomb, 360 and note; see Bede, *In Marci Evangelium Expositio* 4/16 (PL 92/296), and also *Southern Passion* 1837-42. Since Peter is not given news of Jesus' resurrection by Mary Magdalen, let alone informed of the angel's specific reference, it is necessary for him to be convinced in order that his shame at meeting Jesus be dramatised, and John provides here the defence against despair which the angel's reference was held to provide.

Peter's exemplary remorse is treated at length by Ambrose, *Expositio in Lucam* 10 (PL 15/1918-20). With 409-12, compare especially Ambrose 93 (PL 15/1920).

414   *accepted hase* ARBH is to be preferred for meaning and metre to *hase* Hm.

417-20   John 20/10 says the the two disciples then went back to their own home. There is no attempt to seek out Jesus.

417-24, stanzas 55 and 56   The two stanzas consist of two Chester quatrains. *might* 419 does not rhyme; possibly it is an error for the semantically more appropriate *mercy*, although it was apparently the exemplar form and is attested by all manuscripts. Although the two stanzas have the same a-rhyme, there is not the usual Chester link through the b-rhyme, and no alternative rhyme-words are immediately obvious.

420+SD   The play continues with John 20/11-3, which deals only with Mary Magdalen; but possibly the dramatist envisaged the return of all the women at this point, with Mary Magdalen outside the tomb and the others some distance away at first. Such an arrangement seems confirmed by ID/23+SD, which indicates a regrouping after the appearance of Jesus to Mary Magdalen.

424   *sitt* Contrast John 20/11: *Maria autem stabat* (AV "But Mary stood without"). Compare 13/325-6; the detail may be a further point in support of the idea of the sepulchre as tomb-chest.

424+SH–*Finis*   B ends abruptly with the angel's words, while HmA end equally abruptly at 432 and RH continue through Appendix ID.

Deimling cites the ending of the play as evidence that R is not a mere copy of A; he proposes the longest version of the play as original, and draws attention to the additional blank page at the end of the play in B, more than is required for the seven lines by which A is longer than B, for which in any case space remains in B fol.134. B, which omits its *Finis* formula here also, probably has left space for the RH continuation. It is probable that ID was cancelled in the exemplar by a line across the offending passages, and the scribes of HmA and of B had different opinions about where the excision-line ended. A shortened version of the play might better end at 420, or, best of all, at 400, with Peter's affirmation of the resurrection, thereby avoiding the reference to the denial — questionably included at the end of 16 — and of the meeting with Jesus — which contains the explanation, ID/80-95 (see note).

PLAY XVIII

The play could perhaps even have continued to ID/55. But it is clear that no acting version could have ended where HmA or B end.

425   In John 20/11, Mary, weeping, stooped, looked into the tomb and saw two angels who spoke to her. But here Peter and John would see any angels, and it must therefore be assumed that the angels depart after 360–8+SD and return; presumably they return after Mary has entered and sat down. *sonne* 426 reflects *children* 341 and note, and indicates that Mary does not recognise the angel as an angel.

428   The line inaccurately renders John 20/13: *Nescio ubi posuerunt eum* (AV "I know not where they have laid him") — compare 372. AR seek to incorporate this statement in 427 and may perhaps be preferred to HmBH here; for AR, 426–7 would represent a sentence and 428 a direct question.

431–2   The lines are slightly ambiguous — either "To see my lord who once lay here as I wished" or "Just once to see, as I desire, my lord who lay here".

PLAY XIX

Dramatis Personae Lucas, Cleophas, Jesus, Andreas, Petrus, Thomas.

Locations
a castell 99, castellum 111 + SD
in alio loco 143 + SD, castrum 167 + SD
Bethaniae 215 + SD, ad mansionem 239 + SD.

Properties
bread 117, 122, 130, panem 119 + SD; rosted fyshe and honye 194.

NOTE Reference is made to Jesus' wounds 180, 220–4, 243–7.

Costume
Jesus in habitu peregrino 32 + SD.

Sources
Emmaus — Mark 16/12, Luke 24/13–33
Appearance to Disciples — Mark 16/14–8, Luke 24/33–49, John 20/19–23
Thomas — John 20/24–9.

Play-heading
Emaus A village said to be threescore furlongs — about seven and a half miles — from Jerusalem, 24/13. But Eusebius and Jerome identified it with Nicopolis, twenty miles from Jerusalem; see *Glossa Ordinaria*, 'Evang. Lucae' 24/13 (PL 114/351) and Comestor, *Historia Scholastica*, 'In Evangelia' 191 (PL 198/1639). Some indication of this identity may underlie *morne* 115 H — see 112–9, stanza 15 note.

Two appearances by Jesus to his disciples in a closed room are described in the gospels — one on the day of his resurrection and the other on the day of his ascension; Chester seems to conflate the two — compare the treatment of the appearance on the day of resurrection here with that of the appearance on the day of ascension in play 20. Wakefield, York, *Ludus Coventriae* and Cornish *Ordinalia* distinguish the two appearances.

The events in this play are found in other cycles — Emmaus in Wakefield 27, York 40, *Ludus Coventriae* 38/1–240, Cornish

PLAY XIX   293

Ordinalia pp.211–14; appearance to disciples in Wakefield 28/1–167, York 42/1–96, Cornish Ordinalia pp.209–10; Thomas in Wakefield 28/168–355, York 42/97–198, *Ludus Coventriae* 38/241–392, Cornish Ordinalia pp.203–9, 214–20; Shrewsbury Fragment C.

Before 1 SH   Only Cleophas is identified by name in the gospel account, but the fact that the full description of the meeting is to be found in Luke suggests that the other, unnamed disciple is to be regarded as Luke; see, for example, Comestor, *Historia Scholastica*, 'In Evangelia' 191 (PL 198/1639). Despite the SH, the disciple is not identified for the audience; York and Cornish Ordinalia do not name the second disciple, but Wakefield and *Ludus Coventriae* similarly identify him with Luke.

2   Some verb such as *mourn* must be understood; the broken construction, *my owne my mayster* may indicate textual corruption whereby a verb has been obscured.

6   *makes* does not give sense in context and may be an error (for *marres*?). AR and H attempt to supply a meaningful phrase, AR by supplying an infinitive, H by supplying an adjective.

7   ARBH omit *both*. It is possible that Hm included *both* from confusion with *both* 6; if so, the reading would support 6 HmB against 6 ARH.

8+SH   Cleophas, occasionally written Clopas, may be identified with the husband of the sister of the Virgin Mary, John 19/25, and hence with Alphaeus, father of James the Just, Matthew 10/3, Mark 3/18, Luke 6/15, Acts 1/6.

21–2   *that he* 21 ARBH is to be preferred for syntax to *that* Hm, supplying the subject required for *hasse*. An auxiliary, *is*, is required before the past participle *commen* 22; B replaces the past participle by a past (?) tense.

24   "And his death be profitable to us". *gayne* is the infinitive *geinen* MED, dependent upon *may* 23, and *to* is a preposition governing *us*. But H takes *gayne* as noun, regarding the HmARB phrase as *do gayne*, MED "to benefit". B seems not to understand the verb.

32+SD   *in habitu peregrino* Compare 38, and Wakefield 27/97+SD, *in apparatu peregrini*. Luke 24 does not specify Jesus' dress, but Mark 16/12 says that he appeared *in alia effigie* (AV "in another form"), i.e. different from his appearance to Mary Magdalen. *Glossa Ordinaria*, 'Evang. Lucae.' 24/15, 16 (PL 114/351) comments: *Apparuit quidem in specie propria, sed speciem quam recognoscerent, non ostendit*. The pilgrim-dress seems, however, to have been a feature of liturgical drama. Possibly Jesus appeared in the guise of the palmer in the distinctive garb of one who had visited Compostella, with script and staff and a large hat turned up at the front. In Cornish Ordinalia p.218, Thomas makes disparaging remarks about the reliability of palmers.

37–44   Compare Luke 24/18: *Tu solus peregrinus es in Ierusalem, et non cognovisti quae facta sunt in illa his diebus* (AV "Art thou only a stranger in Jerusalem, and hast not known the things which are come to pass there in these days?").

39   *tydinges* ARBH is to be preferred morphologically to *tydinge* Hm; B unnecessarily and inappropriately adds the common collocation *good*.

65–71, stanza 9   In HmARB the stanza contains seven lines instead of the expected eight, lacking a c-rhyme line. The second quatrain corresponds to Luke 24/24: *Et ita invenerunt sicut mulieres dixerunt; ipsum vero non invenerunt* (AV "And found it even so as the women had said; but him they saw not"). H supplies an additional c-rhyme line after 69; the first half of 69 H and the second half of 69 + 1 together constitute 69 HmARB, a fact which might suggest a clumsy cancellation or alteration in the exemplar leading to the combination of the two half-lines in the Group. But the lines are weak, especially the added line, and the correspondence to Luke 24/24 is not close. The final clause of Luke 24/24, which lacks counterpart here, would appropriately prompt the expression of doubt at 70–1, already suggested in 9–31; its omission here might result from the difficulty of reconciling it with the meetings described in Appendix ID.

67–8   See 18/305–400

72–9, stanza 10   No manuscript has the form *laye* for *lawe* 73, required for rhyme. *lawe*, which seems to have prompted *sawe* AR, was evidently the exemplar-reading.

76–9   A somewhat loose rendering of Luke 24/26: *Nonne haec oportuit pati Christum, et ita intrare in gloriam suam* (AV "Ought not Christ to have suffered these things, and to enter into his glory?").

80–95 + Latin   Luke cites no prophets, but says, 24/27: *Et incipiens a Moyse, et omnibus prophetis, interpretabatur illis in omnibus Scripturis, quae de ipso erant* (AV "And beginning at Moses and all the prophets he expounded unto them in all the scriptures the things concerning himself"). The episode of the burning bush, traditionally interpreted as a figure of the immaculate conception, 80–7, is taken from Exodus 3/2 ff; Isaiah's prophecy, 88–95, cited in its Vulgate from at 95 + Latin, is Isaiah 66/13, AV "As one whom his mother comforteth, so will I comfort you: and ye shall be comforted in Jerusalem" — see further Jerome, *Commentaria in Isaiam Prophetam* 18/66 (*PL* 24/687–8). See also 268–70 note.

82   *greave greve* MED n (1), can mean "bush", but has a number of wider senses — e.g. "thicket, copse, shrubbery, undergrowth"; OED records it only to 1612 in the senses of "brushwood, thicket". AR and B either fail to understand the word, or replace it to produce a "more appropriate" meaning.

94   *in better were* OED defines *were* sb[3] as "danger, peril" and "condition of trouble or distress".

better is inappropriate to such connotations and an exemplar-error for *bitter* may be suspected. H substitutes *if* for *in*, making *were* a verb; but the appropriateness of the resulting sentence is doubtful.

99   *a castell* Compare Luke 24/28: *Appropinquaverunt castello quo ibant* (AV "They drew nigh unto the village, whither they went"). See also 14/138 and note.

111   *lore* BH is to be preferred to the scribally erroneous *lord* HmAR, the latter resulting from the confusion of *e* and *d*, perhaps aided by *lord* 110.

PLAY XIX

112–9, stanza 15   *noone* 115 HmARB gives imperfect rhyme with *beforne* 119; *morne* H gives perfect rhyme. Luke gives no indication of the duration of the journey or the time of the encounter with Jesus. Deimling cites *morne* as evidence of H's superiority. But with *noone*, compare *Stanzaic Life* 7613: "The feurthe apering was aftre noon". If Emmaus was regarded as lying only seven and a half miles from Jerusalem, it is unlikely that the journey could be regarded as occupying the whole day, particularly since the disciples immediately return to Jerusalem the same evening and apparently get there within the hour, 201; see further, *Play-heading* note. The references to the visits to the tomb by the women and disciples, 57–71, suggest a departure after the early morning visits, but introduce an inconsistency, since Peter and John do not return home in Chester after finding the empty tomb — see 18/420 + SD note — and there is no indication that the disciples met the women before they had encountered Jesus, Appendix ID — possibly the two remained in Jerusalem long enough to hear the testimonies of women and disciples to the risen Christ, although this is not suggested in Luke. H, however, confers a pleasing irony — since Jesus rose from the dead that morning, he has indeed travelled a long way.

The absence of perfect rhyme may underlie R's erroneous *before* 119.

123 + SD   Compare M. D. Anderson, *History and Imagery in British Churches* (London, 1971), p.161: "On a roof boss in the cloister at Norwich, showing the Supper at Emmaus, a curtain, suspended by rings from a pole behind the table, is carved in the fullest detail. In a sculptural design this is irrelevant, but it explains exactly how Christ managed to 'vanish' on a small raised stage at the breaking of the bread."

128–35, stanza 17   *masse* 132 H is to be preferred for rhyme to *made* HmARB, the latter evidently an exemplar subsitution. *stayde* 133 R seems to be a scribal substitution to restore rhyme, but the attempt is not sustained to 134.

130–1   Luke 24/31 says only: *Et aperti sunt oculi eorum, et cognoverunt eum* (AV "And their eyes were opened, and they knew him"). Here the implication seems to be that only at that moment does Cleophas catch sight of Jesus' face — Luke does not seem to have recognised him, although he acquiesces in the identification. The realisation also follows the disappearance in Wakefield, York and *Ludus Coventriae*; in Wakefield and York it is the act of disappearance that seems to suggest Jesus' identity. In Cornish Ordinalia the recognition precedes the disappearance as the unnamed disciple sees the wounds on Jesus' hands as he breaks the bread.

133   *he* ARBH has been erroneously repeated as *hee hee* Hm. *hee* (1) Hm could be seen as erroneously anticipating *here*, or even lending support to the duplication of *heare* in AR.

135   *luxon* and variants — see 18/315

143 + SD   Luke 24/33 indicates that the disciples returned to the eleven disciples and their companions in Jerusalem.

150–1   See Appendix ID/60–95 and notes. The appearance to Peter depends there upon the statement made here, Luke 24/34, and on 1 Corinthians 15/5.

152–9, stanza 20   The b-rhymes, *knowe* 155 — *thrall* 159, do not rhyme, and *thrawe* AR is to be preferred at 159 for rhyme. The rhyme could have been either *thrawe*—

knawe or *throwe—knowe. thrall* HmBH is not only destructive of rhyme but also semantically inappropriate, but its presence in those three manuscripts strongly argues for its presence in the exemplar. *thraw, throw*, "instant, moment", is last recorded by OED in 1590 (Spenser).

160–7 + SD   Compare John 20/19: *Cum ergo sero esset die illo, una sabbatorum, et fores essent clausae ubi erant discipuli congregati, propter metum Iudaeorum, venit Iesus* (AV "Then the same day at evening, being the first day of the week, when the doors were shut where the disciples were assembled for fear of the Jews, came Jesus"). There is no sense of anticipation of Jesus' coming.

155 + SH   AR have erroneously and inexplicably omitted the SH.

168–99   Compare 20/1–56. The events here are based mainly on Luke 24/36–42, although 168 is found also in John 20/19. A number of passages — 169–71, 178–9, 190–1, 196–9 + SD — lack biblical counterpart.

174   An alternative punctuation would take 172–3 as a completed question and take 174 with 175. Since Peter has previously seen Jesus, the force of *nowe* must be very strong. Luke 24/37 does not specify speakers by name.

176–83, stanza 23   The b-rhymes, *good* 179 — *tree* 183, do not rhyme. Rhyme would result from reading *rood* for *a tree; tree* was evidently the exemplar reading, influenced by the preceding c-rhymes, or by the b-rhymes of the next stanza.

180–1   Compare 244–7, 20/11–12, 20/129–52, 24/305–28; and see the interpretation in *Glossa Ordinaria*, 'Evang. Luc.' 24/40 (PL 114/353–4), and Comestor, *Historia Scholastica*, 'In Evangelia' 192 (PL 198/1640).

182   The line contains three strongly stressed syllables instead of the expected four.

196   Mark 16/14 says that Jesus appeared to the disciples as they sat at meat.

200–15   Based on Jesus' speech in Luke 24/44–47, but omitting its continuation, Luke 24/48–9, where he foretells the coming of the Holy Ghost, a section appropriately utilised in 20/53–6.

201   Compare Luke 24/44: *"Haec sunt verba quae locutus sum ad vos, cum adhuc essem vobiscum"* (AV "These are the words which I spake unto you, while I was yet with you"), which seems to refer to the predictions of the Passion and death made by Jesus to the disciples in Luke, particularly Luke 18/31–4. Here the reference seems to be to Jesus' words on the way to Emmaus, 74–80. See 112–9, stanza 15 note and compare 20/41–52.

204–8   Compare Luke 24/44: *Omnia quae scripta sunt in lege Moysi et prophetis et psalmis de me* (AV "All things .... which were written in the law of Moses, and in the prophets, and in the psalms concerning me"). On the final phrases, compare 20/44–5. The psalm-reference intended may be Psalm 22/11–31. *lawes* 204 B may be rejected as not corresponding to the singular *lege* of Luke; *prophesyes* 205 H may also be rejected as not rendering *prophetis* in Luke.

204–7   It would be possible, and perhaps preferable, following Luke, to treat 204–5 as the concluding clause of the sentence 200–3, and to regard 206–7 as a separate sentence. 205 seems to mean "All other prophets such as have been up to now", but the construction is awkward and H substitutes *then* perhaps as being more appropriate to the verb-tense. 206–7 may suggest "Some of what was said about me has been fulfilled" — compare Luke 24/44: *Necesse est impleri omnia* (AV "All things must be fulfilled"); the implication here may be that more — e.g. 212-3 — still remains.

208–15, stanza 27   *sinne* 212 H is to be preferred for rhyme to *synnes* HmARB, but the latter corresponds to Luke 24/47: *Remissionem peccatorum* (AV "Remission of sins"); compare *synne* 20/50, where only B has a plural form — here the plural form was evidently in the exemplar. *mynes* 213 R possibly suggests an influence from the plural rhyme-word of 212.

212   *preach* The construction in Luke 24/47, *praedicari* (AV "should be preached"), is passive; Jesus is not there saying that he will preach, or the prophets said that he would, but is in effect commissioning his disciples to preach. Unless 212 is taken as a new sentence of address to the disciples, with *preach* as imperative — unlikely, especially in view of 20/49 where *preach* cannot be imperative — the meaning here diverges from that in Luke.

213   *his* So Luke 24/47: *in nomine eius* (AV "in his name"). But Jesus here, unlike Luke, has adopted the first person pronoun at 209, hence *my* is required. The line is improved by the omission of a syllable, as in A or R.

215 + SD   The story of Thomas' doubt in John 20/24–9 follows the description of Jesus' appearance to his disciples; 224–39, 256–75 are without biblical counterpart here. But John does not indicate how Jesus departed from the disciples, nor how they encountered Thomas. *Glossa Ordinaria*, 'Evang. Luc.' 24/36 comments (PL 114/353): *Quod vero dicit Joannes Thomam non fuisse cum illis: cum Lucas dicat istos duos invenisse undecim congregatos, et eos qui cum eis erat, intelligendum est quod Thomas inde exisset antequam Dominus eis hoc loquentibus appareret*; Comestor, *Historia Scholastica*, 'In Evangelia' 192 says of Thomas (PL 198/1640): *Quo egresso*, and in 194 (id/1641): *rediit Thomas*. Mark 16/19 and Luke 24/50, lacking the episode, move from Jesus' appearance to the ascension. Luke says that Jesus led the disciples to Bethany where he ascended.

221–3   Thomas does not here mention his desire to place his hand in the wound in Jesus' side, John 20/25, and Jesus does not refer to it, unlike John 20/27, unless *put in thy hand* 245 is to be understood as such a reference. The wound in the side is indicated in 249 + SD.

226   Some object must be supplied for *have*, and *us* ARBH may therefore be preferred. But the resulting metre is rough and a more acceptable result would be obtained by omitting *and* 227. A semantic objection to ARBH is that the distinction of *us* and *all our fraternitie* is not immediately obvious — is it between the disciples and the others mentioned by Luke as being with them, or between Andrew and Thomas and the other disciples?
   Perhaps *and* was introduced erroneously into the text, and *us* subsequently added for syntactical completeness. If the exemplar indicated that *us* was an addition — e.g. by superscript or caret — the Hm omission would be more readily understandable.

239 + SD   John 20/26 indicates that the second appearance was eight days after the first.

248–9 + SD   Without biblical counterpart — compare 20/129–30, 24/421–8 + SD.

248–55, stanza 32   The b-rhymes, *weeninge* 251 — *see* 255, do not rhyme. *weeninge* reflects the a-rhyme, *see* the b-rhyme, in a stanza rhyming aaaabbbb. A regular stanza would result from reading *weene* 251 — *seene* 255. The error was evidently present in the exemplar.

252   H reflects John 20/29: *Quia vidisti me* (AV "Because thou hast seen me"). *seest in* HmARB presumably means "Look on me".

256–9   The lines affirm Jesus' bodily resurrection, attested by physical signs, in contrast to his refusal to allow Mary Magdalen to touch him, ID/10–12. The issue of Jesus' bodily, as opposed to spiritual, resurrection, was an issue of some theological importance — compare Bede, *In Lucae Evangelium Expositio* 6/24 (PL 92/628–9) and *Glossa Ordinaria*, 'Evang. Luc.' 24/39 (PL 114/353).

260–4   Compare 268–71. The two passages are perhaps influenced by Mark 16/16: *Qui crediderit et baptizatus fuerit, salvus erit; qui vero non crediderit, condemnabitur* (AV "He that believeth and is baptized shall be saved; but he that believeth not, shall be damned"); also John 20/31: *Haec autem scripta sunt ut credatis quia Iesus est Christus, Filius Dei, et ut credentes, vitam habeatis in nomine eius* (AV "But these are written, that ye might believe that Jesus is the Christ, the Son of God; and that believing ye might have life through his name").

268–70   Compare 260–4 note and 24/613–6. Here the lines are somewhat unspecific, suggesting heavenly reward for those who think in any way on God the Father or on the Virgin Mary. The specification of the latter seems to follow upon 80–7, but it may be theologically significant and perhaps indicate a possible reason for the existence of an alternative continuation from the resurrection, via play 20, which omits specifically Marian references.

PLAY XX

Dramatis Personae Jesus, Petrus, Andreas, Johannes, Jacobus Major, Simon, Philippus, Primus Angelus, Minor Angelus/Secundus Angelus, Tertius Angelus, Quartus Angelus.

NOTE Chorus 104+Latin (f) is here held to comprise *Primus* and *Secundus Angelus*, but could suggest a larger company.

Locations
Bethanye 54, in Bethaniam 96+SD, in loco ubi assendit 96+SD in medio quasi supra nubes 104+SD H, in caelum 152+SD, to heaven 158, *to which Jesus ascends* 104+SD ff.

Properties
meate 39
these (bloodye) droppes 129, 137, this blood 133.

Costume
stola sua 104+Latin (d), vestimenta tua sicut calcantium in torculari 104+Latin (f), comely ... in his clothinge 109, thy cloathinge nowe so reedd 122, thy clothes ... bloodye 122-3.

Sources
Appearance to disciples — primarily Luke 24/33-49; cf. Mark 16/14-18, John 20/19-23
Final injunctions to disciples — Mark 16/15-18, Acts 1/4-8
Ascension — Mark 16/19, Luke 24/50-52, Acts 1/9-12.

Play-heading Only the Ascension, 94–*Finis*, is here mentioned. Jesus' appearance to his disciples, 1-56, parallels to some extent 19/168-215 — compare 19/*Play-heading* note and all notes on the scene in 19. The parallels seem sufficiently close to admit the thesis that they might not have been performed together but may represent alternatives. Wakefield 29 presents the appearance and Ascension; York 43, *Ludus Coventriae* 39/1-55 the Ascension.

The biblical quotation is Luke 24/36: AV, imperfectly: "Peace be unto you."

1   *my brethren* Luke 24/33 indicates that there were present the eleven disciples and an unspecified number of others; Mark gives no indication of numbers; John, using this episode as the prelude to the doubt of Thomas, indicates that Thomas was not

present. But the Virgin Mary plays a prominent part in the Ascension plays of Wakefield and York and is present in *Ludus Coventriae*, and was evidently usually included in the preliminary scenes.

sytten in companye The exact location is not clear from the text. Luke 24/33 indicates that the appearance was in Jerusalem, and John 20/19 that it was in a closed room. Wakefield 29/21 is located in Bethany; York 43 has a preliminary dialogue on Olivet before the Ascension; *Ludus Coventriae* 39 indicates movement to Olivet from an unspecified location.

5–8 These lines seem to imply an event immediately after the resurrection when the disciples were still in doubt about what had happened. Luke 24/33–6 indicates that the events took place on the evening of the day of the resurrection, but no further indication of time is given and the appearance is followed there immediately by Jesus' injunctions to his disciples, and by the journey to Bethany and the ascension, as if the events followed immediately. Mark similarly gives no indication of an exact time-scale. John 20/19 indicates that the appearance to the ten disciples was on the evening of the day of resurrection, the appearance to Thomas eight days later, John 20/26; and Acts 1/3 states that Jesus was seen by his disciples for forty days before the ascension. Here, following Luke, the sense of time is lost. Contrast the references to forty days in Wakefield 29/17–8 and York 43/89–95.

9–16, stanza 2   *weet* 12 H is to be preferred for rhyme to *wyde* HmARB. In Luke 24/39–40, Jesus specifies hands and feet — *Videte manus meas, et pedes* (AV "Behold my hands and my feet") and *Ostendit eis manus et pedes* (AV "He shewed them his hands and his feet"), thus confirming the reference at 16. But John 20/20 and 27 specifies hands and side — *Ostendit eis manus et latus* (AV "He shewed unto them his hands and his side") and *Infer digitum tuum huc, et vide manus meas; et affer manum tuam, et mitte in latus meum* (AV "Reach hither thy finger, and behold my hands; and reach hither thy hand, and thrust it into my side"). Only Thomas is asked to feel Jesus' wounds rather than behold them, and no biblical account suggests that they were still bleeding. Hence it is possible that *wyde* HmARB is correct and that *feete* 16, attested by all manuscripts, represents an exemplar change from *syde*. Compare 19/240–7, which similarly specifies hands and feet, though perhaps also intending the side at 243 or 245; and where the wounds are similarly seen as fresh.

9   *you* AR is to be preferred to the erroneous *your* Hm. *you* would be a dative form, giving acceptable syntax and providing a suitable basis for Hm's scribal error. BH probably independently misunderstood the construction and substituted *ther*, which gives acceptable sense.

11   *puttes nowe you froo* A somewhat literal rendering of *affer manum tuam*, John 20/27 (AV "reach hither thy hand"), addressed to Thomas alone. The phrase indicates the composite nature of the account — compare also 9–16, stanza 2 note.

16 + Latin   Luke 24/39: AV "For a spirit hath not flesh and bones, as ye see me have."

17–32   Based on Luke 24/41: *Adhuc autem illis non credentibus, et mirantibus prae gaudio* (AV "And while they yet believed not for the joy, and wondered"). Mark 16/14 indicates that Jesus severely rebuked the disciples for their lack of faith, and York 43/81–101 reflects that rebuke.

18 The line contains five stressed syllables instead of the expected four. A four-stress line would result from the omission of *meethinke*, which may have been anticipated from 19. *me hym* ARBH produces a rough four-stress line, but is syntactically improbable; B produces smoother rhythm by preferring the monosyllabic *seemes*. The ARH form seems to have been that of the exemplar; possibly it represents an "improvement" of an earlier *me seemeth*, which would give good metre and sense.

25–7 Compare 15/193–6, 241–56.

29–32 "Ah, John, what makes us uncertain [about whether it is really Jesus] is that when he keeps appearing and when we most desire to have him [staying] here, he goes away at once." The implication is that Jesus would not go away in that manner, which is more appropriate to a ghost. The two temporal clauses, 30–1, are here taken as parallel and the construction is not broken as the punctuation at 30 might be understood to imply.

The lines seem to suggest other appearances to the disciples, which would not follow from the biblical account of the appearance on the day of resurrection since that was the first appearance to the assembled disciples. It might, however, relate to the appearances in play 19.

33–7 Compare Mark 16/14: *Et exprobravit incredulitatem eorum et duritiam cordis, quia iis qui viderant eum resurrexisse non crediderunt* (AV "And upbraided them with their unbelief and hardness of heart, because they believed not them which had seen him after he was risen"). See also 19/176–7, 20/211–4.

39 The absence of a verb in the line seems to have troubled AR, which supply *is*. A compensates for the additional syllable by omitting *meate*, but R retains the word. *heres* B may represent *here is* in abbreviated form.

meate innough, "food enough". Mark 16/14 states that the disciples were sitting at meat; compare *sytten in companye* 1. Luke 24/42 specifies the food as a piece of broiled fish and a honeycomb. Compare *Stanzaic Life*:

> thenne as thai eten in that halle,
> Crist to hom conne appar
> (8721–2)

and 19/194.

44–50 Compare 19/204–8 note.

53 Compare Luke 24/48: *Vos autem testes estis horum* (AV "And ye are witnesses of these things").

54–7 Jesus' intention to go to Bethany, 54, corresponds to the journey following the appearance in Luke 24/50. But Philip's question and the reply delay the departure until 96 + SD. However, the dialogue following at 57–96 derives from Jesus' reply to a collective question in Acts 1/7–8 where the episode takes place on Mount Olivet just before the ascension. It would therefore be logical to assume that the change of scene to Bethany occurs after 56 and that part of 96 + SD is misplaced. Some support is given to this possibility by 56 + SD, which can only relate to an action following 40 and indicated by 41, suggesting that this SD, if not retrospective, has also been misplaced. Any such error was clearly present in the exemplar, since both SDs are attested by all manuscripts.

The injunction to remain in Jerusalem, 55–6, represents a link between the appearance and ascension accounts, being found in both Luke 24/49 and Acts 1/4. In Luke it precedes the movement to Bethany, thus avoiding the awkwardness of the contradiction in 54–6 where Jesus seems in one breath to tell the disciples to come with him and then tells them to stay in Jerusalem. In fact, however, 54–6 really distinguish the journey to Bethany for the ascension, the present action (*come* 54), from the sojourn in Jerusalem to await the Holy Ghost, the future action (*shall lye* 55).

54 Luke 24/50 states that Jesus led them to Bethany, but does not report a command to the disciples. Compare *Stanzaic Life*:

> thenne when Crist whit hom ete
> he bade hom thai schuld tak the way
> to the mounte of Oliuete
> (8729–31)

The command has more point in *Stanzaic Life*, since Jesus does not accompany the disciples but manifests himself again to them when they reach the Mount.

56 + SH–96 57–72 represent Acts 1/6–8. The remainder of Jesus' reply is based on Mark 16/15–8, with the exception of 93–6, which is without biblical parallel and seems to have been included for dramatic clarification.

68 *shall* BH or *maye* R is to be preferred to the syntactically and semantically inappropriate *wynne* Hm. It may be that Hm omitted the auxiliary verb and that *wynne* is an uncancelled error for *wend*. *mooye* A is evidently a scribal error for *maye* R.

73–80, stanza 10 The rhyme-word *be* 76 ABH has been omitted by Hm. The construction corresponds to *salvus erit*, Mark 16/16 (AV "shall be saved"), and *saved* ABH is therefore also to be preferred to *save* HmR as being closer to the biblical form. The adoption of *save* evidently contributed to the construction in Hm and R; Hm may have omitted *be* as syntactically inappropriate, while R substitutes the syntactically acceptable *yee*. Possibly *save* represented an exemplar error, corrected by ABH; it is difficult otherwise to account for the agreement of HmR, and especially for the refusal of R to follow A in a meaningful reading. See further, 76 note.

73 *in* RH is to be preferred for syntax and meaning to its omission in HmAB; compare Mark 16/15: *Euntes in mundum universum* (AV "Go ye into all the world").

H's omissions of *yee* and *and* — the latter omission shared by B — may be regarded as attempts to produce a smoother metre for an unusually long line.

76 Compare Mark 16/15: *Qui crediderit et baptizatus fuerit* (AV "He that believeth and is baptized"). *fullye*, adverb, seems here syntactically and semantically redundant, and the biblical reading would suggest that it represents a replacement of *fulloght*, "baptism", thereby supplying a noun-object for *hasse* 75, parallel to *beleeffe* 75. The change was clearly present in the exemplar, and would perhaps result from replacing an archaic word; *fullought* is last recorded by OED in c 1450 (Myrc), though the related verb is to be found in *Stanzaic Life* 2310 et seq. . Compare *fullfilled* 102. In corresponding passages in Wakefield and York (*Ludus Coventriae* lacks an equivalent) the meaning is clearer; Wakefield 29/120: "And to all the people preche/Who baptym will abyde"; York 43/132: "Who trowes, if that he baptised be."

Wakefield and York also have plays of Christ's baptism, and Jesus recalls this event in Wakefield 29/147-51, on the authority of Acts 1/5.

80 The Hm*AB* form, meaning "that torment may not leave them", gives acceptable sense and was apparently the exemplar reading. But *they* RH is the form that one might expect, producing the sense "they may not escape that torment".

84 The line contains four strongly stressed syllables instead of the expected three. A reduction of *whersoever* from four to three syllables, i.e. *whersoe'r*, would produce a more regular line.

86 *to putt to*, omitted by R as redundant, serves to mark an infinitive separated from, but dependent upon, *shall* 85.

87 ARH's omission of *yee* is to be preferred as giving better meaning and metre. Compare Mark 16/17, where the third person pronoun is clearly demanded: *Linguis loquentur novis* (AV "They shall speak with new tongues"); the power is given to the converted. ARH assume repetition of *they* 85. B rephrases the line to include the pronoun, but unnecessarily. The Hm *yee* is evidently an error, arising from *ye* 81, *you* 82, and from confusion with the later account of Pentecost, 21/273-4, 367-90.

88 The line corresponds to Mark 16/18: *Serpentes tollent* (AV "They shall take up serpents"). H has an independent and misleading substitution.

95 The detail of blessing is from Luke 24/51.

96 + SD See 54-7 note. The Latin text is Matthew 28/18; AV "All power is given unto me in heaven and in earth." Matthew 28/18-19 is also the basis of 97-104.

102 *fullfilled* corresponds to *baptizantes*, Matthew 28/19 (AV *baptizing*); the verb here seems to represent an exemplar replacement for *fulhtnen*, "to baptize", which still survives in *Stanzaic Life*. Compare 76 note. *fullfilled* gives sense in terms of *fulfil* OED 3 "to make complete". OED *full* v¹ "to baptize", is last evidenced in 1483, the stem-form *folowe* of ARBH is a 15th century variant, and *followed* RBH should be regarded as the preferred reading here.

104 + SD On the mode of ascension, compare Wakefield 29/182 "In a clowde wendende vppe", and 300 "A clowde has borne my chylde to blys"; York 43/175, "Sende doun a clowde, fadir!" and 182 "In a clowde wendande vppe fro me"; *Ludus Coventriae* 39/53 "in a clowde As ȝe hym seyn".

104 + Latin (a) *Ascendo* is sung also in Wakefield 29/254 + ; in York 43, beside line 178, a late hand has added *Ascendo ad patrem meum. Tunc cantent angeli. Ludus Coventriae* 39/47 + SD reads merely *Et in celo cantent etcetera*. H has added a second and redundant *alleluya*. The text reflects Jesus' words in John 20/17 which Mary Magdalen is to take to the disciples; AV "I ascend unto my Father and your Father, and to my God and your God."

(b-g) Based on Isaiah 63/1-3: AV "Who is this that cometh from Edom, with dyed garments from Bozrah? this that is glorious in his apparel, travelling in the greatness of his strength? I that speak in righteousness, mighty to save. Wherefore art thou red in thine apparel, and thy garments like him that treadeth in the winefat? I have trodden the winepress alone; and of the people there was none with me." The rendering at 105–28 differs from the Latin in a number of significant details, giving specific reference to the events of Jesus' Passion and resurrection.

propugnator (e) H is to be preferred to the scribally erroneous readings of Hm, AR and B.

The Latin seems to require only two angels, perhaps corresponding to the two men who address the disciples in Acts 1/10–12. Wakefield and York similarly have two angels, *Ludus Coventriae* one. But the subsequent English version requires four angels in Chester. The dialogue suggests a division of knowledge among the angels, since *Primus* knows of the circumstances of Christ's Passion and resurrection and recognises him, while *Minor* does not.

111 The line has no counterpart in the biblical text and seems inappropriate to Jesus' ascent. Its reference is ostensibly the group of disciples watching the ascent.

113–20, stanza 15   *was* 120 H is to be preferred for rhyme to *were* HmARB. The HmARB reading, presumably also the exemplar reading, may arise from the use of the verb with *people* 117, from a sense that *all* indicates plural, and from a reluctance to repeat *was* 115 in rhyme-position. Deimling cites the form as evidence of H's superiority.

At 122 B has erroneously substituted *rede*, the 121 rhyme-word, for *head*.

123   *ledd* evidently has the force of *leden* MED v (1), 6d, "to wear". MED records it only with reference to armour, but possibly its figurative application here also has an appropriately martial reference.

125–52   Compare 24/421–8.

133–4   At 133 a more regular sequence of strongly and weakly stressed syllables would result from the loss of one syllable, as in H. The consequent syntactical form requires a new subject at 134 which H supplies.

At 134 a more regular sequence of strongly and weakly stressed syllables results from the addition of a syllable, as in H and B.

136   *thee* The pronoun-reference is evidently to the disciples, but one would expect the plural pronoun, *you*. Probably *them* H, referring to *man* 134, should be preferred for meaning; compare *them* 128, referring to *mankynd*.

142–4   *that* 142 introduces a noun clause, object of *knowe* 140; i.e. "That I have created everlasting bliss that they looked for in return for good deeds to prove the virtuous [to be] worthy [of heaven]". H takes *that* 142 as relative and changes the pronoun accordingly.

148   The erroneous repetition of 137–8 after 148 in B may be a cancelled error; see TNs.

149–52   The version in Hm gives acceptable sense, viz.: "I shed these drops on the cross for these reasons (i.e. those rehearsed in 133–48), believe me. All flesh shall be kept for ever, until the last day (when all shall arise in the flesh)." But *freshe* 151 ARBH is a more probable reading, paralleling 130.

152+SD   The basis for the first antiphon is Psalm 20/14; AV 21/13 "Be thou exalted, Lord, in thine own strength: so we will sing and praise thy power." *exaltare* BH is to be preferred to *exaltaremus* Hm in reflecting the biblical and liturgical text; *alleluya* H represents the liturgical text.

The second antiphon is based on Acts 1/11; AV "Ye men of Galilee, why stand ye gazing up into heaven?" *aspicitis* represents the liturgical reading against Vulgate *statis aspicientis*.

With the beginning of the SD, compare 104 + SD. Possibly we are to assume that Jesus moves upwards during the Latin chants of 104–5, stops at the upper level, 112 + SD, to address the angels, and continues — either by mechanical means or by walking upwards and off the stage — at 152 + SD. The chants here would then cover the descent of the angels. Alternatively, a choice exists at 104 between continuing with 105–52 or with 153, the latter abridging an already short action but remaining close to the biblical accounts.

The omission of the SD in AR may suggest unease at the apparent duplication of the ascent in 104–5.

165–6 *sethen* 165 is either an unusual weak form, or an error based on *sithen*, for *sithes*, "times". H substitutes a phrase which, in view of 65–8, seems inappropriate.

At 166 a more regular sequence of strongly and weakly stressed syllables results from adding a further unstressed syllable, as in ARH and B; the ARH version is preferable semantically, but B's inappropriate *to free* seems to derive from a misreading of *so free*, suggesting that ARH represent the exemplar form.

192 *Amen* The word is outside the structure of the stanza, which requires *companye* as rhyme-word, and is therefore omitted in ARH. It is merely the appropriate conclusion to the prayer of 191–2.

PLAY XXI

Dramatis Personae Petrus, Mattheus, Andreas, Jacobus Major, Johannes Evangelista, Thomas, Jacobus Minor, Philippus, Bartholomeus, Mathias, Simon, Thaddeus, Lyttle God, Deus, Angelus, The Second Angell, Primus Alienigena, Secundus Alienigena.

NOTE   Joseph 42 is apparently present in a non-speaking role.

Locations
this wonne 7, this house 258, *in* Jerusalem 86
in heaven 152 + SD, in caelo 238 + SD, to yearth goe downe 167.

NOTE   On a possible movement by the apostles to a separate location, see 65 note.

Properties
lottes 43, sors/sortem 56 + SD
in spetie ignis 238 + SD, ignem 238 + SD, fyre 258, 268, 272.

Costume
None specified.

Sources The election of Matthias and the coming of the Holy Ghost — Acts 1/15–2/12.

There is no biblical authority for the creation of the Apostles' Creed, but the creed takes its name from the tradition of its creation by the apostles under the immediate influence of the Holy Ghost. It is first so termed by Ambrose, Ep. 42/5, and first expounded in its modern form by Pirminius in the early eighth century.

Play-heading The coming of the Holy Ghost at Pentecost is commemorated in the Church calendar on Whit Sunday. Since the Chester Cycle in the sixteenth century was (with the exception of the final production in 1575) performed on the Monday, Tuesday and Wednesday of Whit week, there is particular point in the inclusion in the cycle of the most extensive English dramatic treatment of the events of Pentecost. Elsewhere the election of Matthias is in *Ludus Coventriae* 39 and possibly in York 41/1–12; the coming of the Holy Ghost is in York 44 and *Ludus Coventriae* 40. Neither cycle shows the creation of the Creed, an episode also absent from *Stanzaic Life*; but York had its own independent Creed

Play, as perhaps also Coventry, though the form and content are unknown.

simbolum apostolicum simbolum came to be the term applied to the Creed; see Rufinus, *Commentarius in Symbolum Apostolorum*, para 2 (PL 21/337) and Pseudo-Augustine, Sermo 241 (PL 39/2190).

It may be noted that Whitsun coincides with the Jewish Feast of Weeks, when the first-fruits of the harvest were presented, Deuteronomy 16/9, and the giving of the Law to Moses commemorated; compare episodes in Play 5.

1 *brethren* The play has twelve speaking disciples, together with the non-speaking Joseph 42. Acts 1/13–5 lists the original eleven disciples, together with the women and specifically the Virgin Mary, and Jesus' "brethren", about 120. Compare *Southern Passion* 2433–7, which names the eleven disciples with "Oure lady and hure twey sustren and þe Magdaleyn also", and York 44, where the Virgin Mary is present with the disciples.

7 HmARB presumably mean "Therefore let us who are in this dwelling believe." H, which replaces *trust* 6 by *leeve*, here substitutes *lyve* for *leeve* — "Therefore let us live in this dwelling."

this wonne Acts indicates that the meeting was in an upper room; *Southern Passion* 2431–3 that it was in a corner of the Temple.

17–24, stanza 3 The b-rhymes, *beforne* 20 — *forlorne* 24 HmB, and *before* — *forlore* H are acceptable. AR's *before*—*forlorne* represents an erroneous substitution which destroys rhyme.

20–2 *Davyd* The reference is the quotation from Psalms 68/26 at 32 + Latin below.

towchinge 22, "concerning", may depend upon either *sayd* 20 (in which case 21 is parenthetical), or *all* 21 (in which case no full-stop is required at the end of 21). In either reading, *wytten yee* will also be parenthetical.

wytten 22 ARB is to be preferred to *wrytten* Hm for meaning; the Hm reading perhaps results from a common collocation of *scripture* 18. *witt* H produces a rougher metre.

27–30 The Bible offers two versions of Judas' death. Matthew 27/5 states that after going to the high priests in remorse and casting down before them the thirty pieces of silver, he went away and hanged himself; the priests used the money to buy a field for the burial of strangers, thereafter called the Field of Blood. But Acts 1/18–9 indicates that Peter said that Judas used the money from the betrayal of Jesus to buy a field and that he there fell headlong so that he "burst asunder in the midst" (AV); for that reason the field was known as the Field of Blood. For a reconciliation of the accounts, see Theophylacti Bulgariae Archiep., *Enarratio in Evangelium Matthaei* 27/3–5 (PG 123/459). The title of the fragmentary Wakefield 32, *Suspencio Iude*, indicates the manner of death in that cycle. In York 32/296–315 Judas leaves Pilate and the priests vowing to commit suicide by unspecified means. In *Ludus Coventriae* 39/73 "He hynge hym-self vpon A tre".

29 *hanged* B may be an attempt to overcome the inconsistencies in the accounts of Judas' death. *borsen* AR is a shared scribal error.

32 + Latin Acts 1/20: AV "Let his habitation be desolate, and let no man dwell therein: and his bishoprick let another take." Acts is citing Psalms 68/26: *Fiat habitatio eorum deserta; et in tabernaculis eorum non sit qui inhabitet* (AV Psalms 69/25: "Let their habitation be desolate; and let none dwell in their tents") and Psalms 108/8: *Fiant dies eius pauci, et episcopatum eius accipiat alter* (AV Psalms 109/8: "Let his days be few; and let another take his office").

The form of the quotation here differs from that in Acts in the readings: habitatio] commoratio; eius] eorum; habitet] inhabitet.

sit BH is to be preferred for meaning, and as reflecting the Vulgate reading, to the scribally erroneous *sic* HmAR. *ea* ARBH is to be preferred for reference, and as reflecting the Vulgate reading, to *eo* Hm.

33-4 The distinction of *men* and *fellowes* seems to reflect Peter's opening words in Acts 1/16, *Viri fratres* (AV "Men and brethren"). Compare 1 note and 65 note.

35 *while* H may be preferred to *with* HmAR as reflecting Acts 1/21: *In omni tempore quo* (AV "All the time that"). *with* may indicate scribal confusion with *with* 33, probably in the exemplar; *which* B is erroneous and may result from a faultily expanded abbreviation, a scribal confusion of *t* and *c*, or both — but the error would tend to confirm HmAR as the exemplar form.

37-40 Acts 1/22 merely suggests that the new disciple is to be a witness to the Resurrection.

37 *seene*, "have seen", HmARB is correct; *see* H, the present tense, suggests a misunderstanding of the meaning of the text.

41-2 Compare Acts 1/23: *Et statuerunt duos: Ioseph, qui vocabatur Barsabas, qui cognominatus est Iustus, et Mathiam* (AV "And they appointed two, Joseph called Barsabas, who was surnamed Justus, and Matthias"). There seems no clear reason for reversing the biblical order of names here.

Mathias 41 ARBH is to be preferred to *Mattheus* Hm in reflecting the Vulgate form Hm reads *Mattheus* for *Mathias* also at 60+SH, 104+SH, 298+SH and 354+SH (the last with A); it reads *Mathias* for *Mattheus* at 92+SH, 144+SH, 286+SH and 342+SH. The English form, *Matthewe*, is used at 58.

47 The Hm line is acceptable, but it is notable that ARBH include *all*. By omitting the inflexion of *assenten*, H includes *all* without affecting the number of syllables in the line; but by omitting the inflexion and merely replacing *us* by *all*, AR reduce the number of syllables by one, while by retaining the inflexion and adding *all*, B increases the number of syllables by one. Probably Hm and H represent alternatives in an "emended" exemplar which have been erroneously permuted by ARB.

48+SH In Acts 1/24 the prayer is said by all the disciples together.

56 "And which [is the one] that you will appoint." The line, like 52 and 53, is syntactically dependent upon *shewe* 51; compare the similar construction with *and* *whether* 53 and the similar use of the relative pronoun, *that* 52. With *make*, compare MED *maken* v¹, 14(a), "To appoint or choose (sb) as (bishop, knight, one's heir, one's servant, etc.)", and *apostle thee make* 60.

whither Hm does not give good sense in context and *wheither* A, *whether* RBH are to be preferred. Hm may, however, have been expecting something corresponding to Acts 1/25: *Ut abiret in locum suum* (AV "That he might go to his own place"), a suggestion of motion for which the text here has no counterpart.

The use of *make* evidently troubled AR. A substitutes *take* and R *choose*, both semantically acceptable; but A repeats the 52 rhyme-word, and R destroys rhyme.

56 + SH–96 The usual speaking-order for the disciples is: Petrus, Andreas, Jacobus Major, Johannes, Thomas, Jacobus Minor, Philippus, Bartholomaeus, Mattheus, Simon, Thaddeus, Mathias; see 310 + SD–58 note. Here, however, Mathias speaks out of his usual sequence on the occasion of his election. The order does not correspond to gospel lists of the twelve in Matthew 10/2-4, Mark 3/16-9, Luke 6/14-16.

58–60 + SH *Matthewe* 58, the English form, is given by HmAR, but H continues to use *Mathias* and B has a nonce-form, *Mathi*.

62–3 "Though I be unworthy for that for which you have chosen me"; *that* refers to *ther* in *therto*. But H, apparently unhappy at this construction, rephrases to give parallel clauses: "Though I am unworthy of that, and unworthy of you who have chosen me". Both readings have the disadvantage of suggesting that the election was the responsibility of the disciples rather than God, a difficulty resolvable if *that* could be taken as referring to *God in Trynitie* 61 or *his* 64: "I will die for the sake of him who has chosen me for you"; but *have* 63 precludes a singular reference.

65 *goe we* At this point the twelve apostles apparently withdraw from the others mentioned at 33–4 to another location.

65–120 The comments here continue the idea of constant prayer and supplication in Acts 1/14 and may be considered to occupy the period from the day of the Ascension to the day of Pentecost, ten days later. Acts does not indicate the exact time within those ten days that the election of Mathias occurred.

No set forms of prayer are indicated in Acts; the texts here echo a number of different scriptural passages; viz

69–72 John 14/18: *Non relinquam vos orphanos, veniam ad vos* (AV "I will not leave you comfortless: I will come to you"); and John 14/16: *Et ego rogabo Patrem, et alium Paraclitum dabit vobis ut maneat vobiscum in aeterno.* (AV "And I will pray the Father, and he shall give you another Comforter, that he may abide with you for ever").

75–6 John 14/25: *Haec locutus sum vobis, apud vos manens* (AV "These things I have spoken unto you, being yet present with you").

77–80 John 16/7: *Sed ego veritatem dico vobis: Expedit vobis ut ego vadam; si enim non abiero, Paraclitus non veniet ad vos; si autem abiero, mittam eum ad vos* (AV "Nevertheless I tell you the truth; It is expedient for you that I go away; for if I go not away, the Comforter will not come unto you; but if I depart, I will send him unto you").

All the preceding quotations are from Jesus' address to the disciples after the Last Supper.

85-8 Luke 24/49: *Et ego mitto promissum Patris mei in vos; vos autem sedete in civitate; quoadusque induamini virtute ex alto* (AV "And, behold, I send the promise of my Father upon you: but tarry ye in the city of Jerusalem, until ye be endued with power from on high"). The quotation is Jesus' last words to his disciples before leading them to Bethany in Luke for the ascension; they have no counterpart in Play 20.

89-96 Acts 1/5, quoted in 96+Latin; see note below.

97-112 Acts 1/7-8; compare 20/61-72.

117-120 Loosely, Matthew 7/7-8: *Petite et dabitur vobis, quaerite et invenietis; pulsate, et aperietur vobis; omnis enim qui petit accipit; et qui quaerit invenit; et pulsanti aperietur* (AV "Ask, and it shall be given you; seek, and ye shall find; knock, and it shall be opened unto you: For every one that asketh receiveth; and he that seeketh findeth; and to him that knocketh it shall be opened"). These words represent Jesus' assurances towards the end of the Sermon on the Mount.

81-8, stanza 11   The b-rhymes, *steede* 84 — *highe* 88, do not rhyme. No manuscript has the form *stye* which is required at 84, so that *steede* was evidently the exemplar reading. H provides an acceptable solution in *steight—height*, a reading cited by Deimling in evidence of H's superiority. The ARB form, *stead*, suggests that *heaven-stead* may have been regarded as a noun, "the place of heaven", for which a verb of motion is implied in *to*; but compare 20/158.

82   *there wore* i.e. "were there". H replaced the words by an adverbial phrase, parallel to 83; B seems not to understand the form, apparently construing *wore* as past tense of *wear* and substituting *what* for *that, they* for *there*.

85   The request which prompted Jesus' response is, in 20/57-60, attributed to Philip, hence perhaps the use of the first person pronoun by AR.

96+Latin   Acts 1/5: AV "For John truly baptized with water; but ye shall be baptized with the Holy Ghost not many days hence." The words are spoken by Jesus at his ascension but have no counterpart in play 20.

baptizabimini H is to be preferred to the scribally erroneous forms of HmA, R and B as reflecting the Vulgate reading.

quia B represents the Vulgate reading, linking the text to the statement in Acts 1/4. This was evidently changed to *tunc* in the exemplar in the absence of the preceding Vulgate verse. H, apparently recognising the reason for the change but unwilling to depart from the biblical text, omits *tunc*.

96+SH   *Simon* H rightly identifies this disciple as the *Simonem, qui vocatur Zelotes* (AV "Simon called Zelotes") of Luke 6/15. Compare H's *Simon Ze*, 290+SH, and *Symon Zelot*, 346+SH. In Matthew 10/4, Mark 3/18 he is identified as *Simon Cananaeus* (AV "Simon the Canaanite"). The identification seems to have been the addition of the H scribe. *Symion* A, *Simeon* R represent an error, not repeated by those manuscripts for later occurrences of the name.

98   *some* In 20/56+SH the question is asked by Philip, but in Acts 1/6 it is collectively ascribed, as here.

100+SH   The speaker here is variously characterised in the different gospels as: Matthew 10/3 *Lebbaeus Thaddaeus*, Mark 3/18 *Thaddaeus*; Luke 6/16 *Iudam Iacobi*

PLAY XXI   311

(AV "Judas the brother of James"). He later identifies himself as the author of what AV terms "The General Epistle of Jude". *Thaddeus* HmB was his surname, to which H adds *Judas* and R the anglicised *Jude*, while A uses only the anglicised form. At 294 + SH, 350 + SH AR use only the anglicised form, but other manuscripts, including H, use only *Thaddeus*.

104 + Latin   Acts 1/7: AV "It is not for you to know the times or the seasons, which the Father hath put in his own power."

112 + Latin   Acts 1/8; AV "But ye shall receive power, after that the Holy Ghost is come upon you; and ye shall be witnesses unto me both in Jerusalem, and in all Judaea, and in Samaria, and unto the uttermost part of the earth."

The quotation omits the introductory *sed* of the Vulgate. No manuscript has Vulgate *supervenientis* for *supervenientes*, the latter evidently an exemplar error. *omni* H is to be preferred to its omission in HmARB as reflecting the Vulgate reading.

120 + SD   The hymn *Veni Creator Spiritus*, of which H cites the first two lines, was composed in the ninth century in the Frankish empire, and was used at Vespers at Whitsuntide as well as at the ordination of priests and consecration of bishops. In the latter function it was incorporated into the 1550 Anglican Ordinal and hence into the Book of Common Prayer. The version in *Hymnarium Sarisburiense: Pars Prima* (London, 1871), pp.111–2, has been used for comparisons with 121–45 below. H quotes the first stanza.

In York 44, 135–6 cite the first lines, thus confirming a marginal annotation to 96 in a later hand to the effect that the two angels sing the hymn at the descent of the Holy Ghost. The hymn is also sung by two angels in York 31/154 + SD at the baptism of Christ, and a late hand somewhat unconvincingly proposes it at York 22/91. It is sung in *Ludus Coventriae* 10/110–5 + SD, the play of the betrothal of Mary.

122   *our* ARBH is to be preferred to the scribally erroneous *or* Hm; compare *or* 127, and see 127–8 note.

127–8   Compare:
              Fons vivus, ignis, caritas
              Et spiritalis unctio.
that 128 is evidently a relative pronoun governing *or* 127, "our". Although *lyght* 127 B may represent *igni*, the resulting line does not give sense unless it is taken as a verb — "Shed light upon our misery". H replaces *or* by *of*, giving the attractive phrase *leach of langore*, "healer of misery", but leaving *that* without reference. *lenght* HmAR does not give any meaning, but perhaps represents the exemplar form, an error, corrected in different ways by B and H. A most satisfactory solution would be to adopt H's *leach* for *lenght* as verb, "Heal our misery", an expansion of the second line above.

The H reading confirms *or* as the exemplar form.

129–30   Compare:
              Tu septiformis munere,
              Dexterae Dei tu digitus.
The lines here do not reflect the Latin text.

(1) *hee* 129 Hm seems to be an error for exemplar *yee*, corresponding to Latin *tu*, which is acceptably represented by *ye* B and more ambiguously by *yea* ARH.

(2) *seaven monethes* 129 HmAR seems to stand for Latin *septiformis munere* but can in no way translate it; it was evidently the exemplar form, since *moth* B is a scribal error, and H's *fifty dayes* must derive from the temporal reference. The H scribe evidently decided that the phrase gave sense only in reference to the fifty days which had elapsed between resurrection and Pentecost. Deimling felt this is to be preferable to HmARB, arguing that the Group had simply read *months* for *weeks*, evidently intending to indicate the preceding forty-nine days. But this ingenious suggestion would not account for the basis of the error or the divergence from the Latin text. It is impossible to reconstruct the original form, but three possibilities may be proposed:

(a) the original had no noun and required a referent for *seaven* to be supplied. At some stage, on the mistaken assumption that the reference was temporal, *monethes* was added, to the detriment of metre and meaning;

(b) the original read *seaven might conseyle*, requiring a noun to be understood. At some stage the auxiliary was changed to *would*, but the cancelled *might* remained and was taken as a barely decipherable noun;

(c) *monethes* was a deliberate replacement for some more appropriate noun, such as *gifts* (cf. 169), for reasons which would be obscure.

Accepting (1) and (2a) as the simplest explanation, the line would mean: "You who would give counsel that grace should be distributed about from your Spirit in seven [forms]."

On *seaven*, see 168 note.

134 Compare *Infunde amorem cordibus*. One would expect *love* for *liffe*, *hearts* for *thoughtes* here.

135–6 Compare:
> Infirmans nostri corporis
> Virtute firma perpetim.

A, R and B represent substitutions for *fulsome* HmH, evidently an unfamiliar word to the scribes.

137–52 It is notable that no manuscript has the speeches of the usual final speakers in the speaking sequence of the play, Thaddeus and Mathias. It seems unlikely that they too would not be shown invoking the Holy Ghost. Moreover, A also lacks Simon's speech and its SH, 148 + SH–52; and H transposes 137–40 to follow 152, with corresponding re-ascriptions of the intervening speeches, in contradiction of the sequence in the hymn. The evidence suggests an altered exemplar, with the removal of a final two-speech stanza effected in such a way as to leave two scribes uncertain of the final version intended. The change should be related to problems connected with 153–8 stanza 20, and 159–238; the notes on both should be consulted. It would seem probable, however, that a stanza has been removed, to be replaced by the speech of *Lyttle God*, with perhaps some further re-writing.

143 *and yee* A singular address is used elsewhere, with the exception of 129; and *thou* 144 is a striking change of reference if *Sonne* is indeed the reference of *yee* here. H substitutes *thou*. But it seems more probable that *yee* represents *yea*, an emphatic exclamation. Compare:

> Per te sciamus, da, patrem
> Noscamus atque filium
> Te utriusque spiritum
> Credamus omni tempore.

152+SH   The variants here may reflect dissatisfaction with the HmB reading. *Deus* R confuses the speaker with God the Father, but A and H make explicit the implicit reference of HmB to the second Person of the Trinity. In view of the later problems, it may be significant that the SH in HmAB is in English.

On the use of Jesus here as intercessor, compare John 14/16: *Et ego rogabo Patrem* (AV "And I will pray the Father").

153-8, stanza 20   The stanza consists of six lines, rhyming aabaab, 155 and 158 of three main stresses and the remainder of four. There is no obvious reason for the irregular form and no indication of omission in the exemplar. A erroneously omits 155-8, an omission not shared by R, and B omits 158.

156   *the* RBH is to be preferred to the scribally erroneous *they* Hm.

157   *prosperitye* HmH, "good fortune, success, well-being", does not seem appropriate in context; *posteritie* B gives no sense. *prophesye* R may be preferred.

158   *that* has no antecedent verb. Possibly a verb such as "I pray" is to be understood.

159-238   The long exposition by *Deus* contains two major inconsistencies.

(1) Although at 153-8 *Lyttle God* is distinguished from *Deus* (cf. *gloryous Father* 153), 199-202 suggest the identification of Father and Son in a single godhead, as in the opening speech of Play I.

(2) The speech begins with agreement to *Lyttle God's* request and a promise to despatch the Holy Ghost to strengthen the disciples. 175-98 review God's plan to defeat the devil. But at 199-214 *Deus* seems moved only by the apostles' prayer. He finds them unstable 209, and so pledges, as at the start of the speech, to send them the Holy Ghost 231-8.

It would be possible to move directly from 174 to 239, or to move directly from 152 to 175, thereby eliminating all inconsistencies without detriment to the continuity of the play. The choice would lie between the intercession of Jesus and God the Father's response to it, and the direct petitions of the apostles and the equally direct response of the Deity to them.

With 183-214, compare *Legenda Aurea*, 'De Sancto Spiritu'; ...*ut pater propitiaretur, filius propitiaret, spiritus sanctus igniret.*

161   Deimling (p.xii) says that *to deare* AR "is hardly intelligible". MED does not, however, indicate an appropriate intransitive usage for *areren*, so that an object must be understood in order to produce some meaning such as MED 12(a), "to stir up (hostility, discord, strife, etc.): start (a quarrel, a conflict)". The AR reading may suggest unease at such a procedure. Deimling also does not comment on the omission of *to* in H; this omission may also suggest unease at the verb-construction of HmB and may perhaps represent an attempt to introduce a figurative usage of the adverb *arrere*, as in the phrase *neither avaunt nor arrere*, "neither ahead nor farther back (in a sequence)" — "What you ask is not among the least of my considerations".

168 The seven gifts of the Holy Ghost are based on Isaiah 11/2 and are: wisdom, understanding, counsel, fortitude, knowledge, piety, and fear of the Lord.

169–70 "As theirs to have by devotion, to strengthen them to endure misery." *confyrme* is not clearly defined syntactically, but it may represent an infinitive rather than the imperative indicated in the punctuated text. *ther* is evidently possessive.

176 With *your* HmAR, compare *yee* 179. B and H, perhaps independently, do not seem to have recognised that the speech at this point is one of direct address, and substitute *ther*.

188–90 188 may be taken with 180–7 rather than with 189 — "I assumed human form ... because Man had lost his liberty."

behovedd 190 is an impersonal word whose subject must be understood: "It was fitting to redeem his sin."

195 The repetition of *thus* is acceptable, although the second example has no obvious reference in the context of the speech. *this* H for *thus* (1) seems inappropriate, but the omission of *thus* (2) by AR or its replacement by *have* H may be preferred.

201–6 Compare Jesus' prayer in Gethsemane, John 17/6 and 17/9, and play 15/273–80.

207 Compare Mark 16/15 and play 20/73–4.

215–8 A has erroneously and inexplicably omitted the lines.

220 *languages* here is evidently regarded as a collective noun. A trisyllabic form is required metrically.

223–30 Compare Matthew 28/19: *Euntes ergo docete omnes gentes, baptizantes eos in nomine Patris, et Filii, et Spiritus Sancti* (AV "Go ye therefore, and teach all nations, baptizing them in the name of the Father, and of the Son, and of the Holy Ghost").

233 *glade* ARBH is to be preferred for meaning to the scribally erroneous *gadd* Hm.

238 The phrase depends upon *may be* 236, but R, B and H supply a verb for the line.

238 + SD The antiphon derives from Jesus' words in the alternative account of the coming of the Holy Ghost to that in Acts, namely John 20/22–3: *Accipite Spiritum Sanctum. Quorum remiseritis peccata, remittuntur eis; et quorum retinueritis, retenta sunt* (AV "Receive ye the Holy Ghost: Whose soever sins ye remit, they are remitted unto them; and whose soever sins ye retain, they are retained").

The coming of the Holy Ghost is described in Acts 2/1–4, where it is accompanied by a sound as of a mighty rushing wind. There are no angels, and no explanations are given, but the disciples begin to speak with other tongues.

239–46, stanza 31 A substitutes *dreade* for *deare* 246, destroying rhyme; the substitution seems to arise from the unthinking employment of a common collocation. R corrects A's error but, perhaps misled by the rhyme-scheme aaaabbba, substitutes a b-rhyme, *nye*, at 242. B erroneously substitutes 244 for 240, for no obvious reason.

PLAY XXI

243–6 Compare Matthew 28/19: *Euntes ergo, docete omnes gentes* (AV "Go ye therefore, and teach all nations") and Mark 16/15: *Et dixit eis: Euntes in mundum universum, praedicate evangelium omni creaturae* (AV "And he said unto them, Go ye into all the world, and preach the gospel to every creature").

252 *over* ARBH is to be preferred for meaning to the scribally erroneous *ever* Hm.

268 "Has flown into my heart with this fire". H's replacement may suggest unease at the use of *flee* in this sense, but it is unnecessary. H then avoids duplication of the 269 rhyme-word by reading *truly* for *free* 269. AR "emend" *flee* to *flie*.

269 *dye* ARBH is to be preferred for meaning to the erroneous *doe* Hm.

278 *to* presumably depends upon *can* 277 — "There is no learning but I have understanding in it, and I know how to perfect knowledge." *cunnynge* may, however, be used of the faculty of the intellect rather than the corpus of learning, in which case 278 would have to be understood as "and how to satisfy my intellect".

282 The line contains four strong stresses instead of the expected three. AR's omission of *both* seeks to remedy this excess, producing a three-stress line of rough metre. Perhaps some word other than *languages* is required — compare Acts 2/4: *Et coeperunt loqui variis linguis* (AV: "And began to speak with other tongues"). Some influence from *languages* 273, 289, 297 may be suspected.

288 HmAR require the relative pronoun to be understood. H supplies it, producing a rougher metre. B further expands the sentence by the unnecessary addition of a preposition.

292 *here* ARBH is to be preferred to the scribally erroneous *lere* Hm.

295–302, stanza 38 The Hm stanza rhymes aaababcb, with four stressed syllables insead of the expected three in 302.

steight 299 H is to be preferred for rhyme to *steegh* HmARB, the latter evidently influenced by the a-rhymes of the previous quatrain — compare the reverse confusion in 296 ARH.

dighte 301 AR is to be preferred for rhyme to *drest* HmB, and for rhyme and meaning to *dreight* H. The H form is not recorded by MED and seems to represent a misunderstanding of an exemplar alteration, seen in HmB, from the AR form, due to the influence of the preceding b-rhymes.

No manuscript has a metrically satisfactory form of 302. Such a form would result from the omission of *the love of*. The RB reading does not affect metre or meaning: A adds a further syllable to an overweighted line.

295 Although Hm gives sense, all other manuscripts include the preposition *an/one* before *high*. Such a reading is perhaps syntactically preferable.

303–10 The idea that the Apostles' Creed was composed under the immediate influence of the Holy Ghost, with each apostle contributing one article, is first recorded by Rufinus, *Commentarius in Symbolum Apostolorum*, para.2 (PL 21/337). The idea gained particular currency from a series of sermons, *De Symbolo*, erroneously attributed to Augustine, in which the articles are specifically assigned; compare sermones 240-241 (PL 39/2188–91): *Petrus dixit Credo in Deum Patrem omnipotentem, Joannes dixit Creatorem coeli et terrae* etc. (id.2190).

308 reflects Matthew 16/18–9: *Et ego dico tibi, quia tu es Petrus, et super hanc petram aedificabo Ecclesiam meam, et portae inferi non praevalebunt adversus eam. Et tibi dabo claves regni caelorum; et quodcumque ligaveris super terram erit ligatum et in caelis, et quodcumque solveris super terram, erit solutum et in caelis* (AV "And I say also unto thee, That thou art Peter, and upon this rock I will build my church; and the gates of hell shall not prevail against it. And I will give thee the keys of the kingdom of heaven: and whatsoever thou shalt bind on earth shall be bound in heaven: and whatsoever thou shalt loose on earth shall be loosed in heaven"). The text has special importance for the Roman Catholic Church, in that it represents the basis of papal power, Christ conferring divine authority upon Peter, the first pope, to be recommitted to his successors. The line might therefore have controversial implications for a Protestant audience. No reason is supplied by the Pseudo-Augustine sermons for Peter's responsibility for the first article.

304 *wee* comprehends the apostles, the only ones present at the coming of the Holy Ghost in Acts 2/1. The wider audience of Acts 1/13–5, suggested in 33–4, has receded, presumably from 65.

309 With *lewd* HmH, compare Pseudo-Augustine, Sermo 231 (PL 39/2190): *Symbolum quod vobis tradituri sumus, fratres charissimi, comprehensio est fidei nostrae atque perfectio, simplex, breve, plenum; ut simplicitas consulat audientium rusticitati, brevitas memoriae, plenitudo doctrinae.* A and B seem troubled by the word; B substitutes the formally similar but meaningless *lewte*, while A substitutes the possible *lawe*, at the same time unnecessarily changing the rhyme-word to *leve* and destroying the rhyme. R's *truth*, semantically possible, seems to be an independent substitution.

310 + SD–58 On the ascription of articles to individual apostles, see further Curt F. Bühler, 'The Apostles and the Creed', *Speculum* xxviii (1953) pp.335–9. The order here is that of Bühler's second group, comprising *Ignorancia Sacerdotum* (Bodley ms. Lat. th. c.57. fol.16ᵛ) Pseudo-Augustinus, *Sermo de Symbolo* (PL 39/2189), *Symbolum apostolicum* (third block-book edition), single woodblock no.1759.

310 + SD H anticipates 366 + SD HmARB, allowing the two strangers to be present throughout the recital of the Creed and the following brief dialogue. In HmARB the strangers are not present at this point to hear any of the apostles' words. In York 44, the two doctors eavesdrop throughout; in *Ludus Coventriae* 39 they observe the disciples kissing the ground and, without reference to the gift of tongues, conclude that they are drunk.

311–8, stanza 40 The rhyme *comford* 314 — *lord* 318 is deliberately imperfect, hence the form at 314 HmH, where ARB prefer the more usual *comforte. lore* 318 A represents scribal confusion of *d* and *e* which destroys rhyme and sense.

314 + Latin In conformity with the usual punctuation of the Apostles' Creed, it might be preferable to place the comma after *unicum* rather than after *eius*. It is curious that the important word *unicum* has no counterpart in the following paraphrase.

318 *our elders lord* i.e. "the lord of our forefathers", perhaps in the sense of "promised to our forefathers". The phrase is without Credal counterpart, but

PLAY XXI

compare, e.g., Pseudo-Augustine, Sermo 241 (PL 39/2190), which emphasises the identity of God the Father and God the Son, a purpose which may also be implied in this phrase. Compare play 1/24-31, 286-9.

319 *with* AR is an error, apparently resulting from a desire to make the affirmation more positive. Deimling (p.xii) regards it as "quite senseless."

321-2 The paraphrase has no equivalent to *qui* in the Latin; the relative pronoun must be understood at 321. *was* 322 governs both *conceyved* and *borne*, in equivalence to the *est* of the Latin.

325-6 *was* 326 governs all three past participles in these lines.

326 contains four strongly stressed syllables instead of the expected three. A regular line would result from the omission of *fayre*.

345-6 *sanctorum communionem* has been variously interpreted as "fellowship with holy persons" (either 'saints and martyrs' or 'the faithful, living or dead'), or, as here, "participation in the eucharistic elements" ('a community of holy persons', i.e. as an extension of *sanctam ecclesiam catholicam*). Compare Pseudo-Augustine, Sermo 241 (PL 39/2191): *Credentes ergo sanctam Ecclesiam catholicam, sanctorum habentes communionem, quia ubi est fides sancta, ibi est et sancta communio*. For a full discussion of the issue, see J. N. D. Kelly, *Early Christian Creeds* (3rd.ed., London, 1972) pp.388-97.

348 *sinnes* H is to be preferred to *synne* HmARB in rendering *peccatorum*.

351-8 The interpretation here given distinguishes the *generall resurreccion of ych bodye* 352-3 on Doomsday from the entry of the saint into heaven immediately on death (*after my daye* 356), a distinction of the general and particular judgement which will be developed further in Play 24.

353 *bowne* H is to be preferred for rhyme and meaning to *borne* HmAR, *boone* B. HmARB suggest an obscure exemplar reading; R substitutes a different and inappropriate version of the line. With the rhyme *resurrection—bowne*, compare *boune—devotyon* 3/264-8.

359-66 No such motive of separation follows upon the receipt of the Holy Ghost in Acts 2, where the apostles continue in Jerusalem. 359-62 echo Mark 16/15 (quoted above, 243-6 note).

362 *beede* Hm is required for rhyme. OED records this form of the past tense of *bid* from 14th-15th centuries. *bade* ABH, *byd* R apparently represent the erroneous substitution of more familiar forms.

366+SD On H's omission here, see 310+SD note.

alienigene Acts 2/6 describes those present as *multitudo* (AV "the multitude"). Compare also Acts 2/5: *Erant autem in Ierusalem habitantes Iudaei, viri religiosi ex omni natione quae sub caelo est* (AV "And there were dwelling at Jerusalem Jews, devout men, out of every nation under heaven").

York 44 has two *doctors;* Ludus Coventriae 40 has three Jews, making the identification clear.

367-90 Based on Acts 2/7-12. 371-4 and 389-90 have no biblical counterpart.

The list of places omits the opening, Acts 2/9: *Parthi, et Medi, et Aelamitae* (AV

"Parthians, and Medes, and Elamites"). The account ends with the wonderment of the crowd and does not proceed with the biblical speculation that the apostles might be drunk, or with Peter's eloquent reply which converted many of them. This continuation is found in York 44/155-204, *Ludus Coventriae* 40/14-39.

369 Compare Acts 2/8: *Et quomodo nos audivimus unusquisque linguam nostram* (AV "And how hear we every man in our tongue"). *language* HmARB renders *linguam*, but the absence of an equivalent to *unusquisque* explains H's preference for a plural form.

379 *Ile of Pontus* Compare *Pontum*, Acts 2/9 (AV "Pontus"). Pontus was a large district in the north of Asia Minor, along the coast of the Pontus Euxinus. *Ile* here has the sense of *ile* MED 2b, "In OT usage: a land on the sea coast, a coastland."

380 *Fryzeland* i.e. *Phrygiam*, Acts 2/10 (AV "Phrygia), which vaguely suggested the western part of the central Asia Minor peninsula.

384 *Greece* Compare *Cretes*, Acts 2/11 (AV "Cretes").

389 The line seems to have caused difficulties for all the scribes. It may be significant that all manuscripts except Hm read *folowe* for *fellowe goe*. AR provide the most regular sequence of strongly and weakly stressed syllables, although *spye* A weakens the sequence. BH supplies an object, which improves sense at the expense of metre — B's inversion, *and therefore*, further weakens the metre.

PLAY XXII

Dramatis Personae Ezechiell, Expositor, Zacharias, Dannyell, Johannes Evangelista.

No *Locations, properties,* or *costumes* specified.

Sources
1–260 contain four prophecies with expositions, whose sources are given in the accompanying notes below.
261–340, the Fifteen Signs of Doomsday, present a familiar topic, found in Comestor, *Historia Scholastica,* 'In Evangelia' 141 (*PL* 198/1611–2). L. U. Lucken, *Antichrist and the Prophets of Antichrist in the Chester Cycle* (Washington, 1940) argued that the version in Mirk's homily 'De Adventu Domini' corresponded most closely to the Chester version and might have served as source. This view has been convincingly opposed by W. W. Heist, *The Fifteen Signs Before Doomsday* (Michigan Stage College P., 1952), pp. 167–70, who argues for the direct dependence of the Chester version on the *Legenda Aurea*.

Play-heading The H version includes not only the prophets and the Last Day (presumably the Fifteen Signs) but also Antichrist and Enoch and Elias, characters in Play 23. AR seem to present *Ezechiell* as heading. HmB have no heading. It is possible that the heading had been omitted or cancelled in the exemplar. AR's heading does not describe the play's contents but merely names the first speaker; it possibly represents the SH for the opening speech transferred from before the biblical quotation. There is some variation in the position of the SHs in the succeeding speeches, but the usual position seems to be before the Latin (for exceptions, see 48 + Hm, 172 + A). Here B has the SH before the Latin, but not as heading, and H has the SH to the left of the Latin; but AR, exceptionally, put the SH after the Latin. The BH arrangement could well explain the AR format, and the inappropriateness of AR's heading might have influenced the omission of the SH in Hm. H may represent a scribal description of the content of the play — about prophets prophesying about the Last Judgement, Antichrist and Enoch and

Elias. Alternatively, it may have some significance for the development of the cycle.

No other English cycle has a play on this subject.

Before 1 *Latin*   Ezechiel 37/1-2: AV "The hand of the Lord was upon me, and carried me out in the spirit of the Lord, and set me down in the midst of the valley which was full of bones, And caused me to pass by them round about." *dimisit* H reflects the Vulgate form; *circumduxit* BH is to be preferred to the scribally erroneous *circumdixit* HmAR; no manuscript has the Vulgate *in spiritu* for *spiritus*.

Before 1 SH   See *Play-heading* note.

The sequence Ezechiel—Zechariah—Daniel—John is not biblical, since Daniel should then precede Zechariah. The prophecies present in turn the general resurrection, Enoch, Elias and the martyrs of Antichrist, the coming of Antichrist, and the deaths of Enoch and Elias at Antichrist's hand and their resurrection. In the Fifteen Signs, the play finally reverts to the Doomsday theme.

1-20   Based on Ezechiel 37/1-10, which in context refers to God's revival of the hope of Israel for their homeland. 1-4 have no biblical counterpart, serving here to identify the speaker for the audience.

1-8, stanza 1   Hm rhymes aaaaaaab; line 4 contains four strongly stressed syllables instead of the expected three. No manuscript corrects the rhymes or line 4, but ARH add *or fell* 8, thereby increasing the number of syllables in that line to four instead of the expected three and producing a rhyme for line 4 which results in an aaaaaaaa stanza-form; B's *or shea* 8 may represent a scribal error originating in the ARH form, with confusion of *f* and long *s* and, more obscurely, of *ll* and *a*.

A regular three-stress line would result from the omission of *will* 4; but compare *will I tell* 180. Alternatively, similar regularity would result from the omission of *I*, since the subject is provided by *I*(2) 3; the two *I*'s in 3 might well have influenced an erroneous insertion in 4. *fell* 8 would provide a suitable rhyme but would require the omission of *fleshe or*. Possibly *flesh* was substituted for *fell* but the exemplar contained a note indicating the alternative, *or fell*, which was ignored by Hm but incorporated into the line by ARH and probably B. The preference for *flesh* may have been due in part to the use of *fell* (i.e. *fele*, "many") as rhyme-word at 7. See also 7-8 note.

7-8   Compare Ezechiel 37/1, quoted before 1. A verb must be understood to give sense here — e.g. *were, lay*. The sequence of strongly and weakly stressed syllables at 8 would be improved by the addition of further syllable, which could be supplied either by introducing a verb at the start of the line, or by reading *withouten* for *without*. *wherin* 7 BH may be preferred for metre and meaning to *where* HmAR.

21-4   Compare Ezechiel 37/13-14: *Et scietis quia ego Dominus, cum aperuero sepulcra vestra et eduxero vos de tumulis vestris, popule meus, et dedero spiritum meum in vobis et vixeritis, et requiescere vos faciam super humum vestram; et scietis quia ego Dominus locutus sum, et feci, ait Dominus Deus*. (AV "And ye shall know that I am the Lord, when I have opened your graves, O my people, and brought you up out of your graves, and shall put my spirit in you, and ye shall live, and I shall place you in your own land: then shall ye know that I the Lord have spoken it, and performed it, saith the Lord."). Compare also 23/33-6.

PLAY XXII

29-32 See Comestor, *Historia Scholastica*, 'Liber Ezechielis' 5 (*PL* 198/1445); *Legenda Aurea*, 'De Sancto Spiritu', on Ezechiel 37/4; and *Stanzaic Life*:

> ffor thrugh gostes, As rede we
> Bi Esechiel prophecie
> All þe world shall dee ʒ wykent be
> At domesday þrugh his mercy
> (10, 773-6)

glossing Ezechiel 37/12-14.

40 *mayd* The distinction from *man* and *wyfe* is not immediately clear. Probably the sense "virgin", MED 2(a), is intended, but the reference cannot be to the 144,000 virgins who follow the Lamb in Apocalypse 14 since they have no part in the general resurrection. *maid or wif* is a frequent distinction, between a (usually young) unmarried woman and a married woman — see *maid* MED 1(a) — and the use here may simply be conventional. Or possibly the sense of MED 1(c), "a girl, a young girl", is here intended, to stand for children in general.

41-4 The light-darkness image is commonplace; compare 2 Corinthians 6/14 and Matthew 13/43. *seaven* is perhaps a conventional number — see also 332 note.

AR evidently did not understand *thester* 43 and *underfoe* 44, significantly agreeing in substituting *sorte* and *understand*, to the detriment of meaning and rhyme.

48+ Latin Zechariah 6/1: AV "And I turned and lifted up mine eyes, and looked, and, behold, there came four chariots out from between two mountains."

48+ SH ARBH are to be preferred in placing the SH before the Latin, thus linking the quotation with the vernacular development in 49-72. Hm may have misplaced the SH following the confusion about *Before* 1 SH.

49-72 Based on Zechariah 6/1-5. 71-2 are without biblical equivalent.

54 *sylver hilles* Compare *montes aeri*, AV "mountains of brass", Zechariah 6/1.

56 The question at Zechariah 6/4 is *Quid sunt haec, domine mi?* (AV "What are these, my lord?"), which is the question answered at 67-72 in response to 65.

60-1 Compare Zechariah 6/3: *In quadriga quarta equi varii et fortes* (AV "In the fourth chariot grisled and bay horses"). *they* 61 would therefore refer only to the fourth team of horses, not to all teams, with *biglye* 61 corresponding to *fortes*.

62 *answered* Compare Zechariah 6/4: *Et respondi et dixi* (AV "Then I answered and said"). The word does not presuppose a question here.

63-4 Compare Zechariah 6/4: *Angelum qui loquebatur in me* (AV "The angel that talked with me").

70 Compare Zechariah 6/5: *Coram dominatore omnis terrae* (AV "Before the Lord of all the earth").

71-2 71 Hm gives sense but *fitte may* ARBH may be preferred in its sense "there is not one so fierce as to escape that terrible destiny"; with the collocation of *fit* and *flee*, compare 7/196.

72 seems to mean "nor gain what they desire for themselves from this" — i.e. from the occasion when the four winds blow before Christ.

73-80, stanza 10   No manuscript has the form *lere* for *learne* 80, required for rhyme. The error was evidently present in the exemplar.

81   *see* HmARB is an acceptable past tense form, replaced in H by *saw*; compare *sawe* 3, 89. The uncancelled *se* which follows in H strengthens the possibility that *see* was the exemplar reading which was copied by HmARB and unthinkingly added after the corrected form in H.

85-8   Lucken finds no commentary which might have suggested this or other features of the Chester moralisation. The lines here anticipate the rôle of the two prophets in play 23.

89-90   Some word must be understood within these lines. The simplest approach is to treat *hee sawe* as a relative clause which, by its definitive nature, renders the use of a definite article before *fowre* unnecessary — "the four chariots which he saw". Alternatively, however, a relative pronoun may be understood at the start of 90; or, on analogy with the construction at 81-8, 89 could be regarded as a statement, and a pronoun subject understood in 90. 90 is metrically acceptable, but would also be acceptable if a further unstressed syllable were introduced.

90-3   Omitted by AR, probably an error originating in an eye-slip during the copying of A, whereby *fowre* 89 was confused with *fowre* 93.

93-4   "It is also true that he saw four horses of diverse colours." *certayntee* may here have the sense of *certainte* MED 3(a), "a true account", but also of MED 6, "a specified number; a fixed or guaranteed amount". By this reading, no comma is required after *allso* 93.

By changing the word-order, H avoids the assonantally awkward combination *horses ys*.

95-124   The interpretation in these lines corresponds broadly to that given by Jerome, *Commentariorum in Zachariam* 1/6 (PL 25/1454) *Legi in cujusdam volumine, quatuor quadrigas, in quibus sunt equi rufi et nigri, et albi, et varii, ac fortes, quatuor Evangelia intelligenda et equos Apostolos, per diversitatem colorum diversas gratias possidentes: quorum alii rufi sint in martyrio, alii obscuri, et nigri, et Christi mysteria cognoscentes, de quibus dicatur in Psalmis: 'Caligo sub pedibus ejus". Et: 'Posuit tenebras latibulum suum". Alii albi, gratia virginali; alii varii et fortes, habentes gratiam curationum diversarumque virtutem.* But those converted by Enoch and Elias have no part in Jerome's exposition and seem awkwardly introduced here, at 98-100 and 117-24.

The lines present two difficulties.

(1) The order in which the horses are listed. In 57-60 the order "red—black—white—dyvers" derives from Zechariah 6/2-3. In the angel's exposition, Zechariah 6/6-7, only the black, white and *dyvers* (in two groups) are mentioned, the red being omitted. In 105-24, the order of listing is "red—white—black—*skewed*". The horses were often linked with the four horses of Apocalypse 6/2-8, where the listing order is "white—red—black—pale". The change in order at 105-24 from that at 57-60 seems established by rhyme-schemes and stanza-forms, but no reason for it is obvious. It may be noted that stanza 15 contains only four lines

(2) The identification at 97-104 and its continuation at 105-124 presents difficulties. At 97-104 five groups are listed — martyrs, confessors, the disbelievers

PLAY XXII 323

converted by Enoch and Elias, the virgins and what seems to be a "miscellaneous" group at 102–4. In the subsequent exposition, however, the groups are listed as martyrs 106, those who do not fear death 109–12, confessors 116, and Jews and pagans converted by Enoch and Elias 120. The exposition is thus in different order from that in stanza 13, but for no obvious reason. If the symbolic equation with the horses is extended to stanza 13's listing, yet another sequence results — "red— black—*skewed*—white". The different sequences again seem confirmed by rhyme-schemes and stanza-forms.

Although it seems an unsatisfactory explanation, it does appear that the order of presentation may have been varied to meet the exigencies of stanza-form.

109–12 The white horses are said in Zechariah 6/6 to go into the north after the black ones. These lines seem rather to echo Zechariah 6/7 on the *bay* horses: *Qui autem erant robustissimi exierunt, et quaerebant ire et discurrere per omnem terram, et dixit: 'Ite, perambulate terram; et perambulaverunt terram'*. (AV "And the bay went forth, and sought to go that they might walk to and fro through the earth: and he said, Get you hence, walk to and fro through the earth. So they walked to and fro through the earth"). 111–2 may echo Matthew 16/28, Mark 9/1, Luke 9/27; compare Luke 9/27: *Dico autem vobis: Vere sunt aliqui hic stantes, qui non gustabunt mortem, donec videant regnum Dei* (AV "But I tell you of a truth, there be some standing here, which shall not taste of death, till they see the kingdom of God"), and *Glossa Ordinaria*, 'Evang. Luc.' 9/27 (PL 114/279): *Qui stat cum Christo non gustat mortem, quia nec tenuem mortis aeternae sensum habebit, qui Christi consortia meruerit, cui nec in morte interrumpitur ordo vivendi .... Quia arduum erat animam periculis, corpus morti offerre, sustentat infirmitatem humanae mentis remuneratione praesentium, ne frangatur desperatione vel taedio. Visa enim aeterna gloria, etsi transitu et ad breve momentum, fortiores tamen contra mundi adversa redduntur. Promittit itaque futuram gloriam in transitu videndam in terra, ut certius in coelo speretur aeterna*. The reference may comprehend the 144,000 virgins who are in the company of the Lamb in Apocalypse 14/3–4, who did not 'taste death', being introduced into heaven before the general resurrection. Such significance would extend the sense of *virgens* 101 and explain why the word does not recur in this later exposition as does *marters* 106, *confessors* 116 or, at 119, an equivalent of *men misbeleevinge* 98.

If the link with Zechariah 6/7 is accepted, *above* 110 may be an error for *about*, conveying the sense of *perambulo*.

113–6, stanza 15 The stanza consists of four lines instead of the expected eight and represents a regular Chester quatrain. It may be noted that the statement in Zechariah 6/6 that the black horses went into the north is without counterpart here. Moreover, the triumph of the black and white horses at Zechariah 6/8 is also not reported. Some references to the north might be expected in view of the reference to the south 118. Possibly, therefore, a quatrain required to complete the stanza was omitted in the exemplar.

121–2 Some link with the subject of *shall turne* 122, i.e. with *Jewes and paynims* 120, should be understood, either as a relative pronoun in 121 or as a personal pronoun in 122.

124 + Latin Daniel 7/2–3: AV "I saw in my vision by night, and, behold, the four winds of the heaven strove upon the great sea. And four great beasts came up from the sea, diverse one from another." *Ego Daniell* is without biblical equivalent; compare *I Daniell* 125. No manuscript reads *venti caeli* for *venti*, as in the Vulgate, nor does the word *caeli* have counterpart in the vernacular version. *grandes* ARBH is to be preferred to *gradentes* Hm, the latter evidently an erroneous expansion, and *mari* H to *mare* HmARB, both preferred readings reflecting the Vulgate form.

124+SH   A puts the SH after the Latin. See *Before* 1 SH note.

125–66   An abridgement of Daniel 7; viz., 125–9, 7/1–3; 130–45, 7/7–8; 146–8, 7/20; 149–56, 7/24–26.

125–32, stanza 17   The b-rhymes, *hye* 128 — *leave* 132, do not rhyme. No manuscript presents a rhyme-form, and the error was evidently in the exemplar. Rhyme could be restored by syntactical inversion at 132, reading *leave will I* for *I will leave*.

129   *the* The construction here is parallel to that in 127, where the subject is expressed and immediately taken up in the pronoun *the*, "they". Here, however, by scribal error, concern for metre or unease at the construction, AR omit *the* and B substitutes *ther*.

133–40, stanza 18   The b-rhymes, *fortredde* 136 — *hye* 140, do not rhyme. No manuscript provides a rhyme and the readings were evidently present in the exemplar. It may be noted that 140 has no direct biblical counterpart and may be compared with 128. *fortrade* 136 B is an alternative past form.

137   *of leede* Compare Daniel 7/7: *Dissimilis autem erat ceteris bestiis quas videram ante eam* (AV "And it was diverse from all the beasts that were before it"). The biblical version seems to suggest that it was different primarily from the other three beasts. *of leede* may suggest "known to man", MED *led(e)* n.(2).

143–4   Compare Daniel 7/8: *Et tria de cornibus primis evulsa sunt a facie eius* (AV "Before whom there were three of the first horns plucked up by the roots"). *first* here is taken with *three* rather than *ten*, suggesting a primacy which is unbiblical.

146   "The rest had to be humble towards him." The syntactical relationship of *to bee* to the rest of the sentence is not clear, but 146 seems to represent a result clause dependent upon *so great* 145 and some verb of compulsion must therefore be understood.

149   The vision was interpreted for Daniel by a bystander, Daniel 7/16, identified in St. Cyril's *Catechesis* 15 as *Gabriel archangelus* (PG 33/887).

155   Compare 164, and 164 + Latin note.

157–61   Compare Comestor, *Historia Scholastica*, 'Liber Danielis' 6 (PL 198/1453–4): *Sequitur quarta visio Danielis ... in qua vidit secundum imagines quatuor bestiarum, quatuor regna, quae vidit Nabuchodonosor in statua quadriformi; sed additum est de Antichristo, et die judicii '...Et ecce cornu aliud parvum ortum est de medio eorum.' Hic est Antichristus de tribu Dan ignobilis, in obscuro loco Babyloniae nasciturus.*

164 + Latin   Daniel 7/25: AV "They shall be given into his hand until a time and times and the dividing of times". The explanatory addition is found elsewhere; e.g.

Comestor, *Historia Scholastica*, 'Liber Danielis' 6 (PL 198/1455).

165-8 Compare Comestor, *Historia Scholastica*, 'Liber Danielis' 6 (PL 198/1454).

171 The line can be read with four strong stresses only by regarding *Danyelles* as tetrasyllabic.

172 + SH A places the SH after the Latin; see *Before* 1 SH note.

172 + Latin Apocalypse 11/3: AV "And I will give power unto my two witnesses, and they shall prophesy a thousand two hundred and threescore days, clothed in sackcloth."

et (2) is without biblical counterpart.

173-6 It is usual to identify John, author of Apocalypse, with the apostle John, as, for example, in *Glossa Ordinaria*, 'Apoc. Joannis', Prologus Hieronymi (PL 114/709).

John, Apocalypse 1/9-10, states that he was instructed to write the book while in Patmos. But the ravishing of John's spirit to Heaven traditionally occurred as he slept in Christ's bosom at the Last Supper. See *Northern Passion* 373-82, *Northern English Legendary* 7/16-20, *Glossa Ordinaria*, 'Evang. Joann.' 21/20 (PL 114/426); also F. A. Foster, *The Northern Passion* (EETS os 147) pp.62-3. The reference amplifies 15/80 + SD.

181-210 Based on Apocalypse 11/3-11. The speech has no counterpart to the comparison with two olive trees, 11/4, or to the spiritual designation of the great city as Sodom and Egypt, 11/8.

185-8 The punctuation should correspond to that of 172 + Latin, with comma for semi-colon 186. *clad* HmARH corresponds to *amicti*, Apocalypse 11/3; *sackcloth* 188 B is apparently an unnecessary substitution.

191 Compare Apocalypse 11/5: *Ignis exiet de ore eorum* (AV "Fire proceedeth out of their mouth"). The metre here is rough, and *feight* does not give good sense, or correspond closely to *exiet*. The omission of *the* by R improves metre; B's *send* for *feight* improves meaning but destroys rhyme.

feight cannot represent ME *fighten*, "to fight", but may well have been influenced formally by the word, particularly in this context. We cannot identify the word with any confidence, but it may be an unrecorded variant of a verb-stem in -*t*, such as *feten*, MED 1, "to make or fashion (something)".

199-200 Without biblical counterpart. Compare Apocalypse 11/6: *Et percutere terram omni plaga quotiescumque voluerint* (AV "And to smite the earth with all plagues, as often as they will").

The rhyme-word at 200 was evidently omitted or illegible in the exemplar. HmR retain the omission; B substitutes an adverb for the preposition, destroying any possible rhyme; A and H supply possessive pronoun and noun, of which *their might* H is to be preferred to *their power* A for rhyme. The A reading duplicates the rhyme-word of 202. Deimling cites the variant as evidence of H's superiority.

203 *from beneath* corresponds to *de abysso*, AV "out of the bottomless pit", Apocalypse 11/7.

210   Apocalypse 11/11–2 does not mention the two prophets as speaking after their resurrection, although they are shown to do this in 23/699–714 below.

shall represents a departure from *should* 185, 191, 197, 202, 204, 205, all of which represent the reported speech of God, 180, 189, 196, deriving from the angel's words in Apocalypse 11/1–10. It corresponds to a change at Apocalypse 11/11 from the future tense of the angel's words to the past tense of John's own observation: *Spiritus vitae a Deo intravit in eos; et steterunt super pedes suos* (AV "The Spirit of life from God entered into them, and they stood upon their feet"), and thus indicates John's own prophecy. This subtle distinction is missed by R, which substitutes *shoulde*.

221–8   Compare *Glossa Ordinaria*, 'Apoc. Joannis' 11/3 (PL 114/730) *'Duobus testibus' De Elia et Enoch agitur, per quos praedicatores alii intelliguntur*. On Enoch, see 17/236 + SH note; on Elias, see 17/242 note.

237–40   The beast of Apocalypse 11/7 is identified with that of Apocalypse 13 which conforms to features of the beast described by Daniel. Compare *Glossa Ordinaria*, 'Apoc. Joannis' 13/1 (PL 114/733): *Bestia haec spiritualiter est Antichristus, vel generaliter tota collectio malorum*.

245–52, stanza 32   No manuscript has the form *tome* for *tyme* 248, required for perfect rhyme.

247   A has inexplicably and erroneously omitted the line; R corrects the error.

260 + Latin–66   Lucken, *Antichrist*, p.121 comments: "Bede is the first to acknowledge St. Jerome as his source, and in this he is followed by almost all the writers of either Latin or vernacular versions of the Fifteen Signs of Doom. But there is no treatment of the Signs of Doom to be found anywhere in the extant works of St. Jerome, and this fact makes it impossible to determine which of the many and various versions attributed to him is really his. There is the possibility also that the attribution to him of the authorship of the Fifteen Signs is entirely incorrect." The Latin here serves as a heading and may not have formed part of the spoken text as the previous Latin texts from the Vulgate may have done.

The Signs here follow the prophecies of Antichrist and culminate in the creation of the new earth and heaven, 330. They are therefore properly prophecies of the Judgment and relate to events following the death of Antichrist. *Cursor Mundi* lists them after the death of Antichrist; but *Legenda Aurea* places them before the account of the coming of Antichrist.

Lucken believed that the Chester account, which belongs to a tradition first attested in extant manuscripts by Comestor, derived from Mirk. His belief was influenced by his use of the French translation of *Legenda Aurea* based on earlier manuscripts than Graesse's edition. But Heist notes the close correspondence with Graesse's edition and points out that the earliest version of the *Legenda* was not necessarily the one most widely known.

261–8, stanza 34   The b-rhymes, *doome* 264 — *dwell* 268, do not rhyme; 264 contains four strongly stressed syllables instead of the expected three. These features were probably present in the exemplar, since they are not rectified in any manuscript. The syllables of 264 can be reduced by omitting *to fall*; or by omitting *day of*; or by reading *domesday* for *the daye of doome* (but compare 30). Adopting the last suggestion, rhyme would be restored by reading *stay* for *dwell*.

PLAY XXII

266 *bookes* BH is to be preferred to *booke* HmAR as corresponding to *codicibus* 260 + Latin.

273 Either *wee* HmARB or *I* H is semantically possible. *I* occurs at 277, 289; *we* at 285. It may be noted that Hm originally wrote *I* but cancelled it, and that *wee* might be preferred for rhyme.

276 B's omission here may have been aided by the fact that the b-rhyme of stanza 35 is also the a-rhyme of stanza 36.

277–84, stanza 36   *brene* 282 ARH is to be preferred for rhyme to *burne* HmB, the later evidently a substitution of a more familiar form. The stem-vowel must be short; presumably *kene* 283 A is influenced by the form *brene*, but it should have the short vowel of *kenne* HmRBH.

288 The exemplar was evidently obscure at this point. AR omit the line; Hm is in a different hand. Hm and H are both possible and one can be derived from the other, although it is not clear which should have priority; B seems to support *and* H rather than *a* Hm, but its questionable *main* might support an exemplar *man* or *manie* (with minim misdivision). Deimling wrongly states that B omits the line and cites the omission in support of H's superiority.

The line is without counterpart in Comestor, *Legenda* or Mirk, but compare the fifth sign in *Cursor Mundi*:

> Uggeli sal be þe fift dai,
> Mare þan ani tung can sai;
> All bestes dumb vnder þe lift,
> Vp þan sal þair hefds lift
> Apon vr lauerd for to cri,
> If þae moght spek at ask merci.
> Right to þe air sal þai rin
> For drednes þar to hide þam in,
> An þan cri sal wit stiþer steuen
> Þan nu mai do ten or elleuen,
> All for dred of his cuming
> Þat dome sal deme of alkin thing.
> (22519–30)

313–6 Compare also Apocalypse 6/15: *Et reges terrae et principes, et tribuni et divites et fortes et omnis servus et liber absconderunt se in speluncis et in petris montium* (AV "And the kings of the earth, and the great men, and the rich men, and the chief captains, and the mighty men, and every bondman and every free man, hid themselves in the dens and in the rocks of the mountains").

With *flee* 314 compare *exibunt* Comestor and *Legenda*, *goo* Mirk. With *as the were madd* 316 compare *velut amentes* Comestor and *Legenda*, *so amated* Mirk.

313   *bee* Hm is confirmed by rhyme. *have/hath bene* is attested in the other manuscripts and may well have been the exemplar reading; additional syllable improves the metre, and the original reading may have been *hath be*.

317–24, stanza 41   Rhyme apparently requires *e'en* for *even* 317, a form found in no manuscript, and 318 ARBH, with *bene* as rhyme-word. The form *even* may have prompted the Hm order at 318, giving a short vowel rhyme in *open* which destroys the rhyme of *weene* 319.

317   *elevon* Compare *thirteene* 325 Hm, *foureteene* 327 Hm, *fyfteene* 329 Hm. Possibly the exemplar reading took the form xi^{th} 317 R, xiii^{th} 325 ARB, xiiii^{th} 327 AR, xv^{th} 329 AR, and was then expanded as the ordinal by all other manuscripts except Hm. In all cases, the adjectival form is to be preferred.

321–4   Compare Apocalypse 6/13: *Et stellae de caelo ceciderunt super terram sicut ficus emittit grossos suos cum a vento magno movetur* (AV "And the stars of the heaven fell unto the earth, even as a fig-tree casteth her untimely figs, when she is shaken of a mighty wind"); see also Matthew 24/29, Mark 13/25.

327–8   The sign is partially paralleled by Apocalypse 20/11: *Et vidi thronum magnum candidum, et sedentem super eum, a cuius conspectu fugit terra et caelum, et locus non est inventus eis* (AV "And I saw a great white throne, and him that sat on it, from whose face the earth and the heaven fled away; and there was found no place for them"), but close analogues can also be found in 2 Peter 3/10: *Advenet autem dies Domini ut fur, in quo caeli magno impetu transient, elementa vero calore solventur, terra autem et quae in ipsa sunt opera exurentur* (AV "The day of the Lord will come as a thief in the night; in the which the heavens shall pass away with a great noise, and the elements shall melt with fervent heat, the earth also and the works that are therein shall be burned up"), and 3/12: *Expectantes et properantes in adventum diei Domini, per quem caeli ardentes solventur, et elementa ignis ardore tabescent* (AV "Looking for and hasting unto the coming of the day of God, wherein the heavens being on fire shall be dissolved, and the elements shall melt with fervent heat"). More general references to the fall of heavens and earth are Psalm 102/26 (AV), Isaiah 51/6, Matthew 24/35, Mark 13/31.

329   Compare Apocalypse 21/1: *Et vidi caelum novum et terram novam* (AV "And I saw a new heaven and a new earth"); also Isaiah 65/17, 66/22, and 2 Peter 3/13. In Comestor, *Legenda Aurea*, and Mirk this is linked with the general resurrection from Apocalypse 20/5, 12; Comestor, *Historia Scholastica*, 'In Evangelia' 141 (PL 198/1611) and *Legenda Aurea: Quintadecima fiet coelum novum et terra nova et resurgent omnes*; Mirk: "The xv day heuen and erþ schull be made newe, and all men and woymen and childyrne schull aryse up yn þe age of xxx^{ti} þere and come to þe dome." Since Chester is concerned with the signs before the Judgment, and the general resurrection forms part of the Judgment play, the absence of this detail may be an act of deliberate selection.

332   *his names seaven* The phrase seems confirmed by rhyme, but RB apparently did not understand it and substituted, probably independently, the common collocation *names sake*, meaningful and appropriate to a petition, but destroying the rhyme.

With the reference here, compare Wakefield 13/190: "Now lord, for thy naymes sevyn / that made both moyn & starnes"; Digby *Mary Magdalen* 2044–5
            Lord Iesu, for þi namys sewynne,
            as gravnt me grace þat person to se.
Hemingway, discussing the occurrence in Wakefield, comments (*English Nativity Plays* (N.Y., 1909), p.286, note to 13/190): "In Rabbinical tradition there are seven

sacred names of God, El, Elohim, Adonai, YHWH, Ehyeh-Asher-Ehyeh, Shaddai, and Zebast. In Christian literature I have been unable to find this number. Jerome gives ten names of God in one place [Epistola 25(a), PL 22/428–30] and Junilius gives eight. There seems, therefore, to have been discussion in the mediaeval church on this point, and it is rather strange not to find mention of seven, as seven is the mystical sacred number."

333 + Latin–40 The final stanza draws together the two ideas in the play, *doomesday* 334 and *Antechriste* 339, a summary perhaps necessary because the Fifteen Signs would lead more appropriately to Play 24 than to Play 23. At the same time, 331–2 suggest the finality of a concluding benediction, which is repeated in 335–6. The final stanza may therefore have some significance for the earlier history of the play.

conclusio H recognises both the function of the final stanza as coda, and also its separateness from the preceding list of signs. Since it is absent from the other manuscripts, however, the heading may well be scribal.

336 *them*, apparently the exemplar reading, seems most obviously to refer to *tokens* 334, but does not then yield satisfactory meaning. B and H propose different alternatives, B substituting an auxiliary verb and H a temporal adverb with inverted word-order; and either may be preferred for meaning to HmAR, with H the more probable in view of the probability of scribal confusion between *then* and *them*.

338–40 "In as much as you must assess the accuracy of us and our play of the signs of Antichrist, he comes — you shall soon see!" The inverted word-order has led to the use of *wee* 338 for the syntactically correct *us*. *assaye* 339 seems to have the sense of MED 4(b). The translation given requires a slightly different punctuation from that in the text.

With 340, compare Apocalypse 22/12: *Ecce venio cito, et merces mea mecum est, reddere unicuique secundum opera sua* (AV "And behold, I come quickly; and my reward is with me, to give every man according as his work shall be"), and Apocalypse 22/20: *Dicit qui testimonium perhibet istorum: 'Etiam, venio cito. Amen. Veni, Domine Jesu'* (AV "He which testifieth these things saith: 'Surely I come quickly. Amen. Even so, come, Lord Jesus'"). Both texts refer to Christ's second coming.

339 *Antechristes signes* Presumably in distinction to the Signs of Doomsday; i.e. the prophecies of Zechariah, Daniel and John.

PLAY XXIII

Dramatis Personae Antechriste, Primus Rex, Secundus Rex, Tertius Rex, Quartus Rex, Primus Mortuus, Secundus Mortuus, Enock, Helias, Doctor, Michael Archangelus, Primus Demon, Secundus Demon.

NOTE The parts of *Primus Mortuus/Primus Demon* and *Secundus Mortuus/Secundus Demon* may be doubled.

Locations
this temple 37, 125
terram 149 + SD.

NOTE 1. See also *Properties*.
2. Locations offstage are specified also — *from hell-ground* 654, *in hell* 678, *in a dungeon deepe, right in hell-pytt* 690, *to hell* 691; *to heaven-blysse* 717, *to heaven* 721, *ad coelos* 722 + SD.

Properties
In the temple — tombe 125, 139 (and note), grave 123, 137, sepulchris 104 + SD; tumulo 149 + SD, lowe under the greete 143; up in thy see 171, cathedram 180 + SD, 624 + SD, seate 173
Outside the temple — men buryed in grave 97; trees 82 *with* fruyt 84.
my ghooste...in forme of fyre 131–2, spiritum 196 + SD, animam 678 + SD, soule 679.
our sacrafice 172, lambe and geat 174, this lambe 183; breadd 565, 569, 577.
sword 623, gladio 624 + SD × 2.

Costume
Enoch and Elias — muffeled in mantelles 390.

Sources The legend of Antichrist is not biblical, but it rests upon a number of biblical texts, notably 1 John 2/18–19 and 22, 4/3; 2 John 7; Apocalypse 11, 13 and 20/7; 1 Thessalonians 4/15ff and 2 Thessalonians 2/3–10; prophecies of Daniel, including that in Play 22 together with Daniel 8/8ff and 23ff and 11/21–3; and various gospel passages, especially Matthew 24/24, Mark 13/6 and 22, Luke 21/5 and John 5/43.

PLAY XXIII 331

Lucken points out that the most influential account of the legend is Adso's *Libellus de Antichristo* (PL 101/1291-8), establishing a tradition of the legend to which Chester belongs. Adso is here used as a useful comparison; it is not a direct source. Lucken's claim that Chester depended upon Mirk's account has been refuted by William W. Heist, *The Fifteen Signs*, pp.168-9.

Guild Ascription B omits the guild ascription here as also in the final play. The only previous similar omission by B was in play 4. The omissions at 23 and 24 may be significant in view of the problems of the introduction of these plays into the cycle and their functions; see also 22/*Play-heading* note.

Play-heading
The play survives not only in the five cyclic manuscripts, but also in the Peniarth manuscript, P, printed as appendix IIB, to which reference is made in discussion of the readings of the cyclic manuscripts.

Antechristi Greg, *Antichrist* p. xxiii fn. 2, states: "I believe all manuscripts are consistent in the spelling Antechrist." Although there are exceptions (e.g. 122 + SH A, 188 + SH R), the -*e*- spellings are usual and seem to represent the exemplar reading. Greg may be correct in suggesting "some confusion between Antichrist as the opponent of Christ [*anti*-] and the same as precursor of the second coming of Christ [*ante*-]." The name occurs in the Bible only in John's Epistles (1 John 2/18 and 22, 4/3; 2 John 7) where Antichrist is identified with those who deny the Incarnation. Compare Adso (PL 101/1291-2). The character is not identified to the audience by name until Michael addresses him at 625.

1-8 No source has been found for the Latin stanza. The lines suggest Christ coming in judgment, the role promised, and in their use of Latin recall the opening words of God in plays 1 and 24. A. R. Hohlfeld, ('Die altenglischen Kollektivmisterien unter besonderer Berücksichtigung der Verhältnisses der York- und Towneley-Spielen', *Anglia* xi (1889) p.272) suggested that they might have come from a Latin play; L. H. Martin ('Comic Eschatology in the Chester *Coming of Antichrist*', *Comparative Drama* v, 1971, p.175, note 8) comments: "The Leonine verse, a favorite form in medieval Latin hymns, may imply performance in chant or song, an excess quite in keeping with the character's general conduct." There is internal rhyme in lines 1 and 2.

Legenda Aurea, 'De Adventu Domini', states as the first means of deception used by Antichrist: *Primo per callidam suasionem sive scripturae falsae expositionem.*

Nitetur enim persuadere et ex scriptura firmare, se esse Messiam in lege promissum, et legem Christi destruet et suam statuet.

2 Martin proposes a punctuation: *Age, vobis monstrare descendi, vos iudicare. age* is attested by all manuscripts; *ego* would also be possible.

13–4 Compare Adso (PL 101/1295–6): *Nam sicut supra diximus, in civitate Babyloniae natus, Hierusalem veniens circumcidet se dicens Judaeis: "Ego sum Christus vobis repromissus, qui ad salutem vestram veni, ut vos, qui dispersi estis, congregem et defendam"*; S. Martini Legionensis, *Expositio Libri Apocalypsis* 11 (PL 209/360): *Jerosolymam veniens ... dicens Judaeis: Ego sum Christus vobis repromissus.*

18 *Moyses* Perhaps a reference to Deuteronomy 18/18: *Prophetam suscitabo eis de medio fratrum suorum similem tui, et ponam verba mea in ora eius, loqueturque ad eos omnia quae praecepero illi* (AV "I will raise them up a Prophet from among their brethren, like unto thee, and will put my words in his mouth, and he shall speak unto them all that I shall command him"). Compare John 5/46: *Si enim crederetis Moysi, crederetis forsitan et mihi; de me enim ille scripsit* (AV "For had ye believed Moses, ye would have believed me; for he wrote of me").

Davyd Compare 40+ Latin, 17/185–92 and notes, and 2 Samuel (2 Reges) 7/13: *Ipse aedificabit domum nomini meo, et stabiliam thronum regni eius usque in sempiternum* (AV "He shall build an house for my name, and I will stablish the throne of his kingdom for ever"). See also 2 Samuel 23, and numerous references in Psalms (e.g. 2/6–8).

Esaye Compare 8/317 + Latin–324, 17/25–40, with respective notes, and passages in Isaiah 40–56.

The names chosen suggest the three periods of Old Testament Messianic prophecy in chronological order — that culminating in the time of Moses, that culminating in the time of David, and that from the period of the prophets.

However, warnings of false prophets may also be found from these writings; viz:

Moyses Compare Deuteronomy 13/1–3: *Si surrexerit in medio tui prophetes, aut qui somnium vidisse se dicat, et praedixerit signum atque portentum, et evenerit quod locutus est, et dixerit tibi: Eamus, et sequamur deos alienos (quos ignoras) et serviamus eis, non audies verba prophetae illius aut somniatoris, quia tentat vos Dominus Deus vester, ut palam fiat utrum diligatis eum an non, in toto corde, et in tota anima vestra* (AV "If there arise among you a prophet, or a dreamer of dreams, and giveth thee a sign or a wonder. And the sign or the wonder come to pass, whereof he spake unto thee, saying, Let us go after other gods, which thou hast not known, and let us serve them: Thou shalt not hearken unto the words of that prophet, or that dreamer of dreams: for the Lord your God proveth you, to know whether ye love the Lord your God with all your heart and with all your soul").

Davyd Compare *Legenda Aurea*, 'De Adventu Domini': *Psalm: Constitue domine legislatorem super eos etc. Glossa: id est antichristum legis pravae latorem.*

Esaye Compare Isaiah 14/13–15: *Qui dicebas in corde tuo: In caelum conscendam, super astra Dei exaltabo solium meum; sedebo in monte testamenti, in lateribus aquilonis; ascendam super altitudinem nubium, similis ero Altissimo. Verum tamen ad infernum detraheris, in profundum laci* (AV "For thou has said in thine heart, I will ascend into heaven, I will exalt my throne above the stars of God: I will sit also upon the mount of the congregation, in the sides of the north: I will ascend above the heights of the

PLAY XXIII 333

clouds: I will be like the most High. Yet thou shalt be brought down to hell, to the sides of the pit").

24 + SD The text is from Ezechiel 36/24: AV "For I will take you from among the heathen, and gather you out of all countries, and will bring you into your own land." The text here differs from the Vulgate in *reducam] adducam*. Like the opening and succeeding texts, this Latin was probably uttered to suggest a learned and authoritative basis for Antichrist's vernacular claims.

The text refers most appropriately to 33–6 rather than to 25–32 and may have been misplaced. R's omission may therefore be deliberate.

25–32, stanza 4 The a- and c-rhymes are imperfect, perfect rhyme requiring *fand* for *found* 27 and *bond* for *band* 30. The variants 27 H, 29 B and 31 ARB indicate formal confusion. P's *wende—bende—sende* gives perfect rhyme, but *sende* is a nonce-form.

25 *laykyd him* P is to be preferred to *ligged him* HmH for meaning. HmH might be interpreted "has lied about himself", but *lien* MED v (2) is not recorded in reflexive use. AR therefore substitutes *me*, giving the acceptable "has slandered me", while B omits the pronoun, "has told lies".

here in lande i.e. in the land of Israel, where Antichrist is now standing — compare *this temple* 37 and note. Antichrist was of the tribe of Dan, born in Babylon and trained in evil; compare Adso (PL 101/1292): *Sicut ergo auctores nostri dicunt, Antichristus ex populo Judaeorum nascetur de tribu Dan, secundum prophetiam dicentem: Fiat Dan coluber in via, et cerastes in semita, mordens ungulam equi, ut cadat ascensor ejus retro* [AV, Genesis 49/17: "Dan shall be a serpent by the way, an adder in the path, that biteth the horse heels so that his rider shall fall backward"]. By the opening of the play, he has already won over the rest of the world — witness the lands at his disposal, 241–4 and note — and has come to Jerusalem, as in Adso, *Libellus de Antichristo* (PL 101/1293). See 33–40 note.

28 *fard* See 597 note.

31 Compare 17/129–33.

33–40 Antichrist lays upon Jesus the responsibility for the destruction of Herod's temple; it, and the city of Jerusalem, were in fact destroyed by Titus in 70 AD — compare 14/209–24. Jewish national life was suppressed by Hadrian in 130 AD and the dispersal of the Jews followed. See also the prophecies in Matthew 24/3–24, Mark 13/3–37, Luke 21/7–36, all of which include the coming of Antichrist. The return of the Jews to their homeland and the re-establishment of the temple were accepted signs of the second coming (Adso, *Libellus de Antichristo* (PL 101/1293)). The ruined temple seems, from the reference of 37–8, to be visible on stage and to be somehow restored.

40 + Latin The quotation is from Psalm 5/8; but the total context, Psalm 5/7–8, gives the reference a wider irony, viz: *Odisti omnes qui operantes iniquitatem; perdes loquentes mendacium; virum sanguinem et dolosum abominabitur Dominus. Ego autem, in multitudine misericordiae tuae, introibo in domum tuam; adorabo in templo sancto tuo in timore tuo* (AV "Thou shalt destroy them that speak leasing: the Lord will abhor the bloody and deceitful man. But as for me, I will come into thy house in the multitude of thy mercy: and in thy fear will I worship toward thy holy temple"). The text relates to 37–40. R omits the Latin as it did the Latin at 24 + SD.

42–8 Daniel is cited at 56 + Latin, but the quotation confirms only 49–56. The reference at 42 seems to be to Daniel 11/37: *Et deum patrum suorum non reputabit, et erit in concupiscentiis feminarum, nec quemquam deorum curabit, quia adversum universa consurget* (AV "Neither shall he regard the God of his fathers, nor the desire of women, nor regard any god: for he shall magnify himself above all"). *should* 43 seems to have the force of "would have to", with the implication that Antichrist will be a ravisher of women.

Greg interprets 47–8: "I intend to form repeated unions (*fast* = wed) and have knowledge of (*fand* or *fond* = test) their beauty" but continues: "but this use of *fast* is at least unusual, and the passage appears not to have been understood." Greg regards *fast* 47 as a form of *fasten* MED v (1), 4(a); but one would expect *fasten*. As the lines stand in HmBP, they mean "I intend to hold many fast (i.e. embrace them closely) and make trial of (i.e. sample) their beauty"; A seeks to improve the order by placing *to* beside the verb-form. H, reading *force* for *fast*, and *many fould* for *many hould*, also avoids the separation of the verb-form from *to* and makes explicit the idea of rape. One must agree that the construction is syntactically awkward.

A substitutes 48 for 44. Possibly disconcerted by the repetition of 44; or uneasy at the interpretation of 47–8; or simply miseld by the reference to *Danyell* 42 into moving directly to the quotation at 56 + Latin, R also follows 43 by 48 and then omits 45–46. HmBH agree on the reading at 44, but P offers a different version.

56 + Latin Daniel 11/39: AV "He shall cause them to rule over many, and shall divide the land for gain". The text differs from the Vulgate in reading *et multis*] *in multis*, thereby changing the sense to "He shall give them power and divide the land for gain to many." The same text is cited in *Legenda Aurea*, 'De Adventu Domini', which adds: *Glossa: Antichristus deceptis dona multa dabit et terram suo ex exercitu dividet*.

decimo tertio The reference was evidently incorrect in the exemplar; the same erroneous reference is to be found in P, suggesting that the error may have been present in an exemplar even earlier than the cyclic exemplar. The prefix *un-* and the concluding *nono* have been omitted. R omits the whole reference.

57 *you kinges* Compare Adso (PL 101/1293): *Reges autem et principes primum ad se convertet, et deinde per illos caeteros populos*. But the kings are here clearly the leaders of the Jews — compare 62, 301–8.

68 Compare *Legenda Aurea*, 'De Adventu Domini': *Secundo per miraculorum operationem*; and Adso (PL 101/1293): *Faciet quoque signa multa et miracula magna et inaudita*.

71 *woe* The sense seems to be "distressful doubt"; compare 72–3.

77–104 Compare Adso, *Libellus de Antichristo* (PL 101/1293–4): *Faciet ignem de coelo terribiliter descendere, arbores subito florere et crescere, mare turbari et subito tranquillari: naturas etiam in diversis figuris mutari, aquas contra cursus et ordinem converti, aera ventis commotionibusque multis agitari, et caetera quoque mirabilia et stupenda, mortuos scilicet in conspectu hominum resuscitari, 'ita in errorem inducantur, si fieri potest, etiam electi'* [Matthew 24/14].

Here Antichrist announces his intention to raise the dead, 79–80, but immediately proceeds to announce that he will invert the growing trees; he then repeats his statement of intent to raise the dead, 89–92, after which he proposes his own death and resurrection. Only the raising of the dead and the death and resurrection are clearly indicated in the ensuing text. *nowe wyl I* 81 may be taken to indicate that the dead have been raised — compare *nowe will I* 121; the force of *nowe* is not otherwise clear. It would, however, be possible either to move directly from 80 to 97 or to begin Antichrist's speech at 81, leading from 56; either arrangement would avoid the awkward repetition of intent.

The inversion of the trees is not in Adso. Lucken cites an Irish version of the Antichrist Legend: "And he will pluck the trees up by their roots overhead and they will give fruit out through the roots, by the powers of the devil." Compare also *Piers Plowman* B 20/53–5:

> Antecrist cam þanne, and al þe crop of truþe
> Torned it [tid] vp so doun, and ouertilte þe roote,
> And [made] fals sprynge and sprede and spede mennes nedes.

87 *heresye*, MED 1(a), "opposition to the tenets of Christianity or the doctrines of the Church, the fact of being heretical or a heretic"; and MED 3 "a heretical or pagan practice, conduct inimical to Christianity; falsehood, trickery, wickedness, a sin or vice." Although the exact sense of the word is not clear here, Antichrist's activities parody the basic tenets of Christianity which have been set out in the formation of the Apostles' Creed in play 21. By believing him, the kings become guilty of material heresy, not recognising their error. With the exposure of Antichrist's duplicity by Enoch and Elias, they are required to avoid formal heresy, the wilful and persistent adherence to error, although technically the formal heretic must be a baptised person (the kings go to their deaths unbaptised).

97 *graves* ARB corresponds to *sepulchris* 104 + SD and seems also indicated by *men*; *grave* HmHP may be accepted as a generic term, however: "buried in the grave".

110 The plural *kneene* HmHP seems to have puzzled the other scribes. The singular *knye* A, *knee* B destroy rhyme; R substitutes a nonce-form, *ken*.

112 The line was evidently obscure in the exemplar; it may be significant that it echoes 108 and in HmAR repeats the 108 rhyme-word, suggesting a possible scribal confusion. We have emended *naue* Hm to *knave*, "servant", as the simplest alteration which yields sense and remains reasonably close to the Hm form, but the meaning is not very satisfactory. P is preferable, adding a relative pronoun after *Crist*, and reading *name* for *naue*, *has* for *ys*, *nomen* for *commen* — "Christ who has taken our name", i.e. who has assumed human form. ARB support the reading *name*, and B additionally *that*. AR retain *commen*, but B substitutes *named*, destroying rhyme and meaning; B may have taken the unfamiliar *nomen* as an archaic past participle of *name* or have been influenced by the preceding noun. Hm evidently miscounted the minims in the *m* of *name* and interpreted the resulting *n* as *u*.

The process by which the error arose is not clear. Greg postulates an initial scribal error of *ys* for *has*, rendering *nomen* unintelligible and requiring a new participle and new construction. By this argument P would represent a reading from which the common cyclic exemplar has diverged. But the line in HmARH is metrically defective, requiring the addition of a further syllable after *Crist*, as B recognises. The addition of *in* at this point in AR would produce a metrically and semantically acceptable line, "Christ is come in our name." H, which lacks any addition after *Crist* and retains *ys*, but supports P's *name* and *nomen*, perhaps suggests that the P version existed in the exemplar but had been altered in such a way as to obscure the corrected form.

113 *whollye wrytte* "Holy Writ", the sacred scripture. The Hm form was evidently that of the exemplar, since ARB have taken the phrase as an adverb-verb construction; AR read *wrytten*, destroying rhyme and meaning; B adds a conjunction and construes *write* as present tense, parallel to *fulfill*, although the meaning is inappropriate and perfect rhyme would require a short vowel.

120+ Latin Zephaniah 3/8: AV "Therefore wait ye upon me, saith the Lord, until the day that I rise up to the prey: for my determination is to gather the nations, that I may assemble the kingdoms." The text here omits the continuation, AV "to pour upon them mine indignation, even all my fierce anger, for all the earth shall be devoured with the fire of my jealousy." The quotation omits the opening connective in the Vulgate, *quapropter*, and the ascription of authority, *dicit Dominus*, which follows *me*.

121–88 The episode of Antichrist's death and resurrection is based on Apocalypse 13/3: *Et vidi unum de capitibus suis quasi occisum in mortem, et plaga mortis eius curata est; et admirata est universa terra post bestiam* (AV "And I saw one of his heads as it were wounded to death; and his deadly wound was healed; and all the world wondered after the beast").

128 Greg notes *tent* as apparently "popular only in Scotland" in the sixteenth and seventeenth centuries to explain at least partly AR's curious and meaningless substitution of *teene*. Deimling notes the latter as evidence of a shared inferior reading in AR. The line provides the only example under OED *teen*, sb¹ 5 "Phr. *to take teen?* to take heed. Perhaps a different word (but not an error for *tent*)."

129–41, stanzas 17–8   Stanza 17 consists of a single Chester quatrain, aaab. Stanza 18 contains nine lines instead of the expected eight, rhyming aaaabcccb. H, which numbers the quatrains of Antichrist's speech 113–33 as 1–5 as if to confirm the irregularity, omits 132, thus removing the irregularity in stanza 18. But 132 is justifiable for the blasphemous parody of Pentecost, whereas 133 seems unnecessary, repeats the rhyme-word of 134, and in H is written in red ink as if distinctive or included as a result of a late editorial decision.

In the absence of a source for comparison, it is impossible to determine whether there has been an omission from a regular Chester stanza in stanza 17.

135 "And since his grace is committed to us", echoing the sentiment of 141, 144–5; Greg suggests "The sense seems to be "his grace accompanies us"; but it is not a recognized idiom." R evidently disliked the construction and substitutes *grave* for *grace*; the substitution suggests a formal confusion of *lead* and *lay*, reflected in Hm's use of *leade* for both at 135, 139, 151 — compare *layde* 139 ARBH, *layde* 151 ARH. R does not yield satisfactory meaning.

143 The exemplar evidently contained both *burye* HmAR and *laye* BHP. No priority can be accorded between them. *greete* represents *gret* MED n (3), 2(a) "the earth, ground; 3(b) *leien under* ∼, to bury (sb or sth) in the earth".

158–64, stanza 21   In HmARBP the stanza contains only seven lines, rhyming aabaaab; it lacks one a-rhyme in the first quatrain. The deficiency seems to have been present in the common exemplar and the P-exemplar. H supplies an additional line after 159 but it is of doubtful semantic relevance.

166   "Created in rank as the glorified God." But *greatest* HP may be preferred for meaning in suggesting the uncreated Creator; P may contain an earlier reading, but the substitution is suggested by the HmARB text. Greg argues that the blotting in P (see TNs) suggests an attempt by the re-inker to change the P-reading to *creatyt*.

167–8   The HmHP form of 167 is acceptable. *me* 167 ARB produces a more regular sequence of strongly and weakly stressed syllables, but repeats the 165 rhyme-word.

H apparently misunderstood the phrase *after my wise* 168, "according to my fashion"; it construes *wise* as "wise" and *my* as emphatic, and therefore replaces *my* by *the* and adds an emphatic vocative, "and work as the wise men would" — compare also 212. *will* A is an erroneous substitution which destroys rhyme.

174–6   *Moyses lawe* Evidently the regulations for offerings in Leviticus 3, verses 7 (a lamb) and 12 (a goat); the passage gives detailed accounts of sacrificial procedures. *that lasteth yett* reaffirms the Jewish faith of the kings.

The exemplar reading at 174 seems to have been obscure. AR substitute *lande greate*, while B omits the conjunction; both suggest either that *geat* was the exemplar form and was so unfamiliar as to invite emendation, or that *and* was not clear. Greg suggests loss of *and* in transmission via an intermediate exemplar. *bothe* 174 P may be preferred to its omission in HmARBH in producing a more regular sequence of strongly and weakly stressed syllables, unless *honored* is considered trisyllabic.

176 B may reflect unease at the reference of *hee*. The B version avoids pronoun reference in an awkward construction; but HmARHP is acceptable if we admit the ellipsis: "As Moses has said before in his law that still endures."

181–8   The kings have hitherto spoken in the sequence 1–2–3–4. Stanza 24 is attributed to *Tertius Rex* in HmAB in the absence of any further SH after 180; P makes this ascription clear by repeating *Tercius Rex* before the lines. R attempts to follow the usual sequence by ascribing 181–4 to *Quartus Rex* and, perhaps expecting each king to have one quatrain each, omits 185–8, an omission noted by Deimling. H attempts to re-commence the sequence by attributing 181–4 to *Primus Rex* and 185–8 *Secundus Rex*. See also 196+SH note, 301+SH note.

189–96, stanza 25   The stanza rhymes aaabcbcb. H reverses 193 and 4 and recasts 194 to give the required c-rhyme, but it is significant that H originally wrote *also to you* after *kinges*, then cancelled it to substitute the emended version, indicating that the scribe had the HmARBP form before him. P also reverses 193–4, but without H's emendation. The shared inversion of HP led Greg to emphasise this variant as isolating HmARB as a natural group.

The HmARB order contains an ambiguity resolved in HP, since the lines may mean both "I also tell you kings, I will now send my Holy Ghost" and "I will now send my Holy Ghost to you — you kings — also I say", in the latter case taking *to you* as dependent upon *send*. Antichrist has previously used the second line of a speech rather than the first as vocative — compare 77–8, 113–4 — a practice which might support HmARB here; Greg may also be correct in suggesting the influence in HmARB of the abab quatrain found elsewhere in the plays. It would be unwise to assume that HP necessarily represent an "earlier" or "better" reading than HmARB or that the shared reversal could not result from independent emendations by thinking scribes, preferring to place the vocative at the start of the sentence.

196+Latin   Ezechiel 36/26: AV "A new heart also will I give you, and a new spirit will I put within you". The text here omits the opening *et* of the Vulgate and Vulgate *ponam* (which should follow *novum* (2)).

196+SH   *Severalis* Greg proposes "one of the kings", but the sense may be "each king individually". It would be appropriate for each king to announce the reception of the spirit. P, however, reads *Quartus*, since the last king to speak in P was *Tercius Rex* (see 181-8). H assigned 185-8 to *Secundus Rex*; hence *Quartus* H here does not, as in P, continue the usual sequence. The PH ascription is also suggested by *Primus Rex* 200+SH, the next speaker in sequence.

203   *Moyses* See 18 note and compare Jesus' words in John 5/46: *Si enim crederetis Moysi, crederetis forsitan et mihi; de me enim ille scripsit* (AV "For had ye believed Moses, ye would have believed me: for he wrote of me").

205-36, stanzas 27-30   A omits 217-20 and 225-36, reducing the lines to two stanzas; viz, stanza 27, 205-12, and a composite and non-rhyming stanza of 213-6 with 221-4, aaabcccd. R further reduces the speech to a single composite stanza of 205-8 with 213-6, aaabcccd. Whatever their cause or function, these shared omissions provide further clear evidence of the close relationship of A and R. Possibly the omissions were intended to reduce the degree of blasphemy in the speech. The resulting irregularity of stanza-form may have been assisted by the existence of an isolated quatrain, stanza 31, 237-40, immediately after this section.

207   *Danyell* See 55+Latin and note.

208   *shoulde* ARBHP is to be preferred for meaning to *shall* Hm. The Hm form may be influenced by *shall* 206, 210 and *shalbe* 209.

217   *fayre* HmBH possibly represents a corruption or replacement of *fere* P which gives a more satisfactory rhyme. *fere* would be appropriate to the plural *lordshipes* BHP; the noun seems to be regarded as abstract or collective in Hm, but the plural probably represents the exemplar form.

237-52, stanzas 31-3   As here presented, the stanzas consist of a quatrain (237-40), a Chester stanza (241-8, aaabcccb), and a further quatrain (249-52). But *kynde* P for *kynne* 248 provides a perfect b-rhyme, *kynde* 248—*fynde* 252, thus suggesting that 245-52 is a Chester stanza aaabaaab; a similar arrangement could be adopted for HmARBH, accepting *kynne*—*fynde* as an imperfect rhyme. The relationship of the remaining lines, 237-40 and 241-4, is less clear since they are not linked by rhyme in any manuscript.

At 244 P reads *hyse* for *thine* HmARBH; Greg postulates that: "It seems possible (though it would not give a very good rime) that the original reading in 240 was *prise*. The original sense of this word, 'act of seizing', was developed during XIV c into 'something seized' (= *prize*, booty)." It would, however, seem unlikely that *hyse* is original, since it would necessitate a change in pronoun from second singular at

PLAY XXIII 339

241-3 to third singular at 244. We would prefer to accept *dole* 240, attested (as Deimling notes) by all manuscripts, as the reading more likely to be corrupt, if the lines have indeed been subjected to alteration.

Any reconstruction would be speculative. Possibly *dole* 240 is a substitution for *dome*, MED *dom* 5a (a) "the power to rule or govern, dominion", yielding at 240 the sense "each one shall know his dominion". Such a postulation would require a corresponding change in order at 244
                       and thine yt shalbe Rome
to produce satisfactory rhyme and sense.

At 250 *laye* P is to be preferred to *lawe* HmARBH for rhyme. *lay* OED sb 3, "law, esp. religious law, hence a religion, a faith", is last recorded in 1599; compare 431.

241-4 Although the lands here named seem to have little in common, they may well have had particular connotations for the audience. Compare G. K. Hunter's comment on references in Elizabethan literature: "Geographical exactitude was no part of the literary tradition, and even those writers who 'should have known better' show astonishing carelessness about place-names and modes of transport, using them for their associations, not for their reality" ('Elizabethans and Foreigners', *Shakespeare Survey* xvii (1964), p.40). The references here suggest a composite Antichrist-manifestation embracing Lutheranism, the Turkish threat and the papal involvement in the Franco-Spanish war, all suggestive of events in the 1530s and later.

(1) *Lombardee—Italie—Roome* None of these names had political-national reference. Lombardy is a region of northern Italy; Italy is the land of Italy, then comprising a number of independent states; Rome was the papal city and centre for the papal states. If the references do stand in distinction to each other, they may represent the northern republics and duchies of Italy (*Lombardee*), the southern Duchy of Naples (*Italie*) and the papal states which separated the two (*Roome*). The writer may have had specific aspects of the Franco-Spanish War in mind — e.g. the transference by the Emperor Charles V in 1540 of all imperial rights in Italy to Spain; the sack of Rome in 1527; the hostilities in northern Italy following the death of the Duke of Milan in 1535. Part of Lombardy was held by the Republic of Venice, which for some time during the sixteenth century provided refuge for heretics fleeing from the Italian Inquisition. The phrase "Lombard-Jew", current from the fourteenth century, attests the involvement of the Jews in the banking activities of that region. Even if specific references are excluded, sixteenth-century Italy provided ample evidence of imperial interference and politico-religious warfare which could provide sufficient justification for associating the area with the activities of Antichrist.

(2) *Hungarye—Pathmos* Both areas fell victim to the Turkish advance in the sixteenth century. Hungary was the scene of constant warfare and partition from 1526 — first in the war between Zapolya (the claimant supported by the Turkish Sultan Suleiman) and Ferdinand of Austria, which led to the partition of the country in 1538; later, in further warfare following Zapolya's death in 1549, which led to the tripartite division of the country between Ferdinand, Suleiman, and Zapolya's son Sigismund. Patmos, an otherwise insignificant island in the Aegean, was captured by the Turks in 1537. Patmos was the island on which St. John wrote Apocalypse (Apocalypse 1/9), and a particular irony may be intended in the reference. But, in view of the many other places which could have been cited, it may be suspected that

Patmos was included also because it had received contemporary prominence as another of the holy places which had fallen to the Turks.

(3) *Denmarke* had witnessed the deposition of its king, Christian II, in favour of an absentee Lutheran, Frederick I. Civil war with religious overtones followed the death of Frederick in 1533, ending with the accession of Christian III in 1536 and the implementation of a Lutheran Reformation.

Compare S. C. Chew: "In Roman Catholic propaganda attacks upon Islam were frequently combined with assaults upon Lutherans and Calvinists and it was asserted that Satan worked for the Turks by stirring up the hatred of heretics against the true Church. Conversely, among Protestant controversialists there was a tendency to associate Rome and Islam together as partners in iniquity" (*The Crescent and the Rose*, New York 1965, p.101).

252 + SD *resedet* HmAR, *sedeat* P may perhaps be preferred to *recedet* BH, since 340 + SD suggests that Antichrist remains sitting in the temple.

Enoch et Helias Compare 17/236 + SH and 17/242 + SH and notes respectively, and 17/237-52, 22/86-8, 100, 173-260.

With this action, the first part of the play, the conversion of the Jews, is complete. Antichrist now establishes his rule, and according to Adso 120 years of his reign have passed (PL 101/1296).

262-3 "Who has granted life and heavenly sustenance to whoever dwells in flesh and blood." *longe* is here taken as a form of the verb *leng*; the doubled pronoun *that who* 263 makes it difficult to take *longe* as adverb, as it is in 286.

269-71 R recasts 269 and reverses 270-1, changes which are unnecessary and destroy rhyme. Possibly 269 R is an error in stanza-division, with *begane* an attempt to reproduce the c-rhyme of stanza 35.

272 *paradice* i.e. the earthly paradise of Eden — compare 720 and 17/229-49.

277 *that tyde* No time has been specified previously for Enoch's translation, beyond *sythe the worldes begininge* 269. In fact, Enoch was the seventh generation from Adam and lived on earth 365 years, Genesis 5/23. 269 can only represent an imprecise reference: "From the first eras of the world's existence".

287-8 A relative pronoun should be understood in 288: "Do not let the devil's power [which] this man has within himself spring up." R's *that* may be an attempt to supply the pronoun, giving an interesting emphasis to the line — "Do not let the devil's power which Man has within himself spring up"; but R leaves *his* 290 without clear reference.

300 + SH *Tertius* BHP is to be preferred for reference to *Primus* HmAR. The last royal speaker was *Secundus Rex* 244 + SH, and *Tertius* would be next in order, followed by *Quartus Rex*, attested by all manuscripts at 304 + SH. HmAR seem to believe that a new sequence is about to start at 302. Greg regards this as a major variant in determining variational groups, and argues that "the substitution of *Primus Rex* may have been due to the fact that for some time the kings have been silent, but this motive is too weak to make convergence likely" (p.lviii). But more probably an exemplar *iii^s* was independently misread as *i^{us}* by HmAR through misdivision of minims.

PLAY XXIII

305 *bookes of our lawe* i.e. Genesis 5/21, AV 2 Kings 2/11, both being books of law rather than prophets.

307–8 A distinction seems implied between the translation of Enoch and Elias, which is established by the Books of Law, and their continuation in Heaven (in defiance of the statements of these two claimants on earth) which represents a current rumour that has been recorded in some unspecified work. Possibly the account in the Gospel of Nicodemus is intended; see 17/236ff and notes.

The syntactical construction is here broken: "And it is the common saying [that they] are there yet, as men may find [it] written."

312 The line seems most obviously to mean "if there were any remedy" — i.e. if you renounce the errors which you have unconsciously embraced.

317–24, stanza 42 317 can be read as a four-stress line only by adopting the pattern
ýf thăt wée hēre wýtt món
H provides a more regular sequence of strongly and weakly stressed syllables by reading *anon* for *mon*, and is to be preferred. P reads *redye* for *here*, but fails to resolve the problem of the two final stresses, including stress on the auxiliary verb; Greg notes *redye* as an error for *redelye*.

318 can be read as a four-stress line only by taking *disputacon* as a five-syllable word — dīspūtácīŏn.

319 contains only three strongly stressed syllables.

323 can be read as a four-stress line only by taking *salvatyon* as a four-syllable word:
iń hōpe óf sālvátyoń
P is here to be preferred in including *sawle* before *salvatyon*, thus avoiding any conflict of metrical and sentential stress as proposed above:
iń hópe ōf saẃle sālvátyoń
Greg notes: "The construction was apparently not understood. *sawle* is the OE genitive which survived in phrases till XV c." *sawle* may be a scribal insertion, but it could also be regarded as a form present in P's exemplar but omitted from the common cyclic exemplar.

At 324 ARBHP agree in reading *whatsoever betyde* for Hm's *whatever may betyde*, although either is metrically acceptable.

334 The line in HmARB does not give good sense. The order *doe I* HP is to be preferred, making *doe* imperative, parallel to *be* 333: "And do, I counsel, as I instruct you."

do AR for *you* does not improve the sense and seems influenced by *doe*.

341–8, stanza 45 The b-rhymes, *deceaves* 344 — *wyles* 348, do not rhyme. Perfect rhyme would result from substituting *beguiles* for *deceaves* 344, although the latter was evidently the form in the cyclic exemplar, and also in P's exemplar if different. The word may have been substituted in anticipation of *deceaved* 345.

354 The line contains three strongly stressed syllables instead of the expected four. Greg suggests a possible original form, "Thee the devil's own nurrie", arguing: "The apparent duplication would explain the omission."

358 *lurdenes* A, *lurdans* BP are formally preferable to the scribally erroneous *lardans* Hm, and to *lordens* R, *lordans* H.

361–3 *devyne* 362 perhaps represents MED *divinen* 1(a) "practise divination". If so, *my folke* should be understood as dative: "And needlessly practise divination for my people". H alone reads *denyne*, perhaps *denien* MED 3(a) "to refuse or fail to acknowledge", alluding to the prophets' attitude towards Antichrist's followers. Confusion of u(v) and n may underlie the variation.

At 363 the syntax and metre are improved by regarding *hence*(2) Hm as an erroneous repetition, not found in ARBHP. For the Hm reading, a verb of motion is required after *hence*(1).

365–93, stanzas 48–52 Stanzas 48, 49 and 51 consist of six lines, rhyming aabaab in 48, 51, and aabccb in 49; the b-lines contain three main stresses, the others four. Stanza 50 is a Chester quatrain, aaab. Stanza 52 consists of seven lines, 3 and 7 containing three strongly stressed syllables and the others four, rhyming aabaaab. The a-rhyme of stanza 50 is identical with the c-rhyme of stanza 49, while its b-rhyme is identical with the a-rhyme of stanza 51. Although these identities may be coincidental, they probably influenced the reversal of 382 and 383 in ARBHP; since 383 is a three-stress line, its substitution for 382 would be probable only if 381 had a rhyming line preceding it, in which case 380–6 would become a single stanza aabaaab like stanza 52.

R omits 371–6, for no apparent reason. B erroneously and inexplicably omits 393.

371 *roysard* The word does not seem to occur elsewhere. It may be regarded as an error for *roister* OED sb, "a swaggering or blustering bully, a riotous fellow; a rude or noisy reveller"; compare also OED *roise* v.intr. "? to rave, talk nonsense", evidenced only from York Plays 15/69. *rasarde* A suggests a different scribal reading of the same form. *wiserde* BHP gives sense and may be preferred; OED records its use as "a man who is skilled in occult arts" from 1550, but notes that its earlier reference, "a philosopher, sage", recorded from 1440, is often used contemptuously.

398–401 B erroneously omits these lines. Possibly the omission results from an eye-slip, the scribe moving from *my* 397 to *my* 402.

410–6, stanza 55 In HmARBP the stanza consists of seven lines, differing from a regular Chester stanza in lacking an a-rhyme line in the first quatrain. H supplies an acceptable line after 411, which may be preferred, although it probably represents a scribal invention to correct what was felt to be an exemplar error.

hyngys 414 P, of which *heinges* R might be considered a variant, is to be preferred formally for rhyme to *hanges* HmA, *henges* BH. No manuscript has the word *rings* for *rayngnes* 415, required for rhyme — compare its use at 8/205.

410 See Augustine, *De Civitate Dei* 10/9 (PL 41/286) and 10/13 (PL 41/291).

415 *joye* is parallel to *flower* and the verb must be understood — "so does your joy". The line was either obscure in the exemplar or troubled the scribes. B removes *yt*, making *joye* the subject of *raygnes*, to the detriment of metre. AR omit *nowe*, with no gain in syntax or semantics but to the detriment of metre. P supplies the auxiliary *do*, but omits the pronoun *yt* required for metrical and syntactical completeness.

417–23, stanza 56 The stanza contains seven lines, differing from a regular Chester stanza in lacking an a-rhyme line in the first quatrain. H supplies an acceptable line after 418 and may be preferred; but the line is probably a scribal creation to correct a supposed exemplar error and weakly reiterates the sense of 418.

PLAY XXIII 343

No manuscript has the form *repreve* for *reprove* 419, required for rhyme; *reprove* was evidently the exemplar form found also in P. R omits 419, an error perhaps resulting from the change of page since in R 419 should be the first line on fol.188v.

417 *theeffe* The Doctor is apparently already present on stage, although his entry is nowhere noted. Compare Adso, *Libellus de Antichristo* (PL 101/1293): *Habebit autem Antichristus magos et ariolos et maleficos et incantatores et divinos, qui eum [diabolo inspirante] nutrient et docebunt, et imbuent in omni iniquitate et falsitate et nefaria arte: et maligni spiritus erunt duces ejus et socii semper et comites [Cod.Vat., et commilitones] indivisi*. A more extensive role for the Doctor seems envisaged by the Late Banns 173-4.

421-2 At 421 the manuscripts offer three possible rhyme-words: *knen* HmBH, *kenne* AP, *eyne* R. *eyne* R seems to be a scribal substitution for *kenne*, since a letter has been blotted and cancelled before *e*(1) (see TNs). The choice between the other readings is connected with the interpretation of 422, which seems to mean "Are you now to be told?" Greg comments: "Either it [422] is mere padding, or else it conceals some more relevant expression under an early corruption." It may be significant that the AP rhyme-words for the two lines are formally identical, although if one did influence the other, the direction of influence is not clear. *kenne*, "kindred, parents", is semantically possible and could have prompted exemplar-corruption in *ken* 422; but *knen* HmBH, "knees", may have been original and have been changed to the more familiar *ken* independently in A and P.

424-31, stanza 57 The b-rhymes, *sayen* 427 — *lawe* 431, do not rhyme. Probably *say*—*lay* is required. *saye* is attested by ARBP, but no manuscript has *lay*; *lawe* was evidently the exemplar form. Compare 250 and 236-52, stanzas 31-3 note.

428 *lowlers* HmBP seems to have been an unfamiliar or objectionable term of contempt to AR, which substitute *lossilles*; *loullords* H is probably merely a formal variant. The word, generally *lollard*, "a name of contempt given in the 14th.c. to certain heretics, who were either followers of Wyclif or held opinions similar to his", picks up the emphasis on heresy seen elsewhere in the play. It is attested from 1390 — 20th.c.

431 The line contains four strongly stressed syllables instead of the expected three. A regular three-stress line would result from the omission of *all the*.

436-7 Compare 5/120-4.

446 The line contains three strongly stressed syllables instead of the expected four. It is not possible to establish the nature of any possible omission.

448-53, stanza 60 The stanza consists of six lines, aabccc. 450 contains four strongly-stressed syllables, 452 and 453 three each.

youre P for *in the xx devylles* 450 is to be preferred in producing a three-stress line. H provides an additional four-stress line after 452 which gives sense, although probably a scribal addition, and also recasts 453 acceptably. Deimling acknowledges that there may have been an original six-line stanza, but prefers to argue: "I am inclined to believe that 452, or the closing line of the first half, represents in this reduced form two lines, so that *devills* is to be put in the rhyme with *meeles, heeles, Coelis, wyles, begyles*." He then proposes to read *name* for *waye* 450, and *shame* for *pyne* 453. But the stanza is most readily taken as a six-line stanza, as the Hm indentation-pattern indicates. The absence of b-rhyme is most simply resolved by substituting *agayne* 450.

448 *meeles* Greg takes this as *meal* (OE *mǣl*), "time or repast", as in the phrase "a merry meal", but feels that, if so, the word in alliterative phrases "had come to mean anything or nothing". Possibly the word represents *mel(l)e*, a variant of *medle* MED n(2), 1(a) "quarrel, dispute": an unetymological long vowel would be required for perfect rhyme with *heeles*. *amend* would then have the sense of *amenden* MED 13(c) "to punish (a misdeed)", (d) "to discipline (a person); reprove, chastise."

451 *coelis* The rhyme seems to require a monosyllable, a need perhaps recognised in the AR nonce-word *clisse*. The word may be regarded with some suspicion.

457 The line contains four strongly stressed syllables instead of the expected three. A regular line would result from the omission of *eke the*, which was evidently the exemplar reading. H, apparently independently, omits *the*.

459 *flowers* ARBHP is to be preferred to the scribally erroneous *flowes* Hm.

460 A has erroneously and inexplicably omitted the line, as Deimling notes. The error is corrected in R.

462–5, stanza 62   The stanza is a single Chester quatrain. It is not possible to determine whether there has been any omission.

486 *his* can refer only to *God in trynitie* 484, where, however, Christ is specified as the godhead. H, apparently uneasy at the possibility of *his* referring to *Christe*, omits the verb in 486 and substitutes *Godes* for *his*.

490 *ruled owt of raye* The sense may be "directed out of your appointed place" — compare OED *rule* vb I 4, recorded from 1362, and *ray* sb^3, 2, "line, rank", recorded from 1481 to 1587.

491–512   Lucken comments: "The repudiation of the doctrine of the Blessed Trinity is another element of the legend as given by Adso: *Super omnes istos deos extolletur Antichristus quia maiorem et fortiorem se iis omnibus faciet: et non solum supra hos, sed etiam supra omne quod colitur, id est supra sanctam Trinitatem*; he quotes from Tomás Malvenda, *De Antichristo libri XI* of 1604: *Quia etiam arbitramur Antichristum cum se Deum faciet, negaturum Sanctissimam Trinitatem, ac palam pronuntiaturum falsissimum esse, quod Christiani confingunt tres esse in Divinitate personas, Patrem, Filium, ac Spiritum Sanctum*. The lines reiterate concepts introduced in 1/1–35.

498–504, stanza 67   The stanza consists of seven lines, differing from a regular Chester stanza in lacking an a-rhyme line in the first quatrain. Deimling (p.xxviii) regards this as an omission "which might be taken as an indication that the six-line stanzas were originally in this part of the text, but were afterwards lengthened into eight-liners, to accommodate them to the usual stanza." The supposition seems unnecessary.

501 *madmen* RP is to be preferred for metre to the repetition in HmABH. A compensates for the additional syllables by omitting *therfore*, producing a metrically acceptable line. A's reading suggests that the repetition was present in the exemplar, and that Bellin was dissatisfied with the result. R probably shows an independent omission arising from the same dissatisfaction.

506–7   Compare 1/5–6, 2/1–2, 6/329–32.

513   *gulles* Hm seems to represent OED *gull* sb^3, "a credulous person; .... a dupe, simpleton, fool"; but this is attested only from 1594. Apart from this occurrence, and 13/428, MED *golle* has only one other occurrence of the word in Middle English. The other manuscript forms seem to derive from the same word, but A and B do not appear to have understood it.

522   *his* refers to *my ghoost* 519. ARHP read *maisterye* for HmB's *majestie*; the latter is marginally less probable because of its inappropriate laudatory overtones. Greg may be correct in regarding *majestie* as a substitution deriving from the erroneous assumption that *his* refers to *God almightie* 523; but it is not necessary to regard *his* as an erroneous substitution for *thy*, as Greg also suggests. See also 638 note.

534   *mightie* HmHP, adjective, is to be preferred syntactically to *mightelye* ARB, adverb, although the metre is improved by the additional syllable in ARB. The adverb may also have been influenced by *hastelye* 533.

539–40   *and* 540 does not link clauses of equal syntactical weight. As here punctuated, *and* introduces an infinitive of purpose, *to leere*, dependent upon *common be wee* 538, and 539 interrupts the construction. P is preferable in reading *to se* for *doe* 539 and producing a complementary result clause.

545–60   Lucken cites St. Ephraim the Syrian: "If thou art God, call on the departed, and they shall arise; for it is written in the books of the prophets and also by the apostles, that, when He shall appear, Christ shall raise the dead from their graves" — spoken by Antichrist to Enoch and Elias; and Honorius of Autun, *Elucidarium* 3 (PL 172/1163): *Suscitabit [Antichristus] mortuos vere?* — *M. Nequaquam, sed diabolus ejus maleficiis corpus alicujus intrabit, et illud apportabit, et in illo loquetur; ut quasi vivum videatur.* He also compares St. Hildegard, *Scivias* (PL 197/717), and Hugo Eterianus, *Liber de Anima Corpore Iam Exuta sive De Regressu Animarum ab Inferis* (PL 202/192) on the demonic possession of the dead. But Adso (PL 101/1294), after his account of Antichrist's marvels which concludes with the resurrection, states: *Sed et mendacia erunt, et a veritate aliena: quia per magicam artem et phantasiam deludet homines sicut et Simon Magus illusit illum, qui putans occidere eum, arietem occidit pro eo.*

556   Although *you* H may be an error for *your* in the phrase meaning "if you will amend your life", it is possible that H regarded *lyfe* as the adverb *lief*, "gladly, willingly", and intended "if you will amend yourselves willingly."

560+SH   *Mortuus* ARBHP is to be preferred for morphology to the scribally erroneous *Mortuis* Hm.

585–616   Compare Adso (PL 101/1296): *Tunc mittentur in mundum duo magni prophetae, Elias et Enoch, qui contra impetum Antichristi fideles divinis armis praemunient, et instruent eos, et confortabunt, et praeparabunt [electos] ad bellum.* Chester is unusual in its realisation of *divinis armis* as the power of the Holy Sacrament.

596 *on* and *upon* are strictly equivalent, but may be regarded as an acceptable duplication in an inverted sentence.

597 *feard* is apparently the past participle of *fard* OED v., 2. *trans.* and *fig* "To embellish or gloss over anything", evidenced from 1549; the normal participial form would, however, be *farded*. P, however, reads *that ferde*, evidently identifying the word with MED *faren* 8(b), *faren with* (a thing), "to be concerned or busy with; to engage in, practice, or experience something". *fere* AR may result from confusion of *d* and *e*, but may also show formal and even semantic influence from the past participle of *feren* v MED 2, "to fear", in which case *with* 597 would be parallel to *with* 598 — "you feared imposter, you have led us into heresy with illusion . . ."

602 *trespasse* A smoother metre would result from reading *trespasses*, although this might weaken rhyme. The line seems to echo Matthew 6/12: *Et dimitte nobis debita nostra* (AV "And forgive us our debts") from the Lord's Prayer.

607 *graythes* P is to be preferred for meaning to *greetes* HmARB and *girts* H. *greetes* seems to be a substitution of *greten* MED v 2, 2(a) "to challenge", (b) "to attack (sb), strike"; but the verb cannot be used with *him*, as here. *girts* H seems to represent an attempt to find an acceptable replacement for *greetes*. The variant may indicate that P has an exemplar different from the cyclic exemplar.

608 *slea* ARBHP is to be preferred for meaning to *flea* Hm. Hm seems to have confused *f* and long *s*; *flea* does, however, give sense, albeit weak — cf. MED *fleien* v 1 (a) "to put a flight; drive away; pursue." See 609–10.

611 Either *teache* Hm or *leech*, "heal", attested in various forms by ARBHP, is possible.

613–6 Compare Matthew 5/10: *Beati qui persecutionem patiuntur propter iustitiam, quoniam ipsorum est regnum caelorum* (AV "Blessed are they which are persecuted for righteousness' sake: for theirs is the kingdom of heaven"). The kings seek martyrdom, thereby to join the saints. Compare Adso *Libellus de Antichristo* (PL 101/1297): *Cum per tres annos et dimidium [magna persecutione] totum mundum vexaverit, et Dei populum variis poenis cruciaverit, et in fide permanentes martyrio coronaverit....*

617–24+SD See Adso, (PL 101/1296), who cites also Apocalypse 11/7.

624+SD Compare Adso, *Hic namque Antichristus, diaboli filius, et totius malitiae pessimus artifex, cum per tres annos et dimidium [magna persecutione] totum mundum vexaverit, ... ad ultimum veniet judicium Dei super eum ... Tradunt quoque doctores, ut ait Gregorius papa, quod Michael archangelus perimet illum in monte Oliveti, in papilione et solio suo, in loco illo de quo Dominus ascendit ad caelos; quod utrumque potest esse, quia si Michael Dei faciem venientis, ad judicium praeveniens eum interfecerit, non sua, sed Dei virtus erit et jussio.* (PL 101/1297-8) With the passage of three and a half years, compare 636+1. The change of location to Olivet (with which compare Jerome, *Commentariorum in Danielis* 11/45 (PL 25/573–5)) has no counterpart here.

Michaell Compare 17/213-20 and see 17/212 note. His function here is possibly influenced by Daniel 12/1: *In tempore autem illo consurget Michael, princeps magnus, qui stat pro filiis populi tui; et veniet tempus quale non fuit ab eo ex quo gentes esse coeperunt usque ad tempus illud. Et in tempore illo salvabitur populus tuus, omnis qui*

PLAY XXIII 347

inventus fuerit scriptus in libro (AV "And at that time shall Michael stand up, the great prince which standeth for the children of thy people: and there shall be a time of trouble such as there never was since there was a nation even to that same time: and at that time thy people shall be delivered, everyone that shall be found written in the book").

633–44, stanzas 84–5   The arrangement of lines in P (633–48, stanzas 83–4) is correct. 641–4 represent the second part of stanza 84 and should follow 636. Hm has omitted a quatrain, present in ARBHP, which constitutes the first four lines of stanza 85 and must precede 637–40. The cause of the transposition is a matter for speculation only, but might reasonably be assumed to be the result of attempting to correct in the cyclic exemplar an earlier omission or transposition; or a deliberate reorganisation made in the belief that 644 provides a more appropriate line to accompany Antichrist's death-blow than 640. Hm overlooked a quatrain, but the other manuscripts indicate that all lines were present in the cyclic exemplar. P may have correctly interpreted the exemplar corrections, but may equally have been using an antecedent of the cyclic exemplar which did not contain the error.

633   See 667–74 and note.

636   See Adso, 624 + SD note.

638   Either *majestie* HmARB or *maistry* HP is possible. Greg argues: "The next line, which extends their application to the devil and Antichrist, shows that PH must be correct." But the contrast is between divine and diabolical majesty/mastery and the explicit nature of the contrast permits either word to be used with propriety since no one can assume that *majestie* here imputes divine authority to the devil and his servants without qualification.

639   "Than indeed the devil's and yours by the side of it". *devilles* ARBHP is to be preferred for meaning to the scribally erroneous *dyvell* Hm; a possessive parallel to *Godes* 638, *thyne* 639, is required.

645–7   Antichrist calls upon a number of devils. *Sathanas* and *Lucyfere* 645 are probably equivalent titles for the prince of devils, not separate invocations. *Belzebubb* 646 is the name given in Matthew 12/24, Mark 3/22, Luke 11/15 to one termed *principe daemoniorum* (AV "the prince of the devils"). *Ragnell* 647 is to be identified with *Reynell* (*Ragnell* B) whom Balaam claims as a god, 5/213; see 5/213 note.

651–2   "Now body and soul both together and everything goes to the devil." The sequel is an "anti-Ascension"; as the living Christ was carried bodily up to heaven, so the dead Antichrist is carried bodily down into hell. The devils' dialogue is a counterpart to the ascension hymns of the angels. Antichrist's descent is followed by the resurrection and ascension of Enock and Elias.

659–60   The syntactical construction is broken since *to* 659 lacks a governing verb of perception or volition (e.g. *thought, hoped*, etc.).

661–98, stanzas 88–95   The lines are grouped in a number of different stanza forms with occasionally unusual metrical features; viz:

   stanza 88 — a six-line stanza, rhyming aabccb, with the b-rhyme lines of three stresses and the others of four;

stanza 89 — a Chester stanza, aabaaab;

stanzas 90–95 — quatrains, rhyming abab; the basic line seems to be decasyllabic, although there are variations, particularly in stanzas 93 and 95. At 682 the line contains twelve syllables; a decasyllabic line would result from taking *sorrowe* as monosyllabic, *sorwe*, and omitting *a*, and it may be postulated that the addition of *a* followed on the insistence on *sorrowe* as a disyllabic form, giving symmetry to the two halves of the line. A similar process may be postulated for 688. 689 and 90 contain nine syllables. In stanza 95 695 and 698 contain nine syllables, 696 eleven; 697 contains ten only by regarding *sorrowe* as disyllabic and unelided.

At 682 H has erroneously substituted the 680 rhyme-word *feele* for *keele*; at 698 H recasts the line to increase the number of syllables from nine to eleven.

667–74 So Adso, *Libellus de Antichristo* (PL 101/1292–3).

674 *blynne* Possibly MED *blinnen* 2 (a) "to come to a stand, stop moving" — i.e. his soul will never find rest. Some overtones from the transitive function of the same word, MED 3 (b) "? to deliver or save (sb) from evil", may also be suspected.

675–8, stanza 90 The Hm b-rhymes, *steed* 676 — *hydd* 678, do not formally correspond. The difficulty arises in 678, which must mean: "[Many a fat morsel] from souls that should have been saved [but instead] they are hidden in hell." The final phrase of 678 probably appeared in the cyclic exemplar in the HmH form, thereby allowing *be* to be taken as either verb or preposition ("by"); *the* as third person plural pronoun ("they") or definite article; and *hydd* as verb ("hid") or noun ("head"). It is by no means certain that HmH understood the syntax of the phrase which they copied; P's *be thie hyd* 682 seems more clearly to be a verbal construction; B omits *hydd*, perhaps recognising the problems of rhyme and not understanding the construction; and AR accept the construction as prepositional, although A attempts to clarify its meaning by substituting *hange* for *saved*, while R, with still less satisfactory sense, reverts to *saved*.

The problem of the 678 rhyme-word affects the reading of the 676 rhyme-word. *stidd* BHP is formally preferable to *steed* HmA. *us instead* R, "in our place", seems influenced by a need to identify the rhyme-word formally with *head* 678 R.

The first half of 678 contains seven syllables instead of the expected five. *bene* A, *be* H are to be preferred as reducing the number of syllables to six. The omission of *should* by P suggests that it had the Hm form before it and reduced the line-length (inadequately) by a different omission from A; the result does not give good sense. The agreement of HmRBP strongly argues for the Hm form as original to the cyclic exemplar, and to the P-exemplar if different.

678 + SD   *animam* The soul and body are evidently two separate items — compare 651. The soul is small enough for *Primus Demon* to hold in his hand, 679, and he presumably delivers it to hell during 683–4. The body is then removed at 691–4.

A omits the SD. R and H exclude reference to *animam*. The AR omission/rewording has to be seen in conjunction with other omissions in this section by the two manuscripts — see 679–98 note. H, however, erroneously anticipates 691–4 at this point. P omits the reference to *corpus* here, appropriately, but in a further SD, 702 + SD P, at the point where the body is removed, erroneously uses *animam* again where *corpus* is required. It seems clear that the HmB form of the

SD was in the cyclic exemplar but that scribes were concerned partly at the reference to *animam* as a separate entity and partly because the SD related to two separate actions over a sequence of lines.

678 + SH–98 A omits 678 + SH–90, 694 + SH–8, leaving only the removal of the body, 691–4; the "problem" of *animam* (see 678 + SD note) is thus avoided, and the surviving quatrain makes any SD unnecessary. R shares A's omissions, but also omits 690 + SH–4, thus relying upon the 678 + SD to indicate the clearance of the stage; the reintroduction of the SD in R after its omission in A and the corresponding omission of 690 + SH–4 in R suggest a deliberate policy by Bellin to reduce the scope of the devils' dialogue. It seems unlikely that the omission of 690 + SH–4 in R is influenced by the movement at that point from fol. 193ʳ to fol. 193ᵛ.

H substitutes a metrically unsatisfactory line for 698 HmBP, perhaps desiring greater theological accuracy; compare 711–2.

686 + SD The SD has no counterpart in P and is misplaced; it should follow 698. Possibly a marginal SD in an antecedent of the cyclic exemplar has been incorporated into the exemplar in the wrong position. Its absence from P suggests either that the scribe was conscious of the misplacement or that he was working from an original which lacked the SD; the latter seems more probable.

Compare Adso (PL 101/1297): *Ipsi vero occisi post tres dies a Domino suscitabuntur*, of the resurrection of the two prophets. Compare also 20/209–12. No passage of time is here indicated.

699–706, stanza 96 No manuscript has *releave* for *releaved* 702, required for rhyme. The past tense had evidently been substituted in the cyclic exemplar, and the P-exemplar if different, and may have been occasioned by the misinterpretation of *reade* 701 as past rather than present tense.

710 The BHP omission of *by* is to be preferred to its inclusion in HmAR in reducing the number of strongly stressed syllables from four to the expected three. The error may have resulted from a desire for syntactic completeness, aided by the ambiguity of *be* as verb or preposition here.

711 B has erroneously and inexplicably omitted the line, but has left a line-space blank, suggesting some conscious problem on the part of the scribe rather than carelessness.

722 + SD The text represents Psalm 32/1: AV 33/1 "Rejoice in the Lord, O ye righteous, for praise is comely for the upright."

PLAY XXIV

Dramatis Personae Deus, Angelus Primus, Secundus Angelus, Papa Salvatus, Imperator Salvatus, Rex Salvatus, Regina Salvata, Papa Damnatus, Imperator Damnatus, Rex Damnatus, Regina Damnata, Justiciarius Damnatus, Mercator Damnatus, Jesus, Demon Primus, Secundus Demon, Mattheus, Marcus, Lucas, Johannes.

NOTE 1. The roles of *Deus* and *Jesus* are almost certainly doubled; see *Before* 1 SH note.
2. The instruments of the Passion displayed at 356+SD would seem to require more angels for their display than the two who speak.
3. On the possible presence of prophets and patriarchs, see 362 note.

Locations
quasi in nube, si fieri poterit 356+SD
a lowe 545, the fyre 644, hell 653
blysse 440, 502, my realme 455.

Properties
beames 33, tubas 40+SD
Instruments of the Passion — my crosse 17, cruce 356+SD; crowne of thorne 18, corona spinea 356+SD; speare 18, lancea 356+SD; sponge 18; nayles 19; instrumentis aliis 356+SD.
blood 385, 392, 398, 405, 421-2, 425-8; sanguinem 428+SD.
sepulchris 40+SD
my secke 672, my powche 674.

Costume
Jesus — what weede for them I weare 21 *and note.*

NOTE There are references to costume by the resurrected which suggest what they wore during their lifetime on earth; viz:
   in purple and in rych weede
      (118)
   in softe sandalles [sendal H] amd silke alsoe,
   velvet also that wrought me woe,
   and all such other weedes
      (150-2)
   Fye on pearles! Fye on prydee!
   Fye on gowne! Fye on guyde!
      (277-8)
These costumes may be worn by the resurrected, but not necessarily.

PLAY XXIV 351

Sources The single most significant description of the Judgment for the cycle-plays is Matthew, 24–5. Other details occur throughout the Bible; Chester seems to look particularly at details in the Pauline epistles and Apocalypse. The subject was frequently treated by the Church Fathers; the account in Augustine, *De Civitate Dei* 19–22 (PL 41/622–804), provides a number of analogues and conveniently gathers together scriptural references to the Judgment (e.g. 20/5, 20/20–1 etc.). The subject was also widely treated in medieval painting and sculpture.

Guild ascription On B's omission, for which there is no obvious textual reason, compare 23/*Guild-ascription* note.

Play-heading
judicio extremo The phrase distinguishes the Last Judgment, given collectively to mankind, from other forms of divine judgment. First, there is a continuing judgment upon Man and his deeds in the world, an idea based on John 9/39: *Et dixit Iesus: In iudicium ego in hunc mundum veni, ut qui non vident videant, et qui vident caeci fiant* (AV "And Jesus said, For judgment I am come into this world, that they which see not might see; and that they which see might be made blind"); compare T. Arnold (ed.) *Select English Works of John Wyclif*, vol. I, 'Sermon 118', 392–3: "Al þe liif þat Crist lyvede here was a jugement of þis world, for it was an open mater to juge it at þe dai of dome. For no man may excuse þis, siþ God and man lyvede þus to teche men þe weye to hevene and fle þe falsnesse of þe fend, and ȝit man leveþ Cristis lore, and goiþ þe weie þat þe fend techiþ, þat ne þei leden a liif here to make hem dampned aftirward." The judgment then occurs now, between those attracted to Christ's example and those who do evil, and the judgment after death merely represents the inevitable outcome. This separation, evident throughout the cycle, is seen particularly in play 13. It underlies the warnings of the four evangelists, 24/676–708.

Second, there is the particular judgment of the individual soul at death, a concept resting upon the immediate fates of Dives and Lazarus in Luke 16/22–3, and of the penitent thief in Luke 23/43 — with the latter, compare 16A/323–4, 17/255–72; also upon Hebrews 9/27: *Et quemadmodum statutum est hominibus semel mori, post hoc autem iudicium* (AV "And as it is appointed unto men once to die, but after this the judgment"). See also Augustine, *De Anima* 2/4 (PL 44/498–9). Hence the resurrected souls have already been judged and dwelt in purgatory or hell before the public pronouncement which Jesus justifies at 365–8.

The other cycles also conclude with a play of the Judgment — Wakefield 30 (beginning lost), York 48, *Ludus Coventriae* 42 (ending lost).

Deus Compare 1/*Before* 1 *SH* note. The speaker here is initially the Godhead comprising the Trinity, 5. Possibly at 8–9 he may speak in the person of God the Father (see 7–8 note). From 11 onwards he assumes the role of God the Son, and is therefore probably to be identified with Jesus at 356+SH. The opening therefore restates the opening theology of play 1, establishing continuity; compare York 48/1–64 where God establishes the place of the Judgment by recapitulating the Fall of Man and his redemption.

Before 1 *Latin* See 1/1–2 note. The reiteration of the opening words of play 1 (and play 2) at the start of the final play establishes a structural link, God introducing the first and last plays in the cycle as he instigates and concludes the action of human history. It should be remembered, however, that the words in play 24 were usually spoken on the Wednesday of Whit week and those in Play 1 on the Monday, making the verbal echo less obvious to an audience.

The omission of the redundant and unbiblical *I* Hm by ARBH is to be preferred; the cause or purpose of the Hm reading is not clear.

1–8, stanza 1 The b-rhyme, *preeved* 4 — *meeved* 8 HmB, is acceptable and may reflect the exemplar form. R 'modernises' to the equally acceptable *proved-moved*. But AH, reading *proved* 4, do not make the corresponding change from *meeved* 8. R evidently corrected the inconsistency in A.

1–8 With 1–2, compare 1/5–6; with 3, 1/11; with 5–6, 1/9 and 28–31; with 7–8, 1/16–16+1 and 33–5. The stanza echoes attributes established in the definition of the Godhead with which the cycle began.

1–4 "It shall now clearly be proved that I — God, greatest in hierarchy, in whom there may be no beginning — I am unequalled in power." *I* 3 restates the expanded subject of 1–2; *that* 4 refers to the clause at 3. The syntactical clumsiness of the construction may be dispelled in two ways: (1) by assuming that 1–2 is a complete sentence, with *am* to be understood after *I*; (2) by omitting *that* 4. 4 is metrically rough; *that* is syntactically redundant and could have been introduced into the exemplar by confusion with *that* 3. AH both omit *that* 4, to the benefit of metre. H further improves the metre by omitting *nowe* 4, to give a regular sequence of strongly and weakly stressed syllables.

7–8 "Despite the fact that there are three persons in my Godhead, (*yett*) supreme power, which is within me as Godhead, may rightly be activated." The concern seems to be that the audience should recognise that although actions are carried out by different persons of the Trinity, the power and the motivation for such actions lies in the collective Godhead, not in the individual person. This was a particular difficulty for the discussion of the Judgment, since it was to be conducted by Jesus (see, e.g. Matthew 24/30), yet Jesus claimed that only God the Father knew the hour

PLAY XXIV

of judgment (compare 20/61-4). Compare Comestor, *Historia Scholastica*, 'In Evangelia' 142 (PL 198/1611): *De die autem illa et hora nemo scit, neque Filius, neque angelus, nisi solus Pater. Hic exclamat Arius: Non sunt aequales, qui novit et qui ignorat. Hieronymus respondit in minori breviario super Psalmos: Humanitas Filii dicit se ignorare finem mundi. Quod Gregorius in Registro quasi exponens ait: Novit unigenitus Dei horam judicii, sed non ex natura humanitatis. Tamen etiam sic exponitur: Non novit, subaudi nobis, quibus expedit incertos esse, ut sic vivamus quasi in proximo judicandi.* On the underlying theology, see Augustine, *De Trinitate* 1/13 (PL 42/840-1) and his Sermo 52/2 (PL 38/355). The power of the Godhead therefore finds appropriate expression here in the person of the Son.

lord 7 B is an error resulting from the substitution of a frequent collocation with *soveraygne. mystely* 8 H, "mystically, wonderfully", is a substitution perhaps reflecting scribal unease at the sense of logical justification in *justly*.

9-10 Primus Demon knew of the Judgment at 1/249 and Adam received a vision of Judgment in Eden, 2/465-9, which may suggest God's initial resolve as the reference here. That vision presumably underlies Martha's words, 13/383-4. But Jesus himself foretells the Judgment at 16/45-50, 20/129-52, and it is incorporated into the Apostles' Creed, 21/334 + Latin-8, 350 + Latin-58, and such prophecies may be the reference here. Alternatively, the lines may allude to any one of a range of Old Testament references.

The judgment is here seen as the fulfilment of an earlier resolve. Compare York 48/57-64, where the decision to judge the world arises from God's impatience with Man's persistent sinfulness.

a reckoninge of the right 10 may merely mean "a correct judgment", but seems more probably to mean "a totalling of the righteous". Compare Matthew 24/31: *Et congregabunt electos eius a quattuor ventis, a summis caelorum usque ad terminos eorum* (AV "And they shall gather together his elect from the four winds, from one end of heaven to the other"). The intention is therefore to gather the righteous together as a group. Indeed, priority in resurrection is accorded to the righteous; 1 Thessalonians 4/16: *Et mortui qui in Christo sunt resurgent primi* (AV "And the dead in Christ shall rise first"). Some such consideration may be reflected in the fact that the redeemed speak first, and the damned enter later, 172 + SD.

11 *mee dight* means both "betake myself, go" (MED *dighten* 5 refl) and "prepare myself" (MED 1b (a) refl), "dress, equip myself" (MED 1b (b)). The implication is that the Godhead assumes the form of the Son, as confirmed perhaps by 14, 21-2. B apparently did not understand the reflexive construction and substitutes the inappropriate *thie* for *mee*.

13-4 *angelles* Two angels (24 + SH, 32 + SH) awake the dead, but other would be required to display the instruments of the Passion listed at 17-20, 356 + SD. It is not possible to determine the number and function of angels in the incomplete Wakefield play, beyond the fact that there is more than one. York 48 has two angels to summon the dead, and a third to separate redeemed and damned; *Ludus Coventriae* 42/1-26 specifies as angelic heralds Michael and Gabryell. Both Wakefield and York display the instruments of the Passion. Compare *Doomsday* (Carleton Brown, *English Lyrics of the Thirteenth Century* (Oxford, 1932), 28a/b91): "Four engles in þe dairet blouit here bemen".

15–6 "That I may see before my eyes all for whom I have shed forth my blood". *for* 16 ARBH is to be preferred for syntax and meaning to *forth* Hm. Hm's *forth* may suggest that *that* 16 is regarded as parallel to *that* 15, introducing a result clause dependent upon *wake* 14 and taking *can* 16 as a verb of lexical force rather than an auxiliary indicative of past tense — "so that I can shed forth my blood". But ARBH more logically treat *that* 16 as relative pronoun referring to *all* 15 and governed by a preposition.

17–24, stanza 3 *never* 19 ARBH was evidently the exemplar reading, or at least an exemplar alteration, but rhyme confirms *nere* Hm.

17–24 On the instruments of the Passion, compare 356 + SD and note.

21 *weare* Possibly past tense is intended, in view of the reinforcement of *beare* 22 as present tense by *nowe*. The *weede* must be recognisable from some episode in the Passion or resurrection — perhaps the cloak of 16/195–202, or more probably of 16/322 + SD; or his resurrection gown with the marks of the wounds upon it. The seamless cloak was by the fifteenth century included among the instruments of the Passion; see Louis Réau, *Iconographie de l'Art chrétien* (Paris, 1955–9), 2.ii, 509, and 428 + SD note.

29 B inexplicably omits the line, leaving a space blank for its insertion (see TNs).

29–32 As here punctuated, 31 is a result clause, dependent upon *awake* 29 — "I shall be ready, and that at once, to awaken each worldly creature so that they shall show themselves before you." But 31 could equally be taken as the object of 32 — "You shall see, lord, that they shall show themselves before you immediately." R, adopting the former interpretation, makes 32 a more self-contained statement by reading *that* for *thou* and *be* for *see* — "That shall come about, lord, immediately." B's *that* for *thou* 32 is more difficult to interpret — it may be an eye-slip from *that* 31; or a relative pronoun governing either *them* 31 or *thy* 31, neither yielding good sense.

33 *beames* This is the first indication of the method by which the dead shall be roused. The idea of the trumpets derives from Matthew 24/31: *Et mittet angelos suos cum tuba et voce magna* (AV "And he shall send his angels with a great sound of a trumpet"); see also 1 Corinthians 15/52, 1 Thessalonians 4/15, both of which employ the image of sleep used at 14, 29. But John 5/28 speaks of the dead hearing the voice of Christ. The blowing of the trumpets fulfils the words of Primus Demon at 1/249. The dead are similarly roused by trumpet blast in Wakefield 30 (cf. lines 4, 41, 89–111), York 48/65; but not explicitly in *Ludus Coventriae* 42, where the words of the archangels may be sufficient.

beames HmH seems to have been unfamiliar to ARB, which read *beanes* here and at 46. AB had the appropriate form at 1/249. *beme* is recorded in use by OED only to 1500. It was a long metal horn tapering to a small mouthpiece, and was used for battle and hunting signals.

35–6 "It will soon be evident who can now show a good reckoning." The idea of the judgment as a rendering of accounts derives alike from the parable of the Talents, Matthew 25/14–30, and from the imagery of Apocalypse 20/12: *Et vidi mortuos, magnos et pusillos stantes in conspectu throni; iudicati sunt mortui ex his quae scripte erant in libris, secundum opera ipsorum* (AV "And I saw the dead, small and great, stand before God; and the books were opened: and another book was opened, which is the book of life: and the dead were judged out of those things which were written in the books, according to their works"). In Wakefield 30, the devils go to judgment taking rolls of sins; the image of accounting permeates the morality play *Everyman*.

37–40 Compare clause 40, Athanasian Creed: *Et qui bona egerunt, ibunt in vitam eternam; qui vero mala, in ignem aeternum* the text of the pardon in *Piers Plowman* Passus 7, 111.

A's *evill* for *well* 37 destroys the meaning.

The phrase *withowt mendinge* 39 assumes particular force in relation to the purgatorial doctrine which is manifested in the redeemed souls.

40+SD *omnes mortui* No other cycle has so many resurrected or so closely identified socially. Wakefield 30 has four redeemed and four damned souls, none individualised; York 48 has two redeemed and two damned souls, none individualised; and *Ludus Coventriae* 42 has two groups of redeemed and damned souls who speak collectively. Chester balances redeemed and damned Pope, Emperor, King and Queen, but adds to the damned a lawyer and a merchant. The sequence is apparently in descending order of authority, with the Pope as the greatest under God and source of all legitimate power on earth. The redeemed emperor is presumably the Holy Roman Emperor, directly consecrated by the Pope. Power then descends through the monarchy to the local level of law and trade. Underlying the portraits are a number of concepts. Among them is the special responsibility of those given authority over others; compare Hebrews 13/17: *Obedite praepositis vestris et subiacete eis, ipsi enim pervigilant quasi rationem pro animabus vestris reddituri; ut cum gaudio hoc faciant et non gementes: hoc enim non expedit vobis* (AV "Obey them that have the rule over you, and submit yourselves: for they watch for your souls, as they that must give account, that they may do it with joy, and not with grief: for that is unprofitable for you"). See also Augustine, *De Civitate Dei* 19/19 (PL 41/647). Influence from the parable of the talents, which forms part of Jesus' account of the Judgment, Matthew 25/14–30, is probable, as well as the warning parable of Dives and Lazarus, Luke 16/19–31. The portraits are also influenced by contemporary satire and sermon; see G. R. Owst, *Literature and Pulpit*. The concern with the proper use of worldly authority has been a recurring feature of the cycle as a whole.

40+SH Compare 57–64 note. The inclusion of a pope among saved and damned and the praise of the office of the papacy with its special responsibilities suggests the Catholic orientation for the play. The pope typifies also the special responsibility of all ministers; see Augustine, *De Civitate Dei* 19/19 (PL 41/647). It is unlikely that any specific significance should be read into the reference to 303 years in purgatory, since the reference would require updating on each performance if a historical pope were intended.

47 *in* ARBH is to be preferred to the erroneous *I* (1) Hm in ensuring morphological regularity and syntactical continuity. The Hm reading may have been influenced by *I* (2).

51 *ne* ARBH is to be preferred for meaning to the scribally erroneous *mee* Hm.

57–64 R's omission may be a scribal error, but seems more probably deliberate, censoring the lines which make explicit the identification of the "highest office under thee" 55 with the papacy. It is notable that without these lines the speaker could stand as representative of the clergy without Catholic implications. It may be noted that with the exception of the damned king, who speaks only three stanzas, all the other resurrected souls have speeches of four stanzas in length except the redeemed pope. Possibly, therefore, R's omission was also intended to balance the length of the speech against that of later speakers.

The Petrine reference here derives from Christ's commission at Matthew 16/18–19: *Et ego dico tibi, quia tu es Petrus, et super hanc petram aedificabo Ecclesiam meam, et portae inferi non praevalebunt adversus eam. Et tibi dabo claves regni caelorum; .... et quodcumque solveris super terram, erit solutum et in caelis* (AV "And I say also unto thee, That thou art Peter, and upon this rock I will build my church; and the gates of hell shall not prevail against it. And I will give unto thee the keys of the kingdom of heaven: .... and whatsoever thou shalt loose on earth shall be loosed in heaven"). Peter opens the gates of Heaven in *Ludus Coventriae* 42/49–56.

The reference gains added force in conjunction with the meeting of Christ and Peter in the conclusion to play 18, found only in RH; see Appendix ID/80–95.

57 *grantest* HmAB is a regular form of the past tense of *grant*. H substitutes the equally acceptable *grantedst*, thereby avoiding confusion with the identical present form.

61–4 As here punctuated, the lines require a link to be understood after *lord* 63 — "I furthered my fleshly will that was wicked, which you have now raised, [and it] shall receive its judgment before you." Alternatively, and less probably, *fleshlye will* 61 may be taken as possessive, parallel to *thyne* 60 — "I did not do what you assented to but what my fleshly will, which was wicked, assented to." *I forthered* 63 would then become an archaic past participle, *i-forthered*, in the sense of *furtheren* MED 2, and a pronoun object must be supplied, to continue: "the which, now you have raised [it, have] advanced it, lord, shall receive its judgment before you."

The *fleshlye will* has not, strictly, been resurrected, and the adjective evidently has nominal force here — "the desire of the body ... which you have now raised." But 61 is metrically rough and would be improved by the omission of two syllables; reading *flesh* for *fleshlye will* would produce a more regular sequence of strongly and weakly stressed syllables while improving sense and syntax.

67–8 Compare Wakefield 30/22: "His commaundementys wold we not kepe"; and York 48/150: "His comaundementis wolde we noȝt kepe."

69–72 *purgatorye* This expressly Catholic doctrine may have been the occasion of R's omission of these lines. Purgatory is a place to which are committed after death those souls which have left earthly life in a state of venial, as opposed to mortal, sin, or have not completed temporal penance for remitted sins during earthly life. Most of the redeemed have been assigned to purgatory because their death-bed repentance left no opportunity for temporal penance upon earth; compare 95, 134, 155. It was such a circumstance which led Clement of Alexandria to postulate the existence of purgatory; see *Stromaesis* 6/14 (PG 9/350f). The damned mention no such repentance, but list mortal sins for which they are condemned; see 184, 221–4, 231, 257–8, 273 etc. Purgatory is a place of torment equivalent to Hell, but differing in that its punishments are temporal; see 78, 97–100. The doctrine rests upon the scriptural authority of 2 Maccabees 12/39–45, Matthew 12/31f and the ambiguous

1 Corinthians 3/11-15. It was developed in the writings of the Fathers (e.g. Augustine, *De Civitate Dei* 21/26 (PL 41/743-6)) and was confirmed at the Council of Lyons, 1274. It was rejected by Protestant reformers and is expressly prohibited under article 22 of the 39 articles of faith of the Church of England approved in 1562. It is notable therefore that the play places such emphasis upon the doctrine, and also that it is alone among the cycle-plays in doing so.

It is not clear why the pope is here redeemed, since his description of his life does not seem to qualify him for purgatory. No reference is made to venial sins or late repentance. Instead, his actions fulfil the requirements of mortal sin. His sin is grave, since he neglected his spiritual commission 60; it was carried out in full knowledge of the sin 61, 65-8; and it was done notwithstanding, with full consent 61-3.

69   *yt* has no particular referent but should be understood to comprehend the sin described in 65-8.

77-80   As here punctuated, *to* must be understood after *goe* 79 — "Never let me go back again [to] the pains..."; and 78 is parenthetical. But compare 97-100, where *are* is supplied in a similar comparison at 98, 99. The syntactical difficulties here would be removed by reading *are* for *as* (1) 78, although the latter was clearly the exemplar reading. A change from *are* to *as* would be aided by the presence of *as* (2).

90   The time spent in purgatory is not indicative of any historical personage, but seems merely a precise but conveniently "round" figure.

93   ARB's omission of *that* may be preferred to its retention by HmH as producing a more regular sequence of strongly and weakly stressed syllables. It is unlikely that HmH would insert a metrically detrimental and syntactically redundant word, however, and the omission may reflect independent scribal emendation of the exemplar reading.

97-100, stanza 13   The stanza consists of a regular Chester quatrain. Since stanzas 12 and 14 are complete, it is impossible to tell if there has been any omission in the exemplar at this point.

97   *paines* ARBH is to be preferred for concord with *are* 98 to the collective *payne* Hm.

103   The line is acceptable, but metrically rough. It would be improved by reading *are* for *have binne*, the latter evidently the exemplar reading. A change of tense might have been considered appropriate to the emperor's retrospective wisdom, but the present tense is suitable for the statement of a general principle for the audience.

107   *right hand* Compare 497 and note.

109-16, stanza 15   *minges* 115 H is to be preferred for rhyme to *mynes* HmARB. The H form represents *mingen*, MED 3(a) "to call to mind"; the HmARB form represents *minnen* MED v^1, 1(a) "to call to mind", and was evidently substituted in the exemplar as a more familiar form.

114   "And after torment-time, you bring good tidings." *teene tyde tydinges* seems to restate the *bale-boote* antithesis of 113. OED does not record the compound *teene-tyde*, and an ameliorative sense must be postulated for *tydinges*. It is remotely possible, but unlikely, that *tyde* is an adjective conveying the ameliorative sense of *tight*, as in *tight* OED 5 fig. "faithful, constant"; the form would then be influenced by the first syllable of *tydinges*. B omits *tyde*, to the detriment of metre, perhaps because it did not understand the line.

115 *name* ARBH is to be preferred for meaning to *names* Hm, the latter perhaps influenced by the morphology of the rhyme-words or by the idea of the seven names of God.

125-8 The bodily resurrection and attendant state of physical perfection are discussed by Augustine, *De Civitate Dei* 22/19-20.

129 *bales* HmB and *bale* H are equally possible, but it is difficult to understand the form *balleus*, significantly shared by AR and evidently a conscious substitution.

135 *almes-deedes* Compare Ecclesiasticus 29/14-5: *Pone thesaurum tuum in praeceptis Altissimi; et proderit tibi magis quam aurum. Conclude eleemosynam in corde pauperis, et haec pro te exorabit ab omni malo*. Also Augustine, *De Civitate Dei* 21/27 (PL 41/747): *Propter hoc ergo eleemosynae faciendae sunt, ut cum de praeteritis peccatis deprecamur, exaudiamur, non ut in eis perseverantes, licentiam malefaciendi nos per eleemosynas comparare credamus*.

136 "Has helped to keep me from Hell." The plural subject, *contrytion ... and almes-deedes*, has been regarded as a single reason, hence *hath* rather than *have*. The sense of separation in *from* requires verbal reinforcement today.

137-8 The reference derives partly from the parable of Dives and Lazarus, Luke 16/19-31, where Lazarus is carried after death to Abraham's bosom and Dives appeals to Abraham from Hell. The parable asserts the importance of deeds of charity in the world, a point emphasising the link of penitence and alms-deeds here. But there may also be an echo of Hebrews 11, especially: *Fide qui vocatur Abraham obedivit in locum exire, quem accepturus erat in hereditatem; et exiit, nesciens quo iret .... exspectabat enim fundamenta habentem civitatem, cuius artifex et conditor Deus ..... Iuxta fidem defuncti sunt omnes isti, non acceptis repromissionibus, sed a longe eas aspicientes et salutantes, et confitentes quia peregrini et hospites sunt super terram* (AV "By faith Abraham, when he was called to go out into a place which he should after receive for an inheritance, obeyed; and he went out, not knowing whither he went ... For he looked for a city which hath foundations, whose builder and maker is God ... These all died in faith, not having received the promises, but having seen them afar off, and were persuaded of them, and embraced them, and confessed that they were strangers and pilgrims on the earth").

140+SH The Queen is introduced as the exemplar of the "traditionally female" vices of vanity and lechery rather than as an exemplar of the abuse of authority. This sexual distinction is not so evident in other cycles. On the admission of sexual distinction at the resurrection, see Augustine, *De Civitate Dei* 22/17 (PL 41/778).

141-8 As here punctuated, 141-4 is an invocation, but also represents the subject of *hasse brought* 147. *flesh* 145 and *the soule and bodye* 148 are objects of *brought*: "O peerless prince ... you have brought together my flesh ... [and have brought together] the soul and body also." It would be possible to argue (1) that *flesh* is the object of *raysed* 143, with *mee* either as object or dative: "O peerless prince who has raised me, who has raised my flesh ..." or "O peerless prince who has raised for me my flesh ...";

PLAY XXIV 359

(2) that 145-6 is an extension of *bodye* 148 — "you have brought together the soul and body also — my flesh ..."; neither seems probable. But if ARBH's *the* is preferred to *and* 148, the force of *too* changes from adverb to preposition: "You have brought my flesh together, have brought the soul to the body." It seems probable that *the* 148 ARBH represents the exemplar form.

149-64, stanzas 20-1   The arrangement of lines in H is clearly correct. In HmARB the b-rhymes of the two stanzas do not rhyme and require rearrangement so that the rhyme-pairs *weedes* 152 — *deedes* 164 and *grace* 156 — *face* 160 occur each in one stanza. 161-4 syntactically completes the sentence begun at 149-51, and since 149-51 + 161-4 deals with sensuality and 153-60 deals with the remedy for sin, 153-60 must represent the second stanza.

The cause of the error, which was evidently present in the exemplar, cannot now be determined, but transposition of quatrains may suggest a manuscript in which previously omitted quatrains had been reinserted alongside others, leading to confusion of sequence. H may have emended independently, or have followed a correction not understood by the other scribes, if it did not use an independent exemplar. Deimling cites these lines as evidence of H's superiority.

149-64   The sins of dress and adornment, 149-52, 161-4, seem to look to 1 Timothy 2/9: *Similiter et mulieres in habitu ornato, cum verecundia et sobrietate ornantes se, et non in tortis crinibus aut auro aut margaritis vel veste pretiosa* (AV "In like manner also, that women adorn themselves in modest apparel, with shamefacedness and sobriety; not with broided hair, or gold, or pearls, or costly array"). 1 Peter 3/3 speaks in similar terms of the dress of wives, perhaps also relevant here. Satire on the dress of women was commonplace; see Owst, *Literature and Pulpit*, pp.390-401.

The counterbalancing virtue in good deeds, 154, is echoed in 1 Timothy 2/10: *Sed quod decet mulieres promittentes pietatem per opera bona* (AV "But (which becometh women professing godliness) with good works").

thy byddinge 163 does not seem to refer to any specific injunction.

150   *sendal* H, "a thin rich silken material", may seem more appropriate in collocation with *softe, silke, velvet* and *weedes* than *sandalles* HmARB, "a half shoe of red leather, silk, etc. embroidered and fastened with straps and bands, forming part of the regalia of a sovereign or of the official dress of a bishop or abbot". Either, however, gives sense. *sendal*, in its sense of "fine linen, lawn" is not recorded after 1606; *sandal* is recorded by OED only from 1485.

154   *saffe* introduces a clause, "except that"; *yf any paste* presumably means "if anyone in need passed by".

156   *hath* See 136 note.

162   *perrelles* HmB is a variant of the more familiar form, *pearles* ARH.

167   *warne* OED records *warn* v² in the sense of "to refuse, deny, forbid" only until 1611. H replaces it by *flee*, the word used in the similar context of 159, perhaps having confused the verb with *warn* v¹.

176-9   The pope's soul was adjudged to Hell at the particular judgment, together with the souls of the other damned. His resurrection now has two consequences.

First, his secret vice of covetousness will be made public (*fyled to bee before thy face* 178), in accordance with 1 Corinthians 3/13 and 4/5: *Itaque nolite ante tempus iudicare, quoadusque veniat Dominus, qui et illuminabit abscondita tenebrarum et manifestabit consilia cordium* (AV "Therefore judge nothing before the time, until the Lord come, who both will bring to light the hidden things of darkness, and will make manifest the counsels of the hearts"). Secondly, he will suffer a second death (*and after my death* 179) and return to Hell; compare Augustine, *De Civitate Dei* 20/6 (*PL* 41/666): '*Qui bona*,' inquit, '*fecerunt, in resurrectionem vitae*,' *hi sunt qui vivent;* '*qui vero mala egerunt, in resurrectionem judicii*,' *hi sunt qui non vivent; quia secunda morte morientur . . . ita sunt et resurrectiones duae, una prima, quae et nunc est, et animarum est, quae venire non permittit in mortem secundam; alia secunda, quae nunc non est, sed in saeculi fine futura est, nec animarum, sed corporum est, quae per ultimum judicium alios mittet in secundam mortem, alios in eam vitam, quae non habet mortem.*

182–3   The lines present a number of problems:

(1) *lyvinge* 182 is here taken as present participle — "when I was living"; but it could be a noun, MED 2 "way or manner of living" — "on account of my way of life I was the highest on earth."

(2) *closen* 183 HmB is recorded by MED only as an infinitive form, but cannot be so understood here. It may be an error for the past participle of *closen* MED 8c, "to put (sth) into a surrounding medium, shut in", qualifying *cunynge*. Such an interpretation would require *for* 182 to be preposition governing both *lyvinge* and *cunynge*, and would demand an abstract sense for *cleargye* — "I was highest on earth on account of my way of life and on account of knowledge enclosed in learning."

(3) *chosen* 183 ARH is recorded by MED and would here be a participle dependent upon *was* 182, demanding a concrete sense of *cleargye* and admitting either interpretation of *lyvinge* — "For, when alive, I was the highest upon earth and, being learned, was elected among the clergy."

(4) If *closen* is regarded as an error for some part of the verb *closen*, it could be taken as past tense *closed* as well as past participle — "For when alive, I was the highest on earth and embodied wisdom among the clergy."

184–94   The lines echo 1 Timothy 6/10, partially cited by Chaucer's Pardoner: *Radix enim omnium malorum est cupiditas; quam quidam appetentes erraverunt a fide, et inseruerunt se doloribus multis* (AV "For the love of money is the root of all evil; which while some coveted after, they have erred from the faith, and pierced themselves through with many sorrows"). Hence, for the pope, the consciousness of sin represents an unceasing torment to him.

187   *that* has no nominal referend but comprises the total situation described in 184–6.

197–200   Compare 40 + SH note.

200   "Utterly lost through my laws". It is not clear whether *lawes* implies the actual decrees and decisions of the pope, MED *laue* 1 "a rule or set of rules . . . thought of as promulgated by a rational, authoritative, and powerful lawgiver"; or the way in which the laws were applied during his papacy, MED 7 (a) "the system of administering and enforcing the law; the practical operation of the law". H substitutes *laches*, MED (a) "lack of zeal, laziness, negligence", which OED records

PLAY XXIV

until 1494, although it records the more specific legal sense, "negligence in the performance of any legal duty, delay in asserting a right, claiming a privilege, or applying for redress", from 1574.

202 *or elles to flee* The impossibility of escaping from God is a recurring theme in Scripture — see Psalms 139 AV/7, Jeremiah 23/24. The impossibility of flight is also acknowledged in Wakefield 30/49–50, York 48/121–2.

207 *cease* seems to be present tense plural, perhaps suggesting a collective force for *succour*, although it may be present subjunctive singular. H substitutes *no* to make the line exclamatory.

211 Hm and H are both metrically and semantically acceptable. *hardlye* AR perhaps derives from a desire to make the adverbial force of *hard* morphologically explicit and/or to match the metrical pattern of the previous two lines, where two unstressed syllables intervene between the first and second strong stresses. B seeks to "regularise" the inversion of *bye I* by the use of an auxiliary verb.

217–8 "Alas, who is there that dare do evil? We no longer dare cause injury." *dare* 218 is impersonal. The lines seem to have troubled H, which recasts 218: "Now is there no anxiety to cause injury any more." R merely changes the pronoun from plural to singular, ignoring the collective reference of *we* 219 which indicates that the emperor is speaking on behalf of all the damned.

221 On the revelation of hidden sin, see 176–9 note, and Apocalypse 13/16 on the mark placed by the beast of the Apocalypse on the foreheads of his servants. The latter underlies *Ludus Coventriae* 42/75–8:

> Mercy nay nay they xul haue wrake
> And þat on here fforehed wyttnes I take
> Ffor þer is wretyn with letteris blake
> Opynly all here synne

and the devils read off the sins at 91–130. Similar concern with hidden sin is seen in Wakefield 30/45–8, York 48/129–32.

222 Although *cares* ARBH is well attested, *care* Hm is equally acceptable.

227 *in binne* A rhyme on *e* seems indicated by *teene* 225, *bydeene* 226 and seems to support the HmB order against *bene in* ARH.

229 *knowe* may mean "recognise" or "acknowledge" here. The latter would derive from the idea that judgment reveals the hidden sins of Man — see 176–9 note and 221 note. The former may recall Romans 2/14–6: *Cum enim Gentes quae legem non habent, naturaliter ea quae legis sunt faciunt, eiusmodi legem non habentes ipsi sibi sunt lex; qui ostendunt opus legis scriptum in cordibus suis, testimonium reddente illis conscientia ipsorum, et inter se invicem cogitationibus accusantibus aut etiam defendentibus, in die, cum iudicabit Deus occulta hominum secundum evangelium meum per Iesum Christum* (AV "For when the Gentiles, which have not the law, do by nature the things contained in the law, these, having not the law, are a law unto themselves: Which shew the work of the law written in their hearts, their conscience also bearing witness, and their thoughts the mean while accusing or else excusing one another: In the day when God shall judge the secrets of men by Jesus Christ, according to my gospel"). Hence the Gentile, and here the pagan, finally understands his own condition intuitively, by divine illumination.

233-4 "I always mixed ill-gotten money [with legitimately acquired money]. Now it is repaid by me going to hell." The exact force of *misbegotten* is not clear; the term may even imply debasement of coinage. An impersonal subject must be supplied for *ys* 234; although by omitting *I* 233 and supplying *my*, R makes *money* the subject, leaving *myxed* as past participle, an acceptable reading. *yonge* here could be present participle of *yong*, "to go", agreeing with *me*, dative of respect and governing *hell*; but OED records *yong* only to 1450. The word cannot, however, be the semantically inappropriate *young*. H substitutes *thong*, a reading apparently based on scribal confusion of *y* and *þ*; OED does not record *thong* in any appropriate sense, although it could represent an error for *throng* in the senses of "multitude" and also "pain, affliction".

233 is metrically rough and would be improved by the syllabic reduction in *misgotten* BH and by the omission of *ever* H. *my*, semantically necessary in R's reading, merely increases the irregularity in A.

237-44, stanza 31   *in sett* 239 HmARB does not rhyme. *a sott* H does, but the sense seems unlikely, although Deimling cites it as evidence of H's superiority over HmARB. An imperfect rhyme may have been intended.

243   An ironic echo of Matthew 25/32: *Et congregabuntur ante eum omnes gentes, et separabit eos ab invicem sicut pastor segregat oves ab haedis* (AV "And before him shall be gathered all nations: and he shall separate them one from another, as a shepherd divideth his sheep from the goats"). Here the idea is equivalent to "Better not to have been born at all".

249-60   The major sins of the damned king are oppression — of the poor and weak, and of the Church — combined with lechery and covetousness. Contrast the lifelong charity of the redeemed king, 135, and his final repentance of the worldly presumption of which he was formerly guilty.

256   *keenlye* ARH is to be preferred for meaning to the scribally erroneous *kneelye* Hm. *kinely* B may be scribal error for *kenely*, or alternatively an error for the appropriate *kindly*.

265-72   The lament at 265 is presumably to be considered posthumous. It is the strongest reflection of an understanding of the availability of grace through Christ's Passion expressed among the resurrected.

273-80   Like the redeemed queen, the damned queen committed the sin of lechery; but whereas the redeemed queen mentions her pride in appearance and delight in arousing men's lusts, the damned queen dwells upon her insatiable carnal appetite before cursing the enticements — carnal and sartorial — which led her to damnation. Again, there is no compensating balance of charitable acts and final repentance such as mitigate the vices of the redeemed queen.

276   *my* ARH may be preferred for meaning to *that* Hm and to B's omission. *that* Hm may reflect confusion with *that* (1 and 2) 275; B's omission may represent a desire for metrical improvement.

PLAY XXIV 363

277   *pride* ARBH is formally preferable to *prydee* Hm, where *e* has been erroneously repeated.

280   *harrowe* represents *herien*, MED 3(a) "to torment; chase, pursue"; (b) "to drag (sb or sth), pull". The word ironically reverses its familiar application in collocation with *hell*, MED 2(a) "to rob (hell of souls)". *arrow* B is a nonce-word, perhaps reflecting unease at the irony; *arrow* vb is not recorded by OED until 1627.

285–90   The complaint is reminiscent of laments for lost beauty in lyrics of the *ubi sunt* form. Compare 288 note.

286   *was* ABH is to be preferred for meaning to *ys* (2) HmR. The latter seems to be a mechanical repetition of *ys* (1), whereas the sense seems to be that the lady has lost her beauty on resurrection. But compare Augustine, *De Civitate Dei* 22/20 (PL 41/783): *Quibus omnibus pro nostro modulo consideratis atque tractatis, haec summa conficitur, ut in resurrectione carnis in aeternum eas mensuras habeat corporum magnitudo, quas habebat perficiendae sive perfectae cujusque indita corpori ratio juventutis, in membrorum quoque omnium modulis congruo decore servato.*

291   A relative pronoun must be understood before *I*. R's substitution of *me* for *I am* fails to solve the difficulty.

301–8, stanza 39   *als* 304 H is to be preferred for perfect rhyme to *elles* HmARB. No manuscript has the form *wand*, required for perfect rhyme at 302.

302   *wronge* ARBH is to be preferred for meaning to the erroneous *wrought* Hm; Hm's error is not readily explicable, but may originate in a confusion of *n* and *u* and a resulting substitution of a familiar form.

303   Although *false* ARBH is both the expected form and also well attested, *falsely* Hm is equally acceptable.

305   *sound* is a fifteenth-century variant of *sand*, OED sb¹, 1 "the action of sending; that which is sent, a message, present." OED last records the word in this sense in ?c.1525. It does not seem to have been understood by A or R, neither of which regards it as a noun and therefore substitutes the noun *riches* for the adjective *rych*. A, by deliberate substitution or confusion of long *s* and *f*, reads *founde*, parallel to *sought*; R preserves *sounde* but evidently regards it as an adjective.

309–12   The image of judgment as a trial in which justice will be administered impartially is a recurring theme of the judgment plays.

311   The construction as it stands is syntactically incomplete and metrically rough. The manuscripts suggest two solutions: (1) the substitution of *before* H for *for* HmARB, so that *that* 312 is taken as relative pronoun; (2) the substitution of *is of* AR for *of* HmBH, so that *that* 312 introduces a result clause.

329   *maketh* is to be taken with *to bee* 331 — "Trade causes me to be in the torment of hell." H does not seem to understand the construction and its substitution of *marreth*, while giving the local sense of "Trade destroys me", removes the syntactical link with 331.

329–30   The 'mercator' operates in two areas, in trade and in the acquisition of land and property, neither of which is presented as sinful in itself. But his trading activity is seen as an aspect of cupidity 343-4, which is further manifested in his practice of usury 349 and in the withholding of tithes. His acquisition of property similarly becomes an aspect of cupidity, and leads directly into the oppression of the poor sitting-tenant 335-6. This in turn is linked to the merchant's administration of the law to the disadvantage of the poor 345-6, aided by false oaths 347-8 — perhaps indicating that the merchant, through his wealth and status, was a Justice of the Peace. The effect is a composite picture of evil at local level.

337-40 "But when I died, truly my enemy damned both body and soul by all that I had to the pain of hell for ever." *therebye* 339 takes up *all that I had* 338, a construction apparently not understood by B and H. B adds *was* to 338, making 339-40 an explanatory expansion. H omits *I* 338 and reads *and* for *both* 339 — "My enemy had all that I had, and by it [i.e. the wealth] body and soul [were] damned to the pain of hell for ever."

341-56 R omits stanza 44 and rearranges the lines of stanza 45 to give a new form, aaabaaac, with 356 replaced by another line. The stanza seems to have been a deliberate creation of R; if so, it might also follow that R's omission of stanza 44 was also deliberate. See 351 note.

346 *rayvinge reave* in the sense of 2 trans, "to spoil, rob or plunder" is last recorded by OED in 1567. The word, or its particular form or application here, does not seem to have been familiar to B, which substitutes *ravening*, although *raven* vb is not recorded in a sense appropriate to its transitive use here.

347 *saintes* BH is to be preferred for meaning to *sainte* HmA. As here punctuated, *sainte* is taken as attributive of a personal noun *Hyse* since this seems to be the only way in which HmA could have understood the word; *sainte* is not recorded by OED as a collective noun. But such use is improbable, and *sainte* seems best considered as an exemplar or scribal error for a contracted plural which has been emended or correctly interpreted in BH. Just possibly, the singular *tyme* 348 Hm could have influenced the Hm singular; but A reads *tymes* — see 348 note. *hyse*, attested by HmAH, seems to have been the exemplar form.

348 It seems probable that *sythes* H was the original reading of the exemplar and that *tymes* A was a later substitution. When Hm erroneously copied out the lines after 340 (see TNs) it also wrote *sythes*, but when copying the line in the correct position, it wrote *tyme*, perhaps omitting the inflection because *thousand* conveys the concept of number. *othes* B may represent an attempt to decipher *sythes*.

351 Both A and R read *hyed* for *taythed*, perhaps rejecting the latter reading on doctrinal grounds. It is impossible that a respected member of society, apparently a Justice, could refuse to attend church, and the A reading makes the relevance of 352 less obvious. Possibly these difficulties contributed to R's omissions and rearrangements in this section; see 341-56, stanzas 44-5 note.

355 *the dyvelles bellye* Compare Jonah's prayer from within the whale, Jonah 2/2: *De ventre inferi clamavi* (AV "Out of the belly of hell, cried I"); and Isaiah 27/1: *In die illa visitabit Dominus in gladio suo duro, et grandi et forti, super Leviathan serpentem vectem et super Leviathan, serpentem tortuosum, et occidet cetum qui in mari est* (AV "In that day the Lord with his sore and great and strong sword shall punish leviathan the

PLAY XXIV 365

piercing serpent, even leviathan that crooked serpent; and he shall slay the dragon that is in the sea"). The idea of hell-mouth as a monster's jaws rests on such passages, so that the existence of a hell-mouth on stage here would extend the force of the phrase. The passages also point the confusion between the whale as Hell and Leviathan as the devil which underlies the phrase.

356 + SD *descendet* BH is to be preferred to the scribally erroneous *descende* Hm and the inappropriate *descendit* AR.

in nube Compare 16/50 and note; also Matthew 24/30, Mark 13/26, Apocalypse 1/7 — Matthew: *Et videbunt Filium hominis venientem in nubibus caeli cum virtute multa et maiestate* (AV "And they shall see the Son of Man coming in the clouds of heaven with power and great glory"). See also 20/156-60 and note, perhaps indicating similar staging-devices here; also *Glossa Ordinaria*, 'Apoc. Joannis' 1/7 (PL 114/711): *Cum nubibus, id est cum sanctis; . . . vel, sicut in nube ascendit, ita in nube veniet.*

in aere prope terram The interpretation is based on 1 Thessalonians 4/17: *Deinde nos qui vivimus, qui relinquimur, simul rapiermur cum illis in nubibus obviam Christo in aera; et sic semper cum Domino erimus* (AV "Then we which are alive and remain shall be caught up together with them [i.e. the dead in Christ who rose first] in the clouds, to meet the Lord in the air; and so shall we ever be with the Lord"). For the *doctores* disputing the issue, see Aquinas, *Summa Theologiae* supp.88 art.2. A major alternative to this view is presented by Joel 3/2, where the nations are gathered in the valley of Jehoshaphat for judgment.

cum cruce corona spinea lancea et instrumentis aliis Compare 17–20. The sponge 18 and nails 19 are probably here included among the *instrumentis aliis*. The number of instruments varied considerably; see Louis Réau, *Iconographie de l'Art chrétien* 2.ii, pp.508–9 The justification for the presentation of symbols is Matthew 24/30: *Tunc parebit signum Filii hominis in caelo* (AV "And then shall appear the sign of the Son of Man in heaven"); but early commentators usually restrict the reference to the cross — e.g. Chrysostom, *In Matth. Homil.* 76 al 77 (PG 58/698).

359–60 "If only you knew how it would all turn out and in what way!" This reading follows the punctuation of MED *appenden* 3, "? turn out, come (*to* sth)", for which these lines provide the sole example. The lines imply that God has raised the dead not initially to explain his purpose to them but to set it out before the prophets and patriarchs.

It is, however, tempting to regard *yf* as an exemplar error for contracted *þ*ᵗ, "that" — "So that you may know how it would turn out, and in what way." *but* 361 would then have the force of "but also". Support for such a reading might be found in Aquinas, *Summa Theologiae* (Ottaway 1945: 5 vols) Supp. 88/1: *Dicendum quod universale iudicium magis directe respicit universalitatem hominum quam singulos iudicandorum, quamvis ergo cuilibet homini ante iudicium sit certa notitia de sua damnatione vel praemio, non tamen omnibus omnium damnatio vel praemium innotescet. Unde iudicium necessarium erit.*

362 *prophettes patriarches* Compare Matthew 19/28: *Filius hominis in sede maiestatis suae, sedebitis et vos super sedes duodecim, iudicantes duodecim tribus Israel* (AV "The Son of man shall sit in the throne of his glory, ye also shall sit upon twelve thrones, judging the twelve tribes of Israel"). See also 1 Corinthians 6/2: *An nescitis* *quoniam sancti de hoc mundo iudicabunt* (AV "Do ye not know that the saints shall judge the world?"), which *Glossa Ordinaria*, 'Epist. 1 ad Cor.' 6/2 (PL 114/528), interprets at exemplary level; and Comestor, *Historia Scholastica*, 'In Evangelia' 102 (PL 198/1589): *Ibi contemptores mundi cum Domino judicabunt, non solum cooperatione, sed etiam auctoritate. Duodenarius autem ponitur pro plenitude potestatis, et duodecim tribus Israel pro omnibus judicandis.* The concept derives also from Old Testament references such as Isaiah 3/14: *Dominus ad iudicium veniet cum senibus populi sui et principibus eius* (AV "The Lord will enter into judgment with the ancients of his people, and the princes thereof"). The assumption here may therefore be that the prophets and patriarchs descend with Christ. This seems to accord with Aquinas' second mode of judgment, *Summa Theologiae* Supp 89, art.1. In York 48/185-216 Jesus sits among his apostles to judge.

365-6 *but you but* marks a return of address from the prophets and patriarchs of 362 to the resurrected dead of 359. The judgment is in effect to be a demonstration of the justice of decisions made at the particular judgments.

369-72 See 2/1-424.

371-2 *weare* 372 is established by rhyme. It cannot be a form of the verb "to be" because that function is served by *was* 371 and because it does not show concord with *thou* 371. Syntactically it should be adjective or adverb, but it has no formal counterpart elsewhere in English in this function.

H substitutes *hast* for *was* 371, but the syntax remains obscure; it also substitutes *thou* for *then* 372 to provide a second subject for *weare*, but problems of concord and aspect remain. B substitutes a plural pronoun *they* for *then* 372, giving plural concord but at the expense of the direct address in the second person singular which characterises most of the speech, and without resolving the problem of *was* 371.

377-80 "How might I grant you more grace than by taking that same nature which you have — it [i.e. the human nature or form] is seen clearly here now in this place." The construction is elliptical. *take* is infinitive; a subject must be supplied for *appeareth*.

A inserts *is* in 379 and *as* in 380, changing the impersonal construction but still requiring a subject to be supplied — "Here it is now in this place as it clearly appears." R retains *as* but omits *is* — "Than to take that same nature which you have here in this place [i.e. here on earth], as it clearly appears"; *peareth* for *appeareth* smooths the metre. B reads *as* in 379 for *is* A — "as here now in this place appears clearly" — producing a smoother syntax and metre. H follows B, but omits *this*, to the detriment of metre and sense. Possibly B contains the preferable reading. *is* A could well be influenced by an exemplar *as*, erroneously omitted by Hm; R's omission of *as* would result rather from an attempt to improve the A construction.

381-6 Compare 20/125-8.

385-436 Wilson compares *Stanzaic Life* 9021-40, which contains the last four of the five reasons given by Christ at his ascension; viz. to present the drops to his Father as a prayer for Man; to show how mercifully the righteous were redeemed; to indicate Christ's victory over the devil; to make wicked men acknowledge the justice of their damnation. But the parallels, verbal and structural, with Chester here do not seem significantly close.

PLAY XXIV   367

385–408   Compare 20/149-52. 386 Hm gives sense — "I desired the same blood should be held in flesh till now." But *freshe* ARBH is the expected reading — "I desired the same blood should be kept fresh till now." The line has a rough metre which AR seek to improve at the expense of sense by reading *I shall see* and replacing *tell* by the relative pronoun *that*. Metre would be improved by omitting the syntactically redundant *should* 386, clearly the exemplar form. On the function of this sign, see Aquinas, *Summa Theologiae* Supp.90 art.2.

389–96   Compare 20/137-44. The first cause is that the blood symbolises the redeeming power of Christ's sacrifice, atoning for the sins of man.

396   *to soone* The sense may be that God will withhold vengeance until he is certain of the impenitent state of the sinner. The line indicates that vengeance will be ultimately taken on the impenitent, as the fate of the damned indicates, and hence stands against the view that God will leave sins unpunished because of the perfect nature of Christ's atonement, a view Augustine opposes in *De Civitate Dei* 21/21 (PL 41/734). However, *to* contributes to the metrical roughness of the line and is semantically redundant if *soone* is taken to mean "immediately"; its inclusion may represent a late clarification whereby *soone* was understood to mean "quickly".

397–404   The lines are addressed specifically to the Jews, who deny the divinity of Christ. They correspond to the first cause in *Stanzaic Life* 9007-20 where the blood is displayed to demonstrate the truth of his resurrection:

> lest men hade opet him sto[l]en away
> by coyntys and collusioun
> And that sum other body rose
> that was made be fantasy,
> as was emonge Iewes lose
> hor error for to iustifye.
>   (9015-20)

The charge here is that the Jews were *unkynd*, i.e. acted contrary to the dictates of nature. See also Chrysostom, *In Matthaeum Homilia* 76 al 77 (PG 58/698).

398–401   "[This blood] which the Jews produced in this way should now be displayed here, [so that the Jews] might clearly acknowledge how unnaturally they conducted themselves." The construction requires *that the Jewes* to be again understood at the start of 399. *that* 399 is relative pronoun, but if understood at 400 it would introduce a clause of purpose. *unkynd* 401 may be an adverb — *unkindlye* ARH makes this function morphologically explicit — or alternatively an adjective qualifying *them* — "how they conducted themselves as unnatural people".

405–12   Compare 20/144-8. The third cause is to uphold the justice of God in the final judgment. In so doing, Jesus points a comparison between the unnatural acts of the Jews at the crucifixion and the equally unnatural acts of those who swear falsely and have continued mystically to crucify him thereafter. See 418-20 note.

411–2   The singular pronouns *his* 411, *him* 412, suggest that Jesus is addressing each individual rather than the good and evil collectively. The pronoun is confirmed by rhyme at 411. A subject (e.g. *I*) must be understood for *bought* 412.

413–6 "Yet despite all this great torment that I suffered while I was living here [in earth], you [evil ones] refrained from virtue all the more in your will. I do not look the way I feel."

I 414 is the subject of both *suffered* and *lent*. H makes this explicit, to the detriment of metre. *you* must be understood as the subject of *spared* 415, as indicated by *your*; AR misleadingly supply *I* as subject. The address to the evil-doers follows upon the closing reference in 409–12 but the address becomes collective.

416 is not clear, but it seems to suggest the opposition of a sensory state (*feele*) with some other state of existence (*am*). In view of what follows, the implication is probably that, although Christ appears in his resurrected form, the act of crucifixion has continued mystically and his agony has been perpetuated despite his glorified state.

418–20 Compare *Jacob's Well* cap 23, 'De gula et viciis lingue': "Þe v leef is when men sweryn vyolently, as be god, or be ony of his sayntes, or be his soule, his body, his herte, his flesch, his bonys, his peyne, his deth, his feet, his nayles, or be ony of his oþer lymes. Þanne þei rende god iche lyme fro oþer, and arn werse þan iewys, for Þei rentyn hym but onys, and swiche swererys rendyn him iche day newe." So also Chaucer's Pardoner's Tale VI (C) 472–5 (Robinson ed., p.150):

> Hir othes been so grete and so dampnable
> That it is grisly for to heere hem swere.
> Our blissed Lordes body thay totere, —
> Hem thoughte that Jewes rente hym noghte ynough.

and Parson's Tale 10/591 (Robinson ed., p.246): "For Cristes sake, ne swereth nat so synfully in dismembrynge of Crist by soule, herte, bones, and body. For certes, it semeth that ye thynke that the cursede Jewes ne dismembred nat ynough the preciouse persone of Crist, but ye dismembre hym moore." Robinson's note to Pardoner's Tale 472 ff gives further references and suggests possible influence from Hebrews 6/4–6: *Impossibile est enim eos qui semel sunt illuminati, gustaverunt etiam donum caeleste, et participes facti sunt Spiritus Sancti, gustaverunt nihilominus bonum Dei verbum, virtutesque saeculi venturi, et prolapsi sunt, rursus renovari ad paenitentiam, rursum crucifigentes sibimetipsis Filium Dei et ostentui habentes* (AV "For it is impossible for those who were once enlightened and have tasted of the heavenly gift, and were made partakers of the Holy Ghost, And have tasted the good word of God, and the powers of the world to come, If they shall fall away, to renew them again unto repentance; seeing they crucify to themselves the Son of God afresh, and put him to an open shame").

419 *rente* AR is to be preferred for meaning to *lent* HmB, *hent* H. *lent* is semantically inappropriate and repeats the 414 rhyme-word; it may have been an exemplar error, influenced by the possibility of alliteration with *lymme* 419 and by *lent* 414 in rhyme-position. AR and H would then represent different scribal attempts to make sense of the reading, with AR preferable. Alternatively, *rente* may have been the exemplar-reading, with scribes seeking alternatives because of the echo of *torent* 417.

421–8 + SD Jesus bleeds. A similar effect seems required in Wakefield 30/53: "To se his Woundys bledande, this is a dulfull case". It probably underlies Marlowe's *Dr. Faustus*, Act 5 scene 2, line 150: "See, see where Christ's blood streams in the firmament." The scene owes much to mystical meditations on the Passion; compare Bernard, *Vitis Mystica*, "De Rosa Passionis" 35-41, especially 41 (PL 184/715). From such meditations derives the cult of the Five Wounds of Christ and, in the fifteenth century, the cult of the Sacred Heart of Jesus. The latter may be distantly evoked here, since the SD specified blood-flow only from Jesus' side; traditionally, Jesus was pierced through his left side, since that was the side of the heart.

On production, compare J. W. Robinson ('The Late Medieval Cult of Jesus and the Mystery Plays', *PMLA* lxxx, 1965, pp.510-11) fn. 19: "Again, in the paintings Christ's mantle is draped low so that the wound in his side may be plainly visible."

427 *bleede* Hm is evidently present tense, while *bled* BH is past; *blede* AR may represent either, but seems more likely to be present. Hm means "See the blood flow out that I am still bleeding on the cross because you have constantly re-crucified me by your oaths"; BH "The same blood that I bled for you on the cross now flows out fresh." But on the evidence of 431, past tense is preferable; see 431 note.

431 *bleede* Hm is present tense, while *bled* BH is past; *blede* AR may represent either, but seems more likely to be present. The use of *suffered* 432 as a parallel verb here strongly indicates that the past tense is to be preferred, although either tense would give satisfactory sense, as at 427.

435 "Therefore let each individual make his own assessment, for righteousness must prevail." *reacon* is imperative or subjunctive; on the sense of *goo*, see MED *gon* 8(f). Christ's injunction to each to make his own judgment of the situation and to acknowledge the justice of the decision is in accordance with Romans 2/15.

442 Compare 43 and note. At 90 the emperor specified that he has been in hell a thousand years.

446 *this place*, i.e. purgatory. Previous adverbial references, e.g. *here*, have been to earth; at 441 the emperor uses *therein* rather than *herein*. AR therefore plausibly read *that* for *this* here. Although purgatory might be identified as a place on stage, or as a part of the hell-set, it seems unlikely; at 40+SD the dead came from their graves rather than Hell or purgatory.

448 *yt* has no nominal referent but comprehends *foule and wycket* 444.

450 BH share the erroneous *thisten* for *christen* HmAR, an error perhaps showing influence from the initial digraph in *thrall* and *thy*.

451 *are* AR for *am* HmBH is an error resulting from false concord with *synnes*. The subject is the relative pronoun *that*, which in turn refers to *I* 449.

453-92 The action now turns from justification to the act of judgment itself, resting upon the acts of bodily mercy which are enumerated in Matthew 25. There, in 25/34-46 Jesus states that in Judgment he will address first the saved and then the damned, and will assess them by their six merciful acts of feeding the hungry, giving drink to the thirsty, giving lodging to the stranger, clothing the naked, visiting the sick, and visiting the prisoners. The six acts were traditionally increased to seven by the addition of the burial of the dead — see e.g., Comestor, *Historia Scholastica*, 'In Evangelia' 145 (PL 198/1613) — and the seven acts of mercy became from the thirteenth century a standard part of the Church's programme of instruction.

Here Jesus' dialogue with the two groups occurs in separated passages — to the saved at 453-92 and to the damned at 605-44. The two dialogues are separated by the entry of the devils and their dialogue with Jesus. The acts of mercy are found in the other cycles also — Wakefield 30/442-57 and 482-503; York 48/285-98 and 325-48; *Ludus Coventriae* 42/79-91 (listed only to the damned). In those plays, as here, they are not in the strict biblical order. Here, in addressing the redeemed 453-66, Jesus comprehends visitation of the sick and prisoners under *other deedes to my lykinge* 465, although he includes the visiting of prisoners in his response at 481-4; he reverses the acts of harbouring the stranger and clothing the naked, 462-4. The list to the damned, 621-8, is comprehensive, but the harbouring of the stranger is there placed last.

455-6 Compare Matthew 25/34: *Possidete paratum vobis regnum a constitutione mundi* (AV "Inherit the kingdom prepared for you from the foundation of the world"). But the wording here may owe something to Mark 10/40: *Sedere autem ad dexteram meam vel ad sinistram, non est meum dare vobis, sed quibus paratum est* (AV "But to sit on my right hand and on my left hand is not mine to give; but it shall be given to them for whom it is prepared").

457-8 Compare Matthew 25/35: *Esurivi enim, et dedistis mihi manducare* (AV "For I was an hungred, and ye gave me meat"). The text here does not specify the state of hunger but instead subsitutes a reference which suggests that the acts relate to the period of Jesus' earthly life.

463 Compare Matthew 25/35: *Hospes eram* (AV "I was a stranger").

467-8 Compare 485-6. The lines are without counterpart in Matthew's account but may echo Matthew 19/29, also in a context of judgment: *Et omnis qui reliquerit domum vel fratres aut sorores aut patrem aut matrem, aut uxorem aut filios aut agros propter nomen meum, centuplum accipiet, et vitam aeternam possidebit* (AV "And every one that hath forsaken houses, or brethren, or sisters, or father, or mother, or wife, or children, or lands, for my name's sake, shall receive an hundredfold, and shall inherit everlasting life").

468 + SH In Matthew 25/37 the righteous reply collectively. Here the pope and emperor, the two foremost, represent the redeemed souls.

477-80 Compare Matthew 25/40: *Amen dico vobis, quamdin fecistis uni ex his fratribus meis minimis, mihi fecistis* (AV "Verily I say unto you, Inasmuch as ye have done it unto one of the least of these my brethren, ye have done it unto me"). The biblical point is not made explicit in the text, which merely reverts to the list of merciful acts and hence does not fully resolve the ambiguities of 469-76.

489-92 Without counterpart in Matthew, but looking towards Isaiah 49/10 and its echo in Apocalypse 7/16: *Non esurient, neque sitient amplius, nec cadet super illos sol, neque ullus aestus* (AV "They shall hunger no more, neither thirst any more; neither shall the sun light on them, nor any heat"), taken up again in the promise of eternal joy of Apocalypse 7/17.

493-500 The separation of redeemed and damned occurs in Matthew 25/32 before Jesus' address to the resurrected, and there is therefore no reference to the angels separating and directing the redeemed. Matthew 13/49 speaks of the angels

PLAY XXIV

separating the wicked from the just and casting the wicked into the fire. Here, the earlier speeches suggest a grouping of redeemed and damned from the start of the play, so that the angels would merely shepherd the redeemed souls to Christ to stand at his right hand, leaving the damned to be shepherded to hell by the devils. The opposition, if biblically inaccurate, is nonetheless visually and dramatically effective.

In Wakefield 30/74, York 48/169 the groups are separated before Jesus descends.

493–500, stanza 63   No manuscript has the form *behett* for *beheight* 498, required for perfect rhyme.

508 + SD   As here presented, the SD does not clearly indicate the presence of alternative texts. It should read *Letamini in Domino. Salvator mundi, domine*. On the former, see Psalm 31/11; *Laetamini in Domino et exultate iusti et gloriamini omnes recti corde* (AV Psalms 32/11: "Be glad in the Lord, and rejoice, ye righteous: and shout for joy, all ye that are upright in heart"). In Wakefield 30, the play ends with the ascent of the redeemed to heaven singing *Te deum laudamus*; in York 48 they ascend *cum melodia angelorum*.

demones The presence of devils at the judgment is attested by texts such as 2 Peter 2/4: *Si enim Deus angelis peccantibus non pepercit, sed rudentibus inferni detractos in tartarum tradidit cruciandos in iudicium reservari* (AV "For if God spared not the angels that sinned, but cast them down to hell, and delivered them into chains of darkness, to be reserved into judgment"). But since God had already judged the devils (John 16/11), they were not to be judged themselves. Hence they enter here when effective judgment has been passed. Their presence is, according to Aquinas, *Summa Theologiae* Supp. 89, art.8, required because they have exerted influence over the lives of men: such an idea seems to direct the devils' conduct here. In Wakefield 30 the devils come in response to the doomsday trumpet and enter before Jesus speaks to the resurrected dead. In York 48/217–28 they enter after Jesus has sat on the judgment throne but before he addresses the resurrected dead. In *Ludus Coventriae* 32/31–5 the devils answer the judgment summons with the resurrected dead.

511   *mercye* is the subject of *ys* — "You were the embodiment of mercy, now mercy is denied."

520   The line elaborates *worthye for his trespace* 518, and thus depends upon *that ys* 518 — "who is become mine through sin."

commynne is past participle; H supplies *is* and replaces *myne* by *my hyne*, apparently wishing to make the construction self-contained.

521–4   The lines distinguish the Christian pope who knowingly sinned and hence acted unpardonably, and the pagan emperor who rejected the true faith for *heresye* 535. Both have submitted in their different ways to the direct influence of the devil, 523, 528–9, 534, 536. The king and queen are damned for lack of alms-deeds, 541–2.

540 + Latin   John 3/18: AV "He that believeth not is condemned already." Compare Aquinas, *Summa Theologiae* Supp.89 art.7: *Sicut enim est certa infidelium damnatio, ita et eorum qui in mortali decedunt*.

548   The line contains four strongly stressed syllables instead of the expected three. A three-stress line would result from the omission of *that place*, attested by all manuscripts and evidently the exemplar reading. *passe that place* suggests "pass by that place"; the omission of *that place* leaves *passe* with the sense of "move onwards" with overtones of escape, a usage which today normally requires an adverb, hence perhaps the feeling that some addition was syntactically necessary.

549–56, stanza 70   No manuscript has the form *rightwise* for *righteous* 551, required for perfect rhyme. B's substitution of *thus* for *this* 549 suggests unease at the imperfect rhyme and fully confirms *righteous* as the exemplar reading.

551–2   "And I shall at once test him, if I may see that he may be righteous." The second devil presents his questions as a further trial of Jesus, binding him to his own promises.

556   *us* is dative. A unnecessarily supplies a preposition; *as* B is a scribal error.

564 + Latin.   The Latin at 564 + is Matthew 16/27; AV "For the Son of Man shall come in the glory of his Father, with his angels; and then he shall reward every man according to his works." Hm has erroneously repeated *patris*; *unicuique* B is to be preferred to *unicuiquam* HmARH as reflecting the Vulgate reading. All manuscripts read *opus suum* (*o* A, *opus* R) for Vulgate *opera eius*, although the text reads *mans deedes* 559.

573–80 + Latin   The Latin at 580 + is Matthew 13/49–50; AV "So shall it be at the end of the world: the angels shall come forth, and sever the wicked from among the just, And shall cast them into the furnace of fire: there shall be wailing and gnashing of teeth." No manuscript has Vulgate *ibi* for *ubi*, and only H reads *wher* 578. *seperabunt* BH is to be preferred to the scribally erroneous and semantically inappropriate *sperabunt* HmAR; *part* 576 BH may be preferred to *put* HmAR as a translation of the Vulgate form, *put* perhaps being influenced by *put* 577 (but see 573–80 stanza 73 note).

578 has no counterpart to *erit*, and *is* must therefore be understood; A supplies *is*. Only Hm has *and*, corresponding to *et*, but its omission in ARBH improves the metre of 578. *grennynge* Hm and *grynnyng* BH are variants of the present participle of *grennen*, MED 1(c) "to grind or gnash the teeth" — the form required for rhyme at 583 may support the Hm reading; AR, whether by miscounting minims or by lexical substitution, have instead the present participle of *gremen*, MED "to revile, insult; injure, trouble, disturb". *verey fervent* is evidently intended to convey the force of *stridor*; H substitutes *were* for *verey*, and AR weakly read *veramente*, either not understanding the phrase or seeking to reduce the number of syllables in the line.

573–80, stanza 73   The b-rhymes, *good* 576 — *rehearse* 580, do not rhyme. 576 contains four strongly stressed syllables instead of the expected three; 580 contains only four syllables and would require a stress pattern //x/.

H reduces the number of stresses in 576 to three by reading *part* for *put* (see 573–80 + Latin note) and *for* for *from the*; but this seems an unsatisfactory resolution.

In 580 AR increase the line-length by adding *nowe heare*, producing a three-stress line but no rhyme. BH add *by the rode*, giving rhyme, but also a line more readily read as a four-stress than a three-stress line.

It is impossible to determine the "original" form of the lines from the evidence available, but it is probable that 576 has been refashioned to accord more closely with the wording of the Latin text at 570 +. If so, *from the good* may have been substituted for an earlier monosyllable, and *by the rode* BH for a disyllabic form. Hm seems to have left 570 incomplete because it was unsatisfactory. AR complete it in a way which, if based on an exemplar form, might suggest that 576 could once have read "to put the evyll in fere" — "to put the evil-doers together"; but that is mere conjecture.

581–8, stanza 74   *penne* 582 H is to be preferred for perfect rhyme to *panne* HmARB.

No manuscript has *grenne* for *grynne*, required for rhyme at 583. *grynne* was evidently the exemplar form.

No manuscript has *breme*, "fierce", for *brenne*, required for rhyme at 588. *brenne* appears to be an exemplar error resulting from miscounted minims and from the nature of the context. H's *to* for *and* HmR suggests that *brenne* is an infinitive of purpose; but HmR indicate that it is an infinitive dependent upon *shal* 587 — "they shall all be bathed in bitter torment and [shall] burn." B reads *brune*, moving even further from possible rhyme.

A erroneously and inexplicably omits 585–8; combined with its later omission, the effect is to produce an eight-line 'stanza' of 581–4 + 589–92 rhyming aaabcccd.

581   *men* is the rhyme-word only in Hm; the other manuscripts have readings which suggest that a further word, *henne*, "hence", followed, although no manuscript contains this form. *henne* is the form required by rhyme. The evidence of ARB suggests that the exemplar lacked a minim which lead to readings with three-minim forms, *-ine* and *me*. *hence* H is semantically and syntactically correct but does not rhyme. Hm seems to have emended the exemplar line. ARBH also omit *mee* to compensate for their additional syllable.

585   *chimneye* presumably corresponds to *caminum ignis* 580 + Latin. Its sense is that of MED *chimene*, 3(a) "a contrivance for heating, baking, parching, drying; brazier, stove, oven, kiln, furnace."

593–6   A erroneously omits these lines. There is no obvious reason for the omission, although it may in some way be connected with A's omission of 585–8; see 581–8, stanza 74 note.

593   The line is improved metrically by the omission of a syllable, and R's omission of *all* may be preferred. But an equally acceptable line would result from the omission of *men*.

597–604, stanza 76   No manuscript has *stere* for *styrre* 601, or *lere* for *lure* 603; both are required for perfect rhyme. The forms here evidently reflect the exemplar-readings. *stere* is an acceptable variant of *stir*, OED 4 "Fig. to disturb, trouble, molest" and 8 "to excite to feeling, emotion or passion". MED cites only these lines to exemplify the construction *losen lire* "? let loose one's damnation, earn damnation", but "lose one's allure", taking *lure* as MED *lure* (1), 1(b) "something that entices, an attraction, enticement", seems current and appropriate. Compare the sense 1(a) of *lure*(1), "a bait for recalling hawks", figuratively exended to heaven — "(like a hawk) she has lost her lure (the bait of heaven)"; and see also Wakefield 30/355–8:

> All harlottys and horres,
> And bawdys that procures,

To bryng thaym to lures.
Welcom to my [the devil Tutivillus] see!
lere is not, however, a recorded variant of *lure*.

606 *Sathan* Jesus identifies Primus Demon by name. See also 8/295 and note.

609-18 The question of divine grace for the damned and the efficacy of saintly intercession on their behalf was much debated in the early Church. Aquinas, *Summa Theologiae*, provides useful summaries; e.g. Supp.99 art.2. In 609-12, 618 Jesus stresses that he is constrained — even perhaps against his merciful instinct (*therefore must I for anything* 611) — to act justly rather than mercifully. *Misericordia sapientiae ordine regulatur* (Aquinas). The issue of intercession is discussed by Augustine, *De Civitate Dei* 21/18 and 24 (PL 41/732 and 738) and also Aquinas, *Summa Theologiae* Supp.99 art.3.

Intercession is an important part of Roman Catholic theology; Invocation of Saints is prohibited under article 22 of the Thirty Nine Articles of Faith of the Church of England. The reference to intercession by the Virgin Mary 613 would be particularly appropriate to Roman Catholic belief. In Doomsday poems 28a and 28b of Carleton Brown's *English Lyrics of the Thirteenth Century*, 25-8, the Virgin Mary is seen as present at the judgment in person.

613-*Finis* The end of the play is lost in A.

613-20, stanza 78 The b-rhymes, *late* 616 — *grace* 620, do not rhyme. The readings seem to have been the exemplar forms, but rhyme would result from reading *fate* for *grace; grace* could have been erroneously substituted by the mechanical employment of the common collocation *gaynes grace*.

621-44 Based on Matthew 25/41-6, the completion of the "acts of mercy" passage; see 453-92 note. The sequence at 621-8 is semantically and syntactically confused. *you would not mee clothe* 622 corresponds only to *naked* 622, leaving *hungrye and thyrstie both* 621 without remedy. 626 may correspond to *hungrye*, but the connexion is not explicit. *when I was* 621 must be again understood after *also* 623; *sycke* 623 is remedied in 624, and *in greate woe* 623 therefore suggests the remedy of 625, implying that the *woe* is that of captivity. The infinitives *vysytt* 624 and *come* 625 are therefore parallel and depend upon *would* 624. The use of the *to*-infinitive at 626 signals a change in construction depending upon *in wyll were yee* 628. This interpretation requires a repunctuation of the text as here printed, removing the semi-colon from 624 and replacing the comma at 625 by semi-colon or full-stop.

626 H omits the syntactically redundant *to*, to the detriment of metre.

some RBH is to be formally preferred to the scribally erroneous *somee* Hm, where *e* has been erroneously repeated.

628 + SH In Matthew, the damned reply collectively, but here, as for the redeemed, the pope and emperor are spokesmen for the group.

637-44 The explicit reference to the negligence of the rich 639 towards the poor 642 has no counterpart in Matthew but follows logically from the social emphasis of the opening speeches by the resurrected dead and suggests the 'Dives and Lazarus' theme. Underlying the idea may also be 1 John 3/16-17, where the sacrifice of Christ for Man is set up as a model and the indifference of rich to poor is expressly seen as a denial of divine love: *Qui habuerit substantiam huius mundi, et videri fratrem suum necessitatem habere et clauserit viscera sua ab eo, quomodo caritas Dei manet in eo?* (AV "But whoso hath this world's good, and seeth his brother have need, and shutteth up his bowels of compassion from him, how dwelleth the love of God in him?").

639 OED last records *ryne*, 1 trans. "to touch, to affect", in 1674; B seems not to have understood the word and substitutes a phrase which destroys rhyme and metre. The object must be understood as *the leaste of myne* 637. H supplies a pronoun-object, *them*, which may have a formal counterpart in *then* B, perhaps indicating that the word was in the exemplar; but it is not syntactically necessary and is not in HmR.

642 *lyne* HmR seems to have the sense of MED *line* (1), 9(c) "offspring, posterity". *hyne* H is also possible; *lyve* B is an error probably resulting from confusion of *n* and *u* in an exemplar *lyue*. B destroys rhyme and sense, but its reading seems to confirm initial *l* against H's *h*.

659–60 The lines reinforce the finality and eternity of the judgment, a further issue debated by the early Church. See Aquinas, *Summa Theologiae* Supp.99 art.2 and art.3.

672–4 The sack and pouch of the devil may be distinguished as separate items whose contents in some way correspond to the merchant's sins. In Wakefield 30/141–51 the second devil has a bag of sins and sinners and at 224 Tutivillus has a bag of legal briefs. See also *Jacob's Well* ed. A. Brandeis, EETS, ES 115 (1900), cap.17 'De Accidia': "An holy man ... sey3 a feend beryng a gret sacchell full of thyng .... Þe feend seyde: "I bere in my sacche sylablys & woordys, ouerskyppyd and synkopyd, & verse & psalmys þe whiche þese clerkys han stolyn in þe qweere, & haue fayled in here seruyse.' fforsothe, þanne I trowe þe feend hath a gret sacche full of 30ure ydell woordys, þat 3e iangelyn in cherche in slowthe."

676 + SD–*Finis* Since the devils have removed the damned, the four evangelists speak in front of the tableau of Christ in glory; possibly they have been present among those in glory throughout the judgment — see 362 note. They speak in the order in which their gospels occur in the New Testament. Their speeches constitute a coda to the play outside the 'Creation-Doomsday' timescale, and thus correspond structurally to the start of God's opening speech in the cycle, 1/1–35. The plan formed in God's mind and announced at the start of the cycle is now completed, documented in the scriptures and revealed to the mind of Man. The speeches close the frame of the cycle while reinforcing the sense of logical demonstration characteristic of the whole.

678–80 Perhaps indicative of the dependence of the play upon Matthew's account of the judgment, Matthew 25.

683 *lykinge* HmRB seems to have the sense of MED 3(b), "sensual desire, appetite; esp. sexual desire, lust". H, perhaps conscious of more favourable aspects of the word's meaning, substitutes *lyvinge*, in the sense of "way of life"; compare *lyvinge* 687.

685–92 Alone among the evangelists, Mark does not claim to have warned mankind personally of the consequences of their deeds. Indeed, Mark's gospel received very little critical attention from patristic and medieval commentators because of the brevity of the work and its lack of circumstantial detail, and it similarly contributes less than the other gospels to the content of the Chester cycle.

689–90 *that* 690 parallels *so that* 689 — "so that they cannot excuse themselves, so that they are indeed worthy to suffer ..."

694 Either *workes* HmRB or *words* H is possible, but 680 and 705 indicate that Matthew and John were concerned to record Jesus' words.

695–6 Luke's gospel is the most scholarly of the gospels in its style, construction and documentation, hence perhaps the emphasis on *cunnynge* 695. It is also a gospel for the Gentiles, by a writer who was himself possibly a Gentile (Colossians 4/14) and who chronicled the acts of the apostles also — hence perhaps the appropriate claim that his purpose was to address *all men* 696.

700 Compare 645. Hm gives sense — "This having been done [i.e. that they did amiss against my word, 699], it goes right"; but *dome* RBH for *donne* Hm is equally acceptable — "This judgment goes right." The variation in reading seems to depend upon the counting of minims.

701–8, stanza 89   No manuscript has the form *triste* for *truste* 703, required for perfect rhyme.

705–6 The reference may be to Apocalypse, a major biblical source of information about the judgment; but the influence of John's gospel upon the underlying ideas of the cycle, particularly upon its trinitarian theology and its images of light and life, may also be intended.

APPENDIX IA

Dramatis Personae Noe, Deus

NOTE *tota familia sua* are present also, 47 + SD.

Locations
in nave 15 + SD, archam 47 + SD.

Properties
raven 2,9, corvum 8 + SD
dove 11, 20, columbam 8 + SD, 15 + SD
aliam columbam ferens olivam in ore 15 + SD
ex malo per funem 15 + SD
these beastes 46, animalia et volucres 47 + SD.

Costumes
None specified.

Sources The forty-seven lines of H correspond to Genesis 8/6-20.

1 *40 dayes* The time corresponds to the reference in Genesis 8/6, although it is not there clear from which point the forty days is calculated. Here it seems to define the *little space* of 3/260 + SD — see note.

There is nothing here to suggest, as does Genesis 8/4-5, that the Ark comes to rest on the mountains of Ararat before the birds are despatched.

2–8 Noah's purpose in sending the raven is that given in Genesis 8/8 when he sends out the dove: *Ut videret si iam cessassent aquae super faciem terrae* (AV "To see if the waters were abated from off the face of the ground"). Genesis 8/5 indicates that the tops of the mountains were visible.

There is no reason given in Genesis, as here, for the selection of the raven. In Wakefield 3/479-86 Noah's Wife chooses the raven. In *Ludus Coventriae* 2/244 Noah sends out a crow.

8 + SD–12 Genesis 8/8-9 indicates that Noah sent out the dove on three occasions — first with the raven; second, seven days later, when it returned with the olive; third, a further seven days later when it failed to return. Here it is the second mission which is dramatised, as in all the cycles. Although 8 + SD suggests that Noah sends out the dove as soon as he has sent the raven, 9–10 suggest that some time has elapsed since the raven left.

Only York 9/226 shares Chester's explanation of the raven's failure to return. Wakefield 3/501-4, *Ludus Coventriae* 2/246 and Cornish *Ordinalia* p.31 follow a common explanation in the commentaries, that the raven has settled on the carcasses floating in the water.

9–15, stanza 2   The stanza contains seven lines instead of the expected eight; it lacks an a-rhyme line in the second quatrain, but the manuscript gives no indication of the nature of the omission.

13–5   Compare Wakefield 3/505–6:
> The dowfe is more gentill her trust I vntew
> like vnto the turtill for she is ay trew

The fidelity of the dove in her love was commonplace and served the purpose of Christian example. Compare 'Natura Turturis' in *A Bestiary* (*An Old English Miscellany*, ed. R Morris (EETS os 49) 1872):
> In boke is ðe turtres lif
> writen o rime, wu lagelike
> ge holdeð luue al hire lif time;
> gef ge ones make haueð,
> fro him ne wile ge siðen
> (694–8)

interpreted as the image of the true Christian's love for Christ; see also Tertullian, *Liber de Baptismo* cap. 8 (PL 1/1316–7) and *Glossa Ordinaria*, 'Lib. Gen.' 8/8 (PL 113/109). The explanation is without biblical counterpart.

15 + SD   The birds were evidently models sent and returned by a pulley system.

17   *today* Genesis 8/11 states that the dove returned to Noah *ad vesperam* (AV "in the evening"), presumably on the day on which it was despatched.

21–3   The interpretation of the olive branch is without biblical counterpart; in Genesis 8/11 Noah merely concludes that the waters had receded from the earth. But the interpretation is standard; see Tertullian, *Liber de Baptismo* cap. 8 (PL 1/1317) and S. Maximus Taurinensis, *Sermo* 114 (PL 57/722).

24–30   Noah's motive here is inferred from the biblical text; compare Genesis 8/13: *Et aperiens Noe tectum arcae, aspexit, viditque quod exsiccata esset superficies terrae* (AV "And Noah removed the covering of the ark, and looked and, behold, the face of the ground was dry"). Compare Comestor, *Historia Scholastica*, 'Liber Genesis' 34 (PL 198/1085): *Sed egrediendi exspectabat Domini praeceptum; Genesis and Exodus* 618: "Gede he nogt ut, til god him bad".

32–9, stanza 5   The b-rhymes, *thee* 35 — *soe* 39, do not rhyme. Probably *be soe* 39 represents a reversal of the required order *soe be*.

36   Compare Genesis 8/17: *Tam in volatilibus quam in bestiis* (AV "Both of fowl and of cattle").

46   *that bene hise* i.e. that are "clean" beasts, fit for sacrifice; compare Genesis 8/20: *De cunctis pecoribus et volucribus mundis* (AV "Of every clean beast, and of every clean fowl").

47 + SD   The manner of offering here envisaged seems to be some formal action, suggested by *offeret* (which could correspond to 3/261–8), followed by the slaying of the animals (*mactabit*). Genesis 8/20 is more specific, indicating that the offerings were burned on an altar — the first reference to an altar and to burnt offerings in the

Bible. The burning of the animals has specific point in Genesis because God's relenting is motivated by the smell of the sacrifice, Genesis 8/21.

animalia sua et volucres may correspond to *beastes fowles* 3/267.

APPENDIX IB

Dramatis Personae Deus, Princeps Sinagogae, Moyses, Expositor, Balaack Rex, Miles, Balaam, Asina, Angelus, Esayas, Ezechiell, Jheremia, Jonas, David, Joell, Micheas.

Locations
in loco 24 + SD
montem 32 + SD, the hyll 46, descendet de monte 88 + SD, ex altera parte montis 88 + SD — *identified as* the mownt of Synai 74; on this hill 210, in montem 216 + SD — *the latter having aspects specified as* ad australem partem 216 + SD, ad borealem partem 240 + SD, ad occidentale partem 264 + SD
in supremo loco 136 + SD H.

NOTE It is assumed that the features listed in 265–8 are not realised visually.

Properties
cum gladio extracto 160 + SD, evaginatum gladium 184 + SD.

NOTE 1. It is not clear if Moses is envisaged as actually carrying the tables of stone 77.
2. Some form of "horse" is demanded by *equitando* 88 + SD, *equitabunt* 152 + SD.

Costume
God — with so great lighte 26.
Moses — wondrous bright 42, great lighte 43; horned 45.

Sources
See 5/*Sources* note. The individual prophecies uttered by the prophets are identified in the notes below.

Play-heading The heading, unlike that for HmARB, refers to the Balaam-Balak episode but makes no mention of the prophet sequence, 296 + SH–432.

The prophet-sequence was a liturgical drama which developed from a sixth-century pseudo-Augustinian sermon, 'Sermo Beati Augustini Episcopi de Natale Domini'; for text of caps.11–8, see Karl Young, *The Drama of the Medieval Church* (Oxford, 1933), II, pp.125–32. For a study of liturgical material and a critical text of Play 5, see J. F. Rourke, *An Edition of Play V, "Balaam and*

APPENDIX IB 381

Balack", *in the Chester Cycle of Mystery Plays*, unpublished Liverpool University MA thesis, 1967. Robert A. Brawer, 'The Form and Function of the Prophetic Procession in the Middle English Cycle Play', *Annuale Medievale*, XIII (1972), 88–123, examines the developing function of the episode. Dramatic analogues cited here will be limited to the sermon, to the AN *Adam*, and to episodes in the English cycles — Wakefield 7 (an incomplete prophet play), *Ludus Coventriae* 7 (a 'tree of Jesse' play alternating prophets with kings), York 12 (Annunciation and Visit to Elizabeth, where a *Prologue* recites the prophecies), and Coventry Shearmen (where Isaiah acts as prologue) and Weavers (where two *profetae* recite prophecies).

NOTE   The notes below relate only to material peculiar to the H-version of play 5. The reader should consult the notes to play 5 for passages and material common to HmARB and H.

1–24   Compare 5/1–24 and notes. In the following list of variants, the H reading appears first:

2 the] my

5 honour] have   *have* HmARB reflects *habebis* Exodus 20/3, Deuteronomy 5/7.

6 mawmentrye] false godes   OED last records *maumetry* in the sense of "idols collectively" in 1567; HmARB may not have recognised the word.

7 myn] name   Compare *non assumes nomen* Exodus 20/7, *non usurpabis nomen* Deuteronomy 5/11 (AV "thou shalt not take the name..."). It is tempting to regard the two forms as reflecting *nym*, "take", a form perhaps unfamiliar to the scribes since OED last records it in the sense of "to take" in 1566. H yields sense only by reversing the first and last letters while HmARB substitute *name*, a word of similar form. *nam* A may be an error for *name* or *nim*.

10 also by] yt eke   See 5/9–11 note.

15 abyde] lenge

17 wyves] wyefe   *wyefe* HmARB corresponds to *uxorem* (AV "wife") Exodus 20/17, Deuteronomy 5/21.

17 covettes] desyre   Compare: *Non concupisces domum proximi tui; nec desiderabis uxorem eius*, Exodus 20/17 (AV "Thou shalt not covet thy neighbour's house, thou shalt not covet thy neighbour's wife"); and Deuteronomy 5/21 *Non concupisces uxorem proximi tui* (AV "Neither shalt thou desire thy neighbour's wife"). Although the variants may reflect the variations between *desiderabis* and *concupisces*, the AV forms indicate that *desire* and *covet* could be used interchangeably to render *concupisces*.

18 good] goodes   See 5/18 note.

20 anythinge] nothinge

22 will] love

23 doe] keepe.

24+SD *princeps sinagogae* The "principal of the synagogue" here acts as spokesman for the people, voicing the sentiments which they express collectively in Exodus 20/18–9. The people are prohibited from ascending Sinai by God's injunction in Exodus 19/12, and in Exodus 19/24 the priests are expressly included in the prohibition: *Sacerdotes autem et populus ne transeant terminos, nec ascendant ad Dominum, ne forte interficiat illos* (AV "But let not the priests and the people break through to come up unto the Lord, lest he break forth upon them").

princeps may here be used in an indefinite rather than definite sense — "a principal". The expression "high priest", indicating the senior priest of the Jews, occurs only once in the Old Testament (Numbers 35/25, 28) and in the account of the giving of the Law in Exodus the priests are treated collectively. But alternatively the figure may represent Moses' brother, Aaron. In Exodus 28/1 God reserves the priesthood to Aaron and his sons. Later, in the second giving of the Law, Aaron is distinguished from the rest of the people (Exodus 34/30, *Aaron et filii Israel* — AV "Aaron and all the children of Israel") and from the priests (Exodus 34/31, *Tam Aaron quam principes synagogue* — AV "Aaron and all the rulers of the congregation") in his response. He had previously acted as Moses' spokesman to the people, Exodus 4/14–6. Alternatively, the figure may simply represent the Jews in the manner of *Synagoga* in the Tegernsee *Antichrist* or of *quidam de synagoga* who interrogates Isaiah in AN *Adam*. In the latter play, Aaron is included among the prophets.

25–32, stanza 4   The b-rhymes, *looke* 28 — *wee* 32, do not rhyme. As Deimling notes, rhyme would result from reading *see* for *looke* 28; the error perhaps arose through scribal substitution of a near-synonym.

25–32   *good lord* 25 refers to God; the address changes to Moses at 30.

Deimling (p. xix) considers that the equivalent stanza in HmARB "reminds one pretty much of Deuteronomy ix. 9 and 18" but that "the *mele* (30) in H speaks for this manuscript, and H's stanza might have been meant to relate the events on Sinai according to Exodus xix. 18, etc." Bevington, *Medieval Drama*, compares 30–1 with Exodus 20/19. Compare Exodus 20/18–9: *Et perterriti ac pavore concussi, steterunt procul, dicentes Moysi: Loquere tu nobis et audiemus: non loquatur nobis Dominus ne forte moriamur* (AV "And when the people saw it, they removed and stood afar off. And they said unto Moses, Speak thou with us, and we will hear: but let not God speak with us, lest we die"). There is no equivalent to *with us thou mele* 30 in Deuteronomy.

With 25–8, compare Deuteronomy 5/24: *Ecce ostendit nobis Dominus Deus noster maiestatem et magnitudinem suam* (AV "Behold, the Lord our God hath shewed us his glory and his greatness").

The imminent death of the people, 27–8 and 31–2, is said to be in fear at the wondrous and terrible sights; but the accounts in both Exodus and Deuteronomy indicate that death befalls any mere mortal who hears the voice of God.

33–40   Compare Exodus 20/20: *Et ait Moyses ad populum: Nolite timere; ut enim probaret vos venit Deus, et ut terror illius esset in vobis, et non peccaretis* (AV "And Moses said unto the people: Fear not: for God is come to prove you, and that his fear may be before your faces, that ye sin not").

this 34 refers to *this sighte* 27.

APPENDIX IB

41–8 The transfiguration of Moses occurs when he receives the second set of tables; compare Exodus 34/29–30: *Cumque descenderet Moyses de monte Sinai, tenebat duas tabulas testimonii; et ignorabat quod cornuta esset facies sua ex consortio sermonis Domini. Videntes autem Aaron et filii Israel cornutam Moysi faciem, timuerunt prope accedere* (AV "And it came to pass, when Moses came down from mount Sinai with the two tables of testimony in Moses' hand, when he came down from the mount, Moses wist not that the skin of his face shone while he talked with him. And when Aaron and all the children of Israel saw Moses, behold, the skin of his face shone, and they were afraid to come nigh him").

45 *horned* The detail is based on a common misunderstanding of *cornuta*, Exodus 34/29, 30.

48 *he* Bevington considers this pronoun to refer to God — compare 29. But it seems an unnecessary postulation since *hym* 44, *he* 45, 46, 47 refer to Moses and such reference gives good sense. The attributes of the Deity have become transferred also to Moses.

49–64 Compare 5/81–95 where it rightly follows the second giving of the Law, Exodus 35/1–9. In the following list of variants, the H reading appears first:
  51 doe everye deale] keepe well H is slightly closer to Exodus 35/1: *Quae iussit Dominus fieri* (AV "The words which the Lord hath commanded, that ye should do them").
  52 as] this
  53 boldelye] bodely See 5/85–95 note.
  50 H is different in wording from 5/82 HmARB. For other differences, see below.

53–7 In Exodus 35, Moses utters two separate injunctions — to observe the sabbath and to make offerings for the tabernacle. Here the two injunctions are presented continuously without break, suggesting that the presentation of offerings is part of the observance of the sabbath. The obscuring of this distinction may underlie the confusion in 5/90–2; see 5/90–2 note. H seems to seek to resolve the problem by strengthening the reference of *this* 57 by the addition of *deede*; but it is not clear whether the "deed" is the observance of the sabbath or the offering. Exodus 35/2 contains a sentence which makes the reference clear: *Qui fecerit opus in eo occidetur* (AV "Whosoever doeth work therein shall be put to death").

It may be noted that *deede* 57 has a counterpart in *opus*, and that by reading *any* for *not this* 57 the final sentence of Exodus 35/2 would be rendered adequately. Such a possibility does not exist for HmARB.

57–64, stanza 8   See 5/89–95, stanza 12 note.

58 The line, corresponding to Exodus 35/3, is effectively a prohibition of cooking on the sabbath; see Exodus 16/23. The point of the line seems to have become obscured in HmARB.

61–2 Brass is omitted from the metals offered, 61; *other moe* 62 suggests an awareness of the additional items in Exodus 35/7–9 which are excluded from the list here. *both too* 5/93 HmARB suggests no similar awareness.

65–88 The lines correspond broadly to 5/41–64. The most significant differences are:

65–8, where the specific reference in HmARB to the Decalogue gives place to the more ambiguous *this comaundment*;

72, 81, where the references to the dramatisation of a further episode, the second giving of the Law, in HmARB have no counterpart here since the second episode is not dramatised but has been combined with the first in a composite account. The Expositor here therefore merely adds some further details to the material already presented as *most frutefull*.

89–296 The Balaam-Balak episode corresponds largely to 5/96–327. There are five major differences:

5/124–63, 208–15, 272–9 have no counterpart in H.
241–64, 281–8 in H have no counterpart in play 5.

H therefore lacks the references to pagan deities at 5/124–63 and 208–15 which perhaps detract from the potential dignity and obedience of Balaam and Balak. The pledges of 5/272–9, as distinct from the offer of wealth in 5/268–9, are accommodated in H by 213–4, which differ in wording from 5/268–9. 241–64 H corresponds to Numbers 23/11–24; the lines enhance Balaam's authority over Balak by his stern rebuke and allow him to deliver a messianic prophecy to Balak. 281–4 corresponds to Numbers 23/10–11, to which an unbiblical invitation has been added at 285–8.

A number of minor differences are also noted below.

110 *myselfe* See 5/118–9 note. *my folke* 117 HmARB is to be preferred as corresponding to the sense of the biblical text.

126 *riches* See 5/172–3 note. *landes* HmARB may be preferred for meaning.

135 The line contains three strongly stressed syllables instead of the expected four. The additional syllable supplied by *that* 5/182 is to be preferred in producing a metrically regular line.

140 The line is metrically rough. The omission of the semantically redundant *not* 5/187 is to be preferred.

145 *the folke Balack* 5/192 personalises the issue, but the line is without biblical counterpart and either reading is possible.

189 *thry* is to be preferred to *why* (2) 5/244 as reflecting Numbers 22/32: *Cur, inquit, tertio verberas asinam tuam?* (AV "Wherefore hast thou smitten thine ass these three times"). The HmARB reading seems to derive from a repetition of *why* (1).

199 *tho* The construction here is parallel to 200 — *bade thee tho — saide to thee before*. The reference of *tho* is not immediately clear, since no reference to the earlier dialogue of God and Balaam occurs here to give point to "then"; but the intention is clearly to recall 137–52. *doe* 5/254 is also acceptable, repeating *doe* 5/253. Neither version closely corresponds to the phraseology of Numbers 22/35.

207 "In order to redeem all men, and my own kinsmen." It may be that the distinction intended here is between Gentile and Jew — "To redeem all men, including my kin (the Gentiles)"; but the force of *and* is not clear. *the ende of* 5/262 gives rough metre but attempts to resolve the difficulty.

APPENDIX IB

208   *sure* H is supported in this reading by B at 5/263; but HmAR read *syr*.

230   "I may not have any other reprieve." The line seems to take up the angel's threat at 198–200; it may therefore be an interpretation of Numbers 23/10: *Moriatur anima mea morte iustorum* (AV "Let me die the death of the righteous"), meaning, in effect, "I will not die such a death if I curse the Israelites." But at 5/293 the reading is *reproffe* and the subject is changed from Balaam to the Israelites by reading *shall they none wave* for *may I not have*.

241–64   The lines, without counterpart in play 5, correspond to Numbers 23/18–27 and represent the second "curse" by Balaam. Numbers 23/21–2 have no counterpart in H.

245–8   Compare Numbers 23/23: *Non est augurium in Iacob, nec divinatio in Israel* (AV "Surely there is no enchantment against [*or* in] Jacob, neither is there any divination against Israel"). In Numbers, this comment is quite separate from the earlier comment of 23/20: *Ad benedicendum adductus sum, benedictionem prohibere non valeo* (AV "Behold I have received commandment to bless ... and I cannot reverse it"). One would therefore expect 245–6 to be a self-contained statement: "He sent me to bless his people; therefore I say what I am instructed"; and 247–8 similarly to be an independent comment: "Truly, in this land no idolatry is employed." This distinction is lost by the inclusion of *that* 247, which makes 247–8 a noun clause dependent upon *saie* 246 and indicative of what God has ordered Balaam to say. The omission of *that* would result in closer correspondence to the biblicl text.

249–56   The lines are a Messianic interpretation of Numbers 23/24: *Ecce populus et leaena consurget, et quasi leo erigetur; non accusabit donec devoret praedam et occisorum sanguinem bibat* (AV "Behold, the people shall rise up as a great lion, and lift up himself as a young lion: he shall not lie down until he eat of the prey, and drink the blood of the slain"). The Messianic interpretation seems suggested by a passage in the following "curse", Numbers 24/4–9, which is not dramatised at the appropriate place in H; the passage deals with the coming of God's *king* and also uses the image of the lion.

257–64, stanza 33   *beheight* 259 does not rhyme. If the rhyme was not originally imperfect, some other word (e.g. *betaught*) must be substituted.

265–72, stanza 34   *ryvere* 5/307 HmAB is to be preferred for rhyme to *rivers* 5/307 R, 268 H.
   272 contains four strongly stressed syllables instead of the expected three; see 5/311 note.

279   *twye* i.e. 217–24, 245. It is to be preferred to *thrye* 5/318, which is inaccurate in either version. See 5/316 note.

281–8   Balak does not lament in Numbers, not does Balaam prophesy at this point in response to a further invitation from Balak. Rather, he addresses Balak to inform him of what will happen.

288 + Latin   See 5/319 + SD note.

296 + SH–**340**   The sequence of prophets follows directly upon Balaam's prophecy and has no counterpart in play 5; it occupies the space between 5/327 and 5/328, and constitutes a "play-within-a-play", breaking the chronologically ordered sequence of events in the historical action. H has no counterpart to the final scenes of play 5, the plans to seduce Israel, their execution and consequences, 5/336–455.

The seven prophets appear in the order of the events which they prophesy, with the exception of Micah; Isaiah and Ezechiell (Incarnation and Virgin Birth), Jeremiah (Passion), Jonah (Harrowing of Hell and Resurrection), David (Ascension and Judgment), Joel (Pentecost), Micah (Incarnation). The Expositor's list of prophets, 401–32, characterises the series Isaiah-Joel but omits Balaam and Micah, who thus act as a sort of frame. Balaam's prophecy is not interpreted by the Expositor when it is uttered, but a potential exposition seems implied in 445–8. Micah's prophecy is expounded and is held to indicate both the specific place where Christ was born in the past and also the continuing existence of Christ to the present time.

Various prophets appear in the different dramatic analogues. The pseudo-Augustinian sermon has Isaiah, Jeremiah, Daniel, Moses, David, Habbakuk; AN *Adam* Abraham, Moses, Aaron, David, Balaam, Daniel, Habbabuk, Jeremiah, Isaiah, Nebuchadnezzar; Wakefield 7 David, the Sibyl, Daniel; *Ludus Coventriae* 7 (prophets only) Isaiah, Jeremiah, Ezechiel, Micah, Daniel, Jonah, Obadiah, Habbakuk, Joel, Haggai, with David included among the kings. The Prologue in York 12 cites Amos, the promise to Abraham, Isaiah, Joel, Jacob, Coventry Shearmen present Isaiah, while the two *profetae* at the start of the Weaver's pageant cite Balaam, Isaiah, Malachi, Jeremiah. Even where the same prophets occur, however, different texts are often cited.

296 + SH–304 This is the only instance in which a supporting Vulgate text is not cited. It would be Isaiah 7/14–5: *Ecce, virgo concipiet et pariet filium, et vocabitur nomen eius Emmannel; butyrum et mel comedet, ut sciat reprobare malum et eligere bonum* (AV "Behold, a virgin shall conceive, and bear a son, and shall call his name Immanuel. Butter and honey shall he eat, that he may know to refuse the evil, and choose the good"). The same prophecy is cited in the pseudo-Augustinian sermon, *Ludus Coventriae* 7/1–8, York 12/60 + Latin–68, Coventry Shearmen 20–36, and in Coventry Weavers 40–5.

The speaker is not identified for the audience in the spoken text.

309–10 The prophecy is recalled in Matthew 1/22–3, where the name is similarly interpreted: *Nobiscum Deus* (AV "God with us").

312 + Latin The text is not an exact quotation, but seems to echo Ezechiel 44/1–2: *Et convertit me ad viam portae sanctuarii exterioris quae respiciebat ad orientem, et erat clausa; et dixit Dominus ad me: Porta haec clausa erit, non aperietur, et vir non transibit per eam quoniam Dominus Deus Israel ingressus est per eam, eritque clausa* (AV "Then he brought me back the way of the gate of the outward sanctuary, which looketh toward the east; and it was shut. Then said the Lord unto me: This gate shall be shut; it shall not be opened, and no man shall enter in by it; because the Lord, the God of Israel, hath entered in by it, therefore it shall be shut"). The quotation here is similar to that in *Stanzaic Life* 744 + Latin: *Item dicitur in Ezechiel: vidi portam in domo domini clausam, et dixit angelo: Porta hec non aperietur, set clausa erit...* In particular, one may note the reference to the angel, not present in Ezechiel where the informant is the Lord. Reference is made to the same prophecy in *Ludus Coventriae* 7/43–6.

capitulo 2 The reference is incorrect. It may result from the omission of the chapter number but the inclusion, instead, of the final verse-number.

APPENDIX IB 387

This is the only instance in the prophet sequence in which the Latin text precedes the SH.

321–8 A common interpretation, found in Jerome, *Commentariorum in Ezechielem*, 13/44 (PL 25/430) and in *Legenda Aurea* 'De Nativitate'. Compare particularly *Stanzaic Life*:

> That tokenet Marie ʒ nomo,
> ho was þat ʒate, leue ʒe me,
> ffor bi hit God con com ʒ go,
> As þe prophete in gost con se.
> (753–7)

313–20 Compare *Stanzaic Life*:

> Also þe prophete Eʒechiel
> seʒe a ʒate in heuen on hegh
> closet hit was swith wel,
> that ʒate þer come nomon negh.
> ther told an aungel þe prophet þo,
> that ʒate shuld not oponet be,
> ffor thurgh God wold come ʒ go
> non oʒer ther shuld haue entre.
> (745–52).

328 + SH The speaker is not identified for the audience in the spoken text.

328 + Latin Jeremiah 14/17: AV "Let mine eyes run down with tears night and day, and let them not cease: for the virgin daughter of my people is broken with a great breach, with a very grievous blow." The text differs from the Vulgate as follows:

   deducunt] deducant   lacrimas] lachrimam
   diem et noctem] noctem et diem
   contritione] quoniam contritione   et (3)] *om*
   etct] pessima vehementer

Jeremiah prophesies in general terms in *Ludus Coventriae* 7/31–8. Specific, but different, texts are cited by Jeremiah in the pseudo-Augustinian sermon, the AN *Adam* and the Coventry Weavers 68–74.

337–44 Compare Jerome, *Commentariorum in Jeremiam Prophetam*, 3/15 (PL 24/803): *Dupliciter hic locus intelligitur, vel quod ipse Deus plangat populum suum, et oculi ejus flere non cessent, vel certe imperet ut populorum oculi lacrymis fluant, nec leve esse quod plangendum sit; cum virgo filia populi sui contritione maxima et plaga intolerabili percussa sit. Alii ex persona prophetae haec dici arbitrantur*. The double sense of the suffering God and the God of vengeance is expressed in the passage.

343–4 depend upon *that* 341; at 344 *and that they shall* is to be understood: "The prophet clearly saw ... that they shall cause terror to that maiden, and that they shall receive vengeance for that deed."

344 + Latin Jonah 2/3–4: AV "I cried by reason of mine affliction unto the Lord, and he heard me; out of the belly of hell cried I, and thou heardest my voice. For thou hadst cast me..." The text differs from Vulgate text as follows:

   clamam] clamavi   exaudivit] exaudivit me

The quotation breaks off in mid-sentence — compare 349–50. The same allusion is made by Jonah in *Ludus Coventriae* 7/67–70.

351–2   "But after being in a whale's belly for three days I was saved." The construction contains an adverbial phrase of time, but the syntactical connexion is omitted, perhaps on the assumption that *three dayes* suggests the necessary connexion.

353–60   Compare Matthew 13/40. Although the text suggests the Resurrection, it also suggests the Harrowing of Hell, as in Jerome, *Commentariorum in Jonam Liber*, cap 2 (PL 25/1132–3).

360 + Latin   Psalms 18/7: AV 19/6 "His going forth is from the end of heaven, and his circuit unto the ends of it." The text differs from the Vulgate as follows:
   de] a   occisus] occursus   ad] usque ad
Although prophecies by David appear in the pseudo-Augustinian sermon, AN *Adam*, Wakefield 7 and *Ludus Coventriae* 7, none employs this text. The start of the text is cited in *Stanzaic Life* 9228 + Latin: *Psalmus: A summo celo egressio eius*, as part of the discussion of the Ascension; this derives in turn from *Legenda Aurea*. 'De Adscension Domini': *Coelum autem supersubstantiale est aequalitas divinae excellentiae, de quo Christus venit, et usque ad illud postmodum adscendit. De quo dicitur in psalmo: a summo coelo egressio ejus et occursus ejus usque ad summum ejus.*

361–4   See *Legenda Aurea*, quoted in 360 + Latin note, and *Stanzaic Life*:
        the furth heuen I spek of her
        is aboue all substancial thing,
        ther is the Trinite entere
        Fadur ɀ Son ɀ Gost woonyng;
        from wheche heuen, withouten were,
        com Crist ɀ thider went, bout lesing.
                    (9221–6)

365   No standard commentary seems to extend the interpretation of the text to the Judgment, but reference to the second coming following the Ascension is in standard texts such as the Apostles' Creed. The allusion to judgment is not taken up in the Expositor's comments at 417–24.

366–7   "No man may envisage such events, or think of what is prepared for mankind." *them* has no nominal reference but evidently refers to the two events of the Ascension and Judgment. *shape them of his sight* may then mean "Fashion these events in a form in which he can see them", i.e. form a mental picture of them. Bevington's interpretation: "No man may escape or hide from his sight, or from his judgment that is prepared for mankind", evidently takes *his* 366 to refer to God, *them* 366 as reflexive plural (taking up the collective force of *man*), *shape* perhaps as a form of *scape*, and *deeme* as *dome* sb.

376 + Latin   Joel 2/28: AV "I will pour out my spirit upon all flesh, and your sons ... shall prophesy." The text differs from that of the Vulgate in *de spiritu meo*] *spiritum meum*. An allusion to this prophecy also occurs in *Ludus Coventriae* 7/91–4.

385–92   Compare Jerome, *Commentariorum in Joelem Liber* cap.2 (PL 25/974): *Hunc locum beatus apostolus Petrus impletum tempore Dominicae passionis exposuit,* *quando descendit die Pentecostes Spiritus sanctus super credentes, et omnes loquebantur sicut Spiritus sanctus dabat eis.* As Jerome indicates, the text is cited by Peter in his sermon to the Jews at Pentecost, Acts 2/17–21.

392+Latin   Matthew 2/6. The text is quoted to Herod in 8/310+Latin — see note. There the text is assigned to both Matthew and Micah, but the form, as here, is that of Matthew, not of Micah 5/2. The text here differs from that in the Vulgate in *reget*] *regat*.

399–400   Without biblical counterpart.

403–8   "[This prophecy] informs you truly where Christ will be born; it also informs you that after his cessation from his acts of great mercy he should sit as king in heaven, where he is [now]." The construction is broken. The subject of *certefies* 403 is *this prophesie* 402; *that* 407 is here taken as indicating that the noun-clause 405–8 is dependent upon *certefies* 403, although it could also be taken as dependent upon *see* 402. *certefies* seems to have the sense of *certifien*, MED 4(a) "to inform (sb) as to fact; tell."

411   *six* See 296–440 note.

421   "With our nature into the bliss of heaven", a reference to the bodily nature of Christ's ascension.

429–32   "So, believe you, what we believe about the acts of God, who had pity on mankind when he set them free, is prophesied previously." *beleven* is used parenthetically. Bevington prefers to regard *beleven* as a form of *beleve*, "belief", and translates: "Thus that creed which we believe, concerning the deeds of God....." Although such a reading is unnecessary, the later *leven* could well have influenced the form of *beleve*.

433–40   The stanza is almost identical to 5/328–35. There it is in response to Balaam's prophecy. Here it has behind it the weight of the sequence of prophets, although it is possible, if not probable, that Balak is not aware of the "unhistorical" prophet sequence; the historical action of Balaam-Balak seems suspended while the audience is given confirmatory information.

438   *stryve* 5/333 is to be preferred for meaning to the scribally erroneous *shryve* H.

441–8   Compare 5/440–7. *these prophesies* 445 H seems a logical variation of *this prophecye* 5/444 in view of the variety of prophecies in H's prophet-sequence compared with the single prophecy by Balaam in play 5. But it is strictly only the Balaam prophecy which relates to the coming of the Magi; the others are not connected with that specific event.

With *presented* 447 H, "to give a present to" (*present* OED II, 3b), compare *honored* 5/446.

APPENDIX IC

Dramatis Personae Centurio, Cayphas, Longeus, Fourth Jew, Joseph ab Aramathea, Nichodemus, Pilatus.

NOTE Christ's body remains on the Cross — *a man* 35, *his body* 50, 55, 63.

Locations
super montem 100 + SD.

NOTE 1. *ad Pilatum* 76 + SD, *in sea* 78 suggest a separate location for Pilate.
2. The sepulchre may not be represented on stage, despite references at 73-4, 130.

Properties
spear 13, 17, 27
whott water 28, this water 32
a tree 51
your sea 78
an hundreth pownd of spicery, mirhe, aloes, and many mo 126–7.

Costume
None specified.

Sources See 16A/*Sources* note and 16A/359–*Finis* note.

1–44 The lines are substantially the same as 16A/360–407. Minor differences include:
13 but] *om*   17 take (1)] have   18 do] thou most doe
24 wher] whether   24 ill] evell   27 handes] hand
30 you some] both one   31 the] this   37 very Christ be] be Christ verey
40 done] *om*
Other more important differences are noted below.

1–8 Compare 16A/360–7 and note; compare particularly the different references to *the prophesy* 3 and 16A/365. H does not closely correspond to the centurion's words as quoted in the gospel accounts but emphasises the wrongful nature of the deed, 2 and 7–8 (see 45–100 note). The expression of fear, 5, suggests Matthew 27/54: *Timuerunt valde* (AV "They feared greatly"), the only account to give this detail. See also *Glossa Ordinaria*, 'Evang. Matth.' cap 27/54 (PL 114/176): *Hi in scandalo crucis confitentur Deum*.

13–4 See 16A/370 note. Here Longeus is expressly instructed to pierce Christ's heart.

15 *neithe* seems to be a scribal error for *neither*: compare *ne* 16A/374.

APPENDIX Ic 391

17-24, stanza 3   See 16A/376-84 and note.

25 *call thee here   here* 16A/384 is a verb, "praise"; by supplying *call*, H presents it as an adverb.

28 *whott* does not seem to represent *owt* 16A/388. It may perhaps be intended to represent an exclamatory "what", or, as here punctuated (though perhaps less probably), a form of "hot".

33-44, stanzas 5-6   Compare 16A/392-407, which is to be preferred for stanza-form and meaning. H stanza 6, a Chester quatrain, contains four lines instead of the expected eight. The possibility of omission by H is suggested by the following:

1. A comparison with 16A/392-407. 16A/397-400 have no counterpart in H, although 33-6 H corresponds to 16A/392-6 and 37-43 H to 16A/400-6. H thus lacks the plea for forgiveness by Longeus in 16A/398-9 which echoes Jesus' words at 16A/297-300. 16A/397 and 16A/400-1 are comparable in content and phrasing, suggesting that a scribe may have been led into omission by confusing *that sycke and blynd* 397 and 401.

2. The pattern of rhymes for stanzas 5-7. Treated as one unit, the rhyme-scheme would be aaabbabbcbbcbbc. H rhymes 36 with 40 by reading *affray* 36 where 16A/395 reads *steade*. And, in the only line of the section without close counterpart in 16A, H reads: "And save that on thee call" 44, for 16A/407: "From enemyes Lord I thee praye", thereby making the b-rhyme of stanza 6 conform with the b-rhymes of stanza 7. The changes at 36 and 44 could both either prompt or result from an omission.

3. The abrupt change in pronoun reference from *his* 38 to *thou* 40 in the same sentence. In contrast, 16A separates into different sentences the observer's comment on Christ, 16A/396-7, and the apostrophe to him, 16A/398-408, avoiding syntactical inconsistency. The change in pronoun here may be indicative of an omission.

45-100   The lines correspond broadly to 16A/408-39, but show some expansion in Joseph's speeches, 45-60, 69-84, 96-100, and in Pilate's speech 85-9, which, with the exceptions of lines 45 and 93, are without exact counterpart in 16A. The other parts are comparable with 16A, with the following minor differences:

61 leeve this] saye
62 that he] this
63 to] go   of] at
64 it shall] shall hee
67 wood] horne-wood
68 eke also] all
89 hark] *om*
90 ever] *om*   break] broke   bread] my head
91 is] ther is
93 then take him] take him then

H's additional material emphasises more strongly the belief of Joseph and Nicodemus in Jesus' divinity, 53-9, and intensifies the hostility of the two men to the evil of the Jews, 45-8, 67-8, 72, 82. Also, Pilate shows suspicion of their motives, in his warning to them, 95-6, and his suspicion prompts a further, and prophetic, affirmation of faith, 99-100.

45–76   Joseph seems at first intent only on adoring the crucified Christ, 57–8, and it is Nicodemus who proposes that they go to Pilate to request the right to bury Jesus' body. This does not correspond to 16A, nor does Nicodemus' initiative have support in standard accounts. Joseph's action makes the scene meditational and might have been held to be offensive to some observers in its adoration of a player-Christ.

58   *worshim* seems to be a scribal error for *worship*, influenced by the following *him*.

63–6   "I shall indeed help you to request his body from Pilate — and it shall [indeed] be buried — [and I shall help you] to take him down in reverential manner." The infinitives *to aske* 63 and *to take* 66 are both dependent upon *I shall help* 65; 64 is parenthetical.

67   *wood* H may perhaps give a smoother metre than *horne-wood* 16A/422, but the latter is colloquial and more forceful. *horn-wood* is recorded by OED only from 1500.

73–4   H limits itself to the information given by Mark 15/46: *In monumento quod erat excisum de petra* (AV "In a sepulchre which was hewn out of a rock"). Matthew 27/60 and Luke 23/53 also carry this information, but it is absent from 16A. 16A does, however, contain two other pieces of information found in Matthew — that it was Joseph's own tomb, 413, and that it was new, 442. The additional information that no body had been laid there before, Luke 23/53, John 19/41, is in neither version of the play.

76   The line affirms Jesus' physical death, 87–92, in order that the matter should be put beyond doubt. *his body* therefore limits the force of *he* 75, distinguishing bodily and spiritual death.

78   *sitt in your sea* suggests that Pilate is sitting on his throne at a location other than Calvary. The line has no counterpart in 16A, where Pilate was last seen bringing the superscription, 16A/216+SD-40, and may therefore be assumed to be present thereafter throughout the crucifixion. The line would then convey the force of *introivit* Mark 15/43 (AV "went in"). Pilate's presence at the Cross until Jesus' death is, however, suggested by 18/35–40.

Here the centurion is not merely called over, as at 16A/432, but happens to enter Pilate's hall to bring news of Jesus' death at the very moment when Pilate is seeking confirmation of the death from Joseph — hence the abrupt shift from *thee* 87 to *hark Centurio* 89. Thus, the comparable lines 16A/432 and 88 H have, in fact, different force.

85–92, stanza 12   The b-rhymes, *gone* 88 — *vayne* 92, do not rhyme. 85–9 is presented as a single unit (see TNs), and *vayne* reflects the b-rhyme of stanza 13, perhaps suggesting a replacement resulting from stanzaic misdivision. Although *bone* presents a tempting alternative at 92, it contradicts John 19/36: *Facta sunt enim haec ut Scriptura impleretur: Os non comminuetis ex eo* (AV "For these things were done that the scripture should be fulfilled, A bone of him shall not be broken").

91 contains three strongly stressed syllables instead of the expected four.

101–8   Joseph's adoring meditation has no counterpart in 16A/440–55. H stresses the contemporary force of the event, Christ's knowing sacrifice and the resulting reward from Almighty God for the faithful. 16A confines itself to the historical

APPENDIX Ic

action — the intention to bury Christ 442-3, 449-51; Jesus' previously manifested godhead, 444-7; and his future resurrection, 452-5.

105 *that* The syntactical function of the word is not clear. The change in pronoun from *us* 103, *our* 104, to *they* 105 leads one to expect a causative construction, heralded by *for*. *that* may reflect the unfulfilled expectation of a result-clause after 103-4, or a scribal error resulting from confusion with *that* 106.

109-32 Compare 16A/456-79. H differs from 16A as follows:
 109 sir] *om*   well I] I well
 115 very] wonders   may] might (cf maie AR)
 117 his] all his
 119 never] never before
 120 did cleev then as] clayve that
 121 sepulchrs] graves
 122 rysen] did ryse   ther by night] therefore by right
 123 he is] this was   God] Goddes Sonne
 124 such signes that] that so great sygnes
 125 brought here] here brought
 126 pownd] poundes
 128 will] with (cf will AR)
 132 when he in heaven] in heaven where hee   amen] *om*

115   *very* may be a scribal error occasioned by *very* 114; *wonders* 16A/462 is stylistically preferable in avoiding formal repetition.

Although *may* is supported by *maie* 16A/462 AR, past tense seems required by *yeeld* 116. See 16A/408-*Finis* note.

117-24, stanza 16   See 16A/464-71, stanza 60 note.

128   See 16A/468-9 note. There seems to be no support for the statement that the dead rose in the night.

132   *amen* is not part of the stanza-scheme. Compare also 20/192 and note.

APPENDIX ID

Dramatis Personae Jhesus, Maria Mag, Maria Jacobi, Maria Salom, Petrus.

Locations
None specified.

Properties
baculum crucis *Before* 1 SD.

Costume
Jesus — alba *Before* 1 SD.

Sources Appearance to Mary Magdalen — John 20/14-8 (cf Mark 16/9-10)
Appearance to the Women — Matthew 28/8-10
Appearance to Peter — Luke 24/34, 1 Corinthians 15/5.

Prefatory Note The appearance to Mary Magdalen is also dramatised in Wakefield 26/565-634, York 39, *Ludus Coventriae* 37, Digby *Mary Magdalen* 1055-95, Cornish Ordinalia pp. 201-3. The appearance to the women is dramatised in Digby *Mary Magdalen* 1096-1132.

Before 1 SD   The action continues directly from 18/432 in RH. Compare John 20/14: *Haec cum dixisset, conversa est retrorsum, et vidit Iesum stantem* (AV "And when she had thus said, she turned herself back, and saw Jesus standing"). Since the action is continuous, *in the dawninge of the day* R is unnecessary; the audience is given no verbal indication of time, and no indication is given either in John's account, although the almost symbolic dawn may perhaps be inferred from John 20/1, where Mary's first visit was *mane, cum adhuc tenebrae essent* (AV "early, when it was yet dark").

The gospel does not explain how Jesus came to be present, although it suggests that Mary saw him as she turned and left the tomb.

Jesus' appearance is also not indicated in the gospel, but the description here accords with his normal resurrection-portrayal in medieval art. Compare Réau, *Iconographie de l'Art Chrétien*, 2.ii, p. 545: "La Resurrection": *Quel que soit le parti adopté, le Christ resuscité est toujours caractérisé par une croix-étendard qui est le symbole de sa victoire sur la mort*. Also Gertrude Grace Sill, *A Handbook of Symbols in Christian Art* (p.51): "A triumphant Christ steps out of the sarcophagus clothed in a glowing white garment.... He carries His Resurrection staff, Cross, and banner, sign of His victory over death." This specification is not found in other plays of the

English cycles. It may be noted that Chester has no counterpart to Mary's initial supposition, John 20/15: *Existimans quia hortulanus esset* (AV "Supposing him to be the gardener"), although this idea is made explicit in the other cycles; compare Wakefield 26/563: "Say me, garthynere"; York 39/42: "Therfore, goode gardener"; *Ludus Coventriae* 37/33: "But jentyl gardener"; Digby *Mary Magdalen* 1079: "I wentt ye had byn symovd, þe gardener." The appearance of Christ here may have made the explicit statement of such a supposition seem comically inadequate. The appearance does, however, identify Christ immediately to the audience and perhaps gives added point to Mary's failure to recognise him; see 10 note.

1–23 Based on John 20/15-7. But there is no counterpart to Mary's words, John 20/15: *Dicito mihi ubi posuisti eum; et ego eum tollam* (AV "Tell me where thou hast laid him, and I will take him away"), although perhaps something of these words may have been contained in a line omitted in stanza 1; see 1–7, stanza 1 note. 3–4 are without biblical counterpart.

1–7, stanza 1 The stanza contains seven lines instead of the expected eight; it lacks an a-rhyme line in the second quatrain. A line may have been lost containing material equivalent to John 20/15 — see 1–23 note.

9 The line expands Mary's reply, John 20/16: *Rabboni (quod dicitur Magister)* (AV "Rabboni; which is to say, Master"). It is not immediately clear why Mary is asking for mercy, but the implication is that it is because she did not accept the angel's words and/or did not recognise the risen Christ; see Ambrose, *Expositionis in Lucam* lib 10 (PL 15/1938). The plea for mercy also parallels Peter's first words to the risen Christ, 72, pointing a link between the two penitential scenes. See also 16–23, stanza 3 note, 41–3 note.

10 The prohibition is biblical, but contrasts with the action at 43–7; see notes to 16–24 stanza 3, 41–3, 45–7. Jesus' comment is commonly explained as a rebuke to Mary for her disbelief, but here and in John is without motivation. In the other plays it is often given specific motivation in the desire of Mary to touch Jesus; compare Wakefield 26/588–91, *Ludus Coventriae* 37/38–41, Cornish Ordinalia pp. 202–3, where Mary expresses the wish to touch Jesus' feet — as the other Maries do later, and in distant echo of the earlier anointing scene — and Digby *Mary Magdalen* 1073, where Mary wishes to kiss Jesus.

16–9 Compare 20/104 + Latin (a), where the Latin text is used in the Ascension.

16–23, stanza 3 The a-rhymes, *gone—from—one*, are imperfect. It may be noted that the rhyme-scheme is aaabcccb rather than aaabaaab, the latter the dominant form, and that 18 differs markedly in H and R. *one* 18 H is acceptable as an imperfect rhyme; *alsoe* 18 R destroys rhyme in the H version, but would be acceptable if the manuscript read *go* for *gone*, *fro* for *from*, producing perfect rhyme and yielding the pattern aaabaaab in stanza 3.

It may be noted that 18 R aligns the text with John 20/17: *Ascendo ad Patrem meum et Patrem vestrum, Deum meum et Deum vestrum* (AV "I ascend unto my Father and your Father; and to my God and your God"). *he and I all one* 18 H is parenthetical and requires *are* to be understood; although unbiblical, it could be defended as a continuation of the trinitarian emphasis with which the cycle began and which recurs in the cycle. It also serves as a further affirmation of divinity to Mary, who apparently doubted the resurrection and did not recognise Jesus. See notes to 9 and 10 above, and also Bede, *In S. Joannis Evangelium Expositio* 20 (PL 92/920). Compare also Wakefield 26/595–6: "Tell my brethere I shall be / Before theym all in trynyte."

If an earlier rhyme-pattern, *go—fro—alsoe*, is postulated, it is nevertheless clear that such a pattern could not have existed in the exemplar, which must have been read at least *gone—from—alsoe*. In that case, it might be argued that the rhyme-deficiency may have led H to recast 18.

18 *ther* The message which Mary is to carry has been turned from direct speech in John to reported speech. This has the advantage of making clear the wider reference of *vestrum*, which, if rendered here as "your", would have limited its reference to Mary.

20–3 Without biblical counterpart.

23 + SD In Mark and John Mary, as requested, returns directly to the disciples, as in Wakefield 28/1–64, *Ludus Coventriae* 37/86–101, Cornish Ordinalia p. 203. Here, the meeting and dialogue, 24–39, are unbiblical but are necessary to effect the transition from the appearance to Mary, in John's gospel, to the appearance to the other Maries, Matthew 28/9–10. This is a standard transition, seen, e.g., in Comestor, *Historia Scholastica*, 'In Evangelia' 190 (PL 198/1639). The Maries previously appeared at 18/368 + SD.

39 + SD *mulieres* i.e. Mary Jacobi and Mary Salome. Mary Magdalen plays no further part in the action and should be regarded as continuing on her way to inform the other disciples. Compare *Stanzaic Life*:
>   the secounde tyme aparet he
>   To two Maries hom comyng.
>   (7581–2)

40 The line does not readily scan as a four-stress line. Its form may be the result of adhering closely to Jesus' quoted word, Matthew 28/9: *Avete* (AV "All hail").

41–3 The lines have no biblical counterpart but are necessary to explain why the two Maries can touch the risen Christ but Mary Magdalen could not. She saw only the man, but they saw the risen Lord — compare *Glossa Ordinaria*, 'Evang. Matth.' 28/9 (PL 114/177–8): *Istae tenent pedes quae adorant resuscitatum: sed illa quae nesciebat adhuc resurrexisse Filium Dei, audit merito: Noli me tangere.*

heale 42 H may be infinitive — "You are risen to heal us" — or noun — "You are risen for our health" (with *us* as dative of advantage). But whatever its syntactical function, the word must be regarded as a homophone of *hayle* 40 or the a-rhymes are imperfect. *wayle* R avoids the repetition of a rhyme-form or the use of imperfect rhyme; but it can only be a noun — "You are risen for our joy"; the effect is then to create a phrasal balance with 43 — *rysen to wayle/wayved from were*.

wayved 43 seems best taken as past participle, with *hast* understood. It may be noted that the change in verb-construction would be avoided by reading *hast* for *art* 42, and the possibility of an exemplar-change in verbal auxiliary at 42 cannot be discounted.

45–7 Compare Matthew 28/9: *Tenuerunt pedes eius, et adoraverunt eum* (AV "... And held him by the feet, and worshipped him"). The detail is significantly in contrast to the prohibition of 10; compare *Stanzaic Life*:

APPENDIX ID

>   Then weren hor hertes ful of blis,
>   and touchet his fete deuoutely
>   ther Mavdelayn befor i-wys
>   touchet hym noght, as wel rede I.
>   (7589–92)

Although Matthew does not mention Jesus' wounds, the fact that the feet were pierced, combined with the appeal elsewhere (see 19/190, 244–7, and 20/9–12 and note) to the still fresh wounds as evidence of Jesus' identity could well have suggested this detail here. See also 59.

blessed 45 H is stylistically preferable to *sweete* R, which seems influenced by *sweet* 44 and produces the jingling *sweete feete*.

55   *and* H is syntactically redundant, and arguably its omission in R improves the metre.

55 + SD–95   There is no biblical account of the Maries' report to Peter or of the meeting of Peter and Christ. The latter derives from the evidence of two brief references to the meeting, Luke 24/34 and 1 Corinthians 15/5. Compare *Legenda Aurea*, 'De Resurrectione Domini': *Tertio apparuit Simoni, sed ubi et quando, nescitur, nisi forte, quando redibat a monumento cum Johanne*; so *Stanzaic Life*:

>   Petre twinnet ther from Iohan
>   and turnet by another way,
>   thenne aperet Ih[esu] anone
>   to Petre as mon, leue ȝe may.
>   (7605–8)

Others are more cautious; compare *Glossa Ordinaria*, 'Epist 1 ad Cor.' 15/5 (PL 114/546): *Visus est Cephae: Primus quam aliis viris quibus apparuisse legitur in Evangelio, aliter contrarium esset ei quod primo mulieribus apparuisse legitur*; Comestor, *Historia Scholastica*,'In Evangelia' 190 (PL 198/1639): *Petrus autem surgens cucurrit ad monumentum, ut Lucas dicit. Et tunc verisimile est, quod Dominus apparuit ei in via, et si non legatur in Evangelio*. The meeting here parallels the earlier meeting of the Maries with Peter and John, 18/368 + SD–76. Peter's response continues from 18/401–20.

61   See 16/379–94 and notes. With *forsoke* R compare MED *forsaken*, 7(a) "to contradict (a statement), deny (a fact), refute (an argument)", 7(c) "to deny (an accusation)".

66   *know*, attested by both manuscripts, does not give sense. It may be regarded as an error for either *knowen* or *now*.

69   *runne* R is to be preferred for meaning to the scribally erroneous *rumne* H; the H form seems to result from miscounted minims.

72   The line does not easily scan as a four-stress line. It is an ironic echo of Peter's first denial, Luke 22/57: *Mulier, non novi illum* (AV "Woman, I know him not"); see 16/380. The words lose this echo if the denial is omitted, as in H.

82   The line seems to confuse two different constructions: (1) "This deed have thou in sight"; (2) "Of this deed thou have sight". In its present form, however, the line consists of a regular sequence of strongly and weakly stressed syllables.

84-92 Compare Bromyard, cited by G. R. Owst, *Literature and Pulpit in Medieval England* (2nd edn. Oxford, 1961), p. 251: "God, the highest corrector of men, has permitted Peter, his vicar of Correction on the earth to sin, so that, from the state of his own frailty he might learn to sympathise with the weakness of others"; Owst refers to Chrysostom, PG 50/728. Compare also T. Arnold (ed.) *Select English Works of John Wyclf*, vol. II, 'Sermon 182', p.135. "Men seien how þe gospel telliþ, how Crist apperide speciali to Petre; not oonli for Petre was capteyn, and was beden to conferme his breþeren, but algatis for þis cause, for Petre synnede many weies in denyynge of Crist, and þus he was ny3 despair, and þerfore Petre hadde moost nede to be confortid bi talis of Crist." Mirk, *Festial*, 'De Festo Apostolorum Petri et Pauli et eorum Solempnitate' (EETS es 96) concentrates only upon the second reason given by Wyclif; *Stanzaic Life* 7609-12 presents Peter as a model of obedience. The strong papal overtones of *soverainty* 83 perhaps provide one reason for the excision of the end of play 18 in HmAB.

91 "Then you may have remembrance (on all who shall call to you from now on)." Neither H nor R in isolation gives sense. *thou* R is to be preferred to *then* H; and *minning* H is to be preferred to *meaninge* R. One would, however, expect the preposition *of* after *minning* rather than *to* 89, and some influence from *to* 90 may perhaps be suspected at 89.

93 *more* R is to be preferred to the scribally erroneous *mere* H for meaning.

APPENDIX II

Headnotes

1. *Format*

The reader should consult the notes to the equivalent plays in the cycle-text for the details of *Dramatis Personae, Locations, Properties, Costume*, and the information usually comprehended under *Play-heading*.

2. *Content*

The notes relate to textual matters peculiar to each individual manuscript. For information concerning analogues and other 'non-textual' matters, and also for instances where the reading of the appendix-text is included in the evaluation of readings in the cycle-manuscripts, the reader should refer to the notes to the equivalent plays in the cycle-text.

3. *Other Editions*

Space does not permit detailed consideration of the suggestions of previous editors. The reader is directed to the following editions, to which occasional reference is made:

Appendix IIA: W. W. Greg: 'The Manchester Fragment of the 'Resurrection'', in *Chester Play Studies*, pp.85 – 100.

Appendix IIB: W. W. Greg: *The Play of Antichrist from the Chester Cycle*.

Appendix IIC: F. M. Salter: 'The 'Trial and Flagellation': a new manuscript', in *Chester Play Studies*, pp. 1 – 73.

APPENDIX IIA

8 *escrete* M, like A, confuses *t* with *c*; R emends to *distreite* 18/8. But *estreite* HmBH is to be preferred.

13-4 18/14-20, which one would expect to come between 13 and 14 M, have no counterpart in M and were evidently on the missing portions of the manuscript.

14 The line in M would be metrically improved by the loss of one syllable. This reduction is seen in 18/21, where all manuscripts read *cryed* for M's disyllabic *cryden*. Salter regarded the M form as more archaic and attached some minor importance to the variation — presumably in favour of M's priority in time. But the M form is metrically detrimental and could arise from an uncancelled error whereby the sequence *cryed on* was transcribed as *cryden*. Compare 23 note.

19 *leeve* may be preferred to *beleeve* 18/26 in producing a more regular sequence of strongly and weakly stressed syllables. Greg suggests that "M represents an original reading *welle leeue*, which in the archetype of the cyclic manuscripts was through accident or misreading altered to *welbe leeue...*" (*Chester Play Studies*, p. 99)

20 *beegyn* may be preferred for syntax and meaning to *begane* 18/27, since a present infinitive is required.

23 *ne* 18/30 is to be preferred for syntax and meaning to *nyfe*. The latter appears to be a scribal error, perhaps an uncancelled error resulting from an initial confusion whereby the sequence *ne so* was read as *nefe* (confusing long *s* with *f* and *o* with *e*). Compare 14 note.

24 There is no obvious textual reason for the variation of M and 18/31, both of which are equally acceptable. The two forms are alternatives to which priority cannot be assigned.

25 Either *sore* or *soone* 18/32 is possible. *sore* is a common collocation with verbs of fearing; but this fact would perhaps tend to argue for the authenticity of *soone*. The variation would arise in confusion of *sore* and *sone*. A also reads *sore*, but as part of a total change in the verb phrase, so that the agreement cannot be considered significant.

APPENDIX IIB

24 *hand* Compare *them* 23/24. Either is possible. Greg reads *ham* P.

25 *laykyd* The reading has been crossed out and *lyggedd* inserted above (see TNs); all other manuscripts read *ligged* 23/25. Greg believes the hand of the corrector here is that of the scribe and that the cancellation is a scribally emended error; but he considers (p. lxix) *laykyd* as "quite likely" to be the original reading. This opinion leads him to consider and reject the possibility that the other manuscripts derive from P, preferring to postulate an alteration in the P-exemplar, or an emendation added by the P-scribe to the cyclic exemplar.

27 *confounde* is an erroneous scribal compounding of the correct *can found* 23/27.

35 *then* 23/35 is to be preferred for meaning to the scribally erroneous *they*.

44 *comyn rowland* is less probable, syntactically and semantically, than *come in land* 23/44.

47 See 23/42–8 note.

55 *that* (1) and *hitt* 23/55 are equally acceptable, but the possibility of *that* being influenced by *that*(2) cannot be discounted. Greg suggests confusion of y^t and *yt* as the source of the variation.

56+ Latin *multis* HmBH is to be preferred for meaning to the scribally erroneous *multam* P. *gratuita* is an error for Vulgate *gratuito*.

62 *he*, though syntactically redundant, produces a more regular sequence of strongly and weakly stressed syllables than its omission in 23/62.

67 *some* produces a more regular sequence of strongly and weakly stressed syllables than its omission in 23/67 if *maistrye* is disyllabic, as the form suggests. But if *maistrye* represents a trisyllabic form, *maistery*, the omission of *some* is metrically justifiable, and some such consideration may underlie the variation.

82 *rootes* 23/82 may be preferred to *rote* because it accords morphologically with *trees*; *rote* must be understood collectively.

88 *leede* The word has been emended to *leeve* (see TNs), the 23/88 reading and clearly the form required for meaning.

102 *every* seems to be a scribal error for *verey* 23/102, perhaps a result of the phonological similarity of the two words.

103 *ye* disrupts a regular sequence of strongly and weakly stressed syllables, and its omission at 23/103 may be preferred. It may indicate confusion with *ye* 102.

111 *then* presumably has the force of "therefore", while *there* 23/111 suggests "over there", where the miracle has occurred. Although Greg prefers *then* because he feels that the reference of *there* is not clear, either seems possible.

112 See 23/112 note.

147 *beheight* 23/147 may be preferred to *hyght* in producing a more regular sequence of strongly and weakly stressed syllables.

158 *oure* and *my* 23/158 seem equally possible. With the former, compare *we* 151; with the latter *I* 150, 154. The usage here is, however, particularly comparable with *our* 112.

163 Compare 23/163. Without *and* 23/163, the line in P becomes a petition comparable syntactically with 164.

176 *as*(2) is a formal error for *has*.

189 Either *hyght* or *high* 23/189 is semantically possible. The absence of a verb in 189–90 might explain or justify *hyght*; but Greg argues that loss of *t* is more likely than its addition.

196+SD *spiritum* 23/196+SD is to be preferred for meaning to the scribally erroneous *spritum*.

196+SH See 23/196+SH note.

206 *shall* 23/206 is perhaps stylistically preferable to *will*, since the latter formally repeats *will* 205, which may have influenced a change, and yields the jingling *will fullfill*.

210 See 23/210 note. P omits *and* 23/210, to the detriment of metre.

214 *for* may be preferred to *because* 23/214 in producing a more regular sequence of strongly and weakly stressed syllables, if one also prefers *regions* 23/214 to *regnis*, since a disyllabic form would then be required. The former variation is one of substitution, but the latter may be a result of scribal error based on some form such as *regins*. Or possibly two alternative readings *for—regions* and *because—regnis*, have been wrongly conflated, although this seems less likely. Greg, however, argues that *regions* is "a very forced reading evidently due to unfamiliarity with a use of the original word [*regnis*] that was becoming unusual, though it long survived" (*Antichrist*, p. lxiii); he apparently intends *reign*, OED 1 "kingdom, sovereignty".

218–9 *and* 218 or *as* 23/218 and *and* 219 or *yea* 23/219 are possible, but, as Greg notes, "in P four consecutive lines beginning with *and* look suspicious" (*Antichrist*, p. 77). It is, however, impossible to assign priority to the readings.

237–52 See 23/237–52, stanzas 31–3 note.

247 *good* 23/247 destroys the regular sequence of strongly and weakly stressed syllables and may be regarded as an erroneous addition based upon a frequent collocation. Its omission in RBP may be preferred.

287 *devylls* 23/287 is perhaps preferable as possessive to *devyle*.

295 *thys* can be accepted as a plural, "these". But *his* 23/295 is preferable, and perhaps indicates a form from which *thys* could have derived.

300+SH See 23/300+SH note.

302 *both* 23/302 is semantically redundant in view of *in companye*, "together"; but even in P the line is metrically uneven.

APPENDIX 2B

317 The line is metrically rough. Either *redye* or *here* 23/317 is metrically acceptable, but syntactically the former should read *redelye*, and a trisyllabic form would be still less acceptable metrically.

337–9 See 23/333–40, stanza 44 note.

342 *so* (2) 23/342 produces a more regular sequence of strongly and weakly stressed syllables than its omission in P and may be preferred. Greg argues that, despite P's harsh metre, *so* (2) destroys an alliterative phrase; he proposes a formerly trisyllabic *grissiliche* as the base form.

357 *O* 23/357 may be preferred to its omission by P in producing a more regular sequence of strongly and weakly stressed syllables. Greg speculates that P indicates that the syllabic ending of *ypocrites* was originally pronounced in the line.

440 "You teach me the very thing that I intended." *lerne* is here taken in the sense of MED *lernen*, 4a (a).

444 *donne* 23/444 is to be preferred for meaning to the scribally erroneous *downe*, the latter evidently resulting from scribal confusion of *n* and *u* in *donne*.

459 *freshe* 23/459 is to be preferred for meaning to the scribally erroneous *feshe*.

470 *god* and *godes* 23/470 are equally possible; but the latter may echo Exodus 20/3 (Deuteronomy 5/7): *Non habebis deos alienos coram me* (AV "Thou shalt have no other gods before me"). For the singular form, however, compare *noe God* 5/5. See also 483 note.

480 *mote* 23/480, "to argue, plead, discuss, esp. in a law case", is semantically preferable to *mete*, "to keep an appointment"; but either form is possible. The variation orginates in confusion of *o* and *e*.

483 The addition of *anye* 23/483, perhaps influenced by Exodus 20/3 and its translations (see 470 note), is detrimental to metre. P's omission is to be preferred.

530 P is preferable to 23/530. The omission of *to* produces a more regular sequence of strongly and weakly stressed syllables and avoids the duplication of *to manye on — to the people everychone*, 23/530–1; the construction at 23/531 evidently prompted the introduction of *to* at 530 on the assumption that the constructions were parallel.

589 The function of *and* ARP is not clear; 23/589 reads *A* HmBH.
we 23/589 provides a subject missing from P but apparently required.

613 A stressed monosyllable is required after *I* for a regular sequence of strongly and weakly stressed syllables. *sente* may be preferred, but a possible elision in *I assent* 23/613 would make this reading equally possible. Greg urges the originality of the P-form.

620 *make* 23/620 is to be preferred for meaning to the scribally erroneous *moke*.

625 *Antechriste* 23/625 is to be preferred for meaning to the scribally erroneous *Antecist*.

639 *therefore* 23/643 is to be preferred for meaning to the scribally erroneous *therfo*.

651 The repeated *Ragnell Ragnell* 23/647 is to be preferred for metre to *Ragnayll*. P contains only three strongly stressed syllables instead of the expected four, perhaps because of a simplification resulting from the belief that the repetition was erroneous.

659 The infinitive construction *not to come* 23/655 is to be preferred to the phrasal construction *I wolde not com* in producing a more regular sequence of strongly and weakly stressed syllables. But 23/655 remains metrically uneven.

680 See 23/675–8, stanza 90 note. For a regular sequence of strongly and weakly stressed syllables, P needs a further unstressed syllable, such as that supplied by *in this steed* 23/676 HmABH; *us instead* R also supplies a syllable, but seems based upon a misunderstanding in that Antichrist no longer stands "in our stead" but "lies in this place".

684 *yee* 23/680 is to be preferred for meaning to the scribally erroneous *he*(1), the latter perhaps influenced by *he*(2).

690 *maistries* 23/686 is to be preferred for meaning to the scribally erroneous *maisters*.

702 + SD See 23/678 + SD note.

APPENDIX IIC

Before 1 SD   *Judeus* No other manuscript contains this word, the subject otherwise being supplied by *Before* 1 SH. It is possible that the scribe automatically wrote *Judeus* after *primo* because of the collocation of *primus* and *Judeus* in the SH.

24   *so that* 16/20 may be preferred for meaning to *that soe* C. *soe,* "in this way", is not immediately meaningful in context, whereas as a component of "so that" introducing a result clause it is intelligible and acceptable.

82   *yea yea ye harden* The line is metrically rough and would be improved by the omission of two syllables. HmARBH all lack *yea yea,* although the pronoun form in AR is *yea,* perhaps indicating a source of the C reading. With *harden,* compare *herden* Hm. Hm alone, however, also has a pronoun object, *him,* which overweights the line; *hard* H reduces the number of syllables, to the detriment of metre; *harcken* AR is semantically and metrically as appropriate as *harden.*

119   *hym faye* C follows the erroneous AR reading instead of *in faye* HmBH.

151   See 16/139 note.

176   *lawe* has been erroneously repeated in C and constitutes a unique uncancelled error.

221   A unique C-reading; see 16/209–10 note.

228   Although C has no word not found in another manuscript, its phrase *hase seene ys* seems intermediate between the erroneous *has seene* 16/216 AR and the appropriate *as seene is* BH. *as seemes* Hm is also possible. C perhaps suggests that AR derives from a (possibly corrected) exemplar *hase* for *as.*

234   Only C reads *I will* for *will I,* a unique inversion noted by Salter.

241   Either *therfore* C or *thereupon* 16/229 is possible; the unique C reading is noted by Salter.

272   *suen,* "sue, petition; follow", is a unique C-form. It may be semantically preferable to *shewen* 16/260, "show, demonstrate, vote", although resembling the R-form *shuen.*

301   *have* 16/289 is to be preferred for concord to *hath* C, present singular, since the subject, *them that,* is plural.

314   C erroneously omits the rhyme-word *him.*

330   *slappes* is a unique form, perhaps reflecting scribal confusion of *f* and long *s*; *flappes* 16/318 is to be preferred for meaning and alliteration.

338 + SD   *super caput* See 16/326 + SD note.

345   *bed* See 16/331–38, stanza 44 note.

363-4 C alone erroneously repeats 359-60. The scribe has evidently mistaken the speech-heading, but has recognised his error after two lines and begun afresh without cancelling his earlier lines.

THE IDENTITY OF "DR. MATTHEWS"

The identity of the editor of Part II of *The Chester Plays* (EETS, 1916), who is known from the titlepage only as "Dr. Matthews," has long remained a mystery. R. M. Lumiansky and David Mills, in the "Note to Bibliography" in their edition of *The Chester Mystery Cycle* (EETS, SS 3 (1974), pp.xliii–xliv), thoroughly digest all the information known about this editor. The earliest reference to "Dr. Matthews" seems to have been in the advertisement bound in with EETS, os 113 (1899). But Lumiansky and Mills were unable to locate any further information about Matthews, other than to ascertain to their satisfaction that he was not Brander Matthews of Columbia University (to whom the Bodleian catalogue attributes the edition) nor the medievalist Godfrey W. Mathews and that no such person appeared in English university lists in the late nineteenth century. "We have not searched," they add, "for an appropriate Ph. D. recipient from a German university around 1890. 'Dr. Matthews' remains a mystery" (p. xliv).

We know that a person answering the description of "Dr. Matthews" must have emerged between 1892, when F. J. Furnivall says in Part I of *The Chester Plays* (EETS, ES 62, 1892) that the editor, Hermann Deimling, has died, and expresses the hope that someone will complete the edition (p. vii), and 1899, when EETS could announce the participation of "Dr. Matthews" in the editing of Part II. Since EETS records for this period have not been traced after Furnivall's death in 1910 (see Lumiansky and Mills, p. xliii), we must find another source for people associated with Furnivall in the 1890s. Such a source exists in the *Introduction, Supplement, and Bibliography* to the *New English Dictionary*, which appeared in 1933, and which includes a list of the people who contributed quotations and definitions to the *NED*. (Furnivall had been associated with the *NED* from its beginnings, in 1859.) In this list (XIII, xiii) we find the name of "Albert Matthews (of U. S. A.)." This Albert Matthews, I believe, is the "Dr. Matthews" who edited *The Chester Plays*, Part II.

Albert Matthews was a wealthy gentleman scholar, a native of Boston, Massachusetts, and a member of the Class of 1882 at

Harvard College. Born in 1860, Matthews was a classmate and lifelong friend of George Lyman Kittredge, who was the North American secretary for EETS in the 1890s. Unlike his classmate, who went into teaching and academic research, Matthews never had to take a job in order to live, and so passed his life in genteel editing and antiquarian research; his longest association was with the Colonial Society of Massachusetts, whose secretary he was from the early 1900s until 1924. He outlived most members of his Harvard class, dying in 1946. From the reports that Matthews wrote at intervals from 1885 to 1907 for his Harvard class and from many letters of his that survive in the Kittredge papers at Harvard University, we can reconstruct his interest in the Middle Ages. In the third report of the Class of 1882 (Boston, 1890), Matthews noted, "Under the auspices of the Chaucer Society [which Furnivall had founded in 1868], a 'glossarial Concordance to Chaucer's Works' is being prepared. I am at present engaged in a small share of this task" (p. 58). In the fourth report of his class (Boston, 1896), Matthews says that his studies have "taken the direction of English and American literature; and I have collected a large amount of material in the way of citations for Dr. Murray's 'New English Dictionary'" (p. 52). Matthews's work for the Chaucer Society must have been philological in nature for, in 1897, Alfred W. Pollard mentions such work in the introduction to his edition of *The Towneley Plays* (EETS, ES 71, 1897): "Subject to such corrections as the survey of the dialect now being undertaken by Dr. Matthews may suggest, I think we may fairly regard this Towneley cycle as built up in at least three distinct stages" (p. xxvii). Matthews's presence in England is supported by his own statements. In his 1896 class report, he mentions that he spent portions of the summers of 1890, 1891, 1893, and 1895 in Europe and, in 1901, he added, "Each summer I have spent six or eight weeks in Europe in a successful effort to escape hay fever" (*Class of 1882. Report No. V* (Boston, 1901), p. 53).

From Matthews's correspondence with Kittredge, we learn that he spent much of these European trips in England, both at Oxford and in London, where he habitually worked at Bodley and at the British Museum, often collating manuscripts for Kittredge or checking facts for his classmate in sources unavailable at Harvard. Matthews never mentions the Chester Plays specifically, but he occasionally writes of his interest in late medieval literature and in early drama, and he worked in the very libraries where the manuscripts of the Chester cycle are found. On one occasion, he speaks of attending a performance of a medieval passion play (letter to Kittredge, 30 June 1900). He must have become acquainted with Furnivall by 1890, when he told his Harvard class that he was involved in one of the Chaucer Society's many projects, all of which were arranged by Furnivall. The relationship may well have been a close one, for in 1900 he sent Kittredge "a small check for the fund in commemoration of Dr. Furnivall" (letter, 12 January 1900). Matthews does not mention the amount of his contribution, but his great modesty led him to habitual understatement; his annual contributions to the fund of his Harvard class were always among the largest of any of his classmates. Matthews also contributed an essay entitled "The Word Vendue" to the Furnivall *Festschrift* (*An English Miscellany, Presented to Dr. Furnivall in Honour of his Seventy-Fifth Birthday* (Oxford, 1901), pp. 314–20), so we may certain of his acquaintance with Furnivall in the 1890s. But after 1901, as his correspondence with Kittredge shows, Matthews's interests turned mainly to North American antiquarianism and etymology, so any work that he did on the Middle Ages he must have completed no later than about 1900. Indeed, he seems never to have completed the project he undertook for the Chaucer Society — the Society never published the "glossarial concordance"— or the studies of dialect to which Pollard appears to refer in 1897.

Matthews did not have a doctorate, so it is puzzling that Furnivall should have identified him as "Dr. Matthews" but, in view of his considerable learning, it does not seem unlikely that a British scholar may have assigned such a title to him as a courtesy without actually being aware that he did not hold such a degree. The collations for Part II of *The Chester Plays* that Matthews presumably did in the late 1890s — and which form the bulk of the editorial contributions to the volume — must have existed in Furnivall's papers with a note identifying them as coming from "Dr. Matthews." When, after Furnivall's death, a new generation of medievalists took over the management of EETS, someone who did not know the shy American scholar simply arranged to have his work printed as "edited by Dr. Matthews" without making any attempt to ascertain his correct identity. Indeed, in 1914 Israel Gollancz wrote to W. W. Greg saying that "Dr. Matthews" "cannot be found" (Lumiansky and Mills, p. xliii). Since Albert Matthews's ties had been with Furnivall, and since I have found no evidence to suggest that he made known his early interest in the Middle Ages to Furnivall's successors, we can understand how EETS came to lose touch with him. A definitive statement from Albert Matthews himself that he collated the manuscripts of *The Chester Plays* is lacking, but the circumstantial evidence about his association with medieval studies and with EETS founder and editor Furnivall during the 1890s is so considerable that we can claim to have solved the mystery surrounding the identity of the editor of Part II.

PAUL J. KORSHIN.
University of Pennsylvania
Philadelphia, Pa., U. S. A.

LATIN ERRORS

Space does not permit the inclusion of a complete Latin glossary. Listed below are the erroneous Latin forms in all extant manuscripts with their correct classical equivalent. It is hoped that the list will help the reader to translate tha Latin passages using a standard Latin-English Dictionary.

a = cum 16/242
abiunt = abeunt 18/420
abstreget = absterget 15/160
  abstregit = abstergit 15/160
abstetrices = obstetrices 6/476
ac = ad 23/722
accepe = accipe 11/79
  accepiet = accipiet 6/464
  accipente = accipient 24/40
  accipet, accipetet = accipiet 15/96
  accipett = accipiet 11/150
  accipiet = accipietis 21/112
  accipite = accipit 15/88
ad = et 12/232, 15/104
  ad = ab 16A/423VR
addiscedunt = ac discedunt 18/308
aduxet = adduxit 22/before 1
  addulcentes = adducentes 16/before 1
  addcent, adducente = adducent 12/232
  addcet = adducet 12/128
  adducete = adducet 5/303
admirand = admirando 11/55
adoramus, adoriens = adorans 5/239
adulteriam, adultriam = adulteria 12/268
adventum = adventu 23/ph
age = agere 23/2, IIB/2
agentes = agentis 6/666
agredientes = egredientes 22/48
aholite = attolite 17/152
alablastro, albastro = alabastro 14/40
aliam = alia IA/15
alias = decios 16A/120

alienigene = alienigenae 21/366
alieginarum = alienigenarum IB/288
alleguus, alleluia = alleluya 20/104a
alloquerentibus, alloquerentum = alloquerentur 15/36
altera = altare 11/40
ambulabat = ambulat 13/before 1
amiciti = amicti 22/172
amos = annos 22/164
anelus = angelus 20/104f
angelorom = angelorum 1/ph
  angelus = angelis 24/564
anscendit = ascendit 23/180
antiphonum = antiphonam 21/238
aparent = apparente 19/ph
aparit = apparet 6/547, 7/463
apariet = aperiet 14/56
aplicamini = apostolicum 21/ph
apparebet = apparebit 6/508
  appariet = apparet 7/463
  appariet = aperiet 9/135
appromquat, approquinquat = appropinquat 17/64
aracali = ara caeli 6/712
arbitrum = arbitrium 6/666
arement, arenent = arentur 6/539
armes = armis 15/304
ascendiet = ascendit 21/330
  ascendo = ascendendo 20/104
asendebunt = ascendebant 22/124
asinam = asina 5/223VR
asine = asina 5/271
asine = asinae 5/223
aspiat = aspiciat IC/32
assendit = ascendit 20/96, IIB/180

assendit = ascendent 5/271
assendus = ascendit 20/96
assentione = ascentione 20/ph
asspituit = aspiciunt 18/344
at = ad 23/180
auferitor = auferitur 8/268
aufertur = auferitur 23/678
auriculum = auriculam 15/332, 342
austrem, austrom = austrum 5/279

baptizbamini = baptizabimini 21/96
 baptazuit = baptizavit 21/96
be = de 2/ph
beate, beati = beatae 11/ph
bene = bonae 7/426
bestie = bestiae 22/124
bona = bonae 7/357
 bone = bonae 7/357, 426
borialem = borealem 5/303

caelcis = excelsis 7/371
caena = cena 15/ph
calcantium, calcantrum = calcandum 20/104f
caldet = cadet 10/288
calecem = calicem 4/72
cancabit = cantabit 11/166
canctam = cincturam 6/425-8
cantant = cantabit 7/164
 cancabit = cantabit 11/166
 cantabit = cantabunt 7/447, 18/153
 cantat = cantant 21/238
 cantebit = cantabit 23/722
 cantendo = cantando 21/238
 cantet = cantent 21/120
 cantibunt = cantabunt 24/508
cap = capitulo 22/124, 23/24
 capit = capitulo 22/124
 capitula = capitulo 19/95
 capituo = capitulo 22/48
capieint = capient 23/678
capite = caput 16/326
carnem = carnis 21/350
castellam = castellum 19/ph, 111
 castillum = castellum 19/111
cateros = ceteros 19/143
cath = cathedram 16/322
 catheram = cathedram 16/69

cathelicam = catholicam 21/342
cctlam = ecclesiam 21/342
ceco = caeco 13/ph
cede = caede 4/ph
cela = caeli 6/666
 cela = caelo 20/96
 celes = caelos 21/330
 celi = caeli 1/ph
 celorum = caelorum 17/64
 celum = caelum 20/152, 23/722, IIB/726
celsis = excelsis 7/389, 408
chathedr, chathedram = cathedram IIB/180, 624
cica = dicat 14/40
circumamblant = circumambulant 8/112
circumdixit = circumduxit 22/before 1
circumspetat = circumspectat 13/156
cis = excelsis 7/410
clamam = clamavi 23/644, IB/344
clavem = clavum 16A/200
cocdicibus, codicilus = codicibus 22/260
coesi, coesti = caesi 23/686
cogett = coget 18/193, 201
cognoserittis = cognosceritis 13/35
comedent, commedet = comedet 19/199, 20/56
 commedent = comedent 7/136
 commedit = comedit 19/199
communione = communionem 21/342
condiciplus, condiscipulus = condiscipulos 21/before 1
confringitt = confringit 17/192
confreget = confregit 17/192
congregam = congregem 23/120
consolabom = consolabor 19/95
consulendum = consulandum 5/183
conversus = conversos 23/624
coona = caena 15/ph
creacion = creatione 1/ph
crucis = crucem ID/before 1
crucifixionem = crucifixione 16A/ph
crusifixus = crucifixus 21/322

damnata, damnate = damnati 24/172
 damnatus = damnata 24/260

LIST OF LATIN ERRORS 413

dampnata = damnatus 24/204
dcensum = descensu 17/ph
dctroum = doctorum 22/260
de fores, de fortes = de foris 8/324
dece = de sede 17/176
decendet, decendit = descendunt 8/48
decensu = descensu 17/ph
decimae quarta = decima quarta 14/ph
   decimo tertio = decima tertia 13/ph
decias = decios 16A/120
defindite = defendite 5/131
demidium = dimidium 22/164
demittes = dimittis 17/48
demones = demon 24/508VR
   demones = demonibus 17/96
demonstra = demonstrant 24/356
denittes = dimittis 11/166
dentum = dentium 24/580
descedens = descendens 12/124
   descen = descendi 23/2
   descende = descendet 24/356
   descendes = descendens 14/224
desensum = descensu 17/ph
deseitor = desertum 12/ph
deu = deus 11/166
deum = deus 5/183
dex = dux 8/268
diabolus = diabolum 12/120
dicimo tercia = decimo tertio 23/56
di, diat, dicas, dicatt = dicat 2/252, 10/ph, 16A/216, 21/120
   dice = ecce 22/48
   dicitt, dicitte = dicit 16/117, 23/56
   dicunt = dicat 16/162
die = dei 21/330
discescerunt = discesserunt 8/381
discendunt = discedunt 18/308
discendens = descendens 12/124
   discindi = descendi 23/7
discipule = discipuli 15/264
   discipulis, discipulus = discipulos 15/280
   discipulus = discipulis 19/199
dividitte = dividit 23/56
dixe = dux 8/268
doctori = doctoris 24/356
docuett = docuit 2/ph
domine = domini 1/85

domine = dominum 5/183
domine = domini 14/208
domini = domine 17/48
dominum = domini 20/ph
donet = donec 13/356
dredo = credo 21/ph
duo = domino 24/508

e = et IIB/702
eante = eant 17/276
ed = et IIC/214
effanderet = effoderet 5/80
eius = eis 21/238, 23/56
elivat = elevat 13/441
emittes, emittis = euntes 24/508
emittitte = emittit 24/428
emos = duos 22/164
enim = tuum 23/40VR
eo = ea 21/32
equitand, equitandon, equitandum = equitando 4/ph, 112
eques = equos 8/112
erat = erit 24/580
   erite = eritis 13/35
es = est IB/392
   este = est 5/435, 6/666, 22/before 1, 24/540
et = de 5/80VR, 11/ph, 118, 22/48
et = ei 5/435VR
et = ad 2/312, 10/392, 23/722
et = ex 10/ph, 497
et = it 15/264VR
et = est 21/334
etc = et cetera 5/435, 6/64, 72
etc = ei 4/ph
etct = etc IB/312, 328
et que = atque 23/5
eternam, eternum = aeternam 21/354
   eternus = aeternus IIB/8
eterum = iterum 11/63
evangele, evangeliste = evangelistae 24/676
evaneset = evanescet 19/123
evaquatum = evaginatum 5/239
eviunt, evunt = eunt 15/64, 19/111, 23/141
exaltavit = exultavit 6/72
excellis = excelsis 7/357

exie = exiet 8/310
exputas = exputans IIC/81, 85
extrauntr, extravitur = extrahuntur 17/204
extricto = extracto 5/215
exultabunt = exaltabunt 16A/240

fabicabit = fabricabit 11/40
facient = faciet 10/433
  facitt = faciat 10/497
facibus = fascibus 15/304
facien = faciem 16/89
fatea = facta 22/before 1
fcum = cum 14/260
fiant = fiat 6/666
  fiere = fieri 24/356
filies = filios 19/95
  filius = filiis 17/192
firmantum = firmamentum 7/323
fit obviam = sit obviam 13/372
fiunt = sum 13/356
flagellaverent = flagellaverunt IIC/334
flebet = flebit 14/208
flectantes = flectentes 17/88
  flecten = flectent 21/48
  flectente = flectent 8/84
  flectibus = flectentibus 17/88
flectus = fletus 24/580
foemore = femore 8/268
fores, fortes = foris 8/324
fraget = surget 14/136
fueri = fieri 10/288
fuerust = fuerunt 16A/ph
fuet obviam, fuit obviam = sit obviam 13/372
fugett = fuget 12/256, 264
fumel = simul 5/199
fuorem = furorem 8/324
futrum = futurum 23/120

gaudentes, gaudiens = gaudens 6/64
  gaudet = gaudete 23/722
gentum = gentium 8/268
genu = genua 8/84, 17/88
genuflecten = genuflectent 21/48
giro = gyro 22/before 1
glare, glas, glay, glee, glere, glo, glor, glor glar, glor glor, glore, glore glare,

glori glory, glorie, glorie glare, glorie glora, glorum glarum, glorus glarus, glorus glarus glorius, glory, glory glore, glory glory, glorye, gly, glye, grorus glorus = gloria 7/361-400
glorie = gloriae 17/152
gradentes = gradientes 22/124
gratimo, gratuita = gratuito 23/56, IIB/56
gratius = gartius 7/233, 411
  gertius = gartius 7/279
greges = gregibus 7/ph

habebat = habebit 2/496
habete, habit = habet 20/16
habet, habit = habitu 19/32
habite = habitet 21/32
hac = haec 22/48
  hec, hic = haec 6/666
  hec = hic 22/before 1
hoc = hic 7/463
hodies = hos dies 21/96
horinem = hominem 15/36

ibunt = ibit 7/233
icipiat = incipiat 21/before 1
iit = it 15/264
imprecatorum = imperatorem 6/643
in = is 6/712
  in = tu 8/310VR
incipiant = incipiat 17/276
  incipite = incipit 6/64
indent = induent 16/202
  indeunt = induent IIC/214
  indunt = induunt IIC/334
inferi = inferni IB/344
  inferos = inferna 17/ph
inferne, inferni = infernae 1/ph
ingradientur = ingrediatur 10/264
  ingredetur = ingredietur 10/288
inmittet = immittet 21/56
instrumentes = instrumentis 24/356
introibis = introbit 17/152
ipse = ipsa 24/356
  ipsom = ipsum 4/48
irates = iratus 10/396
irgine = virgine 21/318
ista = iste 20/104d

LIST OF LATIN ERRORS 415

jaceant = jaciant 17/176
jacebet = jacebit 5/215
javenes = juvenes 8/324
judicari, judicas = judicare 21/334, 23/2
judiciri = judicium 22/260
just = justi 23/722
   justus = justorum 24/580
jusu = juxta 13/332

lachrinans = lachrimans 16A/240
lachrymis, lacrinis = lachrimis 14/56
   lacrimas = lachrimas IB/328
lancia, laricia = lancea 16A/383
laternis, laterrens = lanternis 15/304
lavates = levatis 15/96
legabunt = ligabunt 16/314
leposi = leprosi 14/16
liberavit = liberabit 13/35
licencill = licentia 1/19
licramans = lachrimans 16A/240
ligavit = ligabit 4/358
lintheo = lintheolo 15/160
locom = locum 13/372
loquti sunt, loqunti sunt = locuti sunt 23/686
   loqumti fuerint = locuti fuerint 23/686

magistratos = magistros 7/233
magnifacite, magnificate = magnificat 6/64, 69
maiistros = magistros 7/233
males = malos 24/580
manibus = manus 22/before 1
   manibus = manum 15/104
   manus = manu 16A/216
mari = mare 22/124
media = medio 19/167
me = meae 23/120VR
   mee = meae IIB/120
   mei = mea 6/70
   meius, meus = meis 22/172
   meoes = meos 22/48
messus = missus 21/158
misceriacordie, misericordia, misericordiae, misericordie = misericordiam 17/192
   mittendio = mittendus 8/268

mnera = munera 8/338
monstare = monstrare 23/2
mont = montem 5/95
monten = montem 5/95, 271, 8/48
montim = montium 22/48
moriente = oriente 8/212
morientur = morietur 10/433, 23/652
mortuens = mortuorum 24/356
mortum = mortui 23/104
mortuous = mortuos 21/334
mortus = mortuis 18/153, 21/326, 23/164
mos = nos 5/131
muliere = mulieres 18/308
multis = multam 23/56, IIB/56
multus = multam 23/56
mundom = mundum 2/ph

nesessetatem = necessitate 5/131
nichell, nighell, nill = nihil 16/178
   nichill = nihil IIC/190
nock, nocke = nocte 22/124
nonae = nono 8/268
nosse = noscere 21/104
not = non 13/before 1, 18/384, 20/16, 21/32
notam = nota 6/666
noum = novum 23/196
nubens = nubes 20/104b
nundi = mundi 17/72

o = omega 1/1, 2/before 1
o = opus 24/564
obstringit = abstergit 15/160
occisus = occessus IB/360
occuliis, occulus = oculis 15/96
   occulos = oculos 22/48
occumbit = accumbit 15/80
occurrette = occurret 4/ph
oerere = aere 24/356
offerrit = offerit 4/72
omnipotentes = omnipotentis 21/330
omnes = omnium 15/160
   omnes = omnis 20/96
   omnes = hominis 24/564
   omnibus = hominibus 7/420
   omnibus = ovibus 13/21
   omnies = omnes 19/111

onnibus = hominibus 7/420
oo = omega 1/1
opitulamine = opitulamini 5/131
orientoalum = orientalium 8/ph
orient = oriente 8/212

pagena = pagina 3/ph
  pagina, pagine = paginae 22/260
  paginae = pagina 14/ph
palisper = paulisper 18/368
palmar, palmas = palmarum 14/208
pane = panem 4/72, 104
pamos = pannos 14/224
pariet = pariter 13/332
  parie, parietes = pariet 11/24
parmulum = parvulum 8/324
pater familius = pater familias 15/52
patenam = patinam 4/72
patri, patrie = patriae 5/131
patriarici = patriarchi 17/204
pausas = pausans 20/112
peccat = peccata 17/72
  peccatorem = peccatorum 21/346
pedes = pede 18/153
pempora = tempora 21/104
penit = ponit 13/21
penitentia = penitentiam 17/64
percuciet = percutiet 5/223
  percuties = percutiens IIC/113
  percutum = percutiens 16/before 102
peregrinae, peregrine, periogrem, periogrine = peregrino 19/32
perferat = perforat 16A/383
perutrens = percutiens 16/97
perswacione = persuasione 10/ph
phalmo = psalmo 8/338
pinaclo, pinacula, pinoglo = pinnaculo 12/124
platies = plateis 8/324
plocul = procul 11/118
pocula = poculo 4/64
poliabunt = spoliabunt 16/314
policulum = populum 10/497
pones = ponet 16/374
  ponnes = ponet IIC/338
porte, portae = portas 17/152
poste = postea 21/120

posternent = prosternent 14/224
posterma = postrema 24/ph
potent = poterit 24/356
potentes = ponentes 16/322
poteste = potestate 21/104
pre = prae 15/264
preas = aereas 17/192
precinge = precinget 15/144
preco = praeco 4/before 1, 6/273, 280, 373, 417
precucurrent = precucurrit 18/384
prejicitur = projicitur 7/255
presens = praesens IIB/7
primus = primum 10/344
primus = Petrus 14/152
principes = princeps 23/8
procuret = procurret 18/384
procull = procul 11/118
projecient = projicient 21/238
proistiat = projiciat 7/257
prophetica = prophetico 5/319
propungnavor, propugnabor = propugnator 20/104e
proreas = aereas 17/192
protamtem, protantem = portantem 15/36
psal = psalmo IB/360
psalmus = psallemus 20/152
purie = pueri 14/208
purpurea = purpura 16/322, IIC/334

qua = quia 24/356
quadrige = quadrigae 22/48
quarum = quorum 18/185
quassaio = quassatio 5/435
quatuor = quattuor 4/ph, 22/48, 124
que = qui 16A/ph, 17/ph
  que = quae 21/104, 22/260
quere = aere 24/356
qui = quae 21/104
quidam = quidem 20/16
quint, quinto = quinta 5/ph
quorum = duorum 22/48

ragna, ragula = regna 23/120
rames = ramis 14/208
recedente = recedent 16/242
recitanda = recitando 22/260

LIST OF LATIN ERRORS

redebit = redibit IIB/624
rediet = redit 15/296
reges = regis 5/175
regnum = regum 8/ph, 9/ph
reputandum est = reputatum est 5/435
resondet = resonet 16/178
respitiens = respiciens 11/24
resondet = respondet 16/178
   responden, respondentem = respondens 20/104d
resurgens = resurgent 23/686
resureccionis = resurrectionis IIB/120
   resurpens, resurrexones = resurrectionis 23/120
resurrexint = resurrexit 18/185
reticenda = recitando 22/260
revertime, revertuns = revertunt 15/60
rex = regis 5/175

salvata = salvatus 24/40, 468
   salvatus = salvata 24/448
salvator = salvata 24/140
sanctum = sanctus 21/158
sanguiene = sanguinem 24/428
sapiencia = sapientia 1/12
sar = terra 7/410
scedens = sedens 5/183
sciathum, sciatuum = cyathum 9/135
scoko = sancto 21/96
scribenes = scribens 12/240
scripsionem = scriptionem 12/252
scunc = sunt 23/3
secptimo = setimo 22/124
secptrum = sceptrum 8/268
secpulcris = sepulchris 24/40
secrecto = secreto 6/539
seculis = seculi 24/580
secundus = secundum 10/376, 17/48
   2us = secundus 7/263
sedabat = sedebat 14/40
   sedences = sedens 5/183
selsis = excelsis 7/371
seperabunt = separabunt 24/580
septrum = sceptrum 8/268
sepu = sexu 6/539
sepulchis, sepulcor = sepulchris 24/40
   sepulcroum = sepulchrum 13/332

sepulcrum = sepulchrum 13/332, 18/344
sepultro = sepulchro 13/441
sequitur, sequentur, sequntur = sequuntur 24/508
sequitor = sequitur 13/before 1
servam = servum 11/166
sessetatum = necessitatem 5/131
sexagessimo = sexagesimo 8/317
sexagesino sexto = sexagesimo sexto 19/95
sexage, sexagemio = sexagesimo 19/95
sextu = sexto 22/48
sextuagessimo primo = septuagesimo primo 8/338
sic = sit 21/32
simull = simul 16/50
sir = terra 7/410
sites = sitis 23/4, IIB/4
som = sum 13/356
sortiati = sortiantur 16A/88
specium, speciun = speciei 1/ph
sperabunt = separabunt 24/580
spetie = specie 21/238
spina = spinea 24/356
   spinam = spineam 16/326
spinx = sphinx 2/208
spiritum = spiritum IIB/196
stalla = stella 8/64
stan = stans 20/96
   stand = stando 14/136
statine = statim 13/284
statuit = statuet 12/112
stella = stellam 8/212
stellum = stella 7/299
stettet = stetit 5/435
submisse = submissa 7/60
sugent = surgent IIB/702
sua, sue = suae 20/104d
   suae = sua 21/104
   suat = suis 15/88
   suom = suam 13/21
sum = suum 23/164
sunc = sunt 23/3
   sunt = sum 13/356
sumum = summum IB/360
supra = spiritu 21/96

supram = spiritum 23/196
surgit = surgunt 8/97
   surgente = surgent 24/40
   surget, surgete = surgite 5/131

tabulum = tabulam 16A/216
tar, tarre = terra 7/412
   tarram = terram 13/66
tempore = tempora 22/164
tercium = trium 9/ph
terra = terram 5/215
   terra = terrae 21/310
   terre = terrae 21/112, 310
   terre = terra 7/412
3us = tertius 7/278
testacem = testaceum 15/36
tetigent = tetigerit 15/342
tioanica = tirannica 10/ph
torcalas, torculor = torcular 20/104g
   torquilarie = torculari 20/104f
torma = forma 2/208
transient, transiunt = transeunt IIB/172, 192
   transunt = transeunt 23/141
tranfodient = transfodiet 10/376
   trasfodiet = transfodiet 10/344
transformiari, tranfornam = transformari 5/223
trenits = trinitas 1/213
tribulacone = tribulacione IB/344
trin = trium 8/ph
trono = throno IIB/1
tumulu, tunando = tumulo 23/149
tunc = cum 8/289

uncio = unctio 8/289
undcimo = undecimo 22/172

vadint = vadunt 7/459
vece = voce 7/60
velnare = vulnera 19/249
vementes = viventes 23/3

venet = venit *or* veniet 5/215
   venient = veniet 19/167
   veniente = venient IIC/before 1
   veniet = venient 12/216, 13/425
   venint = venient 12/216, IC/76
   venit = venient 21/366, 23/252, 24/172
ventras est = venturus est 24/564
ventrus est = venturus est 21/334, 24/564
veritatibus = veritas 13/35
vestre, vestri = vestro 23/196, IIB/196
   vestrum = vestram 23/24
vestemente = vestimenta 14/208
vestibis = vestibus 16A/88
   vest = veste 16/210
   vestum = veste 16/202
viccionis = unctionis 14/56
vicessima tertia = vicesima tertia 23/ph
vicessima quarta = vicesima quarta 24/ph
vicessima secunda = vicesima secunda 22/ph
vicesimo tertio = vicesima tertia 23/ph
vicessima tertia = vicesima tertia 23/ph
victes = vectes 17/192
videntes = vedentes 14/260
   videntibus = vendentibus 14/224
videtes = videtis 20/16
   videt = vidit 5/215
viragoo = virago 2/150
virtute = viurtutes 20/152VR
vissicima = vicesima 21/ph
vita = vitam 3/246
vite = vitae 13/before 1
vivas = vivos 21/334
viz. = videlicet 21/ph
vocami = vocavi 10/497
vose = vos 23/4
vuanesset = vanescet 11/40

THE ENGLISH GLOSSARY

This Glossary covers the Text (including Stage Directions), the Variant Readings, and the Appendices in Volume I. It is not a complete index of words. For the most part, words are included which (a) have not survived in Modern English — e.g., **buske** prepare, make ready 12/242; (b) have survived but with altered meanings — e.g., **devise** distribute 23/208; or (c) have spellings not easily comprehended now — e.g., **faynest** feign 13/142.

Some inclusions and exclusions, however, are not governed by the three categories listed above. First, a word may belong in one of those three categories and still not be included because its context makes its meaning easily clear. For example, *fellowshippe* 16/38 has survived with altered meanings such as "companionship" and "a stipend for study"; but the older meaning, "company of people" — now more-or-less lost — is quite clear in the context of Pilate's speech. Second, not included are the portions of words, recorded in the Variant Readings, which remain after the damage to MS A — e.g., *thin* 2/38 left from *within*; see pages xv-xvi and xxxviii of Volume I. Third, idiomatic phrases which, as phrases, carry difficult meanings are included, with the key-word in the phrase as head-word in the entry — e.g., **devylles** n. *twentye* ~ *waye* an expression of impatience 3/219; but when a phrase is clarified by defining a single word, that word rather than the whole phrase is entered — e.g., *male intent* 16/213 is clarified by **male** "antagonistic, evil."

Many of the words recorded in the Glossary occur more than once in the material covered. In such cases we have usually recorded the two earliest occurrences which came to our attention from the sequence Text (including Stage Directions), Variant Readings, and Appendices. Additional occurrences are included for two reasons: (1) to illustrate variant spellings — e.g., **gon, gonc, gonne** 3/202, 22/210, IIB/640; and (2) to give a reasonably comprehensive coverage for words which may be particularly misleading — e.g., **the** for **they, to** for **two**. Where an entry for a word includes more than one form — as with **gon** — a single reference for each form is given. Markedly differing variant spellings of words are listed separately with appropriate references — e.g., **weale, wealth** *n.*²; see **wayle**.

Within an entry the variant spellings are presented in alphabetical order. The line-references are given in the sequence mentioned in the preceding paragraph. The system for citing references is as follows:

1. For the spoken lines of the Text, and for their Variant Readings, citation is by play (in Arabic) and line number; e.g., 2/607. 16A/474. Note that the same numerical citation can occur for a word in the Text and a word in the Variant Readings; e.g., **against** 3/80, and **agayne** 3/80 — the latter occurs in the Text, while the former is the ARBH reading in the Variants.

2. For the relatively few words glossed from the Stage Directions, citations are by play, immediately preceding line in the Text, and +*SD*. Thus, **borde** ... 3/260+SD.

3. For words glossed from those passages in the Variant Readings which have no counterpart in the Text, citations are by play, immediately preceding line in the Text, and a superscript *v*. Thus, **apayd** *adj.* 16A/256^v.

4. For words glossed from the Appendices, citations are by Appendix number (Roman) and letter (capital), and line number. Thus, **afright** *adj.* IC/118.

5. In a few instances a word in a given line has a different meaning in one or more of the Chester manuscripts from its meaning in the other manuscripts; in such cases the pertinent manuscript-symbols are included in parentheses after the play and line number. Thus **fyle** *inf.* defile, defame 6/155 (AB), 16/81; place on record 6/155 (HmRH).

A

a *prep.* at 10/470; ~ = **and** 4/61.
above *n. at myne* ~ at my highest point 14/132.
abyde *inf.* submit to 24/282. *OED* abide v. 15.
abye *inf.* pay for, purchase 2/607; pay the penalty 5/223, 13/255.
accompt *n.* account, record 24/35, 199.

accorde *n.* determination 23/100. *OED* accord sb. 5. b.
advoultrye, advowtrye *n.* adultery 12/220, 293.
advyse *inf.* bethink 2/592.
affray, affraye *n.* violence, conflict 19/58, IC/36.
affraye *adj.* afraid 4/349.
affraye, affray, afraye *inf.* disturb with hostilities 5/341, 17/191, IB/343. *OED* affray v. 1. b.

GLOSSARY

affyne, afyne *adv.* completely 18/261, 24/505. *OED* afine adv.
after *prep.* according to 2/232, 322.
afye *inf.* trust, have faith 14/422.
againe, agayn, agayne *prep.* contrary to 10/23, IB/22, IIB/546.
againste, agayne *conj.* before (*temporal*) 3/80. *OED* against VI. B.
agased *pp.* aghast, frightened 18/32. *MED* agasten v. 2.
agayne = **gaine** 6/37.
agaynst *prep.* in preparation for 8/421; **agaynste** toward 4/58; **agayst** = **agaynst** in opposition to 12/263, 24/272.
agrie = **agryse** *inf.* 18/32.
agryse *inf.* shudder with terror 18/32, IIA/25.
aleiche *adv.* alike 7/105.
algates *adv.* nevertheless 8/368.
alledge *inf.* lighten, alleviate 24/288. *OED* allege v.¹
alloes, aloes *n.* fragrant raisins 16A/474, IC/127.
alls, als *adv.* also 16/77, IIB/256.
alowe *adv.* below 7/629
amisse *adj. nothing* ~ without any error IB/338.
amogst, amonghte = **amongest** 24/105.
amonge *adv. have* ~ take part 7/369.
amounte, amounted = **anoynted** 3/75.
amys *n.* deficiency, error 23/456, IIB/456.
amys = **mis** 17/160.
an *conj.* and 9/100, 24/318.
an *prep.* on 7/539, 21/88.
an = **am** 11/105.
and *conj.* if 1/93, 200.
and = **an** 2/596, 5/427, 6/145, 7/76, 539.
and = **as** 5/118.
anker *n.* hermitage 7/667.
annoynte, anoynted *pp.* covered 3/75.
anon, anonne *adv.* immediately 2/73, 4/59; ~ *in hye* in great haste 5/105, 13/369.

anonneright, anonright *adv.* immediately 4/443, 22/220.
anoye, any, anye *n.* harm 2/297, 4/294; distress 2/315, IB/345; dangerous situation 13/370; **anyes** annoyances IIB/272.
any *inf.* annoy IB/109, IIB/475.
anyse = **mis** 17/160.
apartelie, appartlye, appertly *adv.* clearly 4/114, 12/178, 24/685.
apayd, apayde *adj.* contented, satisfied 16A/256ᵛ, 18/353.
apent, appent *inf.* pertain 7/342, 24/359; **appent** *pa. 3 sg.* 6/261. *OED* apent.
appaier *inf.* destroy 1/92; **appayre, appeare** deteriorate 4/155.
appere = **a peer** an equal 16/299.
appreven, approven *pr. pl.* 14/197.
araye *n.*¹ conduct, manner 1/205, 214.
araye *n.*² *of stowte* ~ with large retinues 6/455.
are *conj.* ere, before 18/253.
arere *inf.* stir up, incite 21/161.
arere *adv.* in the background 21/161 (H). *OED* arrear adv. 2.
aright *adv.* correctly IB/47.
arrand *n.* errand, commission 6/289.
arrow = **harrowe** *pr. 3 pl.* 24/280.
as = **has** IIB/176 (2).
ascill = **aysell** 17/131.
aspies, aspyes *imp. 2 pl.* obverse 14/412.
aspine, asspyne *pr. 2 pl.* set a snare 23/359, IIB/359. *MED* aspien v. 2. b.
assaye *inf.* test 2/188; attempt 4/251.
assent *n.* intention 24/60. *MED* assent n. 3. b.
assent *adj. wee be* ~ we are agreed 6/301.
assente *n.* agreement 1/91, 286; *at your* ~ agreeable to you 23/58, IIB/58.
assente *inf.* agree 1/134, 198.
assention = **ession** 1/8.
assyce *n.* assize, judicial body 24/345.
astart *inf.* go away 7/429.
astate *n.* estate, rank, degree IIB/660.
at *prep.* from 2/495, 4/79; with 5/177,

422 THE CHESTER MYSTERY CYCLE

8/100.
atamed *pp.* pierced 7/136. *OED* attame.
attaynt, attaynte *adj.* tainted, corrupted 7/285, IIB/485.
atyte *adv.* at once 3/236.
auncetrye *n.* lineage 16/254.
avaunte *inf.* advance IIB/213.
avowe *n.* protestation, promise 2/283, 5/240.
awayved *pa. t. 3 pl.* avoided 24/407.
awe *n.* terror 24/294.
axe *imp. 2 sg.* ask 7/259.
ayde = **age** 6/393.
ayer *n.* air 7/344.
ayere *adv.* ever 4/445.
aysell *n.* eisell, vinegar 17/131.

B

bab *n.* baby 6/350.
babelavaunt, babelavaunte, babliant *n.* braggart 16/22, IIC/26.
bacheler, bachler, batchelere, batchellere, batchlere *n.* knight 5/164, 6/190, 23/646, IB/117, 133.
bacon *pp.* baked 7/113.
bale *n.* damnation, torment 6/409, 24/113; **bales, balleus** 24/129.
bale, ball, balle = **ballye** 16A/62.
ballamy = **belamye** 8/123.
balleus see **bale**.
ballye *n.* belly, womb 16A/62.
balme *inf.* anoint 9/86, 16A/476.
balmer *n.* coloured cloth 10/2. *OED* balmer.²
bames = **beames** *n.²* 24/46.
ban *inf.* summons, command 7/95.
band *n.* bondage 9/170, 18/177.
bande *n.* bondsman 24/306.
barme *n.* bosom 22/175.
barme-teame, barme-teane, barne-teame, barne-teane *n.* progeny 16A/59, 102. *OED* barm-team.
baron, baronne, barne *n.* child 6/648, 7/569. *MED* barn n.

barro = **borrowe** 10/194.
basenetes, bassnetts *n.* helmets 10/319.
baste = **blaste** 3/91.
baunner = **blaunner** *n.* ermine 10/2.
baylie *n.* bailiwick, dwelling-place 2/203.
baynable *adj.* obedient 6/314.
bayne, beane, beyne *adj.* obedient 3/145, 4/239, 479.
be *prep.* by 16A/201.
beames *n.¹* rays of light, radiance 1/13, 116.
beames *n.²* trumpets 1/249, 24/33; trumpets' 24/46.
beanes = **beames** *n.²* 1/249, 24/33, 46.
beare see **beere** *n.¹*.
beare *n.* bier 13/408.
beare *pr. 1 sg.* give 16/333; ~ *the price* are most esteemed 1/146; *them* ~ *pa. t.* conducted themselves 24/401.
beast *n.* creature 6/25. *OED* beste n. 1. (a).
beawtitude *n.* beatitude, blessedness 1/13.
bed, bede *pr. 1 sg.* offer 16/333, IIC/345.
bede, beede *imp.* speak 16A/225; **beede** *pa. t. 3 sg.* bade 21/362.
bedell, bedill *n.* beadle, herald 6/250, 36.
beeme = **been** 24/438.
beere, bere *n.¹* tumult 6/391, 10/43.
beere, bere *n.²* boast IIC/63, 16/59.
befall *inf.* belong 23/215.
befalles *pr. 3 sg.* takes place 24/202; **befall** *pp.* 1/147, 2/673.
begylus *pr. 2 sg.* beguiles IIB/372.
beheat, beheete, beheigh, beheight, beheit, behett, behette, behighte, behite, behitte *pr. 1 sg.* promise 2/309, 3/282, 305, 324, 10/481, 15/146; **behetes** *pr. 3 sg.* 4/201; **beheight** *pa. t. 1 sg.* 24/9, 650; ~ **behett, behitte** *pa. t. 3 sg.* 4/201, 5/204; **beheight** *pa. t. 3 pl.* 6/174, 10/17; ~ **behight, behyght** *pp.* 2/412, 23/399, IIB/14.

GLOSSARY 423

beinge *vbl. n. full vertuous of* ~ possessed of great talent 8/315.
behoves *pr. 3 sg.* is suitable for 2/122.
beker *inf.* bicker, quarrel 16A/2.
belamye, bellanye *n. bel ami*, good friend 8/123.
beleave = **by leave** (?); ~ *on (of) thee* by your leave 16/209.
belyve *adv.* quickly 10/138, 12/244.
bemased *adj.* bewildered 18/264.
bende *n.* bondage IIB/30.
benesoun, benisonn *n.* blessing 9/150, 15/261.
benne *inf.* be 24/170; **bee** *pp.* 11/3; **bese** *imp.* IIB/9, 333.
bent *pp.* engaged 24/590. *OED* bent ppl. a. 3.
beode *pa. t. 3 sg.* bade 5/92.
bere 10/43, 21/241; see **beere** *n.*[1]
bere 16/59; see **beere** *n.*[2]
bereave *inf.* rob 10/63.
beshitt *pr. 3 sg.* defecate upon 16/98.
beshrewe *pr. 1 sg.* curse 23/421.
best = **hest** 2/482.
betake *pr. 1 sg.* consign, bestow 2/158, 7/284; **betooke** *pa. t. 3 sg.* 17/269, 21/308; **betaken, betakene** *pp.* 6/102, 9/208.
betaught *pa. t. 3 sg.* granted 17/269.
bethought *pp.* decided 5/109.
betokeneth, betokens *pr. 3 sg.* signifies 4/194, IA/22.
bett *n.* better 10/90.
better = **bitter** 19/94 (HmARB).
betyde *inf.* occur 23/324; *pp.* 6/541.
betyme *adv.* soon 3/223, 18/52.
bewrayeth *pr. 3 sg.* reveals 16/389, IIC/403.
beyne see **bayne.**
bibbe, bibble *inf.* drink 7/145.
biglie *adj.* comfortable 1/38. *MED* bigli adj.
biglye *adv.* powerfully 22/61.
bill *inf.* blow 7/155. *MED* bilen v. (1) b.
bine ? 7/156.
bisse *n.* fine fur IB/62.
blab *adj.* swollen 10/197.
blackes, blakes, blak is = **blasses.**

blamner = **blaunner** *n.* ermine 10/2.
blasses *pr. 3 sg.* blazes 7/301.
blaste *n.* strong wind 3/91.
blee *n.* countenance 24/286.
blend *pa. t. 1 sg.* blended 17/295.
blene see **bline.**
blenquyshe *inf.* invalidate (?) 12/296. Not in *OED* or *MED*; a miscopying of **venquyshe**?
blent, blente *pp.* blinded 17/182, 24/357.
blesse *n.* bliss 1/38, 277.
bletinge *pr. p.* bleating 7/403.
bline, blinne, blyn, blynne, blene *inf.* stop 2/103, 173, 6/256, 23/37, IIB/37; **blynne** *pr. 1 sg.* 16A/122; **blyn** *pr. 1 pl.* 16A/88; **blyn, blynne** *pr. 2 pl.* 5/40, IB/40.
bloe *adj.* blue 10/446.
bloe *pr. 1 sg.* heat 10/439. *OED* blow v. 16.
bloting = **bleting** 7/403.
blotles *adj.* pure 12/31.
boade *inf.* proclaim 10/370; **bode** *pr. subj. 2 sg.* 10/315. *OED* bode v.[1] 1.
bode see **byde** *inf.*[2]
bodely, bodelye *adj.* bodily, physical 9/94, 102.
bodely, bodelye *adv.* physically, in human form 5/85, 17/230.
boisters *n.* boaster's 6/391.
bolde, bould, bowld *adj. be thow* (ye, you) ~ be certain 6/133, 8/245, 23/41, 24/487, IIB/41.
bolster = **bloster** *n.* blusterer 17/111. *MED* blusteren.
bond *n.* bondage 5/324, 18/177.
bonde *n.* bondsman 24/306.
bonde *adj.* bound 2/639.
bonere *adj.* debonaire, agreeable 4/454.
bonne *n.*[1] bone 2/146, 8/99; *by my* ~ by my head (?) 8/99.
bonne *n.*[2] bane, punishment 2/422.
boone *n.* favour, prayer 2/651, 5/75.
boone *adj.* ready, prepared 21/253.
boonte = **boote** *n.* 5/115.
booringe, boweringe *n.* a hole made by boring 16A/183.

boote *n.* help, benefit 5/115, 328; *to* ~ in addition 10/356.
boote, boots *pr. 3 sg.* helps 16A/2.
booteles, bootelesse, bootles *adj.* useless, needless 10/420, 24/181, IB/95.
bord = **lord** 1/101, 19/15.
borde *n.* wooden board 3/76; *within the bordes* inside the Ark 3/260+SD; **boord** the floor 16A/88.
bore *n.* ? 7/274; see Explanatory Note.
bore *pp.* born 3/286, 6/202.
borne *inf.* burn 24/355; **borned** *pa. t. 3 sg.* 7/403.
borne *pp.* carried away, drowned 3/263.
borrowe *n.* borough, city 10/194.
borsen = **brosen** *pp.* broken 21/29. OED burst v.
bosiart *n.* buzzard 7/276.
boste *n.* boast 17/98, 21/93.
bosters *n.* braggart's 6/391.
bostes = **bosters** 6/391.
bote *n.*[1] shoe 10/355.
bote *n.*[2] help, benefit IIB/312.
boteles *adj.* useless 5/102.
bought see **buy**.
bound *n.* bondsman 24/306.
bounde, boune *adj.* ready, determined 3/264, 6/273.
boune *imp.* prepare 7/454.
bourdinge *vbl. n.* boasting 11/239.
bout, boute, bowt, bowte, bowten *prep.* 3/75 (see Explanatory Note); without 3/63, 122, 12/76, 16A/199, IIB/507.
bovearte *n.* bullock 7/276.
bow = **bowne** *adj.* 6/273.
bowe *n.* rainbow 3/309, 318.
boweringe see **booringe**.
bowespreete *n.* a large spar 3/93.
bowndly *adv.* readily IB/256. MED boundli.
bowne *adj.* ready, prepared 2/484, 522.
bowt, bowte, bowten *prep.* without 3/63, 122, 16A/199.
boye *n.* servant 8/202.
boyne *imp.* prepare 7/454.
boyst *n.* box 14/69, 18/332.

boyster *n.* boaster 17/111.
brande *n.* torch 23/682.
braste *v.* burst 1/278.
brayde *n.* moment IIB/140, 23/140. OED braid sb.
bread *n. as eate I* ~ , *as ever eate I* ~ , *as ever break I* ~ an expression of certainty 9/73, 21/370, IC/90.
breade *n.* breadth 3/26, 30.
breadeth *pr. 3 sg.* broadens 3/226.
breanes *n.* brains 16/88.
brears *n.* briars 2/331.
breath *n. such a* ~ such an outcry 15/313.
brenne = **breme** *adj.* fierce 24/588.
bren, brenne *inf.* burn 2/538, IIB/686; **brennys** *pr. 3 sg.* 5/129; **brent** *pp.,.* 24/129.
brent *adj.* lofty 10/446. OED brant a.
brewe *inf.* bring about 6/513. MED breuen v. 2.
breynes *n.* brains IIC/92.
brod = **borde** 3/76.
brok, broke, brooke *v. as* ~ *I my head, as* ~ *I my panne, as* ~ *I my crowne* expression of certainty 2/205, 16A/433, 24/582, IB/167.
brond, bronde *n.* brand, sword, torch 8/336, IIB/686.
brune = **breme** 24/588.
bryde *n.* bird 2/194.
bryncke *n.* side 4/288.
buffetes, buffittes *imp.* buffet, beat 16/59, IIC/63.
bundell *n.* collection 4/236+SD.
burges *n.* burgess, freeman of the city 24/306.
burne *n.* burden 4/236+SD. OED burn sb.[2]
bursten *pp.* broken 21/29.
buske *n.* bush 7/498; **buskes** 7/2.
buske *inf.* prepare, make ready 12/242; **buskes** *pr. 3 sg.* 10/271; **buske** *pr. 1 pl.* 21/44; **buskes** *imp.* 10/193, 360.
but *conj.* unless 2/235, 3/206.
but *prep.* except 3/7; without 9/43, 11/13, 16/74; ~ **a were** without a doubt 16/74.

GLOSSARY 425

buxon, buxone *adj*. obedient, submissive 2/589, 24/116.
buy, by, bye *inf*. redeem, pay for 2/400, 4/205; **bye** *pr. 1 sg*. buy 24/211; **bought** *pa. t. 3 sg*. 24/271; *pp*. 18/156, 16A/240.
by and by(e) always 13/216, 274 [*MED* bi and bi (b)]; one by one 21/244 [*MED* bi and bi (c)]; side by side IC/57 [*MED* bi and bi (a)].
bybbe, bybbey *n*. "some kind of herb" (*OED*) 7/22.
bydd, byde *pa. t. 3 sg*. bade 5/92.
byde *inf.*[1] bid, offer 1/82, 10/370.
byde *inf.*[2] abide 1/80; suffer 16A/256, 24/264; **bode** *pa. t*. 18/108.
byde see **beede** *imp*. 16A/225.
bydeene *adv*. quickly, certainly 3/132, 21/108; *all* ~ immediately 4/15, 24/226.
bye = be 2/630.
bye see **buy** .
bylyve *adv*. quickly 3/120.
byse *n*. fine cloth 5/93, 10/2.
byte, bytt, bytte *inf*. cut, bite 3/58, 16/99.
bytlockes *n*. "bits of food" (*MED*) 7/152.
byttoer *n*. bittern, heron 3/182.

C

calde *pa. t. 3 pl*. became chilled IIA/25.
calketh = **talketh** 13/232.
call, coule, cowle *n*. cabbage 3/172.
calvern *n*. calves 3/163.
cambroke, camrocke = **cammock** *n*. stick 10/438.
can *pr. 1 sg*. know 2/261; *pr. 2 sg*. 5/374; *pr. 3 pl*. 18/63; ~ *good* can do well 18/63; **cane** *no good* plans evil action IIC/192.
can, cann, coon *auxiliary* did 2/159, 4/29, 76, 5/426, 8/216, 14/307, 22/94, 139.
canker *inf*. sicken, become cancerous 1/240.
carchaffe *n*. kerchief 4/386, 4/398 + SD.
care *n*. sorrow 1/240, 24/222.
carpe *imp*. complain, cry out 16/87.
carren, carrine, carryen, carryn *n*. carrion 3/290.
carsell = **coysell** 6/218.
caste *inf*. create, devise 1/40; **cast** *pr. 1 pl*. determine 14/314; *pr. subj. 1 pl*. 9/34; *imp*. 1/70; **casten** *pa. t. 3 pl*. planned 12/289; **caste** *pp*. 21/337.
castinge *pr. p*. diluting 17/314. *OED* cast v. 24.
catch *inf*. take, receive 7/283; *pr. subj. 1. pl*. 14/323; **caught** *pp*. received 5/199.
cator-traye *n*. the number 4 on each of three dice 16A/133.
cavlfe = **calfe** 3/163
caytiffe, caytyffe *n*. coward, wretch 2/177, 13/205; **caytiffes** 5/141.
cease *imp*. put to an end 16A/256[v]; *pr. 3 sg*. ends 24/207.
censore = **coursere** 8/41.
certayne *n*. truth 11/285.
certyfie *inf*. assure 8/252; **certefye** *pr. 2 sg*. 8/55; **certefies** *pr. 3 sg*. IB/403.
chaffer, chaffere *n*. trade, merchandizing 14/362.
chance *n*. sequences of events 24/216, 281; *as have I good* ~ as I hope for good luck 12/264.
chandelours *n*. candlesticks 22/189.
chare *in* ~ = **encharre** 18/133.
charettes *n*. chariots, carts 22/52, 67.
charge *n*. instructions 18/123.
charge *in* ~ = **encharre** 18/130.
charged *pp*. instructed 18/130.
charre *n*. turn 18/108. *OED* char sb.[1]
charschaffe = **carchaffe** 4/389 + SD.
chayre, cheare, cheere *n*. chair, throne 1/88, 156.
cheare, chere *n*. attitude, manner 1/220, 4/259; *with (full, right) good chere* happily 4/243; *heavye* ~ sad appearance 4/258.
cheeffe = **cheesse** *adj*. selective

7/179.
cheiste, chest, chiste *n*. ship, Noah's Ark 3/206.
chide, chyde *inf*. debate 23/281, 433.
childer *n*. children 2/433, 3/238.
chiristan = **christen** 24/521.
chitterling *n*. small intestine 7/124^v.
chosen *pp*. allotted 21/156.
chosen = **closen** 24/183.
choyse, chyce, chysse *adj*. selective 2/401, 7/179.
christen, christien *adj*. christened 24/521.
chyffe = **chysse** 2/401.
clam *inf*. smear 3/74. *MED* clammen.
clayve *pa. t. 3 sg*. split 16A/467.
clean, cleane *adj*. pure, undamaged 1/76, 11/27; **clene** complete IIB/672.
cleane *adv*. completely 2/397, 6/237.
cleane = **clam** 3/74.
cleanes *n*. cleanness, purity 24/370.
cleare *adj*. unsullied, chaste 1/76, 11/27.
cleare *adv*. clearly 1/218, 6/237.
cleargie *n*. knowledge of theology 11/242.
cleargye *n*. the clergy 24/183.
cleev, cleeve *inf*.¹ divide, split IC/120, IIA/20; **cleft, clyft** *pp*. 16A/466, IC/119.
cleeve *inf*.² adhere, cling 13/66. *OED* cleave v.² B. 4.
clene see **clean**.
clight *pp*. clutched, held made fast 6/653, 24/258.
clisse = **coelis** (?) 23/451.
clo, cloe, clowe *inf*. claw, scrape 10/438.
clongen *pp*. enclosed 18/320, 430.
closen *pp*. enclosed 24/183.
clough = **clought** 18/430.
clought *pp*. held fast 18/430.
clowt *n*. tripe 7/282.
clowte *n*.¹ 7/52; **clowetes** rags 10/292; **clowtes** baby-clothes 10/209.
clowte *n*.² a heavy blow 7/88.
clowte *inf*. beat 10/438.
clyft see **cleev** *inf*.¹

clylde = **child** 8/348.
clyst = **clyft** 16A/466.
coale, colle *n*. cabbage 3/172.
coarse, corse *n*. corpse 18/73.
cockes *n*. God's; *by* ~ *sowle* a blasphemous expression for emphasis 8/350, 398; *for* ~ *bones* 13/258; *for* ~ *soule* 13/426; *for* ~ *face* 16A/149; *for* ~ *blood* 16/183, IIC/195.
cognisens *n*. identification 16A/220. *OED* cognizance I. 1. b.
cojure = **conger** 24/203.
colle see **coale**.
combe, combes *n*. vat(s), brewing tub(s) 17/314.
comberans, combers, cumberances *n*. troubles 12/147.
comberouse *adj*. distressing 2/445.
come *n*. arrival 14/220.
come = **came** 13/129.
comes *imp*. come IA/45; **commen, common** *pp*. 14/220, 23/295; **come** *of* stop 4/355.
comfort *pp*. comforted IA/17.
comforte *n*. consolation 1/133.
comforture *n*. comforter 1/123.
commen = **congeon** 10/145.
commen, commynne *pp*. become 23/335, 24/520.
commenlye *adj*. jointly 5/366.
commimge = **coming** 12/64.
comon *adj*. common 5/117.
companye n. *in* ~ together 23/302, IIB/302.
compasse *n*. bounded area, realm, scope 1/40. *MED* compas n. 3. b.
comyn rowland = **come in land** IIB/44.
conclude *inf*. put and end 18/299; **concluded** *pa. t. 3 sg*. restrained 17/70.
confounde = **con founde** did try IIB/27.
conge = **congeon** 8/328.
congeon, congion, conine, connion, conjoyne, conioyne, connyon *n*. scoundrel 2/601, 8/328, 10/145, 166, 196.

GLOSSARY 427

conger, congere *pr. 1 sg.* conjure, beseech 1/240, IIC/46.
coninge = **congeon** 8/328.
connynge *adv.* skilfully 21/238.
conseyle *inf.* conceal 21/104; ~ *imp.* 20/57.
conspier, conspyrne *pr. 3 pl.* plot 14/298.
contyse *n.* cunning, guile 2/198, 12/148.
convertes *imp.* convert 23/534, 587.
coon see **can** *auxiliary.*
cordes *pr. 3 sg.* accords, is fitting IB/312.
corne *n.* grain, wheat 2/517, 5/343; **cornes** 2/477.
corrptcion = **corruption** 12/18.
corsett *n.* a laced outer garment worn by both men and women 16A/113.
cossen *n.* cousin, kinswoman 6/45.
cothe *auxiliary* did IIB/33.
cough *n.* pseudo-tuberculosis 7/15.
cought = **cowth** 7/687.
coughte *pp.* secured IB/152.
couintise, countise, countyse *n.* cunning, guile 2/405, 6/364, 12/14.
could *n.* cold 2/504, 24/489.
could *inf.* chill 8/247.
coule see **call.**
counger = **conger** 24/203.
counsaile *imp.* conceal 8/59.
course, curse *inf.* drive with blows 13/168, 228. *OED* course v. 3.
coursere *n.* horse 8/41.
covenante *n.* promise, bargain 1/108.
cover *inf.* recover, redeem 7/471.
covetice, covetise *n.* covetousness 2/405, 12/14.
covettes *imp.* covet IB/17.
cowle see **call.**
cowth *adj.* known *frend and* ~ friend and acquaintance 7/687.
coynt, coynte *adj.* subtle, strange 2/225, 19/18.
coyntly *adv.* subtly 6/620.
coyse *adj.* solicitous 2/401.
coysell *n.* emperor 6/218; *MED* coisel.
cozin *n.* cousin, kinswoman 6/45.

crabbed *adj.* unpleasant 3/105.
crafte *n.* skill 1/70; power 2/8; craftiness 12/148.
crambocke = **cambroke** 10/438.
crape, crapp, crop, croppe *n.*[1] top of a tree [*MED* crop 2 (a)]; ~ *and roote* everything, the entirety 5/330, 18/236, IB/435.
crape, crapp, cropp *n.*[2] a valuable thing 7/427. *MED* crop 4 (b).
cratch *n.* crib in a stable 6/523, 7/491.
creake, creke *pr. 3 sg.* cry out 16/91, IIC/95; **creake, creeke** *imp.* 16/87, IIC/91. *OED* creak v. I. 3.
crocked *adj.* crooked 10/438.
cromes *n.* crumbs, bits to eat 7/639.
crowne *n.* head *by my* ~ 2/603, 3/54.
crowse *adj.* lively 3/178. *OED* crouse 3.
croyse *n.* the Cross IIA/16.
cryn, cryne *pr. 2 pl.* cry out 23/357, IIB/357; **cryden** *pa. t. 3 pl.* vigorously called IIA/14; **crye** *imp.* reveal, make known 16/96, IIC/100.
cubitts *n.* units of measure, about 18 inches 3/25.
cumber *pr. 1 sg.* am overwhelmed 1/240. *OED* cumber v. l. b.
cuninge, cunnynge *n.* skill, knowledge 1/70, 21/221.
cunynge *adv.* skilfully 24/183.
curiouse *adj.* strange, quaint 7/386.
curiously *adv.* unusually 8/420.
cure *n.* care, improvement 5/344, 361.
curs, curse *imp.* excommunicate 23/434, IIB/434.
curse see **course.**
curteise *n.* courtly behaviour 2/198.
curye *n.* parts of an animal thrown to the hounds 7/282. *OED* curry sb.[3].
cuse *n.* excuse 16/143.

D

dafte = **defte** 7/397.
dale *n.* valley 10/51.
dam *n.* mother 2/678, 681; **damys**

mother's 7/68.
dame-kenny, ~ **-kenye,** ~ **-keynn,** ~ **-kin,** ~ **-kynne** *n.* wife (with diminutive suffix) 7/90. *MED* -kin suf.
dangeire, danger, dangere, daungere *n.* domination, control 6/191, 17/92, 19/226, IIC/15; **dangere** opposition 4/71, 16/15.
dare *inf.* frighten 5/286; lie in fear 22/296; do harm 24/218.
dare *pr. 3 sg.* needs 24/218.
dasse *inf.* remain inactive, rest 10/469. *OED* daze v. II. 4.
daster = **daystard** *n.* dastard, coward 10/298.
daunce *n.* course of action 1/209.
dayes, dese, deys *n.* dais, raised platform 6/239.
dayntee *n.* pleasure, enjoyment 2/415; fine quality 14/271.
dde = **Dee** 7/249.
deadem *n.* crown of the blessed 1/34.
deadly, deadlych *adj.* mortal 2/365, 12/27.
deale = **dole** *n.*¹ 2/664, 19/8, 24/236.
deale *n.* part, bit 8/22; *never a* ~ not at all 11/30, 17/82; everye ~ exactly IB/51.
deale *inf.*¹ control, manage, arrange 22/23.
deale *inf.*² provide, present 18/15, 23/24; *pr. 2 sg.* 23/695; **dealt** *pp.* 14/71.
deame see **deeme**.
deare *n.* terror 23/584.
deare, dere *inf.* discipline 2/320; frighten 5/286; challenge 12/5; overcome 7/527, 10/271.
deare *adj.* difficult 21/161. *OED* dear a.² 3.
deare, deere *adv.* expensively 2/607, 16A/240.
deareworth *adj.* beloved 14/34.
dede *n.* dead IIB/518.
dede *adj.* dead IIB/557, 630.
dee *inf.* die IIB/93; **deed** *pa. t. 1 sg.* 11/23.

deed = **dread** 4/167 (B).
deeme, deme, deame *inf.* judge 2/467, 20/132, IIB/704; *imp.* 16/246, 248, 362; *pr. 1 sg.* 7/103; **deemes** *pr. 2 sg.* 14/97; **deeme** *pr. 1 pl.* 10/124; **deemed** *pp.* 16/288.
deeminge *n.* judging 7/315.
deert = **dear heart** (?) 10/486.
defende *inf.* ward off, repel 22/183.
defte *adj.* skilful 7/397.
defyne *pr. 2 pl.* reject 23/361, IIB/361. *OED* defy v.¹ 5.
degree *n.* rank, state 1/194, 2/367; extent 4/289; common ancestry 21/189.
deighter *n.* one who commits treason 10/298. *MED* dighten v. 6.
dele *inf.* distribute IIB/24; *pr. 2 sg.* IIB/699.
delice *n.* delight 2/110.
delyte *n.* undisciplined pleasure 2/191.
deme *n.* judging 24/226, 607.
deme see **deeme**.
demy = **deny** 16/30.
dene (?) = **eyen** 1/179.
dente *n. by* ~ *of sword* by force of arms 5/125.
denyne *pr. 2 pl.* deny 23/362.
deole *n.* grief 19/8, 24/236.
deolful, deolfull *adj.* grievous, sorrowful 4/313, 16A/50.
deolfully *adv.* grievously 16A/267.
departe *inf.* divide 4/39; *pr. subj. 1. pl.* separate 3/229.
deprave *inf.* slander 7/119.
dere see **deare** *inf.*
dereworth *adj.* very worthy 18/368.
derne *inf.* discipline 2/320.
descent *n.* dissent, objection 13/176.
desever *pr. 1 pl.* part 7/357.
despice = **despitte** 16/101.ᵛ
despitte, despytt *inf.* object 16/101ᵛ, IIC/111.
desyringe *pr. p.* asking 5/402.
devise, devyse *inf.* distribute 23/208, IIB/208. *OED* devise 1.
devotly *adv.* devoutly IIB/110.
devour, devoure, devower *n.* service,

GLOSSARY 429

duty 1/44, 22/201.
devyce *n.* devising 10/6.
devyen, devyne *pr. 2 pl.* practise divination for 23/362, IIB/362.
devylles *n. in twentye ~ waye* an expression of impatience 3/219. *OED* devil sb. 19
deyntee *n.* pleasure 2/110.
deys *n.* dais, raised platform 6/239.
deyte *n.* godhead IIB/559.
digges *n.* ducks 3/189.
dight, dighte, dyght *inf.* prepare, arrange 3/79, 5/327, IIB/15; *pp.* 2/416, 18/330; **dight** *pr. subj. 2 sg.* place, assign 15/30; ~ , **dighte** *pp.* 6/220, 21/301.
dightinge *vbl. n.* preparing 7/219.
dignitye *n.* position, station IB/214.
dilfullye *adv.* woefully 14/217.
dinge *inf.* strike 10/200, 235.
dintes, dentes *n.* blows 10/204.
disabeard *n.* idiot, simpleton 16/16ᵛ; see **dosaberd**.
discent *n.* dissent, opposition 12/98
discreeve *inf.* reveal 6/141.
disease *n.* discomfort, trouble 5/369, 23/141.
disobedient *n.* person who disobeys 12/94.
disparcles, dispercles *pr. 3 sg.* disperses, scatters 6/94. *OED* disparkle v.¹ 1.
dispituouslye, dispytuusly *adv.* without pity 6/94, 591.
dissolved *pp.* distended, enlarged 1/34. *MED* dissolve 8.
distaffe *n.* rod for holding wool 10/303.
distance *n.* reserve 2/490, 24/27; ~ , **distaunce** discord 23/352, IID/352.
distresse *n.* pressure 16A/38. *OED* distress sb. I. 1. b.
distrye *inf.* destroy IIB/295; **distryes** *pr. 3 sg.* IIB/276.
diversorye *n.* lodging-place 6/521.
divident *n.* divider 2/19.
do, doe, done, donne *inf.* do 24/28, IB/39; put 15/334; cause 14/337, IB/198; experience 21/269; **dose** *imp.*

do 23/165, IIB/165; **does** *pr. 3 sg.* drives 7/487; **done** *pr. 1 pl.* do 4/130; **do, donne** *pr. 3 pl.* cause, do 16A/298, 300, 24/225; **dyd** *pa. t. 3 sg.* caused 24/184; **done, donne** *pp.* placed, caused 13/422, ID/5; **doe** *away* Stop! 4/351; *have* **donne** stop what you are doing 3/49.
doe see **do, doo**.
dole, dowle *n.*¹ grief 2/664, 7/248.
dole, doule *n.*² portion 23/240, IIB/699.
dolven *pp.* dug 2/495.
dombe, dome, dompe *adj.* dumb, speechless 16/180, 189.
dome *n.* judgment, trial 1/249, 12/240.
dome *inf.* judge 16/132, 23/700.
done see **do**.
done = **dome** *n.* 24/11.
donge *n.* dung, excrement 24/235.
donne see **do**.
donne *pp.* constantly assailed 18/98. *OED* dun v.³ 2.
donne = **dome** *n.* 16/124.
doo *n. a doted ~* a crazed female deer 16/189.
doole *n.* portion IIB/240.
doome *n.* judgment, trial 16/149, 23/662; **doomes** 24/226.
dosaberd, doscibeirde, dosebeirde, doseberd, dosyberde *n.* idiot, simpleton 12/5, 94, 16/16ᵛ, IIC/19.
dose see **do**.
dotardes *n.* fools 8/304.
doted *adj.* insane 5/298, 8/284.
doubt, doubte, dowbte *n.* fear 3/224, 18/31, IIA/24.
doubt *pr. 1 sg.* am uncertain 13/80; fear 21/284; **doubte** *imp.* be hesitant 1/44.
doule see **dole** *n.*²
dowle see **dole** *n.*¹
dowlefull *adj.* sorrowful 24/649.
downe *n.* upland 10/51.
downe *adv. to doe ~* to overcome IIC/162.
downe = **dome** *n.* 16/149; ~ = **donne** IIB/444.
draw *pp.* dragged 18/98; **drawes** =

draw 18/98. *OED* draw v. 4.
drawe *inf.* bring oneself 2/152, 14/307.
draweth = gnaweth 5/118.
dread, drede, dreede *n.* doubt 4/167, 11/260, IIB/511.
dread *inf.* fear 17/116; *pr. 1 sg.* doubt 20/22; *pa. t. 3 sg.* feared 17/106.
dream *inf.* sepculate 16A/101.
dree, dreigh, drey, drighte, drye *inf.* suffer, endure 10/385, 14/213.
dreight = dight 21/301.
dremes *n.* pleasures 7/592.
drent *pp.* drowned 7/249.
dresse *inf.* set in order 18/15; *pr. 1 sg.* present 7/588; drest *pp.* prepared 21/301.
drister *n. a nonce-word* 10/298.
drownes *n.* falls 7/264.
drowpe *pr. 1 sg.* languish 19/8, 24/236.
dryrie *n.* love 7/588. *MED* druerie.
dubletts *n.* the number 2 on each of three dice 16A/130.
duringe *pr. p.* enduring, continuing 22/164.
dwell *inf.* tarry ID/19.
dyd see do.
dynne *n.* noisy debate 16A/199.
dynte *n.* 5/125; *see* dente
dyscreeve *inf.* reveal wrong-doing 6/141.
dyssese *n.* disease, corruption IIB/141.

E

eame *n.* uncle 16A/103.
earles *adj.* ear-less, without kernels 2/541.
earst *adv.* formerly 17/8.
eck see eke.
edder *n.* serpent 2/193, 195; edders 20/88.
edifie, edifye *inf.* build 3/278, 14/255.
ee *n.* eyes IIB/404.
effuscion = effusioun *n.* blood-shed 5/413.
efte *adv.* again 2/611, 23/592.

egallye *adv.* equally 16A/94.
egermonde, egremounde *n.* the plant agrimony 7/22.
eke, eck *adv.* also 1/17, 2/46, 92.
elfe *n.* supernatural being 8/328.
else *adv.* also IIC/81.
elvish *adj.* supernatural 8/326.
enbuxone *adj.* disobedient 2/499.
encharre, encure = encharge *n.* injunction, commission 18/133. *OED* encharge.
enlesse = endless 2/3.
entent *n.* intention 11/263; will IB/67.
entent *adj.* intent, minded 16A/25.
entere *adv.* completely 11/121.
entreate *inf.* concern ourselves 15/67.
errande *n.* message 2/596, 12/108; commission (?) 18/240.
escaped *pp.* deprived 2/700.
eschewe, eshew *inf.* escape, avoid 14/420, 18/128.
espie, espye *inf.* observe 12/34, 14/299; espices = espies *imp. 2 pl.* 14/412.
ession *n.* divine essence 1/8. *MED* essencion.
esshes *n.* ashes 17/295.
este = efte 2/377.
esue = eschewe 18/128.
ever = kever *inf.*² (?) 11/103.
everychone, everye ichone *pro.* everyone 2/25.
every ones *adv.* constantly 4/378.
exalted *pp.* raised 17/312.
example *n.* symbol 4/465; parable, exemplum 14/77.
excelencie *n.* excellence 1/31.
excice, excise, excesse = excite 2/131.
excite, excyte *inf.* cause, arouse 2/131, 306.
excusation *n.* excuse 24/698.
excusse *inf.* investigate thoroughly 13/226. *OED* excuss v. 2.
exelente *adv.* excellently 1/71, 87.
experience *n.* condition, state 1/35, 195.
expresse *adj.* clear, evident 2/16, 81.
expresse *adv.* clearly 6/572, 16/277.

GLOSSARY

eye *adv.* aye, ever 6/88.
eyen, eyne *n.* eyes 1/179, 2/227.
eyer *adv.* ere, earlier 17/8.
eylde *pr. 1 sg.* give thanks 7/681; *pa. t. 3 sg.* yielded, gave up 16A/463.
eylden *pa. t. 3 pl.* = **elden** (?) grew old 17/34.
eyles *pr. 3 sg.* ails IB/233.
eyme-cheare see **yeane-chare**.
eyne = **kenne** 23/421.
eyver = **kever** *inf.*² (?) 11/103.

F

faast *inf.* wed, marry IIB/47. *OED* fast v.¹ d.
fable *n.* falsehood 7/455.
fable *inf.* tell a lie 3/72.
face *n.* presence 3/40, 6/188.
faggot *n.* bundle 4/236 + SD, 243, 257. *OED* faggot sb. 3.
faightest *pr. 3 sg.* fights 6/187.
fall *inf.* occur 22/264.
fall, falles, falleth *pr. 3 sg.* is fitting 4/94, 9/144, 23/218.
fallinge *n.* felling, destruction 11/178.
false = **salfe** 3/263.
falsed = **falshed** *n.* falsehood IIB/27.
fameland, famelande *adj.* faltering, stuttering 16/72, IIC/76. *MED* famelen.
fanne see **fonne** *n.*² 5/170.
fantasye *n.* false presentation 23/28, 526.
fanter *see* **fynter** 7/27.
fare *n.* behaviour 1/238, 11/266; noise, disturbance 14/229; *Frenyshe* - elaborately polite behaviour 3/100.
fare *inf.* travel 7/693; depart 11/308, 18/269; deal 22/35; behave 22/300; **far, fare** *pr. 2 pl.* 23/454, IIB/454; **fard, ferde** *pa. t. 3 sg.* 23/28, IIB/28, 597; **fare amysse** come to grief 8/383.
farr = **fire** *n.* 5/90.
farrely *adj.* strange, curious 11/266.
farse = **false** 10/439.

faste *pa. t. 1 sg.* 24/153; **fast** *pp.* fasted 12/55.
faye, fayth *n.* faith 4/430; *in good* ~ 4/81, 138; *in* ~ 1/158, 4/433, 24/6.
fayle, feale, feele, fell, felle *adj.* many 14/46, 17/83, 22/7, IB/31.
fayle *inf.* lack 22/307. *OED* fail v. 2. b.
fayne, feyne *adj.* happy, eager 2/691, 8/403.
fayne, feyne *adv.* eagerly 3/147, IIC/184.
fayne = **faye** 4/81.
faynest *pr. 2 sg.* feign 13/142.
faynt *adj.* weak 23/489.
fayretest = **faye yet eft** (?) 11/80.
fayture, feature, feayttir *n.* scoundrel I/238, 23/353, IIB/489; **fayteors, faytures** 23/349, IIB/349.
feale *n.* payment 7/48. *OED* feal sb. 3.
feale see **fayle** *adj.*
feard *pp.* embellished, glossed over 23/597. *OED* fard v. 2.
fearder *adj.* more frightened 18/197.
feare, feere, fere *n.* companion, spouse, mate 2/136, 151, 6/461; *in* ~ together 1/85, 2/90, 3/78.
feare, fere *adj.* fair, beautiful 2/254, IIB/217; just 5/454; **fearest** most beautiful 5/393.
feare *inf.* frighten 6/589, 13/300; **feared** *pa. t. 2 sg.* 5/243, IB/188; *pa. t. 3 pl.* 19/61.
fearely, fearly *adj.* wondrous, extraordinary 11/217, 24/296.
feast see **feiste**.
fee *n.* moveable property, reward 14/379, 16A/114.
feeble *adj.* inadequate 6/161.
feeblye *adv.* with weak will 6/142.
feelde, feele, fell *pa. t. 1 sg.* experienced 2/491. *OED* feel v. 9.
feele see **fayle** *adj.*
feeleste *pr. 2 sg.* lack 16A/248.
feere see **feare** *n.*
feerly *adj.* fierce, awe-inspiring 17/100.
feete, fitt, fitte *n.* awesome experience 7/196, 22/71. *OED* fit sb.² 2.
feight *inf.* make (?) 22/191. *MED* feten

v. 1.
feightes *n.* fights 10/47.
feiste *n.* a blow with the fist 16/97ᵛ. *OED* fist sb.¹ e.
fele *inf.* feel, become aware of 7/145, IIB/426; **feld** *pp.* 17/52.
fell *n.* skin, pelt 10/441, 22/8; *fleshe and ~ body* and skin, completely 23/192, 468.
fell *adj.* fierce 5/145, 158.
fell, felle see **fayle** *adj.*
ferd *adj.* afraid IC/5.
ferde see **fare** *inf.*
fere see **feare** *n., adj.*
fere = **freare** 16/72; ~ = feard 23/597.
fervent, fervente *adj.* ardent, eager 1/89, 24/333; vigorous 24/578; searing 24/418.
feshe = **fresh** IIB/459.
fett *inf.* fetch 18/246.
fetterfowe *n.* feverfew, a bitter herb good for sick animals 7/27.
feyles *pr. 2 sg.* lack 16A/248.
feyne see **fayne**. *adj., adv.*
fielle see **fyle**.
figures *n.* symbols 15/72.
fist see **feiste**.
fitt, fitte see **feete**.
flackett, flagette, flaggen, flaggette, flasket *n.* flagon, flask 7/144, 571.
flame *inf.* burn 2/424.
flappes *n.* blows 16/318.
flaterand, flatteringe *pr. p.*; **flattery** *adj.* fluttering 23/376, IIB/376. *OED* flatter vb.².
flea *inf.* flay, strip the skin from 23/608.
flee, fleene, fley, flye *inf.*¹ avoid, escape, fade away 6/188, 10/142, 24/145, 607; **flee** *pr. 2 sg.* IB/138.
flee *inf.*² fly 21/268, 24/145.
flee, fly *inf.*³ hurry ID/38.
flee *inf.*⁴ flow 24/426.
fleene see **flee** *inf.*¹
fleete, flitte *inf.* move 3/281; **fleeting, fleetinge, flittinge** *pr. p.* flowing 3/225.
fleshe-houlden *adj.* kept in the flesh, still bleeding 24/386.
fleshe-likinge *n.* lust 3/6.
fletchinge *vbl. n.* vacillating 15/175; **flechinge, fletchinge, flytchinge** *pr. p.* 20/36, 21/211, 251.
fley see **flee** *inf.*¹
fleytt, flyte, flytt *inf.* quarrel, scold 7/208. 16/101ᵛ, IIC/110; **flett, flyte** *pr. 1 sg.* 7/208; **flite, flytt** *pr. 2 sg.* 7/197; **flyte** *pr. 3 sg.* 16A/3.
flitt = **fytt** *n.*¹ 11/7.
flitte see **fleete**.
flood = **foode** *n.*³ 8/18.
flote *unidentified* 7/589; see Explanatory Note.
flowe *inf.* flood 3/35. *MED* flouen 3 (a).
flowes = **flowers** 23/459.
fly see **flee** *inf.*³
flyche = **slyche** 3/73.
flycker *pr. 3 sg.* moves to and fro 16A/3.
flye see **flee** *inf.*¹
flyre *pr. 3 sg.* grimaces 16A/3. *OED* fleer v. 1.
flyte, flytt see **fleytt**.
flytinge *vbl. n.* quarrelling 15/175; **fleittinge, flettinge, flitting, flittinge** *pr. p.* 20/36, 21/211, 251.
fode *inf.* beguile 10/317. *MED* fode v. (2).
foder = **fother** *n.* further comment 7/425.
folde *n.* times IIB/47.
followed *pa. t. 3 sg.* baptized 17/58. *MED* fulwen (a).
fond, fonde, found, founde, fownd *inf.* attempt 7/319, 8/212, 11/326, 14/324, IIB/48; manage, arrange 4/469; **found, founde** *imp.* prepare 10/148, IIC/68; **foundes, foundeth, fowndes** *pr. 3 sg.* attempts 5/114, 154, IB/107; **fonde, founde** *pr. 1 pl.* attempts 14/208; **founded** *pa. t. 1 sg.* tested 12/146; **fonden, founden, fownded, fownden** *pp.* tested 14/326, 16/317, IIC/329.
fonde see **fyne**.
fone, fonne *n.* enemy 2/423, 3/6, IC/71; enemies 5/170, IB/123.

GLOSSARY

fong, fonge *inf.* undertake 5/45, IB/69; **fonge** seize 17/123, 22/135; proceed 24/231; **fonge** *imp.* take 3/27.
fonne, foone *n.* fool, idiot 11/33, 21/275.
foode *n.* progeny 1/7; creature, child 6/187, 8/18.
for *prep.* against 7/526; for fear of 4/403; because IB/350, IIB/214; despite 14/146.
forby, forbye *inf.* redeem 4/176, 205; **forbought** *pp.* 17/216, 19/87.
forbyar, forbyer *n.* redeemer 20/115, 23/20.
force *n.* no ~ no matter 13/299.
force *inf.* rape 24/47.
forder see **foder**.
fore *num.* four 13/425.
forever = **fire** *n.* 5/90.
forgave *pa. t. 3 sg.* released from debt 14/87.
forgiven *pp.* completely abandoned 16/213.
forgoer *n.* predecessor 21/90.
forgright *pp.* denied 2/392.
forlitte *inf.* forgive 8/40. *OED* forlet v.¹ 4. b.
forlorne *adj.* completely lost, destroyed 8/348, 11/116.
formacion *n.* creation 1/73, 75.
forsake *inf.* avoid 2/212, 252; **forsoke** *pa. t. 1 sg.* denied ID/61; **forsakene** *pp.* 6/101.
forsooth, forsoth, forsothe, forsouth *adv.* truly 2/551, 653, 4/9.
forsware *pa. t. 1 sg.* swore falsely ID/61; **forswere** *pa. t. 3 sg.* 24/671.
forsworne *adj.* perjured 8/350.
for-thee, forthy, forthye *adv.* on that account 2/267, 2/99, 10/309.
forther, further *inf.* further, increase 23/27, IIB/27.
forther = **father** 4/173.
fortrade, fortredde *pa. t. 3 sg.* destroyed by trampling 22/136.
forward, forwarde *n.* agreement 3/301, 4/171.
for-why *adv.* because 21/139

foryeat *inf.* forget, disregard IB/302.
foule, fowle *n.* bird 2/83, IA/5; **fowles** 2/94, IA/14.
found, founde see **fond**.
founder see **foder**.
fowden = **fownden** 16/317.
fowle *adj.* unpleasant, distressing, sinful 1/157, 14/135.
fowle *inf.* betray 14/300; befoul 16/81.
fowle, fowlye *adv.* evilly, foolishly, dirtily 3/4, 6/142; **fowle** *to fare* to come to grief 24/232.
fownd see **fond**.
framed = **fremd** 7/687.
franticke, frenticke *adj.* insane 16/190, IIC/202.
fraught *pp.* be laden 6/187.
fraye *n.* terror 4/430. *OED* fray sb.¹
fraye *inf.* attack 7/306, 10/408. *OED* fray v¹ 4.
fraye = **fayre** beautiful 6/179.
fre, free *adj.* generous, noble, independent 1/260, IC/50.
freake, freike, freyke *n.* fellow, person 6/188, 16/86, IIC/90; **freakes, freekes** 5/175, IB/128.
freare *n.* friar 16/72.
free, freere = **fere** see **feare** *adj.*
freelye *adj.* noble 14/36.
freelye *adv.* generously 21/235.
freight = **feightes** (?) 10/47.
fremd *adj.* unknown 7/687.
frend = **fremd**.
frenticke see **franticke**.
freshe *adj.* unspoiled 20/130; **freshest** healthiest 18/12. *OED* fresh A. I. 9.
freye *n.* fray, battle 7/208.
fro, froe, froo *prep.* from 2/531, 595, 9/84.
froo = **fooe** *n.* enemy 5/578.
froude = **floude** 3/84.
frowarde *adj.* bold, presumptuous 3/194.
fructifye *inf.* produce children 7/522.
fruite *n.* kernels of grain 2/531; ~ , **fruyte** child, offspring 6/4, 16A/245.
fulfill *inf.* populate 2/68, 88; ~ , **fulfyll** carry out 24/67, 476.

fullgens *n.* splendour 1/201.
fulmart, fulmerd *n.* polecat 3/170; **fullimartes** 3/170. *MED* fulmard
fulsome *inf.* bolster, strengthen 21/150; *imp.* 21/135. *MED* fils(t)nen.
further see **forther**.
fyand *pr. 1 sg.* find 22/269.
fygure *n.* person 1/121.
fyle *inf.* defile, defame 6/155(AB), 16/81; place on record 6/155(HmRH); **fyled, fylyde** *pp.* defiled 24/178, IIB/264.
fylth *n.* sin, immorality 14/46.
fynde *inf.* support, sustain 6/426; **fonde** *pp.* 7/463.
fyne *adj.* pure, refined 24/643.
fynter, fanter *n.* "jingling duplication of meaningless sounds" (*OED*) 7/27.
fyrrett *n.* ferret, polecat 3/175.
fyst see **feiste** IIC/105.
fytt *n.*[1] "bodily state that betokens death" 11/7 (*OED* fit sb.[2] 2. b); awesome experience 12/146, 24/296.
fytt *n.*[2] period of time 19/152.

G

gables *n.* cables, ropes 3/90. *MED* gable n. (2) (a).
gadd = **glad** 21/233.
gaine *adv.* swiftly 6/37. *OED* gain adv.[1]
galle *n.* bile 17/131.
gambonns, gammons *n.* smoked or cured hams 7/131.
gammon, gamon *n.* game, activity 6/252, 12/4.
gange *inf.* travel, 7/658; see **goe**.
gate *n.* path, route 9/231, 12/204.
gate *pa. t. 1 sg.* begot 2/434; *pa. t. 2 sg.* got, took 14/101.
gaye *adj.* lively 4/434; **gayer** *comp.* more resplendent 1/104.
gaye, gayle *adv.* spiritedly, brightly 3/171, 11/62.
gayne *n.* profit, help 14/337.
gayne *adj.* well-disposed 9/7. *OED* gain a. 2.
gayne *inf.*[1] profit, help 2/648, 3/146; **gaynes** *pr. 3 sg.* helps, avails 24/167, 620.
gayne *inf.*[2] oppose 8/165. *MED* geinen 2.
gayne *pp.* gone, passed 19/201. *MED* gon 12b (b).
gayne-chare 24/215 see **yeane-chare**.
geat *n.* goat 23/174; **geates** 3/163.
gedling, godlinge *n.* scoundrel 8/307, 326. *MED* gadeling.
geete *pa. t. 2 sg.* got, took 14/101; **geete** *pa. t. 3 sg.* created 22/17; **gett** *imp.* ~ *thee right* receive your just deserts 2/616.
geldinge *n.* castrated man 10/237.
genderyd *pp.* engendered, created IIB/509.
gent *adj.* gentle, noble 10/65, 97.
gere *n.* belongings 7/529.
gete = **geat** IIB/174.
gett see **geete**.
geve *inf.* give IB/263; *pr. 1 sg.* 1/69; **geven** *pp.* IC/110.
ghoost, ghooste, ghost *n.* spirit 6/73, 340, 15/287.
ghoostly, ghoostlye, ghostlie, goostlye *adv.* spiritually 6/370, 17/30, 21/328, IB/388.
ghostly, gostlye *adj.* spiritual 2/169, 15/104.
gibb *inf.* waiver, deviate IB/242. *MED* gibben.
gile *adv.* agilely (?) 3/171.
gilt *n.* sin 12/266.
give = **gif** *conj.* if 16A/294.
gykse = **byse** 5/93.
glade *inf.* gladden 21/233; **glades** *pr. 3 sg.* 23/41.
gladly *adv. do* ~ eat heartily 7/137. *MED* gladli adv. 2 (d).
glee *n.* source of joy 7/332. *MED* glee n. (1). 2 b.
gleett, glette *pr. 3 pl.* discharge 7/247. *OED* gleet v. 2.
glent *inf.* glimmer, shine 22/299.
glent *pr. 3 pl.* vanish, disappear 7/247;

GLOSSARY

pp. moved quickly 8/114, 9/28.
gleoy, gloe, gloo, glye *inf.* stare 7/332. MED glouen v. (2).
gloe = **gole** 7/262.
gloryd *pa. t. 3 sg.* sang of glory 7/401.
glowes see **gulles** 23/513.
goade, god, gode, good *n.* weapon, club 10/313, 371.
goale = **gayle** (?) 3/171.
godlinge see **gedling**.
goe, gon, gone, gonne, goo *inf.* move, walk, go 3/171, 3/202, 8/411, 22/210, IIB/640; **goo** prevail 24/436; **gone** *pr. 3 pl.* 2/75; **goes** *imp.* 6/683, 8/366; **goinge** *pr. p.* 2/78; *as mott I goo, as ever mote I goe* as I hope to continue alive 10/170, 14/258.
gole *imp.* yell, shout 7/262. OED yell v. 1.
golyons *n.* testicles 7/247.
golys see **gowle**.
goo see **goe**.
good, guyde *n.*[1] possessions 2/569, 24/278.
good *n.*[2] righteous people 24/423.
goost, gost, goste *n.* spirit 2/95, 106, 3/5.
goostlye see **ghoostly**.
gossippe *n.* female comrade 3/228, 17/286; **gosseppes, gossippes, gossips** 3/201, 228, 242.
gostlye see **ghostly**.
gotten *pp.* begotten, conceived 4/160, 9/205.
gowle *n.* a stupid fellow 13/428; **golys, gowles, gulles** 23/513, IIB/513. MED golle.
gowne *n.* rich clothing 24/278.
gracyous *adj.* full of grace 24/394.
grane *n.* grain, cereal plant; *his ~ is grounden* his life is finished 16/320.
grantmercye, grauntemercye, grauntmarsye, grauntmercy, grauntmercye *n.* an expression of gratitude 6/281, 16/210, IC/97, IIB/245, IIC/222.
graunt = **graunter** 4/17.
graved *pp.* cut IC/74.

graweth = **gnaweth** eats 5/118.
grayne = **groyne** 7/122.
graynes = **grayn is** 16/320; see **grane**.
graythes *pr. 3 sg.* prepares IIB/607.
great *n.* the mighty 6/246, 9/255.
great *adv.* greatly, very 5/305.
greate *pr. 1 sg.* greet, welcome 20/2; **greete** *pp.* 6/8.
greave *n.* bush 19/82, 84.
gree *n.* rank 6/55.
greene *adj.* fresh 7/116.
greesely see **grisly**.
greet, greete *n.* ground 23/143, IIB/143; **greete** sand 7/75.
greete see **greate**.
greetes = **graythes** 23/607.
greffe, greiffe *inf.* cause distress 10/331; **greivouse** *pr. 3 sg.* grieves 8/390.
greminge *pr. p.* grieving 24/578. OED greme v.
grennes, greonis, greoynes, greynes, groyns *n.* traps, snares 7/262. OED grin sb.[1] 1. b.
grennynge see **grynne**.
greve *n.* burial place IIB/151; **greeves** 22/296; see **grave**.
grimly *adv.* ferociously 7/after 191.[v]
gright *n.* security, peace 23/23, 24/511. MED grith n.
gright *pp.* forbidden, denied 2/397, 420. MED grucchen v. 5. (b).
grisly, grysely *adj.* fierce 23/342, IIB/342, 607; **greesely** grisly, horrible 23/607.
grome, groome *n.* low fellow 23/607, IIB/607; **growme** man-child 8/202.
gronde, grownde, grownden *adj.* sharpened 3/59.
grone *inf.* groan 23/654.
grope *inf.* seize 7/after 191.[v]
grounded *pp.* based, established 1/30.
grounden *pp.* prepared 16/320, IIC/332.
groundes *n.* sorrows, woes 7/262. MED ground n. 6 (b).
growme see **grome**.

growne *n.* groaning 11/222; **grownes** groans 7/262.
growne *pr. subj. 3 sg.* groan 16A/67.
growsinge *n.* eating 7/138.
groyne *n.* swine's snout 7/122.
gryll *inf.* provoke, oppress, torment 3/46, 5/289.
gryll *pr. 1 sg.* tremble with fear 4/340. *OED* grill v. 4.
grynne *inf.* gnash the teeth 24/583; **grennynge, grynnyng** *pr. p.* 24/578.
grysely see **grisly**.
grytch *pr. subj. 3 sg.* begrudge 14/142.
gryth *n.* complaint 11/222.
gryve *inf.* grieve IIB/92.
gulles see **gowle**.
gurd, gurde *imp.* strike, hit 16/65, 16A/9; **gurd** *pa. t. 3 sg.* announced 7/401.
guyde see **good** n.[1]
guyfte *n.* gift 16/210.
gygges = **pigges** 7/128.
gynne *n.* trick, device 2/174.
guyse = **guyfte** 16/210.

H

hacckinge stoccke, hackestocke *n.* chopping block 3/69.
hackney *n.* unimpressive horse 6/282.
halfe *n.* side 16A/42.
halfe *adj.* ~ *tyme yt weare* only half-enough time remains 3/195.
halfe, hals = **hasse** 6/201.
halse *n.* neck IIB/693.
halt *adj.* lame 17/109.
handlinge *n.* treatment, management 20/91.
hannes = **harneis** (?) *n.* personal apparel 7/176[v].
hansed see **haunce**.
hape *n.* chance, fortune 2/673; **happ, happe** good fortune, success 7/253, IIC/72; **hape** favor, liking 7/207; **happes** 7/462.
harbored *pa. t. 2 pl.* lodged 24/464; *pp.* 24/436; **harboringe** *vbl. n.* 24/463.
harborlesse *adj.* without lodging 24/629, 635.
harbour, harboure *n.* lodging 6/454, 24/627.
harkens, hearkes *imp.* listen, pay attention 11/239, IB/50, IIB/220; **harken (herken)** *on* listen sympathetically to 23/251, IIB/251.
harlott *n.* low fellow, scoundrel 8/336, 10/353; **harlottes, harlottys** 23/482, IIB/482.
harme *inf.* take hurt 4/274. *MED* harmen.
harre *adv.* higher 7/414.
harrowe *pr. 3 pl.* drag, pull, carry off 24/480. *MED* herien 3(a) and *OED* harry v. 6.
harrowe *excl.* help 1/266.
harte *n.* male red deer 3/166.
hartles *adj.* dispirited 7/502.
hartye *adj.* fervent 4/222.
hase = **as** IIC/228.
hase, hasse, haste see **have**.
hast *n.* haste 3/226.
hat = **hath** 14/110.
haunce *inf.* elevate, enhance 9/173; **haunshed** *pa. t. 3 sg.* IB/424; **hansed, haunsed** *pp.* 6/98, IB/252.
have *inf.* preserve 6/182; **haste** *pr. 2 sg.* possess 2/115; **hase** *pr. 3 sg.* 2/147; **hasse, haste** *auxiliary* have 24/378; **have** *imp.* ~ *mee* pull me up 7/93.
hayle, heale *n.* health, well-being 3/198, 6/74; *as have I* **heale** as I hope to continue healthy 11/31, 323.
hayle, heale *excl.* hail 16/339, IIC/351.
hayre *n.* heir 4/154, 158.
hayriffe *n.* the herb hairif or goose-grass 7/77.
head *n. as broke I my* ~ an expression of certainty 16A/433.
heades *n.* persons, individuals 6/244.
heale see **hayle** *n.*
heale *inf.* restore to happiness ID/42.
heale see **hayle** *excl.*
health *n.* happiness 1/118, 24/108.
healthfull *adj.* causing well-being

GLOSSARY

21/160.
hear, her *adv.* here 8/56, 23/317, IIB/497.
heare *n.* hair 14/104.
heare *inf.* understand 16/141.
hearkes see **harkens**.
heathen, hethen, hethence, hithen *adv.* hence 7/379, 8/81, 97, 18/356.
heathing *vbl. n.* mocking 16/327. MED hethen v.
heavye *adj.* sad, tired 6/157.
hee (1) = **yee** 7/408.
heeste *n.* promise 3/305.
heigh, height, hie, hight, hye (*soone, anon*) *in, on* ~ at once, immediately 2/88, 5/105, 183, 196, 6/379, 10/22, 13/149, 264, 346, 14/278, 16A/205, 17/136, 21/231, 22/14, 23/637, 24/30.
heighnes *n.* superiority 12/41.
height *n.* sky 2/94.
height, hie, hye *on, one* ~ on high, above, in heaven 2/450, 6/86, 647, 10/73, IB/314.
height *pr. 1 sg.* am named 10/201; *pa. t. 3 sg.* 23/26.
height, heighte see **het**.
heine = **home** (?) 24/581.
heistes see **hest**.
heither *adv.* hither 1/234.
helden *pp.* held to account 24/560.
hell-pine *n.* hell-pain 12/3.
helpe *n.* helpmate, wife 2/130.
helpe = **helped** 12/311.
helpely *adj.* helpful 2/74.
hemlocke *n.* a poisonous plant used as a sedative 7/77.
henbane *n.* a poisonous plant used as a narcotic 7/21.
hend, hende *adj.* courteous 16/376, IA/15.
hend *inf.* take up 7/130; **hent** *imp.* take away 16A/31; *imp.* 7/252; *pa. t. 3 sg.* carried 7/415; *pp.* taken 10/448, 17/183; ~, **hente** *pp.* told, spoken 23/447, IIB/447.
henge *inf.* hang IIB/693.
henge = **gange** 7/658.
her see **hear**.

here *inf.* hear, listen 4/11, 7/47; ~ *tell* learn 5/146.
here *pr. 1 sg.* praise 16A/384.
here = **lord** 4/210.
hereiff, heriff see **hayriffe**.
herken *on* see **harkens**.
hernes *n.* herons 3/182.
herrors *n.* errors IIB/295.
hest, heste *n.* command 2/482, 5/205; **heistes, hestes** 1/139, 10/50.
het *pr. 1 sg.* promise 4/450; ~, **hett** *pr. subj. 2 sg.* 5/172, IB/125; **height, hyght** *pa. t. 3 sg.* 12/182, IIB/147; **hight** *pa. t. 3 pl.* 6/174; **height, heighte, het, hett** *pp.* 6/30, 10/14, IB/157, 282.
hethen, hethence see **heathen**.
hethen-forward *adv.* henceforth 4/177.
hevie = **Hervye** (?) 16/335.
hew, hewe *n.* complexion, appearance 24/279, ID/58.
hewes *imp.* cut, slash 16/343, 344.
hie *on* see **height, hie, hye**.
hie *adv.* highly 1/97; **hye** in elevated fashion, seriously 18/130.
highe = **het** 4/450.
highnes *n.* elevated rank 12/191.
hight *on* see **heigh**.
hight see **het**.
hight = **highe** 2/425, 8/47.
hill *inf.* cover, clothe 2/504.
hilled *adj.* covered, clothed 2/362.
hillinge *n.* covering 2/275.
him = **hem** *pron.* them 2/28.
hime = **home** (?) 24/581.
hinder *adj.* rear 7/272.
hir *pron.* her 2/143, 204.
his *pron.* its 6/618, 24/64.
his, hys = **is** 6/103, 13/94, IIB/294.
hise *n.* bread 17/248. MED hyse *and* hirse.
hise, hyse *pron.* his 2/406, 17/248, IIB/244.
hithen see **heathen**.
hoe *excl.* stop 1/228; see **whoo**.
hollowed = **hallowed** 6/88.
holpen, holpenn *pp.* helped 4/68, 83.

home *pron.* them 17/148.
homely *n.* homily, sermon 12/286.
hommer *n.* hammer 16A/154.
honge *inf.* hang IIB/373; *pr. subj. 3 sg.* 2/539.
honge = **honger** 12/47.
honorys, honoures *imp.* honour IIB/91, 103.
hood *n. by my* ~ an expression of determination 16/84, IIC/196.
hoore *n.* whore 10/397.
hope *inf.* believe 13/275; ~ , **hoope** *pr. 1 sg.* 2/181, 5/298; **hopes, hoopes** *pr. 2 sg.* 16/255, IIC/267; **hopes** *pr. 3 sg.* 6/681, 14/283; *pr. 2 pl.* 23/98, IIB/98; **hopen** *pr. 3 pl.* 10/295.
hoppe *n.* trust, confidence 2/184.
horedom *n.* whoredom, prostitution IIB/672.
horehounde *n.* a plant whose juice is effective against coughing 7/21.
horned *adj.* having horn-like rays of light as a symbol of power IIB/45. *MED* horned 2(a).
horne-wood *adv.* completely insane 16A/422.
horyffe see **hayriffe**.
hould *pr. 2 pl.* keep, observe 5/9.
houlden *pp.* beholden, indebted 14/96.
hoven *pp.* raised 16A/289.
how, howe *excl.* 7/45, 10/57.
howles *pr. 3 sg.* holds 24/192.
howse *n. went over the* ~ was surpassingly excellent (?) 7/385.
hus *pron.* us IIA/18.
husbandes *n.* farmer's 2/475.
hyde *n.* skin 24/279, ID/58.
hydes *pr. 3 sg.* heeds, pays attention 7/505.
hye *inf.* hurry, go 4/382, 5/384; **hyne** *pr. 2 pl.* 23/363, IIB/363; **hye, hyes** *imp.* 3/50, 7/456; **hye** *pr. subj. 1 pl.* 6/422; **hyed** *pa. t. 1 sg.* 24/351; *pa. t. subj. 2 pl.* 3/223; **hyses** = **hyes** *imp.* 10/289.
hye *on* see **height, hie, hye**.
hyer *n. to my* ~ for my use 7/118.
hyght = **hygh** *adj.* IIB/189.

hyght see **het**.
hynde *n.* female red deer 3/166.
hyne *n.* servant 24/520, 642.
hyne see **hye** *inf.*
hyre *n.* punishment, deserts 21/27, 24/650.
hyses see **hye** *inf.*

I

I = it 13/135; ~ = **in** 24/47 (1), 56.
iche *pron.* each 1/112, 2/671.
ichon *pron.* each one 2/34, IIB/60.
idrawe *pp.* drawn 23/306, IIB/306.
ilente *adj.* fallen 2/345.
ilk, ilke *adj.* same 6/570, ID/7.
ilych *adv.* alike 7/105.
image *n.* likeness 1/288.
imbrace see **unbrace**.
iment, imente *pp.* decided 1/288, 6/299.
in = me 24/120.
in chare, in charge = **incharge** *n.* injunction, commission 18/133. *OED* encharge.
incommoditie *n.* discomfort 11/5.
indevoure *doe your* ~ do your duty 1/44.
indewer *inf.* endure, last 1/117.
informer *n.* creator 24/110.
ingendirt *pp.* engendered IIB/633.
insure *pr. 1 sg.* assure 2/304.
inteere *adj.* entire, complete 19/39.
intent *n.* notice, understanding 4/193, 5/43; will 1/93, 284; meaning IB/322; *in no* ~ of no mind 16/241.
iwent *pp.* gone 8/113.
iwis, iwisse, iwys, iwysse, ywisse, ywys *adv.* certainly 2/54, 219, 464, 562, 643, 17/90.
iwrought *pp.* created 1/75.

GLOSSARY

J

jangle, janglen *pr. 3 pl.* babble, chatter 21/378; **janglinge, jangellinge** *pr. p.* 16/9, IIC/9; **janglinge** *vbl. n.* 14/245.
jannock *n.* a loaf of leavened oaten bread 7/120.
javeling *pr. p.* quarrelling, wrangling 16/9. *EDD* javel.
jawce *n.* juice 7/204. *MED* jus 1 (c).
jentyll *adj.* gentle 13/36.
jesayne *n.* gesine, childbed 9/245.
jollitie *n.* sexual power 9/209.
joye = **noye** 6/516.
joye-cheare *n.* joyful attitude 24/215; see **yeane-chare**.
joyen *pr. 3 pl.* rejoice 6/443.
justefie, justefye, justiffye, justifie, justifye *inf.* judge 16/50, 51, 156, IIC/55, 168.

K

keason, keson, keison = **kesar** (?) 10/90.
kedyll = **bedill** 6/36.
keele, kele *inf.* cool 23/682, IIB/686.
keene *adj.* sharp 24/223.
keenlye *adv.* painfully 24/256.
keepe *n.* notice, heed 7/77, 211.
keepe *inf.* guard, pay attention to, observe 2/387, 6/610; *imp.* 23/172.
kempes, kemps *n.* knights, warriors 10/222, 18/10.
ken = **kever** 7/471; ~ = **knye** 23/110.
kenn, kenne *inf.* know 22/283, IIB/422; **kennes** *pr. 2 pl.* 18/10; *pr. 3 sg.* 10/90, 11/240; **kent, kente** *pp.* instructed 2/349, 4/222.
kenne = **knye** 23/421, IIB/421.
kepe *inf.* guard, protect IB/229; *imp.* IIB/172; **kepte, kepit, keped** *pp.* 3/97.

kesar *n.* kaiser, emperor 10/90.
kever *inf.* obtain 2/8; recover, redeem 7/471, 11/103; *pr. 2 sg.* overrun 7/238.
kind, kinde, kynde *n.* race, humankind 2/76, 452, 6/71; **kinde, kynde** nature, natural law 2/34, 36; **kinde** inherited right 6/447.
kindly, kindlye, kyndely *adv.* naturally, by lineage 2/157, 6/435, 9/137.
kinely, kneelye = **keenlye** 24/256.
knave *n.* male child 23/112.
kneene, kneey, knen see **knye**.
knott *n.* a lump from a blow 10/354. *MED* knotte n. 7 (b).
know = **now** ID/66.
knowe *inf.* make known, prove IIB/195; **knoys** *pr. 3 sg.* knows IIB/300; *imp.* IIB/104; **knowe** *pp.* be known 24/400.
knowledge *n.* acknowledgement 6/262.
knowledge *inf.* acknowledge 6/387.
knye *n.* knee 4/192, 23/110; **kneene, kneey, knen, knyes** 4/192, 328, 23/110, 421.
knytt *pp.* knotted *our wyttes were so ~ we were so stupid* 19/154.
kylne *n.* kiln, furnace *burned a ~ caused a commotion* 10/299. *OED* kiln 1. b.
kyne *n.* cows 3/163.
kynne, kythe *n.* relatives, family 7/90, 24/84.
kyrtle *n.* tunic, coat 16A/109, 113.
kyse = **byse** 5/93.

L

lach *inf.* take 7/281. *OED* latch v.[1]
laches *n.* slackness, negligence 24/200. *OED* lachesse.
lackles *adj.* spotless 7/533.
ladd, lade *pp.* led, guided IIB/627, 634.
lafte *pp.* left, remained 7/84, 12/152.
lames = **laynes** 24/166.
langore, langour, languor, languowre, langwore, longer *n.* spiritual darkness, despair, woeful

plight, damnation 2/345, 11/157, 17/6, 21/127, 24/142, 251.
lapped *pp.* enclosed, wrapped 6/524, 7/483.
lardans see **lorden.**
las, les, lesse *n.* lie, falsehood 6/233, 7/418, 17/49.
las *excl.* alas 24/243.
lasse *n.* less; ~ *and more* every detail 21/97.
last *inf.* extend, stretch 16A/184. *OED* last v.[1] 4.
laste = **lafte** *12/152.*
lastlye = **lasteth** 9/92.
late, layte, leate *n.* lightning 18/39, 22/297.
lathes *n.* hostilities 7/194.
latt *adj.* late 19/73.
latter *adv.* later 6/537.
laudacion *n.* glory 1/49.
laude *n.* praise 1/48.
lave = **love** 5/401.
law *adv.* low IIC/176.
lawe *n.* religion 5/405, IIB/431.
layd, lead, leade *pp.* directed, treated 13/373, 16/112.
layde see **leade** *adj.*
laye *n.* law, religion 2/178, IIB/250.
laye *inf.* wager, bet 2/234, 7/232; ~ *on* deal blows vigorously, attack 16/108, IIC/120.
layinge *vbl. n.* levying 24/346.
laykyd *pp.* played, sported IIB/25. *OED* lake v.[1]
layne, leane *inf.* conceal, keep silent 4/283, 8/379; **layne, laynes** *pr. 2 sg.* 9/5, 24/166.
laynige = **layinge** 24/346.
layte see **late.**
leach *n.* perforated vessel 11/252. *OED* leach sb.[2] 1.
lead *n.* a worthless substance 9/76. *MED* led n. 1a. (d).
lead, leade, lede *pp.*[1] laid, placed 23/135, 151, IIB/135.
lead, leade *pp.*[2] continued 2/687, 16A/434.
lead, leade see **layd.**

leade, layde *adj.* of a leaden colour, dirty 15/153. *MED* leden adj. (b).
leade *pp.* worn 20/123. *MED* leden v (1). 6 d.
leadenn, ledden, loden, ludden *n.* refrain, song 3/191, 7/418.
leadge *inf.* lighten, alleviate 24/288. *OED* allege v.[1]
leadinge *adj.* directing, commending 6/206.
leaie = **pleaie** (?) 6/136.
leale *n.* loyalty 14/41.
leale, lele *adj.* loyal, true 21/134, 22/6.
leane see **layne.**
leare, leer, leere, lere *inf.* teach 2/437, 5/62, 16/60, 18/351; **leere, lerr** *pr. 1 sg.* 23/219, IIB/219.
leasinge *n.* falsehood 4/121, 6/349; **leasinges, leasongs** 13/270[v], 16A/239.
leate see **late.**
leav, leaves see **leeve** *inf.*
leave, leve *n.* permission 2/210, IIB/642.
leaver, lever *adv.* rather 23/455, IIB/455.
lech, leche, leech *inf.* heal, cure 11/157, 23/611, IIB/611; **leeche** *pr. 2 sg.* 13/328.
ledd see **leade** *pp.*
ledden see **leadenn.**
lede see **lead** *pp.*[1]
lee *n.* happiness, joy, salvation 2/7, 44.
leede *n.* person, people 16A/230, 22/137; **leedes, ledys** 6/225, IIB/9.
leede = **leeve** *inf.* IIB/88.
leefe *n.* leave, permission 9/205.
leeffe *n.*[1] loved one 16A/241.
leeffe *n.*[2] good will 5/409.
leeffe, lefe, leife, leiffe, leyffe, lief, life, liffe *adj.* dear, beloved 2/249, 251, 493, 6/499, 19/17, ID/6.
leemed *pa. t. 3 sg.* gleamed 7/373.
leeminge *adj.* shining 7/313.
leene *inf.* rest, lie down 11/334. *OED* lean v.[1] 1.
leere, lere *n.* countenance, face 13/407, 19/110.

GLOSSARY

leere, lere *adj.* beautiful 14/33, 18/9. *MED* lere adj. 2.
leer, leere see **leare**.
leere = **lee** 16A/214; ~ = **bere** *n.*[2] 10/43.
leese, lesse *inf.*[1] refrain from 7/155.
leese, lese, loose *inf.*[2] lose, give up 2/528; **leste, lore, loore, lorne** *pp.* 7/148, 18/309, 23/188, IIB/188.
leet *imp.* hesitate 19/245.
leete *pa. t. 3 sg.* let, permitted 22/18.
leeve *had as* ~ would be equally willing 3/99, 4/383.
leeve, leffe *inf.* believe 13/277, IIB/154; **leev, leeve, leve, live, lyve** *pr. 1 sg.* 5/200, 6/47, 8/78, IC/113; **leav** *pr. 2 sg.* IB/445; **leeve, leeven, levon** *pr. 1 pl.* 21/7, 22/256, IIB/508; **leaves** *pr. 2 pl.* 13/276; **leven, levyn** *pr. 3 pl.* IIB/21, IIC/293; **leaves, leeve, leeves, levys** *imp.* 4/131, 5/126, 6/363, IIB/167; **levinge** *pr. p.* 4/46; **leeved, leived, lived, lyved** *pa. t. 3 sg.* 6/62, 24/536; **leeved, levyd** *pa. t. 3 pl.* 23/520, IIB/520; **leeved** *pp.* 23/73.
leeve, lyve *pr. subj. 1 pl.* live, exist 21/7.
leevinge *n.* belief 20/183.
lefe, leife, leiffe see **leeffe** *adj.*
leffe see **leeve** *inf.*
legiaunce *n.* alleviation, relief 16A/256[v].
leinge see **lenge**.
leith *n.* joint of the body ~ *ne lyme* joint nor limb IIC/261.
leived see **leeve** *inf.*
leker = **becker** 16A/2.
lele see **leale**.
lemmon *n.* loved one 18/160.
lend, lende *inf.* stay, remain, abide 6/137, 14/8.
lendeth *pr. 3 sg.* grants 24/142; **lent, lente** *pp.* 2/431, 4/98.
lenge, linge *inf.* linger, remain 2/398, 24/460; **lenge, leinge** *pr. 2 pl.* 5/15; **lenges** *pr. 3 sg.* 4/226; **lenge** *pr. 3 pl.* 2/385; **lenge** *pr. subj. 1 sg.* 2/638; **lenged** *pp.* 17/14.

lenger *adv.* longer 4/232, 6/184.
lenght *a meaningless error* 21/127.
length *imp.* put a long way off, take away 21/128. *MED* lengthen v. 2. c.
lent, lente *adj.* present, in attendance 2/51, 5/388.
lent *pp.* placed 2/18, 6/640.
lere see **leare, leere** *n.* and *adj.*
lere *inf.* learn 8/218, 21/229.
lere = **beare** *n.*[1] 3/109; ~ = **here** 21/292.
lerne = **leeve** *inf.* IIB/440.
les, lesse see **las** *n.*
lese see **leese** *inf.*[2]
lesse see **leese** *inf.*[1]
let *inf.* abandon 3/292.
lething *n.* healing 16/327.
lett *n.* hesitation, obstacle 2/548, 23/61.
lett *adj.* obstructed 10/11.
lett *inf.* halt, prevent, obstruct, hinder 2/446, 3/283; ~ *pr. 2 sg.* hesitate 19/245; **lettes** *pr. 3 sg.* hinders 7/314.
lett *pr. 2 sg.* put 4/387; ~ *bee* put aside 6/161; *of* **lette** let off, excuse 2/310.
lettynge *n.* delaying 4/16.
leve see **leave**.
leve see **leeve** *inf.*
lever see **leaver**.
levinge *n.* believing 24/37.
lewd, lewed *n.* unlearned persons 4/115, 21/309.
lewt, lewte, lewtee, lewtye, lowtye, luteye *n.* loyalty, faith 1/174, 8/225, 10/450, 21/267, IC/113; *by my* ~ an expression of determination 2/638, 6/341.
lewte = **lewd** 21/309.
leyffe see **leeffe** *adj.*
liccoris, licourouse *adj.* wanton, greedy 2/199, 353.
licencill *n.* power, control, authority 1/19. Not in *OED* or *MED.*
licken *inf.* liken, equate 22/96.
lief see **leeffe** *adj.*
liere = **leeve** *inf.* 6/555.
liever, liver *inf.* deliver, produce 2/8.
life, lyfe *n. on* ~ alive 14/315, 344, ID/58.

life, liffe see **leeffe** adj.
lift pa. t. 1 sg. lifted 22/50.
ligged pp. lied, misrepresented 23/25.
light adj.¹ of little importance 24/257; sett at ~ value little 5/205, IB/158.
light adj.² happy, glad 18/326, 23/9.
light inf.¹ alight, descend 2/452, 6/27; pa. t. 1 sg. 18/171; pa. t. 3 sg. 13/109, IB/327; ~ , **lighte** pp. 16/206, IIC/218.
light inf.² gladden 7/521. MED lighten v. (2). 1b.
lighten inf. cause light, brighten 2/44.
lightly adv. leniently 16/112, IIC/124. MED lightli adv. (e).
lightned pp. unburdened, encouraged 20/19.
lightninge n.¹ enlightenment 11/173.
lightninge n.² source of light 2/42; lightninges 2/42.
likeinge, likinge, likynge, lykinge n. pleasure 1/48, 2/79, 696, 23/270.
likest adj. most like 13/86.
liketh, lykes pr. 3 sg. pleases 2/63, IB/8; **lyked** pa. t. 3 sg. 21/185, 24/387.
likinge, lykyng adj. pleasing 5/305, IIB/46.
lille = **lilt** inf. blow, make a sound 7/155.
linge see **lenge**.
list pr. 2 sg. liest, tell a falsehood IIB/462; **lyre** pr. 2 pl. 23/358, IIB/358.
list, liste, listes pr. 3 sg. it pleases 2/144, 3/207, ID/38.
lite n. little 16/102ᵛ, IIC/112.
lither n. wicked person 7/280.
lither, lyther adj. base, deceitful 7/265, 13/201.
litter = **lither** adj. 10/128.
live, lived see **leeve** inf.
liverastes n. a kind of food (?) 7/124ᵛ, 203. See Explanatory Note.
livered = **lived** dwelt 17/239.
liverie n. uniform IIC/217.
liverye n. food, provisions 7/106, 126.
livinge n. life 23/286.
lixom, lixsome, luxom, luxonne adj.

happy, pleasing 18/316, 19/135, 21/135.
loare, loore, lore n. lore, instruction, knowledge 2/516, 5/351, 9/236.
loden see **leadenn**.
logged pp. placed like a log 19/3. OED log v.¹ 3. b.
long inf. remain 24/460; pr. 2 sg. 2/552; **longe** pr. 3 sg. dwells 23/262.
longe adj. attributable 18/253. OED long a.²
longer see **langore**.
longes n. lungs 7/203.
longeth pr. 3 pl. belong, pertain 15/11.
longett pp. languished 17/14. OED long v.¹ 8.
looe, lowe n. flame 24/545. OED low sb.²
looke inf. examine, determine by looking 11/19, 18/379; pr. 1 pl. 16A/119; ~ to take care of 10/382.
lookers n. custodians 14/305.
loore see **leese** inf.²
loos n. renown IB/116. MED los n. (2). 2. (a).
loose see **leese** inf.²
loovesome adj. charitable 24/367.
lord = **lore** 19/111.
lorden, lourden, lurdayn, lurdayne, lurden n. rascal 14/338, 23/274, IIB/374; **lardans, lordans, lordens, lurdans, lurdenes** 23/358, IIB/358.
lordinges, lordings n. ladies and gentlemen 3/328, 5/41.
lore, lorne see **leese** inf.²
lore = **lord** 21/318.
losell n. liar, scoundrel 2/699; **losells, losilles** 5/126, 23/428.
loses = **losells** 5/145.
losinger, losingere n. liar, scoundrel 10/254, IIC/317.
lossayne = **losingere** 10/254.
lost = **leste** 7/148; **loste** = **lefte** 7/398.
lothe n. ill will 5/409.
lottes n.¹ objects cast to decide disputes 21/43.
lottes n.² noises 7/194. MED lot (e) n. 3.

GLOSSARY

loullords, lowlers *n.* rascals, Lollards (?) 23/428, IIB/428.
love = **leve** *inf.* leave 5/364.
loveinge *n.* praise 1/103.
lowd, lowt *n.* loudness, sound 7/164.
lowde *both ~ and stille* at all times 24/66. *OED* loud adv. 1. b.
lowe *n.* low flat land 7/46, 163.
lowe see **looe**.
lowe *pr. 1 sg.* blaze 10/439. *OED* low v.²
lowt, lowte *inf.* bow, grovel, kneel 5/231, 6/615.
lowtye see **lewt**.
ludden see **leadenn**.
luddie *n.* lad 10/158.
lufle *adj.* lovely IIA/9.
lugget *pp.* dragged, pulled 16A/251.
lugginge *n.* pulling 7/201.
lurdayn, lurdayne, lurden, lurdans, lurdenes see **lorden**.
lure *n.* bait, that which is attractive; *lost her ~* earned damnation 24/603.
lurrell *n.* scoundrel, criminal 2/699.
luste, lusts see **lyst**.
luste *n.* enjoyment 2/591.
luteye see **lewt**.
luxom, luxonne see **lixom**.
lye *inf.* remain, be housed 20/55.
lym, lyme, lymme *n.* offshoot, progeny 23/313, IIB/313, 341; **lymme** part of the body 16/249, 306; **lymes** 7/454.
lynde *n.* linden tree 9/205.
lyne *n.* lineal descendants 24/642.
lyne see **list** *pr. 2 sg.*
lyne *pp.* lain 14/29.
lynes = **lymes** 7/454.
lyst *inf.* desire 16A/354; *~,* **luste, lusts** *pr. 3 sg.* 7/244, 20/31.
lyth, lythe *n.* joint of the body 16/249, 306.
lythinge *vbl. n.* easing pain (?) 16/327, IIC/339. *MED* lithen v. (2). 2.
lyvarstes, lyveras 7/124ᵛ, 203; see **liverastes** and Explanatory Note.
lyve see **leeve** *inf.*
lyve = **lyne** *n.* 24/642.

M

madd *adj.* mad, insane 22/292.
madd, made *pr. 1 sg.* go mad, lose one's mind 16A/254.
magistie *n.* majesty 12/182.
maiste = **makest** 3/110.
maister *n.* master 16/13.
maisterye, maistrey, maistrye, maystrye *n.* work of skill or power 12/116, 18/337, 23/86, IIB/86; **maistrie** power, authority 12/182; *~,* **maistrye** control, upper-hand 12/95, 120; **maisters, maistries** victories, conquests 23/686, IIB/690; **maystryes** tricks, deceptions 10/96.
make *n.* mate 2/136(2), 2/142.
makeinge *n.* creation 1/32; **makinge** contrivance 7/299.
male *adj.* antagonistic, evil 16/213, IIC/225.
maleson *n.* curse 2/679.
malmesey, malmesy, malmsme, malnesaye *n.* Malmsey wine 3/233.
mam, mame *n.* mother 2/678, 681.
menace, manece *n.* menace, threat 6/224, 17/159.
mandee, maundye *n.* maundy, washing the feet of the poor on Holy Thursday 4/127.
maner, manere *n.* sort, way 2/193, 438; **maner** custom 16/223; *in all* **manere** by all means 8/138; *for the* **mannere** for the sake of appearances 6/494.
manfulst *adj.* most manly 6/223.
mansuetude *n.* humility, gentleness 1/15.
mar, mare, marre, marye *inf.* destroy, injure, weaken 1/15, 16; **marreth** *pr. 3 sg.* 24/329; **marred** *pp.* 2/690, 10/463.
marchandize, marchandyce *n.* buying and selling 24/329, 342.
maremasett, maremussett, mar-

mosett, marsmosette *n.* small monkey 3/174, 10/15.
marvell *n.* miracle 16A/231.
marvells, mervelles *adj.* marvellous, evilly magical 23/410, IIB/410.
marvlosly *adv.* miraculously IIB/95.
marye *excl.* marry, by Mary 4/315, 16/51.
mas, mase *pr. 2 sg.* make 2/146, IIB/635; **mase** *pr. 3 sg.* 6/580, 21/31.
mase = **manace** 6/224.
mased *adj.* dazed, bewildered 16A/170, 18/264.
mashers *n.* persons who mash malt, brewers 17/317. *OED* masher[1]
maugard, mauger, maugere, maugre, maungere *prep.* despite 8/226, 354, 17/151.
maugere = **nagere** 6/398.
mawmentry, mawmentrye *n.* idols collectively 5/54, IB/78.
may *auxiliary* might, could IC/115.
may *fay excl.* by my faith 11/60.
mayd, maye *n.* maiden, virgin 6/125, 11/71.
mayne *n.* strength 1/98.
mayne *inf.* lead, conduct 23/351. *OED* manye v. 3.
mayster *inf.* control 2/84.
me = **ne** 24/166.
mea = **me** *pron.* 6/118.
meaden *n.* maiden, virgin 11/109.
meane *adj.* humble, of low rank 6/76.
meane *inf.* lament, complain, mourn 11/215, 12/239. *OED* mean v.[2] 2. c.
meanes *n.* man's 5/14.
meaninge, minning *n.* mindfulness, attention IB/91.
meanye, meny, menye, meyne *n.* troop, retinue, family 3/113, 265, IC/68.
meate *n.* food 2/212, 234.
meddest, middest, myddes *n.* the middle, midst 2/217, IB/349, IIC/84.
mediators *n.* messengers, negotiators 5/137; **meditators** = **mediators** 5/137.
medled *adj.* mixed 7/24.

mee = **ne** 24/51.
meede *n.* reward 2/580, 582.
meeke *inf.* humble, subdue 4/76.
meeles, melys *n.* arguments (?) 23/448, IIB/448.
meet *inf.* dream IB/382.
meete *n.* measurement 3/27.
meete, mette *adj.* suitable 3/94, 7/611.
meetinge *n.* meeting, encounter 7/159; but see **mittinge**.
meeve *inf.* move, suggest 12/71; **meeved** *pp.* moved, put in operation 24/8.
meirth see **mirth**.
mele, mell *inf.* speak, discuss, dispute 23/396, IB/30.
mell *inf.* mingle 11/313.
melt = **meete** *n.* (?) 3/27.
members *n.* genital organs 2/275, 280 + SD.
memoriall *n.* example 7/647.
mend, mende *inf.* amend, improve 6/555, IIB/556; *imp.* 16/185, IIC/197; **mendinge** *pr. p.* 1/51; *vbl. n.* 24/39.
mengers *n.* blenders, makers of wine 17/317.
menne, myn *inf.* tell, relate 5/48; **myne, mynne** have in mind 3/272, 7/539; **mynne** take thought 6/360; reflect 15/143; *pr. 1 sg.* tell, relate 2/171; **myne, mynes, mynne** *pr. 3 pl.* remember 19/213, 24/115; **ment** *pp.* kept in mind 1/288, 10/83.
menske, menskie *n.* reverence 9/202, 16A/451.
meny, menye see **meanye**.
merciable *adj.* merciful ID/86.
mere *n.* boundary, landmark 18/151. *OED* mere sb.[2] 2.
mere = **more** ID/93.
mervayles *pr. 3 sg.* causes to marvel 6/6, 11/36.
mesell *adj.* leprous 14/14, 18.
message *n.* errand, instruction 5/375.
messe *n.* portion of food, Mass 18/168.
messie, messy, messye *n.* messiah 8/282, 9/136, IC/81.

GLOSSARY

mete *inf.* meet, encounter IIB/480.
methinke, methinkes it seems to me 1/196, IIB/199; **meethought, methought** *pa. t.* 24/343, 352.
mette see **meete** *adj.*
meven *pr. 3 pl.* move, change, claim 16/44, IIC/48; **mevinge** *pr. p.* 6/588.
meyn see **mayne** *inf.*
meyne see **meanye**.
mich, michell, mickell, mickle, mickles, micle, mikle, much, mych, myche, myckell, mycle *adj.* great, much 2/314, 4/173, 203, 352, 5/152, 7/112, 10/28, 11/25, 299, 13/453, 16/392, 23/425.
middell land, middleyorde *n.* earth 4/267.
middest see **meddest**.
migh = **might** 10/158.
millhook see **nuthooke** 7/640.
minges see **mynge**.
minglers *n.* blenders, makers of wine 17/317.
minning see **meaninge**.
mirhe, myr *n.* myrrh 16A/474, IC/127.
mirrette *n.* merit 17/62.
mirth, myrth *n.* happiness 7/477, ID/29; **meirth** spiritual well-being 1/15, 20; **myrthes** 11/215.
mis *inf.* fail to obtain 17/160.
mis arraye *n.* disarray, confusion 16/139.
miscarye *n.* misfortune (?) IIC/151.
mischeife, mischeiffe, mischeyfe *n.* trouble, harm, suffering 2/314, 335, 12/274.
mischived *pp.* harmed 5/422.
mise *adv.* wrongly, amiss 24/132.
miseraye, misserye *n.* misery 16/139.
mispaye *inf.* anger, irritate 14/114, 16/145.
mittinge, mytinge, mytting *n.* youth 7/159. *OED* miting.
mixen = **myxed** 24/233.
mo, moe, moo *n.* more 1/226, 2/240, 8/316.
moch *adv.* greatly 2/314.
moke = **make** IIB/620.

mombered = **nombred** 4/204.
mon, mone, monne *n.* moan, lament, complaint 4/352, 14/56, 17/86; **mones, monys** 4/377, 7/679.
mon, mone, monn *auxiliary* may 2/658, IIB/317
mon = **anon** 4/190.
mone *n.* moon IIB/223.
mone = **man** 3/5.
mone *inf.* moan, complain 11/215.
mone *auxiliary* must 2/696.
moni, mony *adj.* many IIB/687, 690.
monte *n.* mountain 4/250.
moode *n.* attitude 5/26.
moote *n.* law-suit 24/307, 310.
moote, mote *inf.* debate 5/329, 23/480.
mooye = **maye** 20/68.
most *adj.* highest, most important, greatest 1/50, 7/237, 11/276.
most, moote, mot, mote, moth *auxiliary* must, may 2/259, 401, 4/325, 18/235, 24/242.
mote *n.*[1] talking 3/246. *OED* sb.[1] 4.
mote *n.*[2] note of a horn 7/159.
mote, mott see **thee**.
moth = **months** 21/129.
mould *n.* earth 6/197.
moulde *n.* form, appearance 1/102.
move *inf.* assert, evidence 12/199.
moved *pa. t. 3 sg.* tempted 12/196.
much see **mich**.
multiplye *inf.* populate 1/289.
muted *pa. t. 3 sg.* muffled the sound 7/420.
mutinge *n.* singing 7/360.
mych, myche, myckell, mycle see **mich**.
myddellyarde, myddylarde *n.* earth 4/267.
myddes see **meddest**.
myghtist = **myghtis** powers IIB/195.
mylde *n.* meek persons 6/98.
mylde *adj.* agreeable, meek 4/296, 5/26.
myn see **menne**.
myn = **nym** take IB/7.
mynde *n.* recollection 24/473; **have ~ on** think about, consider 11/1; **makes ~** call attention to 12/170; *full ~*

complete conviction ID/37; ~ *mase* call attention to 6/580, 21/31.
mynd, mynde *inf.* think of, be aware of, give heed 3/272, 7/539, 15/143.
myne *n.* less 1/294.
myne, mynne, mynes see **menne**.
mynge *inf.* remind, remember 21/285; **minges** *pr. 3 pl.* 24/115.
mynne see **menne**.
myr see **mirhe**.
mys, mysse *n.* wrong, sin 7/679, IIB/585.
mys, mysse *inf.* lack, be without 15/230, ID/29.
myse *n.* tribute 24/346. *OED* mise sb.¹ 2.
mystely *adv.* mystically 24/8.
mystie *adj.* unclear 19/25.
myxed *amonge pa. t. 1 sg.* dealt in 24/233.

N

nagere, naugere *n.* auger, carpenter's tool 6/398.
naie *adv.* not 4/425.
nam *imp.* name, speak 5/7.
name *n.* reputation 5/123.
name *unidentified* 23/112.
naue *unidentified* 23/112.
nay, ney, nye *conj.* nor 5/377, 6/147, 24/489.
nay = **may** 6/199.
naye *n.* denial 4/307, 16/221; *this is* (yt ys) *no* ~ this (it) cannot be denied 4/307, 23/593.
ne *adv.* not, no 3/23, 72.
neagromancye, nygnemancye *n.* magic, necromancy 6/613, 23/598.
neare *inf.* draw near, approach 1/106.
near, neare, neere, nere *adv.* never 2/618, 12/7, 16A/385, IC/26.
necessaryes *n.* items needed (for sheep-tending) 7/174.
nedelye, needesly *adv.* necessarily 14/322, 19/202.
neeme = **eame** uncle (?) 16A/103.

neere, nere *adv.* near, close 14/63, IIC/75.
neiled *pa. t. 2 sg.* nailed IC/82.
neithe = **neither** IC/15.
nether, nother *conj.* neither 16A/103, IB/258.
newe *inf.* renew 6/515; **newes** *pr. 3 sg.* 16/345, IIC/357.
newe *pa. t. 3 sg.* knew 24/522.
nexte *adv.* nearest, immediately preceding 2/541, 22/158.
ney *adv.* nigh 15/183.
ney see **nay** *conj.*
niche, nygh *adj.* stringent, severe 16A/64.
nighe *inf.* approach 16/71, IIC/75.
nighe *adv.* near 1/227.
nombred *pp.* numbered, counted 4/204.
nome, noome *pa. t. 1 sg.* took 16A/35, 24/627; **nome** went, came 17/268; **nomen, nommon** *pp.* taken, captured 23/52, IIB/112.
non *pron.* no one, neither 12/307.
non = **not** 6/366.
none *adj.* own IIB/100. *OED* nain.
nones *n.* nonce, occasion *for the* ~ 13/259, IB/278.
norne = **morne** 24/265.
note *n.*¹ profit, benefit 3/246. *OED* note sb.¹ 1. b.
note *n.*² melody 7/159.
nother see **nether**.
nowld *pa. t. 3 sg.* did not wish 2/500.
noy, noye, nye *n.* annoyance, trouble 2/265, 297, 461.
noyce, noyse *n.* clamor, tumult 7/526, 18/22.
numbrer = **nombred** 4/204.
nurre, nurrye *n.* foster-child 4/154, 158, IIB/354.
nuthooke, nutthocke *n.* tool for detaching fruit from trees 7/640.
ny thought = **methought** 24/343.
nyce *adj.* foolish 2/209.
nycke *inf.* deny 16/33.
nydy *n.* persons in need 6/99.
nye see **noy**.

GLOSSARY

nye *inf.*[1] deny 16/33, IIC/37.
nye *inf.*[2] annoy, disturb 5/225, 245.
nye *adv.* near 2/541, 5/354.
nye see **nay** *conj.*
nyf, nyfe *conj.* nor (?) 17/83, 85, IIA/23.
nygh see **niche**.
nygnahe = **nighe** *inf.* 16/71.
nygromancye see **neagromancye**.
nyll *auxiliary* will not 8/192.
nys = **nyf** 17/83.

O

occoure, occurre *n.* usury 24/349, 353^v.
oe, oye *adv.* always ID/20.
of *prep.* off 8/309, 10/158; from 1/7, 2/204, 2/348; in 2/602, 4/416, 7/156; on, upon 4/427, 6/104; over 4/452, 6/388; for 6/548, 16/168.
off *prep.* of IIB/17, 18; from IIB/666, 673.
offers *imp.* offer IB/61.
offpring = **offspring** 8/355.
omd = **and** 12/304.
omipotent = **omnipotent** 13/73.
on *num.* one 4/149, 5/152, 10/211, 24/96.
ondly = **only** 2/6.
one *n.*[1] habitation 2/383; see **wonne**.
one *n.*[2] abundance, expanse 2/26, 3/259; see **won, wone**.
one *n.*[3] one thing 18/42. *MED* on pro. 4a. (a).
one *at* ~ in agreement 6/150.
one *prep.* on 1/178, 2/50; in accord with 5/200; in the future 13/293 (*OED* on 19); ~ sleepe asleep 2/133.
one = **owne** 4/191.
ones, onste *adv.* once 1/43, 2/163.
only, onlye *adj.* alone 2/129, 24/404.
onne *num.* one 6/294.
ont on it 7/126.
onward *adv.* in advance 15/326.
oo *adv.* ever, always 2/22, 47.
operacioun *n.* act 1/69.
or *prep.* ere, before 2/165; ~ *that* before IB/260.

or = **our** 21/122, 127.
ordayne *inf.* carry out, arrange 14/352; **ordayned** *pa. t. 3 sg.* regulated 24/602; **ordeyne** *imp.* prepare 9/31; **ordayned her** dedicated herself 24/602.
osspringe = **offspring** 8/355, 17/206.
oste *n.* host, army 6/610.
ostern *n.* curds: "the curd for cheese before it is taken from the whey" 16/350. *EDD* oast sb. 2.
other *conj.* either 16/300, 24/553.
othes *n.* blasphemies 24/418.
ought *n.* anything 5/203, 540.
ought *pr. 3 sg.* owes 10/94; **oughten** *pa. t. 3 pl.* 14/82.
ought-where *adv.* anywhere 3/296, IA/3.
out, owt *excl.* go away 1/266, 2/569.
overall *adv.* everywhere 2/632.
overpasse *inf.* survive 10/213. *OED* overpass 5.
oye see **oe**.

P

pacialitie = **parcialitie** 9/67.
page *n.* boy 7/225, 8/325.
panch-cloute *n.* the membrane enveloping the bowels, tripe 7/124^v.
panne, penne, pon, ponn *n.* crown of the head, skull 2/205, 537; see **pon** *n.*[2]
pappe *n.* breast 16A/63.
parage *n.* parentage, lineage 8/287.
parcialitie *n.* affection, respect 9/67. *OED* partiality 1. b.
pardee, pardy, pardye, perdee, perdy, perdye *excl.* by God 5/236, 6/281, 7/124^v, 16/358, IB/181, IC/59.
parente *n.* parents 1/7.
parlous, perlouse *adj.* perilous 1/207, 5/395.
parrayle, parrell *n.* peril 18/34, 112.
parte *inf.*[1] divide 4/32, 39.
parte *inf.*[2] depart 1/277.
partie *n.* part, amount 14/95.
pas see **passe**.

pascall *adj.* paschal, having to do with the Jewish Passover 15/7, 27.
pase *n.* pace, step 15/361, 16/82.
passe, pas *inf.* travel 16/82, IB/179; leave 24/548; surpass 1/201; go freely 16/294, IIC/306; **passe** *pr. subj. 2 sg.* experience, undergo 16/353, IIC/367; **past** *pa. t. 3 sg.* experienced 16A/167; **paste** *pa. t. 3 sg.* passed by 24/154.
passinge *adv.* surpassingly, exceedingly 2/254.
pate *n.* head 16/105, IIC/117.
pawlle *n.* cloak, mantle 16A/110.
payde *adj.* satisfied, pleased 6/44, 18/353.
paye *n.* profit, pleasure 1/291, 2/235; result 16/104.
payre *inf.* decrease, diminish 23/284, 24/319; **payred** *pa. t. 3 sg.* 19/84; **payringe** *vbl. n.* 14/64.
peare, pere *n.* peer, equal 1/83, 7/576.
peareth = **appeareth** 24/380.
pearles, perrelles *n.* pearls 24/162, 277.
pearles *adj.* peerless, without equal 1/11, 5/38.
penne see **panne.**
penyble *adj.* painstaking 6/314.
penyegrasse, penyegresse *n.* a plant growing in marshy ground 7/79.
penyewrytte *n.* pennywort, an herb 7/28.
perceive, perceyve *imp.* recognize 16/40, IIC/44.
perces = **perscer** 6/398.
perdee, perdy, perdye see **pardee.**
pere see **peare.**
perlouse see **parlous.**
perlye *adj.* made of pearls 6/577.
perre, perrye, perye, pyrrie *n.* jewelry 4/93, 5/268, 6/577, 10/410.
perscer *n.* carpenter's tool for boring holes 6/398.
pertakers *n.* sympathizers, supporters 8/329.
petrye = **perre** 4/93.
petty *adj.* small-sized 10/41.

pewdras, pewdreas, pewderas = **pewee-ars** 16A/150.
pewer = **pew** a pointed stick (?) 6/591. *OED* pew sb.²
pewee-ars *n.* pissy-arse 16A/150.
pie *n.* magpie *as a* ~ senselessly IB/273.
pigge *n.* pitcher, crock, flagon 8/381 + SD. *OED* pig sb.²
pight *pa. t. 1 sg.* put, cast 24/254; *pp.* placed 9/191, 21/103; made fast, fixed 16A/202, 21/260.
pinches, pinkes, pynckes *adj.* small, scanty 7/224. *OED* pink a.² B.
pine *n.* pain 1/248.
pintell *n.* penis 10/363.
pippe *inf.* whistle (?) 7/189.
pitche *inf.* caulk 3/74.
plainte, playne, playnt *inf.* enter a complaint 10/392, 15/333.
playe *n.* trick, game 1/207, 2/179; sexual intercourse 6/136 (2).
playe, plea *inf.* take part in sexual intercourse 6/127, 136 (1).
playne *n.* flat land 7/169, 23/310.
playne *adj.* full 5/144, 11/253.
plelates = **prelates** 10/1.
plight *inf.* pledge 14/401; *pr. 1 sg.* 6/222, 16A/207.
ploomes *n.* plums 7/637.
plye *inf.* bend 8/207.
poacke, pocke, poke *n.* sack, bag 7/127.
poastye, poostye see **poste.**
poll = **pull** 17/180.
pollicye *n.* strategy 5/125.
pon *n.*¹ domain 23/659. *OED* pawn sb.² 2.
pon, ponn *n.*² skull *by my* **pon** 16A/157; *as broke I my* **ponn** 16A/173. *OED* pan sb.¹ 6.
popelard, popilerde, poplard, poplart, populard, popularde, populart *n.* hypocrite, fool 5/296, 312, 15/362, IB/233.
popelard *adj.* hypocritical 24/589.
possession *n.* goods 24/319.
poste, postee, postie, posty, postye, poastye, poostye *n.* power, strength

GLOSSARY

2/3, 6/185, 672, IC/43, IIB/53, 94, 284.
postee *adj.* strong IIC/10.
pottell *n.* tankard 3/233.
pottle *n.* drink 7/615.
powder *n.* dust 24/146.
power = **powder** 24/146.
powle = **pull** 17/180.
poydrace = **pewee-ars** 16A/150.
poyntes, poyntys *n.* details, subtleties 23/257, IIB/257.
praye *n.* captured goods, spoils of war 4/32, 39; captured person or persons 16/270, 17/120.
preeffe, preff *n.* proof 10/342.
preeve *inf.*¹ deprive 6/519.
preeve *inf.*² prove 6/242; **preeven** *pr. 3 pl.* 14/197; **preeves** *imp.* 10/141; **preeved** *pp.* 6/185, 504.
prepotent *adj.* supremely powerful 8/339.
prese = **priests** 6/220.
present *n.* presence 16/237, IIC/249.
present, presente *inf.* give a present to 4/56+SD, 8/341; **presented** *pa. t. 3 pl.* IB/447.
present *adv.* immediately 6/259.
president *n.* ruler 6/257.
pretty *adj.* astute, cunning 10/41.
prevelye *adv.* privately, confidentially 20/21.
preven see **prive** *inf.*²
preves *n.* proofs IIB/318.
prevytye *n.* secrecy, private plan IIB/257.
price *n.* prize *beare the* ~ *are best* 1/146; *of* ~ of great value 10/1.
pricke *n.* skewer 7/132. *OED* pudding-prick.
principall *adj.* princely, important IC/52.
prive, pryve *inf.*¹ deprive 6/519, 14/312; **pryved** *pp.* 2/407.
prive *inf.*² prove 6/242; **preven** *pr. 3 pl.* 16/40; **prived** *pp.* 6/185.
privelye, privylie *adv.* secretly 6/143, 18/254.
privetie, privetye, privitie *n.* secrecy,

private plan 18/306, 20/62, 23/257.
proctor *n.* procurator 23/683, IIB/687.
proffe *n.* proof 10/342.
promoted *pp.* publicized 17/302.
proose = **proofe** 6/333.
prophecye *n.* foreshadowing, warning 18/132.
prove *inf.* test 5/34.
prove = **preeve** 6/519.
provinges = **province** 6/580.
provydence *n.* foresight 1/23.
prowder *adj.* more vigorous 15/361.
pryce, pryse *n.* value 2/402, 23/425.
prydee = **pride** 24/277.
pryme *n.* the canonical hour: probably 9 A.M. 16A/47.
pure *adv.* completely 6/591, 8/415.
purpur *n.* purple cloth 5/93.
purvaye *inf.* prepare beforehand 15/200, 202.
purye *n.* a kind of food: purée (?) 7/128.
put *pp.* blamed 16/38, IIC/42.
put, pute *inf.* place 24/549.
pyche *n.* food laid or "pitched" out to eat 7/107. *OED* pitch sb.² 8.
pye *n.* magpie 7/417; *as a* ~ senselessly 5/312.
pynckes see **pinches.**
pyne *n.* pain 9/175, 10/397.
pynes *pr. 2 sg.* make an effort 12/65; **pyne** *imp.* 19/238.
pynne *n.* wooden nail 3/61, 76.
pyrrie see **perre.**

Q

quaile, quell *inf.* kill 10/339.
quainte *adj.* strange 19/18.
quaintely *adv.* cunningly 13/286.
quayntyce *n.* cunning, guile 12/14.
queanes *n.* loose women 10/290.
quicke *adj.* living 9/111.
quicken *inf.* come alive 18/114.
quintely, quyntly *adj.* cunningly 8/420, 13/286.
quite *inf.* repay, reward 2/549, 6/312;

pr. 2 pl. 13/267.
quocke, quoked, quooke *pa. t. 1 sg.* quaked, shivered 7/422, 18/272.
quoynt *adj.* quaint, unusual 16/324.
quycke *n.* live persons 21/338, 23/700.
quyte *inf.* pay 9/203; **quitt, quytt, quytte** *pp.* 10/95, 14/295, 24/486; **qwyt** *pp.* repaid 12/145.

R

race, rase *n.* conflict, battle 16/353, IIC/367.
rade, rayde *adj.* ready 2/107.
rade = **red** *inf.* 1/210.
raft, rafte see **reave**.
ragalitie = **regaltye** 8/272.
rake *n.* path 7/40.
rasarde, roysard *n.* talker of nonsense 23/371. *OED* roise v.
raveninge, rayvinge see **reave**.
ravished *pa. t. 3 sg.* carried away by force 17/243.
raye *n.* order, array 23/490, IIB/490.
raygn *n.* reign, ruling power 22/195; **regnis** kingdoms IIB/214.
reacon, reche, recken *inf.* reckon, count 7/26, 24/515, IIB/609; **reacon** *pr. subj. 3 sg.* 23/435; **reconed** *pa. t. 1 sg.* 8/210.
read, readd, reade, redd, redde, rede, reede *n.* advice, counsel 2/263, 14/313, 16/110, 18/285, IIA/17, IIB/366, 438; *hast* **read** are correct 15/131.
reade *n.* lot 2/686. *OED* rede sb.¹ 3. d.
reade *inf.* expound 11/238; *pr. 1 sg.* predict 4/269.
read, reade see **reede** *inf.*
reame, reeme *inf.* weep 13/427, 16A/60; **reamest** *pr. 2 sg.* ID/1; **reemynge** *pr. p.* 24/578; **remynge** *vbl. n.* 17/83.
reane *n.* rain 2/478.
reased *pp.* raised 23/705.
reave, reeve, reve *inf.* rob, plunder, take away 6/519, 16/250, 10/32; **reaves** *pr. 2 sg.* 16/341; **reeves, reves** *pr. 3 sg.* 16/304, IIC/316; **raveninge, rayvinge** *pr. p.* 24/346; **reaved, raft, rafte, reft** *pa. t. 1 sg.* 16/153, 24/255, IIC/165; **rafte** *pp.* 23/416, IIB/416.
reball, reballe *n.* rascall 8/404, 10/31; cf. **ribalde**.
recked = **wretched** *adj.* contemptible 10/31.
red, redd, redde see **reede** *inf.*
redd, redde, rede, reede see **read** *n.*
reddelye, redealye, redelye *adv.* readily, promptly 15/131, 19/66, 22/57.
redshankes *n.* wading birds of the snipe family 3/190.
redye *adv.* readily IIB/317.
reede *inf.* advise 23/334; **read, reade, red, redd, redde** *pr. 1 sg.* 1/190, 210, 2/273, 8/211, 11/120, **reade** *pr. subj. 2 sg.* 7/144; **read** *imp.* 14/89; **reade, rede** *pa. t. 2 sg.* 23/701, IIB/705.
reede *pr. 1 sg.* read 5/53.
reedify *inf.* rebuild 14/255.
reeme, reemynge, remynge see **reame**.
reeve, reve see **reave**.
reformed = **informed** 5/136.
reft see **reave**.
regaltye *n.* kingship 8/272.
regnis see **raygn**.
released *pp.* forgiven 14/112.
relygion *n.* the Church 24/255, 321.
remeeves *pr. 3 sg.* moves 3/249.
remewes, renewes = **remeeves** 3/249.
renne *inf.* run 7/40.
rent *n.* tax 6/263.
rent, rente *adj.* torn 8/351, 24/126; **rent** *pp.* torn apart, defeated 12/127.
repleth *adj.* perfect 1/195; replete, filled 1/211.
repreeve *inf.* reprove 23/430; **reprived, repryved** *pa. t. 3 sg.* 5/421, 12/128.
repreve, reproffe *n.* censure 5/293,

GLOSSARY

IB/230.
reserved *pp.* held over, saved 16/230, IIC/242.
revisible *adj.* again visible 1/124.
rewe *inf.* regret 10/198, IIC/368; *pr. 1 sg.* 7/236; **rewes** *pr. 3 sg.* 16A/228; *imp.* 16/341, IIC/353.
rewkes *n.* knights 10/193.
reysed *pp.* raised 23/546.
rialtye, ryalltee, ryaltye *n.* royalty, royal state 6/23, 8/203, 210.
ribalde, riball, ryball, rybauld *n.* rascal 8/404, 10/309, 13/262, IIC/353; **riballes, rybaldes, rybbauldes** 10/159, 23/490, IIB/490.
ribaldrie, rybaldrye *n.* sacrilegious talk 16/161, IIC/173.
ribbie *n.* an herb: ribwort 7/22. *OED* rib sb.[2]
ribott *n.* rascal 10/309; **rybbattes, rybbottes** 10/159; cf. **ribalde**.
ricked *pp.* twisted 10/31.
right *n.* righteous people 24/10; throughout the ~ with complete justice 23/10, IIB/10.
right, righte *adv.* exactly 5/214, IIC/375; on right certain, correctly 4/49, 8/33.
rightwise, ryghtwyse *adj.* righteous 11/135, IIB/616.
ringes *pr. 3 sg.* rules, governs 8/205.
risynge *n.* resurrection 13/386.
rocked *pp.* swung in a cradle 8/404, 10/31.
rode, roode *n.* the Cross 4/467, 24/580.
rode-tree, roode-tree *n.* the Cross 4/125, IIB/487.
rogge *n.* rogue (?) 18/281.
ronett *adj.* circular 3/34.
ronge *adj.* wrong, prohibited 3/290.
roo, rowe *n.* rest, quiet 7/390, 24/144.
roote *n.*[1] see **crape**.
roote *n.*[2] source 9/109.
roted *pa. t. 3 sg.* rotted 6/719.
rott, rotte *n.* disease of the liver in sheep 7/14, 34.
rotten *n.* rat 3/179.
rought *pp.* wrought, made 7/9.

rowe *n.*[1] deer 10/435.
rowe *n.*[2] on a ~ in succession 7/26, 11/227; upon a ~ in a line 24/547; **rowes** ordered lines 3/186.
rowland see **comyn rowland**.
rowndfull *n.* dicing term, a successful throw (?) 16A/130.
rowte *n.* crowd, troop 5/429, 10/192.
rowtinge *adj.* rotting 9/85.
roysard see **rasarde**.
rufull *adj.* sorrowful 2/686.
rugges *n.* cloaks 7/263.
ruled, rweled *adj.* directed 23/490, IIB/490.
ruler = **ruled** 23/490.
rumne = **runne** ID/69.
ruse *pr. 3 sg.* rues, regrets 1/283.
ruth, ruthe *n.* pity 18/161, 23/230.
ruthfullie *adv.* sorrowfully 24/316.
rwast *pr. 1 sg.* wrest, take away forcibly 16/153.
rybaldrye see **ribaldrie**.
ryball, rybauld, riballes, rybaldes, rybbauldes see **ribalde**.
ryche *inf.* enrich 21/71.
ryffe *adj.* abundant 18/183.
ryne *inf.* touch, affect 24/639.
ryved, ryvyd *adj.* plundered 23/54, IIB/54.

S

sacke, seeke *n.* dry wine 17/316.
sadd *adj.* serious 21/170.
sadlie, sadlye *adv.* earnestly, heavily, seriously 7/409, 18/312, IB/392.
saffe *conj.* but 24/154.
sager, segger *n.* fellow 16A/1.
salfe *adj.* saved 3/263.
salve *inf.* save 11/48; anoint 11/270.
same = **save** 4/489.

sand, sendinge, sond, sound *n.*
    dispensation 1/47, 23/31.
sandalles see **sendal.**
sarrowe *n.* sorrow 5/219.
sarve *pr. 1 sg.* deserve 16A/208; **served**
    pp. 16/111, IIC/123.
saudens, saundence soundens *n.*
    sultans 6/219.
saught *adj.* reconciled 18/121. *OED*
    saught a.
save *prep.* except 2/215, 688.
savely *adv.* safely IIB/12.
saverraye *n.* food: savoury 7/204.
savoure *n.* scent, smell 9/53.
saw, sawe *n.* saying, speech 2/148,
    6/514; **sawes** 11/257, 323.
saye, see *n.* 3/281, IIB/571; **seeyes**
    2/31.
saye, se *inf.* see IA/18, IB/383; **sees** *pr.*
    2 sg. 14/98; **seene** *pr. 2 pl.* 13/243,
    24/606; **see** *pr. subj. 3 sg.* watch over
    6/121; **see, seghe** *pa. t. sg.* 2/449,
    17/162; **see, seene** *pa. t. pl.* 8/213,
    17/35; **seene** *pp.* proved 24/221.
saye, sayne *inf.* inform 14/163, IA/6.
scabbe *n.* skin disease: mange 7/13.
scake *inf.* avoid, flee 23/216. *OED*
    shake v. 1.
scalward = **stalward** 16/181.
scape, skape *inf.* escape 10/211,
    24/216.
scapit *pp.* deprived 2/700.
scatche = **scathe** 10/216.
scathe *n.* harm 10/216.
score = **store** 7/278.
scyence *n.* knowledge 21/277.
se see **saye** *inf.*
sea, see *n.* seat, throne 1/187, IC/78.
seale *n.*¹ prosperity 11/323. *OED* sele
    sb.
seale *n.*² sail 3/197.
seale-yard *n.* spar 3/91.
sease *imp.* cease 7/261.
**secerly, secker, securely, sicker,
    sickerlie, sicurre, sycker, sy-
    curlye** *adv.* surely, securely 2/279,
    584, 5/115, 224, 6/305, 7/209, 12/61,
    17/25.
secke *n.* sack, bag 24/672.
see see saye *n.*, **see.**
see, seene, sees see **saye** *n.* and **sea**
    inf.
seech *inf.* seek 11/210.
seede *n.* race, descendants 1/289.
seemely *adv.* with propriety 6/29.
seemelye *adj.* comely 24/285.
seeminge *pr. p.* appearing 7/312.
seet *inf.* set, place 6/147; *pr. 1 sg.* 7/194.
seeth *inf.* boil 7/73.
**seeth, seithen, seyth, sith, sithe,
    sithen, sithence, sithens, syns** *adv.*
    since 1/86, 2/138, 403, 491, 6/38,
    12/290, ID/92, IIC/224.
seett *of inf.* value, esteem 2/310.
seeyes see **saye** *n.*
segger see **sager.**
seghe see **se.**
seker *adj.* sure 16A/1.
selfe *adj.* same 23/337, 24/378.
semblant *n.* semblance, outer ap-
    pearance 2/575, 578.
sempiternall *adj.* everlasting 13/9.
send, sende see **sent.**
sendal *n.* thin rich silken material
    24/150; **sandalles** 24/150.
sende, sendinge *n.* message, that
    which was sent 4/47, IIB/31.
sended *pa. t. 3 sg.* ascended 21/332.
sendinge see **sand.**
sennyors *n.* gentlemen 1/178.
sent *inf.* send 20/190; **send** *pa. t. 1 sg.*
    21/183; *pa. t. 3 sg.* 21/300; ~ , **sende**
    pp. 15/46, 16/152.
sentence *n.* judgment 23/445.
sente *pr. 1 sg.* assent IIB/613.
served see **sarve.**
sete see **sea.**
sethen *n.* times 20/165.
sett *pa. t. 3 sg.* sat as a judge 24/345.
sett *pr. 1 sg.* ~ *by* put aside 10/219.
sett = **fell** 5/212.
severe *inf.* sever, part 17/208.
seyte see **sea.**
seyth see **seeth** *adv.*
shacke, shake *n.* shaking, shock
    18/276.

GLOSSARY 453

shad, shade *pp.* isolated 7/269. *OED* shed v.¹ 1. b.
shadowe *inf.* "enfold with a protecting and beneficent influence" 6/29. *OED* shadow v.2.
shadowes *n.* foreshadowings 15/70.
shamely *adv.* with shame 2/346.
shape *n.* likeness 2/85.
shape *inf.* ~ *them of* direct themselves from, escape IB/366; ~ *us to* direct ourselves to 7/102.
shapen *pp.* determined 16/236, IIC/248.
shapes *pr. 3 sg.* plans 14/431. *OED* shape v. II.
shappe *n.* human form 2/268.
sharpely *adv.* briskly 6/606.
shaye = **straye** (?) 4/163.
shea *a meaningless error* 22/8.
sheede *inf.* shed 24/121.
sheene *adj.* shining 1/185.
shend, shende *inf.* ruin 6/138, 7/261; **sheindes, shendes, shyndes** *pr. 3 sg.* 7/268; **shent** *pa. t. 3 sg.* 24/593; ~ , **shente** *pp.* 2/346, 354.
shenes = **shendes** 7/268.
shew = **shrew** 7/154.
shewe *inf.* show 1/247, appear 1/281; bear witness 6/514; **shewes, sheweth** *pr. 3 sg.* appears 6/82, 16/340; **shewen** bear witness *pr. 3 pl.* 16/260; **shoo** *pr. subj. 3 sg.* show IIB/157.
ship *n.* sheep 7/3.
shitt see **shutt**.
shoope *pa. t. 3 sg.* shaped 9/260.
shouldarye = **sudarye** 18/387.
shrew, shrewe, shrowe *n.* evil person 7/66, 10/157, 16/164; **shroes** IB/106.
shrewde *adj.* vicious 7/13.
shrews *pr. 3 sg.* curses 16/340.
shryned *pp.* enshrined 5/61.
shryve = **shryne** 5/63; ~ = **stryve** IB/438; **shryved** = **shryned** 5/61.
shunt *inf.* rid, relieve 16/15. *OED* shunt v. 4. b.
shutt *inf.* rid, relieve 16/15, IIC/15; ~ , **shitt** *pp.* 12/149, 24/194; **shutt** *from us* rid of us 15/348.

sibbe, sybbe *adj.* akin 7/555.
siche, syche *adj.* such 10/298, IIB/23.
sicker, sickerlie, sicurlye, sicurre see **secerly**.
sickinge *pr. p.* sighing 6/431; ~ , **sikinge** *vbl. n.* 2/430, 18/311.
sieene *n.* sin 5/36.
sigaldry *n.* sorcery 16/161, IC/95.
sight *n.* appearance 22/43; *in* ~ in mind ID/82.
signe *n.* sign, symbol 11/143; **signes, sines, sygnes, synnys** 15/70, 17/261.
signes *pr. 3 sg.* signifies IB/389.
simnes = **sins** 24/74.
since = **synnce** 16A/147.
sinne, synne *n.* physical decay 9/84; sexual intercourse 9/211; evil use 2/587.
sith, sithe, sithen, sithence, sithens see **seeth** *adv.*
skape see **scape**.
skewed *adj.* skewbald, of various colours 22/117.
skill, skyll *n.* sense, wisdom 13/154, 23/319; **skylles, skyllys** reasoning 23/321, IIB/321; *well can* **skyll** has excellent knowledge 5/374.
skricke *pr. subj. 3 sg.* shriek, screech 16/98, IIC/106.
skylfullye, skyllfullye *adv.* rationally, sensibly 9/106, 14/94.
skyll *n.* matter, topic 18/56. *OED* skill sb.¹ 4. a.
skyll *adj.* reasonable, sensible 4/36, 362.
slake *inf.* reduce effort, moderate 3/303, 4/247; *imp.* 3/118; *pr. 3 sg.* 13/326; *pr. subj. 2 sg.* 3/23; **slaked** *pp.* diminished 3/260.
slee *adj.* sly, wily 2/451.
sleelie, sleelye, sleilye *adv.* cunningly 2/410, 12/196, 14/383.
sleepe *n.* *laye to* ~ kill 10/227.
sleigh, sleight, sleighte *adj.* skilful 16A/178, 21/296.
sleight, sleighte, sleightte, sleyght, sleyt, slight *n.* trick, plot, magic 6/618, 12/114, 145, 14/320, IIB/713;

sleightely *adv.* slily, cunningly 12/196.
slich, sliche, slyche, slytche *n.* mud, slime 3/22, 73, 75.
sliere *inf.* turn away 4/340.
sloparde = **sluggard** (?) 8/305.
slough *n.* skin 18/189. *OED* slough sb.² 2.
slow, slowe *inf.* slay 2/646, 3/35, 4/268.
sluch *n.* sludge, muddy place 7/10.
smale *n.* person or persons of low rank 6/246, 9/255.
smart *adj.* brisk 18/83.
smote, smott *pa. t. 3 sg.* hit 16/96, IIC/100.
smple = **symple** 6/518.
smutted *pp.* characterized by some imperfection 16A/369. *OED* smut v. 1. b.
snell *adv.* quickly 10/338.
soe = **to** 4/173.
soeleme, sollempne *adj.* important, ceremonious 1/36, 287.
solatacion = **solation** *n.* rejoicing 1/37.
solempnitie, solempnitye *n.* ceremony 5/364, 14/354.
solempne, sollempne *inf.* solemnise, sanctify 2/103.
solingere = **losingere** 10/254.
son *n.* sun IIB/223.
sond see **sand**.
sone, sonne, soone *adv.* immediately 1/177, 2/518, 14/144.
songe = **sponge** 24/18.
soone = **son** 8/335.
sooth, soothe, soth, sothe, south *n.* truth 2/253, 269, 6/361, IA/6, IB/411.
soother *adj.* truer 11/69.
soothly, sothlie, sothly, sothlye, southly *adv.* truly 2/295, 3/44, 5/121, 7/310, IB/313.
soothnes, sothnes, sothnesse, southnes *n.* truth 1/26, 16/281, IIC/293, 296.
sope *n.* drink 7/193.
sore *n.* torment, trouble 11/270; afflicted persons 24/250.
sore *adv.* sorely 16/98, 354.

sorye *adj.* unfortunate 15/303.
sose *n.* a sloppy mess of food 7/204. *OED* soss sb.¹ 1. b.
sott *n.* fool 24/239.
sotted *pp.* besotted 3/4.
sought *pp.* found by seeking 7/13; *pa. t. 1 sg.* desired 24/274.
sound see **sand**.
sound *n.* gift, present 24/305. *OED* sand sb.¹ 1.
soundens see **saudens**
soune, sowne, swone, swoone *n.* swoon, faint 10/61, 18/264. *OED* sound v.⁴
soveraignely, soveraignlye, soveraynly *adv.* in a supreme degree 1/78, 283, IB/407.
sowe *inf.* sew 7/50.
sowne = **sownd** *adj.* deep 18/273.
sowse *n.* parts of an animal pickled for food 7/204, 213. *OED* souse sb.¹
space *n.* period of time 4/391, 14/120.
spare *inf.* omit, leave aside 23/360, IIB/360.
spared *pp.* stored up 24/415. *OED* spare v.¹ 8. b.
spart *n.* stalk of coarse grass: spear 10/195.
spede, speede *inf.* fare 2/583; **speede** cause to prosper, prosper 1/237, 13/35; **spede** *imp.* hurry 4/63; **speede, spedd** *pp.* sent away, killed 4/388.
speede *n.* profit 10/79.
speete = **spirit** (?) 16A/358.
spell *n.* speech, statement 5/82, 18/289.
spend *inf.* spread about 11/264; *pa. t. 1 sg.* spent 24/54, 189; *pp.* 2/569.
spewe *pr. 1 sg.* vomit 7/240.
spill, spyll *inf.* kill, destroy, waste 3/43, 308, 4/287; **spilled** *pp.* 9/225.
spine see **spye**.
spinge *unidentified* 16/328.
spould *n.* spittle 16/343. *OED* spold.
spoyle *inf.* take away 17/180; *imp.* destroy 16A/66.
springe, spryng *inf.* grow 2/332, IIB/287; **springes** *pr. 3 sg.* grows,

GLOSSARY

blossoms 23/413, 24/111; **sprong, spronge** *pp.* derived, descended 16/328, IIC/340.
sprite, spryte, sprytte *n.* spirit 15/263, 20/20, 21/218.
spurne *n.* tripping, stumbling, downfall 1/57. *OED* spurn sb.¹
spurne *imp.* disregard 5/211.
spute *inf.* dispute 24/549.
spye *inf.* notice 24/664; **spine** *pr. 2 pl.* spy out 23/359.
stadd *pp.* beset with difficulties 22/312. *OED* stead v. 6.
stales *n.* prostitutes, decoys 5/355.
stall *n.*¹ thief 10/182. *OED* stall sb.² 2.
stall *n.*² standing place 2/674; covered place for animals 3/155.
stallon *n.* stallion 10/314.
stalward, stalwarde *n.* valiant man 18/181, 314.
standinge *n.* stand, collection 2/533.
standinge-cuppe *n.* cup with feet or a base 4/64 + SD.
staneth = **standeth** 24/669.
stanold *n.* a pejorative term? 16/181, 314.
stare see **steare** *inf.*²
starte *inf.* go away 7/429.
state *n.* rank, pomp 12/192.
stature *n.* place, position 1/107.
stea, stee, stye *inf.* rise, ascend 20/96, ID/31; **stayed, stead, steede, steegh, steigh, steight** *pa. t. 3 sg.* 20/158, 21/84, 299, 333, IB/420.
stead, stedde, steed, stid, styde *n.* place 1/186, 4/264, 16A/395, IIB/680.
steake, stecke, steke *inf.* fasten, enclose, shut 3/?57, 16/90, IIC/94.
steare, stere *inf.*¹ rebuke 16/314, 24/23. *OED* steer v.¹ 5.
steare *inf.*² stare, watch closely 6/589; **stare** *imp.* 16/313, IIC/325.
stedde, steed see **stead**.
stee, steede, steegh, steigh, steight see **stea**.
steepe *inf.* soak 7/215.
sterring *pr. p.* stirring, moving 2/93; **sterred, storred** *pp.* moved 9/27;

disturbed 24/205; **sturreth** = **sturred** *pp.* 9/27.
steyne = **strayne**
steyne *pr. 2 pl.* live, reside 16/151. *OED* stay v.¹ 8. b.
stibbon = **stubborn** 10/314.
stiche, stike *n.* a board in a kiln upon which grain is placed 10/299. *OED* kiln sb. 2.
stickt-tode, stuckt-toode, stycktode, styck-toode *n.* frog-piercer 10/314, 369.
stid, stidd, stide see **stead**.
stifflye, stiflye *adv.* steadfastly 12/90, IB/93.
stitche *n. every* ~ every inch.
stonde, stound *n.* moment, time 18/280.
stonne *inf.* be amazed 10/61. *OED* stun v. 2. b.
stoore, store, stowre *n.* time of stress 21/122, 24/86, 205.
stope see **stowpe**.
stopped = **stomped** stamped 7/215.
stopple *n.* stopper 7/613.
store *n.*¹ that which has been saved 6/405. *OED* store sb. 8.
store *n.*² collection (of excrement)? 7/278.
storred see **sterring**.
stout, stoute, stowte *adj.* strong 6/376, 10/379, 11/58; **stowtest** 24/23.
stower *n.* large number IA/47. *OED* store sb. 4.
stowpe, stope *imp.* fall headlong 16/87, IIC/91. *OED* stoop v. 1. b.
stowtly *adv.* strongly 5/100; contumaciously 18/153.
strang, strange *adj.* foreign 8/321, IB/294.
straye *n. one the* ~ in scattered fashion (?) 4/163. *OED* astray adv. or a. *and* straw v.¹ 1.
strayne *inf.* stretch 16A/188.
streake *inf.* strike 16/90.
streat *adv.* severely 22/312. *OED* strait adv. II. 6.
stretlye *adv.* tightly 17/224.

stroacke, strocke, stroke *pa. t. 3 sg.* struck 7/317.
stry *n.* the act of straying 17/223. *OED* stray sb. II. 4.
strynde, strynte *n.* lineage 9/204.
sturreth see **sterring**.
stydd, styde see **stead**.
stye *n.* path 7/671, 24/24.
stye see **stea**.
styffe *adj.* strong, steadfast 18/82, 21/213.
styffned *pp.* made steadfast 21/236.
style *n.* stile, fence 7/671.
stynt *inf.* stop 23/76, IIB/76; *imp.* 7/460.
stytton = **stubborn** (?) 10/314.
subsequence *n.* sequel 1/208.
suche *n.* swampy place 7/10. *OED* sough sb.² (*variant* souch).
sudarye *n.* shroud 18/387.
sue *pr. 2 pl.* engage in 18/127; **sues** *pr. 3 pl.* follow IIC/352.
suen *pr. 3 pl.* petition IIC/272.
suffer *imp.* be passive, stand still 1/295. *OED* suffer v. 4.
suffered *pa. t. 3 sg.* allowed 14/274.
sufferently *adv.* sovereignly, in a supreme degree 1/283.
suffice *inf.* meet the requirements of 21/205. *OED* suffice v. 5.
suffraynty *n.* sovereignty IC/83.
sure *inf.* assure 2/456.
sutte = **shutt** 12/149.
suwes = **sawes** 11/257.
swaine *inf.* swoon 10/61. *OED* sway v. I. 1. b.
swap *inf.* cut 8/401; **swappe, swope, swopp** *pr. subj. 3 sg.* 14/389.
swayne *n.* boy, fellow 8/400, 10/115.
swedlinge *adj.* in swadling clothes 8/400.
sweene = **swem**
sweens *n.* dreams IB/382.
swelling *pr. p.* behaving arrogantly 8/400. *OED* swell v. 9.
swem, sweme *n.* grief 16A/58, 98; think ... ~ be ... grieved 11/8, 16A/144. *OED* sweam sb.
swene, sweyne = swem 11/8, 16A/58.

swone, swoone see **soune**.
swyme *inf.* float 3/83.
swyre *n.* neck 14/389.
syche see **siche**.
sycker, syckerlye, sycurlye see **secerly**.
syde *n.* seed, descendants 6/106.
sygnes, synnys see **signe**.
syke *pr. 1 sg.* sigh 17/299.
sylver *n.* money 24/208.
sym *unidentified* 7/480.
synke *n.* five 16A/147.
synnce, synnes, syyes = **synke** 16A/143, 147.
syns, syth, sythe, sythen, sythenn, sythence see **seeth** *adv.*
syre *n.* father 2/678; man 12/16, 99.
sytt *pr. 1 sg. or that I* ~ before I rest 14/293.

T

taberte, tabret *n.* coat 13/300.
table *n.* tablet; sign 16A/218.
tache *n.* sin 7/285.
takys *imp.* take 4/193; **toke, tooke** *pa. t. sg.* gave 10/394, 21/185; **taken** *pp.* 10/381; **tane, tayne** taken, caught 4/196, 16/266; **take** ... *agayne* withdraw ... 8/163.
talch, talgh *n.* tallow 7/36, 38.
talefull *adj.* full-tailed, fully grown (?) 7/11.
talent *n.* natural ability 2/586; purpose 6/92, 15/358; wish 10/76, 278.
talls = **tayles** 6/275.
tamde, tamed *pp.* reduced in intensity 7/78.
tame *inf.* broach 7/144; **tamed** *pa. t. 3 sg.* began upon 7/432.
tapster *n.* barmaid 17/286; **tapsters** 17/301.
tarboll, tarreboyle *n.* ball of tar 7/175. *OED* tar sb. 4.
tarboyste, tarreboyste, tarbox *n.* container for tar 7/78, 175.

GLOSSARY

tary *inf.* prolong, delay IB/410.
tatch *n.* talent, gift 18/105.
tayle, teale *inf.* mark 7/399; **taylinge** *vbl. n.* 7/36.
tayles *adj.* tail-less (?) 6/275.
tayne see **takys**.
taynt, taynted *pp.* corrupted, rotten 7/285, 18/279; **taynted, tayntyd** attainted, proved guilty 23/594, IIB/594.
taytfull, tytefull *adj.* nimble, lively 7/11. *OED* tait.
taythed *pa. t. 1 sg.* tithed 24/351.
teach *inf.* lead by instructing 14/302.
teare *inf.* destroy, harm 4/446.
teath, teathe, teithe, teythe, tyth *n.* tithe 4/30, 35, 95, 17/151; **tythes, teathinges-makinge** 4/133; **teathinge** *vbl. n.* 4/45.
teene *n.* woe, suffering, torment 1/209, 239; anger 3/319, 8/335; **take good** ~ take close heed 6/720; *take* ~ take heed (?) 23/128; ~ *-tyde* time of suffering 24/114.
teene *inf.*[1] harass, anger 8/171; ~ , **teenen, tynne** *pr. 3 pl.* 10/227.
teene *inf.*[2] endure 11/312.
teight, teighte *pp.* stated 6/30, 22/78. *OED* tight v.[2] 3. b.
teire = **there** 10/446.
tell *inf.* count 7/399; *imp.* 4/162.
tell, tyll *prep.* until 19/231, IA/26; to 3/47, 21/47.
temporalitye, temporaltye *n.* temporal authority 9/67.
tende *pr. 3 pl.* apply oneself 1/72. *OED* tend v. 2.
tendered *pa. t. 3 pl.* administered 5/424.
tent, tente *n.* heed 7/198, IIB/128.
tent *pp.* held 7/511.
teythe see **teath**.
tharf *adj.* unleavened 4/66.
thast = **thrast** 16A/253.
that *pron.* that which 13/296, 21/103; he who IB/107, 271; him who IIC/73; those who 24/540, IC/44.
that *conj.* so that 24/157.

the *pron.*[1] thee 2/142, 579, 13/464, 472, 16/185, 348, 16A/326, 18/281, 23/371, 24/131, IA/40, 43, IB/130, 137, 172, 174, 179, 279, IC/12, 104, ID/9, IIB/184, 186, 201, 241, 242, 246, 549, 551, 658, 710, 715, IIC/357.
the *pron.*[2] they 1/62, 279, 2/27, 31, 51, 186, 392, 421, 3/8, 11, 111, 130, 176, 205, 252+SD, 5/106, 148, 152, 206, 317, 362, 363, 368, 405, 422, 426, 431, 437(2), 6/150, 285, 443, 7/19, 166, 8/151, 152, 393, 402, 10/20, 47, 144, 396, 11/326, 12/289, 309(1), 13/155, 248, 14/223, 301, 16/20, 40, 44, 18/21, 165, 209, 291, 19/247, 20/83, 84, 89, 21/165, 250, 369, 378, 22/27, 68, 127, 129, 185, 191, 197, 222, 316, 23/19, 231, 235, 302, 303, 410, 428, 429, 678, 697, 700, 24/177, 499, 507, 662, 683, 687, IIC/24, 326+SD.
the see **thee**.
the = **he** 4/489; ~ = **we** 18/134; ~ = **them** 5/410.
thedure *adv.* thither IIB/696.
thee *inf.* prosper *never thryve nee* ~ 2/702; *as mote (mot, mott) I* ~, the 2/533, 15/349, IB/102; *soe mott (mote) I* ~ 5/265, 6/425; *yll mote thow* ~ 13/205; *as ever mote I thrive or* ~ 14/397.
theided = **theider** *adv.* thither 5/193.
then *adv.* than 1/104, 165.
thend *contraction* the end 7/132.
ther, there *pron.* their 1/139, 4/43.
theras *conj.* although 2/501.
there *adv.* at that place 24/343, 578.
thereas *adv.* where 6/702, 19/223.
theretyll, thertyll *prep.* there-to 6/200, 21/47.
therfo = **therefore** IIB/639.
therfroe *adv.* away from there 2/230.
ther-throe *adv.* there-through IC/28.
thestearnes, thestearnesse, thesternesse *n.* darkness 2/12, 17/15, 34.
thester *adj.* dark 13/355, 22/43.
theth = **them** I 23/24.
they = **the** 3/37, 10/199, 14/85, 18/238, 20/66, 21/156, 22/109, 237, 253, 257,

24/55, 691.
they = **thy** 11/323; ~ = **then** IIB/35.
thie *pron.*¹ thee 2/144, 4/30.
thie *pron.*² they IIB/682.
thinkes *pr. 3 sg. as* ~ *mee* as it seems to me 6/693, 14/183; **thinketh** *as* ~ *mee* 2/363, 3/168; **thought** *pa. t. 3 sg. mee* ~ it seemed to me 22/4.
thirste, threst *pp.* tormented 17/108.
this *pron.* these 2/274.
this, thys *adj.* these 10/66, IIB/295.
this, thys *adv.* thus 1/277, 2/23, 6/8, 10/146, 12/126, 209, 14/116, 16A/36, 38ᵛ, 347, IB/222, IIC/73.
thisten = **christen** 24/450.
tho *pron.* those 6/586, 12/268.
tho *adj.* those IIB/309.
tho = **the** IIB/594; ~ = **thou** 16A/377.
tho, thoe, thoo *adv.* then 2/22, 295, IB/199.
thoe *adv.* morally, virtuously 11/145. *OED* thew v.²
thoe *conj.* although 7/613.
thole *inf.* suffer 2/660, 15/124.
thonge = **thronge** (?) 24/234.
though = **through** 9/174.
thought see **thinkes**.
thould *contraction* the old 4/196.
thraldome, thralldome *n.* bondage 5/4, IB/4.
thrall *n.*¹ bondage 1/149, 13/50.
thrall *n.*² servant 4/191, 9/39.
thrall *n.*³ time, while 19/159. *OED* thrall sb.²
thrall *adj.* subjugated 6/268.
thrast, throuste, thrust *pp.* pierced 16A/253.
thraw, thrawe, throwe *n.* time, moment, occasion 7/31, 11/185.
three = **thee** *inf.* 2/702.
threepe, threpe *inf.* injure 12/143, 24/218.
threst see **thirste**.
thright *pa. t. 3 pl.* thrust 10/406.
thrise, thry, thrye *adv.* thrice 5/226, 12/144, IB/171.
throe *adj.* stubborn 12/143.
throghe, throwe *prep.* through 18/99,

IIB/31.
throo, throwe *adj.* strong, eager 2/511, 13/307.
thronge *n.* pain, affliction 24/234.
throught = **through** 14/13.
throuste, thrust see **thrast**.
throwe *adv.* strongly 16A/387.
thryfte *n.* prosperity 2/700.
thryve *inf. as mot I* ~ as I hope to prosper IB/439.
thse = **these** 24/581.
thursse *n.* demon 7/37. *OED* thurse.
thus *pron.* this 6/265(1), 21/195(1).
thus *adj.* this 21/195(1).
thy *pron.* thee, you 3/207.
thy = **thou** 10/298.
tibbie *n.* 7/22; see **bybbe**.
tiffer *adj.* tougher 10/164.
tight *pp.* prepared, planned 6/375, 7/235.
till *inf.* farm, cultivate 11/254.
tilt *inf.* to poise, to keep in position for blowing 7/155.
tithe see **tight** 7/235.
to, too *num.* two 2/45, 159, 9/262, 12/234, 21/43.
to *adv.* too 1/71, 6/620, 7/261, 271, 10/293, 14/67, 15/322, 16/109, 21/161(AR), 24/396, IB/70.
to *prep.* as to ID/35; of 5/229, 24/519.
tocken *n.* announcement, news 6/678.
to-draw *pp.* drawn to pieces, killed 18/129.
to-flawe *pa. t. 3 sg.* fell to pieces 24/295. *OED* to-fly.
to-frapped *pp.* severely beaten 13/288.
toke, tooke see **takys**.
token, tokenn *n.* meaning 5/31, 22/231; **token** instruction 5/39.
token, tokyn *imp.* inform 23/226, IIB/226.
tokening, tokeninge *n.* announcement, news 6/678, IIB/273.
tome, toome *n.* time 6/69.
too *adv.* also 16A/161.
too *prep.* to 2/519, 14/386, 24/170, IIB/241, IIC/139.
torent *adj.* completely torn apart

GLOSSARY

12/155, 24/126.
torent *pa. t. 1 pl.* tore completely apart 18/296.
torne *n.* wrestling-bout 7/235.
torne *inf.* turn, change 1/141; *imp.* 1/190.
tornes *n.* deviations 24/225.
totorne *adj.* terribly wounded, torn apart 8/351, 16A/251.
tould *adj.* all-told, in total 14/70, 84.
toylefull *adj.* toil-full, hard-working 7/11.
trace *n.* path, way 1/110, 235.
trame *n.* plot 9/259. *OED* tram sb.[1] II. 2.
travayle, travell, traveyle *n.*[1] toil, work 2/327, 6/280, 11/312.
travayle, travell *n.*[2] travel, trip 6/280.
travayle, travell *inf.* trouble myself 17/82. *OED* travail v. I. 1. b.
travayle *imp.* travel, go 6/256.
travaylinge *n.* suffering 6/527.
traveled *pp.* worked 2/329. *OED* travail v. I. 1. e.
traye, treay *n.* sorrow 1/209, 239.
trayne *n.* delay 9/259. *OED* train sb.[1] I. 1.
treatour *n.* traitor IIC/379.
tree *n.*[1] ship's mast 3/76.
tree *n.*[2] the Cross 15/101, 16A/183.
treeue *adj.* true 3/271.
tremed = fremd 7/687.
troone *n.* throne 7/540.
trowe *inf.* believe 22/231; *pr. 1 sg.* 3/211, 7/630; *pr. 3 pl.* 11/184.
trusse *inf.* pack 14/356, **trussed** *pp.* 7/529.
trust *inf.* expect 2/658.
truste *pp.* trusted 24/703.
tryall *n.* three-ness, triad 1/9; **tryalls** units within a triad 1/28.
trye *inf.* test 13/144; **tryed** *pp.* 5/405.
tugget *pp.* tugged 16A/251.
tup, tupp, tuppe *n.* ram 6/275; **tuppes** 7/11, 399.
turckell, turtle *n.* turtle-dove 11/133.
turn, turne *pr. 2 pl.* convert 23/617, IIB/617; **turned, turnyd** *pa. t. 3 pl.* 23/619, IIB/619.
twayne *pron.* two 14/172.
twayne, twene, twinne, twyne, twynne *inf.* divide, separate 1/292, 2/20, 43; depart 2/175, 7/535; **twynne** *pr. 1 sg.* depart 16A/127; **twyn, twyne** *imp.* separate 16A/336, 24/494; **twyninge** *pr. p.* 1/10; twynned *pp.* 2/11; *in* ~ separated 7/537.
twye *adv.* twice IB/279.
tybbe *n.* 7/22; see **bybbe**.
tycke, tyke *n.* churl, low class person 7/265.
tyde *n.* time 1/180, 10/84.
tydes *pr. 3 sg.* experiences 24/296; befalls 24/323; **tyde** *pr. 3 pl.* happen 20/84.
tyght *pp.* planned, prepared 11/163, 12/222.
tyldes *n.* coverings to protect from the weather 7/6. *OED* teld sb.
tyll see **tell** *prep.*
tyllman *n.* farmer 2/514.
tynne see **teene**.
typpers-tappers *n.* guzzlers, barmen 17/305. *OED* tip v.[2] 5, topper[1] 1.
tyrand *n.* tyrant IIB/505.
tyte *adv.* rapidly 2/189, 16A/65.
tytefull see **taytfull**.
tyth, tythe, tythes see **teath**.
tything *n.* tidings, news IIB/228.

U

umbrace = unbrace 7/437.
unbayen *adj.* disobedient 2/338.
unbethoughte *refl. pa. t. 2 pl.* thought about 24/430.
unboxom, unbuxone *adj.* disobedient 2/499, 8/174.
unbrace *inf.* "free (oneself) from restraint" 7/437. *OED* unbrace v. 4. a.
uncleane *adj.* unchaste 12/238.
uncooth, uncouth, unqouth *adj.* foreign, unknown 4/26, IC/8.

unctions *n.* anointings 8/297.
underfoe *inf.* undertake 3/67; undergo, suffer 22/44; ~ , **underfoo** receive 2/474, 23/632.
underfonge *inf.* accept 4/475.
underfree = **underfoe** (?) 23/632.
undyd *pa. t. 3 sg.* explained 19/153.
unfayn, unfayne *adj.* unhappy 8/162, 23/620.
unhappingely *adv.* unluckily 12/96.
unkindly, unkindlye unkynd *adv.* unnaturally 6/336, 24/401.
unknyt *pp.* opened 2/227.
unkynd, unkynde *adj.* unnatural 6/336, 21/206.
unleeffe *adj.* unloved, unwelcome 2/630.
unlevon *adj.* unwilling 14/219.
unlikynge, unlykeing, unlykinge, *adj.* unpleasant, unhappy 5/189, 24/237, IB/142.
unqouth see **uncooth**.
unrightes *n.* sins 3/142.
unskilfull *adj.* unwise 12/204.
unskylfullye *adv.* unwisely 12/192.
unsought *adj.* irreconcilable 18/328. *OED* saught adj.
unthough = **unthought** 24/430.
unthought *refl. pa. t. 2 pl.* thought about 24/430.
unthought = **umthought** thought about, considered IB/102.
untill, untyll *prep.* unto 15/48, 23/207.
untrewe *n.* unbelievers 11/184.
unwakely *adv.* without warning 10/434.
unwarely *adv.* without warning 10/434. *OED* unwarely 2.
unwynne *n.* distress 24/471.
uppsteyinge *n.* ascending 20/181.
uprise, upryste *n.* resurrection 18/149. *OED* uprist 1.

V

valles *n.* valleys 5/306.

varyans, varyens *n.* variance 12/295, 16A/224.
vayle *adj.* veiled 1/73.
vayne *n.* vein, bloodvessel IC/92.
vayne *adj.* empty 1/73. *OED* vain adj. I. 2.
velanye see **vilanye**.
venged *pp.* avenged 5/124.
verament, veramente, veryment *adv.* truly 4/117, 197, 10/67.
veray, verey, vereye, very, verye *adj.* true 2/423, 467, 16/31, IB/243, IC/37.
verely, verelye, veryly *adv.* truly 6/91, 358, IC/7.
vertue *n.* power, strength, ability 6/192, 14/27.
vervent *adj.* fervent, burning 5/130.
vilanye, velanye *n.* insult 8/164, 14/323.
vilde = **vile** *adj.* 15/362.
villard *n.* villain 8/284.
viragoo *n.* woman 2/150.
vower *n.* duty 22/201; see **devoure**.

W

wache = **watch** *n.* watchman 7/287.
wake *inf.* watch 7/286, 13/329; **wakinge** *vbl. n.* 7/297.
waken *adj.* watchful 16A/72.
wale, wall *n.* well, spring 16A/390, IC/31.
wall *n.* barrier 1/174, 23/115. *OED* wall sb. 3. a
walles = **valles** 5/306.
walson = **maleson** (?) 2/679.
walte, walter *pr. 2 sg. subj.* fall over, tumble 7/257.
wan, wonne *adj.* secure 16A/175.
wand see **wond** *inf.*[1]
wandon *adj.* rebellious 16/316. *OED* wanton A. 1.
wantes *pr. 3 sg.* lacks 9/113; **wanten, wanton** *pr. 3 pl.* 16/63, IIC/67.
warchis *imp.* work, behave IIB/168.

GLOSSARY 461

ware *n.* clothing 16/311, 16A/92.
ware *adj.* aware 2/445; conscious 24/213; prudent IIC/128.
ware *imp.* warn 6/257; *pp.* 2/462.
warne *inf.* defend 16A/12; ~ , **worne** refuse 4/25, 16A/379.
warrand *pr. 1 sg.* guarantee IC/48.
warre *n.* merchandize 14/230.
warre *adj.* prudent 16/116; aware 18/137.
warre *imp.* beware 7/247, 257.
warrye *inf.* curse, afflict with evils 3/273; **warryeth** *pr. 3 sg.* IB/271; **warried, warryed, wearied** *pp.* 2/326, IB/271.
warryson, warrysoun, warysonn *n.* reward 6/278, 16/93, IIC/97.
wast *inf.* overcome, abolish 9/54; **wasted** *pp.* destroyed 3/314.
wave = **have** 5/293, 294.
waves *pr. 3 sg.* overcomes 9/110. *OED* waive v.² 3.
waxe *inf.* become 22/310; ~ , **wax** *pr. 1 sg.* 2/570, 8/415; **waxen** *pp.* 21/276.
way = **was** 24/68.
waye *n.* path, road 2/541, 14/195; *take the* ~ depart 12/309; *in* ~ on the way 15/172, 181.
wayle, weale, wealth, weele *n.* well-being 2/119, 237, 373, 24/108.
wayle-awaye *excl.* wellaway 4/350.
wayshe *inf.* wash IIC/249.
wayte *inf.* watch 7/294; **wayted** *pa. t. 1 sg.* 24/374.
waytinge *pr. p.* awaiting 20/155.
wayve *imp.* banish 14/52; **wayved** *pa. t. 2 sg.* ID/43; **waved, wayved, weaved** *pp.* 2/348, 435, 12/212. *OED* waived v.¹ 1.
weale *n.* splendour IB/251. *OED* weal sb.¹ 1. c.
weare, weer see **were** *n.*¹
weare 24/372; see Explanatory Note.
weare *inf.* guard, defend 2/404, 418.
wedder see **wether**.
weed, weede *n.* garment 16/204, IIC/343, **weedes** 7/507, 24/152.
weend *inf.* go 14/4; **weende** *pa. t. 3 sg.* IIC/178.
weene, wene *n.* doubt 2/139, 22/247; **weeninge** *vbl. n.* doubting 19/251.
weene *inf.* think 14/331; ~ , **wen, wene, wyne** *pr. 1 sg.* 1/183, 2/171, 16/179; **weene, weneste** *pr. 2 sg.* 2/602, 11/219; **weenes** *pr. 3 sg.* 11/240, 18/111; **weene** *pr. 3 pl.* 3/111; **wend** *pa. t. 1 sg.* 6/698, 7/222; **weened** *pa. t. 3 sg.* it seemed 7/374; **wend** *pa. t. 1 pl.* 19/53; **weeninge** *vbl. n.* thinking 23/74.
weet *adj.* wet ID/46.
weete *n.* rain 3/95.
weete, weitt see **witt** *inf.*
weete see **witte**.
weildinge see **welde**.
weined *pp.* detached 2/348. *OED* wean v. 2.
weither *n.* weather 18/38.
welde *inf.* rule, control 10/184; **weld** *pr. 1 sg.* 8/173; **weldinge, weildinge** *pr. p.* 6/111, 17/274; **weldinge** *vbl. n.* power 1/17ᵛ.
welkyn *n.* firmament 2/21, 42.
well *adj.* ~ *is them* they are fortunate ID/53.
wembles, wemles, wemlesse, wymbles *adj.* spotless, without sin 12/28, 16A/256ᵛ.
wemmostlye, wemmouslie = **wemlessly** *adv.* spotlessly 6/626.
wend, wende, wiend *inf.* go away, depart, travel 1/110, 7/473, 24/242; **wend** *pr. 1 sg.* 15/268, IB/160; *pr. 1 pl.* 16/372, 23/339; *pr. 3 pl.* ID/49; **wendinge** *pr. p.* 1/72, 6/111; **wended, winded** *pa. t. 1 pl.* 14/331; **wend, wende** *pr. subj. 2 sg.* 2/608, 23/696; **wend** *pr. subj. 3 sg.* 16/166.
wend = **wond** *inf.*² 16/357.
wende *inf.* alter IIB/29.
wendon = **wandon** 16/316.
wenyng *n.* belief IIB/74.
were, weare, weer *n.*¹ doubt 2/253, 4/65, 10/42, 12/234.
were *n.*² danger, peril 19/94 (HmARB).
were *inf.*¹ wear 21/172.

were *inf.*[2] protect, defend 5/285, IB/222.
were *adv.* where IIB/653.
werrye *inf.* worry 2/637.
wether, wedder, weither *n.* ram 4/440, 7/99; **wedders** 7/4.
wetterlye see **witterlye**.
weyt see **witte**.
whainte, whante, whaynte *adj.* quaint, unusual 16/324, IIC/336.
whall *n.* whale IB/358.
wheither, whether, whither *pron.* which 14/89, 16/255, 21/56.
wheither, whether *adv.* where 22/56, IB/179.
wheither, whyther *conj.* whether 21/99, IIB/101.
wher *conj.* whether IC/24; where 23/483.
whewted *pa. t. 3 sg.* whistled 7/422. *OED* whew v.[1]
which *pron.* who 13/66, 133.
which *adj.* of what sort 2/246.
while *n. the* ~ now 15/147.
white *n.* whit, bit 24/193.
white, witt, whyte *inf.* requite, repay 2/549, 16/100, IIC/108.
white *pr. 2 sg.* blame 24/433. *OED* wite v.[1] 1.
whither see **wheither** *pron.*
wholl *adj.* whole 1/7.
whom, whome *n.* home, dwelling-place 7/217, 10/464.
whon = **whom** 10/464.
whoo *n.* woe 7/375.
whoo *imp.* halt 1/228.
whore *adj.* hoary 7/497.
whot, whott *adj.* hot 5/129, 7/118.
whye *n. do* ~ recompense 14/301. *OED* why adv. 5. c.
whyle *n.* period of time 2/180 (HmRBH).
wiend see **wend** *inf.*
wies see **witt** *inf.*
wife, wiffe, wyefe *n.* woman 15/211, 18/172, 23/405.
wight, wighte, wyght *n.* person 5/99, 24/647, IB/92.

wight see **witt** *inf.*
wilfully *adv.* without reason IC/2.
will *n.* desire, determination 5/215, 9/188, *in* **wyll** desirous 24/628.
will *pr. 1 sg.* wish, order, 2/123, 6/170; *pr. 2 sg.* 16A/29; *pr. 3 sg.* 23/630.
wille, wyle *n.* wile, scheme 5/337, 2/180(A); **wylus, wylys** IIB/348, 452.
willinge *n.* desire 6/230, 12/191.
win, wine, wyn, wynne *n.* joy 2/101, 119; *as I have* ~ , *so have I* ~ as I hope for joy 5/260, IB/205.
winded see **wend** *inf.*
wine *inf.* win 17/192.
wise *n.* manner, custom 23/168, IA/45.
wise *after the* ~ wisely 23/212.
wiserde, wysard *n.* wizard, evil trickster 23/371, IIB/371.
wisse, wysse *adj.* wise 2/225, IIB/424.
wiste see **witt** *inf.*
wisted *pp.* convinced 20/28.
with *prep.* by 16/266, IIC/278.
withou = **without** 2/490, 24/27.
withowte *adv.* outside 3/ph, 220.
withowten *prep.* ~ *naye* certainly 16A/430.
withsayes, withsayth *pr. 3 sg.* contradicts 16/301, IIC/313.
witlie *adv.* knowingly 2/271.
witt *n.* subtle thought 1/246, IIB/713.
witt, witten *inf.* know 1/208, 4/462; **weete** 1/208, 7/74; **weitt** IIC/251; **wight** 10/201; **wot, wott, wotte** 2/231, 449, 10/201; **wyt, wytt, wytte** 2/231, 4/462, 12/223; **wies, wott** *pr. 1 sg.* 2/449, 7/352; **wottys, wytt** *pr. 2 sg.* 2/581, 20/64; **wotte, wotten, wytt** *pr. pl.* 8/221, 15/161, 205; **wyst** *pr. subj. 3 sg.* IIC/142, **wiste, wyste** *pa. t. sg.* 5/242, 6/236; **wiste, wyste** *pp.* 2/140, 18/153.
witte, weyt, weete *pr. subj. 3 sg.* should blame 17/125.
witterlye, wetterlye, wytterly *adv.* certainly 1/60, 5/102, IIB/303.
wold, would *n.* open land 7/229, 286; **wouldes** 7/1.

GLOSSARY

woman = **wonnan** 6/400.
womb-clout *n.* tripe 7/124ᵛ.
wombe *n.* belly IB/358.
woming = **wonning** 2/404.
won *n.*¹ expanse 2/26. *OED* sb.² 3.
won, wone, wonne *n.*² dwelling-place 2/383, 418, IIB/663.
won *num.* one IIB/516.
wond *inf.*¹ refuse, refrain from 4/25, 23/29; **wand** *pr. subj. 2 sg.* IC/14. *OED* wonde v. 2.
wond *inf.*² hesitate, shrink from 5/56, 16A/357; **wondes** *pr. 2 sg.* 16A/283. *OED* wonde v. 1.
wonde = **wende** *pr. 1 sg.* go 5/207.
wonded *pp.* wounded 19/19.
wonden = **wounden** *pp.* IIC/328.
wonder *n.* extraordinary event, miracle 2/139, 11/26.
wonder *adv.* wondrously 5/212, 23/648.
wonderlye *adv.* wonderfully 6/53.
wonders *adj.* wondrous 6/416, 7/62.
wone see **won** *n.*²
wone *n.* abundance 3/259, IB/125. *OED* wone sb.³ 4.
wone, wonn, wonne *inf.* win, gain 17/192; **wone, wonen, wonnan, wonne, wonnen** *pp.* 4/29, 6/400, IIB/52.
wones, wonnes *pr. 2 sg.* remain 16A/283. *OED* won v. 2.
woninge, wonnynge *n.* dwelling-place 2/404, 14/227.
woninge = **wynninge** 5/190.
wonne *n.*¹ habit, custom 7/67. *OED* wone sb.¹ 1.
wonne *n.*² hope 13/290, 19/141. *OED* wone sb.³ 1.
wonne *n.*² belief, religion 14/52, 23/659. *OED* wone sb.³ 2.
wonne *pron.* one, person 18/383.
wonne *inf.* dwell 13/396, 481; **wonnes, wonnys** *pr. 3 sg.* 8/139, 9/29; **wonnynge, wonynge** *pr. p.* 21/178, 200.
wonne, wones, wonnes = **wond, wondes** 4/25, 5/56, 16A/283, IC/20;

see **wond** *inf.*¹
wonne *num.* one 16A/154.
wonne see **won** *n.*², **wone** *n.*, and **wan** *adj.*
woo *adj.* woeful 16/130, IIC/142.
woo = **roo** 7/390.
wood, woodd, woode *adj.* insane 2/570, 8/19, 16/238.
woodlie *adv.* insanely IB/236.
worch *inf.* behave 24/354.
worche *inf.* build 3/51; **worchis** *pr. 3 sg.* works 3/254; **worke** *imp.* 3/29.
wordely, wordly = **worldly** 23/260, IIB/234.
worders = **wounder** 7/397.
wore *pa. t. 3 pl.* were 21/82.
worke *n.* deeds 12/278; **workes** *wilde* acts of sexual intercourse IB/299.
worke see **worche**.
worldes = **wouldes** 7/1.
worne *inf.* warn, instruct 7/507.
worne see **warne**.
worshim = **worship** IC/58.
worth *pr. subj. 3 sg.* **woo ~ thee** may woe come to you 1/274.
worthye *adj.* worth 6/579.
wos *pa. t. 3 sg.* was IIB/14, 17.
wot, wott, wotte see **witt** *inf.*
would, wouldes see **wold.**
would *pa. t. 3 sg.* desire, want 2/500; *pr. subj. 1 sg.* 3/98.
wounde *inf.* refrain, give up 18/94, 23/29; **woundes** *pr. 2 sg.* 16A/283; see **wond.** *inf.*¹
wounden *adj.* wounded 16/316.
wounden *pp.* trussed up 16/319, IIC/331.
wounder *adv.* wondrously IIC/200.
woundes = **wondes** 16A/283.
wracke, wreake, wreck *n.* injury 10/120.
wrang, wronge *adj.* wrong, prohibited 3/290.
wraowe, wrawe *adj.* raw, angry 3/209.
wrast *adv.* strongly 16A/163. *OED* wrast a.
wrath *adj.* angry 5/98, 410.
wrauge = **wrang** 3/290.

wreache *inf.* take heed 23/609.
wreak, wreake, wrecken, wreke *inf.* avenge, inflict 5/170, 259, 14/267, IB/123, IIC/96; **wreake, wrecke** *pr. 2 pl.* 17/104; **wroken** *pp.* 3/320, 5/108.
wreakinge *n.* punishment 7/374.
wreth = **wretch** 16/2.
wreye *adv.* truly 13/281. *OED* vray.
wroken see **wreak**.
wronge *pp.* wrung, tugged 16A/163.
wronge *adv.* wrongly 24/120, 189.
wroth *adj.* angry 2/577, IB/91.
wroth, wrothe *inf.* anger 5/410, IIB/463.
wrothe *n.* anger 5/410, 8/195.
wrough read **wrongh** = **wronge** 16A/236.
wrought *pa. t. 1 sg.* had a care 24/273. *OED* reck v. 1. b.
wrought *pp.* suffered 7/14. *OED* reach v.¹ 4. d.
wrought = **wrong** *n.* evil deeds 24/302.
wrougt = **wrought** IB/236.
wrye *inf.* denounce 8/190, 13/295. *OED* wray v.¹ 1.
wyche *pron.* which IIB/676.
wychyd *pp.* bewitched IIB/347.
wydeweare, wydewhere *adv.* widely 12/6, 16/5.
wyefe see **wife**.
wyght see **wight**.
wyle, wylus, wylys see **wille**.
wyled *pa. t. 3 sg.* misled, tricked 24/120.
wyllynge *n.* desire 2/369.
wyn *inf.* gain, profit IB/156.
wynde *inf.* go, travel 7/473, 24/138; **wynd** *pr. 1 sg.* 5/207; **wynde** *pr. 1 pl.* 23/339; *pr. subj. pl.* ID/37; *pr. subj. 2 pl.* IIB/700.
wyne *n. as drinke I* ~ as I hope to drink wine 10/399.
wyne *inf.* save 2/453.
wyne see **weene**.
wyninge *n.* dwelling-place 2/404; see **woninge** *n.*¹
wynne *pr. 1 sg.* go 16A/127. *OED* win v.¹ 12.
wynninge *n.* gain, profit 5/190, IB/143.
wyste *pp.* managed 18/153. *OED* wis v.¹ 2b.
wyt, wytt, wytte see **witt** *inf.*
wytterly, wytterlye see **witterlye**.

Y

yarde *n.*¹ stick, rod 4/290.
yarde *n.*² enclosed area 5/307; **yardes, yordes** 5/307, IB/268.
yare *adv.*¹ readily 16/312, IIC/324.
yare *adv.*² for a long time, long ago 14/231, 22/33.
yarlye, yerly *adv.* early 19/60.
yche *adj.* each 2/213, 647.
ychon *pron.* each one IIB/128.
yeade *pa. t. 3 pl.* went 22/129.
yeane-chare *n.* turning back, escape 24/215. *OED* gainchare.
yearth *n.* earth 2/29, 33.
yearthly, yearthlye, yeartly *adj.* earthly 2/171, 391, 23/258.
yee *n.* eyes IIB/160.
yeede *pa. 2 sg.* went 19/44; ~ , **yeade** *pa. t. 3 sg.* 16A/231, 22/129; **yeeden** *pa. t. 3 pl.* 17/34.
yeeke, yke *adv.* also 17/88, IIB/457.
yelde *pa. t. 1 sg.* give thanks 7/681; **yeeld** *pa. t. 3 sg.* yielded, gave up 16A/463, IC/116; **yeelded, yeelden** *pp.* repaid 24/234, 560.
yelden see **eylden**.
yendre *adj.* yonder IIB/439.
yerbes *n.* herbs 2/33.
yere, yerre *adv.* ere, earlier 17/8, 18/110.
yerly see **yarlye**.
yerne *inf.* desire, seek 9/189.
yke see **yeeke**.
ylke *adj.* same 2/190, 3/318.
ymbrace = **unbrace** 7/437.
yoare, youre *adv.* yore 20/27, 24/513.
yoe *pron.* you 11/72.
yonge *pr. p.* going (?) 24/234. *OED*

GLOSSARY 465

yong v.
yood, yoode *pa. t. 3 sg.* went away 13/303, 21/79.
yordes see **yarde** *n.*²

yowe *n.* ewe 7/30.
yowle *inf.* shout 13/427.
ywisse, ywys see **iwis.**

The manufacturer's authorised representative in the EU for product safety is Oxford University Press España S.A. of El Parque Empresarial San Fernando de Henares, Avenida de Castilla, 2 - 28830 Madrid (www.oup.es/en or product.safety@oup.com). OUP España S.A. also acts as importer into Spain of products made by the manufacturer.
Printed and bound by CPI Group (UK) Ltd, Croydon, CR0 4YY

20/03/2026

02075328-0004